301.592
M34p

105633

POWER
IN AFRIC

POWER AND CLASS
IN AFRICA

An Introduction
to Change and Conflict
in African Politics

Irving Leonard Markovitz

Queens College of the City of New York

PRENTICE-HALL, INC., ENGLEWOOD CLIFFS, NEW JERSEY 07632

Library of Congress Cataloging in Publication Data

MARKOVITZ, IRVING LEONARD [DATE]
   Power and class in Africa.

   Bibliography: p. 349
   Includes index.
   1. Africa—Politics and government. 2. Social classes—Africa. 3. Elite (Social sciences)—Africa.
I.–Title.
DT31.M34   301.5'92'096   76-49660
ISBN 0–13–686691–3
ISBN 0–13–686642–5 pbk.

© 1977 by Prentice-Hall, Inc., Englewood Cliffs, N.J. 07632

To Amy and Jonatha

Printed in the United States of America

10 9 8 7 6 5 4 3 2 1

Prentice-Hall International, Inc., *London*
Prentice-Hall of Australia Pty. Limited, *Sydney*
Prentice-Hall of Canada, Ltd., *Toronto*
Prentice-Hall of India Private Limited, *New Delhi*
Prentice-Hall of Japan, Inc., *Tokyo*
Prentice-Hall of Southeast Asia Pte. Ltd., *Singapore*
Whitehall Books Limited, *Wellington, New Zealand*

Contents

Chapter III
THE HISTORICAL IMPACT OF
COLONIALISM AND IMPERIALISM   56

Chapter IV
THE STRUGGLE FOR INDEPENDENCE: Tribe,
Tribalism, and the Conditions for Social Development   98

Chapter V
THE STRUGGLE FOR INDEPENDENCE:
The Dynamics of Nationalism   173

Chapter VI
THE CONSOLIDATION OF POWER:
Rise of the Organizational Bourgeoisie   198

Chapter VII
THE CONSOLIDATION OF POWER:
African Business   230

Preface

Caveat emptor! This book has been advertised in some places as a "text." But a text is something that pretends to be definitive, authoritative and objective. Until I bowed to the common sense of wife and friends that a tome of 850 manuscript pages could not rise as a butterfly, I called this work an essay. Montaigne and Emerson wrote short, pithy disquisitions on their way to more important activities. Despite its length *Power and Class in Africa* is at least an "essay" in the sense of something that is tentative, partial and personal—the opposite of a textbook. Not that my aims are modest for I hope to affect not only what people know but how they think, at least in terms of the images people have in their minds as they come to the study of African politics. And as in the poem about *The Past* by Diana Der Hovanessian:

> *Like a drawer of cutlery*
> *dumped in*
> *every which-way*
> *it cuts me when I reach*
> *in to rearrange it*
> *into neat silver settings.**

For aid in this endeavor, I have many to thank. In gratitude for the labor and insights of those scholars upon whose works I have drawn and who have made this study possible, I have tried to deal with their ideas carefully—especially where they differed from my own. For those subtleties of argument, delights of phrase and passions of commitment that I have not conveyed, I am truly sorry.

My intellectual debts go beyond those listed in the footnotes and bibliography. I was fortunate to be able to draw upon friends and scholars learned in many matters. They cautioned that Arabs never completely closed the Mediterranean; that capitalism originated later than the twelfth century (or earlier); that feudalism in southern Europe differed from feudalism in northern Europe; that Adam Smith and John Kenneth Galbraith did not belong together in the same sentence. They provided obscure references to a crucial but little known pamphlet by John Stuart Mill; to medieval Chinese naval policy; to the fine points of democratic theory. They improved this book.

* *The Nation*, September 11, 1976, p. 217

Those who read one or another of the several drafts in their entirety were: Omayemi G. Agbeyegbe, Keith Aufhauser, Martin Kilson, Michael F. Lofchie, Herbert Weiss and Burton Zweibach.

Those who commented critically on one or more chapters were: David B. Abernethy, Frederick S. Arkhurst, Ivo Duchacek, Andrew Hacker, David Kimble, Henry W. Morton, Wentworth Ofuatey-Kodjoe, James F. Petras, Carl G. Rosberg, Roger Sanjek, Phillip Stevens Jr., and M. Crawford Young.

Leonard Pesce did many studies under various lighting arrangements and from diverse angles before he composed the cover photograph that so vividly conveys one of this book's central themes. John F. Povey helped identify the terra cotta Akan funery figure.

Ann Pelner, Minnie Meyers and Anna Hiller typed several drafts carefully and thoughtfully. The personnel of the Word Processing center also contributed significantly to the production of this book, especially: Dorothy Chalek, Wendy DeFortuna, Muriel Devack, Shirley Ladman, Mary O'Shea and Pearl Sigberman.

Part of Chapter IV and Chapter X appeared in different form as "Traditional Social Structure, the Islamic Brotherhoods and Political Development in Senegal" and "Bureaucratic Development and Economic Growth" in the *Journal of Modern African Studies* edited superbly by David Kimble and published by the Cambridge University Press.

My appreciation also goes to the organization that is Prentice-Hall and to Roger G. Emblen who originally signed me; Stan Wakefield, the current Political Science editor, and Kathryn Woringer, a careful production editor. Bruce Fulton, the copy editor whom I never met, read my manuscript thoughtfully. From the woods of Maine, he obliged me to spend one of the lovliest mornings of July seeking a misplaced page number for a quotation from Cabral.

The closing of the City University for two weeks, because of a lack of funds, provided the unasked for leisure for the final revisions and copy editing. At this writing when CUNY still shudders from a policy of "retrenchment" and tuition, I must record my pride at having been part of a great and humane institution of higher learning. The Faculty Research Award Program of the City University provided funds that enabled me to do research in Africa. The material assistance of the Africana Studies Program of Queens College was also valuable. For their support I am grateful. My greatest pleasure, however, has come from my students. My privilege was to see the fires of their minds quicken; to be aggressively challenged by those who were impatient to know, yet who were willing to understand. The imposition of tuition at the City University, which ended a unique system of access to higher education, may be of parochial concern; newspapers in Lomé, Togo or Des Moines, Iowa did not headline the event. But it was, nevertheless a tragedy.

My wife Ruth helped in every way, aided in every task. Her advice and opinions mattered enormously.

Amy and Jonathan helped with the bibliography and with the pagination. They both learned to walk in Africa; and they grew there a little — this book is dedicated to them.

Irving Leonard Markovitz

POWER AND CLASS
IN AFRICA

From C. Gregory Knight and James Newman, *Contemporary Africa: Geography and Change* (Englewood Cliffs, N.J.: Prentice-Hall, 1976).

Chapter I

INTRODUCTION:
On Political Development and
the Value of Conflict

This study seeks out the continuities and conflicts between the African past and the present and asks again those basic questions about African politics: Who gets what, when, where, and how—and who gets left out? Since the achievement of independence by most African states in the late 1950s and the 1960s, significant events and major contributions by so many scholars—particularly the outpourings of African intellectuals—virtually cry out for synthesis. No one person can succeed entirely in organizing this mass of materials and information into a limited amount of space and time, and around a set of problem-focused themes, for the purposes of understanding and teaching.[1] Any such project not only lends itself to failure but invites disaster for the hubris of the endeavor. This effort at an overall interpretation, tentative as it is, has been stimulated by the difficulties I find with the interpretations of others. Having been involved in the study of African politics for more than twenty years, I hope to sharpen a confrontation of basic issues, provoke disagreement over the matters of interpretation, and make manifest the underlying assumptions of different approaches.

Three major currently fashionable political positions that masquerade under an academic façade deserve particular consideration. The first is that African states are falling apart; that the basic problem facing African societies is the need for stability. The second is that African politics are essentially conflictless and classless, a view that originates from two very different sources: romanticism about the unity, the one-for-all and all-for-one nature, of the "African people"; and Western liberal and conservative social sciences that reject class interpretations in any context. The third, which stems from a bitter overreaction to wildly optimistic expectations at the end of the Second World War that independence would bring some new panacea for mankind, is a devasting pessimism as to the possibilities for future African state building and economic development.

To refute these contentions requires examining contemporary

---

[1] In part, this study continues the attempt I began in my reader, *African Politics and Society: Basic Issues and Problems of Government and Development* (New York: Free Press; London: Collier-Macmillan, 1970).

2

developments on the continent within two types of frameworks: first, Africa's present in terms of her own past; but second, an avoidance of regional parochialism, a comparison of similar problems elsewhere in the world, both today and in other periods of history. The necessary perspective then, from which we will attempt to view the problems of contemporary African societies, originates with the rise of nation-states in sixteenth-century Europe and with the beginnings of capitalism in the twelfth century—for a better understanding of the difficulties of creating unity and socialism in Tanzania and Zambia—and extends to the technology of computers and cybernetics in the twentieth century, to better comprehend problems such as the horrifying, historically unique nature of the "permanently unemployed" in modern African cities. A comparative and historical perspective enables us to better determine the nature of stability and instability; to understand the development of class structures; to explore sources of disunity; to examine the thrust of the revolutionary changes wrought by mass nationalism; to see more realistically how far African nations have "progressed"; and not to look backward nostalgically nor dwell on the terrors of yesterday, but to realize the uses of history as a spur for the future and as a weapon for a new freedom for ancient peoples.

"Instability" preoccupies social scientists concerned with developing countries in the same way that "law and order" concerns establishment politicians. Disorganization, dislocation, breakdown, regression, anarchy—words such as these constitute the vocabulary of this social science. Samuel Eisenstadt maintains that the major problem facing "modernizing nations" is the necessity to develop an institutional structure capable of preventing "breakdown."[2] Arnold Rivkin argues that "the endemic political instability, the widespread economic stagnation, and the epidemic in military coups d'état in the decade of the sixties are direct manifestations of the African institutional gap. They testify to the need for new institutions. . . ."[3] Aristide Zolberg warns that we have to look forward to "periods of substantial disorder," which will permeate entire regimes. We can expect a sort of institutionalized instability, just as occurred over many decades in Latin America. Zolberg asks, "Does Africa suffer from too much authority or from too little authority?" and answers that the dramatic danger of disorder imposes itself upon our attention. He cites President Houphouet-Boigny of the Ivory Coast as saying, quoting Goethe, "I prefer injustice to disorder: one can die of disorder, one does not die of injustice; and injustice can be repaired."[4] Samuel Huntington,

---

[2] Samuel Eisenstadt, *Modernization: Protest and Change* (Englewood Cliffs, N.J.: Prentice-Hall, 1966), p. v.

[3] Arnold Rivkin, ed., *Nations By Design* (Garden City, N.Y.: Doubleday, Anchor Books, 1968), pp. xii–xiii. See also Rivkin's *Nation-Building in Africa* (New Brunswick, N.J.: Rutgers University Press, 1969).

[4] Aristide Zolberg, *Creating Political Order* (Chicago: Rand McNally, 1966), p. 42. See also the approach of Henry L. Bretton in *Power and Politics in Africa* (Chicago: Aldine, 1973). Stability is a central concern of Henry Bienen in his *Kenya: The Politics of Participation and Control* (Princeton, N.J.: Princeton University Press, 1974). Bienen maintains that he doesn't argue "that stability is a good

one of the most influential writers in modern political science, carries this concern to one logical conclusion when he writes that "the most important political distinction among countries concerns not their form of government but their degree of government."[5] The United States, Great Britain, and the Soviet Union are all in the same category because in all three countries "the government governs."[6] Communist one-party dictatorships and Western liberal states lie together along Huntington's axis of categorization because "the primary problem is not liberty but the creation of a legitimate public order."[7] Lest we worry too much about what is "legitimate," Huntington assures us that one of the functions of existing government, any existing government, is to define what philosophers have long debated: the public interest.[8] He, like Goethe, assures us that "men may of course have order without liberty but they cannot have liberty without order." Too rapid mobilization of too many formerly subjugated new groups constitutes the primary problem of the politics of these states because political institutions have not developed at a comparable pace. Institutionalization, then, according to the most eminent theorists of the social science, must, for the foreseeable future, be our central concern.

Would we, however, value the stability of a concentration camp or torture chamber? Stability for whom and in whose interest? These questions must accompany any premium that we place on the value of maintaining systems and power structures. Conflict, dissent, revolution—the politics of the oppressed and of struggle—sometimes move men and weigh more heavily in the balance of desirable social goals. Indeed, from any perspective, why does "instability" strike so worrisome a tone? Does "instability" mean the lack of institutions, and an accompanying potential for "anarchy," or is the problem simply one of temporary disarray? Is "instability" in modern Africa equivalent to the disintegration of government during epochs such as the great plagues of the early fourteenth century? Or only to the *apparent* chaos of times such as the French Revolution in the eighteenth century? Marc Bloch, writing on the strength of government in medieval times, notes; "One of the common features of all the governments was not exactly their weakness, but the fact that they were never more than intermittently effective; and this blemish was never more strikingly

---

thing per se," but he does find that in Kenya "it has been associated with economic development." He also finds that "the poor and marginally employed do not constitute an organized political force," and he does say, "I argue that Kenya remains stable because classes have not formed in any clear fashion." (pp. 22, 23)

[5] Samuel Huntington, *Political Order in Changing Societies* (New Haven: Yale University Press, 1968), p. 1. Cf. the somewhat different concern for "democratic stability" in Seymour Martin Lipset, *The First New Nation* (London: Heinemann Educational Books, 1963). Ira Katznelson points out in *Black Men, White Cities* (New York: Oxford University Press, 1973) that stability depends not only on the strength of institutions but also on the terms of the participation they make possible: these can require "temporarily destabilizing decisions" (pp. 202, 203).

[6] Huntington, *Political Order in Changing Societies*, p. 1

[7] *Ibid.*, p. 7.

[8] *Ibid.*, p. 6.

manifest than where ambitions were greatest and the professed sphere of action widest."[9] Here there was a problem of an institutional framework that was insufficient to achieve the declared objectives of the holders of power.

In the contemporary African states, however, the most striking political development since independence, I would argue, is not the lack of stability but indeed, from any long-range historical perspective, the rapidity with which stability has been achieved. Coups, rebellions, civil wars, racial conflagrations, and riots notwithstanding, in less than two decades African states have settled into a pattern that is in large measure predictable. However, this is not necessarily a cause for rejoicing, not without first determining who in fact is in charge, and not without first establishing the connection between the present rulers and those of previous regimes. An understanding of the continuities between the post-independent African governments, the colonial regimes they replaced, and precolonial African societies is absolutely essential for a judgment. Alexis de Tocqueville, describing the connection between the old regime and the revolution of 1789, wrote:

> Those who saw the Revolution overthrowing all the institutions and customs which had hitherto shored up the social hierarchy and prevented men from running wild were naturally inclined to think that the Revolution spelled the end of all things; not merely of the old order, but of any order in the state, not merely that of any given form of government, but of any government at all—that in fact the nation was heading toward sheer anarchy. Yet, in my opinion, those who held this view were misled by appearances. . . . beneath the seemingly chaotic surface there was developing a vast centralized power which attracted to itself and wielded into an organic whole all the elements of authority and influence that hitherto had been dispersed among a crowd of lesser uncoordinated powers. . . . Never since the fall of the Roman Empire had the world seen a government so highly centralized. This new power was created by the Revolution, or, rather, grew up almost automatically out of the havoc wrought by it. True, the governments it set up were less stable than any of those it overthrew; yet paradoxically they were infinitely more powerful."[10]

The new African governments, heirs to colonial regimes, have already succeeded mightily in creating central administrations strong enough to unite, in a variety of social projects and economic enterprises, traditional societies and vast assemblages of peoples whose many tongues and cultures differ from each other as much as those of the Russians and Scandinavians. The military coups d'état and civil wars, appearances of anarchy notwithstanding, have furthered this process of consolidation. Every major historical event strengthens the centralizing powers further, but to what purpose, to what end?

[9] Marc Bloch, *Feudal Society* (Chicago: University of Chicago Press, 1961), p. 409.
[10] Alexis de Tocqueville, *The Old Regime and the French Revolution* (Garden City, N.Y.: Doubleday, Anchor Books, 1955), pp. 6–9.

James Coleman, in the introduction to his impressive work on Nigeria, had the courage to state, "A student of African nationalism finds it difficult to contribute original conclusions regarding the nature of colonial nationalism. . . . The most he can do is to show that the African response to alien rule . . . follows a historic pattern. . . ."[11] Can historic patterns, discernible elsewhere, be applied to the study of African politics and society? Academic training gears us to detect nuances of difference, to sort out subtleties, to make fine gradations. Yet sometimes cutting through subtleties to focus on the broad strokes of the larger picture, seeing the forest as well as the trees, finding the broad universal elements, are the most important tasks. One of my former professors in a graduate course on economic development, to the astonishment of the class, impatiently admonished a languidly equivocating student, "I know, I know, everything is in between, everything is a shade of gray. Well let me tell you, that is for sophomores. Sometimes things are black and sometimes things are white. Now which is this?" The marvel of complexity, from an intellectual point of view, should not obscure the simplicity of recurring patterns of basic divisions, such as that, for example, between the holders and the victims of power.

Marx knew of the existence of lawyers, clerks, engineers, fishermen, and students as well as factory workers and factory owners, yet he wrote: "Our epoch, the epoch of the bourgeoisie, possesses, however, this distinctive feature; it has simplified the class antagonisms. Society as a whole is more and more splitting up into two great hostile camps, into two great classes directly facing each other: bourgeoisie and proletariat."[12]

With similar intent to delve into the underlying causes of political evolution, de Tocqueville discovered that

> there are periods in a nation's life when men differ from each other so profoundly that any notion of 'the same law for all' seems to them preposterous. But there are other periods when it is enough to dangle before their eyes a picture, however indistinct and remote, of such a law and they promptly grasped its meaning and hastened to acclaim it. In fact, the most extraordinary thing about the Revolution is not that it employed the methods which led to its success or that certain men should have conceived the ideas which supplied its driving force. What was wholly novel was that so many nations should have simultaneously reached the stage in their development which enabled those methods to be successfully employed, and that ideology to be so readily accepted.[13]

De Tocqueville went on to say that he had had the occasion to study the political institutions of medieval France, England, and Germany

---

[11] James Coleman, *Nigeria: Background to Nationalism* (Berkeley and Los Angeles: University of California Press, 1958), p. 409.

[12] "The Communist Manifesto," in *Marx and Engels: Basic Writings on Politics and Philosophy*, ed. Lewis S. Feur (Garden City, N.Y.: Anchor Books, 1959), p. 8.

[13] de Tocqueville, *The Old Regime and the French Revolution*, p. 13.

and that the more deeply he went into the subject the more he was struck by the remarkable similarity between the laws and institutions in all three countries. He found a "family likeness" among them, and of their inhabitants "one might almost say that they were not different men, but essentially the same men everywhere."[14]

Every African country is unique. East, West, North, South, and Central Africa all have special problems peculiar to their region. Yet every passing year brings out more emphatically common elements in their political developments. All these nations of Africa belong, in de Tocqueville's sense, to the same family. What is it that makes for this "family likeness," that creates "not different men but essentially the same men everywhere"? Coincidence can hardly explain the arrival of independence to most African as well as Asian states at approximately the same time, nor can it account for the similarity of their evolution toward increasingly one-party or military-led authoritarian regimes. Obviously, similar forces are at work. During the 1950s the most fashionable explanation focused on the forces of international communism. Marx's warning of 1848 that the specter of communism was haunting Europe found renewed credence in the West after the Second World War in the anticolonial revolution of third world countries. In Africa, Nyerere, Touré, Nkrumah, Kenyatta, Keita—all the leaders of the new national movements claimed the mantle of socialist philosophy, ranging from the mildest sort of Christian democratic socialism to an intense commitment to orthodox scientific materialism. Yet Eric Wolf appears much closer to the truth when, in analyzing the peasant wars of the twentieth century, he quotes Bertolt Brecht: "It is not Communism that is radical, it is Capitalism."[15] Capitalism brought with it a quadruple alienation: of men from the process of production, which had previously guaranteed their livelihood; of men from the products of their work, which became transformed into commodities; of men from themselves, insofar as they lived only in order to work at meaningless labor; and of men from their fellows, whom they met as competitors on the marketplace. Everywhere, Wolf maintains, "the dance of commodities brought on ecological crises" because of the changing balance in the combination of resources necessary to eke out a livelihood. Equally serious, capitalism threatened the material base of the traditional power brokers, and precipitated a crisis in their authority as the cocoa farmer, cloth merchant, and civil servant confronted the obas, asantehenes, bours, guers, and warriors. As the market, along with "western" education, culture, technology, and religion, spread unevenly, vast new interests rose, commingled, and conflicted, frequently resurrecting and reinvigorating ancient commitments and alliances. In Wolf's words,

> Commitments and goals point in different directions: the old is not yet overcome but remains to challenge the new; the new is not yet victo-

[14] *Ibid.*, p. 15.
[15] Eric Wolf, *Peasant Wars of the 20th Century* (New York: Harper & Row, 1969), p. 275.

rious. The dislocations caused by rapid change are still visible to all; the wounds caused by them, raw and open. New wealth does not yet have legitimacy and old power no longer commands respect. Traditional groups are not yet strong enough to wield decisive power. This is especially marked in colonial situations, where capitalism has been imported from abroad by force of arms. . . . Inherited control mechanisms fail, but the new mechanisms engage only rarely, with considerable slippage.[16]

To maintain that capitalism is revolutionary, however, is not to allege the simple predominance at all times of economic forces over all other factors—particularly in Africa, where race and ethnicity overlay and complicate class and economic interpretations. Traditional identifications and communalism rank among the most important elements we must consider.[17]

Nevertheless, we cannot be blind to the inequalities that characterize African societies: farmers and slum dwellers have a life expectancy of thirty-eight years, diets of starch three times a day, seven days a week, extraordinary rates of infant mortality, and all the debilitating diseases known to man; ministers earn more in a month than peasants in a lifetime; millions are budgeted for civil servants' salaries and a pittance goes for agricultural innovation. We are compelled to seek out the structural sources of such inequalities.[18]

In the United States the great social discovery of the 1960s was the persistence of enormous poverty. The persistent impoverishment of large minorities in the developed countries of the West belies the once optimistic expectations of mainstream thinkers from Adam Smith to Milton Friedman that increased industrialization would bring equality and affluence for all. How much worse a situation should we expect in the third world countries? In a remarkable study, *Economic Growth and Social Equity in Developing Countries,* Irma F. Adelman and Cynthia Taft Morris ask, "Who benefits from economic development?" They write, "Egalitarian philosophies stimulated by the industrial revolutions of Western Europe have produced widespread expectations that economic growth will equalize wealth and earnings opportunities as well as raise the average level of economic welfare. *These expectations have not been borne out.*"[19] Adelman and Morris report that they discovered, to their great surprise, that "economic structure, not level of income or rate of economic growth, is the basic determinant of patterns of income distribution."[20] The top 5 percent of the population in the Ivory Coast, for example, absorbed 29 percent of

---

[16] *Ibid.,* pp. 283, 284.

[17] See Richard L. Sklar, *Nigerian Political Parties* (Princeton, N.J.: Princeton University Press, 1963), p. iv, where he argues that the key elements in understanding power in the emerging African nations are "the interplay of three converging social forces—the thrust of nationalism, the persistence of cultural particularism and the crystallization of emerging class interests."

[18] On problems of health in Africa, see Marc Sankale and Pierre Pene, *Medicine sociale au Senegal* (Dakar: Afrique Documents, 1960), p. 41.

[19] (Stanford, Calif.: Stanford University Press, 1973), p. 141 (emphasis added).

[20] *Ibid.,* p. 186.

the national income; the top 20 percent in Sierra Leone accounted for 64 percent of the national income. Only 8 percent of the national income was distributed to the bottom 40 percent of the population of Gabon, and 14 percent to the bottom 40 percent in Nigeria.[21] A closer look must obviously be taken at the concept of community in Africa.

Classes exist in Africa today, and they have existed, except for some communitarian societies, in the past. "Class" implies a system characterized by conflict, not simply a hierarchy of inequalities. Objectively, classes can exist regardless of whether or not the people that compose these various groups are conscious of their situation. This is not to say that a common interest in the face of a threat posed by a common external enemy cannot emerge and temporarily override internal divisions. A builder of high-rise apartments can precipitate the consolidation of a "community" interest by his intrusion into a neighborhood of one-family houses. For some time, colonialism created a "community" in the sense that all groups suffered and stood to benefit from the expulsion of this foreign intrusion.

One of the major reasons for studying the African past is to stress the revolt against colonialism; one of the major elements of continuity is that the resistance against colonialism did not occur simply with the birth of mass nationalism but was a characteristic of major traditional systems as well. This continuity is masked by the westerner's too often technical definition of nationalism as something determined by scientific capacities to build communications and distribution systems over large areas. The study of African history is also important as a means of demonstrating the greatness of precolonial societies; this greatness is often downplayed by those who argue that the lack of great civilizations became a significant weapon in the hands of the colonial ruling classes.[22] European colonialism, we must also keep in mind, occupied surprisingly few decades of the continent's existence, despite the millions of words written by Europeans. Few historians will go as far as Ouologuem, who downgrades European colonialism into a "mere historical incident that had no serious impact on African society."[23] In a chronological sense, Ouologuem is certainly correct. To determine the substance of his claim necessitates a closer look at key developments in this precolonial period and here we find a different type of continuity, one of class domination that carries over from the "traditional" to "modern" societies.

Conflict and struggle marked the perpetuation of the hegemony of the ancient ruling classes. If traditional leaders began their relations with external forces in bitter struggle, they equally often reached an accommodation that insured the perpetuation of their reign. Status

[21] *Ibid.*, p. 152.

[22] Cf. Robert Rotberg and Ali Mazrui, eds., in their *Protest and Power in Black Africa* (New York: Oxford University Press, 1970); and of Michael Crowder, ed., in his *West African Resistance* (New York: Africana Publishing, 1971). See also my discussion of African history in Chapter II.

[23] J. Mbelolo Mpiku "From One Mystification to Another: 'Negritude' and 'Négraille' in 'Le Devoir de violence,'" *Review of National Literatures*, 2, no. 2 (Fall 1971), p. 143.

reversals occurred; important new elements were introduced into the dominant groups; in particular, the middle levels of power were expanded. All of these developments varied considerably from one traditional society to the next and from one part of the continent to another. They are all caveats against too mechanistic a view of the linkages between Africa's past and present. Yet there are patterns of domination–subordination that endure.

During the advent of independence, when almost all attention was either focused upon the struggle of colonialism or given over to a general euphoria over the foreseeable birth of the new regimes, Frantz Fanon startled not only Western audiences with his discussions of the necessity of violent struggle but African political activists as well, by looking beyond the struggle with colonialism into the post-independence period to show how splits would arise within the "African community."[24] He warned that African "ruling classes" would take over the roles of Europeans in the colonies and that these new governments would remain dependent internationally on their past and continuing masters. For Fanon, the crucial historical event was the killing of the sense of self-worth of the colonized by all the various instruments of oppression—social, economic, cultural, political, military, and psychological—of the foreign colonial power. With the establishment of colonial control, history for the African comes to an end. No longer do significant events occur. Development stops. For the European killing machine zombiaized the African into the living dead. History begins again with a shot—actually fired or symbolically demonstrated by a willingness to engage in violence to attest human dignity. History, therefore, in terms of Fanon's discussion in *The Wretched of the Earth* and elsewhere, begins with the struggle for independence. (Fanon is also concerned with the future, the creation of a new society and a new culture, which requires revitalized political instruments, the new man, and the new humanism.) To complete Fanon's investigation, however, we must relate the analysis of precolonial history to the consolidation of power after independence. Thus will we be able to see linkages between those ancient African empires, the slave trade, the growing trade in commodities of primary products and the rise of African business, and the emergence of the "new class" that Fanon warns against.

The Historical Case for Optimism

After the decimation of Biafra, prolonged civil war in the Sudan and Chad, racial confrontation at almost every point along the edge of the Sahara, the chaos of the Congo during the early 1960s, the eclipse of one parliamentary system after another by military regimes—to say nothing of economists' dire predictions about the failure of economic growth, surging rates of population increase, and unbreakable cycles

---

[24] *The Wretched of the Earth* (New York: Grove Press, 1968).

of poverty — pessimism about the future of Africa's social development would not appear unreasonable. Yet what other nations and regions have undergone in terms of their Hiroshimas, Nagasakis, Auschwitzes and Dachaus of present times, as well as the devastations wreaked in their pasts, finds no parallels in African history. Where was the hope in Europe's past? Marc Bloch begins his account of the origins of feudalism with a statement by the bishops of the province of Rheims assembled at Trosly in 909: "You see before you the wrath of the Lord breaking forth. . . . There is naught but towns emptied of their folk, monasteries razed to the ground or given to the flames, fields desolated. . . . Everywhere the strong oppresseth the weak and men are like fish of the sea that blindly devour each other." Bloch discovers in this incessantly recurring theme of the ninth and tenth centuries "the proof of a state of affairs regarded as intolerable even in those days. Certainly it was a period when those who were capable of observing and making comparisons, the clergy in particular, felt themselves to be living in a hateful atmosphere of disorder and violence."[25]

The constriction of the Mediterranean to "westerners" as a result of the expansion of Islam in the seventh century caused the rapid decline of European commerce. Merchants virtually disappeared in the eighth century and urban life collapsed. With the decline of merchants and townsmen, contact between western Europe and the outside world almost came to an end. Henri Pirenne tells us that "the object of labor was not to grow wealthy but to maintain oneself in the position in which one was born, until mortal life should pass into life eternal."[26] Nothing, however, could have prepared Europe for the death and stagnation of the fourteenth century. Famine laid waste the whole of Europe from 1315 to 1317. Thirty years later the Black Death, the most horrible of all reported epidemics from 1347 to 1350, helped carry off a third of the population of Europe. Plague and famine followed each other in intermittent outbursts for the whole century. Political holocaust no less cruel accompanied natural devastation. Civil war and banditry were endemic, surpassed in their toll finally by the Hundred Years War, which ruined France and exhausted England.

Could there ever have been a worse time to live? What makes choosing "the worst epoch of European history to live in" difficult is that so many periods offer so much competition. Consider, for example, Britain at the advent of the industrial revolution. Plumb describes this time as follows:

> Britain in the third quarter of the 18th century was a strange mixture
> of privilege and liberty, elegance and filth, and antiquated habits and

---

[25] Bloch, *Feudal Society*, p. 3.

[26] Henri Pirenne, *Economic and Social History of Medieval Europe* (New York: Harcourt, Brace and World, 1937), p. 13. Cf. Fernand Braudel, *The Mediterranean and the Mediterranean World in the Age of Philip II*, 2 vols. (New York: Harper & Row, 1972), for an interpretation that emphasizes the continuities and comprehensiveness of these contacts; see especially Part Two of Volume I, pp. 355 and passim.

new inventions; the new and the old were jostled uncomfortably together; fabulous riches mingled with dire poverty. Posh country clubs and sleepy market towns witnessed strict bannings, rick-burnings, machine smashing, hunger riots . . . death came so easily. A stolen penknife and a boy of ten was strung up at Norwich; a handkerchief, taken secretly by a girl of fourteen brought her the noose. . . . Vile slums in the overcrowded towns bred violent epidemics; typhoid, cholera, smallpox, ravaged the land. . . . Children died like flies; most men got through two or three wives. Disease scourged the land and the stink of the common paupers' graves at Manchester grew too foul even for that tough age. . . .[27]

Closer to our times, consider the observations of John J. Johnson on developments in the postindependence stage of the new countries of Latin America:

There is a well-worn phrase in Spanish America to the effect that the expulsion of the Spaniards in 1825 marked "the last day of despotism and the first day of the same!" . . . Spanish America became a morass of anarchy, a perpetual theatre of civil war. Anarchy and violence became the universal pattern of political development and force an accepted political instrument. . . .[28]

Even closer to home, how many people in this country realize that over a million fellow North Americans met their death in this century as a result of prolonged civil war and revolution directed toward creating a new society? Frank Tannenbaum, writing in the 1930s about Mexico, notes that after the 1910 revolution,

rebellion and murder are still elements in political technique. The last 120 years were almost constant turmoil . . . the acceptance of death by violence was almost passive. One who has travelled in Mexico and has talked to the people will have learned this simple fact. Political life is still lived with guns at hand. . . . as long as politicians and soldiers can, at will, shift public policies, change laws, betray aspirations, make promises meaningless, the old habits will be employed for old ends and politics will continue to be what they have been: the threat of murder, pillage, force, fire and treason until the end, which is death.[29]

Nations do not, however, fall apart. Power is consolidated, reforms fashioned, policy formulated. To take one final historical example, one of the greatest social scientists also cried out for the need for stability: in the middle of the seventeenth century, Thomas Hobbes believed that his description of the life of man as "solitary, poor, nasty, brutish, and short" was a literal description of the condi-

---

[27] J. H. Plumb, *Men and Places* (Harmondsworth: Penguin, 1963), p. 20.

[28] John J. Johnson, *Political Change in Latin America: The Emergence of the Middle Sector* (Stanford, Calif.: Stanford University Press, 1958), p. 62.

[29] Frank Tannenbaum, *Peace by Revolution: Mexico after 1910* (New York: Columbia University Press, 1966), pp. 104–5.

tions of the age. If, as has been claimed, the great merit of Hobbes was to have raised more vigorously and systematically than any before him the problems of order—to recognize that the existence of order is problematic, and to ask how social order is possible—was his answer really one that we would like to live with today? Or is Hobbes's prescription one that we would like simply to reserve for the "less-developed" countries? Carl Friedrich finds that the search for power in the seventeenth century parallels a similar quest in our own time:

> The statesmen of this age made a cult of power and of its adornments: the vast spectacle, the impenetrable intrigue, the gruesome murder. Power has always been one of man's dominant ends, in the search of one of his great passions. But probably no age allowed this passion to become so all-engulfing, unless it be our own, in many ways so strangely akin to the baroque period. Hence, Thomas Hobbes, self-styled "child of fear," in his uncompromising adulation of power, coined perhaps the age's most revealing phrase: "so that in the first place I put for the general inclination of all mankind, a perpetual and ruthless desire of power, after power, that ceaseth only in death."[30]

Friedrich goes on to maintain that there was a common core to the political and economic thought of the seventeenth century, and this core was man's new sense of power to shape his own society and his own destiny. Friedrich questions only whether the modern state emerged in this period because its most important representatives were filled with a sense of power, or whether they were filled with a sense of power because modern states emerged. He brooks no doubt that the two developments molded the mental outlook of the time.[31] The seventeenth century increasingly understood the state as a secular organization with "practical and expedient rather than moral objectives," an organization directed to the acquisition of stability. To the modern social scientist concerned with stability, nothing is more self-evident. Yet we must remember that even during the seventeenth century, John Lilburne and Gerard Winstanley argued programs that were quite different from those of Thomas Hobbes. The Levelers proposed programs of political equality, and the Diggers argued for radical economic communalism, a program that the time considered Utopian, the object of a miniscule minority of fanatics. But these programs echoed down through the ages. Their followers considered these matters of much greater import than the seeking out of stability. Then as now, some persons wanted more than stability and asked, "Stability for whom and in whose interest?"

In comparison with the historical experiences of Europe, as well as with other, non-Western "underdeveloped" countries, the condition of African societies does not suffer. Indeed, one of the foremost modern spokesmen for Latin America, Celso Furtado, in comparing African and Asian countries with those of the Southern Hemisphere, ar-

[30] Carl J. Friedrich, *The Age of Baroque, 1610–1660* (New York: Harper & Row, 1952), p. 36.
[31] *Ibid.,* pp. 12–13.

gues that "in Latin America there is a general feeling of living through a period of decline, that 'easy' development based on exporting primary products or of 'import substitution' has run its course," that the "margin of self-determination . . . is going to be reduced as the 'security' measures of the United States require a greater alienation of the sovereignity of national government." On the other hand, one can find that in Africa the "memory of recently achieved victories injects optimism into the behavior of these people even to the point of their overestimating their resources and possibilities in their effort to overcome underdevelopment."[32] There are, therefore, good reasons for the cry of Mtshali:

> Have hope, brother
> Despair is for the defeated.[33]

Phases of African Political Development

Clearly discernible patterns of political evolution in the political history of Africa's new states enable us to distinguish among events and to foresee possibilities for future development. One purpose of our analysis is to create or to at least suggest the framework that would give us a clearer idea of the significance of these events. If we can also indicate a patterned response and a systematic handling of the major problems of new countries, we would be well on the way toward showing the difference between mere "change" and "development" rooted in political, economic, and technological-bureaucratic structures.

Since the end of the Second World War, virtually all African states have undergone or are experiencing three phases of political development: (1) the winning of formal independence; (2) the consolidation of power—that is, the founding of the basic framework, institutions, and political parameters of the new state—and (3) the restructuring of society and the forging of a new bureaucratic apparatus necessary to establish the psychological and technological framework for development.

The First Stage: The Winning of Formal Independence

Nkrumah warned his countrymen, "Seek ye first the political kingdom and all else shall be granted."[34] In the French territories it wasn't until the late '50s that most African political leaders sought independence as the prerequisite for self-determination. We can, therefore, in examining the evolution of African states, begin with the fundamental distinction between those countries that have gained their formal independence and those (such as areas of southern Africa) that have not.

[32] Celso Furtado, *Obstacles to Development in Latin America* (Garden City, N.Y.: Anchor Books, 1970), pp. 3–4.

[33] Oswald Mbuyeseni Mtshali, *Sounds of a Cowhide Drum* (New York: Third Press, 1972), p. 64.

[34] See his autobiography, *Ghana* (London and New York: Thomas Nelson, 1957).

Confronting the colonial regime was not the only difficulty of African leaders in the late '50s. Indigenous social forces contended for strategic positions from which to take control at the dawn of independence, and often basically disagreed on the framework and nature of the future state. In Algeria the FLN (Front de Libération Nationale) fought the colonial regime in the bloodiest fighting on the continent for many years, before the French relinquished their hegemony. Violent confrontations took place also in the Cameroons, the Ivory Coast, and the Sudan. Demonstrations against colonial institutions flared up in Senegal, Ghana, and Nigeria. In Kenya and in the Congo peasants and farmers, more radical than their western-trained civil servant allies, exploded in anti-European movements of great violence and bitterness.

We can discern two very different processes by which political independence occurred. In one case, a nationalist leadership succeeded in forging an organizational weapon composed of masses of citizens who either engaged in direct action or prepared to do so. In the second case, a coalition of indigenous notables reached an agreement with the colonial establishment for the *de jure* transfer of the symbols of sovereignty. *De facto* power remained, as both sides knew it would, in the hands of the overseas establishment. Nothing substantial changed, or even had the potential of changing, but to remain draped in the bunting of the metropole flared too embarrassingly old-fashioned. Virtually all of the francophone states—Guinea and Mali the exceptions—acquired independence in this fashion. Throughout their political history the French sought two objectives: to inculcate into every faction in France and abroad the idea of a universal civilization that could change, but whose head remained forever in Paris; and second, to create a class, a handful of faithful African allies that would constitute their handmaidens in rule. In this they succeeded. Their "new" governments offered neither immediate novelty nor the promise of significant innovations after formal independence. Except for their turnout under the auspices of traditional religious leaders at elections and on various other politically festive occasions, the vast mass of the population did not belong to what Robert Dahl has called "the politically relevant strata of the population."[35] Their wishes could be safely overlooked, for they were not true participants. Extended political mobilization did not take place, and politics remained in the hands of technicians, western-educated members of the liberal professions, Muslim marabouts, Catholic converts, and traditional princes, who after being bitter antagonists worked out an accommodation with the Europeans.

Latin American countries gained their independence 150 years ago. They have lost their original political momentum. Their bourgeoisie succeeded in achieving their political goals and have little taste for the socialist "liberation struggles" of today.[36]

[35] See, for example, Dahl's *Who Governs; Democracy and Power in an American City* (New Haven: Yale University Press, 1961).
[36] See Regis Debray, *Revolution In the Revolution* (New York: Monthly Review Press and Grove Press, 1967).

In Africa, where leaders declared both independence and socialism their objectives, the possibility existed for simultaneous political
and social revolutions. Nationalist movements promised to rise on the
broadest social base by merging the bourgeoisie with a mass following.[37] Yet since independence the ruling African bourgeois elements,
particularly in most francophone countries, have made spare attempts
to direct themselves to the rule of urban majorities, to engage the
mass of the population in direct action, or to participate in a communal endeavor. No wonder that a sense of self-consciousness and class
grievance has not evolved. The leaders of these francophone
countries have, instead, isolated and fragmented their populations on
the bases of every nuance of religious, tribal, ethnic, and communal
separateness. No wonder, then, that they have succeeded in creating
only governmental coalitions balanced and counterbalanced by so
many ordinarily incompatible personalities that constructive action,
even should it be desired by most progressive elements, cannot be undertaken lest the whole fragile structure crumble. Labyrinthine alliances punctuated frequently by purges, cabinet changes, and sometimes coups—a variety of devices to rotate personalities without
fundamentally altering the status-quo orientation of such regimes—
are often accompanied and reinforced by labyrinthine ideologies. For
example, negritude and some versions of African socialism are doctrines meant to entertain by their erudition but not to forge an organizational unity or stimulate the throwing off of "false consciousness."[38]

Obviously, then, the period of the struggle for independence is
directly related to that of the consolidation of power. The way in
which independence comes about determines who controls the mechanisms of coercion and in large part channels the subsequent content
of the policies of the "independent" administration. These states cannot attempt to move directly on to the third stage of development—
technical encadrement. No wonder, then, that Fanon takes note of the
existence of a mass discontent that is "like the smoking ashes of a
burnt down house after the fire has been put out which still threaten
to burst into flames again."[39] Fanon tells us that, in 1789 "after the
bourgeois revolution, the smallest French peasants benefited substantially from the upheaval. But it is a commonplace to observe and
to say that in a majority of cases, for 95% of the population of underdeveloped countries, independence brings no immediate change."[40]

---

[37] Regis Debray, *Strategy for Revolution* (New York: Monthly Review Press, 1970), pp. 76–77.

[38] Among the works that insist on the cultural unity of Black Africa from different perspectives are
Deuxieme, Congres des Ecrivains et Artistes Noirs, L'unité des cultures Negro-Africaines (Paris: Presence
Africaine, 1957); and Jacques J. Maquet, *Africanity: The Cultural Unity of Black Africa* (New York: Ox-
ford University Press, 1972).

Negritude is a doctrine that argues the essential unity of all black civilizations. For an extended bibliography and critique, see Irving Leonard Markovitz, *Leopold Sedar Senghor and the Politics
of Negritude* (New York: Atheneum, 1969; London: Heinemann Educational Books, 1970).

[39] *The Wretched of the Earth*, p. 75.

[40] *Ibid.*

In this phenomenon there is an element of continuity, for as we shall argue below, not only are there direct links between the ancient and modern rulers, but in these past and present African states the mass of the farmers and peasants were and continue to be mute, objects manipulated by their "betters." Whether this manipulation is for fraternalistic or exploitative purposes, leaders in positions of great power exercise unilateral control of the inhabitants' opportunities in life. Even those sincere in their endeavors to increase economic growth rely upon the authority and manipulation of "experts" in social engineering as well as upon the know-how of agricultural technicians in expanding production. Improved seeds and fertilizers, they feel, will eventually wither away the supernatural and feudal bases of the traditional leaders' strength. They do not call upon the people as the mechanisms for their own improvement.

The Second Stage: The Consolidation of Power

The struggle for power never really comes to an end. Regimes long in office are frequently overthrown. Ethnic loyalties long dormant can again come to the fore. Within the last few years conflagrations in Ireland, Belgium, Greece (is Greece ready for self-government?), and France hurl this consideration into our faces. Yet consolidation does not necessarily imply "cementification," the freezing of one force into control forever. What does occur are patterns of settling down into *systems* of government. The different types of objectives and opposition constitute two distinct subphases of this process. Distinguishing "opposition" into different categories provides one dramatic way of looking at the consolidation of power.

Three patterns and styles of opposition differentiate types of regimes within the emerging stability of the new African states. First, we find an "external" opposition, one usually espousing a *Weltanschauung* type of politics—that is, a fight to the death for a world view—a political position that immediately places this opposition outside the possibility of compromise with the governing constellation. Total systems confront each other unable or unwilling to give in because they define issues in moral terms. The exceptional bitterness engendered by all *Weltanschauung* confrontations is intensified during transitional periods, where the "rules of the game" have not been laid out, where methods for nonviolent coming to terms do not exist in the national legacy, and where the political world must be created anew.

To create the symbols of a common loyalty and to extend the reach of the central government over the extent of a given territory are the basic goals of this period of the consolidation of power. Issues very similar to those debated at the Constitutional Convention of the newborn American states—strong centralized government versus decentralized confederation, direct versus indirect systems of elections, regionalized administrations versus concentrated administrations, secular versus supernatural bases of legitimacy—stir the greatest turmoil.[41]

The second type of opposition, more familiar to American readers, operates within the perimeters of the extant framework of government. Knowing how to keep the peace better than anything else, this opposition poses no fundamental challenge to the reigning authorities. Content to work within the stipulated areas of agreement and disagreement, this "constructive" opposition shores up the given establishment. It differs over specific pieces of legislation, argues over procedure, disagrees possibly on matters of emphasis or on the pace of instituting various proposals or reforms, but seeks above all to replace the reigning set of individuals with its own people. It hopes for a share of the spoils rather than alternative, radically different proposals.[42] Since the conditions for the existence of democracy as well as its definition will be discussed in Chapter IX, let me simply point out here that in all underdeveloped countries, "me-too" parties as well as those built around "single issues" or personalities have a rough time surviving—not because of the risk of physical annihilation, but simply because when they are out of power their sugar is less sweet. Parties that offer a real choice to the Tweedledee and Tweedledum parties of the establishment are seldom tolerated.[43]

If "me-tooism" won't work because most people feel that it is better to have a bird in the hand than a bird in the bush, desperation might well drive even this "good" opposition beyond the pale of both public esteem and government toleration. This dilemma helps explain why so many legitimate opposition groups choose to combine voluntarily with the prevailing powers. In richer lands with longer historical experience, the rotation of at least lesser offices, or even merely the promise of the prospect of the rotation of office, often suffices to buy off those dissenters who have sufficient confidence in the system to foresee that their time will come. What grounds do members of the "outs" in new countries have for such a belief, particularly when they know that those in power might welcome a minority in parliament as window dressing but would certainly reckon again should their worthy opponents win unexpectedly at the polls?[44] This second type of constructive opposition generally functions as the process of state consoli-

---

[41] For examples of this type of opposition, see Chapter IX for the discussions of Ghana in 1966 and particularly that of the United Party and National Liberation Movement. See also the discussion of how the Marxist-Leninist parties of Senegal and the Cameroons were squelched. One of the worst clashes of race and class occurred between landless African peasants and a politically dominant Arab landowning minority, leading to revolution in Zanzibar in 1964. See also the discussion in Chapter IX of the class-based social revolutions in Burundi and Rwanda.

[42] For a further discussion of these points in third world countries, see Asoka Mehta, *Democratic Socialism* (Bombay: Bharatiya Vidya Bhavan, 1959); and Angela Burger, *Opposition in a Dominant Party System* (Berkeley and Los Angeles: University of California Press, 1969).

[43] See, for example, the case of Dennis et al. v. The United States, 341 U.S. 494 (1951).

[44] No leader of the third world has better analyzed the dilemmas of a "constructive opposition" than Asoka Mehta, formerly of the Praja Socialist Party in India, in a series of publications. Practically every governing party in Africa has a long history of mergers; consider, for example, the history of the UPS in Senegal, where every change in name marked the swallowing up of the various opposition parties.

dation becomes more advanced. Toleration comes more willingly when the governing party becomes more secure and feels less threatened, either because they have secured consensus about the framework of the state or because they have built up the mechanisms of coercion. Knowing they have the power to crack down should dissenters become threatening, they can more easily open new doors of freedom. Overseas, trained intellectuals may sometimes remember their Magna Charta or momentarily respond to international pressures, but pressures such as these do not endure—particularly when the chances are great that this "constructive opposition" will be popularly discredited (for various reasons, discussed especially in Chapter IX).

The stage is then set—again, let me emphasize that there is nothing ironclad about this—for the emergence of still another qualitatively different type of opposition. This opposition emerges from the mass base of the governing party. This is its major characteristic. Often this emergence is spontaneous, caused by the withering of the channels of communication between the organization leaders and followers at the same time that the "legitimate" opposition became discredited. All political parties in Africa are and have been "reconciliation" parties—that is, nonmonolithic, nontotalitarian conglomerates of a variety of interests.[45] Often directed against neither the policies nor the outstanding leaders of the ruling administration, this spontaneous internal opposition is sometimes simply born of frustration and desperation, even though a specific event or piece of legislation might have stimulated its coalescence. What is involved here is more than just factional disputes or parochial disagreements by disgruntled elements of the coalition. The challenge raised, though within the rubric of the given legitimacy, cuts to the heart of the system. Class issues, matters of felt betrayal, or government unresponsiveness can be at stake. One outstanding example of internal opposition occurred in 1961 in Ghana when the dock workers and the railway and municipal employees wildcatted in despair over aspects of the government's austerity program. The workers stayed out despite appeals by both their government-controlled union and the Convention People's Party that they had helped found and bring to power. The emergence of such an opposition frequently signals the government's loss of legitimacy. In such a crisis, the regime is often faced with the choice of whether to seek compromise or turn the guns of its armies against its own supporters and have the revolution consume its own children.[46]

Directed first against the *Weltanschauung* opposition and then against commonly accepted "threats to the public quarter," the coercive as well as bureaucratic apparatus can grow strong enough to give

---

[45] See David Apter's distinction between reconciliation systems, mobilization systems and modernizing autocracies, in "Systems, Process and the Politics of Economic Development," in *Industrialization and Society,* ed. Bert F. Hoselitz and Wilbert E. Moore (The Hague: Mouton, 1963), pp. 135–59.

[46] See Irving Leonard Markovitz, "The Three Stages of African Post-Colonial Development," in *African Politics and Society,* ed. Markovitz, pp. 1–13.

the new regime strength that was missing at the advent of independence, an ominous option that may evolve into systematic repression.
The striking rise of huge new office buildings and government
centers, the marked presence of tens of thousands of new civil servants on the streets of the cities, and the skyrocketing sums poured
into the administrations indicate that the African regime has reached
a new stage of development, one that is unlike any known before.

The Third Stage: Technology, Democracy, and the Problems of Encadrement

For development to occur, certain material and psychological requisites must be instituted. Economic growth requires not only tractors,
improved seed, and technical know-how, but a willingness on the part
of the population to utilize the fruits of Newtonian science. The organizational capability of integrating the exchange of goods, services,
and information on a nation-wide basis is also necessary. These needs
and goals necessitate bureaucracy and an expanded state apparatus as
well as new types of membership associations. In traveling through
rural areas, the presence or absence of the regional and local
branches of various departments and corporations differentiates African countries. Returning to the same village over a number of years,
one notes in the build-up of the *"fonctionnaires"* some of the most visible physical changes. What is needed, therefore, is a "web of activity"
linking together diverse people in multiple activities and reinforcing
networks of interaction. "Encadrement" conveys the sense of this activity strikingly, for it connotes the reorganization of the population
into a "cadre," a framework for development.

Within the last twenty years, an incredible expansion of the size
and activities of the bureaucracy and the number of civil servants at
all levels has occurred, in response to three major developments: (1)
"Africanization" as the result of progress toward independence; (2)
the expansion of governmental activities in response to the rising demands of an expanded, "politically relevant" population; and (3) an
extension of the bureaucracy into rural areas and to other social
groups that are lower in the hierarchal structure of governmental activities and programs. Until recently in the twentieth century, the basic philosophy of virtually all Western governments was: "That government is best that governs least." Colonial regimes in particular
engaged in only the basic tasks of maintaining law and order and contented themselves with maintaining a classic Hobbesian framework in
which private interest—religious or economic—could operate. Expanded education, increasing independence, and "the revolution of
rising expectations" changed all that. The emergence of all the new
civil servants and politicians responding to these changes is part and
parcel of a web of historical trends that Weber saw as the "rationalization" of societies and that others have called "modernization."[47]

[47] See Max Weber, *The Protestant Ethic and the Spirit of Capitalism* (New York: Scribner's, 1958), pp. 13–31.

The major differences among African countries have to do with where they stand in the process of bureaucratization. Most regimes have already "Africanized" their administrative apparatus, but to different degrees. Vast differences in levels of technical competence exist. In some countries, even key policy makers remain European. In other parts of Africa, the major difficulty is the creation and expansion of vitally necessary organization. However, the central problems of African bureaucracy increasingly revolve around its effective operation, not only in terms of its rational, predictable, and intended day-to-day workings, but also in terms of its responsibility to a nonprofessional popular constituency.

Every regime in Africa, no matter what its political complexion, has attempted encadrement. Increasingly, every political party, no matter how conservative, must do something, if not about the misery of the mass of the population, then at least about the fact that fewer and fewer social groups are willing to accept their "historical lot." Different political systems have claimed two ways of mentally and physically restructuring their population: either by a commitment to some sort of ideological system, or through an allegedly nonideological pragmatic endeavor to manipulate the environment on wholly technical grounds that I have dubbed "technicity." Ideological commitments ranging from African socialism to African capitalism define the political and social paths of most governments. The technical approach to encadrement claims to be above politics and leaves matters of ideology for the soothsayers. Technicians espousing their nonideological expertise have advocated every type of policy in every country of the world from Communist China to Eichmann's Germany. An inquiry into who the technicians are, and an examination of their claim to objectivity are among the purposes of the present study. Although no one can quarrel with objectivity as an ideal, this study argues that the technicians represent one aspect of the rise of an organizational bourgeoisie in Africa; "technicity" constitutes a major element in the ideology that justifies their rule.

The army-led coups that overthrew the first generation of leaders and parties that brought their countries through the first period of independence represent in great measure the logical culmination of this tendency. Insofar as organization, hierarchy, efficiency, innovation, and the mobilization of men and resources are characteristically highly prized goals sought by the technocrats, these objectives are also shared by the army commanders. Yet whether the professionals wear uniforms or not, among the difficulties associated with "technicity" that we must consider is the failure of development that stems from an unwillingness on the part of farmers to heed the advice of those who by their mental set as well as their style of life proclaim themselves foreigners, even when these "foreigners" want to do their job and not simply fill their pockets. A serious question also arises as to whether the job will in any event be done. The "invisible hand" of classic capitalism cracked its wretched "economic whip" in the marketplace, threatening starvation to those who would not compete to their utmost. Socialism holds forth a communal ethic and prospects for a nonalienated future. What will prevent the workings of bureaucratic paycheck cashers from degenerating into chaos and corruption? Above all, we must see if the new professionals acknowledge the distinction between economic growth and economic development. Economic growth means simply the increase of the total amount of goods and services produced in any particular country. This measure tells us nothing about how the material goods of society are distributed. Most African leaders, particularly the first generation at the advent of independence, have spoken knowingly and carefully about economic development. They wish to produce a high standard of living and a good life for all of their people, not just the talented tenth or the civil servants or the lawyers, doctors, and intellectuals. Many social scientists don't know enough to make this distinction. Many economists argue that the distinction is not necessary because with sufficient economic growth economic development will take place automatically. From the time of Adam Smith, "bourgeois" economists have maintained that wealth would eventually trickle down to even the bottom strata of a developing society. Today, the technological determinists maintain the same type of argument: with the systematic application of Newtonian science and sufficient capital, the same pattern of development that occurred in the United States will happen everywhere. Over an extended period of time, previously deprived groups—following, for example, the classic case of the American labor movement in the past and blacks today—will be bought off and incorporated into a fantastically abundant producing economy. Yet even in the United States the "invisible poor," the "permanently unemployed," the "forgotten third" persist. In African cities today, marks of affluence are apparent. Skyscrapers, four-lane highways, supermarkets, and villas attest that some economic growth has occurred and that some Africans have benefited. Incredibly, however, in a number of African countries the absolute—not relative—standard of living of large numbers of farmers has declined since independence. In Senegal, for example, and in Ghana, commodity farmers in the '70s returned to the raising of subsistence crops because they could not live on their income from the marketplace. Improvements in scientific techniques and increases in agricultural and industrial production have resulted frequently in widening the gap between the rich and the poor. Even those social scientists most reluctant to acknowledge the existence of classes have on occasion admitted that "patterns of restratification" and the solidification of inequities have accompanied the rise of the gross national product.

Systematic mobilization of the mass of the population bears certain possibilities for a more humane society. One such possibility is a quicker awakening of the population to new opportunities. Peasants and village dwellers are not idiots; when they discover that the new technology is for *them,* they will be quick to absorb innovations and increased opportunities. A second possibility is social equity in the distribution of the benefits of development. The historical evidence for this possibility is not sanguine. The term "new class," after all, came out of Communist Yugoslavia. Yet if devising systems of meaningful popular participation taxes our imagination, the failure of the trickle-down mechanism for the distribution of benefits and the narrow-based social origins of those who today are the prime beneficiaries of development impose upon us the necessity for additional efforts in this direction. Third, without the creation of a mass-based political alternative to many of the existing backward-looking coalitions, real social progress is impossible. An alternative power base is essential for undertaking the radical reorganization and restructuring of these societies. As long as extensive social mobilization does not take place, this stipulated objective of many of those African parties that desire to create a more humanistic form of African socialism cannot be accomplished. Those regimes that are most successful in aligning their goals and philosophy with the appropriate social base will succeed best in forging the type of stability that will enhance and push forward their social objective.

Before concluding this overview and introduction, two additional aspects of the consolidation of power and the political development of these new African states must be emphasized. First, my use of the term "stages" does not imply "inevitable progress." The days of Condorcet are long gone. That economically underdeveloped African countries will follow the path of industrialization toward the high standard of living of the richer nations remains an open question.[48] My foremost concern in this introduction has been to indicate that stability is not necessarily the primary problem of the African states and that historically there is certainly a basis for optimism. Second, although a certain logic links the three major problem areas of the struggle for power, consolidation, and encadrement, many of the tasks that I have discussed do not in fact take place in a strict chronological order. Amilcar Cabral, for example, leader of the PAIGC (Independence Movement of Portuguese Guinean Cape Verde Islands), insisted in theory as well as in the practical administration of areas controlled by the guerillas that he led, that encadrement take place simultaneously with the conflict against the Portuguese. He set up a political and social administration that included health services and educational facilities, and he encouraged a more scientific farming for the peasants in the region, while he held himself and his men responsible to the people that he presumed to lead. With renewed poignancy, Cabral brought into Africa the idea that the ends are contained within the means sought for their achievement; that the beginnings of the type of African socialism he hoped to achieve were to be sought right there in the heat of the revolution against the Portuguese.[49] Considering the perversion of the original goals of revolutions despite the

[48] See the discussion on Andre Gunder Frank and W. W. Rostow. See also Rheinhard Bendix, *Nation-Building and Citizenship* (New York: John Wiley, 1964), pp. 8–9.

[49] Amilcar Cabral, *Revolution in Guinea* (New York: Monthly Review Press, 1969). See also Edgar Snow's description of the Chinese Communist agricultural organization at the time of their civil war against Chiang Kai-shek, *Red Star Over China*, rev. and enl. ed. (New York: Grove Press, 1968).

best effort of their leaders, Cabral's understanding and insights provide an important warning against a too schematic anticipation of future developments.

Development is a cruel process with no great happy ending, no limitless progress. "Developed" societies are not "happy" societies. Neither are they necessarily rich, at least in the sense that all things can be done and all interests accommodated easily. Developed societies are still cruel societies in their treatment of ethnic minorities, the aged, and criminals. Yet as the new African countries settle into patterns that will prevail for generations to come, the process of development might become crueler still. To explore some of these problems is the purpose of this study.

Chapter II

AFRICA'S DUAL HERITAGE:
Imperialism and
Precolonial Greatness

Political Reasons for the Study of Africa's Past

Magicians who did tricks with the past, colonial overlords caused African history to vanish so that their own rule would be more lasting. This is the first reason why the reassertion of the *fact* of African history is so important. The denial of an African past was part of an effort at dehumanization. Colonialism turned people into objects in order to facilitate their manipulation. Colonialism sought to eliminate that inner tension of men possessed of a critical intelligence by denying them their ability, and their "right," to question. All repressive systems use ideology and psychological coercion in addition to physical violence to buttress their rule. All governments, regardless of their ideological content, seek to establish their "authority" as well as their power. They seek to convince their subjects that the state has the *right* to command and the people are morally *obligated* to obey. The state, they maintain, fulfills suprahuman tasks necessary for the common good. History is a weapon for these purposes.

Colonialism used the denial of African history to establish the necessity of the "white man's burden" and to argue that it was advancing the cause of mankind. From that vast majority of Africans who could not be bludgeoned or brainwashed into active support of the *mission civilatrice*, colonialism sought acquiescence and apathy. The colonizers insisted on a division between private activities and the affairs of society. Africans were not worthy to deal with public matters. Africans must dig only in their own gardens. To the extent that colonialism succeeded in inducing this schizophrenia, it isolated individuals in their own world of mundane concerns. Collective action became more difficult; resistance, harder to organize. Yet resistance to the colonial regimes appeared everywhere on the continent. To better understand the *fact* of this early resistance and its connections with modern nationalism is a second important reason to investigate African history.

Architects of unity, African political leaders through the ages have sought seriously to discover elements of a common past that once linked now hostile ethnic groups. African nationalists wish to bind these peoples together with the threads of this history. Their task is a double one: (1) to fight the colonizer, the outsider; and (2) to unify, consolidate, and maintain their newly won power.

African nations seek to remake their past, and in the sense of Renan's warning, "every nation must forget its past before it can begin to reconstitute it," they forge a new myth of a common previous identity. In this sense, African nationalist movements also forget in order to remember.

Yet the truth of the past is vital for our better understanding of contemporary African politics. History helps us better grasp the nature of "tribalism" as well as of empire. Tribal identities, then as now, changed as peoples came into contact with one another and parted. Urban areas, centuries ago, performed the same melting-pot functions they do in Africa today. Important connections still remain between the great societies of the past and those of the present. But not all of these links and not all of the memories are of glory.

A third reason for an inquiry into the political development of previous centuries is to better recognize the stratified nature of many of even the most famous traditional systems. Their structures of rule are related to the organizational bourgeoisie of present regimes. All African societies were not communitarian or egalitarian; many were based on developed class structures. The ruling families of these kingdoms differed fundamentally from ordinary men: in the vital resources of land and labor; in their eating of meat rather than millet; and in the adornments of body and home. The development of trade is instructive because it illustrates the connections between the men of commerce and the political system—persistent links cemented over the years. Those in command could endure when the economic basis of African societies changed from feudalism to slavery and then again to "legitimate commerce." Trade associated with the rise of great African empires also helps explain resistance to colonialism. European and African empires collided as competitors and fought over the division of territory and spoils. Black Islam was associated with the rise of new African empires, with resistance to colonialism, with trade, and with the emergence of new social classes. A reforming Islam overthrew in their *jihads* (holy wars) feudal lords' and warriors' aristocracies. Islamic movements during the eighteenth and nineteenth centuries facilitated the rise of capitalism and the social transition from caste to class, processes that were essential for modern political development to take place.

For all of these reasons we must look to Africa's past—not as chronicles of antiquity but because of our interest in who is in control in the present. Systems of stratification continue to reflect earlier social divisions. Patterns of land ownership and control of scarce resources that were developed over the centuries still endure. An inquiry into African history will thus demonstrate not only the elements of greatness in civilizations but also that the mass of people—then as now, in Africa as everywhere—passively accepted a fate that was dealt to them not by the deities but by men of greater power. From resistance to colonialism to the consolidation of the power of the organizational bourgeoisie, the *facts* of African history are vital.

Ancient Great Kingdoms of North, West, Central, and East Africa

A leading anthropologist has written of African states that "in the thoroughness of their political institutions and in the skill with which social institutions were utilized to lend stability to the political structure, they far exceeded anything in Europe prior to the 16th century."[1] Any study of African traditional societies must emphasize their variety and complexity as well as their greatness. In the precolonial era, many traditional societies numbered 100,000 people or more, and a few passed the million mark. For example, Ganda in the nineteenth century comprised between 500,000 and 1,000,000 people.[2]

Nok culture flourished in northern Nigeria as early as the fourth or perhaps even the fifth century B.C., working iron and producing terra-cotta sculpture of great beauty and sophistication.[3] Despite allegations that writing did not occur south of the Sahara before the European and Arab intrusions, recent discoveries show that the priests of the African state of Meroe invented an alphabet toward the third century B.C.[4] The Meroites, who presided over a distinctive civilization that flourished for 700 years, originally used Egyptian hieroglyphics, but at the height of their power — in 300 or 200 B.C. — they invented an alphabet of their own. Over 800 fragmentary texts have been found in this Meroitic script, but scholars have thus far deciphered practically none of them. Other wholly African-invented scripts, such as the recently unveiled Mandingo, indicate the extent of our previous ignorance.

The first known written record bearing on sub-Saharan Africa comes from the pen of an Egyptian seafarer, who in about A.D. 60 published a mariners' handbook for the Indian Ocean coast. The author of this account, entitled *Periplus of the Erythraean Sea*, briefly described the hazards and advantages of sailing on the East African coast as far south as Tanganyika. He pointed out that a voyage would normally take twenty-three days from a point just south of Cape Guardafui on the horn of Africa to as far as Rhatta, the last market town on the East African mainland. (The exact location of Rhatta is now unknown. At that time the town was probably very important as an exporter of ivory to India.)[5] An even earlier record of trade between Egypt and sub-Saharan Africa, found on the tomb of an Aswan

---

[1] Ralph Linton, *The Tree of Culture* (New York: Vintage Books, 1959), p. 170.

[2] Margaret Chave Fallers, *The Eastern Lacustrine Bantu* (London: International African Institute, 1960), p. 52; quoted in Gerhard E. Lenski, *Power and Privilege* (New York: McGraw-Hill, 1966), p. 148.

[3] Frank Willet, *African Art: An Introduction* (New York: Praeger, 1971), p. 68.

[4] Basil Davidson, *The African Past* (New York: Grosset & Dunlap, 1967), p. 65.

[5] *Ibid.*, pp. 20–21. See also Davidson's *The African Genius* (Boston: Little, Brown, Atlantic Monthly Press, 1969); and Roland Oliver and Brian M. Fagan, *Africa in the Iron Age: c 500 B.C. to A.D. 1400* (London: Cambridge University Press, 1975).

nobleman of the sixth dynasty, or about 2340 B.C., tells of a forty-day overland journey to bring back ebony, ivory, and frankincense from Darfur.[6]

If African societies were so great in the past, where is the evidence for this today? skeptics demand. Evidence does in fact exist, but we must also keep in mind that not all social developments, even in technology, have been in the direction of "progress." One of the most striking examples of this is the apparent disappearance of writing in Greece between 1100 and 800 B.C.[7] Whatever the final explanation for the eventual "decline" of the great African empires, the phenomenon is similar to the rise and fall of great empires elsewhere in the world. On a universal scale, historians and social scientists from Aristotle to Toynbee have critically assessed and argued this problem. How great an impact Egyptian civilization had on the lands to her south remains an unexplored frontier in history. No one questions that the impact was extensive. Cheikh Anta Diop, taking the archaeological evidences of contact, boldly reverses the usual hypothesis of culture contact and argues that African states and peoples influenced Egypt, rather than vice versa. Moreover, Diop maintains, Egyptian civilization at its origins was black.[8] Though still controversial, Diop's central thesis has gained support over the years. For example, Frank Willet, one of the leading authorities on African art, describes the art of predynastic Egypt as showing essentially African characteristics dating from 3100 B.C. Willet maintains that far from being a potent source of influence on African Art, "Egyptian art is seen to be a local manifestation of a wide-spread African tradition."[9] The ancient Egyptians called the land to their south Kush. This, the most ancient of the independent king-

---

[6] Basil Davidson, *op. cit.,* p. 44.

[7] Jack Goody, *Technology, Tradition and the State in Africa* (London: Oxford University Press, 1971).

[8] See Cheikh Anta Diop, *Nations Nègres et culture* (Paris: Presence Africaine, 1955); *L'unite' culturelle de l'Afrique Noire* (Paris: Presence Africaine, 1959); *Les fondements culturels, techniques et industriels d'un futur etat federal d'Afrique Noire* (Paris: Presence Africaine, 1966); and *Anteriorité des civilisations Negrés: mythe ou vérité historique?* (Paris: Presence Africaine, 1967). See also Leopold Sedar Senghor, *Les fondements de l'Africanité ou Negritude et Arabité* (Paris: Presence Africaine, 1967); and Frank Snowden, *Blacks in Antiquity* (Cambridge, Mass.: Harvard University Press, 1970).

Obenga Theophile, a student of Cheikh Anta Diop, provides further linguistic, paleontological, and physical anthropological evidence in support of Diop's thesis in his *L'Afrique dans l'antiquité: Egypte pharonique—Afrique-Noire* (Paris: Presence Africaine, 1973). See also John Strong, "Egypt Under the Rule of Kush, Racism and Historiography," *Pan-African Journal*, 6, no. 4 (Winter 1973), 397–408.

Selections from Diop's works have recently been translated into English as *The African Origin of Civilization: Myth or Reality* (New York and Westport, Conn.: Lawrence Hill, n.d.). John Henrik Clarke, in his review of this translation (*Presence Africaine*, No. 90, 2nd Quarterly [1974], 280–83), discusses some of Diop's difficulties in having his thesis accepted.

Diop also argued that African societies did not develop because they had reached a "stage of perfect equilibrium." He maintains that in Senegal his own people, the Wolof, even though separated into castes, had achieved a harmonious and cooperative division of labor. Boubacar Barry in *Le royaume du waalo: Le Senegal avant la conquete* (Paris: Francois Maspero, 1972), disagrees. He maintains that Wolof castes facilitated exploitation of the peasantry by using the state for this purpose; rather than stability, castes also produced stagnation (see p. 322.)

In 1966, Diop gained recognition from the Festival of Negro Arts meeting in Dakar as the "Black intellectual who has exercised the most fruitful influence in the 20th century." See also my assessment of Diop in *African Politics and Society: Basic Issues and Problems of Government and Development*, ed. Irving Leonard Markovitz (New York: Free Press; London: Collier-Macmillan, 1970), p. 15.

[9] Willet, *African Art*, p. 112.

doms of Africa, covered most of what is today known as the Republic of the Sudan. Linked closely to the history of Egypt since about 2000 B.C., Kush was at times a province under forced occupation. But at other times, when the Egyptians had to withdraw to confront invaders such as the Libyans or to settle their own internal disputes, it stood relatively unencumbered by external control. Around 1100 B.C., Egypt's control over its empire began to disintegrate. A Kushite king named Kashta not only broke away but invaded and conquered Egypt as far north as Thebes, the capital of Upper Egypt. Soon after 700 B.C., the son of Kashta, Piankhy, completed the conquest of Egypt and became the African ruler of a land that extended over almost a quarter of the African continent—from modern Ethiopia to the shores of the Mediterranean. Kushite kings ruled over Egypt as the Pharaohs of the twenty-fifth dynasty.[10] Forced to leave Egypt some 200 years later, the Kushite rulers moved their capital south to Meroe (whose ruins can today be found about 100 miles north of modern Khartoum), where they presided over a distinctive civilization that flourished for another 700 years. The Axumites, who were originally from the southern tip of Arabia, created a kingdom on the west coast of the Red Sea and absorbed the wealth and trade of Meroe as the power of the Kushites declined. About A.D. 350, the army of King Aezanes of Axum finally crushed the remnants of Kush.[11] Trade and military connections with Axum form part of the heritage of the modern state of Ethiopia. Ethiopia ranks among that rare group of world states that possess a history of more than 2,000 years. This heritage includes a dynasty that traces its origin to the Old Testament depiction of the visit of the Queen of Sheba to Solomon's court in Jerusalem. Ethiopian kings conquered a large part of southern Arabia as well as dominions on the continent. An Ethiopian army pushed back the Western colonial powers in a major defeat at the battle of Adwa.

In West Africa, the black kingdoms of Tekrur and Ghana date back to the third and fourth centuries A.D. Ghana lasted until the eleventh century, forming an empire that stretched from the Niger north to the Sahara and expanding its trade to the southern port of western Morocco. It was defended by an army of over 200,000 men, including 40,000 archers and huge cavalry forces. In the twelfth century, Ghana gave way to Mali, which had an existence of thirteen centuries. The period from the eleventh to the seventeenth century was a time of exceptional activity in Mali. The great emperor Sundiata Keita (1230–1255), ancestor of Modibo Keita, a former president of contemporary Mali, erected magnificent palaces and mosques and again extended the caravan trade. One of the fourteenth-century emperors of Mali voyaged to Mecca with a caravan of over 60,000 people and

---

[10] P. L. Shinnie, *The African Iron Age* (Oxford: Clarendon Press, 1971), pp. 24–25.

[11] Some scholars have speculated that the Kushites fled and settled in the area around Lake Chad. When Thor Heyerdahl wanted to build a reed boat for his transatlantic voyage, he found a weaver and maker of such boats not in Egypt but among the people of the Lake Chad area. See his *The Ra Expeditions* (Garden City, N.Y.: Doubleday, 1971).

80 camels; each of the latter was loaded with 300 pounds of gold dust. Also during this time, Malian rulers expanded the University of Timbuktu. Mali declined in the fourteenth century, and Songhay replaced her as the mightiest of the West African empires. Originally vassal to Mali from its origins in 700, Songhay eventually absorbed both Mali and Ghana before it fell in 1591. By the sixteenth century, Songhay had produced complex systems of laws and administration, created banking and credit arrangements to finance commerce, built systems of irrigation that brought water to the desert sector of the kingdom, instituted an official policy of toleration of religion that brought together Mohammedans, Christians, and Jews, floated great fleets of ships, and supported great intellectual centers not only at Timbuktu but also at Goa, Walata, and Jenne.[12]

By the end of the first millennium A.D., the great kingdoms of Buganda, close by Lake Victoria, Bunyoro, near Lake Albert, and Ruanda and Urundi, north of Lake Tanganyika, all incorporated extensive territory, large populations, permanent bureaucracies, and well-functioning judicial and executive systems.

In Central Africa the ruins of Zimbabwe reveal the existence of a great stone wall dating from the end of the fifteenth century, created probably by the Shona Bantu coming from the great lakes region. To this day, we know little about the great civilization necessary to have produced the city revealed by these ruins.

If we then examine either the black empires of the western Sudan or those kingdoms that emerged in the grasslands that stretch between the Niger and the Nile—especially Kanen, Bornu, the Hausa emirates, Darfur, and Sennar—we discover social and political systems at least as sophisticated as those of medieval Europe. They possessed courts that were "theatrical in their ceremony and splendor" and retinues of armored knights and quilted cavalry. As in Europe, the ruling dynasties amassed power, leeched tribute from peasants, expanded the use of metals, and thirsted after trade.[13]

These African kingdoms expanded their contacts beyond the continental limits of Africa. Exchange with China, for example, is well

[12] See, for example, Desmond J. Clark, *The Prehistory of Africa* (New York: Praeger, 1970); Lester Brooks, *Great Civilizations of Ancient Africa* (New York: Four Winds Press, 1971); J. F. Ade Ajayi and Jan Espie, eds., *A Thousand Years of West African History* (Ibadan: Ibadan University Press, 1965); Harry A. Gailey, *History of Africa from Earliest Times to 1800* (New York: Holt, Rinehart & Winston, 1970); J. D. Fage, *A History of West Africa*, rev. ed. (Cambridge: Cambridge University Press, 1969); and J. D. Fage, ed., *Africa Discovers her Past* (London: Oxford University Press, 1970). See also Roland Oliver and Anthony Atmore, *Africa Since 1880* (New York: Cambridge University Press, 1967); G. T. Stride and C. Ifeka, *Peoples and Empires of West Africa: West Africa in History, 1000–1800* (New York: Africana Publishing, 1971); J. F. Ade Ajayi and Michael Crowder, eds., *The History of West Africa*, Vols. I and II (New York: Columbia University Press, 1972, 1973; London: Longman, 1972, 1974); Basil Davidson, *A History of West Africa to the Nineteenth Century* (Garden City, N.Y.: Doubleday, Anchor Books, 1966); Robert I. Rotberg, *A Political History of Tropical Africa* (New York: Harcourt, Brace & World, 1965); and Nehemia Levtzion, *Ancient Ghana and Mali* (London: Methuen, 1973).

[13] See Alvin M. Josephy, Jr., ed., *The Horizon History of Africa* (New York: American Heritage, 1971); and Basil Davidson, *The Lost Cities of Africa* (Boston: Little, Brown, Atlantic Monthly Press, 1959), pp. 89–91.

documented, beginning with a report of an African ambassador in China in A.D. 1083. Twelfth-century porcelain in great quantities, as well as coin of the thirteenth-century Sun Dynasty, has turned up on East African beaches. By the fifteenth century, huge fleets of Chinese ships and tens of thousands of men had visited African coastal ports. By around 1450, however, these visits had ceased. From a study of science in China, Sinologists have revealed conflicts within the imperial court between sea-based and land-based factions. By 1500, these conflicts had forced the closing of the great shipyards and had eliminated a Chinese interest in ocean trade with Africa.[14] The Chinese were not again present in Africa until they participated in the Tanzanian-Zambian railway of our own time.

Pre-Columbian Transatlantic Voyages

Of all the hypotheses concerning the scope of activities of these early African empires, perhaps the most enticing concerns the possibility of Africa's discovery of the New World.[15] The argument for the existence of pre-Columbian African expeditions to the Americas is based on early travelers' reports that were previously treated as nonsense and on recent archaeological and anthropological findings. Columbus apparently had been informed when he stopped at the Cape Verde Islands, off the coast of Africa, that blacks had been known to set out for Guinea and other areas on Africa's Atlantic coast in canoes loaded with merchandise. Indians in the West Indies told Columbus that they had obtained gold from black men who had come from across the sea. Amerigo Vespucci claims to have witnessed the return of these sailors to Africa when he was in mid-ocean. Spanish conquistadors in the fifteenth and sixteenth centuries found small tribes of black men dispersed all over the New World. In 1513, for example, Balboa reported a large permanent settlement at war with the Indians. This was before the founding of Spanish colonies and the first importation of African slaves. Other colonies of blacks were discovered in northern Brazil, St. Vincent Island in the Gulf of Mexico, Venezuela, with the Zunis in New Mexico, and elsewhere. Indian legends recall the coming of black men from far-off lands. Peruvian tradition recounts how black men from the east had penetrated the Andes Mountains. Ancient Indian religions bear resemblances to those of peoples of the

---

[14] On African contacts with China during the medieval period, see Teobaldo Filesi, *China and Africa in the Middle Ages* (London: Frank Cass, 1972).

[15] The following account is drawn from Harold G. Lawrence, "African Explorers in the New World" *Crisis,* June/July, 1962. See also Heyerdahl, *The Ra Expeditions;* Roger Bastide, *African Civilization in the New World* (New York: Harper & Row Torchbook ed., 1971): Brooks, *Great Civilizations of Ancient Africa;* Ivan Van Sertina, "Bad News for Columbus Perhaps," *New York Times,* Op-Ed Page, December 4, 1975; and Legrand H. Clegg II, "Who Were the Americans", *The Black Scholar,* 7, no. 1 (September 1975), 33–41.

west coast of Africa. The Mayas, Aztecs, and Incas all worshipped black gods. Quetzalcoatl, a serpent god and god of trade, was black and woolly haired. Serpent worship still exists today in the Mandingo occupied areas of modern Mali. Various sculptured figures with black morphology have surfaced in various parts of South America, including five heads in Vera Cruz, Mexico. Archaeologists have also uncovered burial mounds, in an area ranging from the southwestern United States through Central America, that contain fossils and cowrie shells similar to West African varieties. Pre-Arabic writing systems comparable to Mandingo existed in American Indian settlements. Yams, taro, and cotton from West Africa were found in America by Columbus and Spanish explorers, just as maize from America turned up in Africa.

The wealth, power, and knowledge of Mali would have made these voyages possible in the twelfth, thirteenth, and fourteenth centuries. Books on all subjects were available, written in both Mandingo and Arabic; Djenne, Mali's second most important city, had over 4,200 teachers in the twelfth century. Mali's agricultural techniques included crop rotation, irrigation, and soil conservation. Well-kept roads, rest houses, and a postal system added to the high degree of security represented by 200,000 warriors—all this at a time when bubonic plague, famine, and constant warfare shrouded Europe. No wonder Ibn Battuta, a fourteenth-century Moorish traveler, claimed that Mali possessed the world's second highest civilization, surpassed only by that of his own Morocco. Under the Malian emperor Sakura (1285–1300), knowledge of advanced maritime techniques—including the concept of the earth as being round and an understanding of longitude and latitude, the compass, and the sexton—provided the scientific basis upon which 400 ships equipped with men, food, water, and gold were sent across the Atlantic. After Songhay established its hegemony over Mali in the fifteenth century, these transatlantic voyages resumed under Askia Mohammad Toure (1492–1529). Most of the reports from Columbus, Vespucci, and their contemporaries date from this time. The availability of scientific technology, the existence of political systems capable of great endeavors, a constantly expanding commerce and empire, a variety of reports by European explorers, legends from South America, religious beliefs traceable to Africa, and sculpture and other discoveries of archaeology—all of this evidence is capped by the physical possibility of such transatlantic voyages. Only 1,600 miles separate Africa and South America; the route is punctuated with islands and supplied with favorable currents. Belief in these transatlantic voyages remains a minority position. Nevertheless, this matter will channel great research efforts in the future. At present it at least challenges our imagination. The mere possibility of such voyages tells us a great deal about the material magnificence of the precolonial civilizations.

Precolonial Trade and How It Evolved

Who raised the provisions for the sailors of Mali and equipped their ships? Who fed the warriors of Ghana, collected the gold for the emperors of Songhay, and allowed the kabakas, asantehenes, bours, and damels the leisure and functionaries necessary to administer their kingdoms? Peasants trembled when their lords approached. In some societies common men prostrated themselves in kowtowing; in others they could come near the throne only by throwing dust and ashes on their heads. The class divisions that were as much a part of the great empires as the bronzes of Benin and the gold weights of Asante deepened with the expansion of trade and were strengthened by the quickening tempo of the dance of commodities.

Trade routes preceded and paralleled the rise of empires. A shift in trade from the interior to the coast occurred concurrently with the decline of old African empires and the rise of more recent ones. The rise and fall of empires demonstrates the essential connections developed over long centuries between parts of Africa that the colonial regimes arbitrarily separated into discrete units. For example, close bonds developed across the Sahara between governments and trading classes. The historical development of trade also tells us a great deal about the evolution of African social stratification.

Around 3,000 B.C. the Sahara began drying out, a process that has continued to the present day, resulting in recent drought and famine. The benefits of the neolithic revolution had reached both Britain and the central Sahara by that time. In Egypt the Bronze Age civilization was just beginning. The drying out of the Sahara created an increasingly great obstacle until the introduction of the camel into common commerce about the time of the birth of Christ.[16] At no point, however, was contact between the Mediterranean coast and the interior completely severed. Horses, chariots, raiding, trading, and migration parties—even before the camel—crisscrossed and linked major entrepôts. The magnitude of the massive Sahara Desert—the world's largest arid waste, stretching from the Atlantic to the Red Sea, nowhere less than 1,000 miles wide—blinds us to the fact that geographical features must always be viewed in terms of (1) the technology available at the time and (2) the political factors. Whether a desert or ocean is a highway or barrier depends on whether the sextant, compass, camel, or airplane is present to provide a new technical capacity. And whether that capacity, if present, will be utilized depends on a political will. Kwame Nkrumah, for example, stated, "If in the past the Sahara divided us, now it unites us. Today, we are one."

From ancient times, caravans pulled the continent together. The Roman city of Laptis Magna, adjacent to modern Tripoli, prospered

---

[16] See Thurstan Shaw, "The Approach Through Archaeology to Early West African History," *A Thousand Years of West African History,* ed. Ajayi and Espie, pp. 23–38.

from its location at the head of a major trans-Saharan trade route, as did the Carthaginian settlement of Lixus on the Atlantic coast of Morocco. Herodotus, writing in the fifth century B.C., was the first historian to depict regular contact across the desert waste.[17] Above all, the early trans-Saharan trade concerned salt and gold. The gold trade with Ghana was well established before the coming of the Arabs—that is, before the seventh century. By the eighth century, Arab explorers had commented profusely on the expense and organization of this trade.[18] Only those who have suffered its absence can understand the willing exchange of gold for an equal weight of salt. Bovill claims that in the western Sudan, salt was a luxury that only the rich enjoyed regularly.[19] Later, especially from the seventeenth to the nineteenth century, the same routes, particularly the road from Fezzan to Bornu, became essentially slave networks, although they continued to carry a great deal of salt—which to this day is available in great blocks in the markets of Bamako. Bovill tells us of the recorded horror of travelers along the bloodstained Fezzan-Bornu highway at "the thousands of human skeletons with which it was strewn," skeletons mainly of young women and girls, the weakest and first to fall.[20] From the earliest times, the rulers of the North African littoral used these routes to satisfy the demand for black slaves, some of whom were used locally but the majority of whom were exported to Egypt and Turkey—a trade that expanded its burden of human misery continually until the middle of the 1820s.

At first, the coming of European sea traders had little impact on the trans-Saharan trade: first, because of the size and nature of that trade, and, second, because of the sophistication and power of the African kingdoms.[21] West African empires began to import cowrie not later than the beginning of the fourteenth century. Merchants could have used cowrie shells effectively as a medium of exchange only if some sort of state organization had existed to regulate this use. Karl Polanyi has pointed out that cowrie in fact "gained the status of a currency by virtue of state policy, which regulated its use and guarded

---

[17] Fage, *A History of West Africa*, p. 60. J. B. Webster and A. A. Boahen describe the major trans-Saharan caravan routes in their *History of West Africa* (New York: Praeger, 1970), p. 66. For a slightly different version of the establishment of long-distance trade routes, see Peter Morton-Williams "The Influence of Habitat and Trade on the Politics of Oyo and Ashanti," in *Man in Africa*, ed. Mary Douglas and Phyllis M. Kaberry (Garden City, N.Y.: Doubleday, Anchor Books, 1971), pp. 82–88.

[18] E. W. Bovill, *The Golden Trade of the Moors*, 2nd ed. (New York: Oxford University Press, 1968), p. 69.

[19] *Ibid.*, p. 239.

[20] *Ibid.*, p. 245.

[21] See e.g. *Technology, Tradition and the State in Africa*, p. 24. See also A. G. Hopkins, who argues, "The pre-colonial economy was complex, efficient and adaptable, and it had reached a relatively advanced stage of commercial capitalism long before the impact of the Western world was felt in Africa" (*An Economic History of West Africa* [London: Longman, 1973], p. 293); and Ralph A. Austin, who in a review of recent historical studies stresses the continuities among various pre-colonial economies ("Economic History," *African Studies Review*, 14, no. 3 [December 1971], 425–38).

against its proliferation by preventing shiploads from being freely imported. Neither in primitive society nor later under modern conditions was such a handling of cowrie possible."[22] Polanyi then showed how the cowrie currency disappeared with the coming of the French administration and the expanding use of metallic currencies as a means of exchange.

The third reason for the relatively minor disturbance of the trans-Saharan trade was that preindustrial Europe required either luxury manufactures such as silks, drugs, and perfumes or specialized tropical crops such as spices and sugar, none of which African societies were organized to produce on a large scale for export. Indeed, some historians have argued that the primary British interest in Africa was as a source of way stations along the route to India.[23] By the eighteenth century the African supply of the two commodities in greatest demand in Europe, ivory and gold, had greatly diminished. From the seventeenth century on, expanding European capitalism, followed by the demands of the new factories sprouted by the industrial revolution, changed outside interest in Africa dramatically. Not until the nineteenth century, however, did the trans-Saharan caravan trade suffer its most serious damage, and not until the beginning of the twentieth century did the final remnants wither away.

Three main factors lay behind the final disintegration of this pattern of trade, which had lasted well over a thousand years: first, the decline in the slave trade; second, the expansion of the more attractive and richer trade along the coast to Europe; and, third, changing political conditions in the interior. By the mid nineteenth century, slaves accounted for almost half of all exports across the Sahara. Britain officially abolished the slave trade in 1807. In 1842 the bey of Tunis agreed to do the same, as did the Ottoman government fifteen years later. The French advance to Timbuktu cut off exports from the Soudan, but not until the Italian occupation of Cyrencia in 1911 was the slave trade as a commercial enterprise finally abolished.[24]

Most authorities have agreed that what finally dealt a death blow to the slave trade was not the enforcement of legalistic provisions but the competition of more attractive alternatives and commercial opportunities. According to Webster and Boahen, "Once European goods began to reach the markets of Hausaland [and other inland marketplaces], from the late 1850's onwards, at relatively cheaper prices, and in greater quantities, it was obvious that the caravan trade was bound to collapse. The camel was obviously no match for the

---

[22] Karl Polanyi "Archaic Economic Institutions: Cowrie Moneys" in *Primitive, Archaic and Modern Economies: Essays of Karl Polanyi*, ed. George Dalton (Boston: Beacon Press, 1971), pp. 298–99.

[23] This is the argument of Ronald Robinson and John Gallagher, *Africa and the Victorians* (New York: St. Martin's Press, 1961).

[24] See Bovill, *The Golden Trade of the Moors*, pp. 248–49. Also, Webster and Boahen point out in their *History of West Africa* that although the slave trade across the Atlantic was legally abolished by most of the European powers between 1807 and 1820, the attack on the slave trade across the Sahara and the Mediterranean was not even begun until 1840 (p. 64).

steam vessel!"[25] Bovill points out that the new trade routes were not only cheaper and swifter but also involved a demand for new agricultural products. For example, "the unromantic groundnut [peanut] has provided a greater and more reliable source of wealth than all the gold and all the slaves, the bundles of ostrich feathers and the loads of ivory carried by camel caravan across the Sahara."[26]

Political conditions in the Sahara and the western Sudan also changed drastically after the overthrow of the Songhay by the Moroccans at the end of the sixteenth century. Strife and insecurity continued throughout the seventeenth and eighteenth centuries and into the nineteenth. Kingdoms and empires fought for supremacy. In the middle of the eighteenth century, the slave trade to the European colonies revolutionized West Africa and contributed to the move of the centers of wealth and power away from the Sudan and toward the coast. While European powers remained confined to negligible enclaves along the coast, many of which were simply leased from African chieftains, the most impressive African political development of the seventeenth and eighteenth centuries—the expansion of the new group of major African states—took place a short distance inland.[27] Eventually, the European coastal establishments combined with that thin layer of "coastal Africans who are partly European in their outlook" and with the chiefs of the coastal traditional societies to confront the leaders of these new African empires.

J. D. Fage precipitated a major debate among African historians by arguing that slave trading in West Africa did not have a disastrous effect on its population. According to Fage, slavery was not a flourishing institution before European intervention, nor was it simply imposed by foreigners. Rather, commercial slavery developed along with a growth of African states; it was a system of labor organization that met the demands of a growing system of foreign trade. Although the European demand for slaves for the West Indian plantations' economies peaked from about 1650 to 1850, the slave trade was one aspect of a much wider process of African political and economic growth. Fage maintains that slavery was necessary for social development even before the Europeans, because the abundance of land meant that without slavery there was no effective inducement for the organization of labor.[28]

In contrast with Fage, this study agrees with Walter Rodney who argues that after the fifteenth century, economic initiative, especially in terms of the slave trade, came from Europe. European capitalism expanded to embrace the various economies of underdeveloped

---

[25] *History of West Africa*, p. 65.
[26] Bovill, *The Golden Trade of the Moors*, p. 250.
[27] See Fage, *A History of West Africa*, p. 123; and Maxwell Owusu, *Uses and Abuses of Political Power* (Chicago: University of Chicago Press, 1970).
[28] See Fage's *A History of West Africa*, especially Chap. 8.

countries, including the African barter economy, in a global network.[29]

The Dynamic Expansion of the Asante Empire
and the Fante Kingdom

As an example of the process of the development of inland states and
the parallel rise of coastal kingdoms, consider the rise of power after
1500 of the Asante Empire and the Fante Kingdom of modern
Ghana. The proliferation of firearms during the second half of the
seventeenth century facilitated the assimilation of weaker states by
more powerful ones. And the Ghanaian historian Daaku has maintained that this "territorial expansion by force of arms became the
means to gain economic power and the new order."[30] In Asante, the
architects of these unions are known and revered today in the same
way that George Washington and James Madison are in the United
States. Osei Tutu and his advisor and chief priest, Okonfo Anokye,
created a national religion, the Asante national army, a constitution,
an oath of allegiance, and symbols of unity, including "the golden
stool" and the myth that this stool embodies the soul of the Asante
peoples—a myth believed by many to this day.[31] By the beginning of
the nineteenth century, the Asante Empire had grown to include
practically all of contemporary Ghana as well as parts of the Ivory
Coast and Togo.[32]

[29] See Rodney's *How Europe Underdeveloped Africa* (Washington, D.C.: Howard University Press,
1974). Cf. Ivan Hrbek, "Toward the Periodization of African History," in *Emerging Themes of African
History*, ed. T. O. Ranger (Nairobi: East African Publishing, 1968), pp. 37–52. Hrbek finds a large
number of major happenings between 1805 and 1820—among them the jihad of Osman Dan Fodio, the rise of the Chaka, the eclipse of Bunyoro, and the rise of Buganda—that pointed to the
growth of unified and highly centralized states. For Immanuel Wallerstein, the key question in any
effort at periodization is not how many "mini-systems" are self-sufficient but how many "*worlds*" were
there—that is, arenas in which there were systematic sustained exchanges of goods. Wallerstein goes
on to argue that the first world economy was the capitalist economy that originated in the sixteenth
century. This proposition forms a base of Wallerstein's subsequent categorization of periods of African history. Between 1450 and about 1750, West Africa remained essentially outside even the periphery of the European world economy and engaged in nonessential long-distance trade that left
the two social systems essentially separate. However, after 1750, with changes in the industrial nature of European capitalism, there began a process of steady incorporation of Africa into the world
economy. The first stage of "this historic process" was "*informal empire*," the second stage was "*colonial rule*," and the third and final stage was "*decolonization*." Immanuel Wallerstein, "Africa in a Capitalist World," *Issue, 3*, no. 3 (Fall 1973), 9. Cf. Wallerstein's, *The Modern World System: Capitalist Agriculture and the Origins of the European World-Economy in the Sixteenth Century* (New York: Academic
Press, 1974).

[30] K. Y. Daaku, *Trade and Politics on the Gold Coast: 1600–1720* (Oxford: Clarendon Press, 1970),
pp. 5–6.

[31] A British army commander precipitated a major war by his unthinking demand for the golden
stool's surrender. The English anthropologist R. S. Rattray, in one of the most remarkable of all anthropological accounts, sets forth the story, as told to him by various Asante elders, of how traditional religion and legends brought together diverse Akan-speaking peoples under a common political umbrella. See Rattray's *Ashanti* (London: Oxford University Press, 1923). See also his comparison
of European feudalism with the Asante system in *Ashanti Law and Constitution* (London: Oxford University Press, 1929); and his remarkable account of the funery rites for Asante kings in his *Religion
and Art in Ashanti* (London: Oxford University Press, 1927).

[32] J. K. Fynn, "Ghana-Asante (Ashanti)," in *West African Resistance: The Military Response to Colonial
Occupation*, ed. Michael Crowder (New York: Africana Publishing, 1971), pp. 20–22. See also Web-

At the beginning of the eighteenth century, Fante, located along the coast of contemporary Ghana, also began to expand, responding directly to the new economic demands of trade with the Europeans. By the end of the eighteenth century, Fante had conquered most of the coastal kingdoms to the east and west, placing almost the entire coast from the mouth of the river Pra to the borders of the Ga kingdom under its control. In addition, fearing political subjugation by the Asante, the Fante acted to stop the Asante expansion to the sea; they strove to maintain their middleman position in the trade between the interior and the Europeans. The Asante asserted that they required enormous amounts of guns and ammunition in order to maintain their huge empire; the Fante responded with laws prohibiting the sale of guns, powder, iron bars, lead, and pewter to Asante traders.[33] The Fante added to this provocation by granting sanctuary to criminal refugees from Asante and by fomenting rebellion among various Asante vassals.

The Asante were willing to go to war to keep open the trading routes by which they obtained their guns and powder from the Europeans on the coast, in much the same way that the United States threatened intervention over oil in the Middle East and acted with force on many occasions to maintain its so-called vital resources. On numerous occasions, war broke out between the Asante and the Fante as a result of the Fante's persistent refusal to allow Asante traders direct access to the overseas merchants.

During the nineteenth century, limitations on the access of the Asante to the markets of the coast inhibited the emergence of a wealthy mercantile class, which had already been thwarted by the anticommercial traditions of a warrior nation. However, the creation of the "Cult of the Golden Stool" and other devices symbolizing the identity of the nation strengthened the power of the state. These symbols of national allegiance also acted, by design, as effective barriers to Islamization, which was considered an anathema as well as a political threat to the traditional chiefs. Because integration and ready assimilation of "foreigners" also characterized the Asante political system, "men of talent" from conquered areas could enter the administration and rise to high office.[34]

---

ster and Boahen, *History of West Africa*, p. 116. Ivor Wilks recently introduced an intriguing new interpretation of Asante historical development in the nineteenth century. Previous authorities, including Rattray and political scientists who relied upon his data—for example, David Apter—had maintained that Asante consisted essentially of a confederation of almost wholly autonomous local units. In fact, Apter made this the essential point of difference between the so-called pyramidal and hierarchical traditional systems, the Asante serving as an example of the former, and Buganda, the latter. See Apter's "The Role of Traditionalism in the Political Modernization of Ghana and Uganda," *World Politics*, 13, no. 1 (October 1960). Wilks argues that the characteristic feature of the Asante system was its centralized and largely appointed bureaucracy, which had to be destroyed if the colonial regime was to consolidate its rule ("Asante Government," in *West African Kingdoms in the Nineteenth Century*, ed. Daryll Forde and P. M. Kaberry (London: Oxford University Press, 1967), pp. 206–7.

[33] Fynn, "Ghana-Asante (Ashanti)," in *West African Resistance*, ed. Crowder, pp. 20–22.

[34] Peter Morton-Williams, "The Influence of Habitat and Trade in the Politics of Oyo and Ashanti," in *Man in Africa*, ed. Douglas and Kaberry, p. 95.

During this period the previously separated Asante and Fante—
and kingdoms in Nigeria, the Congo, and elsewhere—united in new
societies. Their rulers consolidated power, remaining atop complex hierarchies. By inventing or rediscovering symbols, myths, and religions,
the chiefs and their high priests succeeded in creating a new sense of
national identity among men of diverse cultures. At the same time colonialism helped strengthen those African states that acted as procur-
ers of export commodities in their confrontations with other African
states. A class of African traders also developed along the coast that
acted as middlemen between the Europeans and those who controlled
the trade of the inland states.[35]

In addition to the infusion of a sense of national identity, therefore, no wonder that Ivor Wilks stated about the Asante at this time
that "the characteristic feature of their system was a centralized and
largely appointive bureaucracy, capable of exercising a high degree of
social control and of organizing the manpower and other resources of
the area under the king's authority."[36] Political power and "commerce" thus marched hand in hand to create increasingly stratified societies. In Nigeria a similar process marked the Fulani "revolution":
During the nineteenth century, the Fulani managed to impose the authority of a single government over a large region formerly occupied
by a number of competing states. Again, parallels between the Fulani
and British Empires are striking. Similar confrontations between expanding Belgian, Portuguese, and French empires and rising African
political systems occurred throughout the continent.[37]

Trade and the Spread of Islam

In addition to trade, the expansion of African kingdoms such as the
Asante Empire and their links to contemporary history cannot be understood without a knowledge of the role of Islam. Reforming Islamic
holy men succeeded in their divine missions by appealing to oppressed peasantries who knew that the decadence and corruption, the
unfair taxes and luxurious living of their feudal lords—so bitterly denounced by the marabouts—were possible only at their expense. After
the first shock of the reformers, traditional authorities reestablished
their power—much as the European establishments came to terms
with the Protestant Reformation after the first convulsions of the sixteenth century—but on a new basis. Islam in the eighteenth and nineteenth centuries shook feudal social structures and opened caste so-

[35] Cf. I. Wallerstein in "The Colonial Era in Africa," in *Colonialism in Africa 1870–1960.* Vol. 2, *The History and Politics of Colonialism, 1914–1960,* ed. L. H. Gann and Peter Duignan (Cambridge: Cambridge University Press, 1970), p. 400.

[36] Wilks, "Asante Government," p. 206.

[37] Jan Vansina, for example, analyzes the development of a Luba-Lunda culture in east Central Africa and a Kongo and colonial Portuguese culture in west Central Africa. *Kingdoms of the Savanna* (Madison, Wisc.: University of Wisconsin Press, 1966), p. 5.

cieties to new opportunities, new mobility, and new social classes. By so doing, Islam brought radical changes — but it did not bring revolution. Classes remained. The relative power of rulers and ruled persisted. The conditions of life of the majority of peasants stayed unaltered. The trans-Saharan trade routes constituted the first major channel for the spread of Islam. Two other major paths followed by large organized forces were (1) directly south from Egypt — an adventure that came to defeat because of the military powers of the Christianized Nubians — and (2) direct voyages across the Arabian peninsula to the east coast of Africa. Among the Muslims who followed the second route were a major group from Oman in the seventh century, refugees from a revolt against the caliph. These Arabs — many of whom settled on the island of Zanzibar and established hegemony over a large black majority, a hegemony that lasted until the revolution of 1960 — eventually became the first slave hunters to operate on a large scale in East Africa.[38] Islam, as it finally came into Black Africa, was not borne by Arabs. The peoples of North Africa, overrun by the united tribes of the Arabian peninsula, themselves comprised many diverse groups, which were lumped together under the name "Berber" by outside observers. Only after Islam had become integrated into North African culture did it descend more deeply into the continent — through the agency of North Africans, not Arabs.

One hundred years after the death of Mohammed, in A.D. 632, Islam extended from India to the Atlantic coast in North Africa.[39] From North Africa, this converting religion crossed over into Christian Europe and soon covered most of Spain, Portugal, and part of southwestern France. Europeans called the invaders Moors, or people from Morocco. Trade, empires, and Islam become increasingly intertwined. The political development of the African empires had gone hand in hand with the growth of the trans-Saharan trade, as African rulers endeavored to extend their authority. Then, according to Nehemia Levtzion, "the Arab conquest of North Africa gave the trans-Saharan trade a new impetus by linking it with the vast empire, anxious to obtain as much as possible of its gold, on which the monetary system of the Muslim world depended."[40] Everywhere among the earliest converts to Islam were traders and merchants. From the eighth century on, most of the traders that traveled the trans-Saharan routes were Muslims. Froelich calls the traders "the most active promoters of individual conversion." This is because Islam was a "pass-

---

[38] See Zoe Marsh and G. W. Kingsnorth, *An Introduction to the History of East Africa* (London: Cambridge University Press, 1965). See also Michael F. Lofchie, *Zanzibar: Background to Revolution* (Princeton, N.J.: Princeton University Press, 1965).

[39] See, for example, the discussion in Jacques Baulin, *The Arab Role in Africa* (Baltimore: Penguin, 1962); Vincent Monteil, *L'Islam Noir* (Paris: Editions du Seuil, 1964); I. M. Lewis, ed., *Islam in Tropical Africa* (New York: Oxford University Press, 1966); and James Kritzeck and William H. Lewis, eds., *Islam in Africa* (New York: Van Nostrand Reinhold, 1969).

[40] Nehemia Levtzion, "The Early States of the Western Sudan to 1500," in *The History of West Africa*, Vol I., ed. Ajayi and Crowder, p. 122.

port to welcome from abroad." Traders also tried to enter the entourage of chiefs and convert them for their own protection.[41] When kings and members of the aristocratic classes converted, large groups of dependents frequently followed their lead. Islam supported the authority and prestige of the conqueror and served as a framework for judicial and administrative unification. It provided a system of common beliefs as well as an ultimate set of common ends for the society. Islam failed to penetrate segmentary, stateless societies and did not have much of an impact on "commoners" until centuries after its first appearance in Black Africa.[42]

The earliest African empires, most notably Ghana, resisted the coming of Islam mightily. However, for hundreds of years Muslims, particularly traders, were accepted as individuals and lived in a special section of town set aside for them. Muslims also sat in court, acting as interpreters and even holding offices as ministers. Yet in the middle of the eleventh century, Ghana's ruling classes still wished to maintain their allegiance to their ancestral religion.

In the eleventh century, however, a puritan revivalist Islamic movement, the Almoravids, swept out of the desert in the western Sudan in two great wings, driving north and south. The northern wing overran Morocco and by 1103 dominated all of Muslim Spain. The southern branch collided with ancient Ghana about 1062 and did not overcome serious resistance until 1076 when the Moslims captured and sacked the Ghanaian capital. Although Ghana eventually reasserted its independence, its rulers never were able to reassert the empire's former power. After this Muslim invasion, the Ghanaian Empire disintegrated into its various "tribal" components.[43] Once a religious split occurred between a ruling class that was Muslim and the commoners who remained pagan, the rulers attempted to moderate their beliefs. Consequently, Smith tells us, "most of them were neither real Muslim nor complete pagans." Built into this situation, therefore, was a twofold conflict: religious, in that some rulers turned more to Islam and others turned back towards traditional animism; and social, in that the distinctions between rulers and ruled that had existed prior to and independent of Islam were accentuated by cultural life styles.

[41] J. C. Froelich, "Essai sur les causes et methods de l'islamisation de l'Afrique de l'ouest du XIᵉ siecle," in Lewis, ed., *Islam in Tropical Africa*, p. 173. See also Abner Cohen, *Custom and Politics in Urban Africa* (Berkeley and Los Angeles: University of California Press, 1969), for a modern version of the same process.

[42] See Levtzion, "The Early States of the Western Sudan to 1500," p. 124; Froelich, "Essai," p. 173; and Fage, *A History of West Africa*, p. 80. This is why Levtzion states, "The history of the Western Sudan revolves, therefore, around three things: trade, states and Islam" ("The Early States of the Western Sudan to 1500," p. 124).

[43] See Fage, *A History of West Africa*, pp. 82–85. The word "Almoravid" derives from the practice of the founder of the movement, Ibn Yasin, a puritan who withdrew to an island retreat, an "aribat," and later brought there with him an elite group of disciples whom he trained both in theology and military discipline. The Almoravids were then known as *al-mura-bitum*, "people of the Ribat," (*Ibid.*, p. 81).

One resolution of these dilemmas came with the resurgence of Islamic puritans, who directed themselves against what they denounced as the superficiality of the Islam of the traditional rulers. They called on the oppressed peasants and members of the lower castes to form the vehicle for a simultaneous social revolution and spiritual rejuvenation. One of the early leaders of the Almoravids, Yusuf, proclaimed himself the "champion of the masses, the liberator of the people from the cruel tyranny of corrupt princes."[44] The peasantry rallied to him. They eagerly joined the overthrow of the local tyrants and swelled the ranks of his army.

When religious rejuvenation accompanied the spread of empire, Islam acted as a supertribal ideological cement. The routes of the Muslim traders' commerce acted as sinews that bound together the empire. Islamic learning also facilitated the growth of an educated class, which formed the bureaucratic cadres necessary to tie these new centralizing states into a new world of power and prestige ranging from India to France.[45]

In summary, from the eleventh to the thirteenth century Islam was a religion for nobles and chiefs. At first it was mainly of political and cultural significance, but later it gained historical note because of its commercial impact. From the thirteenth to the fifteenth century Islam became the religion of the intellectual elite, as well as the belief system of kings, administrators, and military leaders. Increasingly, Islam was valued as an aid to unity because of the prestige associated with its learned scholars and because of its many intellectual links with the Maghreb, particularly as the caravan trade with the north increased and commerce spread further south. From the eighteenth to

---

[44] Bovill, *The Golden Trade of the Moors*, p. 75. On the links between the Africans and the Arabs, P. R. Makonnen, one of the pre–World War II founding fathers of pan-Africanism, said, in 1966, "the Egyptians look down at us because of our color. Look at their historic policy: look at the color of those hauling the stones of the pyramids, and the color of those with the whips. That was the beginning." Quoted in W. Scott Thompson, *Ghana's Foreign Policy 1957–1966* (Princeton, N.J.: Princeton University Press, 1969), p. 8.

Going as far back as the Pharaohs of the sixth dynasty (2423–2242 B.C.), records exist of how these early rulers of Egypt dominated the black peoples to the south. We know the name of the first Egyptian subruler over the region: Harkhuf, of the sixth dynasty. Basil Davidson comments, "Harkhuf and his fellow lords of the South were the earliest known precursors of all that long line of imperial pioneers who have penetrated continental Africa from the outside."

Davidson, *The Lost Cities of Africa*, pp. 29–30. See also Ras Makonnen, *Pan-Africanism From Within* (New York: Oxford University Press, 1973).

See also Basil Davidson, "The Niger to the Nile," in *The Horizon History of Africa*, ed. Josephy, p. 220; and Abdullahi Smith, "The Early States of the Central Sudan," in *The History of West Africa*, Vol. I, ed., Ajayi and Crowder, pp. 122–23.

[45] Scholars differ in their categorization of the different phases of the impact of Islam in Africa. J. S. Trimingham marks off four phases. The first period of expansion involved two separate cultural zones in North Africa, Egypt and the Maghreb, where Islam integrated every aspect of existence. In the second phase, "traditional African Islam," Islam was fitted into the indigenous system and toleration and "religious dualism" characterized all relations with existing authorities. In the "theocratic phase," Islamic law prevailed over the entire pattern of social life, becoming increasingly intolerant not only of "pagans" but also of less zealous adherents. The fourth phase, "the secularized Islam of neo-Islamic communities," occurred simultaneously with the spread of western secular attitude and the continued progress of Islam. "The Expansion of Islam" in *Islam in Africa*, ed. Kritzeck and Lewis, p. 330.

the end of the nineteenth century a newly militant Islam stirred a revolutionary fervor in once quiescent masses and created empires of ever growing strength that clashed head-on with Europe overseas.[46]

The Jihad of 1804: Rise of the Sokoto Empire

One of the most important events of African history is the Jihad of 1804. This marked the conquest of the original Hausa states of northern Nigeria by the Fulani under Shehu Usman dan Fodio. The Sokoto empire that he founded determined the historical development of contemporary northern Nigeria. This holy war of Usman dan Fodio belonged to a wider movement of political renaissance in the western Sudan that included the Torobé revolt of 1776 in the Futa Toro of Guinea as well as the religious wars of Al Haj Omar in Upper Niger and Senegal. (In addition, news of the Sokoto Jihad was credited with triggering the revolt of the Hausa slaves in Brazil.)[47] The roots of these developments lay in the rising consciousness of an oppressed peasantry who sought to overthrow the domination of their overlords.[48]

Before beginning his crusade, the Shehu wrote a book (the *Kitab al-Farq*) drawing up an indictment against the traditional leaders. He classified their offenses under headings such as "oppression," "corruption," and "self-indulgence." Among the charges of oppression were the allegations that the ruling classes both "abducted the women they wanted without offering marriage, and mis-appropriated the possessions of women who were wards of the court; they forced levies of goods and money in the markets, commandeered pack animals without paying for them, sequestered the goods of strangers who died in their territories, levied tolls on merchants and travelers, and conscripted men to their armies allowing those who wished to buy themselves out to do so."[49] Foremost among the Shehu's priorities was his demand that the burden of taxes on the peasantry be lightened.[50]

---

[46] J. Spencer Trimingham, "The Expansion of Islam" in *Islam in Africa*, ed. Kritzeck and Lewis, p. 330. Cf. Gouilly's *L'Islam dans l'Afrique Occidentale Francaise* (Paris: Larose, 1952).

For an idea of the complexity of the spread of Islam about the tenth century, consider this account: ". . . at the Western end of the Mediterranean [was] a great Arab kingdom of the Ummayads, known to Europe as the Moors, [and] at the Eastern end an even greater empire of the Abbasids, known to Europe as the Saracens. . . . Islam came to Kaenknem from Egypt and Mecca, but to Ghana from Morocco and Tunis." S. J. Hogben and A. H. M. Kirk-Greene, *The Emirates of Northern Nigeria* (London: Oxford University Press, 1966), p. 137.

[47] *Ibid.*, pp. xvi–xvii.

[48] H. A. S. Johnston, in *The Fulani Empire of Sokoto* (London: Oxford University Press, 1967), argues that the expansion of trade and the establishment of Islam can be attributed to a series of improvements in communications that had the effect of converting Hausaland from a "backwater to a center of commerce and industry." The orthodox interpretation of the jihad characterizes it as primarily a religious movement. There are also those who believe that religious manifestations were only a justification for *ethnic* clashes—in the present case, an attempt on the part of the Fulani to dominate the Hausa and other peoples among whom they had settled. See *Ibid.*, pp. 96–98, for a refutation of these positions.

[49] *Ibid.*, pp. 30–31.

[50] *Ibid.*, p. 37.

After the war began and the forces of the Shehu gained an advantage over their adversaries, adventurers and opportunists took advantage of the situation to join his ranks. They then plundered and oppressed under cover of the war the very peasantry the Shehu sought to convert. The Shehu recognized this as a problem, but the peasantry, unsurprisingly, withdrew more and more from contact with their religious masters. After the Fulani victory, the great mass of the Hausa peasantry nevertheless accepted the new regime without protest. When the ruling classes of the Hausa, Kanuri, and their allies fled, the Fulani took over their houses and the public offices that they had occupied. All this explains why the seizure of power was so thorough and far-reaching and why what began as a class-based reform eventually ended in the reconstruction of a social structure much like the one against which the Shehu had originally harangued.[51]

In northern Nigeria revolt had spread by 1809 to Zaria, Katsina, and Kano. Eventually, the conquering Fulani marched as far south as the once powerful Yoruba empire of Oyo, killing the Alafin and continuing the jihad until their armies were finally halted in 1843 by Ibadan. During the nineteenth century, Islamic reforming movements with similar social import spread over large parts of North Africa, most of the Arabian peninsula, and large areas of Black Africa in addition to Nigeria.

In the western Sudan a new Islamic brotherhood, the Tijaniyya, emerged simultaneously with the efforts of the great reformers to attract a mass following. The formerly dominant brotherhood of the Quadiriyya had emphasized study and intellectual activity, and because of this they appealed to the chiefly classes. The Tijaniyya maintained that the basic means for salvation could be comprehended by a faith that was basically simple and easily understood by all men. All brothers of the Tijaniyya were equal under a moral law that should be demonstrated in action, not reflection.[52]

By the middle of the nineteenth century, Islam had become the official religion of the majority of the peoples of the Sudan.[53] Islam undermined local tribal traditional loyalties and replaced them with new national, imperial, or global ties of loyalty. The intrusion of western colonialism with all of its white man's burden and caravans and missionaries did not stop its spread. Indeed, the colonial expansion promoted Islam, sometimes voluntarily for political reasons—for in-

[51] See also Webster and Boahen's analysis of the primacy of class in their *History of West Africa,* p. 20 and further.

[52] See, for example, the authorities on Islam in Africa cited in footnote 41. See also Lucy Behrman, "The Political Significance of the Wolof Adherence to Muslim Brotherhoods in the Nineteenth Century," *African Historical Studies,* 1, no. 1 (1968), 60–78; Lucy Behrman, *Muslim Brotherhoods and Politics in Senegal* (Cambridge, Mass: Harvard University Press, 1970); Martin A. Klein, *Islam and Imperialism in Senegal* (Stanford, Calif.: Stanford University Press, 1968); Donal Cruise O'Brien, *The Mourides of Senegal* (New York: Oxford University Press, 1971); Markovitz, *Leopold Sedar Senghor and the Politics of Negritude.*

[53] This appeal of Islam has continued to the present: nine to ten conversions to Islam occur for every convert to Christianity. (Kritzeck and Lewis, eds., *Islam in Africa,* p. 2).

stance, to form advantageous alliances with an established class—and sometimes involuntarily, through the creation of an economic interest structure and the establishment of pacification, which mixed populations who welcomed a new common basis of identity in new urban centers.

Resistance to Colonialism

Muslims and non-Muslims, members of great empires and citizens of egalitarian communes, Africans rose up against colonialism. This resistance provides another element in the continuity of African history, again disproving the colonial myth of the disappearance of an African past. In addition, this resistance paved the way for the many African countries today.

In the history of great African empires extending over 3,000 years into the past, European colonialism is but a short episode. The relative brevity of this epoch must be emphasized along with three other characteristics of European colonialism: (1) the relative recentness of the occupation; (2) the resistance that rose virtually everywhere on the continent in one form or another; (3) the fact that in some cases the colonial regime never did conquer African establishments, but reached an accommodation according to terms that satisfied both sides. The neat boundary lines of maps drawn up and painted by European geographers obscured this situation.[54] Distance, poor communication, and a general lack of interest promoted our misunderstanding. Even colonial offices frequently did not know what was happening and left decisions in the hands of "men in the field." Yet if African regimes were not simply overwhelmed and conquered, one could logically expect that some of the ruling elements from the traditional regimes would carry over into the colonial-dominated present as largely autonomous systems. In fact, this did occur; some "traditional" societies did continue to function. This in turn raises certain questions about the nature of "tribal societies"; these questions will be analyzed in Chapter IV.

The actual European conquest took place primarily in the quarter-century from 1880 to 1905. Resistance continued in Mali, Niger, the Ivory Coast, eastern Nigeria, northern Nigeria, Mauritania, and elsewhere until the second decade of the twentieth century. Resis-

---

[54] One day when I was a graduate student doing research for the first time in the archives of Le Building Administratif in Senegal, a Nigerian scholar also working on his dissertation came rushing over to me in great excitement saying, "Look at that, look at that." Since the manuscript in question was in Arabic, I could only express my bewilderment. His great excitement resulted from his uncovering of the correspondence between Faidherbe and his African opponent, which revealed that at precisely the same time Faidherbe was sending dispatches back to Paris claiming definitive victories, he was in fact simply reaching mutual accommodations that underlined the limits of his power. Clearly, the events that took place differed radically from all of the conventional European textbook accounts. Cf. Boniface I. Obichere, *West African States and European Expansion: The Dahomey-Niger Hinterland 1885–1898* (New Haven: Yale University Press, 1971), who notes the piecemeal ways kingdoms were conquered (p. 252).

tance was not only bitter but skillful, ranging from the well-developed armies of states such as Dahomey and Asante to prolonged guerrilla warfare. Michael Crowder points out that

> a good majority of the States of West Africa, large and small, as well as most of the people living in segmentary societies opposed European occupation with force. . . . Since each village offered its resistance, there was no identifiable army to defeat among the Ibo as there was, say, among the Tukulör, the Emirates of Nigeria or Samori's Mandingo Empire. Each village or federation of hamlets had its own war leader. These societies conducted what was, in effect, guerrilla warfare against the invading armies, quite the best tactic that could have been adopted under the circumstances.[55]

Crowder also points out that even where the colonial regimes appeared to have won clear-cut victories, new outbreaks occurred continually, particularly during the 1914–18 war. Large areas of the western Sudan reasserted their independence at that time. The Shona and the Ndebele in Central Africa rose against the British at the turn of the century; the people of Tanganyika rose against the Germans in the Maji Maji in 1905–06. In their dealings with the Sokoto caliphate, the English worried constantly about a revolt that they would not be able to put down.

No wonder, then, that the African historian J. F. A. Ajayi wrote: "In any long-term view of African history, European rule becomes just another episode. In relation to wars and conflicts of people, the rise and fall of empires, linguistic, cultural and religious change, . . . the cultivation of new ideas and new ways of life, [and] new economic orientation . . . , colonialism must be seen not as a complete departure from the African past, but as one episode in the continuous flow of African history."[56] It is also helpful in placing colonialism in its proper historical perspective to realize that Germany and Italy, though powerful colonial empires of the twentieth century, did not even exist until the second half of the nineteenth century except as a group of independent or semiindependent states: Italian unification did not occur until between 1860 and 1870; the German state came under a single flag in 1871.[57] Lamine Gueye, the first African deputy to the French National Assembly, delighted in teasing General De Gaulle that his commune of St. Louis in Senegal became "part of France" earlier than the region of De Gaulle's origin. Focusing on East Africa

---

[55] Michael Crowder, ed., *West African Resistance*, pp. 1–2. Cf. T. N. Tamuno, *The Evolution of the Nigerian State: The Southern Phase, 1848–1914* (London: Longman, 1972), pp. 33–94.

[56] "The Continuity of African Institutions Under Colonialism," in *Emerging Themes of African History*, ed. T. O. Ranger (Nairobi: East African Publishing, 1968), p. 194. As evidence of the long continuity among the traditional rulers of northern Nigeria, see the case studies in Hogben and Kirk-Greene, *The Emerates of Northern Nigeria*. In Mali the same dynasty, the Keitas, ruled the empire for at least the four centuries of its reported history, "The Early States of the Central Sudan" in *The History of West Africa*, Vol I., ed. Ajayi and Crowder, p. 148.

[57] W. E. F. Ward and L. W. White, *East Africa: A Century of Change 1870–1970* (New York: Africana Publishing, 1971), p. 13.

as it existed in 1870, Ward and White point out that all the peoples of
East Africa, from the swamp of the Nile right down to the river Lim-
popo, were independent of any European control. They governed
themselves as they pleased, whether it was through powerful chiefs or
kings like the Buganda or clan elders like the Kikuyu.[58]

Ethiopia has existed for over 3,000 years, but not until the 1840s
did there begin a "thin but continuous and increasing trickle of European visitors to the chiefs, kings and later emperors of Ethiopia."[59]
When the Italians attempted to establish themselves on the Red Sea
coast during the nineteenth century, the Ethiopian general Ras Alula
soon defeated them, at the Battle of Dogali in 1887, the first major
humiliation of a European state at the hands of an African army,
though only a sample of what was to come. The Emperor Menelik's
modernized army crushed the Italians at Adowa on March 1, 1896,
one of the most important bench marks in the history of African resistance to modern imperialism. At the beginning of this century Menelik created modern Ethiopia, incorporating a larger area than had
any of his predecessors of the previous 400 years. The armies of Menelik, in occupying the traditional kingdoms of Jojjan, Begender-
Amhara, Tigre, and Shoa, as well as parts of Somali country, curbed
rival Italian expansionism in the same way that the Fulani stopped the
British in Nigeria.[60]

In West Africa, the Asante generated the longest period of resistance to take place against European occupation. After clashing with
the British forces in 1823, the Asante in 1824 defeated a British army
and killed the British governor. Through a succession of great battles,
the Asante prevented the British from entering Kumasi until 1896. At
that point the Asante still did not consider themselves conquered, and
as late as 1900 they arose in the bitterest struggle of the entire series
of encounters.[61]

The resistance of the coastal forest people of the Ivory Coast
from 1891 to 1918 was also unprecedented. Operating on a small
scale and lacking the organization of the Asante and Dahomey, they
nevertheless immobilized the superior weaponry of the French by utilizing the forest for hit-and-run tactics.[62]

One of the leaders in the Niger-Senegal area, the Tukulör char-

[58] *Ibid.*, p. 1.

[59] Robert L. Hess, *Ethiopia: The Modernization of Autocracy* (Ithaca, N.Y.: Cornell University Press, 1970), pp. 54–55.

[60] *Ibid.*, pp. 58–59.

[61] Fynn, "Ghana-Asante (Ashanti)," in *West African Resistance*, ed. Crowder, pp. 19–20. In regard to resistance in West Africa, see also Marvin Harris, "Portugal's Contribution to the Underdevelopment of Africa and Brazil," in *Protest and Resistance in Angola and Brazil*, ed. Ronald H. Chilcote (Berkeley and Los Angeles: University of California Press, 1972), pp. 209–23. Harris analyzes why Africans fought off the Portuguese so much more effectively than did the Indians in Brazil. Cf. David Bir-mingham, *Trade and Conflict in Angola* (Oxford: Clarendon Press, 1966), on how resistance led to a series of successively dominant African kingdoms—the Kongo, the Ndongo (or Angola), the Ka-sanje, the Lunda, and the Ovimbundu.

[62] Webster and Boahen, *History of West Africa*, p. 233.

ismatic divine al-Hajj Umar, brought revolution and reorganization; he founded the Tukulör Empire in 1852. In his travels, Umar witnessed two of the greatest Islam reform movements of the nineteenth century, the Wahhabi movement against the Turks in Arabia and the organization efforts of Mohammad Ali in Egypt. He had also lived in the emirates of northern Nigeria and participated in their reform efforts. When Umar called for the support of the peasantry, the chiefly classes of the entire region were said to fear for their positions, particularly when a large number of literate and skilled artisans from St. Louis, Senegal came to help him build stone forts and operate sophisticated weaponry. Umar pursued a sophisticated policy of political development that included a willingness to cooperate with the French in opening trade routes. As Catholics the French feared Umar because he was a Moslem holy man, and as colonialists they feared him because he was a radical popular leader. Webster and Boahen maintain that the "common fear of Umar began to bring the French and the chiefly classes of the Futas into alliance."[63] After a series of great battles against the "creator of modern Senegal," General Faidherbe, Umar was finally killed at Macina in 1864, a year before Faidherbe left Senegal. Webster and Boahen speculate that before Faidherbe's departure, events began to turn against the French and in favor of Umar and Senegal: "Had Umar not lost his life in Macina he might have swept to the coast and overturned the work of Faidherbe who had alienated many by his methods."[64] Shortly thereafter, in 1870, France suffered a crushing defeat by Bismarck's Germany, which forced the French to cut back their colonial adventures. By this time, however, because of Umar's death and internal strife, the Tukulörs could not take advantage of France's difficulties.

Further south, between the Tukulör Empire on the north and the Mossi and Asante kingdoms in the east, Samori Touré created the Mandingo Empire, which clashed almost from its foundation in 1870 with French imperialism. Building upon a tradition of the greatness of a common past under the empire of ancient Mali, Samori articulated a common religious, commercial, and national spirit and by 1886 had united all of the small states of the area under a central authority. Samori not only reorganized long-distance trade with the help of wealthy businessmen, but created new political bureaucracies and industrial enterprises. This commercial network insured the supply of horses and firearms, including over 6,000 repeating rifles. To guard against a cutting off of his sources of supply, Samori's blacksmiths and artisans set up their own workshops to produce ammunition and armaments. They completely modernized the Mandingo army. Eager to learn from all sources, Samori even sent soldiers to enlist in the colonial armies in order to learn their methods. Between 1870 and 1898,

[63] *Ibid.*, p. 23.
[64] *Ibid.*, pp. 24–25.

Samori fought the French with skill and determination. He created an empire that replaced established hereditary castes with a new Mandingo fraternity of common membership.[65]

In Central Africa during 1896 and 1897 the Shona rose in armed resistance. This revolt created a new unity among clans that only a few years previously had fought one another consistently. Bloodily suppressed by the colonial authorities, this great uprising conditioned the development of the mass nationalists' movements of the late 1950s and the 1960s in the Rhodesias.[66]

Where conflict came to an end by negotiated treaties, leaders of the African kingdoms continued to maintain a partnership relation with the Europeans. "Partition" had virtually no significance for hundreds of thousands of Africans. "Indirect rule," frequently more indirect than rule, often kept the Europeans out of the way. Riots in the 1930s and 1940s among the Yoruba, Ibo, and Urhobo of Nigeria, the Mende and Temne of Sierra Leone, and the Baoulé of the Ivory Coast, in response to European efforts to collect taxes, did not result from an unwillingness to pay taxes per se, Webster and Boahen point out; rather, they represented the refusal of Africans to accept a status that payment of tribute symbolized.[67]

The End of Resistance

Resistance against the colonial oppression ultimately foundered because of the superior weaponry of the Europeans and internal divisions among the Africans. Kanya, for example, points out the reasons for the ineffectiveness of Tukulör military resistance:

> In Africa the vast economic and technological resources of a modern European state can always be translated, when necessary, into an overwhelming military superiority. The Tukolörs were hopelessly outgunned. Their motley collection of muskets and obsolete rifles were no match for French artillery and the latest repeaters. The stone walls of

---

[65] A conflict exists among the authorities, however, as to the extent of Touré's anti-traditional-establishment direction. Webster and Boahen write, "Samory was the commonest of commen men, and like the other great nineteenth century reformers he had been born into the scholar class. He was born poor and he went much further than Umar in attacking and destroying the worldly position of the chiefly class" (*History of West Africa*, p. 43). Yves Pearson, on the other hand, writes of Samory, "his conservatism, however, surprises us—for example, his scrupulous respect for the established local chiefs and other notables" ("Samori and Resistance to the French," in *Protest and Power in Black Africa*, ed. Robert I. Rotberg and Ali A. Mazrui [New York: Oxford University Press, 1970], p. 112).

[66] T. O. Ranger, *The African Voice in Southern Rhodesia* (London: Heinemann Educational Books, 1970), pp. 3–4.

[67] Webster and Boahen, *History of West Africa*, p. 234. See also Michael Crowder and Oharo Ikeme, eds. *West African Chiefs*, where Atanda describes how the Nigerian alafin considered the British governor simply an advisor and himself master in his own empire. The British did not interfere, on the grounds that the wisest policy would be to wait for the alafin's death. This did not occur, however, until 1944.

their imposing fortresses provided some protection, but all of them were breached in the end.[68]

As in the Middle East today, or Spain in the 30s, the major European powers tested their new weapons on the bodies of the "others." The Maxim and Gatling guns spawned by western technology, along with other such experimental devices as flairs, searchlights, and special incendiary shells, had their effect. More far-reaching yet, this weaponry reflected an industrial society with more resources at its command than economies based solely on subsistence agriculture.[69] Yet as Vietnam and China, Cuba and Algeria have proved, superior technology, weaponry, and industrial resources do not automatically or necessarily produce victory. Africans did develop effective defenses and counter-tactics, mobilizing impressive mass-based resistance. The Baoulé of the Ivory Coast, the Mandingos of Guinea, and the Tukulórs of Mali utilized a variety of stratagems ranging from hit-and-run tactics to scorched-earth policies.

Kanya reveals another reason for the decline of resistance when he notes that "after 1890 the Tukolors did not even enjoy a significant advantage in numbers."[70] Why? Because the French were able to recruit and train African troops on the spot. The French succeeded in this because the Tukulör Empire "did not possess the necessary support, active or passive, voluntary or coerced of the mass of the population. Rent by rebellion and turmoil the Tukolör rulers found an establishment of their authority amongst their own subjects increasingly difficult."[71] Webster and Boahen argue bluntly that "Africa was conquered by Africans trained and officered by Europeans and fighting with European arms."[72] To begin their conquest of Africa, the British first used West Indian troops and stationed them permanently in Freetown, the Gold Coast, and Lagos. These troops fought against Bai Bureh, the Asante, and the Ijebu. Later, Lord Lugard used troops born in Hausaland to combat the Sokoto caliphate. One of the "lasting contributions" of General Faidherbe was the *Tirailleurs Senegalaises* (Senegalese sharpshooters). Founded in 1857, these were recruited from among local Africans, officered by Frenchmen, used first against al-Hajj Umar and deployed by the hundreds of thousands in every major French European war, including the wars of 1870, the First World War, and the Second World War.[73]

Their success in recruiting African troops led the European in-

---

[68] A. S. Kanya-Forstner, "Mali-Tukolor," in *West African Resistance,* ed. Crowder, p. 73.

[69] See the discussion of the failure of Turkish nationalists in the late nineteenth century to recognize that modern weapons could not simply be imported and used effectively without the reorganization of their entire society, in Robert E. Ward and Dankwart A. Rustow, eds., *Political Modernization in Japan and Turkey* (Princeton, N.J.: Princeton University Press, 1964).

[70] Kanya-Forstner, "Mali-Tukolör," in *West African Resistance,* ed. Crowder, p. 73.

[71] *Ibid.*

[72] *History of West Africa,* p. 228.

[73] See Abdoulaye Ly, *Mercenaires Noirs* (Paris: Presence Africaine, 1957).

vaders to interpret the people's resistance as being due to the oppression of their rulers. This in turn led the Europeans to overestimate their acceptance by the Africans—demonstratively an erroneous interpretation. Again, we see the importance of a close analysis of the structure of African societies.

African Acolytes

Around 1607, a powerful Southeast African feudal lord, Monomotata, faced with the revolt of powerful vassals, called in the Portuguese to help him. When they did, the traditional ruler agreed to the following terms: "I, the Emperor, Monomotata, think fit and am pleased to give to his Majesty all the mines of gold, copper, iron, lead and pewter which may be in my empire, so long as the King of Portugal, to whom I give the said mines, shall maintain me in my position. . . ."[74] From this time on, a constant theme in African history, as everywhere else, concerns those traditional leaders occupying shaky political positions who welcomed allies, including overseas adventurers, wherever strong opponents appeared.[75] Given the multiplicity of kingdoms and rival states in West Africa, the French and British had no difficulty in aligning, for example, with the Fante against the Asante, the Ibaban against the Ijebu, and the Bambara against the Tukulör.[76]

In Tanganyika at the turn of the century, the established traditional authorities became willing to cooperate once they learned that the Germans had no objection to their continued use of slaves and were equally eager to protect the caravan routes. Over time, the Germans became proficient in winning the support of various factions. They defeated the resistance movement by breaking down the original "tenuous compromise of many contradictory elements—commoners and notables, slaves and owners, coast and interior, . . ."[77]

In addition to the "national" conflicts that prevented, for ex-

[74] Basil Davidson, *The African Past* (New York: Grosset & Dunlap, 1967), p. 164.

[75] See, for example, Ayandele's discussion of the Egba of Yorubaland, who in the 1840s welcomed missionaries as strong allies to buttress their position against the hostile neighbors, especially Ibadan and Dahomey, who surrounded them and were dedicated to their destruction. The missionaries in turn urged the British government to protect the Egbas against all of their enemies. Ayandele argues that originally the Egba and Ibibio chiefs did not have the least interest in the white man's creed per se. See E. A. Ayandele, *The Missionary Impact on Modern Nigeria 1842-1914* (New York: Humanities Press, 1967), pp. 6–9.

[76] See Crowder, ed., *West African Resistance*, p. 14. See also Olatunji Oloruntimehin, who provides fascinating details on the negotiations between officials of the French and African empires and analyzes the diplomatic relations between rising African states in his "The Western Sudan and the Coming of the French, 1800–1893," in *History of West Africa*, Vol. 2, J. F. Ade Ajayi and Michael Crowder (New York: Columbia University Press, 1973), pp. 344–79. Cf. Oloruntimehin's monograph, *The Segu Tukulor Empire* (New York: Humanities Press, 1972).

[77] Robert D. Jackson, "Resistance to the German Invasion of the Tanganyikan Coast, 1888-1891," in *Protest and Power in Black Africa*, ed. Robert I. Rotberg and Ali Mazrui (New York: Oxford University Press, 1970), p. 77. Perhaps the most sanguine assessment of these internal African conflicts comes from J. M. Lonsdale, who in evaluating the resistance movement in western Kenya claims, "It is more useful to see both those who resisted the colonial rule and those who exploited it as two groups of innovating leaders" ("Political Associations in Western Kenya," in *Protest and Power in Black Africa*, ed. Rotberg and Mazrui, p. 589).

ample, the Tukulör and Mandingo Empires from uniting in a way similar to the great unity forged in Ethiopia and East Africa, two types of internal dissension should be noted. First, many African traditional political systems lacked clearly defined rules of succession to the throne. To this day, bitter disputes frequently ensue between members of royal families. Contenders for the offices often become leaders of opposition factions willing to engage in intense struggles for power. Sometimes such candidates accepted external aid. The French supported a number of pretenders to the head of the Tukulör Empire. In Dahomey, the colonial governor placed the brother of the dismissed king on the throne. Lugard managed to install a royal rival in Nupe. Similar stratagems were applied to the Wolof, the Bambara, and the Mossi.

A second type of internal division occurred not simply within the "royals" but involved class conflict. For example, one of the smallest African armies—which nevertheless engaged in some of the bitterest fighting with the colonial power—was that led by Bai Bureh of Kasseh, a tiny Temne state in northern Sierra Leone. Bai Bureh, who is today hailed as a national hero in Sierra Leone, became a chief in May, 1887. Previously, his father, a professional warrior, followed family tradition by sending him to be schooled in his craft. The other chiefs called upon Bai Bureh, as a war chief, to help them reclaim their lost privileges from the British. Among these former privileges were the enslaving of prisoners taken in battle, the slave trade in general, judicial authority—including the right to use the "ordeal" (physical torture used to determine guilt or innocence)—and flogging. Without the threat of flogging, the chiefs complained in particular, even "domestic slaves and women would disobey them." Many of the frontier police employed by the British were runaway slaves who had gained their freedom at Freetown. The chiefs resented their vulnerability to arrest by men who had once been their slaves—a situation that exacerbated the loss of a major source of income. The ultimate defeat of Bai Bureh was therefore not bemoaned in all African quarters.[78]

Finally, in many cases resistance did not so much collapse as prove unnecessary, primarily because of the increasing incorporation of leading members of the African establishments into the colonial administrative structure. These individuals were co-opted not just into the system of indirect rule by the native authorities. The sons of the traditional leaders also became important members of the westernized bureaucracies. A most dramatic instance of this occurred in Matabeleland in Central Africa, where, upon recognition of the inevitability of defeat, the senior chief sued for peace. Cecil Rhodes gave status and salaried positions to the "officially recognized chiefs."[79] Absorbed into the "underlying incentive system of the colonial powers," this vested

---

[78] See La Ray Denzer and Michael Crowder, "Bai Bureh and the Sierra Leone Hut Tax War of 1898," in *Protest and Power in Black Africa*, ed. Rotberg and Mazrui, pp. 178–83.

[79] Ranger, *op. cit.*, p. 26.

African local interest in the colonial bureaucracy created an effective channel for the direct expression of discontent.

African resistance, therefore, involved the dignity of proud men struggling to be free, acting to assert their prowess. Over time, these early struggles with colonialism also revealed much about the stratified nature of African societies.

Conclusion

A number of African writers have warned against "glorification" of the African past. Seydou Badian avers that

> the unconditional glorification of the past leads inevitably to confusion: heroes must be those who incarnate those virtues useful to the revolution and every revolution needs its own heroes, its own values. One need not, in a revolutionary environment, enlarge and magnify those men whose past action, in every way, is found contrary to the objectives for which we want to prepare men's spirits. It is in the pursuit of this that we find a fundamental contradiction, a non-logic. These men in their time obeyed a logic which is not necessarily the one of today and which is often in conflict with it.[80]

Eldred Jones asserts:

> Generally, . . . in looking back on the African past, writers felt the need to divert their eye from whatever was wrong and concentrate on showing what was good in African society. . . .
> The African writer can now, I feel, shake himself free of this indirect limitation and take a total non-embarassed view of his Africa — the Africa of the present and the past. The resulting picture may be unromantic, it may be disillusioning. The only rule should be that it must reflect the total situation.[81]

J. K. Obatala, while pointing out that there are many positive aspects of the African-American past, goes on to warn that

> for the average African-American familiar with the rigid social stratification of Egyptian and other ancient Black societies, there would hardly be for him anything romantic about them, since their ways of life were based upon the drudgery and ignorance of the common man. Still less appealing would be the tyranny of the long Islamic oppression in sub-Saharan Africa, which has been romanticized by certain westernized Africans and African-American intellectuals.[82]

---

[80] Seydou Badian, *Les Dirigeants d'Afrique noire face a leur peuple* (Paris: Francois Maspero, 1965), p. 102.

[81] Eldred Jones, "The Decolonization of African Literature," in *The Writer in Modern Africa*, ed. Pere Wastberg (New York: Africana Publishing, 1969), pp. 71–78.

[82] J. K. Obatala, "El Dorado, Africa," *New York Times*, February 10, 1974. Cf. Chinweizu, *The West and the Rest of Us: White Predators, Black Slavers and the African Elite* (New York: Vintage Books, 1975).

Sembene Ousmane, the Senegalese film maker and writer who most recently has depicted the ravages of colonialism in his film *Amitai,* is one of the foremost critics of the organizational bourgeoisie in Africa. In an extensive analysis of why it is necessary to consider the past frankly, he stated, "We have to have the courage to say that during the colonial period sometimes we were colonized with the help of our own leaders, our own chiefs and our own kings. We mustn't be afraid of our lacks, of our faults and our errors. We have to recognize them in order to fight against them."[83]

If this chapter began, then, with an extended catalogue of the proud accomplishments of great African civilizations and discussed how this should be an added spur to future unity, it ends by introducing the necessity of investigating historical social conflicts that still have not been overcome.

European commerce and administration offered a "carrot" for a minority of "qualified" Africans as well as a "stick." Opportunities for status and mobility within the Western system created new attitudes that acted as an acid upon dissent. This development became particularly marked as the colonial establishments became more sophisticated in their understanding of local factions, and especially after an accommodation was made with Islam—to the point where European governors frequently curtailed missionary activity stringently in the Islamic areas of the interior. It is therefore within this framework of increasing cooperation between the colonial establishments and the African bourgeoisie that we must go on to examine more specifically the policies of the various colonial powers, how they evolved, and how they differed.

[83] Quoted in Harold Weaver, "Interview with Ousmane Sembene," *Issue,* 2 (Winter 1972), 58.

Chapter III

THE HISTORICAL IMPACT
OF COLONIALISM
AND IMPERIALISM

"Without the grain of Africa," Marc Bloch tells us, "the existence of Imperial Rome is as little conceivable as Catholic theology without the African Augustine."[1] Even earlier than Rome, overseas empires began to drain the African continent of her raw materials. The Phoenicians, sailing in the twelfth century B.C. from the biblical cities of Sidon and Tyre, established their main base at Carthage, near Tunisia, and spread settlements over the whole of the western Mediterranean coast of Africa. At approximately the same time, Greek city-states founded colonies at Cyrenaica, opposite the Iberian Peninsula. Later, in 596 B.C., Phoenician sailors under the orders of Pharaoh Necho of Egypt circumnavigated the continent in three years—landing for three months each year to grow crops. After Rome destroyed Carthage in the Third Punic War in 146 B.C., Romans became masters of the Mediterranean from Morocco to Egypt. All of the interior below the Mediterranean they called Ethiopia. As far south as Kenya, Rome shook loose Africa's ivory, precious stones, gold dust, ostrich feathers, slaves, and animals for the amphitheaters—and spurred caravan trade forward with the introduction of the camel at about the time of Christ.[2] But then the disintegration of the Roman Empire, the spread of Islam, and the chaos and decline that led to the small-scale organizations characteristic of Europe throughout the Dark Ages broke contact between Europe and Africa until the Renaissance.

Western Europe's rediscovery of Africa did not occur until the end of the fifteenth century, when Prince Henry of Portugal, seeking silk and spices, ventured around the African coast in an effort to reach India.[3] From the sixteenth to the twentieth century, the European powers of the Atlantic led the world.[4] The relations of these

[1] Marc Bloch, *Feudal Society* (Chicago: University of Chicago Press, 1961), p. xix. See also Fernand Braudel, who writes, "Without Africa [Europe] could not have developed the New World for thousands of reasons, notably the climate, but also because it could not divert too much manpower from its own labour force" (*Capitalism and Material Life, 1400–1800*, [New York: Harper & Row, 1973], p. 22).

[2] Frank Snowden, *Blacks in Antiquity* (Cambridge, Mass.: Harvard University Press, 1970).

[3] See Ronald Robinson and John Gallagher with Alice Denny, *Africa and the Victorians: The Climax of Imperialism* (New York: Doubleday).

[4] Among the general histories of European colonialism in Africa, see Raymond Leslie Buell, *The Native Problem in Africa*, 2 vols. (New York: Macmillan 1928); Lord Hailey, *An African Survey*, rev. ed. (London: Oxford University Press, 1957); Donald L. Wiedner, *A History of Africa South of the Sahara*

powers with Africa fall into three main periods.[5] First, the slave trade dominated economic relations from the sixteenth to the eighteenth century, after which it was replaced by "legitimate commerce" — palm oil, gold dust, timber for firearms, tobacco, beads, and rum.[6] Then, private "traders" functioned as governments until the mid nineteenth century, when metropolitan legislatures inaugurated "crown colonies." Then, in the third period, colonies gained economic value as a result of exploding industrialization in Western Europe which required major new supplies of raw materials (such as manganese and bauxite) and expanding markets for manufactured goods.[7] To encourage exports and imports, colonial powers imposed their equivalent of a Pax Britannica. They improved transportation, introduced new systems of communications, and established governments that were strong but limited in scope.

Colonialism was only one expression of an ever more encompassing capitalism. Only the post-Vietnam 1970s era of detente with the Soviet Union and accommodation with China has clarified the parameters and nature of capitalism as a world system. Ranging from the chartered company to the multinational corporation, the instruments of this ever more encompassing system have varied over time, reflecting changes in the productivity, organization, and structure of international capitalism. Political forms and relations have also changed, from negotiated treaties between equal powers, to colonies, to independent states. The social structure of African societies responded to these changing forms of commodity production and exchange. If African societies did not necessarily undergo restratification, at the least capitalism and colonialism changed the basis of the economic and political power of the traditional ruling classes.

Contact with "the West" in the final analysis produced a growing dependency, an other-directed, outer-directed alienated development.

(New York: Random House, 1962); Robert I. Rotberg, *A Political History of Tropical Africa* (New York: Harcourt, Brace & World, 1965); Joseph E. Harris, *Africans and Their History* (New York: New American Library, 1972); Jean Suret-Canale, *Afrique Noire*, 2 vols. (Paris: Editions Sociales, 1961, 1964); Roger Owen and Bob Sutcliffe, eds., *Studies in the Theory of Imperialism* (London: Longman, 1972); and John D. Hargreaves, *West Africa Partitioned*, Vol. 1, *The Loaded Pause, 1885–1889* (Madison, Wisc.: University of Wisconsin Press, 1974).

[5] For other efforts to periodize African history, see Chapter II of the present text.

[6] For figures in the slave trade, see Philip Curtin, *The Atlantic Slave Trade: A Census* (Madison, Wisc.: University of Wisconsin Press, 1969). See also Curtin's important analysis of the development of African traders in the precolonial era, *Economic Change in Precolonial Africa: Senegambia in the Era of the Slave Trade* (Madison, Wisc.: University of Wisconsin Press, 1975).

[7] Export figures for primary crops reveal the extent of this shift in the nature of the economic relations between the European powers and their colonies. For example the amount of cocoa exported by the Gold Coast rose from five tons per year in the period 1891–1895 to the hundreds of thousands of tons by the early 1930s. See G. B. Kay, ed., *The Political Economy of Colonialism in Ghana* (Cambridge: Cambridge University Press, 1972); and A. G. Hopkins, *An Economic History of West Africa.* (London: Longman, 1973). Immanuel Wallerstein, in *The Modern World-System: Capitalist Agriculture and the Origins of the European World-Economy in the Sixteenth Century* (New York: Academic, 1974), builds brilliantly upon the work of Braudel (*Capitalism and Material Life, 1400–1800,* and *The Mediterranean and the Mediterranean World in the Age of Philip II,* 2 vols. [New York: Harper & Row, 1973]) in showing the changing relations among core, semiperiphery, periphery, and external areas. Also, cf. Samir Amin, *Accumulation on a World Scale* (New York: Monthly Review Press, 1974) with Arrighi

We must keep the nature of this dependency in mind when we consider the contribution of imperialism, of international capitalism to economic growth and to the political development of African states. Even the most dramatic rise in the gross national product or even an absolute rise in the standard of living would occur within this context.

Objectives and Methods of Imperialists in Africa: Differences in Colonial Rule before the Second World War

Colonial policies and structures of rule differed among the European powers and over time. These policies conditioned the nature of the nationalist movements that emerged in Africa before independence, and also guided the type of economic development and social policy characteristic of different African territories. The objectives and methods of imperialism also affected the continuities between ongoing African indigenous systems and postindependence regimes. In the following pages we will delineate the basic premises of each of the major European colonial powers before and after the Second World War, the great watershed in recent African political history that marked the advent of mass nationalism.[8]

British Policy

The primary goal of British policy in Africa at this time was to maintain a long period of external control over its possessions. Britain sought to justify this policy in two ways: first, through the notion of trusteeship; and, second, by alleging that self-government was the ultimate objective of its administration. Trusteeship, which was concerned with "less advanced," "backward" peoples, was rooted in English political theory—not in the most conservative political philosophers but rather in "liberals" such as John Stuart Mill. Mill, in his famous work, *On Representative Government,* argued at great length the necessity of tutoring peoples who were not familiar with the conduct of their own affairs. They were "made ready" for self-government.[9] Mill was talking about "natives" of North America, but this doctrine lay at the heart of the use in Africa of the notion of the "white man's burden"— not simply in terms of bringing Christianity to the heathen (although this is certainly one important root), but also in terms of the belief growing out of English constitutional history that only after prolonged experience could a people manage their affairs properly. Although the English established colonies in Africa only at the end of the nine-

Emmanuel, *Unequal Exchange: A Study of the Imperialism of Trade* (New York: Monthly Review Press, 1972).

[8] See especially Thomas Hodgkin, *Nationalism in Colonial Africa* (New York: New York University Press, 1957).

[9] John Stuart Mill, *Considerations on Representative Government* (1861). That Mill was "far ahead of his time" on racial issues and that he is emphatically clear that the problem is one of social conditions does not gainsay the importance he attached to a period of tutelage. Cf. his *The Negro Question* (1850).

teenth century, the long history of their confrontation with Ireland produced stereotypes as blatantly racist as any that marked subsequent English colonial domination.[10]

Although self-government might have been the ultimate objective of English rule, two unwritten conditions existed. First, the colonial governors thought of the achievement of independence as only a "remote possibility," something to be instituted after generations and generations, hundreds of years. Second, independence was not to be achieved by a sudden revolutionary thrust, but by a gradually increasing degree of participation in the political decision-making process set up by the colonial regimes.

The central questions, therefore, became these: What were the mechanisms for the conduct of self-government to be, and who was to man them? Here, a basic ambiguity in British policy manifested itself in the form of two institutions: the legislative council and the system of indirect rule. Ultimately, however, institutions functioned to entrench and consolidate the power of the emerging African organizational bourgeoisie.

The British established legislative councils in all their territories. In countries without a permanent European population, especially in West Africa, the councils followed a definite pattern of evolution, expanding the number and the powers of African members as well as continually democratizing their mode of selection. At the beginning, the governors selected "unofficial members" at their whim. Usually, however, the governors sought out leading members of the African establishment. As their number grew, the legislative council expanded into a legislative assembly with both elected and appointed members. Over time, the proportion of elected members expanded and the method of their selection became increasingly "democratic" as restrictive qualifications such as education, property, and income were removed. The British did away gradually with electoral systems and indirect systems of election based, for example, on tribal elders descended from traditional ruling families. With Westminster as their model, the British offered a system of universal suffrage based on "one man, one vote"; the voters would choose between contending political parties; and the leader of the majority party would become prime minister. Western-educated Africans, members of the liberal professions, some businessmen, and a few chiefs, accepted the legislative council as this "parliament in embryo." They foresaw that through this system, they and their heirs would govern their countries. They contented themselves with working within the stipulated channels. They pressured for an increase in the number of elected members and for the assumption of ministerial responsibilities in more significant areas of legislative jurisidiction.[11]

[10] See Richard Ned Lebow, *White Britain and Black Ireland: The Influence of Stereotypes on Colonial Policy* (Philadelphia: ISHI Publications, 1976).

[11] See, for example, Martin Wight, *The Gold Coast Legislative Council* (London: Faber & Faber, 1947); Joan Wheare, *The Nigerian Legislative Council* (London: Faber & Faber, 1950); Kalu Ezera, *Constitu-*

This legislative council system originated during a time when colonial regimes in Western settled areas, such as the United States and Canada, consisted of "kith and kin" whose model of government had always been the English Parliament. In Africa and Asia, when confronted by peoples whose social, economic, and political systems they did not understand, the "founders of Empire" developed a new theory that incorporated a new institution. This was the "native authority system," more commony known as "indirect rule."[12] The British administration declared they would recognize and support the customary authorities in African tribal society, the chiefs and elders, even though these authorities differed from any the British had previously encountered. The British accepted the notion, at least in theory, that each people possessed their unique genius, their own social and political customs, traditions, and institutions. Out of different historical backgrounds and material situations would come vastly different institutional expressions of political authority. Unlike the other colonial regimes, therefore, the English did not commit themselves to imposing a single political form over the traditional political structures. The native institutions should maintain their uniqueness. However, the British insisted that they be "purged of excesses," as well as adapted to new conditions. What were excesses? Usually, anything contrary to British traditions and customs; for example, polygamy. Clitoridectomy especially stirred the English sense of repulsion. Not realizing that clitoridectomy had symbolic significance for the Kikuyu in Kenya, as did circumcision for the Jews, the British forbade its practice. One of the major causes for the Mau Mau uprising in the 1950s was resentment over this abolition: the Kikuyu saw this directive as threatening their existence as a people.[13] The theory of indirect rule placed great emphasis upon slow change: ideal systems were those that least disturbed the rural life of Africa. Yet at the same time—especially in the absence of white settlers—colonial authorities encouraged Africans to grow cash crops such as cocoa, coffee, or cotton, unaware of or unconcerned with the disruptions of the traditional basis of material life that this might cause.

Native authorities varied in size from the great, well-organized

tional Developments in Nigeria, 2nd ed. (New York: Cambridge University Press, 1964): and Francis Agbodeka, *African Politics and British Policy in the Gold Coast, 1868–1900* (London: Longman, 1971).

G. B. Kay offers a brillant interpretation of the dynamics of colonialism in the Gold Coast. He argues that the key for an understanding of the evolution of colonial policy was the emergence of a capitalist class. The British failed to promote the *trade* of the colony—a goal to which they were formally committed—because this would have meant encouraging the African cocoa farmers. This could have been done, Kay maintains, only at the expense of British mining interests. Miners and cocoa competed for scarce resources and, therefore, for a favorable government policy in fields as diverse as transportation—feeder roads for isolated farms versus railroads for gross tonnages—sea-education, and fiscal policy. See Kay, ed., *The Political Economy of Colonialism in Ghana.*

[12] The classic formulation of indirect rule is found in Lord Lugard, *The Dual Mandate in British Tropical Africa* (Edinburgh: Blackwood & Sons, 1922). See also Lucy Mair, *Native Policies in Africa* (London: Routledge and Sons, 1936).

[13] See L. S. B. Leakey's *Mau Mau and the Kikikuyu* (London: Methuen, 1952) and *Defeating Mau Mau* (London: Methuen, 1954).

emirates of northern Nigeria with budgets in the hundreds of thousands of dollars, to small groups of a few hundred who scarcely possessed separate political institutions. Among the Ibo, the British established "warrant" chiefs; that is, in the absence of recognized political leaders, a local administrator would simply sign a piece of paper that "warranted" that so and so was the chief. In other territories, slaves or people of low status were put forward as chiefs. In some cases, genuine status reversals took place over time. Other systems became mere facades. While their power was ascending, the British did not worry if these native authority systems they set up did not work. In particular, they were not too concerned if they did not win African political allegiances.

French Policy

Throughout the incredible array of regimes ranging from divine right monarchy to the French Revolution, from Bonapartism and military dictatorship to socialist governments and popular fronts, certain basic principles nevertheless characterized French colonial policy before the Second World War.[14] To begin with, all the regimes, no matter what their ideology, shared principles that they believed provided an "obvious" and "unquestioned" basis for the conduct of their administration. Foremost among these, nobody questioned the notion of "permanent association with France": unlike the British, the French, no matter which regime was in power, never held out independence as an eventual goal. Who would want to break the connection with the mother country? Both socialists and monarchists found the idea unthinkable. Not that they felt the government of France was perfect—far from it. Every faction strove to change the basic structures of rule—but in the motherland itself. They advocated the reforms of France into a divine right monarchy, a socialist Utopia, or a bourgeois democracy, and then they would change the rest of the world under the light of the French sun.

The second principle of French colonial policy was that politically, rule came from the "center" in a unified and uniform system.

[14] On the history of French colonial policy, see, for example, Charles-Andre Julien, *Les technicians de la colonisation* (Paris: Presses Universitaires de France, 1947); George Hardy, *La mise en valeur du Senegal de 1817 a 1854* (Paris: Emile Larose, 1921); William B. Cohen, *Rulers of Empire: The French Colonial Service in Africa* (Stanford, Calif.: Hoover Institution Press, 1971); Robert Delavignette, *Freedom and Authority in French West Africa* (New York: Oxford University Press, 1950); Bernard Schnapper, *La politique et le commerce Francais dans le Golf de Guinée de 1838 a 1871* (Paris: Mouton et Cie, 1961); Felix Brigaud, *Histoire traditionnelle du Senegal* (Saint-Louis, Senegal: C.R.D.S., 1962); Virginia Thompson and Richard Adloff, *French West Africa* (Stanford, Calif.: Stanford University Press, 1957); Andre Delcourt, *La France et les etablissements Francais au Senegal entre 1713 et 1763* (Dakar: Memoires de l'Institut Francais d'Afrique Noire, 1952); Doudou Thiam, *La portee de la citoyennete Francais dans les Territoires d'Outre-Mer* Paris: Societé d'Editions Africaines, 1953); H. O. Idowu, "The Establishment of Elective Institutions in Senegal, 1869–80," *Journal of African History*, 9, no. 2 (1968), 261–77; Lamine Gueye, *Etapes et perspectives de l'union Francaise* (Paris: Editions de l'Union Francaise, 1955); Jacques Charpy, *La foundation de Dakar* (Paris: Larose, 1958); and Bruce D. Marshall, *The French Colonial Myth and Constitution Making in the Fourth Republic* (New Haven: Yale University Press, 1973).

Local differences were not taken into account in the colonies, just as regional or provincial administration in France itself had not mattered through a long history of continual centralization of power. In true Cartesian fashion, logical principles provided a philosophical justification for the uniform formulation of laws and policy and their universal application. When coupled with the third basic principle — complete juridical and administrative integration of the dependencies into the metropolitan institutions — the French system incorporated a type of unity and wholeness unique for the size and variety of its empire. De Tocqueville long ago took note of this centralization of political power and unification of bureaucratic authority when he highlighted the patterns of continuity between the old regime and the revolution designed for its overthrow.[15] In France, all roads led to Paris, a domestic pattern that was extended to the empire. To this day, the basic division in France is that between Paris and the rest of the country. Everything outside of the capital city is the provinces, the backwoods. To give one example of French administrative unification: until the educational reforms brought on by the student-led rebellion of Nanterre in 1968, the great goal of administrative integration was for a visitor to be able to walk into any classroom in any school in any part of France and find every student in every classroom on exactly the same page in exactly the same book. No wonder the French had no interest in the political genius of the Mossi or the administrative brilliance of the Wolof.

No matter what the fundamental underlying assumptions, colonial *practices* did differ depending upon the type of regime in power in France. One can, however, again broadly distinguish between the principles of "identity" and "association" as threads that connect and crisscross a variety of administrations. Originating in the French Enlightenment, the principle of identity held that all Africans were to be completely assimilated and made equal citizens of France. Eighteenth-century philosophes replaced the Christian notion of equality before God with the belief that all men had the capacity of reason. Rousseau declaimed that men were born free, yet were everywhere in bondage. Beneath the artificial encumbrances of property, culture, and religion, men possessed a sameness that would enable them not only to communicate but to create a great society, if only the superficial barriers could be shed. The French Revolution expressed these ideals in its clarion call for "liberty, equality, and fraternity." The armies of the French Revolution attempted to carry this messianic message by force of arms throughout Europe. The radical left continued to maintain these ideals as ultimate goals. Although in modern political terms assimilation translates into "Uncle Tomism," the original bearers of the ideal postulated a harmonious community that would bar differences in class between citizens and colonial natives. Periodically, political movements in France proclaimed themselves heirs to that tradition

---

[15] *The Old Regime and the French Revolution* (Garden City, N.Y.: Doubleday, 1955), pp. ix and x.

and sought to identify themselves with the welfare of overseas peoples. Again, however, practice differed from the ideal, and the achievement of the principle of identity seemed quite as remote a possibility as the goals of self-government in the British territories. Only a tiny minority ever did achieve French citizenship. Only Senegal in the pre–World War II period enjoyed representation by deputy in the French National Assembly.[16] No French government made social and economic equality a reality to the vast mass of African subjects.

Those regimes that favored a policy of association worried primarily about the immediate practicalities of administration. From the beginning, they maintained that it was necessary to deliberately create an African elite who would accept the standards of the West and then become "associated" with French rulers in the work of colonial development. They did not even attempt to pretend to elevate the condition of the mass of the population. In any event, the method of development, if any was to occur, assumed a common universe of discourse between elevated members of African and French establishments who were united in a common disdain for the untutored.

Under every regime, no matter what its form of government, the French were more willing than the British to accept social and economic change. The British wanted traditional societies to "maintain their uniqueness" and, therefore, stay the way they had always been. The French objective, however, was not that the African should develop on his own lines but that he should become "civilized"—that is, a black Frenchman. Again, even this was accepted as being possible only in the remotest future.

Belgian Colonial Administration

Belgian rule possessed the following distinctive characteristics:

1) No pretense or promise of either theoretical or symbolic equality for Africans;

2) a vital role for the Catholic Church and the Congolese clergy the church created;

3) the "density" of administration, the numbers of civil servants and officers and the extent of its occupation and organization of the countryside;

4) the reliance on big business and their corporate organizations for commercial and industrial "exploitation" and development.

The Belgians prided themselves on not possessing basic philosophical principles. Rather, they maintained that their own colonial administration should be pragmatic and "empirical;" that is, they pos-

---

[16] Idowu, "The Establishment of Elective Institutions in Senegal, 1869–80." pp. 261–71. See also G. Wesley Johnson, Jr., *The Emergence of Black Politics in Senegal* (Stanford, Calif.: Stanford University Press, 1971).

tulated neither a national philosophy of self-government, nor eventual political integration. They concerned themselves supposedly only with bureaucratic "integrity."

Yet despite these allegations of "pragmatism" and disavowals of ideology, as Herbert Weiss points out, Belgian rule inadvertently was the most assimilationist of all the colonial systems, because the impact of their rule was greatest on those social structures and belief systems that really mattered. Unlike the French stress on the absorption of the metropolitan "culture," the Belgians in the Congo stressed "Christian monogamy, and the adoption of an essentially Western way of life."[17]

Without ideological pretensions, Belgian colonial administration meant direct rule by Belgians; that is, no local governments of Africans; no African representation in Belgian institutions; no Africans in any form of political activity whatsoever. Policy makers proclaimed themselves unabashedly paternalisitic. When criticized for not involving Africans in political affairs, or for their preoccupation with economic development, the Belgian colonial administrators replied that this was just nonsense. They were indeed mindful of the social and political evolution of the Congolese, but this growth was based on creating a solid economic foundation. They proclaimed quite bluntly their objective in colonial administration to be efficiency and profitability—an objective that was to be free of the financial and "other" scandals of the old Leopold regime. Even more than the French, the Belgian rulers completely accepted the necessity for rapid economic development, as well as its consequences, such as "detribalization" and the breakdown of the old system of authority. The single-mindedness with which economic development in the interest of business profitability was pursued had ramifications in social policy. For example, unlike the Republic of South Africa or Rhodesia, the Belgians refused in theory to tolerate industrial color bars. With fewer settlers, and because of the importance of the Catholic Church, they were willing to train Africans to do the work of higher paid Europeans and avoid the expense involved in organized apartheid.

Because of their labor requirements, and in order to insulate Africans from "subversive" elements, Belgian colonialism limited Africans to practical education, mainly at the primary and technical levels. In contrast, the British and French encouraged the formation of an African elite educated in social studies at higher levels, including

[17] Herbert F. Weiss, "Comparisons in the Evolution of Pre-Independence Elites in French-Speaking West Africa and the Congo," in William H. Lewis, ed., *French-Speaking Africa: The Search for Identity* (New York: Walker and Company, 1965), p. 134. On the history of Belgian colonial administration see Crawford Young, *Politics in the Congo* (Princeton, N.J.: Princeton University Press, 1965); Georges Brausch, *Belgian Administration in the Congo* (London: Institute of Race Relations, 1961); Raymond Leslie Buell, *The Native Problem in Africa*, 2 vols. (New York: Macmillan, 1928); *Le Congo Belge*, 2. vols. (Brussels: Infracongo, 1958); Robert Cornevin, *Histoire du Congo-Leo* (Paris: Editions Berger-Levrault, 1963); Lord Hailey, *An African Survey*, rev. ed. (London: Oxford University Press, 1957); L. P. Mair, *Native Policies in Africa* (London: Routledge and Sons, 1936); Edmund D. Morel, *King Leopold's Rule in Africa* (New York: Funk & Wagnalls, 1905); Ruth Slade, *King Leopold's Congo* (London: Institute of Race Relations, 1962); and Joseph Conrad, *Heart of Darkness* (New York: Signet Books, 1950).

the university. The Belgians foresaw the potentially explosive effects of exposing Africans to the challenging environments of overseas universities. They did not relish the prospects of a situation that had occurred in British and French territories, where Africans returned from universities demanding to know why the goals of Magna Carta and the ideals of the French Revolution were not for them.

Nevertheless, because of the Catholic Church, a considerable percentage of the Congolese leadership received the equivalent of a college education. In addition to 400 post-secondary school graduates of technical institutes which included medical assistants, agricultural technicians, and administrative specialists, over 3,000 Congolese, who did not become priests, received the advanced training available through the seminaries. The Belgian state, in an undertaking unparalleled in the annals of African colonialism, subsidized the Catholic mission schools (about 700, by independence) and paid for the maintenance of the missionaries, including 6,000 Europeans aided by 500 African priests and 25,000 catechists. Unlike the French and British, the Belgians who monopolized politics and commerce offered the Congolese only one channel of upward mobility, the Church. The Belgians ordained the first African priest in 1917; they graduated the first Congolese university student in 1956.[18]

Church activities supported the most intense reorganization of the rural areas undertaken in colonized Africa. Belgian agricultural officers, for example, at least one per district, brought the central authorities into direct contact with the remotest village; several African agricultural assistants and a network of sub-assistants backed up each Belgian civil servant in a far-flung system. Among other duties, they carried out a program of legally authorized, compulsory labor. Administrative control of the Congo remained much freer from the constraints of domestic politics than had occurred in France or Britain. The Belgian parliament voted the Congo budget as a ritual, without debate; virtually all other matters could be settled through a decree of the king.

Large corporations, themselves generally the subsidiaries of a handful of giant holding companies, dominated business in the Congo, and along with the Church and the administration, composed a trinity of power. Whether based on plantations or on mining, at least one major enterprise dominated the area around it. The administration took extraordinary measures to secure the investments of these concerns by making available land and securing food and labor. Retired at an early age, army officers and high civil servants often joined the private sector. Colonial administrators came mainly from the middle and upper classes and shared with business an antipathy towards "poor whites."

---

[18] Weiss, "Comparisons in the Evolution of Pre-Independence Elites," op. cit., p. 131. See also Ruth Sloan Associates, *The Educated African,* ed. Helen Kitchen (New York: Praeger, 1962).

Portuguese Colonies

Of all the major powers, Portugal has both the longest history of sustained contact with Africa and the least to show for it in terms of political and economic developments.[19] In theory, Africans with the necessary education and European cultural attainments were entitled to the same legal status as the citizens of Portugal. Although more social contact probably occurred between Europeans and Africans in the Portuguese areas of dominion than in any other colonial zone, in reality few Africans were ever legally assimilated and thereby given rights of education and law.

Portugal practiced the crudest form of direct exploitation, including forced labor, which lingered to modern times. Portugal itself, the poorest nation in Western Europe, subjected its own people to a most severely repressive authoritarian regime. No wonder, then, that political development did not occur in the Portuguese territories and that Portuguese rule was marked by an absence of economic development—and an absence even of basic educational facilities.

In examining the colonial policies of the major powers as a whole during this pre–World War II period, and in attempting to summarize their major qualities, one finds certain assumptions and practices that all regimes held in common. Kenneth Robinson has pointed out that the policies of identity were myths, whether they were policies of assimilation under the French policies or of self-government under the English.[20] Second, when confronted with political or administrative difficulties "in the field," every regime did follow pragmatic policies. The French, in particular, accommodated themselves to powerful indigenous systems when those systems could not readily be overthrown.[21] A third characteristic of all systems was that Africans occupied roles that were subordinate to those of Europeans.[22] Despite talk of creating indigenous elites or of allowing au-

---

[19] On the history of Portuguese colonial policy see, for example, James Duffy, *Portuguese Africa* (Cambridge, Mass.: Harvard University Press, 1959); William Minter, *Portuguese Africa and the West* (Harmondsworth: Penguin, 1972); John Davis and James K. Baker, eds., *Southern Africa in Transition* (New York: Praeger, 1966); Eduardo Mondlane, *The Struggle for Mozambique* (Baltimore: Penguin, 1969); and Allen F. Isaacman, *Mozambique: The Africanization of a European Institution* (Madison, Wisc.: University of Wisconsin Press, 1972).

[20] Kenneth E. Robinson, "Political Development in French West Africa," in *Africa in the Modern World*, ed. Calvin Stillman (Chicago: University of Chicago Press, 1955).

[21] Michael Crowder argues that although in practice both the British and the French had little alternative to the use of existing political authorities as a means of governing the vast African empires, there was nevertheless a vast difference between the French system of native administration and the British indirect rule. Fundamentally, what was important was not that chiefs were used, but how they were used. See Crowder's article, "Indirect Rule—French and British Style," *Africa*, 34, no. 3 (July 1964), pp. 197–205; reprinted in *African Politics and Society*, ed., Markovitz, pp. 26–36.

[22] For a remarkable, unintentionally self-revealing portrait of the colonialist as liberal patron, see Isak Dinesen's much-praised *Out of Africa* (New York: Modern Library, 1952), the colonial novel equivalent to Alan Paton's novel about South Africa, *Cry, the Beloved Country* (New York: Scribner's, 1948). The book is about Dinesen—not about Africa and certainly not about Africans. Even though

tonomy for "native authorities," in the end the Europeans expected to give orders and demanded that Africans obey them. Finally, all regimes emphasized merely their negative duties (that is, the maintenance of law and order and the prevention of extortion) rather than promoting large-scale social trends, such as economic development and social welfare. For laissez-faire bourgeois regimes that were committed to the philosophy that "that government is best that governs least," this might not appear surprising. Yet in furthering the interests of private business, early colonial policy under the aegis of mercantilism went far beyond simply creating a "political arena."

Objectives and Methods of Imperialists in Africa: Differences in Colonial Rule after the Second World War

After the Second World War, with the rise of nationialism clearly limiting the days of empire, great changes took place in the colonial policies of all the major powers. British policy had to change the least, since the development of self-government within the commonwealth had always been basic policy. Changes within the British colonies were also facilitated because from the beginning the British had treated each territory as a distinct unit with its own laws, budget, public service, and legislative council. Two basic changes, however, did take place. First, the Labor government in England for the first time accepted the interest of the black majority in the multiracial territories of East and Central Africa as dominant. This meant independence on the basis of "one man, one vote," without a specially protected status for Europeans. Second, after the example of the French in Indochina and Algeria, prolonged encounters in India and Ceylon, and movements of rebellion and revolution in Black Africa that threatened to accelerate, the British accepted an immense change in the pace towards autonomy—particulary in West Africa, where no settled European population existed. Nevertheless, the British insisted to the end on granting independence through the established insitutions of the

she describes objects, others, and happenings, her novel is really about her inner life, how she reacts in a remarkably introspective manner. The primary features of her existence are isolation and unconnectedness. She floats on a cloud of cool that cushions her sense of self-importance. She "understands" the Africans around her, she sympathizes, yet she remains basically uninvolved, aloof in the same floating sort of way; there is only a surface contact. Her deepest feelings don't engage; her inner self stays shelled. The object world overhanging her is secondary. Even when adversity breaks this serenity and she has to sell her 6,000-acre estate because of rising expenses, this becomes a matter of regret but not of tragedy. One can easily imagine that her life will go on albeit in a different house and a different country. Dinesen's story reveals how the magnitude and even the possibility of tragedy and adversity are of a different nature for the settler than for the native. For Dinesen there is no question of her or her family starving or dying. When one has 6,000 acres one also has a small inner space of peace. Out of this peace emerges that classic paternalism, that restrained superiority that enables Dinesen—the model of the sensitive liberal European—to be aware of blacks as human beings far earlier and more deeply than her compatriots but at the same time to remain Baroness—and Robber Baron—on her coffee estate. See also E. M. Forster's *A Passage to India* (New York: Harcourt, Brace & World, 1924); and the Cameroonian writer J. Oyono's novel *Houseboy* (London: Heinemann Educational Books, 1966).

legislative council. In every case, therefore, independence was negotiated with an African leadership that had accepted the procedures and structures of government laid down by the colonial system. Even the most radical of these leaders, therefore, operated "within the system."

The British allowed quick practical results in this era: first, they greatly increased African representation in the legislative council; second, they developed African cabinets with responsibility; third, popularly elected local governments replaced native administrations; and finally, there was a speedup in the pace of economic development, including the use of public monies for the expansion of the "infrastructure," which comprised such things as roads and harbors. The British colonial establishment also encouraged private business to invest in industries rather than to engage simply in commerce. They also expended some effort on social administration; for example, they undertook mass-education and social-welfare projects.

French Policy

After the defeat of the Axis, three political parties of the French left—the Christian Socialists, the Democratic Socialists, and the Communists—jointly assumed power for a short period and established one of the most radical regimes since the time of the Great Revolution. Even then, the French government did not grant independence. They did abolish the system of forced labor, and they even extended citizenship to large "categories" of Africans, but they didn't allow universal suffrage. Under the constitution of the Fourth Republic, all territories acquired the right to seat representatives in metropolitan institutions, including the French National Assembly, the Council of the Republic, and the Assembly of the French Union. Under one common electoral roll, the number of eligible voters expanded by well over 500 percent from 1946 to 1952. Popularly elected local assemblies rapidly gained additional powers, and thereby quickly acquired the status of territorial legislatures. This status was legitimated by the *Loi Cadre* of 1956. A *loi cadre* within the French system establishes the basic framework for the carrying out of a stipulated policy. This 1956 legislation marked a radical departure in French colonial policy because it announced that the basic objective of overseas policy would henceforth be autonomy—no longer integration.

When General De Gaulle was catapulted into office by the threat of a right-wing military takeover in Algeria, he held a referendum in each of the territories of French West Africa and French Equatorial Africa. The referendum provided a choice between independence and continued "association" within the French overseas framework. General De Gaulle campaigned throughout the territories; he made clear that a vote for independence meant a complete and immediate rupture of all connections with France, including technical assistance, educational facilities, preferential markets for stipulated commodities, backing for currency, and economic aid. Only one country opted for independence—Guinea under Sekou Touré. De Gaulle, true to his word, pulled everything that was French, including medicines and telephones, out of that country. Not until 1960, after prolonged negotiation and the creation of both formal and informal agreements, did France's African colonies gain their "formal" independence in an amicable manner.[23]

Belgian Policy

The Belgians did the most radical turnabout of any of the colonial regimes in the post—World War II period. Until the last minute before the granting of independence to their colonies, no major changes of policy took place. The Belgians introduced more secondary education, established the University of the Congo in 1954, and began a new system of local councils, but they announced no fundamental changes of philosophy.

Not until 1957 did Belgian officials begin to realize that "emancipation" was on the historical agenda. But even so, they still thought they could rule for several decades to come, that they could control this development, and that they could continue to manipulate pliant African subjects. King Baudoin could still declare in 1955 that Belgium and the Congo formed a single nation. The most daring Belgian administrators envisaged a Belgium-Congolese community in which the Congo would possess internal autonomy with the two states linked by the Crown.

Widespread demonstrations and "riots" in Leopoldville during January of 1959 for the first time forced the rulers of the Belgian establishment to come to grips with the aspirations of an African leadership. British and French administrators limited political expressions in their colonies, but after World War II recognized a widening sphere of activity as legitimate. When the colonial establishment finally permitted the establishment of political parties, Congolese political leaders built their organizations on a base of pre-existing and largely spontaneous working class and "peasant" protest. More clearly than elsewhere, the official "leaders" did not create the anti-colonial protest; at most they directed dissent into formal channels. The mass base clearly provided a more violent impetus and pointed to a more radical solution. The anti-colonial protest that resulted in independence in 1960 began with the spontaneous uprisings of January 1959 in Leopoldville that then spread to the rural areas of the Lower Congo, Kwango and Kwila provinces. The "official" Congolese leaders at that time were either in jail or otherwise indisposed.

The Belgians then, consistent with their "pragmatic commitment," turned about and resolved to vacate very quickly. They at-

---

[23] For an account of what happened to the huge numbers of colonizers who remained in Africa after independence, see Rita Cruise O'Brien, *White Society in Black Africa: The French of Senegal* (London: Faber & Faber, 1972).

tempted two stratagems: first, to continue to govern behind a facade of the newly sovereign indigenous administration — for example, keeping Belgian officers in charge of the army and Belgian higher civil servants in key positions within the bureaucracy; second, to concentrate their efforts in the mineral-rich province of Haut Katanga, where they had every reason to expect that their Congolese acolytes under Provincial President Moise Tshombe would rule in their favor.

Portuguese Policy

After the Second World War, the Portuguese, while paying lip service to political reform and economic development, did virtually nothing concrete to improve the standards of living of the people within their huge territories. Only under the continual pounding of the African guerrilla movements in each of the three Portuguese territories, only after the expenditure of millions of dollars and untold lives, did the Portuguese turn to political and economic reforms, which were facilitated by funds from Portugal's NATO allies — foremost among them, the United States. Portugal's Organic Law of 1885 had established units of local government in African areas and increased the responsibilities of the Legislative Council, a white advisory board. Thereafter, the Portuguese made efforts to correct the most serious abuses in the "contract labor" system — which was openly criticized in Portugal as well as in the rest of the world. Also, the number of Africans in Angola and Mozambique that were bestowed Portuguese citizenship was greatly increased.[24]

Finally, Portugal's own army officers, in frustration at waging useless and debilitating wars of attrition, turned against the despotic Portuguese government and in 1974 staged a coup d'etat. As quickly as possible thereafter, Guinea, Mozambique, and finally Angola gained full independence.

On September 10, 1974, Portugal formally recognized the independence of the Republic of Guinea-Bissau in accordance with an agreement signed with the PAIGC on August 26. The accord also provided for a referendum on the future of the Cape Verde Islands, which became a separate country in 1975. Africans in Guinea-Bissau date the country's independence from September 24, 1973, when they unilaterally asserted their freedom. Luis Cabral, brother of Amilcar Cabral, became the first president of the Republic.

On September 7, 1974, Samora Machel, leader of FRELIMO (Front for the Liberation of Mozambique) signed a cease-fire agreement that ended 500 years of Portuguese domination. The date selected for the new nation's independence, June 25, 1975, marked the

---

[24] For accounts of these matters and also of Portugal's 1953–1964 Overseas Development Plan, see James Duffy, "Portuguese Africa, 1930 to 1960," in Peter Duignan and L. H. Gann, eds., *Colonialism in Africa, 1870–1970*, Vol. 2, *The History and Politics of Colonialism, 1914–1960*, ed. Duignan and Gann (Cambridge: Cambridge University Press, 1970); Duffy, *Portuguese Africa;* and David Abshire and Michael Samuels, eds., *Portuguese Africa, A Handbook* (New York: Praeger, 1967).

thirteenth anniversary of the founding of the front. FRELIMO, founded under the leadership of Eduardo Mondlane, originated in the shots fired by Portuguese troops into black demonstrators in Lourenco Marques in 1960 and early 1961.

Angola, after fourteen years of guerrilla warfare, became independent on November 11, 1975. Based on great resources of oil, diamonds, iron, and coffee, Angola's 1973 gross national product of $1.5 billion far surpassed that of Portugal's other colonies. With a more diverse population and more varied geographic regions, Angola also had three major guerrilla movements. The other two territories each possessed a single strong nationalist organization that took over administration from the Portuguese. The MPLA won a prolonged civil war and moved to consolidate its power after a struggle in which foreign interventions had threatened to produce an African Vietnam.[25]

Neocolonialism and Dependency

Political independence clearly did not mean economic independence for the new African states. These new countries still depended on the colonial powers, both for development funds and for the technology necessary to achieve a higher standard of living for their peoples. The conditions of exploitation remained: the new states were still producers of raw materials; they still had little industry; they were still markets for more sophisticated goods. The former colonial powers— although threatened by powerful competitors such as the United States, Japan, and West Germany—nevertheless had established basic trade patterns. The price of modern warfare and the cost of troops meant that most western nations could not afford to maintain a siege of occupation, but they still could dictate the conditions of aid. Under these changed circumstances, Lord Palmerston's dictum that he did not have to own an inn in order to sleep in it made a good deal of sense.[26]

[25] See Immanuel Wallerstein, "Luanda is Madrid," *The Nation*, January 10, 1976, pp. 12–17. For background on the fighting in the Portuguese territories, see Thomas Okuma, *Angola in Ferment: The Background and Prospects of Angolan Nationalism* (Boston: Beacon Press, 1962); Richard Gibson, *African Liberation Movements* (New York: Oxford University Press, 1972); Basil Davidson, *In the Eye of the Storm: Angola's People* (Garden City, N.Y.: Anchor Books, 1972); *Portugal and Africa: The Struggle Continues*, special issue of *Africa Today*, 21, no. 1 (Winter 1974); *Portugal and Africa: A New Day Dawns*, special issue of *Africa Today*, 21, no. 4 (Fall 1974); *Mozambique*, special issue of *Issue*, 4 no. 2, (Summer 1974); and Mondlane, *The Struggle for Mozambique;* Christine P. Potholm and Richard Dale, eds. *Southern Africa in Perspective* (New York: Free Press, 1972); Basil Davidson, *The Liberation of Guine* (Baltimore, Penquin, 1969); Kenneth Grundy, *Guerrilla Struggle in Africa* (New York: Grossman, 1971); and John Marcum, *The Angolan Revolution*, Vol. I, *The Anatomy of an Explosion, 1950–1962* (Cambridge, Mass.: M.I.T. Press, 1969).

[26] On neocolonialism, see, for example, Alphaeus W. Hunton, *Decision in Africa* (New York: International Publishers, 1957); Stuart Smith, *U. S. Neocolonialism in Africa* (New York: International Publishers, 1974); Kwame Nkrumah, *Challenge of the Congo* (New York: International Publishers, 1967); Kwame Nkrumah, *Neo-Colonialism: The Last Stage of Imperialism* (New York: International Publishers, 1965); Abdoulaye Ly, *Les masses Africaines et l'actuelle condition humaine* (Paris: Presence Africaine, 1956); Abdoulaye Ly, *L'etat et la production paysanne* (Paris: Presence Africaine, 1958); Edward M. Corbett, *The French Presence in Black Africa* (Washington, D.C.: Black Orpheus Press, 1972); Walter Rodney, *How Europe Underdeveloped Africa* (Washington, D.C.: Howard University Press, 1974); Richard D. Wolff, *The Economics of Colonialism: Britain and Kenya, 1870–1930* (New Haven: Yale University

Not everybody agrees that "the history of Africa's relations with the West has been a history of robbery."[27] The most sophisticated of those theorists who stress the "positive contributions" of colonialism agree that the mother countries might have benefited from "an unusually high" rate of profit, particularly from colonies with easily extracted mineral wealth. One such writer argues, nevertheless, that European colonialism "did not impoverish the colonies in any fundamental way."[28] Another commentator maintains that the only "core of truth in the Leninist theory of imperialism" is that traditional economic systems have become disrupted as a result of being "integrated into the international capitalist economy" and that this breakdown of "pre-modern" societies has provided the background of "all successful twentieth century revolutions."[29] Social scientist W. W. Rostow speaks of "competitive compulsions" and "power ploys" on the part of "national political actors" to "advance a national interest negatively by denying a source of power to another nation."[30] A monopoly of trade in a given underdeveloped area is one way of doing this. Rostow alleges, nevertheless, that the creation of colonies was caused basically by the "societal condition" of the colonial areas themselves. In his view, traditional societies had shown themselves incapable or unwilling to organize themselves for modern import-export activity. European governments therefore had to "initiate the process," even though they were perfectly willing to have engaged in "normal trade between equals."[31] While Rostow voices irritation at the "native societies," which virtually forced European capitalist regimes to reorganize their economies at a modest fee, African traditional systems have their own defenders. J. D. Fage, for example, defends African chieftains against what he calls the racist implication that they were economic ignoramuses. Fage argues that the slave trade was organized basically by traditional ruling classes who recognized a good thing when they saw it. He contends, in addition, that the African traditional systems as a whole benefited. The slave trade stimulated economic growth and caused a rise in the standard of living of "the mass of the popu-

Press, 1974); Justinian Rweyemanu, *Underdevelopment and Industrialization in Tanzania: A Study of Perverse Capitalist Industrial Development* (Nairobi: Oxford University Press, 1973); Colin Leys, *Underdevelopment in Kenya: The Political Economy of Neo-Colonialism, 1964–1971* (Berkeley and Los Angeles: University of California Press, 1974); Constantine V. Vaitsos, *Intercountry Income Distribution and Transnational Enterprises* (London: Oxford University Press, 1974); Richard L. Sklar, *Corporate Power in an African State: The Political Economy of Multinational Companies in Zambia* (Berkeley and Los Angeles: University of California Press, 1975); and Carl Widstrand, ed., *Multinational Firms in Africa* (Uppsala: Scandinavian Institute of African Studies, 1975). Edward H. McKinley, in *The Lure of Africa: American Interests in Tropical Africa, 1919–1939* (New York and Indianapolis: Bobbs-Merrill, 1974), discussing the atrocities of King Leopold in the Congo, states, "The bicycle craze of the late Victorian era was then at its height, and rubber was in constant demand. . . . Prim and proper cyclists were shocked to learn that they were pedaling through life on the 'red rubber' of the Congo stained with the blood of the hapless Africans who had gathered it." (pp. 13–14)

[27] Jack Woddis, *Africa: The Roots of Revolt* (New York: Citadel, 1962).

[28] C. E. Black, *The Dynamics of Modernization* (New York: Harper & Row, 1966), p. 125.

[29] John Dunn, *Modern Revolutions* (Cambridge and New York: Cambridge University Press, 1972), p. 249.

[30] W. W. Rostow, *Political Stages of Growth* (New York: Cambridge University Press, 1971), p. 109.

[31] *Ibid.*, p. 110. See also Rostow's *The Stages of Economic Growth: A Non-Communist Manifesto*, 2nd ed. (New York: Cambridge University Press, 1971).

lation"—except, presumably, for those unfortunates who were the essential commodity.[32] Other writers have defended imperialism against charges of race prejudice. For example, L. H. Gann and Peter Duignan, in their book with the revealing title *Burden of Empire*, assure us that "race prejudice is much older than capitalism; race prejudice moreover transcends color."[33]

No western scholar has done more than Rupert Emerson to facilitate the study of third world countries, encouraging both westerners and the many leaders of these nations who were his students at Harvard. Emerson also advocated rapid independence when that was an unpopular position. Yet even Emerson, although he does not claim that imperialism was the ideal instrument for the spread of civilization, has argued that

> a plausible case can . . . be made for the proposition that the future will look back upon the overseas imperialism of recent centuries, less in terms of its sins of oppression, exploitation, and discrimination, than as the instrument by which the spiritual, scientific, and material revolution which began in Western Europe with the Renaissance spread to the rest of the world. . . . The importance of more peaceful and egalitarian processes of cultural diffusion may not be minimized in order to identify the positive role which imperialism has played.[34]

Eventually, the non-European societies strove to acquire new means of transportation and communication, modern medicine, and higher standards of living, and damned colonial governments, "not so much because they had ruthlessly upset the old order of things—although they were damned for that too—as because they had so inadequately carried through the work of industrializing ancient societies and dragooning them into the modern world."[35] Why couldn't these gains by non-European societies have been accomplished without imperialism? Because, Emerson believes, "there remains good reason to doubt that the non-European peoples could have been induced, without compulsion, to undertake in any comparable span of time a revolutionizing of their societies which involved abandonment of their established way of life."[36] Therefore, Emerson concludes, out of the colonial experience came not only education along western lines but also "the acceptance of individualism," "a far greater measure of egali-

---

[32] See Fage's *History of West Africa*, rev. ed. (Cambridge: Cambridge University Press, 1969). In refutation, see, for example, Martin Klein, "Social and Economic Factors in the Muslim Revolution in Senegambia," *Journal of African History*, 13, no. 3 (1972), 419–41; and Edward A. Alpers, *Ivory and Slaves in East Central Africa* (Berkeley and Los Angeles: University of California Press, 1975), p. 266.

[33] L. H. Gann and Peter Duignan, *Burden of Empire: An Appraisal of Western Colonialism in Africa South of the Sahara* (New York: Praeger, 1967), p. 144. However, cf. Woddis, *Africa: The Roots of Revolt*, and especially Winthrop Jordan, who in his *White Over Black* (Baltimore: Penguin, 1969) details a coincidence between the rise of mass prejudice and increasing economic exploitation and political domination.

[34] Rupert Emerson, *From Empire to Nation* (Boston: Beacon Press, 1960), pp. 6–7.

[35] *Ibid.*, p. 11.

[36] *Ibid.*, p. 8.

tarianism," and "a sense that the introduction of Western-style parliamentary democracy symbolized the attainment of political maturity."[37]

In the final analysis, the logic of the above assessments is bizarre, their premises about the cultural and material level of precolonial African civilizations in comparison with that of the West are false; and their theories of the causes of development are fundamentally mistaken.

Two African Assessments of Colonialism

From the earliest days of contact with European traders and explorers, Africans welcomed the possibility of the exchange of ideas, inventions, and culture, as well as trade and commerce. They denied, however, that imperialism was the medium necessary for this exchange to take place. Africans pointed out that any so-called benefits of Western civilization were side effects, produced reluctantly. Jomo Kenyatta wrote, in one of the first anthropological studies by an African of his own people,

> There certainly are some progressive ideas among the Europeans. They include the ideas of material prosperity, of medicine, and hygiene, and literacy which enables people to take part in world culture. But so far the Europeans who visit Africa have not been conspicuously zealous in imparting these parts of their inheritance to the Africans, and seem to think that the only way to do it is by police discipline and armed force. They speak as if it were somehow beneficial to an African to work for them instead of for himself, and to make sure that he will receive this benefit they do their best to take away his land and leave him with no alternative. Along with his land they rob him of his government, condemn his religious ideas, and ignore his fundamental conceptions of justice and morals, all under the name of civilization and progress.[38]

Aimé Césaire, the founder of the doctrine of militant negritude, poet and dramatist, and one of the most articulate fighters for the rights of France's overseas empire, has discussed how colonialism turned the colonizer into a pawn, a guard, a whip, and the colonized into an instrument of production. For Césaire, colonization equals "thingafication." In reply to the "storm of protest" of those who would emphasize "progress and 'accomplishments,' sickness conquered, higher standards of living," Césaire speaks of "societies emptied of themselves, of trampled cultures, undermined institutions, confiscated lands, of assassinated religions, annihilated artistic masterpieces, of extraordinary possibilities suppressed." What resulted from the contact between the West and Africa?

[37] *Ibid.,* p. 11.
[38] Jomo Kenyatta, *Facing Mt. Kenya* (New York: Random House, n.d.), p. 305.

Security? Culture? Law? While waiting I look and I see that wherever the colonizers and the colonized meet face to face there is force, brutality, cruelty, sadism, violence. . . .

Between colonizer and colonized there is only room for forced labor, intimidation, pressure, policing, taxes, theft, rape, forced farming, scorn, distrust, arrogance, roguery, and conceit towards the deranged elites and downtrodden masses.

There is no human contact, but only the relationship of domination and submission. . . .[39]

Césaire admits that the contact of differing *civilizations* is good, because whenever any civilization looks only upon itself and loses contact with external worlds, it becomes enervated. The great opportunity and advantage of Europe was that it acted as a crossroads of civilizations, incorporating many ideas, philosophies, and beliefs. However, as Césaire maintains, the "distance from civilization to colonization is infinite."

The Dual Economy and Other Propositions of "Modernization" Theories

Among the propositions that most mainstream economists hold incontrovertible regarding the impact of colonialism on African societies are the following, which we do *not* accept:

1) Subsistence economies of the traditional societies coexist in a pattern of uneven "development" with the commodity-exchange economies introduced by "westernization." Eventually, the commodity-exchange system will take over in an expanding network of economic relations, but until that time a dual economy will continue. A key point of this proposition is that essentially the two systems are not interrelated; each develops along its separate path.

2) Some variation of "feudalism," or some variation of "traditional" or "primitive" economies and technologies, is the primary cause for the lack of development.

3) All societies will eventually follow the same path. There are "higher" and "lower" civilizations, and some of the "lesser" peoples have not as yet caught on. Given enough time and the proper tutelage, they will eventually become "just like us." In the most sophisticated version of this thesis, "higher" and "lower" supposedly have no moral or judgmental qualities attached, but simply have to do with "fortuitous" or "different" characteristics or circumstances. The key to development is contained in "Western" or (again, to escape the

---

[39] Aimé Césaire, *Discours sur le colonialisme* (Paris: Presence Africaine, 1966), pp. 7–13; reprinted and excerpted as "On the Nature of Colonialism," in *African Politics and Society: Basic Issues and Problems of Government and Development*, ed. Irving Leonard Markovitz (New York: Free Press; London: Collier-Macmillan, 1970), pp. 37–42.

value connotation) "Newtonian" technology. Disagreement occurs among the various subschools over whether this evolution will follow definite stages of growth or be marked by less precise progressions. Science, properly applied, propels the whole process of development.

4) Foreign aid, including massive transfusions of capital coupled with technical assistance of all types, is the essential mechanism for growth. Given the pressures of rising demands and expectations, no country can hope to pull itself up by its own bootstraps. Given the enormous size and expense of modern means of production, faithful overseas allies require major commitments.

5) Capitalism in some form is the most efficient means of economic growth. Capitalism is not incompatible with some type of centralized controls or with a large role played by the state. Indeed, these are essential. However, socialism of any sort cannot succeed, for a variety of reasons. Either the necessary bureaucratic arrangements are too complex for a poor country to handle, or human nature makes the task impossible.[40] Even when a government calls itself socialist, it is in fact practicing capitalism.

6) The nationalist bourgeoisie is a social class that is necessary for economic reconstruction, and in the newly independent African states it will once more play the constructive role in amassing capital and building industry that it has played historically.

7) No difference exists between "neocolonialism" and simple "interdependence." Once a country has achieved independence, to talk of neocolonialism is to view common economic realities through ideological blinders. Not all countries are superpowers. Even the superpowers cannot go their way in complete independence. Complex technology and rapid communications bind all governments to one another in a sometimes unsatisfactory manner. Why complain about the inevitable?

To evaluate these propositions and to better understand the realities of European intervention and the connections the European powers established with African regimes requires, to begin with, changing the commonly held notion that African traditional societies simply disintegrated under the "Western" impact. African social and economic structures did not disintegrate or disappear. European economic systems might have undermined or disrupted traditional productive capacities, but this is quite different from asserting a breakdown in the relative positions of power of social strata in African systems. Although the economic basis of power of the governing classes changed, the relative positions of power of social strata often remained comparatively unaltered. Disruption of the traditional economies, therefore, as well as the new opportunities offered, created

---

[40] One of the strongest critiques of the possibilities of establishing Socialism in Africa is Elliot Berg, "Socialism and Economic Development in Tropical Africa," *Quarterly Journal of Economics*, 67, no. 4 (November 1964).

powerful alliances between the European and African dominant groups. The major traditional political and economic interests were the precursors of today's "new class." The term "new class," therefore, is to a large extent a misnomer. In reality, the ruling group is an "old class"; it now governs a politically relevant populace that is much expanded, and it governs with the aid of a greatly increased number of auxiliary bureaucrats and technocrats. We need a new image to reinforce our theoretical understanding of the realities of imperialism. No longer do we believe that colonial regimes simply entered African occupied areas and conquered at will. The image of a map of Africa with nice neat boundaries is very misleading. Our new image must also take into account the processes of mutual accommodation characteristic of "indirect rule."[41]

Traditional capitalist interests have always persisted in Africa but sometimes in a modernized form.[42] Consider labor and the unexpected dependence that occurred with expanded educational, even higher educational, facilities. Imperialism has always looked to dependent areas for cheap labor. The definition of cheap labor has changed in ways that might at first appear qualitatively significant, but that in fact simply reproduce previous patterns of exploitation.[43] To turn out skilled engineers and technocrats might appear essential to launch new countries on the road to "true" independence. However, we must ask additional questions about why these technicians are being turned out and for whom they go to work. To take one example, in Ghana, Kaiser Aluminum's Valco hires almost all of the graduate engineers from the Kumasi Technical Institute, paying them a beginning salary of $3,500. In a country where the average per capita income is less than $300, such a salary would seem incredibly generous. However, in comparison with United States standards, Kaiser is simply taking advantage of another cheap commodity.[44]

New forms of entangling alliances buttress the influence of the metropolitan centers. Edward Corbett alleges that following years of nominal sovereignty, the French presence still pervades the former French territories of Western and Equatorial Africa and Madagascar.

[41] See G. C. Z. Mhone, "Economic Exploitation and African Economic Development: A Comparative Critique of Marxist and Traditional Views of Imperialism" (unpublished paper read before the African Studies Association meeting, Syracuse, N.Y., February 31, 1973).

[42] Frank Bonilla, *The Failure of Elites* (Cambridge, Mass.: M.I.T. Press, 1970), p. 321.

[43] Henry Bretton, certainly not given to materialist interpretations, has noted that the reality of bread-and-butter politics limits the options of the new leadership of African countries and forces them to serve at least two masters, their own constituents and the source of their outside support: "the precarious financial position of the regimes in middle Africa is not such to require much effort by world centers of economic power to make things quite uncomfortable for mavericks" (Henry L. Bretton, *Patron-Client Relations: Middle Africa and the Powers* [New York: General Learning Press, 1971], p. 23).

[44] "Bloodsucking imperialist" has long been an epithet hurled poetically at Western corporate exploitation. The *New York Times* on January 27, 1973 carried the story of an American company in Haiti that bought blood plasma from impoverished Haitians who needed the money, exporting 5,000 to 6,000 liters of it every month to the United States. See the story for the detailed connection between leading ministers in the Haitian government and various overseas business interests that created an industrial empire based in part upon "bloodletting."

France has maintained "special relationships" with these states, relationships defined by detailed treaties that validate her preeminence in cultural, political, economic, and military affairs and reinforce the French "mind-set" of the African establishments. To consider just one country, Corbett lists ten separate French-Cameroonian treaties signed between 1960 and 1963. The "comprehensive range of cooperation" encompassed by these accords included a diplomatic convention; a cooperative agreement on economic, monetary, and financial matters; a convention regulating relations between the French and Cameroonian treasuries: a general technical-cooperation agreement on matters of personnel; a cooperation agreement on matters of civil aviation, aerial navigation, air bases, and meteorology; an agreement on military technical assistance; a convention on the role and status of the French military mission in Cameroon; a cultural convention; a consular convention; and a legal convention. The agreements on personnel included three protocols, covering military personnel on detached duty in the public service of Cameroon, teaching personnel, and judicial personnel put at the disposition of Cameroon.[45]

American policy in Ghana provides another example of the mechanisms of neocolonial intervention in an African country as well as a glimpse into the reasoning of American "liberal" administrations. Towards the end of his regime, Kwame Nkrumah not only hosted huge foreign investments, particularly from the United States and Britain, he also began to investigate the possibilities of associate membership in the European Economic Community. This was after years of fighting even the idea of such a connection between Africa and former colonial countries. In an about-face, he also accepted the conditions under which the International Monetary Fund and the World Bank would give Ghana their support. Within his government, Nkrumah conspicuously increased the power of avowedly pro-Western economists. W. Scott Thompson tells us, however, that "this was all done too late." Western governments thought that these moments of rationality were, at best, only short hesitations on a steep downward slide. For years, Nkrumah had hidden his real intentions, they believed. While professing friendship with the West, he had led his state on a reckless and ultimately calamitous course. Now, guarding their hand, they played his game: "If there is no evidence of their collusion in the 1966 coup, there is reason to think that Western economic pressures would, by the spring of 1966, have made the regime's survival very unlikely."[46] As an illustration of "subtle" economic pressure, Thompson cites the probability that in the absence of the 1966 coup, credit for consumer goods, "on which the stability of the regime depended," would not have been extended by the large expatriate firms,

---

[45] Corbett, *The French Presence in Black Africa*, p. 4.

[46] W. Scott Thompson, *Ghana's Foreign Policy, 1957–1966* (Princeton, N.J.: Princeton University Press, 1969), p. 363. See also my review of Thompson in *Africa Report*, 15, no. 3 (March 1970), 32–35; and Richard J. Walton, *Cold War and Counter-Revolution: The Foreign Policy of John F. Kennedy* (Baltimore: Penguin, 1972).

and "Nkrumah could [not] have survived the riots and demonstrations that would ensue from the food shortages."[47] To satisfy the needs of foreign governments, moreover, required not simply safeguards against confiscation, but guarantees that overseas business could plan investment rationally. British concerns in particular feared not so much nationalization as a general deterioration of Ghana's economy to the point that would render their investments worthless. American government officials were particularly sensitive to Nkrumah's decision to hold an anti-Vietnam War conference in Winneba. Growing ill feelings were mutually inflamed, by the daily American bombing of North Vietnam and the American invasion of the Dominican Republic on the one hand, and increasingly vitriolic antiimperialist attacks in the Ghanaian press and radio on the other. The decision to hold this conference marked the point at which American diplomats "gave up on Nkrumah."[48] Although these same diplomats recognized that Nkrumah had a long record of "compromise with imperialism," they believed that there would be "less compromise in the future." Side by side with Nkrumah's antiimperialist rhetoric, however, was his acknowledgment that Ghana's "need of the West" had increased. For example, the seven-year Ghanaian development plan that was to begin in January, 1963 projected heavily increased Western investment as the basis for further industrialization. In 1963 the Ghanaian government passed a new investment law that offered still greater inducements for Western businessmen to come to Ghana. Central to Ghana's whole national development program was the building of the Volta Dam, which relied on American capital and expertise. In 1963 the Kaiser Aluminum Company had still not committed itself to constructing the huge aluminum smelter that was to use the dam's electricity. Dean Rusk, in testimony before the Senate Foreign Relations Committee, made it very clear that the United States would not provide additional capital for the all-important Volta scheme if Nkrumah were to "steer Ghana down a road that is hostile to the United States or American interests there."[49] Since his pro-Algerian independence speech as a senator, President Kennedy had been considered a friend of nationalist regimes. He pursued a foreign policy that was distinguished by its sophistication from the crude anticommunism of the Dulles-Eisenhower era. Yet he sent several missions to Ghana headed by men such as Henry McLoy, head of the Chase Manhattan National Bank, to find out whether Nkrumah was or wasn't a communist. When Western intelligence sources discovered that Communist China had sent "experts" to Ghana, "the last stage of Ghanaian subversion had begun. From this time on Chinese (and East German) assistance might have led to a level of competence which would have made Nkrumah's regime very dangerous indeed had the 1966 coup not in-

[47] Thompson, *Ghana's Foreign Policy, 1957–1966*, p. 363.
[48] *Ibid.*, p. 408.
[49] *Ibid.*, p. 272.

tervened."[50] If this was the attitude of America's most sophisticated leaders, it was obvious that more than personalities mattered in the formulation of policies in the era following Ghana's independence.

Postcolonial imperialism involved subtler forces than direct or even indirect political intervention. As the economies of African states became increasingly intertwined with those of the industrial states, as their need for capital and more sophisticated technology grew greater, as they found the overseas markets for their products controlled more tightly by "private" corporations, their dependency grew greater, the forces beyond the control of African national governments loomed even more formidable, and "correct behavior" became largely self-induced. African governments—especially those of the organizational bourgeoisie, but socialist regimes also—sought to discover, without being commanded, the "proper" course of conduct to attract the apparently indispensable agents of profit and progress.

These considerations in turn raise issues that have bitterly divided social scientists. First, does growth originate from superior Newtonian technology or from an exploitative relation that denies the wealth of colonies? The conflict here is between the theories of "modernization"—a term that we must consider no longer neutral or technical but ideologically shaded because it has historically been associated with and assumed the evolutionary-diffusionist approach—versus the theories of "dependency."

The second issue turns on how theorists view impoverishment, in relative or absolute terms, in comparison with an African country's own past or with the gap between the underdeveloped and developed countries. Frequently, even the most sophisticated analysts leave this basis of comparison unclear or unexamined; their assumptions and predictions about the future development and evolution of underdeveloped countries do not ring true or are blatantly erroneous.

Third, no one doubts that African societies have undergone and continue to undergo processes of restratification. Whether the social groups are strata, elites, masses, classes, or castes are hotly disputed, as is the ultimate scope and source of political and economic power and control. In terms of development the problem is not only whether the gross national product can be increased but whether the standard of living of the mass of the population—and not just that of a small organizational bourgeoisie—can be raised within a capitalist framework, and if so, what, if anything, would be wrong about that.

Finally, persons argue about the degree of independence and competence of the African bourgeoisie: whether it is simply a comprador class or truly nationalist; whether it is parasitic, living off artificially raised prices but incapable of productive investment or technological innovation; whether it derives from and depends on a new political or bureaucratic class or whether it will become the economic

---

[50] *Ibid.*, pp. 360–61.

class that will provide the foundation for the most enduring African regimes of the future.

This study shares the perspective of the dependency theorists. Newtonian technology, enormously productive, operated within a capitalist framework that, historically, has guided the most important outcomes for the most important parts of the material lives of most people, most of the time. This study, however, assumes that capitalist development can produce economic growth in African countries; that the GNP can increase; that the fortunes of the African bourgeoisie will soar—largely at the expense of the mass of the rural population—that the absolute standard of living of the mass of the population may well sink to historically unprecedented depths as the exploitative mechanisms of a market economy are added to those of traditional systems; but that because of the qualitatively higher productivity inherent in Newtonian technology and modern industry, coupled with the changing requirements of corporate capitalism, the absolute standard of living of large sections of African populations in certain countries may well improve over the long run.

However, African societies will pay the price of a "perverted development." Their dependency on the transnational capitalism of the industrialized nations will increase. Even as the African bourgeoisie becomes more aggressive in pursuing its historical role of searching for profit, and more nationalistic in its use of the state to squeeze additional concessions from the multinational corporations—thereby acting far differently than a mere comprador class—its dependency, its incorporation as an active agent fulfilling a vital role in the international division of labor—the role of the national wing of an international institution—will become more complete.

Outer-directed development based on the maximization of profits means that the general welfare of the population is provided for indirectly, at best; that the benefits of growth are left to a "trickle-down mechanism"; that the interests of the small farmer, the unskilled worker, the unemployed, the sick, the uneducated, and the illiterate village dweller can safely be ignored; and that if economic development takes place at all, hundreds of years will pass before the descendants of the wretched of the earth will benefit. And even if these descendants finally do become true members of the society, the society will still possess values of materialism and individualism that are characteristic of all capitalist civilizations. The rest of this chapter and subsequent chapters will attempt to develop these propositions.

Imperialism and Theories of Dependency

In tracing the rise of the modern nation-state, Carl Friedrich has examined the connections between a greatly strengthened political system and the rise of a new mercantile commerce. The growth of the West was fed by nonwestern civilizations. Friedrich quotes Sombart's assertion that "the modern state emerged from the silver mines of Mexico and Peru and the gold mines of Brazil."[51] Whether we look at Europe in its connections with the New World during this period, or at Great Britain, France, Belgium, and Portugal in their relations with Africa today, the central thesis of Andre Gunder Frank appears to hold true: "Underdevelopment is not due to the survival of archaic institutions and the existence of capital shortage in regions that have remained isolated from the stream of world history. On the contrary underdevelopment was and still is generated by the very same historical process which also generated economic development: the development of capitalism itself."[52] For example, after the destruction of the Spanish Armada by the English in 1588, Great Britain, through a series of commercial treaties and exploitative trade relations, virtually eliminated the Iberian countries from participation in world capitalist development. The inequitable trade relationship between the English and the Iberians was exemplified by the exchange of textiles, an industrial product, for Portuguese wines, an agricultural product. Although classical economists such as Ricardo might have justified this exchange on the basis of a supposed natural or comparative advantage, Frank concludes that underdevelopment is what happens when an initial competitive edge is magnified over centuries.

Thus, in contrast with the "evolutionary-diffusionist" theory, which maintains that development occurs in advanced cultures because of a superior technology which can then be donated to the "backward" areas, Frank argues that development occurs because of an exploitative relationship between countries that originally were virtually equal. Thus, economic development occurs simultaneously with underdevelopment. Only when the "advanced countries" suffer catastrophe, depression, or world war do the "poor countries" loosen their dependent ties with the world metropolises and begin to enjoy spurts of economic growth. When the metropolis recovers and resumes its position of domination, it restores and intensifies the satellite status of the "poor" country, rechannelling it into underdevelopment.[53]

In assessing the obstacles to development in "poor" countries, Celso Furtado argues similarly that after beginning on planes of comparable equality, the "dominant centers reserved for themselves the economic activities that concentrated technological progress." By controlling the spread of new technological processes through political domination, the rulers of the "advanced" countries created a worldwide economic system. Underdevelopment, therefore, cannot be studied as a "phase" of the development process: "Since the underdeveloped countries are contemporaries of — and in one way or another dependent on — their developed counterparts, the former cannot re-

[51] Carl Friedrich, *The Age of the Baroque, 1610–1660* (New York: Harper & Row, 1952), p. 6.

[52] Andre Gunder Frank, *Capitalism and Underdevelopment in Latin America* (New York: Monthly Review Press, 1967), p. 9. See also Frank's *Lumpenbourgeoisie: Lumpendevelopment* (New York: Monthly Review Press, 1972).

[53] Frank, *Capitalism and Underdevelopment in Latin America*, p. 28.

trace the experiences of the latter. Therefore, development and underdevelopment should be considered as two aspects of the same historical process."[54]

The Dual-Economy Myth

Frank argues that the universally accepted, common-sense notion of a "dual economy" is a myth.[55] Slavery and feudalism did not come to a precipitous end. Neither did dual societies and economies exist side by side for a long period of time. Economists have long maintained the theory of "creeping capitalism," according to which a network of changed relations involving more and more workers in a cash economy spread only gradually and coexisted with a subsistence economy. Marked by evident inequalities of income and differences in culture, each of the two economies and societies was supposed to have had separate histories, social institutions, and political and social dynamics. Supposedly, only the exchange sector interacted consistently and systematically with the "outside capitalist world," and because of this contact it became "modern" and "developed." The other sector, which was characterized as feudal, precapitalist, or subsistence, supposedly was isolated, primitive, and therefore more underdeveloped. The strongest attack against this thesis comes from Frank who maintains that the entire theory is false:

> A mounting body of evidence suggests, and I am confident that future historical research will confirm, that the expansion of the capital system of the past centuries effectively and entirely penetrated even the apparently most isolated sectors of the underdeveloped world. Therefore, the economic, political, social, and cultural institutions and relations we now observe are the products of the historical development of the capitalist system no less than are the seemingly more modern or capitalist features of the national metropoles of these underdeveloped countries.[56]

According to Frank, therefore, no part of the economy of third world countries is feudal; all of it is integrated fully into a single capitalist system.[57]

Eugene Genovese has criticized Frank's theory on the grounds that the strength of capitalism in an underdeveloped country lay in its ability to cut the peasant off from access to "a market mentality and a bourgeois ethos while forcing his labor into a market economy." But this is pre-

---

[54] Celso Furtado, *Obstacles to Development in Latin America* (Garden City, N.Y.: Doubleday, Anchor Books, 1970), p. xvi.

[55] For discussions of the concept of the dual economy see, for example, W. Arthur Lewis, *The Theory of Economic Growth* (Homewood, Ill.: Richard D. Irwin, 1955); Gerald M. Meier and Robert E. Baldwin, *Economic Development* (New York: John Wiley 1957); and Andrew W. Kamarck, *The Economics of African Development*, rev. ed. (New York: Praeger, 1971).

[56] Andre Gunder Frank, *Latin America: Underdevelopment or Revolution* (New York: Monthly Review Press, 1969), p. 5.

[57] See also Frank, *Capitalism and Underdevelopment in Latin America*, p. xiv.

cisely Frank's point. Contrary to Genovese's fears that viewing economic development in exploited poor countries as a capitalist rather than a feudal process will "play into the hands of the counter-revolution by obscuring the need for the revolution as opposed to reform of the capitalist system," Frank's argument leads to a better appreciation of the exact way in which capitalism has indeed incorporated preexisting feudal organizations into a new structure for its own ends, thus subverting their essential nature while maintaining those aspects and attributes that enable it to exploit a peasant work force more effectively.[58]

Discussing African patterns of rural social stratification, Claude Meillasoux shows how the introduction of capitalism resulted in integrated economies and intensified divisions between rich and poor farmers. Big farmers bought grain during the harvest and sold it back to the poor peasants during the hungry period. Social inequality among the peasants was linked directly to the urban trade:

> The studies of the mechanism associated with the markets show . . . the subordination of the peasant communities to a trade, always induced from outside, and the subsequent deterioration of the rural sector for the benefit of the commercial and industrial capital sector. In other words, it demonstrates the irrelevance of the notion of a dual economy made of two distinct sectors, traditional and modern, foreign to each other.[59]

James Coleman describes how Nigerian industry, once freed from the controls of overseas capitalism, spurted forward during time of war, and how this helped create an awakening nationalist consciousness:

> The lack of shipping, plus wartime shortages of imported foods and consumers goods resulted in a remarkable growth of local industries (shingles, furniture, butter, potatoes, sugar, and later, cigarettes, beer and soap). Moreover, the local products were cheaper than the imported ones. It was the proof that the nationalists had been waiting for; here was conclusive evidence that the only bar to industrialization in Nigeria was the desire of the British administration to protect home manufactures. The nationalists believed that the evidence gave substance to the charge of exploitation. The growth of local industries not only increased the urban labor force but also created new tastes and new wants.[60]

---

[58] Genovese, "The Slave Systems and European Antecedence," *In Red and Black,* Pantheon, 1968, Vintage Books, New York, 1972, p. 63.

[59] Claude Meillassoux, ed., *The Development of Indigenous Trade and Markets in West Africa* (London: Oxford University Press, 1971), p. 85. Meillassaux bases his arguments, in large part, on the findings about rural stratification made by Polly Hill in her *Migrant Cocoa Farmers of Southern Ghana* (Cambridge: Cambridge University Press, 1963).

[60] James S. Coleman, *Nigeria: Background to Nationalism* (Berkeley and Los Angeles: University of California Press, 1958), p. 253. Furthermore, the Nigerian economist O. Aboyade argues that "the notion that Nigeria exhibits a dualistic economy profile must be revised" if dualism "involves a parallel system of two basic, usually independent sectors of an economy" (*Foundations of an African Economy* [New York: Praeger, 1966], pp. 14–15). This view is reinforced by R. Olufemi Ekundare, *An Economic History of Nigeria, 1860–1960* (London: Methuen, 1973).

A critique from the "left," of Frank's interpretation as it applies to Africa, comes from E. A. Brett, who attempts to assess the relative truth of the "diffusionist" and Marxist theories on the impact of colonialism.[61] Brett acknowledges that colonialism accelerated the integration of African society into the system of international exchange dominated by the leading capitalist powers. He also shows how colonialism provided these societies with the infrastructure required for the simplest forms of export production, and hence with the base for continued exchange with other sectors of that system. Nevertheless, he argues that "although colonialism induced a rapid expansion of the cash economy in East Africa, it has also left behind an economy characterized by continuing and perhaps intensifying structural imbalances, massive and growing inequalities, apparently irreducible dependence on external sources of technological innovation, and a tendency towards political authoritarianism and instability."[62] Brett attacks Frank's analysis on the grounds that "the classical capitalistic revolution had hardly begun to work itself out and that no genuine basis had been created for a socialist revolution of the kind that Frank assumes to be possible for Latin America."[63] Brett nevertheless shows clearly how African society was integrated into the capitalist system precisely because labor was not completely free to become a steadily employed proletariat. Colonialism maintained the seasonal character of the African labor force. This forced wages down to subsistence levels and transferred a major portion of the costs of production to ongoing rural "traditional" societies that sustained workers when they had no commercial employment. Obviously, the character of these rural societies did not remain the same insofar as they were called upon to subsidize a new wage-earning work force.[64]

A similar phenomenon occurs today in that many African governments refuse to even count (and thus recognize as unemployed) the so-called migrant or casual laborers who come to the cities, live off relatives, and then, driven by desperation or disappointment, return to the rural areas. African governors seek to push under the covers a problem of unemployment that can range from 20 to as high as 60 percent of the labor force. They force an already burdened peasantry to shoulder the additional task of maintaining an exceptionally mobile class of cheap labor.

Despite a radical change in appearance, neocolonialism retains the basic features of profiteering. The change from the slave trade to commerce during the nineteenth century occasioned strong dis-

[61] E. A. Brett, *Colonialism and Underdevelopment in East Africa: The Politics of Economic Change, 1919–1939* (New York: Nok Publishers, 1973). Cf. James F. Petras, "Sociology of Development or Sociology of Exploitation," *Le Tiers Monde*, in press.

[62] Brett, *Colonialism and Underdevelopment in East Africa*, p. 305.

[63] *Ibid.*, p. 307.

[64] See also Brett's analysis of differences in the agricultural development of Kenya, Uganda and Tanganyika. He shows how diverse colonial policies, coupled with diverse traditional systems and differences in the ecological environment, affected the social structures and the nationalist movements in each of these countries. (*Ibid.*, pp. 290–310.)

agreement in the interpretation of motives and motivations. The changing economic requirements of capitalist industries were more subtle than might first appear. Why didn't European governments, for example, allow the slave trade to continue simultaneously with the search for new markets, if humanitarian or broader political considerations were not at stake? Part of the answer was that national capitalists sought not only to enrich themselves but also to simultaneously prevent access to the prized goods by competitors. Thus, when Britain stopped the slave trade, it denied labor to the French West Indies. This forced the French to raise sugar prices so that the British might once again be competitive. By the middle of the nineteenth century, Great Britain no longer wanted a triangular trade, but rather a direct exchange of English cotton cloth for palm oil from West Africa, sugar and coffee from Brazil, raw cotton from the United States, and so forth. In West Africa, limited supplies of labor created competition between the slavers and those who grew cotton and produced palm oil. Scarcity of labor was a problem at every stage of production, from the actual growing of the crops to the loading of the ships. "Raw labor" could not function except in an organizational framework. As long as the commercial interests of the traditional leadership revolved around the slave trade, European commerce lacked the political framework necessary for an expansion of the new trade.[65] Only when the capitalist nations brought slavery to an end could the new commerce flourish. As an example of the rapid and successful transition in the commercial basis of African economies, in 1899 the entire cocoa exports of the Gold Coast were valued at no more than £16,000; twenty-five years later they were worth well over £9,000,000.[66] Yet questions about economic exploitation persist, particularly in regard to neocolonialism.

On the Economic Nature of Modern Imperialism

When General De Gaulle landed in French Somaliland on his way to China on what he thought was to be an historic mission to end the war in Vietnam, he found himself to his great chagrin facing a completely unexpected demonstration demanding immediate independence. Hastily calling a press conference, De Gaulle announced in his haughtiest manner that if the Somalis really wanted their independence they were free to take it, for after all, who needed Somali, "a

[65] See also Kwame Yeoba Daaku, *Trade and Politics on the Gold Coast, 1600 to 1720* (Oxford: Clarendon Press, 1970), for a comparison of European economic interests in seventeenth-century Africa with those of later periods.

[66] See *The History and Politics of Colonialism, 1914–1960*, ed. Duignan and Gann, pp. 15–16, for comparable trade figures comparing Liberia and the Gold Coast, Nigeria, Kenya, Tanganyika, Northern Rhodesia, and Southern Rhodesia, as well as French Equatorial Africa, French West Africa, and the Belgian Congo. See also the excellent collection of studies in the other volumes of the series: Vol. 1, *The History and Politics of Colonialism, 1870–1914*, ed. Duignan and Gann (Cambridge: Cambridge University Press, 1969); and Vol. 3, *Profiles of Change: African Society and Colonial Rule*, ed. Victor Turner (Cambridge: Cambridge University Press, 1971).

land of dust and cows." Rather, the Somalis needed France with her magnificent culture and capital.[67] General De Gaulle would have no patience with generalizations about "dependency."

Sophisticated social scientists have at least taken the effort to argue that theories of economic imperialism missed the mark. Capitalist countries, they have maintained, were not driven by economic necessity to exploit or in any other way subjugate "colonies." One of the most sophisticated refutations of this thesis comes from Harry Magdoff, who rejects the oversimplifications of the "pure economic determinist formula," stating that the "search for unadulterated economic motives of foreign policy decisions will serve as a useful hypothesis for a large number of cases. But it will fail if one expects to find such for each and every act of political and military policy."[68]

Among the reasons why crude theories of economic determinism do not work, Magdoff points out, is that military and political policies are not based on strict cost-accounting rules. Even business corporations, as their size and skill multiply, need concern themselves only with the ultimate balance sheet—not necessarily with each and every adventure. The ultimate purpose, critics and supporters of Western imperialism agree, is "nothing less than keeping as much as possible of the world open for trade and investment by the giant multinational corporations."[69] Magdoff points out, for example, that "small Latin American countries that produce relatively little profit are important in United States policy making because control over all of Latin America is important."[70] The problem is to prevent the expropriation of American capital and to guard against revolution—possibly because even a vote at the United Nations or the Organization of American States is important. What matters to the United States is not the isolated expenditure on any particular action of theirs, but rather, again, the overall context and structure in which that action takes place.[71]

Two other critics of traditional theories of economic inperialism, Ronald Robinson and John Gallagher, argue that the pursuit of economic advantage in Africa cannot itself explain British colonial policy. Africa was important to Britain only insofar as coastal way-stations facilitated travel to India. Political motivations—not economic ones— were what counted.[72] A. G. Hopkins argues that economic motives were

---

[67] See "A la Conference de Press de l'Elysee," *Le Monde,* October 27–November 2, 1966, pp. 5–6.

[68] Harry Magdoff, *The Age of Imperialism* (New York: Monthly Review Press, 1969), p. 10.

[69] *Ibid.* The label "open-door policy," which describes American foreign policy in China at the turn of the century, was not coined by a Marxist.

[70] *Ibid.,* p. 14.

[71] *Ibid.,* p. 15. See also my discussion of "interstitial imperialism" in *Leopold Sedar Senghor and the Politics of Negritude* (New York: Atheneum, 1969; London: Heinemann Educational Books, 1970), pp. 98–99.

[72] Robinson, Gallagher, and Denny, *Africa and the Victorians.* For various criticisms of Robinson and Gallagher, see the *Journal of African History,* 3 (1962), 469–501. John D. Hargreaves refuted Robinson and Gallagher in part by noting dryly that European policy makers "did show some awareness that the free enterprise capitalism of their countries was running into economic difficulties" (*West Africa Partitioned,* Vol I, p. 22).

a central feature of the partition of West Africa, but that they do not provide a complete explanation of it.[73]

According to Magdoff, one of the reasons frequently given for downgrading economic interpretations of imperialism is that only a small segment of a nation's business seems "vitally concerned" with military affairs or foreign economic activities. The "realities of economic concentration" suggest, however, that this is not the case. To cite only one example, the 100 largest corporations in the United States own 55 percent of the total net capital assets of the American manufacturing industry. Magdoff shows that even within this small group, conflicts of interest and disagreement over particular policies occurred on numerous occasions. However, when there is a community of ultimate interests, a small number of firms concentrate their power. Through finance, and control over mass media, they can "wield an overwhelming amount of economic and political power."[74]

This concentration of economic power creates "a structural difference" that distinguishes the "new imperialism" from the old. In recent years this concentration has reached the point where competition among groups of giant corporations and their governments takes place over the entire globe. The multinational corporations compete for the markets of the advanced nations as well as those of the semi-industrialized and nonindustrialized nations. Magdoff maintains that, "the struggle for power by the industrialized nations for colonial and informal control over the economically backward regions is but one phase of this economic war and only one attribute of the new imperialism."[75]

Even in Magdoff's theory, the emphasis is on a struggle for power among *nations* that happen to house the giant corporations. What is most startling about the newest stage of capitalist development, however, is precisely the transnational character of the multinational corporation and the further integration of Africa into a world system. Samir Amin has argued that the Second World War accentuated underdevelopment by transferring whole regions of Africa from the stage of a "primitive reserve," virtually outside the world market, to the stage of an "underdeveloped economy," dominated by and integrated into the world economy.[76] Between 1960 and 1970 the rate

---

[73] Hopkins, *An Economic History of West Africa*, p. 124.

[74] See Magdoff, *The Age of Imperialism*, pp. 191–202 for numerous illustrations of this concentration of industry—a phenomenon well documented in general social science literature from Berle and Means to J. K. Galbraith.

[75] *Ibid.*, p. 15. See also James Hudson, *Super Imperialism* (New York: Holt, Rinehart & Winston, 1972), for a discussion of the financial realities involved in this new concentration of capital. For the best critique of Magdoff's position, see Benjamin J. Cohen, *The Question of Imperialism* (New York: Basic Books, 1973). In support of Magdoff's position, see Mhone, "Economic Exploitation and African Economic Development." This paper contains a fairly extensive selection and discussion of anti-Marxian critiques of materialism. See also Steven J. Rosen and James R. Kurth, eds., *Testing Theories of Economic Imperialism* (Lexington, Mass.: Heath, 1974), for an interesting set of studies that attempts quantitative verification of some of the basic propositions of economic imperialism in a variety of circumstances.

[76] Samir Amin, *Neo-Colonialism in West Africa* (New York: Monthly Review Press, 1973), p. xiv. Cf. Robert Scheer, *America After Nixon: The Age of the Multi-Nationals* (New York: McGraw-Hill, 1974).

of real growth of West Africa hovered at 4.3 percent a year, compared with a population growth rate of 2.3 percent. Amin argues that in consequence, the gaps between this region and the developed world grew sharper. Since the growth rate of the industrial sector and of urban employment was too low to absorb the huge migration into the cities, unemployment grew rapidly.[77]

Norman Girvan has also argued that because imperialism was interested in the "periphery" mainly as a source of primary products, its involvement in the economies of underdeveloped countries could not lead to substantial economic improvement, but only to the "continuous impoverishment of the mass of the population, peasants, workers, underemployed and unemployed."[78] The continual involvement of Senegal in the world economy, we can see, resulted in the drastic impoverishment of the Senegalese peasant, as well as in the rise of an increasingly significant "trader" class. In recent years, a precipitous fall in the international price of peanuts, a drought in Senegal, and certain policies of the Senegalese government have resulted in a decline of as much as 40 percent in purchasing power of Senegalese rural society.[79]

Amin points out that the volume of foreign investment has not been negligible. He complains that investments went into "not directly productive infrastructure."[80] Yet, earlier in his study he acknowledges such investments as necessary foundations for future growth. The dependence on outside stimuli and the lack of "internal dynamism" may prove to be only temporary, and not based upon any irremediable structural impairment—particularly should the national bourgeoisie step up its entrepreneurial enterprises.

A fundamental problem of economic growth, Amin maintains, is that the "relative and absolute gap between this region and the developed world is growing sharper."[81] Thus, even Amin does not maintain that Africa has not experienced any growth *in comparison to previous periods in its history,* or that some types of investment have not in fact occurred, or that even certain types of industrialization have failed to result in greater and more diversified products.

Too much pessimism leads to complete paralysis. When Amin alleges that the overriding obstacle to development in West Africa is the division of the area into nine states, and that fragmentation into micro-regions means that "any development policy is therefore bound to fail," he acts to foreclose options.[82] This contention of Amin's rests heavily upon his assumption that the only effective means to achieve

---

[77] Amin, *Neo-Colonialism in West Africa,* p. 267.

[78] Norman Girvan, "Economic Nationalists versus Multi-National Corporations: Revolutionary or Evolutionary Change?" in *Multinational Firms in Africa,* ed. Widstrand, p. 38.

[79] See, for example, International Bank for Reconstruction and Development, *Senegal: Tradition, Diversification and Economic Development* (Washington, D.C., 1974).

[80] Amin, *Neo-Colonialism in West Africa,* p. 269.

[81] *Ibid.,* p. 267.

[82] *Ibid.,* p. 273.

development is heavy industry, which requires an extensive market, which in turn can be possible only through unified, centralized political government.

From Bill Warren on the left, to Elliot Berg, a wide spectrum of opinion has attacked as a "myth of underdevelopment" the impossibility of absolute growth. We must recognize both the actual growth that occurred in the past and the potential for future development if we are to understand previous patterns of exploitation. Although we cannot underestimate the difficulties of obtaining absolute growth and further investment, it is crucial to examine the increasing integration of African economies into the world economy, and the nature of the chief instrument used for these purposes — the multinational corporation (MNC).[83]

The Multinational Corporations and African Dependency

What are the multinational corporations? What purposes, and whose interests, do they serve? Can they further the development of African countries, or are they what they appear on their face, nothing more than the most sophisticated form of profiteering the world has ever known? Are the MNCs merely expanded colonial trading companies, a continuation of the past, or are they part of a new, independent future? Are they the vanguard of advanced technology, or the merchants of overpriced, obsolete equipment? Are they the exploiters of raw materials and labor they have always been? Are they allies of the African *petit bourgeoisie*, or are they true friends of "progressive" governments? Are they sources of capital, or the major agents of profit repatriation?

In his capacity as secretary of state, Henry Kissinger, on September 1, 1975, delivered a remarkable address to a special session of the United Nations General Assembly.[84] He declared that the "transnational enterprise" has been possibly the most effective "engine of development." Often, he asserted, there was "no substitute for their ability to marshall capital, management, skills, technology, and initiative." "Thus," he concluded astoundingly, "the controversy over their role and conduct is itself an obstacle to economic development." He warned that host governments must treat transnational enterprises "equitably without discrimination," and not as "objects of economic warfare." Kissinger stated, furthermore, that "the capacity of the international community to deal with this issue constructively will be an important test of whether the search for solutions or the clash of ide-

[83] Cf. Bill Warren, "Myths of Underdevelopment," *New Left Review*, 81 (September-October 1973), 3–45, the analysis of Ivory Coast development by Amin, in his *Neo-Colonialism in West Africa*, pp. 41–47; and Elliot J. Berg, "Structural Transformation versus Gradualism: Recent Economic Development in Ghana and the Ivory Coast," in *Ghana and the Ivory Coast*, ed. Philip Foster and Aristide Zolberg (Chicago: University of Chicago Press, 1971), pp. 137–230.

[84] Reprinted in *The New York Times*, September 1, 1975, p. 20.

ologies will dominate her economic future. The implications for economic development are profound."

What are these remarkable "engines for development"? The multinational corporations are more than businesses that happen to operate in more than one country. Girvan points out that they are part of a large and rapidly expanding sector of the *world* economy and are based on a revolutionary system of production and accumulation. The main features of this new system are diversified internationalized production under centralized control, massive size, and huge financial resources.[85] These forces have increasingly produced a single, dominant world economy that includes socialist as well as capitalist nations, developed as well as underdeveloped countries, all of which are merging in a continual enlarged and intensified sphere of action that absorbs, subordinates, or liquidates all other systems of production and accumulation.[86]

American MNCs account for 62 percent of American exports, 35 percent of American imports of manufactured goods, and at least one third of American domestic economic activity. At the end of 1971, they controlled at least $268 billion in short-term liquid assets. The world's largest MNC, General Motors, outgrosses the GNP of most of the countries of the world, including developed countries such as Switzerland and Denmark. General Motors' annual turnover is approximately $36 billion. Forty of the largest 99 "economies" of the world are multinationals, and they have a higher growth rate than most nations. In addition to size, the extent of their activity is striking. Operations involving over twenty products in more than a dozen foreign countries are not uncommon. Product diversity and global range have created a unique flexibility and independence from any one country or product. The MNCs possess the most creative technology, and they spend great sums on research and development. Although their activities are dispersed and decentralized, the most important decisions are made at global corporate headquarters by a small group of senior officers. These decision makers can determine the size of employment, the distribution of products, the amount and value of exports and imports, and the quality of life of a growing number of the world's peoples.

Although corporations had overseas investments in the past, these were generally in the form of other nations' corporate stock portfolios. Today, the MNCs themselves as Girvan points out directly organize production in the less developed countries. They provide themselves directly with primary products and penetrate foreign markets by producing the entire range of goods abroad, rather than by

---

[85] Girvan, "Economic Nationalists Versus Multi-National Corporations," p. 29.

[86] Cf. Constantine Vaitsos, who, in his *Intercountry Income Distribution and Transnational Enterprises* (London: Oxford University Press, 1974), questions whether the term "multinational" is correct. Although the MNCs may operate across national boundaries, key activities such as the development of productive knowledge, decision-making, ownership, and control are concentrated in the home country. Vaitsos, however, does point out that the firms do not always act in the interests of their country of origin, since "their ultimate objective is corporate and not national" (p. vii).

exporting finished goods turned out from plants in their home country. Thus, as national companies have become world corporations, interlocking directorates and financial ties, coupled with market interpenetration, result in extensive cooperation and the promise to replace the national rivalries that helped produce two world wars. The most dramatic post–World War II change in political form was the replacement of political imperialism by neocolonialism. But there is a further movement beyond both colony and "client state": the power of transnational capital to withhold investment and technology is becoming so overwhelming that the threat of physical coercion—to discipline national capital and labor, for example—is no longer necessary. Increasingly, compliance occurs "naturally" as capital flows by "sheer force of circumstances" to those countries that provide "the necessary investment climate." The ghost of communism vanishes as the specter of economic decline and technological stagnation haunts the socially radical. Ever more free to select the potentially most profitable investments wherever these may be, able to favor the most cooperative governments, the transnational corporations *denationalize capital* as the inevitable corollary of their global reach.

In recent years, MNCs have greatly increased their investments in Africa. The total world stock of foreign direct investments was about $165 billion (not including the Republic of South Africa) in 1971; this represents an increase of 60 percent over 1967. Nigeria, with a stock of foreign investments of $2.1 billion in 1972, was the largest single investment market. Nigeria nearly doubled its stock of investments from 1967 to 1971, making it the fifth most important area of investment in the underdeveloped world, after Brazil, Venezuela, Mexico, and Argentina. Nigeria, with 22 percent of all foreign investments in Africa (again, excluding the South African investments), was followed by Libya, Zambia, and Zaire, in that order.[87]

As one example of the operations of the multinational corporations in Africa, after Zambia gained her formal independence, her economic dependency on copper and the copper industry increased. From 1965 to 1970, copper accounted for 45 percent of her net domestic production, 60 percent of government revenue, and 95 percent of the value of exports. A huge percentage of revenues received went to foreign skilled labor and "organizational entrepreneurship." The 29,000 non-Africans were paid a total of Kwacha 120 million, only Kwacha 25 million less than the amount paid to all 307,000 African employees. Non-Africans were paid about ten times as much as the average paid African.[88] Zambia proceeded to nationalize her copper enterprise. This nationalization would have done her little good unless

[87] Hveem Helge, "The Extent and Type of Direct Foreign Investments in Africa," in *Multinational Firms in Africa,* ed. Widstrand, p. 66. Cf. Colin Leys, *Underdevelopment in Kenya: The Political Economy of Neo-Colonialism: 1964–1971* (Berkeley and Los Angeles: University of California Press, 1974); Justinian Rweyemanu, *Underdevelopment and Industrialization in Tanzania* (New York: Oxford University Press, 1973); and Richard L. Sklar, *Corporate Power in an African State: Multinational Mining Companies in Zambia* (Berkeley and Los Angeles: University of California Press, 1975).

[88] Sklar, *Corporate Power in an African State,* p. 204.

the copper could be sold overseas. As long as the copper MNCs could continue to profit from these sales, it was not in their interest to undermine the producer — the government of Zambia. By the same token, Zambia did not seek a showdown either. Sklar argues that the "market relationships that transcend nationalism and nationalization may prove to be the most enduring ties between the capitalist powers and their colonies. Thus, this perpetuates imperialism."[89]

The National Bourgeoisie as a Comprador Class

The experience of the international copper-mining companies in Zambia clearly reveals the difference between a national bourgeoisie and a *comprador* class. A *comprador* class sits in power at the pleasure of foreign corporations and governments. Tool and puppet, its loyalties and policies are determined by these outside forces. Without an independent domestic base, its autonomy is severely circumscribed, as are its national loyalties. The multinational corporation cannot doubt the patriotic intensity of the national bourgeoisie. Although the government in Zambia, for example, must still employ foreign managers and engineers, the Zambian bourgeoisie insists upon achieving self-management as quickly as possible. It regards foreigners as temporary employees and servants. As a matter of self-interest, the national bourgeoisie needs the state to protect and further its personal and economic interest.

From the perspective of the MNC, the national bourgeoisie is only the local segment of a transnational class. Its nationalism can be understood and tolerated, despite conflicts. The national bourgeoisie and the multinational corporations cooperate because both are in the business of business. What is good for American Metals Climax Corporation is good for all of her suppliers, Zambian corporate officials, and Zambian supervisory personnel.

Conflicts may develop between the Zambian national bourgeoisie and the Zambian local bourgeoisie who are not employed by the MNCs or otherwise involved as business associates. In the past, there were conflicts between the MNC and smaller European concerns. The gigantic, technologically intensive undertakings of the MNCs, however, afford local African capitalists not only training and economic and technical support, but also entry into a web of relations that ordinarily would be beyond their grasp. The national bourgeoisie, like its counterparts throughout history, benefits from the strengthening of the capitalist forces of production, distribution, and exchange. Sklar argues that state participation in the mining industry has introduced a new era in which "citizens of the Republic of Zambia are now collectively able to choose between alternative paths of development."[90] "From the standpoint of class analysis," he maintains, "power may be said to lie with the managerial bourgeoisie."[91] As evidence, he cites the

[89] *Ibid.,* p. 86.
[90] *Ibid.,* p. 180.
[91] *Ibid.,* p. 209.

unilateral repudiation of the nationalization agreement of 1973 by President Kaunda, who was determined to increase state control over the copper companies.

The power of the MNCs, however, cannot be underestimated — not only because of the scale of operations and amount of resources at their command, but because the MNCs are the "driving point" of capitalist development. They represent the forces that have created the world market system. It is the bourgeoisie of the African countries that must fit itself into the MNCs' framework. The role of ITT in the overthrow of the Allende government in Chile, bribery and extortion by Lockheed and the oil companies of political notables in Italy, Japan, and the Netherlands, indicate the magnitude of extralegal means these businesses have at their command. Assassination attempts by the CIA and the poisoned needles, darts, guns, and gasses directed at the political foes of the MNCs are only the most dramatic evidence of how the governments of the industrial world can support their business enterprises.[92]

The power of the MNC, however, does not automatically exclude the possibility of the emergence of a well-developed national bourgeoisie with an internal material base. Indeed, the endeavors of a national bourgeoisie can go far beyond "such parasitic activities as commerce and real estate and light manufacturing industry."[93] Alliance with a national bourgeoisie gains the MNCs higher profits and more freedom for long-range corporate planning. The nationalist bourgeoisie acts to protect itself against complete domination, and insofar as it is dissatisfied with a weak, dependent, or junior position, it will continually assert its independence and continue to develop an internal base.

The nationalist bourgeoisie will, therefore, operate increasingly within the framework established by the MNCs. The nationalist bourgeoisie will not be able to affect the structural arrangements outside national, or at the most, regional boundaries. If the nationalist bourgeoisie desires to engage in substantial international trade, the degree of its dependency will increase. It might indeed conclude, however, that the development of internal industries and a domestic market are more important priorities.

But from the perspective of both the national bourgeoisie and the multinational corporation, the fundamental problem is not an either-or situation — either complete dependence or complete autonomy. The issue, rather, is one of the *degree* of cooperation and integration. Indeed, a high degree of national autonomy would produce mutual benefits — increased profits for the indigenous bourgeoisie, and increased efficiency through decentralization for the MNCs. The MNCs can afford to let loose the native mice on an island with no place to run, especially when the mice cannot swim.

[92] Alvin Wolfe, "The African Mineral Industry: Evolution of a Supra-National Level of Integration," *Social Problems*, 2 (Fall 1963), 163.
[93] Girvan, "Economic Nationalists versus Multi-National Corporations," p. 38.

A most dramatic example of a conflict of loyalties involving MNCs took place in September and October of 1975, when the Gulf Oil Corporation paid $116 million in oil royalties to a bank controlled by the MPLA at the same time that the United States government was channeling $32 million in covert support to the two other competing Angolan political movements. After consultations with officials of the State Department on December 22, Gulf announced the suspension of further oil operations in Angola and declared that it would place an additional $125 million, still due as royalty payments, in an interest-bearing account "for the benefit of the State of Angola."[94] No wonder that the MPLA's prime minister, Lopo de Mascimento, declared that the United States was "waging economic war on Angola."[95]

Nationalist governments pay a high price for accommodationist policies. To safeguard their economic relationships with the MNCs, Zambia, for example, became more flexible and tolerant toward the policies of its neighboring states. In the past, Zambia had militantly expressed its determination to advance the interest of antiapartheid revolutionary movements. As the degree of her dependency on international firms increased, not only did Zambia become more "responsible" in her actions towards the Republic of South Africa, but she called for American intervention against the MPLA on behalf of UNITA and the FLNA, and even supported the South African invasion.

Widely heralded for their "message of industrialization," for their know-how, their Newtonian technology, their capital, their contacts and world-wide marketing arrangements, their management skills and their inventory prospecting, the multinational corporations are supposed to find oil in the ocean and uranium under the sand. They allegedly turn empty beaches into tourist havens, make deserts bloom, crisscross swamps and jungles with ribbons of concrete, and bound over hills and mountains with jumbo jets and helicopters. Alchemists sought only to turn lead into gold. What chagrin, then, when the MNCs fail to find work for the rising number of unemployed with their labor-saving machinery, when they fail to purchase local products from the national bourgeoisie, and when they inculcate a sense of inferiority in the indigenous creators of technology.

The MNCs pour asbestos into drinking water, sulphur dioxide into the air, hormones into cattle, mercury into fish. The MNCs pollute, they corrupt. They buy prime ministers and pay the 10 percent to administrative officials. The willingness of indigenous nationalists to accept bribes should not divert attention from the bribers. If the MNCs can, as alleged, bribe the Dutch royal family and arrange payoffs to Japanese prime ministers, they can do it to anybody.[96]

---

[94] *The New York Times,* December 23, 1975.

[95] *The New York Times,* February 1, 1976.

[96] Reginald Green has pointed out that the belief in powerlessness in the face of the MNCs is self-fulfilling. See his discussion of the potentialities and limits of the MNCs' contributions to economic development in "The Peripheral African Economy and the MNCs," in *Multinational Firms in Africa,* ed. Widstrand, pp. 92–124.

Whether the MNCs have contributed in any satisfactory manner to a qualitative improvement in the lives of the vast majority of the peoples of the continent remains debatable at the very least. There is no question, however, that the multinational corporation represents the latest chapter in the long story of the continued expansion of national capitalism.

Conclusion

This chapter has focused on the nature of international imperialism and the theories of dual economic development. We have considered the theory of the coexistence of traditional and capitalist economies. We have rejected the notion of a uniform pattern of historical evolution in which poor countries were considered "lesser civilizations" that would eventually follow the same route of the Western civilizations to ever increasing prosperity. Ultimately, the situation of the new African countries is rooted in their own domestic conditions. Although the parameters of choice are limited by the multinational giants of the capitalist world economy, choices are nevertheless available to leaders of new countries and, equally to the point, have been over the centuries.

Barrington Moore criticizes Magdoff and other "radicals" for the "huge dose of provincialism and even reverse chauvinism" in their claim that imperialism "bears the main responsibility for misery and starvation in the economically backward parts of the world."[97] The whole thrust of Moore's work, particularly in his *Social Origins of Dictatorship and Democracy*, is to show how Chinese, Indian, and African societies contain enormous internal obstacles to modernization, obstacles with which these societies are contending even today.[98]

To understand more about these domestic constraints on development, we must examine the nature of "traditional society." This is necessary in order to contrast "traditional" with "modern", and "developed" with "underdeveloped," and in order to understand better the "forces of stability" and the beginnings of internally generated growth.[99]

[97] Barrington Moore, Jr., *Reflections on the Causes of Human Misery and Upon Certain Proposals to Eliminate Them* (Boston: Beacon Press, 1972), p. 114.

[98] (Boston: Beacon Press, 1966).

[99] See Samuel P. Huntington, "The Change to Change," *Comparative Politics*, 3, no. 3 (April 1971), 283–322.

Chapter IV

THE STRUGGLE
FOR INDEPENDENCE:
*Tribe, Tribalism, and
the Conditions for Social
Development*

Traditional social structures in new African states have not withered away according to the plans of modernizing African leaders or the projections of Western social scientists.[1] Leaders and social interests of long ancestry continue to count, and often determine the policies of so-called modern governments. Many chiefs and religious figures have succeeded in maintaining their positions of power vis-à-vis their former subjects.

In order to clarify these contentions and to further our understanding of traditional societies, this chapter again focuses on class as a crucial political factor. The primary criterion for distinguishing classes is the relationship of the class to the "means of production," which usually entails, as a subsidiary characteristic, variations in styles of life. A distinction must be made among class, elite, and stratum. A stratum is a descriptive category that includes persons who occupy a similar position on a hierarchical scale of certain situational characteristics, such as income, prestige, style of life. Classes emerge from certain structural conditions and function as interest groupings to effect structural changes. Although class consciousness may be absent, classes are "objectively" in conflict because of their "productive relations." In this sense, classes are social conflict groups.[2]

Although the differences in science and technology available to traditional and modern society must not be overlooked, or the psychological meaning of tribalism in rural and urban settings ignored, the continuity of economic and political powers stretches from the present to the past and cannot be grasped without an understanding of class relationships in traditional societies. How social-class relationships

[1] Parts of this chapter, especially the section dealing with caste, are based on my article, "Traditional Social Structure, the Islamic Brotherhoods, and Political Development in Senegal," *Journal of Modern African Studies*, 8, no. 1 (1970), 73–96.

[2] Cf. Ralf Dahrendorf, *Class and Class Conflict in Industrial Society* (Stanford, Calif.: Stanford University Press, 1959). For an elaboration of the concept of "political stratum," see Robert A. Dahl, *Who Governs: Democracy and Power in an American City* (New Haven: Yale University Press, 1961), pp. 91–94. For a distinction among class, elite, and stratum, see C. Wright Mills, *The Power Elite* (New York: Oxford University Press, 1956), especially pp. 3–30. Cf. Mills, "The Power Elite: Comment on Criticism," *Dissent*, 4, no. 1 (Winter 1957), 22–34, which contains the author's defense of his methodology, as well as a general discussion of the conceptual and ideological problems involved in the analysis of social strata.

have been extended and transformed in modern times is of crucial importance.

Traditional Social Structure and the Nature of Tribal Society

In respect to traditional social structure, this study attempts to establish four propositions:

(1) Classes—and not merely strata—existed. Historically, traditional societies were beset by internal as well as external conflict. African society was never simply a harmonious, mutually beneficial hierarchy, but at times contained bitterly competing interests united characteristically on an essentially domination-subordination basis.

(2) "Conservative" classes existed in traditional society in the sense that they held commanding positions within a social hierarchy and sought to perpetuate themselves, as well as their values and their relations of dominance, within the community.

(3) These traditional conservative classes could adapt to change and continue to exist as powerful, if not predominant, forces within the community; they have not changed and will not change essentially in purpose, nor will they wither away.

(4) Throughout the history of many of Africa's traditional societies, caste has been of paramount social and political importance, and continues to be to the present day.

Caste involves five characteristics:

(1) a hierarchically organized system of occupations;

(2) entrance into an occupation determined by birth;

(3) endogamous marriage within occupational and status groupings;

(4) "objective" conflict between the interests of the different castes; and

(5) subjectively, a situation where even the lowest, most debased castes may assert no grievance, but may attest to the rectitude of the moral order and maintain the rightfulness of their own positions in society.[3]

Although caste rituals were not developed in Africa to the extent that they were in caste societies outside of the continent (India is the obvious example), "caste" and not merely "classes" did and do exist. Caste self-affirmation—a belief in the "rightness" of the caste system and one's place in it, no matter how "lowly"—in traditional societies such as those in Senegal, furthermore, was vital for the individuals

[3] See Joseph Bensman and Bernard Rosenberg, *Mass, Class and Bureaucracy* (Englewood Cliffs, N.J.: Prentice-Hall, 1963), p. 246.

concerned. These individuals implicitly consented to the caste system in a way that westerners sometimes cannot understand without changing their preconceived images of such societies.

Neither the existence of classes nor even the most wretched condition of exploitation depends upon, or even calls forth, open class conflict or a self-conscious sense of grievance. The secure status and power of the privileged strata allow them to adopt a stance of benevolent paternalism towards those grateful for protection from still higher authorities. When neither side seeks to question the legitimacy of the existing relationship of domination and of subordination, each stratum accepts the hierarchy as authoritative.[4] In European feudal societies as well as in traditional African caste societies, the absence of a sense of self-consciousness and grievance did not mean that exploitative relationships did not exist. Class "in itself" did not become class "for itself," but rather was an objective reality.

Patterns of Traditional Authority

Behind the conflict of opinion on the nature of traditional African societies often lies the failure to specify which kind of traditional society is meant. Before proceeding further, therefore, we shall attempt to distinguish among basic categories of African traditional political systems.[5] One preliminary distinction is the basic difference between "state" and "stateless" societies. "State" societies possess centralized authorities, administrative machinery, separate judicial institutions, and cleavages of wealth, privilege, and status that correspond to the distribution of power and authority. Examples of this type of society are the Zulu, Bemba, and Ankole. On the other hand, stateless societies in Africa characteristically lack centralized authority, administrative machinery, constituted judicial institutions, and sharp divisions of rights, status, and wealth. Examples are the Tallensi and Nuer, as well as many Ibo groups. The basic criterion distinguishing the two types of systems is the absence or presence of "government"—that is, the presence or absence of organized force.[6]

Another distinction to be made is among kinship, lineage, and administrative systems. *Kinship systems* are very small societies in which

[4] This self-acceptance by the inferior castes resembles the way in which the lower orders of feudal society accepted a system under which they had few material advantages and still fewer rights of any type. See Alexis de Tocqueville's explanation of this phenomenon in his *Democracy in America* (New York: Vintage Books, 1960), Vol. 1, pp. 8–9.

[5] For efforts to categorize African traditional political systems, see M. Fortes and E. E. Evans-Pritchard, eds., *African Traditional Political Systems* (London: Oxford University Press, 1940). Cf. John Middleton and David Tait, eds. *Tribes Without Rulers* (London: Routledge & Kegan Paul, 1958). See also Paula Brown, "Patterns of Authority in West Africa," *Africa*, 21, no. 4 (October 1951): 261–78; reprinted in Irving Leonard Markovitz ed., *African Politics and Society: Basic Issues and Problems of Government and Development* (New York: Free Press; London: Collier-Macmillan, 1970), pp. 59–80. Herbert S. Lewis provides an excellent survey of relevant anthropological literature in his bibliography, "African Political Systems: A Bibliographical Inventory of Anthropological Writings," two parts, *Behavioral Science Notes*, 7, nos. 3 and 4 (1972), 209–235, 331–47.

[6] Fortes and Evans-Pritchard, eds., *African Traditional Political Systems*, pp. 14–15.

even the largest political unit embraces a group of people who are all united to one another by ties of kinship. Political relations are, therefore, coterminous with kinship relations, and political structure and kinship organizations are completely fused.

In a *lineage system,* the lineage structure is the framework of the political system. There is a precise coordination between the two; they are consistent with each other, yet each is distinct and autonomous. Rulers and their key advisors are selected from well-defined key families. Other families traditionally provide important leaders and key functionaries; frequently, there is considerable choice among the cousins and brothers contending for key offices.

In *administrative systems* family background may still be important, yet an administrative organization is the cement that binds people together politically. The power stemming from a hierarchical organization constructed according to principles of rationality and efficiency, such as Max Weber has described, overcomes ties of blood. The system is qualitatively different from one based on lineage.

There are marked variations in the number of people and the territorial range associated with these three types of systems: fewer people can be united by kinship into a single organization than by lineage or administration. There is simply a limit to the size of government that can hold together without some kind of centralized bureaucracy. The state systems characteristically engage in complicated economic activities and bring together many culturally diverse groups. A centralized authority in an administrative organization seems necessary to accommodate these culturally diverse groups within a single political system. (The Zulus, however, possessed a homogenous culture.)

In the state system, political rights and obligations are territorially defined. That is, the chief is the administrator and the judicial head of a given territorial division; everybody living within a particular area is considered a subject; each individual accepts certain obligations. In stateless societies, territorial units defined by administrative systems do not exist; local communities are bound together simply by ties of lineage and bonds of direct cooperation; and, thus, membership is defined by ties of kin and not by residence.

Every traditional society, no matter how complex or simple, possessed a balance of forces—elements that helped support the system as well as elements that worked against it. Among the key maintaining factors, a genealogical restriction on the succession to key offices often eliminated the threat of unrestricted competition; kin or dependents carried out key functions; frequently, a society was organized along the lines of an army and maintained an armylike discipline; and, finally, there were the "mystical sanctions of office." Fortes and Evans-Pritchard have commented on the mystical values associated with political office in African traditional systems:

> An African ruler is not to his people merely a person who can enforce his will on them. He is the axis of their political relations, the symbol of

their unity and exclusiveness and the embodiment of their essential values. He is more than a secular ruler; in that capacity the European government can to a great extent replace him. His credentials are mystical and derive from antiquity. Where there are no chiefs, the balanced segments which compose the political structure are vouched for by tradition and myth and their interrelationships are guided by values expressed in mystical symbols. Into these sacred precincts the European rulers can never enter. They have no mystical or ritual warranty for their authority.[7]

Among the forces tending to undermine privileged position that every African ruling group had to contend with was, to begin with, a council either of elders or of regional notables — some group whose advice had to be sought. A king was also limited in that he generally could not choose his own successor. A special group of investiture officials had the right to that task. Other leading members of the society might also have a right to exercise power in particular realms. For example, the queen mother could often maintain a separate court. Power in the various regions devolved into the hands of subchiefs, who were often autonomous in their regional or local powers. This autonomy always posed the threat of revolt to the various suballiances that were formed among these local leaders. Poor transportation and communication systems guaranteed that no matter how rigid the hierarchy or how strong the desire for centralization, power would always be dispersed.

Every African traditional ruling group assumed duties as well as possessing rights. Among the latter, the chiefs enjoyed tribute labor and various taxes. But in return, chiefs had to provide protection, dispense justice, and insure the general welfare. Often, when these duties were not fulfilled even common farmers could rebel. They did so, directing themselves not against the system of rule but rather against the particular occupant of the office (thus, incidentally, confirming the essential "rightness" of the institution as a whole).[8]

In their assumption of duties, all African rulers attempted to manifest their authority. When their authority was undercut, their power was threatened. The example of the Asante of Ghana shows how the power of the traditional authorities suffered the threat of dis-

---

[7] *Ibid.,* p. 16.

[8] On the distinction between rebellion and revolution, see Max Gluckman, *Custom and Conflict in Africa* (New York: Barnes & Noble, 1967). Paula Brown finds that "West African states . . . provided the rulers with goods by taxation, levies on trade, trade monopolies, death duties, compulsory labor, and rights over war captives. Slave labor maintained the rulers in Dahomey, Mende and Nupe at a superior standard of living; the kings of Bono and Asante grew rich through the gold trade. . . . The ruling group and especially the king, possessed prestige symbols in the form of horses, elaborate regalia, entourage, etc." Brown, "Patterns of Authority in West Africa," pp. 72–73. Another effort to categorize African state systems was undertaken by Gluckman. He found them to range from the symbolic ritual kingship of the Shilluk, which lacked administrative powers but represented the unity of the nation, to the great states of West Africa with their large capitals and slave plantations. *The Ideas in Barotse Jurisprudence* (Manchester: Manchester University Press, 1972), pp. 68–69. Cf. the categorization of Jack Goody based upon technology and geography. Goody finds a dichotomy between the "gun states of the forest (where the horse could not operate, partly for trees, partly for tsetse) and the horse states of the Savannahs." *Technology, Tradition, and the State in Africa* (London: Oxford University Press, 1971), p. 55.

integration, at least temporarily, from the "new forces of Westernization." Who was the chief in Asante society? What role of a chief was of primary significance? According to K. A. Busia,[9] above all the chief was "he who sits upon the stool of the ancestors." The major political significance of the chief stemmed from a cosmological belief. The Asante believed that they composed an ongoing community of the "dead," the living, and those yet to be born. The "dead," though unseen, nevertheless influenced the course of the living: they could cause crops to fail and prevent women from conceiving. They could be offended and therefore had to be "reached." The chief, as successor of the royal ancestors, acted as a bridge for the tribe between the living and the dead. The second major source of the chief's power was his ability to allocate tribal land. Again, this was related to his mystical role, for the chief was custodian of the tribal land insofar as the land belonged to the ancestors and the community. The third source of his powers—his judicial functions and his arbitration of disputes—was also mystical, because all offenses were considered religious in nature. Disputes threatened the relationship among the community, the ancestors of the chiefs, and the gods, and therefore could not be decided simply on the basis of personal interests.

The main threat to the Asante chief's position came from Christianity. Christian subjects did not believe that the crops would fail or that misfortunes occur if the sacrifices to the ancestors were not performed. They thereby ripped away a most important basis of the king's legitimacy. Only secondarily did the colonial administration undercut the power of the chiefs, by bringing them under the control of secular authorities. Third, not only did the colonial administration appear more powerful, it also preempted various functions and duties of the traditional leaders, including the provision of social and welfare services, a functioning treasury, roads, wells, and schools. Fourth, new demands arose for services, jobs, and a standard of living that could not be fulfilled by the traditional system. These new demands required "Western" technology and vast sums of capital for their fulfillment. Fifth, a growing centralization necessary for the maintenance of peace and various services undermined the old system, which had consisted of autonomous decentralized units based to a very large extent on kinship. Sixth, the economic position of the chief changed. The fundamental change was that land was no longer the primary source of revenue or the primary way of earning a living. People could go to towns and enter a market economy. Temporarily at least, the personal position of the chief also changed. For in the past, no attempt had been made to distinguish the chief's personal property from that of the "stool." The chief was not expected to own property or to engage in trade. He could command goods and services, and he could determine the livelihood of the other members of the tribe.

With new economic opportunities, however, men became less

[9] K. A. Busia, *The Position of the Chief in the Modern Political System of Ashanti* (London: Oxford University Press, 1951).

and less inclined to perform their customary services. Fewer and fewer sanctions were left under the control of the traditional authorities. Which customs and beliefs were legitimate and which were not became increasingly confused in a society in transition. Competition among "royals" for vacant stools indicated a weakening of lineage systems and a breakdown in the old morality and in the acceptance of custom.

In summation, among the causes of the chief's insecurity were, one, rivalry among royals; two, lack of definition of the chief's functions; three, loss of economic resources; four, the emergence of educated commoners, successful cocoa farmers, or others who were able to "make it" in a new economic system; five, the presence of a superior authority; and six, the undermining of the religious authority of the traditional leaders.

Ultimately, the difficulties experienced by the Asante traditional authorities were rooted in the centralization of administration on a territorial basis by a superior outside power, and in the progressive secularization of the chief's office as well as of society as a whole.[10]

The Nature of Traditional Society and Newtonian Science and Technology: The Ability of Traditional Rulers to Adapt

Different definitions of traditional societies emphasize different key variables. For instance, the element of class is emphasized in Marx's distinction among feudalism, capitalism, and socialism. Max Weber considered the key variable to be the increasing rationalization and organization of societies; he considered that bureaucracy was a key institution in this process.[11] Daniel Lerner regards expanded "emphatic" participation through the use of the mass media and through broader communications as paramount.[12] Karl Deutsch has discovered mass mobilization of the population and the development of communication grids as central to the rise of a qualitatively different type of political participation.[13] W. W. Rostow leads the "diffusionist" school,

---

[10] See Apter's "The Role of Traditionalism in the Political Modernization of Ghana and Uganda," *World Politics,* 13, no. 1 (October 1960), pp. 54–68.

David Apter distinguishes between "consummatory-Pyramidal" and "instrumental-Hierarchial." The latter political systems have an ability to innovate readily, recognizing that various innovations have no higher purpose but are simply necessary to the attainment of particular ends. Apter argues that Buganda's ready adaptability in contrast to the Asante stemmed from this traditional organizational characteristic. Although enticing, Apter's analysis neglects more significant variables—namely, national income among the Asante was double that of Buganda; Ghana possessed a much more extensive transportation and communication network; in Uganda, Asians and Europeans monopolized both commerce and the civil service to a much greater extent and at a much earlier stage, Buganda traditional rulers—practically the entire ruling elite—were gifted by the British government with fee-simple title to land over which they had previously ruled by virtue of their traditional positions, an action that changed overnight the economic basis of their power.

[11] See Weber's *The Protestant Ethic and the Spirit of Capitalism* (New York: Scribners, 1958).

[12] See Lerner's *The Passing of Traditional Society* (New York: Free Press, 1958).

[13] See Deutsch's *Nationalism and Social Communications* (Cambridge, Mass.: M.I.T. Press; New York: John Wiley, 1953).

which locates the fundamental turning points in history at the times of basic new scientific discoveries about the universe. According to Rostow, the decline of traditional powers, such as the Asante, and the ultimate "conquest" by colonialism originated in the nature of the technology available to each type of system.[14]

According to Rostow, a traditional society is one "whose structure is developed within limited production functions, based on pre-Newtonian science and technology and on pre-Newtonian attitudes towards the physical world."[15] By Newtonian, Rostow means a belief that the world is subject to a few knowable laws, and is therefore systematically capable of "productive manipulation." In the context of this definition, the central fact about traditional society was that a "ceiling existed on the level of attainable output per head." This was because the potentialities of modern science and technology simply were not available. Ultimately this lack of ability to overcome perpetual poverty affected the value system: "No idea of progress characterized such a society, only a long-run fatalism in which everybody believed that the possibilities of one's children were virtually the same as for oneself." Above all, Rostow argues, development requires the widespread belief that man need not consider his physical environment as something given by nature and providence, but rather as an "ordered world which, if rationally understood, can be manipulated in ways which yield productive change and (in one dimension at least) progress." The rise of individualism also accompanies this change in values and production, because men increasingly become valued in society not for connections with their clan or caste but for their individual ability to perform certain increasingly specified functions. Development also requires structural changes. Income above the minimum levels of consumption, previously concentrated in the hands of those who controlled land, must, Rostow argues, be shifted into the hands of those who will spend it on productive facilities, such as roads, railroads, schools, and factories, rather than on country homes, mistresses, and personal luxuries.

Rostow's definition of traditional society does not appear to be ideologically or politically directed. Yet Rostow has subtitled his book *A Non-Communist Manifesto.* In addition to loathing communism, Rostow believes that he has found an alternative mode of political and social development, one that distinguishes between the legitimate *nationalist* aspirations of diverse peoples, and the *class*-founded critique of Marx and the Marxists. Revolution is not necessary to achieve economic development, according to Rostow's schema, if only the traditional ruling classes have enough sense to alter the economic foundations of their power. Additional strata of the population will at least have to be taken into account by the rulers in their decision making,

[14] See Rostow's *The Stages of Economic Growth: A Non-Communist Manifesto,* 2nd ed. (New York: Cambridge University Press, 1971).

[15] This and the other arguments of Rostow cited in this paragraph are found in his *Stages of Economic Growth,* pp. 4–19.

yet the relative positions of power of the diverse social groups need not be basically altered. Nationalism, coupled with capitalism, can provide a "legitimate alternative" to both socialism and communism. Economic development can occur under any political system, provided sufficient use is made of Newtonian science. Under all systems, the benefits of economic growth will then eventually trickle down to even the lowest social stratum. Rostow implies that this has been the historical pattern in the West, where the material abundance of an expanding economy sufficed to "buy off" formerly discontented groups, ranging from trade unions to blacks to women, and co-opt them into "the system." The winds of economic change, therefore, may rock the boat but not necessarily overturn it. Rostow sees clearly the necessity to distinguish between traditional ruling *classes* or elites and traditional *societies* on the grounds that the latter are ongoing social systems. The traditional *society*, therefore, may disintegrate, yet the traditional leaders possess every possibility of becoming "modern leaders" who are still in control and still the ultimate source of key decisions for the whole society.[16]

Rostow's approach differs fundamentally from those social analyses that recognize that traditional authorities still have power in the modern political setting, but attribute this simply to a failure of the "processes of modernization" to have gone far enough. For example, Norman Miller maintains that "rural traditional authorities survive in modern times as local political leaders. They do so by serving as intermediaries between modernizing bureaucratic authorities and the custom-bound populace. . . . Moderate neo-traditionalism continues . . . because the Government is not yet in a position to withdraw totally the powers of headmen and a few chiefs."[17] Elliot Skinner, commenting on what Miller finds to be a paradox of modernization and traditional authorities, continues basically in the same vein of analysis as Miller, except that he is not as astounded: "The survival of the traditional leadership in African societies is not paradoxical, given the financial and technical inability of the modern African states to 'implant new rural institutions,' etc. Moreover, it is doubtful whether any new political leaders could successfully supplant older ones without the economic power and institutional apparatus with which to do so."[18] Skinner goes on to point out that in the area with which he has the greatest familiarity, the Mossi country of Upper Volta, the rural chiefs, who in the period of the transference of power, 1955–7, were apprehensive of the new political leaders of the Upper Volta, were

[16] *Ibid.*, p. 19. See also Rostow's *Politics and the Stages of Growth* (New York: Cambridge University Press, 1971).

[17] Norman H. Miller, "The Political Survival of Traditional Leadership," *Journal of Modern African Studies*, 6, no. 2 (1968), 187, 197; this article is reprinted in Markovitz, ed., *African Politics and Society*, pp. 122–32.

[18] Elliot P. Skinner, "The 'Paradox' of Rural Leadership: A Comment," *Journal of Modern African Studies*, 6, no. 2 (1968), 199; this article is reprinted in Markovitz, ed., *African Politics and Society*, pp. 133–36.

able by 1964 to resume effective control over their people, a result very much like what Miller found among the Nyamwezi in Tanzania. Skinner attributes this resumption of power to the failure of the new states to provide modern institutions. Events such as these were

> the direct result of uneven development or, if one wishes, of a transitional development stage for which there is a lack of congruence between the political ideology of the state and the existing political organization in the rural areas. There is no doubt in my mind that conditions in the rural areas of modern Africa will change. Chiefs may continue to provide leadership for rural Africans but only until the modern bureaucratic nation-state can afford to create and effectively use its own local institutions.[19]

The difference between Skinner and Miller on the one hand and Rostow on the other is that Rostow can envisage a situation where "the chiefs" attain control in the "modern nation-state." Whether local agencies of government would then continue to be run by elders or various subchiefs deriving their authority from an ancestral past, or whether they would be run by elected agents of town and local government, would be relatively immaterial. The nation-state concentrates and centralizes power. Those in charge of the new administrative — including military — apparatus make the key decisions in "modern" societies. What is there to preclude either the "chiefs" of the traditional ruling class or their sons from taking over these new institutions? Rostow thus indicates how those who governed the former kingdoms can shift the basis of their political power as well as the material source of their wealth and maintain themselves as a class.

In a study of caste in Indian society, Susanne and Lloyd Rudolph request that we alter our conception of the distinction between traditional and modern societies, demanding that we see them "as continuous rather than separated by an abyss."[20] They argue that in India "in its transformed state," caste has helped make a success of representative democracy and fosters the growth of equality. Whether this is true is highly debatable. Equally debatable is the Rudolphs' allegation that "a strategy more likely to achieve modernization with stability, effectiveness, and liberty is one that provides those who represent natural associations with conditons and incentives that enable them to foster the interest of their groups in ways and contexts that also lead toward modernity."[21] Who are those that represent "natural associations"? What is the "interest of their groups" that will be fostered "in ways and contacts that . . . lead toward modernity"? The major difficulty seen by the Rudolphs is the establishment of separate as-

[19] Skinner, "The Paradox of Rural Leadership," in Markovitz, ed., *African Politics and Society*, p. 134.

[20] Lloyd I. Rudolph and Susanne Hober Rudolph, *The Modernity of Tradition* (Chicago: University of Chicago Press, 1967), p. 10.

[21] *Ibid.*, p. 66. Aristide Zolberg exhibits a similar perspective about ethnic groups in Africa in his "Mass Parties and National Integration: A Case of the Ivory Coast," *Journal of Politics*, 25 (February 1963), 36–48.

sociations and political structures, the results of which may extend even to political instability and civil war. Divisiveness must therefore be balanced by integrating forces:

> Overcoming the tendency of ascriptive associations to formulate separate political identities and establish separate political structures requires powerful integrative forces. Strong leadership, naturalist ideology, and viable state structures may not be enough. Extended and socially penetrating experience of modern political culture and institutions along with broadly recognized economic interdependence can be critical. So too can the capacity to maintain a balance between the claims of the nation state and those of ascriptive solidarities.[22]

As general propositions, the necessities of recognizing "economic interdependence," "modern political culture," and so forth face no quarrel. However, what do these propositions mean in terms of specific states and interest groups? The Rudolphs allege that "Nkrumah's Ghana represented a pathology of national integration, the pursuit of unity without regard for ascriptive local quarrelism, whereas Balewa's Nigeria represented the pathology of diversity, a nation state with too limited a sense of citizenship."[23] Obviously, differences would occur over strategies of integrating diverse "natural associations." However, entirely different ideological approaches to these "traditional associations" are also involved. Nkrumah, for example, considered the traditional rulers of Asante a life-and-death threat to his regime. He had no romantic notions of "the natural community" of these age-old associations. Neither did Balewa have simply a rosy picture of "the traditional community." Rather, in a manner readily comprehensible in Rostow's terms he possessed the financial, organizational, and moral backing of the most powerful emirs of northern Nigeria. The "traditional community" remains an idyllic abstraction in the same sense as Abraham Lincoln's definition of a democracy as a government of, by, and for the people: each of these lovely abstractions makes a good deal of sense until one attempts to define "the people" and how they are to rule.[24]

If ever a community did exist, the advent of capitalism in Africa proved disintegrating to it, as it did everywhere capitalism confronted

---

[22] Rudolph and Rudolph, *The Modernity of Tradition*, p. 66.

[23] *Ibid.*

[24] This view is reinforced by Angus Maddison in his description of the Indian village as a traditional community. Maddison points out that although the social structure within villages in traditional communities may have been fairly egalitarian because income differentials were probably smaller than they are now, nevertheless "the top groups in the village were allies of the state, co-beneficiaries in the system of exploitation," *Class Structure and Economic Growth: India and Pakistan Since the Moghuls* (London: Allen & Unwin 1971), p. 27. See also, in Julian H. Steward ed., *Contemporary Change in Traditional Societies*, Vol. I, *Three African Tribes in Transition* (Urbana, Ill.: University of Illinois Press, 1967, 1972) the studies by Edward H. Winter and T. O. Beidelman of the Ukaguru in Tanzania; Robert A. Manners of the Kipsingis of Kenya; and Stanley Diamond of the Anagula of Nigeria. Joan Vincent, in her study of the Gondo in Uganda, discovered "an equalitarian myth that permitted leadership to pass unresented" (*African Elite: Big Men of a Small Town* [New York: Columbia University Press, 1971], p. 3).

traditional societies. George Lefebvre describes the corrosive effects of capitalism centuries ago upon feudal France. He tells of the rise of a possessive individualism, of social disintegration, of the breakdown of traditional societies, and of the rise of a new class society:

> The increase of wealth swelling private incomes, broadened interest and stimulated the desire to satisfy new tastes. Individualism chafed at restrictions: the contagious example of material success encouraged all those who judged themselves capable of enjoying the rewards offered during this life. The family disintegrated as each child demanded his rightful inheritance, and conventional standards of conduct were challenged and evaded. Urbanization acted as a catalyst—life in the city undermined social restraints, placing a greater part of existence outside traditional groups; . . . capitalism . . . hastened social differentiation, enriching some and impoverishing others. It created a dynamic and unstable society in which power, based on money and always threatened with sudden destruction, could inspire only transitory respect. It added glamor to this life and obscured the afterlife. It reduced the importance of personal ties which bound the individual entirely and emphasized contractual relations dealing with objects and thus limiting obligations. . . . In a hundred different ways the individual who had lain dormant beneath feudal, despotic, and corporate restrictions was awakening to independence and dreaming of freedom.[25]

Under these circumstances, what are the "traditional leaders" to do? If they are to withstand competition from new social groups geared to the new economic arrangements—merchants, "financial experts," labor bosses, foremen—as well as the pressures of the petty officials of the state bureaucracy, the professionals, and the school teachers, they must adapt and retrain themselves and their children. To argue that they must change, however, is to assert that they might indeed maintain their position of social control. This is to deny again the imminence of their eventual disintegration as leaders within a rapidly changing society.

The Tribe and Tribalism as Cultural and Psychological Rallying Points

Anthropologists have defined a tribe as "a community which believes that it is culturally different from all other communities around it, a belief shared by the surrounding communities."[26] In addition to the difficulties in defining the "traditional community" discussed above, Jan Vansina points out that the notion of "the perennial tribe" is meaningless: "It can easily be shown that tribes are born and die,

---

[25] George Lefebvre, *The French Revolution*, Vol. I, *From its Origins to 1793* (New York: Columbia University Press, 1962), pp. 56–57. N. B. Lefebvre emphasizes class, not simply the rich against the poor, which *is* the focus of Pierre Goubert, *The Ancien Regime: French Society, 1600–1750* (New York: Harper & Row, Torchbook ed., 1973), who produces a very different assessment.

[26] Jan Vansina, *Kingdoms of the Savanna* (Madison, Wisc.: University of Wisconsin Press, 1966), p. 14.

sometimes without displacement of populations or even without changes in the objective cultures of the communities involved."[27] Vansina discusses as an outstanding example of this phenomenon the case of the Lulua in what was then the Congo. Before 1890, he points out, there was no such tribe; there were only Luba Kassai. Yet by 1959, the Lulua and Luba Kasai had developed such diverse interests and were so different that they engaged in bitter fighting. Angolan and European traders who first entered Kasai named the people they found there the Lulua, even though the people called themselves Luba, as did the groups further to the south. However, when as a result of slave raiding thousands of Congolese sought protection at a "state post," they were settled by the Europeans and entered into mission schools and hospitals. "Very soon they began to feel themselves to be different from the original inhabitants and this feeling, which was shared by the latter, crystalized in the use of the terms Luba and Lulua."[28]

In contrast, the capacity of one tribe to absorb others is illustrated by the Asante in West Africa. The Asante insisted upon assimilating groups of strangers. Ivor Wilks tells us that the adoption of Asante ethical and cultural standards was not only permitted but enjoined. Communities of slave origin merged within a generation or two with the free Asante commoners, and their new status was given full protection in Asante law.[29] The English anthropologist R. S. Rattray revealed that an Asante legal maxim of the greatest import was, "One does not disclose the origins of another!" According to Asante law, "Whoever dares tell his son: these people were from such and such a place, conquered and translocated to this or that town, were sure to pay for it with his life. Neither were such people themselves allowed to say where they had been transported from."[30] Wilks maintains that the entire organizational resources of the Asante state were used to resettle strangers and captives in a program of rapid and planned growth so as to avoid the emergence of a class of unassimilated and underprivileged subjects.[31]

The multi-tribal character of the great Sudanic empire was well known. In the conquered territories an effort was made to retain the local chiefs, even though the rulers of the empires appointed their own governors or commissioners as overseers and sometimes kept the sons of the local chiefs as hostages in a central court. Given even a vast, uniformly administered and integrated state organization, many self-contained societies survived for centuries within a broader imperial framework.

Because most outsiders have pictured "traditional society" as

[27] Ibid.

[28] Ibid., p. 15.

[29] Ivor Wilks, "Ashanti Government," in West African Kingdoms in the Nineteenth Century, ed. Daryll Forde and P. M. Kaberry (London: Oxford University Press, 1967), p. 229.

[30] C. C. Reindorf, quoted in Wilks, "Ashanti Government," p. 230.

[31] Wilks, "Ashanti Government," p. 230.

static and unchanging, this evidence for the shifting composition, changing definition, and persistent psychological commitment to the tribe is of the greatest significance. Another obstacle to understanding the nature of tribalism, however, comes from a failure to distinguish between the tribe as a continuing organizational structure and "tribalism" as a focal point for psychological and other "modern" needs.

Tribalism as a Psychological and Ethnic Phenomenon

Tribalism in towns differs from tribalism in rural areas. According to Max Gluckman,[32] in rural areas a tribe consists of a working political system incorporating an active social life based on kinship. It is an ongoing social system based on existing economic and social needs. *In this sense, the tribe and "tradition" represent not merely "conservatism," in the sense of the preservation of a hierarchy and values based on outmoded social sanctions and forces, but also constitute a realistic response to the environment.*

In the towns, on the other hand, tribalism serves primarily as a means of classifying the multitude of Africans of diverse origins who live together. In this respect tribalism performs a number of functions, the first of which is social. One's tribe of origin forms the basis of new groupings. Coming into a threatening and strange environment, bewildered by strange phenomena and overwhelmed by a sense of one's own insignificance amidst the whirling energies of the city, strangers often discover that the major element they immediately have in common with other urban dwellers is a common traditional origin. Among the first groups founded by all immigrants in every society on every continent were burial societies. Mutual-help and self-improvement organizations were among the quickly growing panoply of groups designed to meet the most pressing needs of urban life. They came to exist side by side with political pressure groups and economic interest organizations.

Second, tribalism fulfills a number of psychological needs. Among these, tribal identity offers a basis for the assertion of personal identity in the towns, providing a psychological rallying point and — along with family and village identity — giving answers to the questions that come with the breaking of the ties of a close community, "Who am I?" and "Who is my brother?"

The significant influence of tribalism on behavior stems from the fact that Africans now live in towns — not that they come from tribes. Being town dwellers, they will earn their livelihood in a fundamentally different fashion than they did in their old environment. They will acquire new face-to-face associates, new ways of looking at the world, and new customs, habits, and philosophies. With the constant movement between rural and urban areas, with the presence of relatives in

---

[32] Max Gluckman, "Tribalism in Modern British Central Africa," *Cahiers d'etudes Africaines*, 1 (January 1968), pp. 55–70; reprinted in Markovitz, ed. *African Politics and Society*, pp. 81–95.

both settings, and with the recent migration from a society in which one was born and raised, tribal characteristics will obviously endure, but with the change of the fundamental economic, social, and political context their significance will also change.

A. L. Epstein in his study of African miners in Lusaka,[33] highlights the impact of social context in two ways. First, he presents the example of how a case of assault is decided in a traditional and in an "urban" setting. In an urban setting, the basic judicial inquiry is directed at determining who is at fault. The judge will ask who started the fight, whether there was unnecessary force or provocation, what the physical conditions of the two combatants were, whether drunkenness was involved, and so forth. In a traditional community, the judges would more likely be interested in the family background of the two parties. Who were their fathers? Their brothers? Did they have many children? To whom were they married? Such an inquiry would be necessary because the fate of the entire community would be at stake, particularly in a strongly mystical society where conflict between persons might also be believed to affect the gods—and hence the fecundity of the harvest, among other things. The two legal systems, then, reflect the societies of which they are an integral part.

Second, Epstein examines the nature of the organizational base of a copper miners' strike, thereby providing additional insight into the nature of tribalism. During the 1950s, tens of thousands of Africans came from British, Belgian, and Portuguese territories to Luanshaya to work in the mines. The mine owners provided food, lodging, and relatively high pay for workers who stayed on contract for several years. They also attempted to provide a system of social services and government that conformed to the "traditional system" For this purpose, the European mine owners brought in tribal elders to represent the tribes and provided them with special houses and clothing. The elders were related to the royal families and attempted to project the authority of the tribe into this urban, industrial setting. The mine management related to the workers only through the elders. Apparently, this system worked well for a very long period. A variety of disputes occurred between miners but were settled in accordance with customary procedures. The traditional elders maintained respectability and authority, as they had in the rural areas.

Then some of the miners began to demand better pay and improved working conditions. They acted as miners have everywhere, and for the same reasons. The elders tried to prevent discord. They demanded that the workers go back to work. The miners stoned the elders, who proved to be completely powerless in the face of the strike. The miners' accusation of collaboration with the Europeans completely destroyed any vestige of authority the elders possessed. Epstein points out that as *tribal representatives whose authority was based*

---

[33] A. L. Epstein, *Politics in an Urban African Community*, (Manchester University Press, Manchester, 1958).

on the political system of the tribe, these elders had no legitimate connection with the work situation of the mines. The workers, organized in departments and work gangs in an industrial situation, occupied roles in which the previous tribal situation was irrelevant.

Many of the mine workers came from tribes that had historically been enemies, raiding each other and warring, often for hundreds of years. Tribal divisions and allegiances did not, however, operate in industrial action. What counted ultimately was whether a person was a worker in the mines or part of management. In the administrative system the elders had become representatives of the mine owners in dealing with the workers, and, therefore, the elders became the enemies of the workers. When, eventually, a trade union of Africans was formed, 97 percent of the miners supported the abolition of the system of tribal elders as one of their primary demands.

All of this is not to deny the significance of tribal identification. Indeed, tribal affiliation was of particular significance in matters between Africans. Elections within the miners' union, like elections everywhere, brought out the need for balanced slates of candidates to run on opposing tickets. Tribal affiliations and background provided a pivotal point for rousing workers' loyalty and stimulating their interest in working for particular candidates. On the other hand, however, conflicts among the workers cut more and more across tribal lines as more jobs involving better pay and requiring more skill opened to Africans—thus precipitating additional differences between, for example, skilled and unskilled Africans. In this sense, tribalism in Luanshaya or Lusaka compares with tribalism in New York City or Boston. In Gluckman's words, "Tribalism in the Central African towns is, in sharper form, the tribalism of all towns."[34]

Retribalization

A similar point is made by Abner Cohen: the same tribal group may be going through a process of "detribalization" on one political level and "retribalization" on another level; "Many tribal groupings in central Africa might have been 'detribalized' in their collective struggle with white employers but 'retribalized' in the struggle for power within their own camp."[35] Focusing on the Hausa community of Sabo in the Yoruba city of Ibadan, Cohen studied the mechanisms of long-distance trade. This trade involves substantial amounts of money and goods, the latter usually of a highly perishable nature, such as kola or cattle. The trade conducted within a traditional indigenous framework does not have recourse to modern banking or insurance institutions or to the police or civil courts, even though extensive credit arrangements are necessary. To a very large extent, this trade requires mutual trust between individuals located hundreds of miles apart, per-

[34]Gluckman, in Markovitz, ed. *African Politics and Society*, p. 90.

[35] Abner Cohen, *Custom and Politics in an Urban African Community: A Study of Hausa Migrants in Yoruba Towns* (Berkeley and Los Angeles: University of California Press, 1969), p. 196.

sonally unknown to each other, yet about whom a great deal can be taken for granted because of a confidence in background and upbringing.

Even though the Hausa are located in the middle of a modern city and carry on trade within a modern commercial context, the assertion of a tribal identity acquires a vast new significance. This is what Cohen means by "retribalization":

> When a Hausa man from the North comes to live in Sabo he does not automatically become a citizen of the Quarter. Settlement in the Quarter is a complex process which involves passage through a series of roles, ranging from that of a stranger to that of a permanent settler. As the migrant becomes more settled, by being drawn into active participation in the social life of the Quarter—economically, politically, morally, and ritually—he becomes increasingly more "retribalized." His Hausa identity becomes the expression of his involvement in a web of live social relationships which arise from current, mutual interests within a new social setting.[36]

The pressure on the Hausa immigrants to maintain an exclusive, inward-looking relationship with the Sabo community extends to a virtual prohibition on marriage between Sabo men and Yoruba women, precisely because the community recognizes that such intermarriage can be highly subversive of Sabo ethnic exclusiveness and thus ultimately fatal to Hausa economic interests, especially because Yoruba wives have relatives living nearby in Ibadan and the surrounding area. When such a marriage does occur, a Hausa man will not be trusted by northern Hausa dealers to conduct their business in Ibadan.[37]

Cohen sums up his assessment of the ethnic solidarity of the Hausa in contemporary society by arguing that they have "retribalized" themselves by insisting on speaking their own language even in their dealings with the Yoruba, on dressing and eating differently, and on cutting off all intercourse with their host community, and by inhibiting by all possible means "the development of moral ties and loyalties across the lives of tribal separateness." The Hausa's ethnicity illuminates their political organization, an important weapon in their control of the cattle business. For these reasons, Cohen declared that "tribalism is basically a political and not a cultural phenomenon, operating within a contemporary political context and is not . . . an archaic survival arrangement carried over into the present by conservative people."[38]

---

[36] *Ibid.,* p. 29.

[37] *Ibid.,* p. 53. That the difference between the Hausa of Sabo and the Yoruba is not simply one of religious differences between Muslims and Christians may be seen from the efforts by the Hausa to cut themselves off from the Yoruba Muslims. The Hausa have nothing to do with the *Central Mosque* of Ibadan the city, and for their directives for the beginning and ending of Islamic feasts and the fasting in Ramadan, they look to Kaduna in the north rather than to the Central Mosque. (*Ibid.,* p. 154)

[38] *Ibid.,* p. 190. Cohen also makes the very important point that whether class stratification will in the future become more significant than ethnic divisions will depend in large measure on whether the new lines of stratification cut across or overlap with tribal cleavages (*ibid.,* pp. 193–94). See also a

Class, Tribe, and Communal Interests

Class interests can cut across ethnic groups and create new primary loyalties. If the "deprived" from one ethnic group cooperate with the less privileged from other ethnic groups, those in positions of power will also close ranks to protect their interests. One can imagine, then, the continual development of a new, class-conscious interest, along with different life styles, norms, values, and ideologies of increasingly polarized economic strata.

An entirely different scenario could occur, however, if the new class cleavages coincide with tribal groupings. Consider what would happen if the new top social classes coincided with one particular ethnic or tribal group, and the underprivileged with another group. Under these circumstances, cultural differences become not only consolidated and strengthened but also embittered. Old antagonisms are strengthened by the new class lines: "Old customs will tend to persist, but within the newly emerging systems they will assume new values and new social significance."[39] This type of coincidence among ethnic group, economic position, and solidarity group explains why some commentators have analyzed the Zanzibar revolt primarily in communal and ethnic terms. On the face of the events, a clearly economic-founded revolution appeared to pit the landless African laborers against a dominant Arab minority that not only controlled the land but ruled in an undiminished hegemony that extended back hundreds of years. Michael Lofchie points out that on the purely subjective level, however,

> most of the Zanzibaris perceived the pattern of political conflict primarily in communal rather than in economic terms. For Africans and Arabs alike, the emotive stimulus of solidarity and the symbolic ingredient of self-identification was to the ethnic community rather than to the economic class. . . . In the case of the African community, economic subordination generated a sense of collective grievance against Arabs, but, once established, that grievance came to be defined almost entirely in racial terms. . . . thus to the extent that the basic character of a political conflict can be defined in terms of the subjective perceptions of its participants, the Zanzibari Revolution was primarily a racial phenomenon.[40]

One need not, however, accept the definition of a political conflict in terms of the "subjective perceptions of its participants." One may well turn to "objective criteria" such as wealth or class position to understand the basis of those communal ethnic and racial factors involved in the conflict. What counts in politics is not simply how people "feel"

similar discussion in David Truman, *The Governmental Process* (New York: Knopf, 1959), on overlapping interest groups and the theory of pluralism.

[39] Cohen, *Custom and Politics in an Urban African Community*, pp. 193–94.

[40] Michael Lofchie, "The Zanzibari Revolution: African Protest in a Racially Plural Society," in Robert I. Rotberg and Ali A. Mazrui, eds., *Protest and Power in Black Africa* (New York: Oxford University Press, 1970), p. 966.

about themselves or their neighbors but under what circumstances they are driven to action.[41]

Dennis Austin in his studies of politics in Ghana, also delves into the interrelationships among class, ethnicity, and various other factors that attract political loyalties. Austin points out that the Asante farmers union succeeded in certain areas not because the villages were cocoa-farming communities, but because they were Asante. The National Liberation Movement (NLM), of which the Asante farmers union was a part, combined an economic appeal to cocoa farmers with an ethnic cry for allegiance by the Asante to the Asanthene, their leader. Austin maintains that had the NLM limited its campaign to the simple issue of the price of cocoa, many farmers would have joined forces. When, however, the NLM appealed to the traditional allegiances of the Asante, Brong and Colony farmers viewed the NLM not as the farmers' friend, but as the spearhead of the new Asante invasion to the south.[42] On the other hand, Austin has pointed out that for the most part practically all interests in Ghana were willing to work within a national framework and economy. Thus, demands based upon local or parochial interests could not be seen simply in terms of tribal conflict or as evidence of a major threat to the stability of the state: "The multiplicity of conflicts may make the life of the central government complicated; it must maneuver endlessly among local groups and distribute its prizes so as not to offend too many interests. But the competition that it has to control is for favors within the general framework of the powers of the central government."[43] Austin maintains that the conflict between the NLM and the CPP (Convention Peoples Party), was not simply a tribal struggle or even a regional one. Rather,

> minor skirmishes constantly upset the main battle lines, between rival Muslim groups, between Catholics and Protestants, between competing lineages of an Akan stool or a Northern Skin, and between families whose ancient feuds were enlarged and recast in party form until the political scene was a bewildering, whirling pattern of alliances and counteralliances which the national leaders constantly had to try and maintain in some sort of working order. The rival parties reached into local disputes in their search for allies.[44]

Austin convinces us that politics is deeply imbedded in local conflicts of diverse origins. People worry about the coming of the rains, where their cattle graze, and who will be the target of village gossip—much

---

[41] Cf. Michael Lofchie, "The Uganda Coup: Class Action by the Military," *Journal of Modern African Studies*, 10 (May 1972), 19–36. Two critical replies are contained in the same volume of that journal: John D. Chick, "Class Conflict and Military Intervention in Uganda" (pp. 634–37); and Irving Gershenberg, "A Further Comment for the 1971 Uganda Coup" (pp. 638–40).

[42] Dennis Austin, *Politics in Ghana, 1946–1960* (Oxford: Oxford University Press, 1970), p. 344.

[43] Dennis Austin, "Opposition in Ghana 1947–67," in *Studies in Opposition*, ed. Rodney Barker (New York: St. Martin's, 1971), p. 254.

[44] *Ibid.*

as they always have. But *now all of this happens within the nation, under capitalism, and under the eye of a powerful bureaucracy.*

In another case study, this of a miners' strike in Nigeria in 1964, Robert Melson and Howard Wolpe found a situation where economic and ethnic factors were intertwined. No matter how bitter tribalism might have been at the time, it did not cause the strike. To understand the causes, Melson and Wolpe examined the relationship between political elites and the miners. Here the differences were not tribal, but of status and class.[45] Melson has tried elsewhere to show how "objective differences in income and life style between workers and political elite were perceived by workers and how this affected their willingness to strike."[46] In a survey of workers by Melson, more than 90 percent said that the cause of the strike was low salaries; more than 70 percent stressed the difference between the salaries of the workers and the salaries of the senior civil servants and politicians as a major precipitating factor.[47] As the strike progressed, organizers cloaked themselves in appeals to traditional loyalties. For this reason, Melson and Wolpe maintained that "men become tribalists not only out of insecurity but also out of the many opportunities created by social mobilization in a communal milieu."[48]

Amilcar Cabral wrote about the "economic tribe" in Western countries and contrasted it with the "ethnic tribe" of Africa. In the common struggle of Guineans against the Portuguese, Cabral felt that ethnic differences could be overcome because they did not constitute structural barriers to unity, although many problems stemming from traditional loyalties did exist:

> We consider the contradictions between the tribes a secondary one; . . . we consider that there are many more contradictions between what you might call the economic tribes in the capitalist countries than there are between the ethnic tribes in Guinea. Our struggle for national liberation and the work done by our party have shown that this contradiction is really not so important; the Portuguese counted on it a lot but as soon as we organized the liberation struggle properly the contradiction between the tribes proved to be a feeble, secondary contradiction. This does not mean that we do not need to pay attention to this contradiction; we reject both the positions which are to be found in Africa — one which says: there are no tribes, we are all the same, we are all one people in one terrible unity, our party can comprise everybody; the other saying: tribes exist, we must base parties on tribes. Our position lies between the two, but at the same time we are fully conscious that this is a problem which must constantly be kept in mind; structural, organizational and other measures must be taken to insure that this con-

---

[45] Robert Melson and Howard Wolpe, "Modernization and the Politics of Communalism," *American Political Science Review*, 64 no. 4 (December 1970), 1112–30.

[46] Robert Melson, "Nigerian Politics and the General Studies of 1964," in Rotberg and Mazrui, eds., *Protest and Power in Black Africa*, p. 772.

[47] *Ibid.*, p. 786.

[48] Melson and Wolpe, "Modernization and the Politics of Communalism," p. 1115.

tradiction does not explode and become a more important contradiction.[49]

"Tribalism" in modern African countries—in job distribution, for example—does not, then, involve a conflict between ongoing social systems but rather the type of ethnic quarreling over spoils distribution that is so much a part of every Western city and nation. In a study of Kenya, Donald Rothschild points out that "time and again . . . spokesmen for the less advantaged African peoples have alleged that tribalism is a significant factor in determining appointments and promotions in the civil service."[50] He goes on to quote a minority-group member of parliament, who substantiates this type of contention by pointing to the staffing of various government ministries, describing them as predominantly Kikuyu in composition:

> Today, when we look at the top jobs in the government, we find that in most of the ministries including certain cooperatives, practically all of these have been taken over by people from the central province. . . . if one tribe [the Kikuyu] alone can take over about 72% of the Kenya jobs, and they are less than two million people, how can you expect 25% of the jobs to go to more than eight million people who belong to other tribes?[51]

Rothschild also tells how in Kenya a parliamentary committee was set up to investigate allegations of tribalism. The committee's report argued at length for the "principle of group equity: namely, that positions should be distributed so far as possible according to the group's numerical proportion in the total population." Although Parliament rejected this motion in the end, during the debate grim allusions were made to the role of ethnicity in the Nigerian Civil War.[52]

Clearly economic interests are not always paramount. In Africa as everywhere else, ethnic, religious, racial and communal considerations may be periodically at the fore, regardless of their origin or precipitant causes. Equally clear, today's tribal confrontations are not those of ancient times but take place within the framework of nation-states and are bounded by the realities of capitalist economies, rationalizing bureaucracies and Newtonian science.

---

[49] Amilcar Cabral, *Revolution in Guinea* (London: Monthly Review Press, 1969), pp. 64–65.

Thomas Turner, in his discussion of the mixture of ethnic and economic conflict in the Congo points out that the "traditional" enmity between Kongo and Yaka or between Lega and Bembe appears relevant in contemporary politics mainly as it fuses with current grievances—for example, those involving competition for jobs. Particularly interesting is his discussion of the rise of the myth of the kingdom of the Kongo, which practically all of the Bakongo people believe today, even though the original kingdom ceased to exist by the eighteenth century. Thomas Turner, "Congo-Kinshasa," in *The Politics of Cultural Sub-Nationalism in Africa*, ed. Victor A. Olorunsola (Garden City, N.Y.: Doubleday, Anchor Books, 1972), pp. 204–62.

[50] Donald Rothschild, "Kenya," in *The Politics of Cultural Sub-Nationalism in Africa*, ed. Olorunsola, p. 303.

[51] *Ibid.*

[52] *Ibid.*

On the Absence of Class Consciousness in Traditional Society: Objective Exploitation vs. "Knowing One's Place"

Western observers allegedly sympathetic to the cause of African civilization have maintained, among other things, that even though African traditional communities might be "more exposed to outside environmental dangers," Africans have "less anxiety"; they "get along better with each other." The authors of an anthropological-psychoanalytic study called *Whites Think Too Much* maintain that the Dogon, a people in modern Mali, have "community."[53]

In the case of societies—traditional as well as modern—that are complex and demand the cooperation of people doing all sorts of jobs, some commentators have contended that "all roles [are] equally important to the maintenance of the body politic. . . . the emphasis on inequality of status combined with equal participation by all in public discussions are among the bases for present political patterns."[54] Lawyer, doctor, chief, emperor, garbageman, king, and slave—all of these roles are vital to the maintenance of an ongoing social system.

Still another view is that although in the past Africans were born into the position that they would fill throughout their lives, and although members of a chief's family were assured higher status than members of a commoner's family, because people lived at the subsistence level their economic situation was more or less equal: "A chief might have larger fields and larger herds of cattle than a commoner, but he could only eat sufficient to satisfy his hunger; he had no means of storing his surpluses for long periods. What he produced in excess of what was brought to him in tribute he had to redistribute among his followers. Consequently, the standard of living among the people did not differ significantly."[55] An observer in Central Africa points out, however, that even where there was "equality in economic scarcity" there still existed "inequality in social and political rank."[56] Weinrich argues that with the greater educational advantages of children of educated parents, this stratification is likely to be perpetuated and to develop, in time, into a class structure resembling that of European society.[57]

Finally, in an examination of Hausa society, rather than accepting the distinction between the peasantry on the one hand and "the royal classes" and "those holding office" on the other, Kirk-Greene prefers a distinction among the "rich," the "comfortably off," and the

---

[53] Paul Parin et al., *Les blancs pensent trop: 13 entrentiens psychoanalytiques avec les dogon* (Paris: Payot, 1966).

[54] Nicholas Hopkins, *Popular Government in an African Town* (Chicago: University of Chicago Press, 1972), p. 26.

[55] A. K. H. Weinrich, *Black and White Elites in Rural Rhodesia* (Manchester: Manchester University Press, 1973), p. 226.

[56] *Ibid.*, p. 103.

[57] *Ibid.*, p. 226.

"poor"—that is, a classification that eliminates the "power distinctions" of a "Marxist-type class struggle" in preference for "the more valid assumptions of wealth."[58]

In much the same way that De Tocqueville argued that every great historical event and every major invention contributed to the spread of equality, it might be argued that every great invention contributed to the development of more complex systems of stratification in Africa, thereby enabling the strong to consolidate their power and become even stronger. The invention of iron, for example, so crucial in the development of civilization, contributed to the emergence of classes. The earliest iron-using communities yet discovered in West Africa were those of the Nok culture of about 500 B.C. Shinnie tells us that "the working of iron gave its users improved weapons, more control over their environment, and was instrumental in enabling them to establish trading centers which in time developed into an important feature of the Western Sudan."[59] She then spells out the ways in which the incorporation of iron into a civilization contributed to its further stratification, enabling the ruling class to further consolidate its power. Jack Goody, in a fascinating essay relating technology to the state of civilization in Black Africa, shows how the invention of the plow, the introduction of the horse, and the adoption of the stirrup added to this process.[60]

It might also be argued that with each new invention and each great historical event, inequalities within the emerging traditional African states seem to have increased. From ancient times to the present, poets and playwrights have cried out their pain at the loss of power and at the economic exploitation of the common people. This is not to deny, however, that traditional rulers might well have retained the respect of their subjects even when they were most repressive and exploitative.[61]

The strengthening of the powers of those at the top of the social pyramid has not been confined only to Africa:

> The outstanding feature which emerges from any comparison of simple and advanced horticultural societies is a striking development of social inequality [which is] carried to a level far beyond anything ever observed in less technologically developed societies. . . . the separation of

---

[58] A. H. M. Kirk-Greene, "The Merit Principle in an African Bureaucracy: Northern Nigeria," in *Nations by Design*, ed. Arnold Rivkin (Garden City, N.Y.: Doubleday, Anchor Books, 1968), p. 262.

[59] Margaret Shinnie, "Civilizations of the Nile," in *The Horizon History of Africa*, ed. Alvin M. Josephy, Jr. (New York: American Heritage, 1971), p. 65. Frank Willett dates Nok sculpture from at least the second half of the first millennium B.C. (*African Art* [New York: Praeger, 1971], p. 24), whereas Shinnie uses the date 300 B.C.

[60] See Goody's *Technology, Tradition and the State in Africa*, particularly his discussion of the stirrup (pp. 34–35). The stirrup enabled men to bear with the great weight of highly expensive armor and to mount their steeds.

[61] On this phenomenon, see, for example, Barrington Moore, Jr., *Social Origins of Dictatorship and Democracy: Lord and Peasant in the Making of the Modern World* (Boston: Beacon Press, 1966), p. 470; and Donald Zagoria, "The Ecology of Peasant Communism in India," *American Political Science Review*, 65, no. 1 (March 1971), 58.

the political and kinship systems and the resulting development of the state are necessary preconditions for the development of marked social inequality. . . . the power, privilege and prestige of individuals and families is primarily a function of their relationship to the state. In short, the inequalities of government provide the key to the solutions of the major questions concerning distribution and stratification in societies at this level.[62]

The Organic Image of Society and Class Consciousness

The historical development of social inequalities was attended by the development of an organic image of society as a major component of the prevailing ideology of the powers in control — in Europe as well as in Africa during the Middle Ages. R. H. Tawney tells us, for example, that from the twelfth to the sixteenth century the "fundamental and commonplace" analogy by which society was described was that of the human body:

> The gross facts of the social order are accepted in all their harshness and brutality. . . . What they include is no trifle. It is nothing less than the whole edifice of feudal society — class privilege, class oppression, exploitation, serfdom. . . . these things must be given some ethical meaning, must be shown to be the expression of some larger plan. The meaning given them is simple. The facts of class status and inequality were rationalized in the Middle Ages by a functional theory of society. . . . society, like the human body, is an organism composed of different members. Each member has its own function, prayer, or defense, or merchandise, or tilling the soil. Each must receive the means suited to its station, and must claim no more.[63]

Cheikh Anta Diop explains the caste society of the peoples of Senegal in terms of natural harmony. Every caste has a particular function to perform. All peoples are happy in their knowledge of the successful fulfillment of their duties, and all groups are unified in a harmonious whole. Diop argues that the enormous success of West African societies in achieving harmony, both with one another and with their environment, was the major reason for their demise at the hands of more conflict-ridden, exploitative, but dynamic societies of the West. European societies, in their constant groping for economic and political advantage, succeeded in creating a technologically more advanced, but grasping and morally bankrupt, social organization.[64]

Some anthropologists and political scientists have argued that in African societies, no clear correlation exists among economic power, control of the political system, and stratification.[65] Others hold that

---

[62] Gerhard E. Lenski, *Power and Privilege: A Theory of Social Stratification* (New York: McGraw-Hill, 1966), pp. 154–60.

[63] R. H. Tawney, *Religion and the Rise of Capitalism* (New York: New American Library, 1947), p. 27.

[64] C. A. Diop, *L'Unite Culturels de l'Afrique Noire* (Paris: Presence Africaine, 1959).

[65] See, for instance, Arthur Tuden and Leonard Plotnicov, eds., *Social Stratification in Africa* (New York: Free Press, 1970), p. 8. Tuden maintains that "in a number of cases — Amhara, Galla,

nonindustrial societies to a greater degree offer different types of rewards to different social groups. Ownership of land, military abilities, claims to ritual and religious knowledge, commercial enterprise, being able to read and write — all have been distinct bases for access to material, social, and symbolic privileges in traditional societies. Parkin argues that the institutional separation in feudal societies among the powers of the landed nobility, the church, and the merchant classes is "perhaps one of the best documented examples of a diversified multi-based reward system" in which rewards do not flow from a single primary source and in which "almost inevitably, discontinuities are to be found between wealth and status positions."[66]

Georg Lukacs, in comparing industrialized and nonindustrialized societies, alleges that the various parts of precapitalist societies are much more self-sufficient and less closely interrelated than those of capitalist societies. "Commerce plays a smaller role in [a precapitalist] society, the various sectors are more autonomous (as in the case of village communes) or else play no part at all in the economic life of the community and in the process of production. . . . in such circumstances the state, i.e. the organized unity, remains insecurely anchored in the real life of society."[67] Under these circumstances, Lukacs goes on to argue, "class consciousness is unable to achieve complete clarity" because "class interest in pre-capitalist society never achieved full [economic] articulation. Hence the structuring of society into castes and estates means that economic elements are *inextricably* joined to political and religious factors."[68] Only later, with the development of the rule of the bourgeoisie, did society reorganize along class lines and abolish the "estates system." Despite the ideology of society as a self-reinforcing organism, therefore, we can understand the reasons for, and the error of, the view held by leading social scientists that "social classes did not traditionally exist in Africa."[69] A brief case study of a caste society in Senegal will help illustrate some of these propositions.

Ancient Reigning Families: The Caste Structure in Senegal

In 1961, the population of Senegal was estimated at 3.4 million. The Wolof, with more than a million people, are the largest ethnic group in Senegal, as well as the most important political and economic entity. The Serer, with 16.5 percent of the population, are slightly less numerous than the Peul (17.5 percent), but much more important socially and politically because of their location and history. The Tuku-

---

Marghi — the superior strata neither control economic power systematically nor consistently receive honor." Data from the articles in his own book, however, suggest the contrary. See also the critique of Tuden by William Derman, *Serfs, Peasants and Socialists: A Former Serf Village in the Republic of Guinea* (Berkeley and Los Angeles: University of California Press, 1973), p. 29.

[66] Frank Parkin, *Class Inequality and Political Order* (New York: Praeger, 1971), pp. 38–39.

[67] Georg Lukacs, *History and Class Consciousness* (Cambridge, Mass.: M.I.T. Press, 1971), p. 54.

[68] *Ibid.*, p. 55.

[69] Tuden and Plotnicov, eds. *Social Stratification in Africa*, p. 17.

lör (9 percent) and Mandingo (6.5 percent) have social structures similar to those of the Serer and Wolof.[70] The Diola, the major tribe of the Casamance, represent about 9 percent of the population of Senegal; they have a tradition of common origin with the Serer, but their social structure is more egalitarian and lacks castes. Though numbering less than 1 percent of the population, the Lebou—often counted as a faction of the Wolof—are another group far more important than their numbers would suggest. Territorial concessions negotiated with the French have made the Lebou owners of much of the most valuable property in Dakar. In addition to these peoples, there are many minor ethnic groups in Senegal.[71]

In Senegal the history of the Wolof is a history of the ruling families and of their roles within each of the states. The exact beginnings of the Wolof are uncertain. Broadly, the founding of the Wolof state can be dated somewhere during the thirteenth or early fourteenth century.[72]

The extent of the Wolof kingdom varied greatly over time, including at one point part of Fouta, Sine, and Saloum. Four regions—Walo, Cayor, Baol, and Jalof—were the heart of the kingdom, which was headed by a ruler with the title of *bour*. Election of the *bour* from the royal lineage of the respective states was by a council of the highest ranking nonroyal chiefs. In Walo, these were primarily descendants of the three chiefs who had first given their allegiance to the legendary founder of the kingdom, Ndiadiane Ndiaye. The kingdom was divided into fiefs controlled by vassals called *kangame*.[73] Three of the *kangame*, called *samba linguere*, belonged to the royal family and

[70] The Tukulör caste system involved several more gradations than that of the Wolof and Serer. Abdoulaye Diop describes in considerable detail the class nature of Tukulör society in his important study, *Societé Toucouleur et migration* (Dakar: Institut Francais d'Afrique Noire, 1964). A study of the social structure of the Serer provides additional insight into the caste and class system of traditional Senegal. See also Martin A. Klein, *Islam and Imperialism in Senegal, Sine-Saloum, 1847–1914* (Stanford, Calif.: Stanford University Press, 1968). See also Pathe Diagne, "Royaumes sereres: les institutions traditionnelles du Sine-Saloum," *Presence africaine* (Paris), 54 (1965), 142–72. For legends on the origin of caste, see Felix Brigaud *Histoire traditionnelle du Senegal* (Saint-Louis, Senegal: C.R.D.S., 1962), p. 239; and A.-P. Angrand, *Manuel Francais-Oulof* (Dakar: Institut Francais d'Afrique Noir 1963), p. 81. J. Copans et al., in *Maintenance sociale et changement economique au Senegal* (Paris: Travaux et Documents de L'LRSTOM, 1972), suggest that the Mouride movement resulted from a peasant economy trying to absorb the forces of the market without ceasing to be a peasant economy.

[71] *Senegal: faits et chiffres* (Dakar, 1965), pp. 1–9; the figures above are taken from the still unpublished 1961 census.

[72] On the history and social structure of the Wolof, see Victoria Bomba Coifman, "Wolof Political and Social Organization until the Nineteenth Century," paper presented to the 1965 meeting of the (American) African Studies Association; Brigaud, *Histoire traditionnelle du Senegal*, especially pp. 312–31 for a further bibliography; and Ousmane Silla, "Le systeme des castes dans la societe Ouolof," *France-Eurafrique*, 148 (January 1964), 38–46. Cf. Charlotte A. Quinn, *Mandingo Kingdoms of the Senegambia: Traditionalism, Islam and European Expansion* (Evanston, Ill.: Northwestern University Press, 1972).

[73] Every year in Walo at the *gamou* festival of the birth of Mohammed, all the *kangame* were obliged to appear before the ruling *brak* and present him with tribute consisting of one third of their year's income. The nonauthorized absence of a *kangame* could result in his destitution and sometimes death. An annual *gamou* is still held at Linguere in memory of the Wolof emperor Bour Djoloff Bouna N'Diaye. It is interesting to note that the presiding officers in 1965 were grand marabouts rather than descendants of the emperor (*Dakar matin*, February 10, 1965).

were the only ones who had the right of succession to the throne. This council, like those in other kingdoms, also had some power to depose the king.

Wolof society was a hierarchy based on divisions consisting of families, upon which were superimposed the further divisions of caste. The caste structure comprised the nobility, the commoners (*badolo*), the "men of caste" (*gnegno*), and the slaves. The nobility was composed of:

> *garmi*—royal families with a right to the throne
>
> *tagne*—princes with a direct but imperfect link to the crown, who had a voice in the final selection
>
> *kangame*—chiefs whose families had the right to a regional command; certain other families furnished canton and village chiefs
>
> *tara*—sons of a prince and a slave, who had the right to the command of certain villages; also called *dom-i-bour* ("sons of the king").

After the nobility came the *badolo*. Although their status is still unclear, it would appear that they were not unlike the commoners of the Middle Ages, with the difference that they only worked the land. *Badolo* itself is said to mean "not having any power." Together with the nobility, the *badolo* form the *diambour* or *guer*, who are called the "free caste"—free, that is, of the blood of slaves, artisans, and *griots* (praise singers). The *guer* do not consider themselves upper caste and the others lower caste, but see the basic division as one between those who are free of caste and those who are bound into castes. This terminology suggests a subjective attitude of being "trapped" among the lower castes. Recently, various occupational groups in Dakar were interviewed; in the absence of a question about their father's caste, people who were of possible lower-caste status answered that they were now *guer*. To them this meant that in urban, westernized society they were rid of status and occupational restrictions—that is, free of caste—rather than members of the nobility or yeomanry.

Gnegno, "people of caste," referring to artisans and *griots*, is said to come from a Peul word meaning "flatterer," because their one common function was supposed to be to flatter the *diambour* to obtain presents. Included among the occupational groups were:

> *teug*—blacksmiths and jewelers
>
> *oude*—leatherworkers and shoemakers
>
> *tamakat*—players of a type of drum
>
> *khalmbane*—singers accompanying a guitar
>
> *mabo and bambado*—weavers who also sing and play the drum
>
> *segne and laobe*—different types of woodworkers
>
> *griots*—praise singers and musicians

Between the *guer* and the *gnegno* was an intermediary class, forbidden to intermarry with either, called the *gnole*. Among their functions was that of *diaraf*, overseer of land rents. At the bottom of the social pyramid were the slaves, also called the "captives," who were subdivided into house slaves and crown slaves. A further distinction was made between slaves who were born into captivity and slaves who were bought or captured in a raid or war.

Taxation was a fundamental manifestation of a state's authority. Symbolically, the right to levy taxes was so important that the *bours* protested vigorously against any infringements of it. This power—and the practice of taxation—should be kept in mind whenever assertions are made that Senegalese traditional states consisted of well-integrated social strata, each having its own rights and obligations, with power dispersed throughout the society and individual rights universally respected.

Taxation united the various castes in a comprehensive system, but it did not do so democratically or harmoniously. Most of the taxes were collected by the ruling warrior class from the commoners. Martin Klein quotes an early missionary who wrote that the wise peasant never displayed his wealth for fear that it might be confiscated. Klein goes on to analyze the importance of collecting these taxes:

> The wealth collected from the peasants played an important role in the operation of the state. It was not just the prize. The political power of a Bour, or of any other chief, depended on his ability to support an entourage and maintain a certain position. It was imperative that he be well-dressed, ride fine horses, and have griots to chant his praises. . . . At the same time, loyal followers had to be rewarded. It was by the distribution of his wealth and the key positions he commanded that the Bour maintained his power.[74]

This analysis of the procedures of maintaining and rewarding a loyal entourage in traditional society helps explain the basis of the clan system of modern Senegalese politics, wherein clusters of individuals follow a man of status who is able to offer rewards.

One may also theorize that pressures were particularly great upon social leaders in Senegalese traditional society to meet the demands of their followers because of two factors: caste and an abundance of land. In a caste society, the division of labor placed those who did not work at the top of society. The injunctions of "noblesse oblige" reinforced a pattern of gift and alms giving that required more elaborate generosity in keeping with the status of the givers and recipients. Moreover, where land was plentiful, to provide new land alone was not sufficient; those lords who aspired to the highest positions also had to provide goods and services—actual wealth, the finished product.

Slavery added a further dimension to conflict within the society.

---

[74] Klein, *Islam and Imperialism in Senegal*, p. 21.

There may have been some happy slaves, and there may have been some who were powerful, but on the whole the lot of slaves was scarcely likely to support the image of a society in any way "balanced." For example, in a conflict with the French over rights to several villages just inland from Joal, the Bour of Sine sent a letter to Gorée threatening to kill every "toubab" (European) in Sine if he were not permitted to exercise his traditional rights: "We wish neither gold, nor silver, nor diamonds. We wish only the inhabitants of Diavolo and Fadioudj; we wish to do with them as we have always done. . . . These people are my slaves. I will take their property, their children, and their millet."[75]

Peace is hardly the preoccupation of a professional warrior class. The warrior classes of the Wolof and Serer were no exceptions. With the advent of the Europeans, profits soared from the export of slaves, and raiding for prisoners became the main motive for war. The new slave trade played an important role in the Wolof, Serer, and other highly stratified West African states. Not only was the power of the *bours* strengthened, but hostility increased between the warriors and the *badolo*, because the latter received none of the income of the trade and became themselves the potential objects of raids by neighboring states. Increased conflict between states provided another rationale for European forces to intervene and impose peace upon lesser, "warlike" peoples.

The official view of the government of modern Senegal is that in the cities there is practically no observation of the traditional hierarchy, and that marriages between persons of different castes are quite common. This does not in fact seem to be the case. Even the government admits, that the "rural world" is still strongly structured, and that the old social stratification still persists, although it is constantly being weakened.[76]

A striking study by Luc Thoré shows that in both city and country, caste differences constitute virtually insurmountable barriers to marriage. In the past, Wolof and Serer rulers married quite frequently into the leading families of the other society. They took refuge on each other's lands, and formed other types of allegiance. Other classes within these societies sought corresponding links with their homologues. Traditionally, therefore, marriages across tribal lines were permitted and, indeed, helped in the formation of mutual interests and unity between these two ethnic groups.

Historically, cross-religious marriages have also constituted no great difficulties. According to Thoré, however, those who violate the taboos of caste meet an unyielding opposition from their families. When Thoré tried to determine the effect of education on his respondents—to the extent of distinguishing between literate and illiterate—a considerable difference in attitude was manifested. Whereas

[75] *Ibid.,* p. 58.

[76] *Senegal: faits et chiffres*, p. 8.

less than 5 percent of the illiterate population expressed a willingness to marry people of different castes, three times this proportion (but still only 16 percent) of the literate could tolerate such unions.[77]

This is not to suggest that the caste system has remained intact in contemporary Senegal. Status reversal involving nobles, commoners, and men of caste became a widespread phenomenon as the power of traditional leaders declined, and as new ways of making a more profitable livelihood became increasingly available to artisans and those best capable of skillful individual effort.[78] In politics today, several cabinet members and high administrative officials are of low-caste origin. This, however, is not surprising in traditional terms. For under the *bours*, positions of the greatest responsibility were held by slaves, who by virtue of their lowly status had no recourse to a life other than complete dependence on and obedience to their king. Systematic interviewing of administrative officials, university students, and high politicians reveals, however, that an insignificant proportion of them are of low castes.

Today, the consequences of caste origins are more indirect, but nonetheless quite real. Slaves cannot be bought or sold like chattels, or in any way treated like commodities. Yet their social status and life opportunities remain low. Similarly, it is hardly surprising that the men at the top of traditional society seem by and large to have come out not too badly in their modern relationships as well. Caste is still of great significance in modern Senegal. In Senegal, as elsewhere in Africa, different classes follow different ways of life, whether they do so self-consciously or unconsciously.

Life Styles and Class Consciousness in Traditional State Societies

Wole Soyinka has a character in a play of his say, "The accumulated heritage—that is what we are celebrating. Mali. Chaka. Songhi. Glory. Empires. But you cannot feel it, can you? . . . this is the era of greatness. Unfortunately, it is for those who cannot bear too much of it to whom the understanding is given."[79] Soyinka goes on to present on stage a resurrection of the dead ancestors, but "instead of being the

---

[77] Luc Thoré, "Mariage et divorce dans la banlieue de Dakar," *Cahjers d'etudes Africaines* (Paris), 4, no. 16 (1964) 492. See also Ousmane Silla, "Persistence des castes dans la societe Wolof contemporaine," *Bulletin de l'I.F.A.N.* (Dakar), 28 (B), no. 3–4 (July–October 1968), 731–70.

[78] Detailed facts about status reversal among the Tukulör, as one example of a general phenomenon, are given in "Les budgets familiaux," mimeographed (Dakar, 1958); see especially pp. 22, 23, and 27. In 1957, when this study was carried out by the Mission Socio-Economique du Fleuve, the average income of fishermen and artisans was about 25 percent higher than members of the *torobe*, the highest traditional caste of the great landed proprietors. The authors of the report attribute this primarily to differing attitudes towards work in a changing social situation. It is not clear from this document how extensive and universal a status reversal there was. My interviews among the many influential Tukulör members of the National Assembly in Dakar in 1965 indicated that they were universally of high-caste origin. Unpublished findings by Abdoulaye Diop tend to confirm this. See also Diop's *Societé Toucouleur et migration.*

[79] Wole Soyinka, *A Dance of the Forest* (London: Oxford University Press, 1963), p. 8.

idealized figures of the tribal imagination they turn out to be full of ancient bitterness and resentment and are shunned by everyone as 'obscenities.' " Soyinka is concerned that the ancient animosities and conflicts in "traditional communities" and empires might be detrimental to the development of national unity and greatness.

An even more sustained attack on the traditional rulers comes from the Malian writer Ouologuem, who in his *Bound to Violence*[80] shows how the Saif (the African emperor), a descendant of a dynasty stretching back thousands of years, maintains himself in power in the mythical western Sudan state of Maken and continues to control "his people" as slaves, serfs, and industrial workers. Ouologuem goes so far as to demonstrate how the Saif dupes the French by sending the son of a slave to the University in Paris, training him to eventually become a deputy in the French National Assembly. What is most shocking in Ouologuem's account is the ruling class's sense of power and of place and its willingness to maintain itself in power at any cost.[81]

Throughout the continent, styles of life as well as objective economic and political positions differed enormously among diverse castes, classes, and ethnic groups. Describing relations between caste-like groups in the Great Lakes area of Central Africa, Jacques Maquet tells us that

> the Twa group was . . . seen as inferior to the Hutu: Twa ate any kind of meat, even the meat considered disgusting such as mutton, whereas Hutu, like decent beings, had many food interdictions; moral and physical stereotypes of Hutu were more flattering than those of Twa; for Tutsi, to marry a Hutu girl was 'not done,' but to marry a Twa girl was unbelievable . . . a Hutu could (and would) push away very rudely a Twa for forgetting to keep the distance becoming to his low rank. . . . Simply because he has ancestors who conquered the country, because he has friends as accorded a king, because he has cattle, that precious wealth, because he is a warrior, a Tutsi inspires respect in his Hutu neighbors, and they do not dare to refuse an occasional service he asks, some agricultural produce he wants, the right to graze his cattle where the soil is good and fertile even during the dry season, etc. . . . it was not a question of coercion, not even of pressure but the utilization of the prestige linked to membership in a superior group.[82]

Maquet shows how the Tutsi were able to "translate status into profit," first through power-winning elections in the modern political arena and, second, through economic influence, by taking advantage of the new opportunities of modernization. Maquet sums up the traditional social structure as follows:

[80] (New York: Harcourt Brace Jovanovich, 1971).

[81] For a critique of Ouologuem, see J. Mbelolo Ya Mpiku, "From One Mystification to Another: 'Negritude' and 'Negraille' in *Le Devoir de violence*," *Review of National Literatures*, 2, no. 2 (Fall 1971), 124–47.

[82] Jacques Maquet, "Rulers and Superiors," in *Social Stratification in Africa*, ed. Tuden and Plotnicov, p. 115.

Inequality was seen as innate and natural. . . . The higher ranking individuals at least saw the differences between strata in a light which today we would call "racist." In their eyes the Iru, Hutu and Ha were born lacking the potentiality for certain qualities (largely intelligence, self-control, sense of responsibility, etc.) and could never acquire them. Social inequality simply translated the inequality of nature.[83]

Ronald Cohen describes the differences in style between members of different classes of Kanuri society in the Bornu territory of West Africa:

[Lower-class] people are engaged in the productive sector of the economy, wear a different style of dress for everyday work, have dialect distinctions in their speech, and are dependent upon the upper class for protection and the adjudication of disputes. Through their connections along hierarchical chains of political relations they link themselves to upper class members.

Upper class members dress more elaborately in long flowing robes, and their speech is different in that they do not drop *g* and *s* as consonants in the middle of words—a widespread, lower class custom. The most important distinction is one of power and authority. Upper class people hold office in the political system of Bornu. They can exert power over others in many ways because Kanuri society is identifiable primarily as a political unit. Thus a very wealthy trader who has never had any political office describes himself as a commoner, even though many of the people he regards as upper class members are much less wealthy than he himself. Within the upper class tradition there has always been a distinction between   a) Royals and non-Royals and   b) slaves and freemen.[84]

From an entirely different type of source—not a Western social scientist—additional insight is provided into the nature of society in Bornu: From the late fourteenth century the Bornu became a major force in the trans-Saharan trade, importing horses and exporting mainly slaves. The "Song of the Bornu Slaves," transcribed in the 1840s, "reflects the desperation of generations of Bornuan slaves as they trekked their way to servitude in unknown lands":

Where are we going? Where are we going?
Where are we going, Rubee?
Hear us, save us, make us free;
Send our Atk down from thee!
Hear the Ghiblee wind is blowing,
Strange and large the world is growing!
Tell us, Rubee, where are we going?
Where are we going, Rubee?
Bornou! Bornou! Where is Bornou?
Where are we going, Rubee?

[83] *Ibid.*, p. 153.
[84] Ronald Cohen, "Social Stratification in Bornu," in *Social Stratification in Africa*, ed. Tuden and Plotnicov, p. 254.

Bornou-land was rich and good,
Wells of water, fields of food;
Bornou-land we see no longer,
Here we thirst, and here we hunger,
Here the Moor man smites in anger;
Where are we going, Rubee?[85]

On the other side of the continent, in Uganda, a "noble" exclaimed his happiness in being able to sing;

Listen,
My father comes from Payira,
My mother is a woman of Koc!
I am a true Acholi
I am not a half-caste,
I am not a slave girl;
My father was not brought home
By the spear, my father was not exchanged
For a basket of millet.[86]

The unequal application of the law to peoples of diverse social classes also characterized many African state societies. Barnes tells us that in Central Africa, "Ngoni society was not egalitarian, and status differences were reflected in differences in penalties . . . derived from the enduring structure of Ngoni society. . . ."[87]

The Nigerian historian Atanda points out that Yoruba society in the precolonial period contained gradations not only of individuals but also of families—a general characteristic of state organizations:

Apart from the members of the royal families, there were important families of nobles and commoners. Correspondingly, there were gradations of individuals into princes, nobles and commoners. To a larger extent, law and Oyo-Yoruba society was "a respecter of persons," or more correctly, a respecter of families. It was an accepted philosophy of the society that while the Alafin was under obligation to respect the rights of members of royal families as well as those of nobles and members of their families, he could trample with impunity on the rights of commoners. This is epitomised in the saying:
(Literally: the poor man's mouth is a cutlass. We shall use it to clear the forest.)

---

[85] Josephy, ed., *The Horizon History of Africa*, p. 235. Reprinted from *The Languages and Peoples of Bornu Being a Collection of Writings of P. A. Benton*, London: Frank Cass & Co., Ltd., 1968

[86] Okot P. Bitek, "Song of Lawino," in *Coming of Age in Africa*, ed. Leon E. Clark (New York: Praeger, 1969), p. 44. An analysis of praise songs that shows the exploitative and ruthless nature of Habe rulers, "the burners of villages and forgers of chains," may be found in Mervyn Hiskett, *The Sword of Truth: The Life and Times of Shehu Usuman Dan Fodio* (New York: Oxford University Press, 1973), pp. 74–75.

[87] J. A. Barnes, "The Politics of Law," in *Man in Africa*, ed. Mary Douglas and Phyllis M. Kaberry (Garden City, N.Y.: Doubleday, Anchor Books, 1971), p. 106.

(Idiomatically: the poor man's rights do not matter. They can be trampled upon.)

Thus, in his dealings with the commoners, the Alafin could be, and was often, autocratic. . . . The Alafin could order the execution of any of his subjects in these areas without trial.[88]

Evidence exists that over the years the cost of maintaining those in power in the African states continued to grow as "pomp and majesty kept pace with military reinforcement." In Kano from 1703 to 1731, for example, "tradition says that taxes and tribute . . . increased to such a point that 'Arabs left the town and went to Katsina, and most of the poorer people fled the country.' "[89] Basil Davidson finds that this is perhaps an exaggeration, but the fact that many Hausa freemen "did indeed become acutely discontented with their lot" is strongly suggested by the relative ease with which the Fulani Jihad, launched in 1804, would succeed.[90]

These aspects of traditional societies have direct significance for contemporary African politics. Modern nationalist politicians, however, differ profoundly in their assessment of the meaning of these conditions.

Contemporary African Political Leaders' Views of Stratification in Traditional African Societies

Four different concepts of class in traditional and modern societies are held by contemporary African political leaders.[91] First, some leaders contend that no classes at all existed in either traditional or modern societies. Julius Nyerere argues that:

> there was not complete equality; some individuals within the family, and some families within the clan or tribe, could own more than others, but in general they acquired this through extra efforts of their own, and the social system was such that in time of need it was available to all. Fur-

---

[88] J. A. Atanda, "The Changing Status of the Alafin of Oyo Under Colonial Rule and Independence," in Michael Crowder and Obaro Ikime, eds., *West African Chiefs* (New York: Africana Publishing, 1970), p. 214.

[89] Basil Davidson, "The Niger to the Nile" in *The Horizon History of Africa*, ed. Josephy, p. 229.

[90] *Ibid.*

[91] For an earlier—indeed, one of the earliest—analysis of the division of traditional tribal societies into classes, see William Bosman, who in 1701 described indigenous societies along the Ivory and Gold Coasts. An extensive excerpt may be found in Leslie H. Fishel, Jr. and Benjamin Quarles, eds., *The Black American: A Documentary History* (Henview, Ill.: Scott, Foresman, 1970). For a discussion of precolonial social classes, see Osende Afana, *L'economie de l'Ouest Africain, perspectives de developpement* (Paris: Francois Maspero, 1966), pp. 158–73. See also Szymon Chodak, "Social Stratification in Sub-Saharan Africa," *Canadian Journal of African Studies*, 7, no. 3 (1973), 401–17. One virtue of Chodak's article is that he discusses the anthropological literature, particularly that following the lead of early British functionalists who promoted a picture of precolonial Africa composed essentially of kinship groups, lineages, and extended families that were basically free from internal strife, exploitation, and social stratification. Chodak goes over the early controversies stimulated by Max Gluckman's attack on the schools of Malinowski and Radcliffe-Brown (p. 402). Cf. Gluckman, *Custom and Conflict in Africa;* and Ladislav Holy, *Social Stratification in Tribal Africa* (Prague: Academia, 1968).

ther, the inheritance systems were such that in almost all places debt led to the dispersal of, for example, a large herd of cattle, among a large number of people. Inequalities existed, but they were tempered by comparable family or social responsibilities, and they could never become gross and offensive to the social equality which was at the basis of the communal life.[92]

A second group maintains that African societies can become classless once certain exploitative groups are eliminated. Sekou Touré maintains that once the chieftaincy in Guinea, which had grown apart from the people under the aegis of the French, was overthrown, Guinea could again become the kind of communal society that it had once been somewhere in the mythical past.[93]

The third interpretation, though continuing to maintain the essentially communitarian nature of traditional society, warns of the possibility of "incipient classes." Leopold Senghor has created a whole new vocabulary that emphasizes the emergence of "socio-technico-professional" groups, but he maintains that they are differentiated simply by different degrees of possession of wealth and by the performance of different functions. Groups possessing these characteristics have always existed, even in ancient traditional society, and although Europeans might have mistaken them not only for classes but also for castes, they were in error since neither conflict nor class consciousness exists. Nevertheless, Senghor, in some of his writings, has warned that unless the government takes a strong role in guarding the evolution of modern societies under a plan aiming ultimately at the creation of "African socialism," "true classes" can become a reality.[94]

The fourth interpretation is that classes exist, did exist in the past, and are amenable to analysis. This is the perspective of the present study. Kwame Nkrumah reached this conclusion only gradually and most reluctantly. The evolution of his thinking about class is one of the most interesting aspects of the development of his whole political thought.[95] During the struggle for independence, when his major

[92] Julius K. Nyerere, *Ujamaa — Essays on Socialism* (New York: Oxford University Press, 1968), p. 108. On the whole, then, Nyerere maintains that inequalities in traditional systems were not serious — with one major exception: the role of women. Not all women were alike. Annie M. D. Lebeuf, for example, tells us that in political systems . . . characterized by a pronounced hierarchical structure, those women who either belong to, or have affinal ties with, the royal lineage, enjoy various prerogatives which often have political implications. They're frequently given positions of territorial authority, having one or several villages under their control or full powers over a district. . . . The rights usually assigned to them place them apart from the rest of the female population, and enable their behavior to approximate more closely to that of the male sex than that of their own. "The Role of Women in the Political Organization of African Societies," in *Women of Tropical Africa*, Denise Paulme (Berkeley and Los Angeles: University of California Press, 1971), p. 107.

[93] Sekou Touré, *Guinean Revolution and Social Progress* (Cairo: Societe Orientale de Publicité, N.D. [1963]).

[94] Cf. Senghor's concept of class and class conflict in my *Leopold Sedar Senghor and the Politics of Negritude* (New York: Atheneum, 1969; London: Heinemann Educational Books, 1970).

[95] See, for example, the change in Nkrumah's thinking about class from *Ghana: The Autobiography of Kwame Nkrumah* (London: Nelson and Sons, 1957) to *Africa Must Unite* (London: Heinemann Educational Books, 1963) to *Class Struggle in Africa* (New York: International Publishers, 1970).

effort was devoted to consolidating his power and establishing national unity, he was, like most African leaders, interested above all in stressing those elements within African society that would strengthen the bonds of common interest. Later, when faced with continuous opposition, and then when he was thrown out of power, he dwelled on the internal conflicts of African societies and traced their roots into the past. He maintained that the "peoples of Africa" passed through the "higher stage of communalism characterized by the disintegration of tribal democracy" and became imbedded in the "emergence of feudal relationships, hereditary tribal chieftaincies and monarchal systems." Under the impact of imperialism and colonialism, "communalist socio-economic patterns" collapsed as the result of the introduction of export crops and the interconnection of the economies of the colonies with world capitalist markets, which stimulated capitalism, individualism, and tendencies to private ownership.[96]

Amilcar Cabral, faced with the necessity of creating a mass-based guerrilla movement in rural areas, critically examined the social structure of the peoples of Guinea to see which groups would be most amenable to political organization. His political position necessitated the most hardheaded assessment:

> In the rural areas we have found it necessary to distinguish between two distinct groups: on the one hand, the group which we consider semifeudal, represented by the Fulas and on the other hand, the group which we consider, so to speak, without any defined form or state organization represented by the Balantes. . . . I should now like to give you a quick idea of the social stratification among the Fulas. We consider that the chiefs, the nobles and the religious figures form one group; after them come the artisans and the dyulas, who are itinerate traders, and then after that come the peasants properly speaking. . . . Among the Balantes, which are at the opposite extreme, we find a society without any social stratification: there is just a council of elders in each village or group of villages who decide on the day to day problems. In the Balante group property and land are considered to belong to the village but each family receives the amount of land needed to insure subsistence for itself. . . . In general, the peasants have no rights and they are the really exploited group in Fula society.[97]

On African Feudalism

King Idris Alooma of Kanem-Bornu and Queen Elizabeth I of England, Basil Davidson tells us, certainly talked different languages, but their basic administrative and political problems were not very dissimilar: "Both, after all, were much concerned with the overweening

---

[96] Nkrumah, *Class Struggle in Africa*, p. 13.
[97] Cabral, *Revolution in Guinea*, pp. 56–57.

power of nobles and the need for loyal servants; both had a great deal of trouble with each."[98]

If African leaders disagree about the existence of class in traditional societies, Western scholars argue even more fiercely about the existence of feudalism in these societies, and even about the meaning of the term when used to describe them. Some historians have heatedly denied that European feudal political systems can be compared with the precolonial states of Africa. They have alleged that the term "feudal" has no application whatsoever to Africa.

Our purpose here in examining this term is to try again to determine—as one of the basic purposes of this study—who rules, for what purposes, and in whose interests. Our concern is not simply with taxonomy. We seek an understanding of the sources of power and of the use of social arrangements for the implementation of power. We therefore welcome comparisons with European experiences insofar as they provide insight into the basic underlying social and economic processes that led to present power constellations. From this perspective, what is significant about the term "feudalism" is not that it was created by lawyers and antiquarians in the seventeenth century and applied to a previous era, but that many of the laws and institutions described as "feudal" protected the privileges of the landed aristocracy and permitted them to exercise arbitrary powers over the mass of peasants.[99]

The fundamental features of feudalism in Europe between the tenth and the thirteenth centuries, as defined by Marc Bloch, are

> a subject peasantry; widespread use of the service tenement (i.e. the fief) instead of a salary, which was out of the question; the supremacy of a class of specialized warriors; ties of obedience and protection which bind man to man, and within the warrior class, assume the distinctive form called vassalage; fragmentation of authority leading inevitably to disorder; and in the midst of all this, the survival of other forms of association, family and state. . . .[100]

On a variety of grounds, Africanists have attacked the applicability of even Bloch's definition of feudalism to "tribal" society. If European

[98] Davidson, "The Niger to the Nile," in *The Horizon History of Africa*, ed. Josephy, p. 231.

[99] According to Peter Duus, many academic historians in France, England and the United States restrict [the meaning of feudalism] to a much more narrow sense. They use it to describe a system of military and political organization in which armed warriors or knights rally to leaders who give them grants of land in return for personal service. Most of these writers regard feudalism not as a universal phenomenon but as a set of institutions peculiar to a limited area of Western Europe in the middle ages. Duus also points out that in the early stages of feudalism, a lord might have supported a warrior in his own household or provided him with an office that gave him some income; within later stages, the benefice conventionally took the form of a grant of land or rights over land. This was the fief or feudum, from which our term "feudalism" derives. By using an adaptation of Marc Bloch's definition of feudalism, Duus is able to find key elements of comparison in feudalism in Europe and feudalism in Japan between 1300 and 1600. Peter Duus, *Feudalism in Japan* (New York: Knopf, 1969), p. 6.

[100] Marc Block, *Feudal Society* (Chicago: University of Chicago Press, 1961), p. 446.

feudalism began with the breakdown of the state and the distribution of powers from large-scale organizations to private individuals, in most African states the characteristic trend was toward rather than away from centralization.[101] Jack Goody declares that "words like tribalism, feudalism, capitalism—these abstractions make for too crude a level of analysis [and contain] little meaning except for polemical purposes."[102] In one of the most sophisticated denials of the existence of feudalism in Africa, Goody maintains that in precolonial Africa land was not scarce, because of low population densities, and it was of little economic importance because "its tenure could hardly provide the basis of differentiation for the class system."[103] Land scarcity, however, does not by itself create an economic system; rather, the central problem is the organization of land as a means of production. Henri Pirenne points out that the essence of feudalism was the return to agriculture—*as opposed to movable property and commerce*—as a source of livelihood: "Land was the sole source of subsistence and the sole condition of wealth. All classes of the population, from the emperor, who had no other revenues than those derived from his landed property, down to the humble serf, lived directly or indirectly on the products of the soil, whether they raised them by their labor, or confined themselves to collecting and consuming them."[104]

Goody himself admits that "though there were no landlords, there were of course lords of the land—the local chiefs of centralized states, who, from the standpoint of food production, were in a sense carried by the rest of the population."[105] Furthermore, he allows that being "carried by the rest of the population" may be looked at either as "a return for services rendered or as the exploitation of the weak, for there is, I think, no real test." "No real test" indeed! "Exploitation" obviously involves a political theory of men's relations in society, but so does the notion of "fair pay for services rendered." How easily are even the facts of inequality swept away.

Vast differences in "styles of life," Goody tells us, were to be found in the "trading states of the coast, in the empires of the Niger Bend and in the Emirates of Northern Nigeria." He finds other "exceptions" in the "coastal strips," where ruling and merchant groups financed themselves out of the European and Asian trade; "there were certainly some sumptuary distinctions reported by travelers from Dahomey and Asante; in Ethiopia a series of sumptuary rules confined to the nobility the playing of certain musical instruments, the brewing of honeywine, and similar forms of behavior that were by definition of high prestige." Yet even if great wealth and flamboyant

[101] See J. Beattie, "Bunyoro: An African Feudality," *Journal of African History*, 5, no. 1 (1964), 25–36.

[102] Goody, *Technology, Tradition and the States in Africa*, pp. 16–17.

[103] Jack Goody, "Feudalism in Africa," *Journal of African History*, 4, no. 1 (1963), p. 63.

[104] Henri Pirenne, *Economic and Social History of Medieval Europe* (New York: Harcourt, Brace & World, 1936), p. 7.

[105] The quotations by Goody in this and the following three paragraphs are from Goody's *Technology, Tradition and the State in Africa*, pp. 31, 32, and 76.

gaps in styles of life had not separated social strata—as in fact they did—"differences" were "marked" if they merely placed the chieftaincy or "nobility" in a superior position of access to increasingly frequent and productive innovations. In a footnote, Goody, though not directly measuring "a return for services rendered or the exploitation of the weak," tells us that

> in Ethiopia the church was the largest land owner after the emperor. Some of these lands were worked by the monks; others were farmed by peasants. The landlord's rent, lay or ecclesiastical, could be enormous. At the end of the eighteenth century Bruce noted that the tenants of Tigre usually surrendered at least half their crop, the landlord supplying the seed. But it was 'a very indulgent master that does not take another quarter for the risk he has run'.

In another ingenious argument, Goody disputes the contention that social differentiation in the means of agricultural production was of major significance: "Much more important was the ownership of the means of destruction, since on this depended political overlordship in the production of booty." In the grasslands of Africa the major "means of destruction," the basis of political supremacy, was the horse: "The commoners . . . opposed the horse because it was the instrument of their oppression. The rulers identified themselves with it because it was the instrument of their domination." Goody here recognizes a self-conscious sense of class on the part of both the "commoners" and the "rulers," but he does not see that *acquisition of the "means of destruction" on a systematic basis was made possible precisely by control over the means of production.* Not that a reciprocal relationship didn't exist; rather, again, the major question here is which factor was dominant. And in regard to the argument, "The chief himself was rich not in land, but in goods and services," what was the source of these "goods and services" if not the social organization of land?

Goody's final argument is that the "so-called feudal systems of Africa lacked a feudal technology." That is, "in the absence of wheel, plough and all the concommitant aspects of the 'intermediate technology,' Africa was unable to match the developments, productivity and skill, stratification and specialization, that marked the agrarian societies of the early medieval Europe." That doesn't mean that stratification in Africa was "unable to match" stratification under the feudalism of early medieval Europe. Were these differences of degree or only of kind? The only time that Goody suggests the basis for distinction is when he maintains that African chiefs, under the changes introduced by colonialism, found the retention of their high status much more difficult than in parallel situations in Europe: "Consequently, the emerging system of stratification in Africa has less to contend with in the shape of traditional authorities, anyhow in the economic sphere. The new 'class' structure is relatively open." Nowhere does Goody offer any evidence to support this contention. Although status reversal occurred, apparently with great frequency in country after country, the traditional leaders and their descendants appear to have done quite well.[106] That there were sharp social differences and that these differences were often felt keenly by both the rulers and the "commoners" Goody does not, in any event, deny. In the final analysis, all that appears to be at issue are the extent of these differences, particularly in terms of the European experience, plus a theory, based on allegations concerning technological differences, that is designed to facilitate the comparison of Europe and Africa. What concerns us, however, are the differences among social layers within African society. Comparisons of power, wealth, and status must be in terms of indigenous standards.

Lloyd Fallers argues that feudalism was absent in Africa because there was "no high-low culture difference."[107] African villagers, he maintains, don't feel the same degree of ambivalence towards the "political superstructure" that peasants in Europe, Asia, and Latin America do, because they don't feel themselves in contrast with "the possessors of a differentiated high culture" and, therefore, they don't "to the same extent feel judged from above by a set of standards which they cannot attain." Fallers goes on to say that "Africans very commonly perceive themselves as being differentiated in terms of wealth and power but they do not often, except in the few real composite conquest states, view their societies as consisting of 'layers' of persons with differential possession of a high culture."[108] Thus, even though the African villager might have been a "peasant economically and politically," he was not one "culturally." However, Fallers refutes himself. A "court art" certainly did exist in Benin, Asante, Kongo, and Dahomey. Any major museum abounds with concrete evidence against Fallers's thesis—namely, that *cultural* criteria are crucial. What matters for our purposes are questions of political, social, and economic domination and subordination. In terms of "class consciousness," Fallers informs us that whenever a literary culture has entered Africa it has made the African more fully a "peasant": "Thus Muslim Swahili peoples of the East Coast and the Hausa of the Western Sudan were traditionally more peasant-like than their non-literate, pagan neighbors; and the modern Baganda and Asante, with their imported Western Christian high culture, are more fully peasant than were their great-grandfathers."[109]

[106] See this chapter, section on the "Continuity Between Chiefs and Modern Elites."

[107] Lloyd Fallers, "Are African Cultivators to be Called 'Peasants'?" in *Economic Development and Social Change: The Modernization of Village Communities,* ed. George Dalton (Garden City, N.Y.: Natural History Press, 1971), p. 176.

[108] *Ibid.*

[109] *Ibid.*, pp. 176–77. Raymond Apthorpe presents a critique of Fallers's conceptions of feudalism and especially traditional state bureaucracies in his "The Introduction of Bureaucracy into African Politics," *Journal of African Administration,* vol. XIII, July 1, 1960, pp. 125–34.

Fallers carries his analysis to an extreme conclusion in his last publication, *Inequality: Social Stratification Reconsidered.* In this work he rejects concepts of social stratification as well as of class. Fallers stated not only that "objective" inequalities must be understood in their cultural contexts, but that

I do not mean to allege that European and African feudalism are identical. On the contrary, Eugene Genovese is correct when he maintains that "every social class is unique. The terms 'bourgeoisie,' 'proletariat,' 'slaveocracy,' or 'slave class' are essential in historical investigations, for they provide a starting point in underlying common characteristics that lead us directly to the mainstreams of social change."[110] Genovese warns, however, that the "promiscuous application of class labels" is no substitute for "historical specificity." If in the modern world "the uniqueness of social classes usually must be understood in a national context," and if no two national classes are exactly alike, still the "significance of their universality relative to their particularity depends entirely on the problem under investigation for each has its own legitimate sphere of relevance."[111]

Max Gluckman, though employing the word "feudalism," in his discussion of certain African traditional systems pointed out that "these systems were not feudal in terms of rights to land. Most of the villagers were seemingly able to obtain land by right, possible because it was 'plentiful.' . . . These West African states were tribute-organizing states, in which much use was made of the labor of slaves."[112]

The essentials of feudalism were not matters of legalistic jargon but the social condition of those who lived on "seigneurial soil": what mattered was that feudal society was divided, and that the "dependents" were at once exploited and protected. As Pirenne tells us,

> What was the *Seigneur* (Senior) if not the elder, whose authority extended over their *familia* whom he protected? Unquestionably he did protect them. In times of war he defended them against the enemy and sheltered them in the walls of his fortress, and it was clearly to his own advantage to do so, since he lived by their labor. . . . Unable to produce for sale owing to the want of a market, he had no need to tax his ingenuity in order to rend from his men and his land a surplus which would merely be an encumbrance, and as he was forced to consume his own produce, he was content to limit it to his needs.[113]

what really matters are "interpersonal relations of superiority," which can have many bases—race, ethnicity, occupation, regionalism, age, sex, and so on. In his demonstration of the complexity of human relations, Fallers virtually reduces the scope of our ability to generalize to dyadic connections. (Chicago: University of Chicago Press, 1973); see especially pp. 3–29.

[110] Eugene Genovese, *The World the Slave Owners Made* (New York: Vintage Books, 1969), p. 19.

[111] *Ibid.* In his work in the Western hemisphere Genovese uses the term "seigneurialism," which is roughly equivalent to "serfdom" though not exactly so, for "it includes regimes in which the lords' claims on the economic surplus are met by payments in money or kind as well as in labor services" (*ibid.*, p. 111).

[112] Max Gluckman, *Politics, Law and Ritual in Tribal Society* (New York: New American Library, 1965). See also Gluckman's *The Ideas in Barotse Jurisprudence*.

[113] Pirenne, *Economic and Social History of Medieval Europe*, pp. 7, 15. In *Saints and Politicians: Essays in the Organization of a Senegalese Peasant Society* (Cambridge: Cambridge University Press, 1975), D. B. Cruise O'Brien claims the Mouride brotherhood has been a vehicle for upward mobility (p. 64). See also Cruise O'Brien's exceptionally fine study, *The Mourides of Senegal* (New York: Oxford University Press, 1971). Cruise O'Brien finds to his great amazement that the marabouts, though "taxing" an enormous portion of the income of their *talibés*, nevertheless offered solace and "protection." The unexpectedness of his finding tempers Cruise O'Brien's critique, as if any political system, no matter how repressive, did not provide "something" in benefits, if only circuses. For a sympathetic assessment see Cheikh Tidiane Sy, *La confrerie Senegalaise des Mourides* (Paris: Presence Africaine, 1969).

The situation of the Hutu in Rwanda illustrates these propositions. Jacques Maquet tells us that the function of the Hutu institution of *buhake*—a word meaning "to pay one's respects to somebody"—"was to provide the upper stratum with agricultural goods without significant reciprocity, and without the obligation to participate directly in the productive processes—that is to say to work."[114] Until 1959, when they revolted and overthrew the feudal caste system, Helen Codere states that "the Hutu were oppressed and terrorized and accepted what they had to accept as they did what they had to do."[115] To Western social scientists who ask, If the system was so exploitative why did those on the bottom tolerate it for so long? Codere demonstrates clearly how the system repressed dissent.

Traditional systems in Ethiopia have probably been described as feudal more frequently than any other systems on the continent. Among the many writers using the term to describe the Amhara of Ethiopia, Hoben writes:

> It would seem then, that insofar as the term *feudal* is detached from its historical setting and used to describe a type of societal organization in which the polity is based on a hierarchical network of personal, diffused, and contractual ties between patron and client and in which sovereignty is bound to rights and land, the Amhara patterns may be called a feudal one.
>
> Similarities between traditional Amhara and European feudalism go beyond these similarities in the pattern of political and land relations. There are similarities in the ideology of social stratification also, in the ways that people conceptualize and justify the major divisions or "estates" that make up society.[117]

As in Europe, increasing centralization of the power of the king at the expense of his nobles caused an evolution of the African state systems. Many of the same elements that marked the evolution of England and France characterized these developments, including the

---

[114] Jacques Maquet, "Rwanda Castes," in *Social Stratification in Africa,* ed. Tuden and Plotnicov, p. 117. See also Maquet's *The Premise of Inequality in Ruanda* (London: Oxford University Press, 1961); and his "The Power of Tutsi Domination," in *Economic Development and Social Change,* ed. Dalton, pp. 81–88.

[115] Helen Codere, "Power in Ruanda," *Anthropologica,* 4, no. 1 (1962), 63.

[116] *Ibid.,* p. 63. Codere maintains that because Maquet analyzed social roles and social strata without highlighting the inherent exploitative nature of the vassals and overlords, he completely missed an understanding of the bitterness that eventually led to the revolution in Rwanda and produced some of the greatest slaughters in Africa—thus, her conclusion that "Ruanda has been undergoing a genuine social and political revolution. . . . The Hutu wished to end Tutsi domination and to govern Ruanda" (*ibid,* p. 63). Across the continent, from the West Coast to Central Africa to the East Coast, the comparability of African and European feudalism can be argued. See for example A. A. Boohen, "Kingdoms of West Africa," in *The Horizon History of Africa,* ed. Josephy, p. 183; and H. A. S. Johnston, *The Fulani Empire of Sokoto* (London: Oxford University Press, 1967), cf.

[117] Allan Hoben, "Social Stratification in Traditional Amhara Society," in *Social Stratification in Africa,* ed. Tuden and Plotnicov, p. 191. See also Robert L. Hess, *Ethiopia: The Modernization of Autocracy* (Ithaca, N.Y.: Cornell University Press, 1970); Richard Greenfield, *Ethiopia, A New Political History* (New York: Praeger, 1965); and Richard Pankhurst, *An Introduction to the Economic History of Ethiopia from Early Times to 1800* (London: Sedgwick and Jackson, 1961).

playing off by kings of commoners against the nobles, the use of religion as a state-building device, and the intertwining and expansion of commerce and politics along the lines of new trade routes. Finding parallel developments across the continent from Buganda to Asante, Bradbury, in his study of Benin, recounts how "the kings were able to subvert descent-group-based claims to authority, and to appropriate to themselves a large measure of control over the means of administration. . . ." In the late eighteenth and early nineteenth centuries, the political consolidation of power by the Asante over extensive and culturally heterogeneous territories was possible because of a "differentiated and professional administrative organization" that accompanied military expansion. Bradbury argues that "the main structural outlines of the nineteenth century Benin polity were established as a result of broadly similar developments taking place in broadly similar circumstances as far back as the fifteenth and early sixteenth centuries."[118]

On the Differences Among Serfdom, Slavery in the Traditional State Systems, and Commercial Slavery

Feudalism could not develop in Africa as it did in Europe, the argument has been advanced, because land was plentiful, even if so unproductive as to require the frequent movement of peoples when fertility soon declined. The social consequences, Goody maintains, encouraged the development of slavery, insofar as chiefship tended to be over people rather than over land:

> In slavery, labor is controlled by political force; in serfdom, economic controls, such as land tenure, are of equal importance. . . . In Africa, labor requirements led to slavery but not serfdom; trading towns like Kano and Bida in Northern Nigeria, or Salaga in Bole in Northern Ghana, were surrounded by villages of slaves which supplied the ruling and commercial groups. Domestic slaves, dependent kinfolk and clients filled other servile roles, but the supply of land and the degree of control made it difficult to exploit labor by anything other than slavery.[119]

---

[118] R. E. Bradbury, "Patrimonialism and Gerontocracy in Benin Political Culture," in *Man in Africa,* ed. Douglas and Kaberry (Garden City, N.Y.: Doubleday, Anchor Books, 1971), pp. 28–29. Early in the sixteenth century, the fifteenth Oba quelled the powerful nobles with the aid of guns provided by European visitors. One device used by obas was to install an "open court," to which "many prominent commoners" were invited. *(Ibid.)* But cf. Ivor Wilks who argues that the high degree of control established over the patterns of socioeconomic and ideological organization, coupled with the range of "its propriatory and managerial functions over land, manpower, and production" far removed the Asante state in the nineteenth century from the "feudalities to which many scholars, following Rattray, have been inclined to assimilate it." "Ashanti Government," in *West African Kingdoms in the Nineteenth Century,* ed. Forde and Kaberry, p. 232. Two factors nevertheless must be noted: (1) as we pointed out above, the states did evolve and growing centralization was a fundamental aspect of their political development; and (2) the relative positions of domination and subordination of rulers and ruled did not change but were strengthened.

[119] Goody, *Technology, Tradition and the State in Africa,* p. 30. As Goody himself admits, in Latin America despite ample land the Spanish conquerors "imposed on the population a system of peonage, which was something less than slavery" *(ibid.).*

In fact, different types of precommercial slavery existed in Africa. Claude Meillassoux distinguishes three different forms in West Africa. The first, domestic slavery, involved the slave in a work relationship alongside other junior members of the lineage into which he was assimilated economically: "He works lands owned by the lineage of the family and shares in return a common product distributed by the elders." Under these circumstances, "exploitation is not obvious . . . the slave, after generations have elapsed, loses his inferior status, marries within the master's family, and becomes a full member of the community." In the other two types of slavery, more direct production for the market evolved. Under one system the master allocated a plot of land to the slave to provide for himself and his family, but the slave also worked for his master, allocating for his benefit a certain number of days of "labor rent." The status of a slave descended to his children. In the third type of system, the slaves became so numerous that they had to be grouped into separate hamlets and the stigma of a separate and lower status intensified.[120]

Many authorities point out that slaves in African kingdoms frequently had many privileges, ranging from the holding of important offices — in which they were trusted, because freemen could hope to seize power for themselves — to becoming heads of important commercial houses.[121]

In the eleventh century, merchants on the edge of the savanna possessed more than one thousand slaves, a figure that was surpassed by some slave owners of later centuries. Men such as these, A. G. Hopkins points out, could afford expensive items — meat, wheat, yams, salt, and luxuries from abroad. On the other hand, "the poor, who are often presumed not to have existed in pre-colonial West Africa, had to content themselves with carrion, inferior grains or cassava and imperfect salt substitutes, and at times of extreme need freemen had to place themselves or a member of their family in pawn to wealthy creditors."[122]

On the Slave Trade and the African Ruling Class

The European Atlantic slave trade didn't begin until the sixteenth century, reached its maximum during the eighteenth century, and was

---

[120] Claude Meillassoux, *The Development of Indigenous Trade and Markets in West Africa* (London: Oxford University Press, 1971), p. 63. See also Phillip Curtin, who points out that "although Africa and Europe in the Middle East all had traditions of slavery going back from millennia, the form of slavery differed so much from one society to another that it can be misleading to talk of slavery as a single institution." He goes on to argue that in different parts of Africa, similarly huge distinctions occurred. Phillip D. Curtin, "The Atlantic Slave Trade, 1600–1800," in J. F. A. Ajayi and Michael Crowder, eds. *History of West Africa* (New York: Columbia University Press, 1972), pp. 242–43.

[121] See, for example, J. B. Webster and A. A. Boahen, *History of West Africa* (New York: Praeger, 1970), p. 69.

[122] A. G. Hopkins, *An Economic History of West Africa* (London: Lougman, 1973), p. 27. Hopkins asserts that West African rulers did not concern themselves with expanding markets or economic de-

abolished at the start of the nineteenth century. The Arab slave trade across the Indian Ocean, on the other hand, began before the birth of Christ and didn't stop until the end of the nineteenth century.

Although the volume of the Arab slave trade in any one year did not reach the highest figures of the European commerce, the total number of persons removed during two millennia may well have exceeded 15 million. The treatment of slaves was terrible in both cases: the most reliable estimates are that "about one-half of those captured in West Africa reached their destination, [and] only one-fifth of those captured in East Africa and shipped to Arabia and the East, survived."[123] Even in West Africa, the export slave trade dates from early antiquity:

> Already in the late ninth century, slave merchants, even from Asia, were established in Fezzan, dealing with suppliers to the south. Later in the eleventh century, al-Bakri mentioned slave exports from Fezzan. Ibn Battuta, in the mid fourteenth century, commented that Bornu was renowned for its exports of excellent slave girls, eunuchs, and saffron-dyed fabrics. Leo Africanus gave an interesting description of trade in Bornu at the beginning of the sixteenth century of Barbary merchants bringing war horses for the king, and receiving slaves in exchange. Although the king was very wealthy—his spurs and bridles, tableware, even dog chains were said to be true gold—he preferred to pay only in slaves.[124]

Marsh and Kingsnorth, in assessing the motives of the Arab slave trade, maintain that the Arabs were

> by far the most important outside traders who promoted the slave trade in East Africa. . . . They were Muslims, and the Koran, although it did not explicitly forbid slavery, lay down strict rules for the treatment of slaves and positively forbade any Muslim to enslave another. It was, therefore, necessary for the Arabs to look outside their own country for slaves, and East Africa became their source of supply. From the ninth century a stream of slaves left the East African ports for the markets of Turkey, Arabia, India and Persia.[125]

The same authors also point out that "ivory and slaves were the commodities on which the wealth of the Arab settlements of East Africa was based."[126] Although Islamic law forbade the enslavement of free Muslims, it nevertheless tolerated the continued enslavement of peoples who converted after their capture.[127] Although Europeans might

---

velopment: "Politics in a pre-industrial society is largely the art of redistributing a relatively fixed national income with a degree of inequality which is sufficient to make life luxurious for the rulers without at the same time provoking discontent on such a scale as to endanger the existence of the state" (*ibid.,* p. 25).

[123] See Zoe Marsh and G. W. Kingsnorth, *An Introduction to the History of East Africa* (London: Cambridge University Press, 1965), p. 39.

[124] *Ibid.,* p. 71.

[125] *Ibid.,* p. 33.

[126] *Ibid.,* p. 33.

[127] John Ralph Willis, "The Spread of Islam," in *The Horizon History of Africa,* ed. Josephy, p. 141.

well debate whether slavery in Africa was comparable to slavery elsewhere, the Fishers point out that Muslim law is quite specific in defining slavery and applied different treatment to slaves and freemen: the evidence of a slave was not admissible in court; the legal penalties inflicted upon slaves differed from those applied to freemen; slaves could not inherit; a slave not only was not required to make the pilgrimage to Mecca, but his pilgrimage was considered invalid should it be done without his master's permission; and so on.[128]

The Slave Trade Under Capitalism

Although slavery existed under indigenous systems, a qualitative change occurred with the huge expansion and demand stimulated by the growing trade of a burgeoning European capitalism. As the Ghanaian historian Daaku points out,

> Debt, captivity and war, and criminal offenses could easily lead people into slavery, and these appeared to have been the means whereby the rich secured slaves. But the outright sale of others as slaves was as incidental as it was irregular, because people did not normally set themselves up as slave dealers. . . . The slave trade that followed in the wake of the Europeans was completely different and foreign to the norms of society. Henceforth, in the trans-Atlantic trade, human beings were considered as ends in themselves. They were commodities. The introduction of the new trade in slaves brought significant far-reaching changes in the values and organizations of states. It is not without significance at the beginning of the era that the intensive slave trade coincided with the growth of sizeable political entities in the forest regions of the Gold Coast. *The correlation between the growth of Empires and the European trade, especially the slave trade, is one of the most important phenomena in the history of the Gold Coast in the seventeenth century.*[129]

To argue the fundamental difference between slavery in indigenous African traditional systems and slavery under the impact of Western commercialism is not to deny the precolonial significance of slavery or to allege that slavery had merely an "ephemeral intransitory status." One commentator, for example, maintains that slavery

> has had no major influence on the systems of stratification that have since emerged and which exist today, with the possible exception of South Africa. This is true even where slaves were important as labor and commodities for trade. . . . It is true that some slaves were regarded as only and purely economic commodities, but these were marked for sale and export, and their sojourn in any one place was short. They cannot be taken into consideration in our discussion, for they were to-

---

[128] See Allan G. B. Fisher and Humphrey Fisher, *Slavery and Muslim Society in Africa* (Garden City, N.Y.: Doubleday, 1971; Anchor Books ed., 1972), pp. 7–49.
[129] Kwame Yeboa Daaku, *Trade and Politics on the Gold Coast, 1600–1720* (Oxford: Clarendon Press, 1970), pp. 20, 29 (emphasis added).

tally dehumanized and were no more a part of any social system than any item of trade or wealth.[130]

These contentions are simply contradictory and nonsensical. Although Daaku confines his remarks to developments in the Gold Coast, similar trends occurred throughout the continent. Slaves captured in war were generally reserved for the kings and their elders, who benefited the most from them because of their privileged positions. Sustained by custom as well as political and social organization, as Daaku points out, "the Europeans always sought an understanding with the rulers, since by virtue of their position they were the greatest potential traders."[131] Walter Rodney argues that as early as 1448,

> The Portuguese decided to take part in commerce with the Africans rather than try to hunt them. That was the year . . . in which they set up Arguin in Mauretania as the first European "factory" in West Africa. From then onwards, the Europeans generally *bought rather than captured* Africans to be used as slaves. . . . With the exceptions of the Portuguese in Angola the Europeans never went inland to obtain captives. In fact, the Africans on the coast prevented the Europeans from going into the interior, so that they themselves could bring down the slaves and receive as many European goods as possible.[132]

A similar point is made by Boahen:

> Throughout West Africa and the Congo it was the ruling aristocracy — the kings and their nobles — who were ultimately responsible for supplying these slaves, for they waged the wars, organized the raids, tried the criminals and debtors, and passed the judgments. The French factor Jean Barbot was correct when he wrote that "the trade in slaves is a business of kings, rich men, and prime merchants."[133]

To say that Africans took part in the slave trade is not, however, to deny the permanent responsibility of external forces, because the systematic organization of African states who were geared to a new market situation created a more horrendous enterprise. As Rodney declares,

> Some historians go so far as to say that the Africans took the major part in the slave trade. Any enemy of the African people would happily take this view, as a way of excusing the inhuman behavior of the Europeans

---

[130] Arthur Tuden, "Introduction," in *Social Stratification in Africa*, ed. Tuden and Plotnicov, pp. 12, 15.

[131] Daaku, *Trade and Politics on the Gold Coast, 1600–1720*, p. 32.

[132] Walter Rodney, *West Africa and the Atlantic Slave Trade* (Nairobi: Historical Association of Tanzania Paper, 1967). One of the earliest documents illustrating cooperation between European slave traders and African chiefs describes Hawkins's slaving voyage in 1562 to Sierra Leone. An agreement was drawn up in which the Europeans provided weapons and other aid in the war between the "King of Sierra Leone" and a neighboring chief in exchange for slaves. See Basil Davidson, *The African Past: Chronicles from Antiquity to Modern Times* (New York: Grosset & Dunlap, 1967), pp. 199–200.

[133] A. A. Boahen, "Kingdoms of West Africa," in *The Horizon History of Africa*, ed. Josephy, p. 317.

by placing the blame and responsibility on the Africans. Nothing could be more incorrect and ridiculous, because what happened in Africa was only one side of the whole story. The Atlantic slave trade was organized and financed by Europeans, who had already reached the capitalist stage of development. Africans had absolutely no control over the European side or the American side of the slave trade. Only the European capitalists had such world-wide power, and they used Africans for their own purposes. [134]

"Stateless societies," which did not have central governments or ruling elites, did not acquire slaves for the benefit of the Europeans, nor did they war with their neighbors for the purpose of acquiring captives.

Once begun, the slave trade produced its own momentum: rulers constantly found new uses for the windfall profits that came from abroad—if only to use those new monies against the foreign intrusion. For example, Samory Touré relied on the sale of slaves to buy horses, almost 2,000 annually, from the north.[135] Slaves were sometimes paid to soldiers on active service as a bonus.[136] The military, in fact, became more and more autonomous and self-conscious as a class, as the value of slaves as commodities sold to foreign merchants increased. According to Meillassoux,

> the interest of the military class became more and more estranged from those of the people. In extreme cases, when this separation became complete, the warrior class, as a declared enemy of the people, attempted to reduce them to slavery, as in Kayor [in Senegal]. It loses thereby its justification as arbitrator and protector. Even though it might have reinforced its position through the part played in an international economy, it loses the political control of the people it claims to dominate. Its weakness can only be mitigated by embarking on more and more wars; or by an increased repression. External warfare or social warfare, such are the alternatives open to the military class if it wishes to continue in power.[137]

Reportedly slavery continued into the twentieth century. According to Fisher and Fisher, "colonial governments, even in the twentieth century, found the sale of slaves accompanying pilgrims, and disguised as servants or fellow pilgrims, particularly difficult to check. . . . In 1960 some Maure or Tuareg notables were reported to have covered part of their pilgrimage expenses by selling slaves in Arabia."[138] Similarly, Robert L. Hess, noting the existence of slavery in modern times in his history of Ethiopia, points out that after Ethiopia became a member of the League of Nations in 1923, the Regent found it nec-

---

[134] Rodney, op. cit., p. 7.

[135] Webster and Boahen, *History of West Africa*, p. 50.

[136] See Fisher and Fisher, *Slavery and Muslim Society in Africa*, p. 111, for a number of examples, including the wars of the Bornu in West Africa, the Mirambo in East Africa, and the Bello in Northern Nigeria.

[137] Meillassoux, op. cit., pp. 66–67.

[138] Fisher and Fisher, *Slavery and Muslim Society in Africa*, p. 146.

essary to emancipate all slaves in the country in order to render Ethiopia less susceptible to criticism from abroad.[139] In East Africa, slavery remained legal until this century, with Swahili society recognizing a slave hierarchy based on length of service of ancestors, employment, reputation, and the owner's status.[140] As late as 1903, slavery continued in certain emirates of northern Nigeria. The Emir of Kontagora was reputed to have said, "Can you stop a cat from mousing? When I die I shall be found with a slave in my mouth."[141]

The Devastation and Economic Effects Wrought by the Slave Trade

The destruction and devastation, demoralization and disinvestment wrought by the slave trade have been frequently described. For example, the noted economist Andrew Kamarck writes:

> Unfortunately, the slave trade, in addition to being an inhuman and in a real sense, an immoral activity, was a particularly destructive type of commerce. It drew off from the continent human beings at the most productive ages. Worse still, it encouraged tribe to fight tribe and encouraged conflict within tribes. Finally, and perhaps most important, any advantages that Africa derived from contact with the rest of the world—the learning of some skills, the introduction of new foods, such as maize and manioc—were more than offset by the slave trade plunging vast stretches of Africa into anarchy. Whatever else economic development requires, it does need a basic minimum of personal security. The fact that rulers along the West African coast were successful in building up states on the middleman traffic in slaves did not mitigate the disastrous impact of the trade on the peoples further inland.[142]

Recently, however, a new school of historians has sought to prove that the slave trade enhanced the economic development of the state societies concerned. Fage, the leader of this school of thought, argues that not only was Africa not seriously depopulated (his evidence is that the areas that produced the most slaves—for example, Iboland—remained among the most overpopulated on the whole continent), but, under the stimulus of external commerce, the standard of living

---

[139] Hess, *Ethiopia*, p. 65.

[140] See Willis, "The Spread of Islam," in *The Horizon History of Africa*, ed. Josephy, p. 144.

[141] Quoted in Walter Schwartz, *Nigeria* (London: Pall Mall, 1968), p. 17. A problem persisted apparently down to independence. Dr. Azikiwe, renowned African nationalist leader and former Nigerian head of state, spoke in the then Nigerian Federal Parliament on a bill to abolish the Osu system: "This bill seeks to do three things: to abolish the Osu system and its allied practices including Oru and Ohu systems, with prescribed punishments for their continued practice, and to remove certain social disabilities caused by the enforcement of the Osu and its allied systems." The bill defined the Osu system to "include any social way of living which implies that any person who is deemed to be an Osu or Oru or Ohu is subject to certain prescribed social disability and social stigma." An Osu is a "slave who is dedicated to a shrine, or deity, or the descendants of such a person." Quoted in Ikenna Nzimiro, *Studies in Ibo Political Systems* (Berkeley and Los Angeles: University of California Press, 1972), p. 40.

[142] Andrew Kamarck, *The Economics of African Development*, rev. ed. (New York: Praeger, 1971), pp. 7–9.

of the peoples in the entire area rose (excluding, of course, those who were deported). African traditional leaders, Fage maintains, were just as able to calculate their economic best interests as anyone else; to allege otherwise is to assert a racist doctrine of African ignorance or incapacity.[143]

To speak, as Fage does, of "Africans" benefiting from the slave trade blurs fundamental distinctions between the African rulers who carried out this commerce and the mass of the population, to say nothing of the slaves themselves. Even here, a further distinction must be made between the slave-raiding societies and the societies that were raided, for it could possibly be argued that even the lower strata in the enslaving societies benefited on a trickle-down basis, from the blood of their brothers, just as in industrial countries large segments of the working class enjoy indirectly the fruits of increased productivity, no matter what its ultimate source. Fage also does not take into account the changing international commercial picture, which would have produced a growth in the standard of living even in the absence of slavery. To say that slavery caused any improvements is possibly to mistake a coincidental event with a fundamental cause.

In a case study of the effect of the slave trade and commerce on traditional structures, conducted in Senegal, Martin Klein concludes "that the slave trade contributed to the development of military structures and to the polarization of Senegambian societies between a warrior elite and an industrious Muslim peasant population."[144] The slave trade, Klein tells us, was "conservative because it put wealth and weapons in the hands of those who commanded military forces and could enslave other men. The only other groups to profit materially from the increased wealth were artisans and griots in client relationships to the elite, and the middleman groups in and around the factories." The development of a class of warriors and nobles separate from the mass of the peasants created an elite with values that radically differed from those of the mass of peasants and fishermen, based on a monopoly of their weapons and trade.[145] Later, with the development of cash crops based on peanuts and oil production, the same warriors and artisans were the first to become the city dwellers and formed the cadres for the French colonial commerce and administration. Thus, the old ruling class merged quickly with the new.

What is certain, moreover, is that when the British and French ultimately abolished the slave trade—for reasons intrinsic to their own industrial development—the same African chiefs bitterly resisted ef-

---

[143] See J. D. Fage, *A History of West Africa*, rev. ed. (Cambridge: Cambridge University Press, 1969), particularly Chapters 8 and 9.

[144] Martin A. Klein, "Social and Economic Factors in the Muslim Revolution in Senegambia," *Journal of African History*, 13, no. 3 (1972), 441.

[145] *Ibid.*, p. 422. See also Paul Pelissier, *Les paysans du Senegal* (Saint-Yrieix, France: Imp. Fabregue, 1966); and Boubacar Barry, *(Le royaume du Waalo, le Senegal avant la conquete* (Paris: Francois Maspero, 1972).) Cf. Edward A. Alpers, *Ivory and Slaves in East Central Africa* (Berkeley and Los Angeles: Univeristy of California Press, 1975), who also shows how disruptions and loss of manpower were not made up by technology or manufactured products (p. 266).

forts to end the slave trade: "African chiefs found new ports from which to ship slaves, they made plans with the slave traders to outwit the British warships, and they were very hostile to any person who came telling them to stop trading in slaves. The position of the African slave trading chiefs was in reality quite straightforward. Capturing and selling people as slaves was their main function ever since the fifteenth and sixteenth centuries.[146]

The slave trade was replaced by the introduction of "cash crops," which were necessary as raw materials for the burgeoning industries of western Europe. By the middle of the nineteenth century in Nigeria, for example, so much palm oil was produced that the several outlets of the Niger came to be known as the "oil rivers." Webster and Boahen rank the replacement of the slave trade by the palm oil trade as one of the three most significant events in nineteenth-century West Africa, along with the Islamic revolutions of the western Sudan and the later partition of Africa by European powers. Indeed, the introduction of cash crops led ultimately to the partition of West Africa, because of the difficulties the Europeans found in introducing systematic large-scale agricultural production for the marketplace. The African rulers of the coastal kingdoms of West Africa objected that the Europeans had forced abolition on them without provision for substitute revenues. Eventually, far greater profits came from peanuts and coffee beans than ever accrued from slavery, but the majority of African chiefs attempted to straddle the interim by introducing palm oil and other cash crops while still holding on to the slave trade. Until the potentialities of the new system became clear, African princes, not surprisingly, resisted abolition with every weapon at their command.[147]

Slave Revolts

If in some traditional African societies slaves were treated familiarly, slave conditions in general were by no means idyllic—particularly in those areas so poor in resources that even freemen suffered from want. If the condition of slaves in many cases was so miserable, why did they not revolt? There are good reasons to explain the difficulties any oppressed people have in rising up against their lot, but slave revolts did in fact occur in virtually every area of the continent. These revolts were much more frequent among newly captured or bought slaves than among those born in captivity. As in every society, the prevailing institutions indoctrinated all members with a psychological and religious orientation designed to induce passive acceptance. Slave society itself comprised many gradations of formal ranking that diverted attention from the governing structures and splintered opposi-

---

[146] Rodney, p. 24.
[147] See Webster and Boahen, *History of West Africa*, p. 79. Cf. E. M. Chilver and P. M. Kaberry, "The Kingdom of Kom in West Cameroon," in *West African Kingdoms in the Nineteenth Century*, ed. Forde and Kaberry. Slavery enabled the king of Kom to "consolidate control along his borders, brought wealth into the country, and strengthened his hold over his own people . . ." (p. 133).

tion. Close ties often did exist between masters and slaves, particularly in agricultural societies, where slaves often engaged in occupations similar to those of their masters. Slaves engaged in agricultural production or artisanal work did not produce only for the market or only for their master's account; often, they could earn a good living for themselves, and sometimes they became wealthy. For a variety of reasons, slave status did not prevent the progressive integration of slaves into society, at least as "minor citizens."[148]

Slave revolts nevertheless occurred. They occurred among the Itsekiri and Urhobo in the mid nineteenth century.[149] In the eighteenth century, slave "administrator-soldiers" overthrew the Kulibali dynasty of the Bambara kingdom of Segu.[150] Slaves rose up under a leader from their midst, Afonja, in the Oyo Empire. In 1838 the Koranko rose against the Susu of Sierra Leone; Bilale, their leader, built a fortified town offering freedom to runaways. Slave revolts were a threat to sixteenth-century Songhay.[151] In 1890 Lugard described the towns of Fuladoyo, Mogogoni, and Nwaiba in East Africa as "large stockaded villages, colonies of runaway slaves," and added that he understood that they had beaten the Arabs in battle some years before. In the late nineteenth century, slaves armed by Arab traders who directed them to put down a revolt led by the African chief Mirambo in Tanganyika ran away and fought instead against the Arabs.[152]

Goody makes the interesting point that slave revolts were related to technology because with the introduction of the gun, kings could depend upon slaves rather than freemen: "However, to do so is to sow the seeds of one's destruction. By placing one's trust in slaves, the way is open for revolution as well as rebellion, a slave revolt of the kind that worried the Asante king . . . and that usurped power in the Bambara state of Segou in the eighteenth century."[153] Goody goes on to summarize discussions between Asante kings and a series of travelers, Dupuis,

[148] Meillassoux concludes that all of this shows that "a social division of labor had not yet been achieved," but he nevertheless admits that "the germs of a class society were there insofar as masters objectively exploited slave labor and gained profit from their production for the market" (Meillassoux, ed., The Development of Indigenous Trade and Markets in West Africa, p. 65). In addition to physical differences that distinguished slaves from other classes, and social differences such as dress, slaves were frequently branded with facial and body markings that marked them off from the rest of the population and showed hierarchal differences among the slaves themselves. Cf. Bradbury, "Patrimonialism and Gerontocracy in Benin Political Culture," in Man in Africa, ed. Douglas and Kaberry, p. 21.

[149] Obaro Ikime, Niger Delta Rivalry: Itsekiri-Urhobo Relations and the European Presence, 1884–1936 (New York: Humanities Press, 1969), pp. 30, 39–40.

[150] Phyllis Ferguson and Ivor Wilks, "Chiefs, Constitutions and the British in Northern Ghana," in West African Chiefs, ed. Michael Crowder and Obaro Ikime (New York: Africana Publishing, 1970), p. 326.

[151] Webster and Boahen, History of West Africa, p. 70.

[152] Fisher and Fisher, Slavery and Muslim Society in Africa, p. 111. The Fishers provide many other instances of slave revolts, including the 1756 uprising in Futa Jallon that resulted in the building of a fortified town, Kombeeah. Similar fortified towns were built as a result of the 1838 revolt of the Koranko slaves, and Kukuna and the village of Ganon emerged as a fugitive slave fortress between the upper Senegal and upper Gambia rivers. Cf. K. O. Dike, Trade and Politics in the Niger Delta, 1830–1885 (Oxford: Clarendon Press, 1956), pp. 153–65.

[153] Goody, Technology, Tradition and the State in Africa, p. 3.

Clapperton, and Hutchinson. In one of the discussions the Asante king was quite explicit about the possibility that too many slaves might lead to a revolt.

One of the most interesting slave movements occurred in old Calabar. The slaves began by attacking the customs of the Efik nobility, which required the sacrifice of slaves, servants, courtiers, and wives upon the death of a king or prominent person.[154] Drawing their membership from all those "who were in need of protection against the oppression of the Ekpe," the slaves founded the "Order of Bloodmen." The name came from an oath sworn on the mingled blood of their members designed to create solidarity and trust amongst themselves.[155] In 1851, when the Ekpe arrested some slaves preparatory to funeral rites, thousands of bloodmen poured into Calabar and threatened to destroy the town if their comrades were harmed. So well organized and numerous were they that they were able to secure new rights for their members. Under the British colonial administration, and with the turn to cash crops, they were able by 1863 to gain added protection and win court cases against the nobility.[156]

With increasing political, social, and economic development, with the introduction of capitalism, and with the imposition of democratic parliamentary forms of government, slave-based systems in Africa, as elsewhere, disintegrated. Wole Soyinka has a traditional ruler exclaim in one of his plays, when faced with a recalcitrant soldier, "Slaves: can't they forget they once had lives of their own? How dare they pester the living with the petty miseries of their lives! . . . What does it mean? Why should my slave, my subject, my mere human property say, unless he is mad, I shall not fight this war. Is he a freak? . . . Will there be more like him, born with this dark cancer in their heart?"[157] Slaves, and peasants as well, became increasingly rebellious as their belief in the "authority" of the traditional leaders declined and as their own lives gained an autonomous significance.[158]

---

[154] R. S. Rattray describes similar practices among the Asante, including the ritual sacrifice of retainers to follow the king, in his *Religion and Art in Ashanti* (London: Oxford University Press, 1954), p. 106.

[155] See Kannan K. Nair, *Politics and Society in South Eastern Nigeria, 1841–1906* (London: Frank Cass, 1972), p. 48.

[156] See Robin Horton, "The Political Organization of Old Calabar," in *Man in Africa*, ed. Douglas and Kaberry, p. 58.

[157] Soyinka, *A Dance of the Forests*, p. 60.

[158] The conditions not only of slavery but between rulers and ruled in general varied tremendously from one African state to another as well as changing over time. Melvin L. Perlman compares peasants living in neighboring East African states in his "The Traditional Systems of Stratification Among the Ganda and the Nyoro of Uganda," in *Social Stratification in Africa*, ed. Tuden and Plotnicov, p. 157. Max Gluckman tells us that "according to an unpublished manuscript by Southwold, of the 33 kings from the traditional history [of Buganda] records as having reigned up to the establishment of the British protectorate in 1894, fourteen came to be overthrown through rebellion. . . . Although the population of the capital must have run to tens of thousands, there is no sign that a city mob took any part in rebellions, as it may have done in some West African states. This is doubtless because very stern measures were taken to control the population of the capital. Periodically, and especially at times of political dissention, or when there were large numbers of rowdy men abroad in the street, the royal executioners were sent out to ambush the streets of the capital and to seize and kill all persons who could not give a good explanation of their presence. Those arrested

On Unrestrained Power and the Loss of Authority

Every political regime, no matter what its ideological complexion, seeks to establish among the people it governs a sense of legitimacy, as well as to demonstrate the force of its power. Force is a gun held to the head. The classic symbol of the state is the uniformed policeman with a gun. However, to rule by force is, if nothing else, costly and inefficient. Every government, from Nazi Germany to Stalin's Russia, seeks to instill in its people a sense that they should obey because in some way obedience is morally right: the state has a right to demand that citizens comply with its policies, and people will want to follow the government's edicts without a studied analysis of the possibilities of punishment.

In precolonial traditional African states, a sense of legitimacy accrued to rulers because (as we pointed out above) their positions required an exchange of services and obligations in return for taxes and duties exacted from the citizens. In addition, the power of the traditional authorities was limited by institutional restraints as well as by convention and custom. Remedies were available for violations of these restraints and in fact were exercised.

Under colonialism, a paradoxical situation occurred: traditional rulers were incorporated into the overarching political structure. Many chiefs were reduced to mere auxiliaries; at the same time, the removal of all customary restraints by an often unknowing superior administration thrust absolute power into the hands of the traditional rulers vis-a-vis their subjects. Now the chief could command without fear of popular retaliation, backed up as he was by the troops and police, as well as by fines and other economic sanctions of the Europeans. As long as the chiefs met their quotas of conscripted labor and collected the required taxes in money and in kind, the colonial authorities did not overly concern themselves with the methods used or with the possibility that an unauthorized portion of the taxes might be pocketed by the chief. As a result, the chieftaincy in many areas became an empty shell — all-powerful on the outside but empty of legitimacy. No one has documented this phenomenon better than Jean Suret-Canale in his study of chieftaincy in Guinea. Suret-Canale points out that on December 31, 1957, the African-led government of Sekou Toure put into effect a decree suppressing the "so-called customary chieftaincy." What made this decree a reality, however, was a deep-seated popular movement begun well before independence. Although Toure and the democratic party of Guinea contributed to the

---

had not necessarily committed any crime: they are described as people who had no employment in the capital, and included innocent peasants who were bringing in food. It is, therefore, not surprising that the common people went in fear of their lives in the streets of the capital, and if they had to go there hastened home again as soon as their business was completed."

Politics, Law and Ritual, in Tribal Society, pp. 184–85. See also E. V. Walter, *Terror and Resistance* (New York: Oxford University Press, 1969), the best analysis of the use of terror, secret societies, and other techniques of repression utilized by African rulers to maintain themselves in power.

development of this movement, the disintegration of the chieftaincy was initially accomplished before they came to power. Its legal suppression was only the final act.[159]

In Nigeria, Chief Awolowo, a founding father of nationalism, expressed "the prevailing view of the educated minority" that the root cause of "most tensions between Yoruba communities and their paramount chiefs was the excess of power which had been vested in those chiefs by the British in disregard of customary limitations."[160] And yet, if the office of chief as an agent of local government suffered, this did not necessarily mean that the influence of the chiefs disappeared or that they were unable to pass on advantageous control over resources to their heirs.

Continuity Between Chiefs and Modern Elites

Traditional leaders, having preferential access to overseas education and economic advantages enabling them to become powerful in the new commercial systems, shifted more easily than any other social stratum into positions of dominance. "Blood ties" between the old and new governing classes facilitated an essentially peaceful evolution of power.[161] Growing numbers of traditional rulers traveled abroad, earned university degrees in France, England, and occasionally the United States, practiced the new professions, and pinned down positions of influence in the new regional, federal, and centralized national governments. The large number of positions in exploding bureaucracies and governmental institutions required an expansion beyond the ruling members of the historical state systems, and new opportunities afforded by Western education and a burgeoning capitalism led to the rise of new classes filled with "commoner" men of ambition.

From the beginning, the organizational bourgeoisie was recruited in no small part from high-ranking traditional families. This gave spe-

---

[159] See Jean Surete-Canale, "The End of the Chieftancy in Guinea" in Markovitz. Reprinted in abridged form in *The Journal of African History*, vol. 7, no. 3, 1966 in *African Politics and Society*, ed. Markovitz, p. 99.

[160] Quoted in Richard L. Sklar, *Nigerian Political Parties; Power in an Emergent African Nation* (Princeton, N.J.: Princeton University Press, 1963), p. 232. See also John N. Paden's account of the increase in the powers of the emir of Kano for similar reasons in "Aspects of Emirship in Kano," in *West African Chiefs*, ed. Crowder and Ikime, pp. 162–86. Martin Kilson analyzes how the chiefs' exercise of customary rights to labor in Sierre Leone under the authority of the native administration became very oppressive and was a major factor in the peasant tax riots as late as 1955–56 (*Political Change in a West African State* [Cambridge, Mass.: Harvard University Press, 1966], p. 58).

Lonsdale, describing the situation in Central Africa among the Luyia and Luo peoples, puts the point this way: "The chief's position became much more secure as it depended upon government approval rather than popular consensus. Furthermore, with the growth of the cash economy and opportunities for education, new opportunities developed for the long-term consolidation of the chief's family position. There is no doubt that many chiefs became petty despots." J. H. Lonsdale, "Political Associations in Western Kenya" in *Protest and Power in Black Africa*, ed. Rotberg and Mazrui, pp. 591–92.

[161] See, for example, Hugh H. Smythe and Mabel M. Smythe, *The New Nigerian Elite* (Stanford, Calif.: Stanford University Press, 1960), p. 166.

cial legitimacy to the continuing political activities of this ancient dominant class and strengthened its position in the new society.[162] Being joined together in central institutions under a common administration also helped create a sense of corporate identity for the traditional leaders. This new interest transcended the limits of different ethnic groups. Over the years, in different territories and different countries, traditional leaders had formed unions (syndicates in the French territories) to defend their interest. Territorial syndicates in the francophone areas joined together in 1966 in the *Union Federale des Syndicats des Chefs Coutumiers*, which covered all of French West Africa.[163] Ruth Schachter Morgenthau tells us that a corporate identity developed most keenly among the chiefs in Mali, Niger, the Plateau and Savannah regions of Guinea, and somewhat in Senegal. The chiefs' class consciousness became the basis for major "patron parties," including those that brought Niger and Mauritania to independence. According to Morgenthau, patron parties dominated Mali and Guinea also, until defeated in 1956 when Keita and Toure, themselves the descendants of chiefs, succeeded in creating "mass" parties.[164]

Not all traditional leaders felt threatened by innovations: some saw both the material and political opportunities in the changes brought by the new systems and methods. The central conflicts did not occur, therefore, "between traditionalists and modernizers" but rather on the basis of more complicated alignments and calculations of interest. From the beginning, numerous chiefs rushed for profit and pleasure, taking advantage of the amusements as well as the instruments of power offered by the new system. To take only the case of the traditional rulers in northern Nigeria as an example; the emir of Zinna made the pilgrimage to Mecca across the desert by car in 1934.[165] The emir of Gwandu, who journeyed to England with his entourage in 1933, later encouraged projects such as the UNICEF malaria control scheme and innovative agricultural research projects. (The present emir, incidentally, traces his ancestors' line of direct rule back to 1744.)[166] Clapperton, the great English explorer, wrote in 1929 of his having found the sultan of Sokoto reading an Arabic copy of Euclid sent to him by the king of England and reported how grateful the sultan was for this present, since his family's copy, procured in Mecca some years earlier, had been destroyed when part of his house burned down the previous year.[167] As early as 1912, the shehu of Bornu dispatched the first consignment of cattle by rail from Kano to

[162] Cf. Martin Kilson, "The Emergent Elites of Black Africa, 1900–1960," in *Colonialism in Africa, 1870–1960*, ed. Peter Duignan and L. H. Gann, Vol. 2, *The History and Politics of Colonialism, 1914–1960*, ed. Duignan and Gann (Cambridge: Cambridge University Press, 1970), p. 377.

[163] Ruth Schachter Morgenthau, *Political Parties in French Speaking West Africa* (Oxford: Clarendon Press, 1964), p. 333.

[164] *Ibid.*

[165] S. J. Hogben and A. H. M. Kirk-Greene, *The Emirates of Northern Nigeria* (London: Oxford University Press, 1966), p. 453.

[166] *Ibid.*, p. 427.

[167] Davidson, *The African Past*, p. 67.

Lagos.[168] The emir of Sika made history in the early 1920s by driving his own motor car.[169] Muhammad Tukur, at the age of 34, gave up a brilliant career as a Hausa professor at the University of London and then as commissioner for Northern Nigeria in the United Kingdom to assume the emirship upon the death of his father.[170] Traditional ruling families competed with one another and boasted about the disproportionate share their sons had in eminent positions of leadership. Bornu, for example, rejoiced greatly at the selection of Sir Kashin Ibrahim, a Kanuri, as the first Nigerian governor of the North.[171]

The Traditional Rulers Versus "Westernized Elites"

Many Africanists have depicted a growing cleavage between the chiefs and the "educated African community" insofar as Western education provided a skill necessary for advancement in the institutions introduced by colonialism. David Kimble, for example, asserts:

> Educated Africans . . . found it increasingly difficult to fit into the traditional order, where religious and secular authority rested with the chief, where the social hierarchy ascended and descended in clearly defined stages, and where status depended on birth and lineage rather than individual qualifications or achievements. Thus there emerged a growing cleavage between the chiefs and the educated community. This became more acute as some of the politically conscious staked their claim to leadership on a national scale, transcending the local authority of the chiefs.[172]

Yet as Kimble himself points out, from the earliest days of intensive colonial concern with education — a period well into colonial rule — the chiefs were intimately involved with educational policy. When Governor Guggisberg of the Gold Coast set up an "Educationists' Committee" during the period 1921–1930, he was careful to associate the chiefs as far as possible with his new plans. A member of the committee, the paramount chief Nana Ofori Atta, urged upon the governor that "the student should be imbued with the true ideals of his country *. . . to enable him to adapt himself to the customs, manners and institutions of the place to which he belongs."[173] Kimble describes the claim of the "natural rulers" to participation in the central government: "against opposition from the educated elite who consider that their training for the problems of the modern world gave them a prescriptive right

---

[168] Hogben and Kirk-Greene, *The Emirates of Northern Nigeria,* p. 339.

[169] *Ibid.,* p. 361.

[170] *Ibid.,* p. 259.

[171] *Ibid.,* p. 338.

[172] David Kimble, *A Political History of Ghana: The Rise of Gold Coast Nationalism, 1850–1928* (Oxford: Clarendon Press, 1963), p. 62.

[173] Quoted in *ibid.,* p. 111.

to leadership on a national scale. This problem was to remain unresolved for many years with the scales becoming increasingly weighted against the chiefs."[174]

Another interpretation of the role of chiefs, however, maintains that the traditional ruling families were able to maintain influence in a double way:

(1) as a collective group — that is, *chiefs as chiefs united as a type of pressure group, able to exert themselves as a powerful political force behind common objectives* — and

(2) through their descendants, who acted in leadership roles in the new systems but who did not occupy the official position or act in the office of chief.

An outstanding example of a combination of these two approaches may be found in the person and attitudes of Colonel Afrifa, leader of the group that overthrew Nkrumah and, until the voluntary transfer of power to civilians, head of the military- and police-directed National Liberation Council of the Ghanaian government. Afrifa has written:

> In all our history our chiefs are known to be our natural rulers. . . .
> Chieftaincy is an institution that must be respected and protected. It is the embodiment of our souls. The chiefs are traditional focal points of the people's collective activity. They are the rallying points of our national endeavors. It is in these roles that the chieftaincy provides the momentum for our people's advancement.[175]

Afrifa goes on to lambaste Nkrumah for having made a mockery of the role of chief under the old regime and for having been nothing but an "upstart": "None of his ancestors ever led an army before the white man came. To the outsider, this might seem insignificant, but to us, particularly the Asantes, our battle honors mean a lot. . . . I come from a long line of chiefs who had served in positions of command in the Asante army. . . ."[176] The 1969 constitution, instituted after the Af-

---

[174] Kimble, *A Political History of Ghana*, p. 139.

[175] A. A. Afrifa, *The Ghana Coup, 24th February 1966* (London: Frank Cass, 1966), p. 115.

[176] *Ibid.,* p. 43.

[177] La Ray E. Benzer, "The National Congress of British West Africa: Gold Coast Section" (unpublished M.A. thesis, University of Ghana, 1965), quoted in Martin Kilson, "The National Congress of British West Africa, 1918–1935," in *Power and Protest in Black Africa*, ed. Rotberg and Mazrui, p. 574. Kilson states "these data go far to explain the perpetual ambivalence displayed by the Ghanaian emergent elites or its chiefs, supporting them and cooperating with them in some circumstances and opposing them in others." See also Kilson "The Emergent Elites of Black Africa, 1900–1960," in *The History and Politics of Colonialism, 1914–1960*, ed. Duignan and Gann, pp. 375–76 where the extent of chiefly influence in the "new" political systems is detailed. Cf. Sklar, *Nigerian Political Parties*, p. 353.

Clement Moore also has discussed continuities between traditional and modern elites in North Africa. He shows how the "old families" took advantage of Western education and came to dominate the bureaucracies brought by colonialism, as well as business and the major offices in the new political parties. Moore analyzes causes for variations in the structure of elite in Tunisia, Algeria, and Morocco. Time was one variable. In Morocco, for instance, the impact of colonialism did not allow newcomers to emerge in large enough numbers to challenge the old families, whereas conditions in Tunisia engendered a more open society. *Politics in North Africa* (Boston: Little, Brown, 1970), pp. 46–49.

rifa coup, recognized the "continuing importance of traditional leaders" by providing that two thirds of the district councils comprise "traditional members" and that each of the nine regions have a regional house of chiefs, thereby recognizing a "re-emergence and solidification" of the interest represented by the "intellectuals and chiefs."

As an example of the double role of chiefs, consider the occupational background of representatives to the West African Congress, the leading proto-nationalist organization in the years 1918–1935. Of thirty-five members of the Ghanaian delegation, fifteen were lawyers, eight were merchants, and many of the rest were journalists, doctors, and educators. Clearly, the congress represented the "emergent bourgeois." The three chiefs—as chiefs—made up only 8 percent of the membership. However, another 40 percent of the Ghanaian delegation also showed close kinship ties with high-ranking traditional families and chiefs. This, then, reveals an entirely different aspect of the situation.[177]

The Chiefs and Education

In practically every territory, almost every colonial administration took special steps to insure the education of the chiefs and their sons, giving them special preference in a clear effort to create an ongoing indigenous ruling group bound closely to its interests. At first, the chiefs, as a result of their suspicion, often refused to participate, or they would send the sons of slaves or other low-status persons. In most areas, however, the traditional rulers quickly perceived the utility and advantages of these "schools for chiefs." At the Conference of Chiefs of the northern provinces of Nigeria in 1938, for example,

> When it was asked if the Emirs would like the school for their sons to be made "open," the general feelings of the chiefs was expressed by the following two Emirs. The Emir of Kano considered that "association with the children of common people would be inclined to inculcate the outlook of the peasant," while the Emir of Kontagora thought that "the character of the chief's children was adversely influenced by association with the children of ordinary people."[178]

When in 1906 the Sierra Leone government opened Bo School "solely for the sons and nominees of chiefs," the local district commissioner remarked at the inauguration, "It should not be open to all and sundry, but only to selected pupils chosen from a stratum slightly, but not much beneath those eligible for Bo School. The upper and leading classes must be educated before the lower or working classes."[179] In modern times the sons of chiefs attend universities as well as secondary and primary schools far out of proportion to their numbers. At

[177] Billy J. Dudley, *Parties and Politics in Northern Nigeria* (London: Frank Cass, 1968), p. 16.
[179] Kilson "The Emergent Elites of Black Africa, 1900–1960," in *The History and Politics of Colonialism, 1914–1960*, ed. Duignan and Gann, p. 359.

the University of Ghana, for example, over one fourth of the students surveyed were the sons of holders of traditional titles.[180] The authors found that "even traditional tribal elites were represented at [University of Ghana] Legon." Twenty-eight percent of the students mentioned one or more traditional titles held by members of their immediate families.[181] No wonder, then, that continuities exist between the traditional and "new" classes.

The Chiefs and Politics

To understand properly the role of traditional ruling authorities in modern African societies, we must make two basic distinctions. First, not all chiefs or their descendants will act in a cohesive, self-serving, or class-serving manner. Just as most revolutionaries have historically come from the class they wish to overthrow — and not from the peasantry or proletariat — so too can chiefs in modern dress lead nationalist movements or push for African socialism. No one can predict automatically on the basis of class membership or origin the action of particular individuals or groups; special study of each particular set of circumstances is necessary.[182]

Second, we must distinguish the evolution of chiefs along two lines: as a pressure group — one among many others, such as the *fonctionnaires* or civil servants — and as ongoing elements of the ruling class — that is, not as one among many equally powerful competing interest groups but as the political arbitrators of society. As members of this latter dominant stratum, the chiefs might not exist as chiefs, for ruling might very well necessitate radical changes of appearance and expertise. What matters are not so much the formal instruments of power, but the relative position of dominance vis-à-vis other social strata.

Many chiefs under the colonial administration became merely "professional bureaucrats" trained in colonial schools. These chiefs could still be very powerful, particularly in guaranteeing their own prerogatives, but as minor bureaucrats they lost all control over basic policy, thereby revealing how far down the political ladder they had actually come.[183] Even the French, despite their commitment to direct rule, recognized the traditional aristocracy where large-scale pre-European empires existed. European field administrators often found their

---

[180] G. Jahoda, "The Social Background of the West African Student Population," *British Journal of Sociology*, 4, no. 4 (December 1964), 361–62.

[181] David J. Finlay, Roberta E. Koplin, and Charles A, Ballard, Jr., "Ghana," in *Students and Politics in Developing Nations*, ed. Donald K. Emmerson (New York: Praeger, 1968), p. 100. Note, however, that comparable figures for the general population were not given either in this study or in the Jahoda study.

[182] Cf. Seymour Martin Lipset, *Political Man* (New York: Doubleday, 1960).

[183] For an illustration of this point, see Martin Klein's discussion of the evolution of the role of chiefs in Senegal in his "The Evolution of the *Chefferie* in Senegal" in *Nations By Design*, ed. Rivkin, p. 201.

task of governing easier and more effective when they named the heirs of the customary ruling class as the local administrators.[184]

The realities of power underlay even matters that appeared to be broadly ideological or philosophical in nature. Thus, the reason why the parties of "chiefs" from both Mali and Guinea had parliamentary ties with the French socialists at the end of the Second World War was that the French administrative officials who intervened directly in the organization of the first election were socialists.[185]

Some modern political leaders still rule as the direct descendants of ancient aristocratic families. They may continue to rule for the same interests for whom they always ruled, even though they may have changed their manner. But today there are also "modern" politicians who know how to make use of hangover loyalties for virtually unique purposes, including the restructuring of their ancient institutions. In Mali, for example, one of the most radical African socialist parties, the Union Soudanaise under Modibo Keita, drew much of its support from the Malinke areas, the base of the ancient Mali Empire. In Guinea, the PDG (the Parti Démocraique de Guinée) under Sekou Touré appealed to the historic supporters of Samory in obtaining the support of the ruling families of Timbuktu, Gao, and other ancient cities. In a sense, the strategy of the Union Soudanaise was to create a coalition between the descendants of the Malian and Songhai Empires, previously dominant in the area.[186] Despite their connections with leaders of the ancient past, however, neither Keita nor Touré depended upon traditional social groups and organization—the ancient nobility, bureaucracy, and priests—for their real political clout. They turned instead to an entirely new form of mass political organization involving a new concept of the political role of the peasant, as well as social appeals to new economic and social interests. On the other hand, Ahmadu Bello, Sardauna of Sokoto and great-grandson of Sultan Bello—great founder of the best-organized, longest enduring emirates of Northern Nigeria—ruled within essentially the same framework as did his forebears, relying on the same social forces brought together during the last century by a ruling class that had successfully transferred its power into modern institutions.[187]

[184] See Morgenthau, *Political Parties in French Speaking West Africa*, p. 251.

[185] *Ibid.*, p. 250.

[186] Morgenthau, illustrating the strength of Toure's appeal in the areas of his forebears' major strength, quotes a descendant of one captured in Samory's Wars who asked, "You will not sell us into slavery?" To which Touré replied, "I am against all slavery." PDG political organizers also propagandized, "If Samory Touré can make you slaves, Sekou Touré can make you free." (Quoted in Morgenthau, *Political Parties in French Speaking West Africa*, p. 254)

[187] For an exceptionally thorough analysis of the "factors that promoted the condition of political continuity in Northern Nigeria," see C. S. Whitaker, Jr., *The Politics of Tradition: Continuity and Change in Northern Nigeria, 1946–1966* (Princeton, N.J.: Princeton University Press, 1970), pp. 317–467. See also Sklar, *Nigerian Political Parties;* Johnston, *The Fulani Empire of Sokoto;* and M. G. Smith, *Government in Zazau, 1800–1950* (London: Oxford University Press, 1960). Murray Last, *The Sokoto Caliphate* (New York: Humanities Press, 1967), is particularly important for his genealogies of emirs, which illustrate the process of intermarriage between ruling families. R. A. Adeleye's *Power and Diplomacy in Northern Nigeria, 1804–1906* (New York: Humanities Press, 1971) is a fine overview.

Remarking on this resiliency of traditional ruling elements to endure which is present in many places throughout the continent, Bakari Traore notes:

> In effect down to our own days neither the uprooting of the structures of traditional society by colonization nor the development of a modern political life has definitively broken the traditional framework and freed the masses from the grip of the notables and religious chiefs. Even in Dakar on the edge of the strictly political organizations of the U.P.S. there exist all sorts of organizations that group people who originated from the same town or village or belong to the same ethnic group or who simply have the same family name. All these organizations are apparently apolitical and their avowed aim is to battle against the "depaysement" of their members in a big city like Dakar and at the same time to promote amongst themselves a spirit of solidarity and cooperation. In reality these diverse organizations are nothing other than the carryover into a politicized urban milieu of the survival of traditional ancient forms of authority. In effect the leaders of these organisms are often the descendants of those who formerly exercised traditional authority. In these urban centers which are nevertheless found on the margin of the traditional political frameworks the influence of the traditional chiefs is not always excluded. They continue even there to play a role.[188]

As an example, Traore cites the notables of the Lebou collectivity in the Cape Verde region. The present head of the Lebou community is the direct descendant of Dial Diop, founder of the Lebou Republic. Also, the supreme chief of the Tukulör in Dakar and in all of Senegal is El-Hadj Seydou Nourou Tall, the great-grandson of El-Hadj Omar, founder of the great Tukulör Empire.

The case of the Tukulör in Senegal is also interesting because it reveals a situation where an organization was created with an ethnic base to meet the purely modern and urban needs of newly arrived lower-class immigrants in the city; later, this organization was used by the traditional ruling classes as a weapon to gain a position of political eminence in the modern government. Abdoulaye Diop tells us that the oldest and most important political organization of the Tukulör was the Union Genérale des Originaires de la Vallée du Fleuve (UGOFS), founded in 1947. At the beginning, the only objective of this association was the defense of the interests of people coming from the Fouta area, interests such as the construction of schools, dispensaries, and roads, improved methods of garden farming and animal husbandry. But very quickly, as a result of competition between the political parties, it took on a clearly political character, becoming an instrument in the hands of the parties during the electoral campaigns. Once the organization became politically involved, traditional

---

[188] Bakari Traore, Mamadou Lo, and Jean-Louis Alibert, *Forces Politiques en Afrique Noire* (Paris: Presses Universitaires de France, 1966), p. 124.

social realities—namely, the stratification of Tukulör society into castes and family hierarchies, reasserted themselves immediately. According to Diop,

> It was in this way that the first President General of the association was overthrown and replaced because he was of an inferior caste by a clan of the descendants of a "great family." This in turn precipitated a split with a group of young Turks who broke away to form another organization. The new organization in turn also came under the control of one of the leading great traditional families. The political struggle that ensued demonstrated not only conflicts between the major traditional ruling families and their followers but also that it was possible—as had been the case historically—for differences to arise within the same family. At the same time the grand Marabouts and traditional notables at elections supported candidates belonging to modern elites, lawyers, teachers, doctors, etc., but were careful to choose members of their own families or trustworthy allies.[189]

In Nigeria, the founders of the Northern Peoples Congress, the dominant political organization, were careful to stipulate at their inaugural conference that they "would not usurp the authority of [their] natural rulers." Instead, their "ardent desire" was to enhance that authority and help the rulers in the "proper discharge of their duties . . . in enlightening" the peasants. They went out of their way to demonstrate how a desire for change could be accommodated with a respect for tradition.[190] In contrast the minor opposition party, the Northern Elements Progressive Union (NEPU), in their 1952 declaration of principles, "decried the 'shocking state of social order' caused by the 'autocratic' rule of the native authorities and their 'unscrupulous and vicious system of administration.' It saw a class struggle, supported the depressed peasant class, the Talakawa, and therefore, stated it was 'diametrically opposed to the interest of all sections of the master class' and 'hostile to the party of the oppressors.' "[191]

After citing numerous calculations that demonstrated that up to 90 percent of the Northern Peoples Congress members of the regional and federal Nigerian legislatures were the sons, brothers, nephews, or cousins of chiefs, or in some other way their direct affines or affiliates, Kirk-Greene declared, "It would be otiose to seek further proof of the perpetuation of traditional Hausa special patterns in the modern political system. The case appears amply proved. The inference is inescapable that the power pattern of contemporary Hausa society reflects as much continuity as it does change."[192] No wonder eminent authorities have concluded that leadership in the far North

---

[189] Abdoulaye Diop, *Societé Toucouleur et migration*, pp. 171–79. See also Barry, *Le royaume du Waalo.*
[190] Schwartz, *Nigeria*, p. 75.
[191] Quoted in *ibid.,* p. 76.
[192] Kirk-Greene, "The Merit Principle in an African Bureaucracy," in *Nations by Design*, ed. Rivkin, p. 270.

was and is primarily a "function of one's status in the society, which is determined largely by birth and wealth."[193]

Since the Nigerian-Biafran Civil War, and before his overthrow during the summer of 1975, the military government of General Gowon instituted reforms that one commentator maintained created a "quiet revolution which . . . transformed the political system of the former Northern region to an extent which in 1966 almost nobody would have thought possible."[194] Allegedly, the major props of the emirs' power were taken away. That is, the emirs' law courts and the former Native Administration police were incorporated into the national Nigerian systems, as were the Native Authority prisons. Although military rule precluded fully elected councils, local authorities were said to be more representative than they had been before 1966. Whatever the "major changes" undertaken, they were initiated by elements in the military who had close connections with the traditional aristocracy. Brigadier Hassan Katsina, the military head of the Northern region and the man under whose auspices these "innovations" occurred, was himself son of one of the North's most important rulers. (Brigadier Hassan's chief advisor was the late Alhaji Ali Akilu, a son of Sokoto, "the very center of Northern Nigerian traditionalism.")

After a discussion of other leading roles assumed by other members of the Northern ruling class and their sons, the leading journal of the area, *West Africa*, concluded that other rulers, great and small, have come to terms with the silent revolution. By their wisdom the rulers may have ensured long life for the institution of chieftaincy in the Northern emirates.[195] This is why other analysts have maintained that the Northern aristocracy, which had always taken particular pride in its tradition of administrative competence, will be able to continue to rule, except possibly indirectly and with more discretion. Richard Sklar summed up the relationship between the traditional authorities and the new "Westernized" elites in Nigeria before the great civil war by stating, "In the Western region, traditional authorities bowed to the political leadership of the rising class of businessmen, professionals, civil servants, educators, and so on. In the North, businessmen generally defined their interest in terms of collaboration with the politically dominant chiefs and administrative elite."[196]

Among the Ibo and Yoruba in Nigeria, leading chiefs took important roles in sponsoring the two cultural societies—the Egbe Omo Oduduwa of the Yoruba and the Ibo State Union—that were the pre-

---

[193] See Dudley, *Parties and Politics in Northern Nigeria*, p. 118. See also John P. Mackintosh, *Nigerian Government and Politics* (Evanston, Ill.: Northwestern University Press, 1966), pp. 88–92, for a study of the family background of members of the Federal House of Representatives. See also the detailed family portraits in Sklar, *Nigerian Political Parties*, pp. 505–506.

[194] "The North's Revolution," *West Africa*, No. 2819 (June 25, 1971).

[195] *Ibid.* See also S. K. Panter-Brick, *Nigerian Politics and Military Rule* (London: Athlone Press, 1970), p. 134. A study of the government in Zaria in 1950 relates that even as late as 1950 "the Native Administration ruled the population of the emirate without much fear of effective British supervision." M. G. Smith in *Government in Zazzau: 1800–1950* (London: Oxford University Press, 1960).

[196] Sklar, *Nigerian Political Parties*, p. 353.

cursors of the Eastern and Western regions' two major political parties, the Action Group and the National Council of Nigeria and the Cameroons, later called the National Council of Nigerian Citizens (NCNC). According to Sklar, "Both associations were created by representatives of the new and rising class—lawyers, doctors, businessmen, civil servants, and certain farsighted chiefs—who perceived that the locus of economic and political power was not local or regional but national."[197] The Yoruba traditional rulers developed one of the most flexible and ingenious systems for incorporating the *nouveau riche* and other up-and-coming men of newly acquired power and significance. When they founded the Action Group, for example, the traditional rulers developed their strategy on the assumption that the chiefs were destined to play a major role in local and national politics. The Yoruba chiefs, for their part, were with few exceptions "not averse to political cooperation with those members of the new elite who were prepared to observe the traditional proprieties."[198] As in the historical development of England, the Yoruba had developed a procedure whereby successful men could acquire honorary chieftaincy through due process and by paying heavily. Awolowo himself was among those acquiring a chieftainship in October, 1954, following his becoming the premier of the Western region.[199] A similar idea spread to the Edo and Ibo, who bounded the Yoruba areas and whose heads of state were usually called *obi, eze* or *Atamanya* and were supported by a hierarchy of subordinate title chiefs. Titles such as these were acquired by payment of fees or were granted to men of special ability.[200] The development of a highly stratified corporate structure among the Ibos is particularly noteworthy because of the prevailing anthropological view that *rules* rather than *rulers* were the essential mechanism of social order in what had been pictured as stateless societies in which there were "no individuals of outstanding power or authority."[201]

Martin Kilson has further documented this important role of the "neotraditional elite" in the immediate post–World War II political

---

[197] *Ibid.,* p. 10. Kenneth W. J. Post and George B. Jenkins, in their *The Price of Liberty: Personality and Politics in Colonial Nigeria* (London: Cambridge University Press, 1973), present a remarkable case study of Adegoke Adelabu, the leader of the opposition to the government of Awolowo, the leader in the West of the NCNC and the unchallenged political boss of Ibadan. Adelabu's traditional background is discussed, as well as the conflict among the various clans and their descendants. See, for example, p. 35.

[198] Sklar, *Nigerian Political Parties,* p. 110. On the traditional history and social structure of the Yoruba, see Robert S. Smith, *Kingdoms of the Yoruba* (London: Methuen, 1969), and A. L. Mabogunje, "The Pre-Colonial Development of Yoruba Towns," in *The City in the Third World,* ed. D. J. Dwyer (New York: Barnes & Noble, 1974), pp. 26–33.

[199] Sklar, *Nigerian Political Parties,* p. 234.

[200] See G. I. Jones, "Chieftaincy in the Lower Eastern Region of Nigeria," in *West African Chiefs,* ed. Crowder and Ikime, p. 315.

[201] See, for example, M. M. Green's "classic" account, *Ibo Village Affairs* (New York: Praeger, 1964). See also, C. K. Meek, *Law and Authority in a Nigerian Tribe* (London: Oxford University Press, 1937); and T. Olawale Elias, *Nigerian Land, Law and Custom* (London: Routledge and Kegan Paul, 1953). More recent studies, some by anthropologists who were themselves Ibo, have indicated that in different areas Ibo communities evolved in diverse patterns, including monarchies. See, for example, Nair, *Politics and Society in South Eastern Nigeria, 1841–1906;* and Nzimiro, *Studies in Ibo Political Systems.*

systems of the nation-states. His evidence reveals that the British were successful during the 1950s in their deliberate efforts to include elements of the ancient ruling classes in the new political systems:

> In Sierra Leone, for example, the neo-traditional elite has held 25% of the seats in the legislature, a position enshrined in the constitution since 1951. . . . In French Africa . . . between 1947 and 1952, they won 29% of the seats in the territorial assembly of Mali, 15% in Upper Volta, 30% in Niger and 23% in Guinea. . . . The neo-traditional elite . . . likewise benefited from kinship ties with other politicians. Between 1947 and 1952, for instance, about 33% of the new elite legislators in the Ivory Coast were related to traditional ruling families. (By 1959, the proportion increased to 43%.) In Mali, 35% of the legislators were kinsmen of chiefs, 45% in Upper Volta, 70% in Niger and about 50% in Guinea. The neo-traditional elite gained a comparable position for itself in British Africa. For example, in 1957, 84% of the politicians in the Sierra Leone legislature had chiefly kinship ties.[202]

Describing the intermixture of chiefs and professional elites in Uganda, their high status and existence as a class apart, Lloyd Fallers notes:

> The high status of civil servant chiefs—particularly the county and subcounty chiefs—may be seen in the deference which they are granted by ordinary people and in their position as part of a national elite for purposes of social life. . . . Such persons share an elite style of life, based upon higher incomes, and in general speak each other's language—the language of high-level politics and of events beyond the ken of peasants.[203]

Fallers goes on to demonstrate convincingly the continuities between the descendants of the traditional chiefs and modern high administrative officials. "Objective" civil service examinations do not disintegrate class advantages because "qualifications always include more than simply native ability. Normally, they include training, to which there usually is differential access. In addition where means other than objective examinations are used as the basis for selection, factors of ascribed status may be involved."[204] Fallers also points out that access to education in a poor society was itself a great privilege and therefore an important factor in determining who entered the service.[205]

[202] Kilson, "The Emergent Elites of Black Africa, 1900–1960," in *The History and Politics of Colonialism, 1914–1960*, ed. Duignan and Gann, p. 375. See also Morgenthau, *Political Parties in French Speaking West Africa;* and Simpson's analysis of the occupational and social backgrounds of African members of the Sierra Leone Legislative Council in his "Ethnic Conflict in Sierre Leone" in *The Politics of Cultural Sub-Nationalism in Africa*, ed. Olorunsola.

[203] Fallers, "Are African Cultivators to be Called 'Peasants'?" in *Economic Development and Social Change*, ed. Dalton, pp. 189–91.

[204] *Ibid.*, p. 191.

[205] See also Fallers's *Bantu Bureaucracy* (Chicago: University of Chicago Press, Phoenix Books, 1965). Cf. the analysis by John Markakis, *Ethiopia: Anatomy of a Traditional Polity* (Oxford: Clarendon Press, 1974), especially pp. 73–142 and 182–94.

The power and persistence of traditional rulers throughout the continent are demonstrated most strikingly in the following case studies of the ancient dynasty of Ethiopia, Uganda, and the radically committed socialist country of Tanzania.

The Traditional Rulers and the Organizational Bourgeoisie in Ethopia

Haile Selassie ruled Ethiopia as absolute monarch, tracing his descent back to the Queen of Sheba. No room was included in the traditional Ethiopian political system for serious or systematic opposition, certainly not from the nonnobility. Periodic outbursts and assassination attempts have been hurled against government officials, including the emperor, but not until 1974 did widespread demonstrations at every level shake the entire structure of the society.

Yet, the emperor himself attempted a process of modernization that was directed at the elimination of "feudal recalcitrants" who opposed the policies of centralization, and that could have shifted their power to a more enduring base. As Hess states,

> The educated classes . . . are a product of a policy deliberately decided upon by the emperor. They are his creations, conceived for the purpose of staffing and expanding and centralizing modern government. Until 1960 they appeared far more loyal to the modernizing emperor than the old nobility who had a regional basis of power that had to be subordinated to the government of Addis Ababa. Haile Selassie succeeded in breaking the power of the regional lords to discover that the educated classes, created to further the modernization of the state and to introduce Western ideas of progress, harbored some of his sharpest critics. They repeatedly criticized his political conservatism and preferred to ignore his solid accomplishments.[206]

The development of Ethiopian traditional state structures appears to have followed closely the pattern of evolution of European feudalism from centralized empire to small-scale units to a reconsolidation of widespread political institutions. (See the discussion on the comparability of African and European feudalism on pp. 134–141.) From 1769 to 1855 the ancient Ethiopian Empire disintegrated. Brawling claimants to the throne laid desolate ancient lands. Hess points out that as in the Holy Roman Empire, power evolved to local nobles. Only at the turn of the century did Menelik institute the beginnings of centralized ministerial government, consolidating imperial power and authority within an enlarged Ethiopia. His victory at Adowa highlighted both Ethiopia's military power and its limited success in the military aspect of its modernization. Under Menelik, not only were recalcitrant regional feudal lords curbed but European advisors were brought in to modernize Ethiopia's army, introduce modern commu-

---

[206] Hess, *Ethiopia*, p. 164.

nications systems, and develop technologically more sophisticated instruments of production. The key to the modernization plans of Theodore II, Menelik II, and Haile Selassie I over the past hundred years has been the breaking of the power of the old nobility. Even today, however, they continue in many cases to exercise virtually sovereign rights in the still remote provinces.[207] Modernization might have enabled the old ruling class to strengthen the foundation of its power, but it certainly did not lead necessarily to democracy or increased egalitarianism.

In a statement entitled *Repression in Ethiopia,* written before the military coup that overthrew the emperor, the Ethiopian Students Union in North America declared, "Beneath the picturesque medievalism of kings and queens lies the overwhelming reality of the misery of our people who have born the burden of this pageantry. . . . Politically, Ethiopia remains a despotism. Power is exclusively held by the feudal nobility. . . ."[208] The authors go on to quote at length from the official guide to Ethiopia:

> There have as yet been no basic changes in the structure of Ethiopian society. The Emperor is a hereditary ruler. Then there are the great landowning families whose heads bear titles of nobility and who serve as ministers, officers of state, governors of provinces, military leaders and church officials. Below the imperial family and the nobles are the Amhara and Galla landed gentry who have been the major beneficiaries of educational opportunities abroad and make up much of the government personnel.[209]

In 1971 a bill was proposed in the Ethiopian Legislative Assembly, itself dominated by landlords and their representatives, that would limit to 33 percent the amount of the annual crop that a landlord could take from a sharecropping tenant. Under the existing law, landlords could legally take as much as 75 percent. The new bill would also have provided some restrictions on the right of landowners to evict tenants, by establishing security of tenure for a year and by outlining specific grounds for eviction. As modest as the reforms proposed by this bill were, they stimulated passionate debate, including fistfights and pistol brandishing. In the end, the measure was tabled without a vote because it was clear that it would not have passed.

In 1973, between 50,000 and 100,000 people were thought to have died in the drought that spread over northern and central Ethiopia as well as clear across the continent at the edge of the Sahara. The Ethiopian government's apparent reticence to take remedial measures, including the elimination of corruption, prevented early aid from reaching the right people and earned the government a great mea-

---

[207] See also Hess, *Ethiopia*, pp. 57–79, and note especially the contrast between Hess's interpretation of the significance of the monarchy's effort to modernize and the one offered here.

[208] (New York: Africa Research Group, 1971), p. 1; the statement was originally issued in January 1971.

[209] *Ibid.,* p. 2.

sure of responsibility for tens of thousands of apparently needless deaths. Patrick Gilkes has pointed out that Ethiopia's land system encourages a famine situation when climatic disaster strikes. In the worst hit areas, for example, there were 375,000 landless peasants, of whom more than 150,000 were tenants who paid at least 50 percent of their produce to their landlords, many of whom were absent or deceased. The land tenure system renders peasants who are already on the verge of subsistence virtually defenseless when any added burden such as drought strikes.[210]

Socialism and Rural Inequalities in Tanzania

Although the difficulties of the peasantry in the ancient monarchy of Ethiopia might be expected, rural inequalities exist in Tanzania despite a rhetoric that proclaims the classless nature of traditional societies. Such inequalities have become a prime target for Julius Nyerere's government.

Under a single united nationalist party, the Tanzania African National Union (TANU), Tanzania's prospects for a democratic form of African socialism appeared aided by the absence within the country's boundaries of structured historical African kingdoms. Internecine rivalries and conflicts that tore other African states, as well as sharply differentiated and competitive social, economic, and political interests, have been largely absent thus far. Also, all the people of Tanzania share a common national language, Swahili.[211] TANU has nevertheless attempted to fundamentally alter the traditional system of authority. Before independence, TANU exploited certain dislocations in traditional life for political ends; after independence, however, it attempted to incorporate traditional leadership into national social plans.

As an organized system of government under TANU, chieftaincy dissolved slowly, as it did everywhere else in Africa.[212] During 1960 and 1961, leading government officials defended traditional chiefs against harassment by overeager local politicians; but the ministries moved toward popular election of local authorities, thus making the position of the chief anomalous. At a meeting with representatives of the Tanganyika Chiefs' Convention in October, 1961, Nyerere told the chiefs that their identification with the colonial government during the struggle for independence had resulted in "popular opposition to chiefs in certain parts of Tanganyika at present" and that "democracy demanded that the chairman of local councils should be

---

[210] Patrick Gilkes, "Ethiopia: It Takes More Than Aid to End Starvation," *African Digest*, December, 1973, p. 136.

[211] See G. Andrew Maguire, *Toward "Uhuru" in Tanzania* (Cambridge: Cambridge University Press, 1969), p. xix, particularly for information showing the small percentage of the total population that each ethnic group represents.

[212] See, for example, Miller, "The Political Survival of Traditional Leadership," in *African Politics and Society*, ed. Markovitz.

elected but this would clearly place the chief, who in the past had been the sole ruler in his chiefdom, in an anomalous position." If Nyerere—the son of a chief—was "telling the chiefs as gently as possible that there was no room for them as chiefs in modern local government"—he held before them the possibility of even better positions in modern government for their sons, as the ancient offices—now only affairs of local government, in any event—slowly died out: "The problem was whether to allow the post of chief to die a natural death or to plan their transition. ... The problem was likely to be a temporary one as the educated sons of chiefs would not wish to inherit so insecure a post and would prefer to serve the country in other ways. Government hoped that chiefs would be replaced on their voluntary resignation when local conditions were suitable."[213] Evidence of the strong role played by members of the traditional hierarchies in modern politics may be seen within both grass roots political organization and the highest levels of the new Tanzanian elite. TANU is built entirely on a division of the rural and urban population into units of a small number of people (usually ten) called cells. The role of cell leader in contemporary Tanzania and that of headman during the colonial period are virtually identical and entail many of the same functions as did the role of the chief under the traditional organization.[214]

In a study of the background of members of the modern elite in Tanzania, Raymond Hopkins found that although most members of the elite were born and raised in a rural setting, the vast majority described their families as "above average" in terms of wealth in the community. Not coincidentally, traditional status was a key factor in their backgrounds. Children of the traditional nobility attended special schools provided by the colonial government; education more than any other factor differentiated the modern elite from their kinsmen, and was the single most important factor that made possible the attainment of modern elite positions by the sons of the nobles.[215] Thus, even in the most egalitarian and socialistic of African countries, traditional class membership played and continues to play a key role in determining the membership of the new elites.

New Economic Opportunities for the Traditional Rulers

Besides their preeminence in politics, traditional rulers were from the beginning in an advantageous position to take advantage of the new opportunities in an expanding commerce and a new technology, and

[213] Nyerere quoted in Maguire, *Toward "Uhuru" in Tanzania*, p. 330.

[214] Cylde J. Ingle, *From Village to State in Tanzania* (Ithaca, N.Y.: Cornell University Press, 1972), p. 179.

[215] Raymond F. Hopkins, *Political Roles in a New State: Tanzania's First Decade* (New Haven: Yale University Press, 1971), pp. 70–71. Cf. Issa G. Shivji, *Class Struggles in Tanzania* (New York: Monthly Review Press, 1976).

in fact they did so.[216] The chiefs benefited at first as free agents, then under colonialism, then as those who controlled important sectors of the newly independent African states. Although their role in local colonial administration appeared to be the most striking manifestation of their new power, equally significant were the new colonial-sponsered rules of commercial exchange, which enabled the chiefs to gradually convert their positions of traditional eminence and ancient right to services into outright title over land and agricultural development:

> Gradually and in total disregard of traditional concepts of land use, changes were effected that figuratively, and eventually literally, removed the ground from beneath the feet of the peasantry, wiping out what little power they once had over traditional rulers and setting them up for final assault by the new but wholly impersonal state landlord. Land value was converted to money value, and traditional society was rendered vulnerable to money-related power plays.[217]

The Sierra Leone Protectorate Native Law Ordinance of 1905 sanctioned the chief's rights to customary tribute and upheld as mandatory the chief's rights to free labor:

> Every paramount chief in his capacity as chief . . . shall continue to have the same powers with respect to obtaining labor that they had heretofore possessed, that is to say, the farms of such chiefs . . . shall be worked by the laborers of such chiefs and by all the people respectively recognizing each such chief . . . and such people respectively shall continue to supply labor sufficient to enable the farms of their chief to be properly worked.[218]

What ensued was the commercialization of the chief's customary economic rights: tribute and labor were converted into money and capital. This enabled the traditional rulers to be among the first groups in African society to raise cash crops for the money economy.

One of the continent's most dramatic cases of the wholesale conversion of the economic basis of power of the traditional ruling class occurred in Uganda, through special colonial legislation. Over time,

---

[216] Terence Ranger in his *The African Voice in Southern Rhodesia* (London: Heinemann Educational Books, 1968), pp. 20–29, presents one of the most interesting and best-documented case studies showing connections between early resistance movements against colonialism and the development of modern nationalism in Southern Rhodesia. This study illustrates how the Ndebele aristocracy came to have a vested interest in the colonial system. "Loyalists" among the chiefs were well rewarded with cattle, and even recalcitrants and ex-rebels among the royal family were able to build up large herds at a time when a large demand for meat meant that the chiefs were in an advantageous position to become major capitalists.

[217] Henry L. Bretton, *Power and Politics in Africa* (Chicago: Aldine 1973), p. 155.

[218] Quoted in "The Emergent Elites of Black Africa, 1900–1960," in *The History and Politics of Colonialism, 1914–1960*, ed. Duignan and Gann, p. 57. Among the other sources of new wealth Kilson notes as having been available to chiefs were (1) direct money payments by governments, (2) tax extortion, and (3) salary payments by native administrations. The colonial administration, in an effort to maintain the support of the chiefs between 1949 and 1956, virtually doubled their salary payments.

the chiefs' actions and attitudes had created a profound sense of grievance in the public. The chiefs treated the peasants in a "derogatory and contemptuous" manner.[219] Land was the most important source of economic grievance, and no wonder. The Uganda Agreement of 1900 established freehold land tenure; it made 1,000 senior chiefs and notables freehold landowners over so much of their birthright land that not enough was left for commoners. This resulted in a situation where "a hierarchy based largely on political control was reinforced by economic wealth in land which could be inherited. This introduced the potentiality of a political economic class system which had hitherto been alien."[220] Apter, however, concluded that "enough social mobility persisted to avoid the establishment of an economic ruling class. Moreover, some chiefs were inept and some commoners were wise and could buy land." Futhermore, Apter argues, "even though such institutions as Mengo High School were set up to cater to the sons of chiefs, mostly the sons were less satisfactory than the fathers and in the civil service chieftaincy merit was important. Hierarchy thus came to be based on merit rather than family."[221] Apter offers no substantiation for these later contentions, which fly in the face of his own evidence. Indeed, all of Apter's reasoning and evidence point to the increasing development of precisely the type of class society he himself predicts as a possibility still later in his book: "It was the economic factor which helped the chiefs become an effective solitary grouping . . . economic status helped to weld them into a party anxious to protect its own heritance against those who would take it away from them. A political party with economic class as its underpinning represents something deep and fundamental in a society."[222] Other analysts have described how one of the major political parties in Uganda, the Kaba Yeka, descended from a series of political organizations within Uganda that "emphasized the common man's struggle against the chiefs."[223]

In Uganda, then, we see the ability of a traditional ruling group to convert the economic basis of its power and to manifest this new power in politics and in every other aspect of life. Subsequent revolutionary developments within Uganda, including the putsch of General Amin, cannot override the major significance of the traditional "natural rulers" or their ability to survive in the modern arena at least as

---

[219] David Apter, *The Political Kingdom in Uganda: A Study in Bureaucratic Nationalism* (Princeton, N.J.: Princeton University Press, 1961), pp. 122–23.

[220] *Ibid.*, p. 110.

[221] *Ibid.*

[222] *Ibid.*, p. 120. See also J. C. D. Lawrence, "A Pilot Scheme for Grant of the Land Titles in Uganda," *Journal of African Administration*, 12 (July 1960), 135, which details the development of in fee simple ownership of the traditional Ugandan aristocracy.

[223] See Nelson Kasfir, "Cultural Sub-nationalism in Uganda," in *The Politics of Cultural Sub-Nationalism in Africa*, ed. Olorunsola, pp. 89–90, for a discussion of the conflict between the traditional ruling classes and the commoners in the political development of Uganda.

well as any other "modern class" faced with rising mass discontent and the unbridled power of a newly self-conscious military.[224]

Summation:
The Conservative Classes' Ability to Change

"Traditional leader" is a shorthand phrase in widespread use among social scientists dealing with underdeveloped countries, a phrase that immediately conjures up the image of those opposed to change or innovation. Distinctions have nevertheless been made among traditional systems on the basis of their adaptability to the forces of modernization.

Many of the chiefly leaders of contemporary Africa are not a traditional class in the sense of opposing innovation, change, or modernization. Rather, they can best be understood as part of a conservative class, in the sense that they seek, at a minimum, to maintain their social, political, and economic power. From this perspective, change need not necessarily be viewed as a threat; it may even be welcomed as a means of consolidating power.

From their vantage points of power and prestige, wealth and information, the ruling classes of rural society are in a strategic position to see the opportunities, as well as the dangers, of modernization. This is not to suggest that radical changes will not take place in the basis of power of these classes; or that their power is not threatened. Obviously, the sources of power and legitimacy differ in feudal and capitalist societies, and among the religious brotherhoods. What is asserted, however, is that in the face of change, the traditional governing classes have greater opportunities to shift the basis of their power and reconsolidate their position.

Objections have been raised that the problem is not the process of change itself, but the speed of change and economic development.

---

[224] A number of recent studies of the history of East African kingdoms provide additional strong evidence for the complexity and continuity of their social arrangements. See, for example, D. A. Low, *Buganda in Modern History* (Berkeley and Los Angeles: University of California Press, 1971), which covers the historical conflict between peasants and chiefs and its persistence in modern politics; especially Chap. 5. M. S. M. Semakua Kiwanuka, in *A History of Buganda* (New York: Africana Publishing, 1972), warns that in the era he covers, A.D. 1200 to 1900, there was never a complete break with the past, no sharp division between colonial and precolonial Kiganda society. Similar arguments are maintained about the neighboring kingdoms in J. N. Nyakatura, *Anatomy of an African Kingdom: A History of Bunyoro-Kitara*, ed. Godfrey N. Uzoigwe (Garden City, N.Y.: Doubleday, Anchor Books, 1973); David William Cohen, *The Historical Tradition of Busoga* (Oxford: Clarendon Press, 1972); and Samiri Rubaraza Karugire, *A History of the Kingdom of Nkore in Western Uganda to 1896* (Oxford: Clarendon Press, 1971). In East Central and Central Africa, comparable studies that analyze the rise of states are H. W. Langworthy, *Zambia Before 1890* (London: Longman, 1972), on the Chewa, Bemba, Lozi, Lunda, and Ngoni kingdoms; Alpers, *Ivory and Slaves in East Central Africa*, which contains an important discussion of the profits reaped by the Yao, Bisa, and Makua chiefs from the slave trade; and Mutumba Mainga, *Bulozi Under the Luyana Kings: Political Evolution and State Formation in Pre-Colonial Zambia* (London: Longman, 1973). See also Stanley Diamond and Fred G. Burke, eds., *The Transformation of East Africa* (New York: Basic Books, 1966), especially Gordon Wilson's "The African Elite," pp. 431–62.

In England, the conservative classes had hundreds of years to adapt. In underdeveloped countries, the change from feudalism to the modern nation-state can occur in a single generation. If the "conservative" classes are going to change, then the change will have to come about fairly quickly. A "telescoping of stages," the skipping of years of evolution, is brought about by the emulation and adoption of the most modern techniques of machinery and organization, as well as of styles and values.

Equally important questions concern the great scarcity of both the number of positions of wealth and power and the number of qualified individuals available to fill them. This means that in any event there is going to be a class structure; but for what purpose? and with what degree of control and responsibility?

In respect to both these factors, the rapidity of change and the scarcity of opportunities, the "conservative" classes who are established at the top of an allocation system of scarce resources, manipulate to their own advantage men and materials—using the loyalties, values, skills, and connections that established their previous positions for the purpose of transforming the new institutions and relationships. Leaders who had a monopoly over the allocation of land, based on obligations of fealty, are in a better position to acquire the freehold ownership of that land than are most other classes in society. This is so, regardless of any supposed reciprocal rights. A peasant may not have much luck in asking for a piece of land if his lord now holds legal title in his own name. There is always a lag in carrying out mutual obligations at times of social transition. In a similar fashion, insofar as higher education is important for the proper functioning of modern society and especially of its bureaucracy, leaders of the old oligarchy can, better than anyone else, send their sons to college and entrench them in the administrative and governing hierarchy.

The dimension of class thus provides a better understanding of "tribalism" as an ingredient of contemporary mass-based politics, and of the integration of tribal leaders and their sons into the governing strata of Africa's organizational bourgeoisie. Neither traditional rulers nor traditional systems, however, remained unaffected by the rise of nationalism, itself stirred by great social and political movements.

Chapter V

THE STRUGGLE
FOR INDEPENDENCE:
The Dynamics
of Nationalism

To understand contemporary African politics, we must examine not only how and why independence came when it did, but how and why self-government brought disappointments as well as opportunities. This understanding requires an analysis of the class character of African nationalism and nationalist movements. The class character of African nationalist movements helped determine policy outcomes in the postindependence period. Classes rooted in traditional social structures continued to mold the power relations of the contemporary era. New classes rose as a result of the spread of capitalism and the rise of new bureaucracies. These class interests clouded the prospects of independence.

African students studying in France eloquently articulated the meaning independence had for them in a survey conducted during the late 1950s. The students believed that independence meant "life itself," the "end of alienation," the raising of the standard of living, gaining control of both personal and national destinies of oneself and one's country.[1] Frantz Fanon, less exuberant, argued the necessity of a more critical analysis of independence. One must distinguish, he maintained, between different types of regimes. During the early 1960s, at a time when most African countries had just gained independence, Fanon declared that the masses had been frustrated.[2] Neither their material nor moral conditions had improved. They still did not eat meat, nor did they have peace of mind. They had discovered to their shock that the fighting had yielded no fundamental change. The French Revolution, Fanon declared, benefited the smallest farmer, but in Africa the flames of discontent threatened to burst out again. Africans sat in the national assemblies, in councils of state; they manned the bureaucracies and ran corporations. All of this looked new, yet seemed familiar. Why was there this discontent?

Alexis De Tocqueville concluded that the most amazing thing

---

[1] Jean Pierre N'Diaye, "African Students and the Ideology of Independence," reprinted in abridged form from *Enquete sur les etudiants noirs en France*, Editions realitées africanes Paris, 1962 in Irving Leonard Markovitz, ed., *African Politics and Society: Basic Issues and Problems of Government and Development* (New York: Free Press; London: Collier-Macmillan, 1970), pp. 199–206. Cf. Martin Minogue and Judith Molloy, eds., *African Aims and Attitudes, Selected Documents* (Cambridge: Cambridge University Press, 1974).

[2] Frantz Fanon, *Wretched of the Earth* (New York: Grove Press, 1968), p. 75.

about the French Revolution was not so much the inauguration of a "new order," but the continuities established with the ancient regime. Critics had alleged that the revolution brought chaos, disorder, and instability; that "things were falling apart"; that the new regime simply regularized anarchy. De Tocqueville replied that the revolution did not intend, "as some have thought, to change the whole nature of our traditional civilization, to arrest its progress, or even to make any vital change in the principles basic to the structure of society. . . . On the contrary, it sought to increase the power and jurisdiction of the central authority."[3] Building up the power of the central authority meant continuing the process brought to high achievement by the old regime. The revolutionaries girded the basic institutions of a strong central government with the additional fortifications of powerful bureaucracies. They used the strengthened institutions of state and bureaucracy to further the elimination of "those political institutions commonly described as feudal." The kings of France had themselves begun this process. They had sought a new power and authority by replacing the institutions of feudalism "with a new social and political order, at once simple and more uniform." De Tocqueville reminds us that other ages despaired of "instability" and "chaos," yet the elements of continuity quickly reasserted themselves. A Robespierre and a Louis XVI were men of two different worlds, almost races apart. The tundril and the guillotine, like the scepter and mace, dealt death to individuals. But cobblestone missiles did not dissolve society. The country endured. Men ruled. People went about their affairs. But to what end? There was a tension between promise and reality similar to that that marked Africa at the time of the rise of nationalist movements. The result was an ever more powerful central government capable of ever stronger manifestations of its will over the entire countryside.

After two world wars, Korea, Vietnam, Marx, Freud, the civil rights movement, Watergate, and the Plumbers, few Americans believe that the concept of the equality of all people has found political or social implementation. But if the possibilities for a just social order seem so impossible and the forces of "the establishment" so overwhelming, why do people even attempt to radically change their social situation?

Most people are less astounded than De Tocqueville at the continuities between regimes, at least in the sense that governments are remote; that "they" continue to govern. What surprises are the challengers, the reassertion of hope. How did the Nkrumahs and Nyereres dare dream of repulsing the forces of mighty industrial empires? Given all the resources at the command of those in power, no wonder the colonial rulers convinced themselves of their own invincibility.[4]

---

[3] Alexis De Tocqueville, *The Old Regime and the French Revolution* (New York: Doubleday, Anchor Books, 1955), pp. 19–20.

[4] See Chalmers Johnson, *Revolutionary Change* (Boston: Little, Brown, 1966), pp. 10–11. Johnson maintains that revolution can be avoided by all social classes and interests, no matter what the cir-

Why should it ever be the case that large numbers of people become so dissatisfied with their existing social arrangements that it is worth their while to create chaos in order to give "the revolutionaries" this chance.[5] Wretched material conditions are not enough.[6] The evidence of every great revolution in the past in France, the Soviet Union, and China reveals that massive poverty and exploitation are themselves not enough to precipitate revolution. Marx in his famous cry "Workers of the world unite, you have nothing to lose but your chains" could not have been more mistaken, because men do not revolt out of despair or out of a sense of desperation that they can no longer bear their suffering. Rather, the oppressed rise up when an improvement in their material condition gives them hope and sustenance for gaining even greater advantages, but some reversal or failure has frustrated these newly aroused expectations.[7] A new awakening on the part of the people to the fact of their oppression, a feeling of injustice and of being victimized, a conclusion that the old demands of the previous rulers are no longer justifiable is necessary before any fundamental challenge can be hurled against either colonial or indigenous authorities.

"Nationalism" sometimes provided a set of ideas that pulled together these sentiments, that aroused people already deeply discontented, that clarified the source of their problems, that provided a solution, and that legitimated by a high moral purpose Africans' assumption of their political destinies. "Nationalism," however, sometimes brought nothing but more of the same — new flags but old faces. What was involved in these processes?[8]

---

cumstances, if only people are willing to sit down and reason together. Such a view of rationality appears to overlook both the intensity of interests and the fact that the reallocation of scarce resources is not always simply a matter of rational calculation.

[5] John Dunn's response is that in this century, revolutions have generally occurred under conditions in which a large measure of chaos already existed from the point of view of the mass of the population, as a result of war, invasion, and so forth (*Modern Revolutions* [Cambridge and New York: Cambridge University Press, 1972], p. 13).

[6] *Ibid.*, pp. 14–15.

[7] As De Tocqueville pointed out long ago, "It is not always when things are going from bad to worse that revolutions break out. On the contrary, it oftener happens that when a people which has put up with an oppressive rule over a long period without protest suddenly finds the government relaxing its pressure it takes up arms against it. . . . For the mere fact that certain abuses have been remedied draws attention to the others and they now appear more galling; people may suffer for less, but their sensibility is exacerbated." De Tocqueville, *The Old Regime and the French Revolution*, p. 22.

[8] Barrington Moore has argued that it is not hard to tell when a peasant community does not receive real protection or a real return on services rendered:

"The objective character of exploitation seems so dreadfully obvious as to lead to the suspicion that the denial of objectivity is what requires explanation. . . ." (*Social Origins of Dictatorship and Democracy:* pp. 470–73).

During periods in Europe as far apart as the eighteenth and fifteenth centuries, Charles Tilly, in *The Vendee: A Sociological Analysis of the Counterrevolution of 1793* (Cambridge, Mass.: Harvard University Press, 1964), and Rodney Hilton, in *Bond Men Made Free: Medieval Peasant Movements and the English Rising of 1381* (New York: Viking, 1973), relate political activity to rural social structures undergoing urbanization and commercial and industrial change. Hilton states that the most radical social forces in medieval peasant movements were "those elements most in contact with the market, those who in suitable circumstances would become capitalist farmers" (p. 235). Cf. Charles Tilly, ed., *The Formation of National States in Western Europe* (Princeton, N.J.: Princeton University Press, 1975), especially pp. 84–164.

The Definition and Social Base of African Nationalism

Nationalism in Africa changed over time, and its objectives, social base, philosophy, and leadership differed greatly from one country to another.[9] At the same time, all nationalist movements shared certain common features and owed their successes to similar underlying social and economic forces. There are three reasons why a discussion of the rise of nationalism is important:

1) To distinguish between countries that have gained independence and those that have not. Different sets of priorities and problems are paramount in these two very different situations.

2) To examine the forces of change that produced a new political consciousness and set of demands among newly politically relevant groups and to realize that these currents of change have not abated; to see the continuities between the pressures that gave rise to independence and those that confront the indigenous ruling groups.

3) To recognize that the manner of achieving independence was all-important because it helped to determine the composition and relative position of the contestants in the political arena. The forces that brought the country to independence had the greatest opportunity after independence to consolidate power in their favor.

What then was African nationalism? Social scientists have expended a great deal of energy attempting to define "nation" and "nationalism." Thomas Hodgkin, dean of European Africanists, uses the term in the broadest sense to describe any organization or group "that explicitly asserts the rights, claims and aspirations of a given African

---

[9] An enormous literature exists on African nationalism and its causes. See, in addition to works previously cited, Frantz Fanon's *A Dying Colonialism* (New York: Grove Press, 1965) and *Toward the African Revolution* (New York: Grove Press, 1967). Two of the earliest African expressions of anticolonial sentiment may be found in the novel, Rene Maran's *Batouala* (Rockville, Md.: New Perspectives, 1973); and George Simeon Mwase, *Strike a Blow and Die*, ed. Robert I. Rotberg (Cambridge, Mass.: Harvard University Press, 1967). Cf. Stanlake Samkange, *On Trial for My Country* (London: Heinemann Educational Books, 1966); Ndabaningi Sithole, *African Nationalism*, 2nd ed. (New York: Oxford University Press, 1968); Jomo Kenyatta, *Facing Mt. Kenya* (New York: Random House); Patrice Lumumba, *My Country* (New York: Praeger, 1962); Thomas Kanza, *Conflict in the Congo* (Baltimore: Penguin, 1972); Kwame Nkrumah, *Ghana: The Autobiography of Kwame Nkrumah* (London: Nelson and Sons, 1957); Nkrumah, *Revolutionary Path* (New York: International Publishers, 1973); and K. A. Busia, *The Challenge of Africa* (New York: Praeger, 1962).

See also Henry S. Wilson, ed., *Origins of West African Nationalism* (New York: St. Martin's 1969); Norman Robert Bennett, *Mirambo of Tanzania* (New York: Oxford University Press, 1971); Immanuel Wallerstein, *The Road to Independence: Ghana and the Ivory Coast* (Paris: Mouton, 1954); Hodgkin, *Nationalism in Colonial Africa*; Hodgkin, "A Note on the Language of African Nationalism," in *St. Antony's Papers, No. 10*, ed. Kenneth Kirkwood (Carbondale, Ill.: Southern Illinois University Press, 1961), pp. 22–40; Kenneth Little, *West African Urbanization* (New York: Cambridge University Press, 1965); Richard Wright, *Black Power* (New York: Harper & Brothers, 1954); William McCord, *The Springtime of Freedom* (New York: Oxford University Press, 1965); Pierre Bonnafe, *Nationalismes Africaines* (Paris: Fondation Nationale des Sciences Politiques, 1962); Michael K. Clark, *Algeria in Turmoil* (New York: Grosset & Dunlap, 1960); William G. Andrews, *French Politics and Algeria* (New York: Appleton-Century-Crofts, 1962); Donald C. Hodges et al., *NLF National Liberation Fronts, 1960–1970* (New York: Morrow, 1972); and Conor Cruise O'Brien, *To Katanga and Back* (New York: Grosset & Dunlap, 1962).

society (from the level of the language group to that of Pan-Africa) in opposition to European authority, whatever its institutional form and objectives."[10] James Coleman confines the term to organizations that are essentially political—not religious, economic, or educational—and whose objective is the realization of self-government or independence. He maintains that

> nation is not a loose catch-all term denoting a larger grouping of tribes ... rather it is a post-tribal, post-feudal terminal *community* which has emerged from the shattering forces of disintegration that characterized modernity. ... there must be a greater awareness of a closeness of contact with "national" compatriots as well as with the "national" government. This closeness of contact on the horizontal and vertical levels has been a distinctly Western phenomenon, for the obvious reason that it is the result of modern technology.[11]

The difficulty with these definitions is that they automatically exclude the possibility that the precolonial African empires created a sense of common identity among the diverse peoples of their area;[12] moreover, they do not distinguish differences in the class origin of the leaders and of the followers of various movements.

The nationalism of African kings and nobility of the medieval states differed from, for example, the nationalism of the bourgeoisie. Bourgeois nationalism evolved through two separate stages: (1) the genteel nationalism carried on as a leisure activity by the small class of petty bourgeois Africans aspiring to the upper status of the colonial establishment; and (2) the nationalism of the large group of intermediary civil servants, aspiring politicians, striving merchants, and other members of a mobile lower "middle class" who stood at the vanguard of the exploding numbers of semiliterate and socially mobilized and were located in a peripheral social position, marginal to the holders of power yet conscious of the possibilities of change. This lower middle class was not content with its relative share of social and political rewards, yet was secure enough to work for something better. As the benefits of economic development begin to trickle down, this group found its appetite whetted, yet remained the most sensitive group to shifts in

[10] Thomas Hodgkin, *Nationalism in Colonial Africa* (New York: New York University Press, 1957), pp. 24–25.

[11] James S. Coleman, "Nationalism in Tropical Africa," in *African Politics and Society*, ed. Markovitz, pp. 153–78.

[12] David Kimble, in his massive study of nationalism in the Gold Coast, traces the changing meaning of the word "nation." He notes a range of state organizations from the tribe to an area that includes virtually all of modern Ghana: "It is evident, in any case, that the words 'nation' or 'national' have meant very different things at different times; hence, our study ... is concerned with a constantly chaning phenomenon. Yet there was an essential continuity of development, as the center of loyalty shifted from the small independent State (e.g. Adansi) to the tribe (e.g. Fantis), to the Confederacy of States (e.g. Ashanti) or the wider ethnic or linguistic group (e.g. Akans). Each in turn was credited with the title of Nation; but eventually, after many vicissitudes and internal rivalries, it became possible to think of "the Gold Coast Nation" as a unit, and to demand for it the status appropriate to a modern nation state. *A Political History of Ghana: The Rise of Gold Coast Nationalism, 1850–1928* (Oxford: Clarendon Press, 1963), p. 554.

the economy. The most exposed, the most vulnerable, increasingly politically aware—this is the most disappointed and the most bitter group in the population.[13] Finally, there is a mass-based nationalism, whose major thrust comes from rural areas and whose main support is a militant peasantry. A growing literature has analyzed this social base in Sierre Leone, Zaire, Kenya, the Cameroons, and other nations.[14]

The types of nationalism and the classes upon which they were based determined the outcome of the move from colony to nation. We must therefore distinguish whether independence resulted from mass organization and pressure, the weight of numbers, and the promise of turmoil, aggravation, and expense—the major weapons of the poor, the exploited, and the oppressed—or whether it resulted from "an arrangement" between colonial and African establishments that recognized each other and proposed no radical alteration of previous arrangements.

Soon after the end of the Second World War, colonies became an international embarrassment; the political styles of the day had changed even if the economic and political realities had not. New political forms could hide old patterns of domination. Legal and symbolic independence, a flag and a constitution, neither filled bellies nor breathed life into puppet regimes. Where independence resulted from the organizational weapon of a mass movement ready to use violence if necessary, and demanding, not requesting, immediate self-government, at least there was greater potential for social reforms.

Analysts distinguish between pre–World War II and postwar nationalism, yet a chronological division can be misleading. For it was not simply the passage of time that was significant but rather whether or not the colonial power had succeeded in creating an African "elite" and had reached an understanding with it about independence. In some countries, true mass nationalism has yet to develop.

Early Bourgeois Nationalism

To find a precise term characterizing early nationalism is difficult. Although an "elite" may be defined in terms of (1) differences in degree of possession of scarce resources and (2) differences in kind in the control of skills and instruments of power, including the ability to

---

[13] Cf. Eric Wolf's treatment of the middle-level peasant in his *Peasant Wars of the Twentieth Century* (New York: Harper 1969), pp. 289–90.

[14] Herbert Weiss, *Political Protest in the Congo* (Princeton, N.J.: Princeton University Press, 1967); Martin Kilson, *Political Change in a West African State* (Cambridge, Mass.: Harvard University Press, 1966); Donald L. Barnett and Karari Njama, *Mau Mau from Within: Autobiography and Analysis of Kenya's Peasant Revolt* (New York: Monthly Review Press, 1966); Victor T. Levine, *The Cameroons, From Mandate to Independence* (Berkeley and Los Angeles: University of California Press, 1964); and John Saul and Roger Woods, "African Peasantries," in *Peasants and Peasant Societies*, ed. Teodor Shanin (Harmondsworth: Penguin, 1971), pp. 103–14. Cf. G. Ionescu and Ernest Gellner, *Populism* (London: Macmillan, 1969); Joseph Mwangi Karuiki, *Mau Mau Detainee* (Baltimore: Penguin, 1963); and Gerard Chailand, *Armed Struggle in Africa: With the Guerrillas in "Portuguese" Guinea* (New York: Monthly Review Press, 1969).

mobilize or control the persuasive and coercive mechanisms, organizational terms are nevertheless inadequate because they do not convey a sense of conflict of interest between classes. "Bourgeois nationalism" better conveys a sense of this reality.

The original Westernized African elite consisted of interpreters, clerks, lower civil servants—all those who linked the colonizers and the masses. In reality, this group possessed poor education and little power. Not a classic bourgeoisie because it was defined not by ownership of the means of production but rather by its position in commerce, bureaucracies, and the service professions, this group nevertheless changed and developed as more Africans entered the wage labor force and the system of commodity exchange. With the Europeans on top, the limits of an African "ruling class" were clearly circumscribed. Nevertheless, its power—in combination with that of the traditional ruling class—vis-à-vis the vast majority of Africans was great.

Even though limited in wealth, poorly educated, and politically powerless in the face of the military superiority of the colonial regime, the original African privileged class felt itself a group apart from the majority of their countrymen. Numerically weak, they could associate with the European population and aspire to fill its functional roles. A belief in colonialism's alleged policy of assimilation lessened the leadership role of this African privileged class with the masses. Envisaging only a limited field of political action for themselves, and certainly for "the natives" in general, the lawyers, doctors, teachers, and lesser bureaucrats who sought a modicum of European prestige could only *hope* for some of the outsider's power. Although they might have been the first element aware of the "colonial situation," few questioned the system itself. These original African elites were too often aloof and paternalistic towards their own people. For them, politics was a part-time affair, a hobby, or an aid to their major preoccupation—pecuniary gain or individual prestige.[15]

Every social class that has not been integrated into the political system poses a revolutionary potential. Every group, until it is so absorbed, goes through a phase in which it develops aspirations leading to either symbolic or material demands upon the political system. If these demands are frustrated, the group threatens the establishment. Cultural nationalism provided symbolic outlets.

Cultural Nationalism and the Crises of Identity

To a large extent, the nationalism of the privileged African strata consisted of demands for cultural and not political autonomy. In the

[15] In some respects the nationalism of the pre–World War II African privileged class is reminiscent of similarly situated classes in the American colonies at the time of American independence. Barrington Moore, however, declares about the American Revolution: "Since it did not result in any fundamental changes in the structure of society, there are grounds for asking whether it deserves to be called a revolution at all." *Social Origins of Dictatorship and Democracy*, p. 113.

French colonies, the development of the ideology of *negritude* is an outstanding example of this.[16] At the beginning, this class did not so much seek to lead "the people" in forging a unique identity; it wanted more to continue to enjoy its advantages of status, prestige, and arrogant superiority to "the natives."

This class did, however, react intensely to the assimilationist policies of previous African privileged interests and personalities as well as to foreign domination. The first bourgeois nationalist leaders proclaimed a revival of African cultures even as they immersed themselves in the day-to-day problems of business. George Shepperson has remarked that a "historical introversion, a kind of turning in upon themselves to find elements in their national heritage which are of indigenous not foreign origin," has occupied their national consciousness and has led to a rediscovery of African history and to a new culture.[17]

Combating the colonial establishment, dominated by strange men of an alien culture and civilization, these Africans wrote of their crisis of identity—both in personal terms and in the sense of a conflict of cultures. This concern was largely the luxury of small minorities of intellectuals. Leopold Sedar Senghor, for example, described how, as a product of two cultures, he did his exercises every morning and every evening while listening first to the music of Brahms and then to the enchanting tones of the balafon; first to the poetry of St. John Perse and then to the musical refrains of the *griots*.

The identity crisis suffered by nonintellectual Africans had to do with their sense of personal autonomy and social power. There was no conflict between cultures, no "split minds," no wars between tribal gods and the dictates of the church. The real problems of ordinary people had to do with physical and material insecurity, and were compounded by the additional insecurities wrought by an authoritarian and strange political machine. The people described by Margaret Field in her *Search for Security* are burdened with real conflicts of work and society.[18]

Nevertheless, the reactions of the intellectuals and African bourgeosie were important in creating cultural and other organizations that became the bearers of early nationalism. In 1889, one of the first West African cultural associations, the Mfantsi Amanbuhu Fekuw, was formed in Cape Coast by leading West African intellectuals to "counteract excessive Western influence." One of the first African lawyers, J. Mensah Sarbah, in summing up their guiding principles, said

[16] See Irving Leonard Markovitz, *Leopold Sedar Senghor and the Politics of Negritude* (New York: Atheneum, 1969; London: Heinemann Educational Books, 1970).

[17] George Shepperson, "External Factors in the Development of British Nationalism," in *African Politics and Society*, ed. Markovitz; Cf. Thomas Hodgkin, "Background to A.O.F., The Metropolitan Axis," *West Africa*, 2 January-20 February, and 6 March, 1954; and Robert G. Weisbord, *Ebony Kinship: Africa, Africans and the Afro-American* (Westport, Conn.: Greenwood Press, 1973).

[18] See Gordon MacKay Haliburton's *The Prophet Harris: A Study of an African Prophet and his Mass Movement in the Ivory Coast and the Gold Coast, 1913-1915* (New York: Oxford University Press, 1973), in addition to Field's *Search for Security: An Ethno-Psychiatric Study of Rural Ghana* (Evanston, Ill.: Northwestern University Press, 1962).

that "it was better to be called by one's own name than be known by a foreign one, that it was possible to acquire Western learning and be expert in scientific attainments without neglecting one's mother tongue, and that African dress, closely 'resembling the garb of the Grecian and Roman,' should not lightly be cast aside."[19] Before the turn of the century, Africans began to assert their identity by discarding European names. A newspaper advertisement published in 1892 reads, "To all whom it may concern!! Two gentlemen of intelligence having pluckily dropped their foreign names have encouraged me to do the same. . . . I am no slave so nobody must call me *Ebenezer* Weldu *Cole* Eshun anymore. My real name is Esuon Weldu."[20] Sarbah in his major study, *Fanti National Constitution*, written to redirect attention to the "shamefully neglected" history of the Gold Coast, quoted Gladstone as saying, "Unhappy are the people who cut themselves from their past."[21]

This resurgence of a national identity could, and in some cases did, lift the veil covering the hideous face of colonial society. Cultural concerns could lead to political action. As Lukacs wrote,

> The veil drawn over the nature of bourgeois society is indispensable to the bourgeoisie itself. For the insoluble internal contradictions of the system become revealed with increasing starkness and so confront its supporters with a choice. Either they must consciously ignore insights which become increasingly urgent or else they must suppress their own moral instincts in order to be able to support with good conscience an economic system that serves only their own interest.[22]

Not in every instance was the veil ripped off, for sometimes cultural nationalism became a substitute for political nationalism. This was not always an intentional ideological maneuver. Members of the African bourgeoisie reclaimed their own personal identities and were content to cogitate upon the past rather than concern themselves with the social problems involved in a political reorganization of a national future. As the Camerounian philosopher Martien Towa states,

> When we present our past culture as something marvelous that is absolutely necessary to safeguard, and when we insist upon holding it up for international admiration, we work to maintain the status quo. . . . African philosophy must be an effort to elucidate our present situation in the world, a condition mainly of dependence and of weakness. We must adopt a critical attitude toward the past as well as the present . . . in order to take our destiny into our own hands.[23]

Focusing on the past and on their cultural personalities had the effect — regardless of the motivations of the intellectuals involved — of diver-

[19] Quoted in Kimble, *A Political History of Ghana*, p. 518.

[20] *Ibid.*

[21] *Ibid.*, p. 523.

[22] Georg Lukacs, *History and Class Consciousness* (Cambridge, Mass.: M.I.T. Press, 1971), p. 66.

[23] Quoted in *Jeune Afrique*, No. 560 (September 28, 1971).

ting attention away from immediate radical political change.[24] Cultural expression proved insufficient to meet persisting and intensifying political difficulties.

Problems of the African Bourgeoisie Persist

Those educated Africans who aspired to top positions in the civil service and government bureaucracies received a severe jolt in the early twentieth century when both the French and British drastically changed their programs of Africanization and instead began rapidly to reintroduce their own nationals. Turning away from their declared intention of training Africans to assume the role of Europeans in preparation for self-government, the British brought in European administrators as quickly as their budgets would allow, and abruptly halted the advancement of Western-educated Africans already in service. In 1910, the colonial office announced that "Englishmen naturally expected to enjoy the fruits of their conquest and that it was logical that they should be preferred over Africans in senior positions.[25] At approximately the same time, the French abruptly brought to a halt their program of training an African administrative elite to join them in their "work of empire" and *mission civilatrice.*

The real flood of French migration to Senegal, for example, did not occur until after 1900. French administrators tightened their system of direct rule in all the urban areas and attempted to eliminate urban Africans from the electoral rolls and the communes established since 1848. Frenchmen also increasingly resented African successes in business. Paradoxically, conflicts over commerce increased even as the production of cash crops expanded. As Wesley Johnson noted, "Economic conditions, increasingly favorable to urban Africans as the communes grew, contributed a new spirit of independence to African traders; but the growth of peanut culture also brought larger French trading companies, which threatened many African middlemen."[26] This combined threat to African political participation and economic opportunities changed the African attitude towards local politics and helped mobilize Africans into new political organizations.

Decades before World War II, a burgeoning African bourgeoisie had organized in various regional and hinterland centers in Senegal, as well as in the capital city, and created networks of alliances among members of their class.[27] The "surprising" victory in 1914 of Blaise Diagne, the first black African deputy to the French National Assembly, was one major result and this in turn further stimulated extensive political organization throughout the country, and provided the model for the urban "elitest parties" that flourished until the Sec-

---

[24] See, for example, the analysis of Senghor in Markovitz, *Leopold Sedar Senghor and the Politics of Negritude.*

[25] Webster and Boahen, *History of West Africa* (New York: Praeger, 1970), p. 241.

[26] G. Wesley Johnson, Jr., *The Emergence of Black Politics in Senegal* (Stanford, Calif.: Stanford University Press, 1971), p. 123.

[27] *Ibid.,* p. 39.

ond World War.[28] The point must be emphasized again, however, that Diagne's election, like other manifestations of early nationalism, was by and large the part-time concern of small numbers of Western-educated members of the liberal professions or merchants who sought— often vigorously—"understandings" with the colonial regime rather than the creation of an "organizational weapon" based upon mass support.

Conflicts occurred between Africans of the lower and upper strata of the middle class because the total income available to urban Africans not only was limited but shrank. Following each world war the size of the lower stratum grew as real income fell because of the destruction of trade and inflation. Squeezed by these pressures, the lower- and middle-class elements vented a more militant, and often more radical, nationalism. They demanded an expansion of education, suffrage, and representation in political institutions. The African administrative and professional bourgeoisie, as well as the traditional ruling chiefs, appeared to them an oppressive class responsible for thwarting their just aspirations. A growing African merchant class felt thwarted by a colonial regime that monopolized the leading centers of commerce, and by privileged African groups that lived off government and administrative revenues. These aspiring middle-class elements turned to the rural areas to seek support for their struggle, hoping to channel the quiescent, but periodically erupting, long discontented peasantry.[29]

A major reason for the failure of widespread social revolution to occur in African countries attempting to throw off colonialism was a lack of harmony between the frustration of the urban middle class and the frustration of the peasantry.[30] The peasants wanted out of the economic as well as political system introduced by colonialism and capitalism. Like peasants everywhere, they desired a return to the status quo that had existed before the European advent; they wanted to return to the "traditional" way of life. The budding bourgeoisie wanted to enter more fully into the promising materialist civilization. They demanded a greater share in a new standard of living. They un-

[28] Cf. Irving Leonard Markovitz, "The Political Thought of Blaise Diagne and Lamine Gueye: Some Aspects of Social Structure and Ideology in Senegal," *Presence Africaine*, 72, no. 4 (1969) reprinted in *Black Leaders of the Centuries*, S. O. Mezu and Ram Desai, eds. (Buffalo: Black Academy Press, 1970), pp. 202–218. See also K. W. J. Post, "British Policy and Representative Government in West Africa, 1920–1951," in *Colonialism in Africa, 1870–1960*, ed. Peter Duignan and L. H. Gann, Vol. 2, *The History and Politics of Colonialism, 1870–1914*, ed. Duignan and Gann (Cambridge: Cambridge University Press, 1970), pp. 31–57. Like Johnson, Post pushes the origins of nationalism back to the pre–World War II period.

[29] Cf. Immanuel Wallerstein, "Class, Tribe and Party," in *The History and Politics of Colonialism, 1870–1914*, ed. Duignan and Gann, pp. 310–11.

[30] Samuel Huntington reminds us that it takes more than one revolutionary group to make a revolution: "The probability of revolution in a modernizing country depends upon: a) the extent to which the urban middle class—intellectuals, professionals, bourgeoisie—are alienated from the existing order; b) the extent to which the peasants are alienated from the existing order; and c) the extent to which urban middle class and peasants join together not only in fighting against 'the same enemy' but also in fighting for the same cause. This cause is usually nationalism." *Political Order in Changing Societies* (New Haven: Yale University Press, 1968), pp. 276–77.

derstood the nature of the new mechanisms of state power and reached for its control. Patterns such as these that marked the historical evolution of colonialized Africa still prevail in contemporary Rhodesia. A. K. H. Weinrich finds that the "top stratum" of Africans in Rhodesia receive high salaries, are well educated, try to preserve elite status for their children by sending them to the best schools, and otherwise attempt to follow a European way of life that distinguishes them from lower-class Africans:

> Members of this top stratum who are employed by government try to reduce their contact with uneducated Africans. . . . The ordinary concerns of African peasants are practically alien to them. . . . Politically, they are often neutral, or at least inactive, their economic rewards blind them to submit passively to a social order which discriminates as much against them as against the less educated members of their race. . . .[31]

Weinrich goes on to argue that "middle-stratum" Africans in Rhodesia are unable to afford the luxuries of high-priced cars and expensive hotels enjoyed by African members in the top stratum. Because they face visibly insurmountable barriers that exclude them completely from European society, because their loss from the ouster of the white establishment would be less than that of the members of the African elite, because the potential advantages would indeed be enormous, a significant number of this intermediate black bourgeoisie are willing to participate in political actions and organizations that seek to bring about fundamental social change. Like their historical counterparts in Nigeria, Kenya, and the Congo, they are a fundamental social force that provides a basic drive towards nationalism. They are part of the movement towards a more radical nationalism that occurred after the Second World War.

Causes for the Rise of
Mass Nationalism after World War II

The Second World War speeded the movement of additonal tens of millions of Africans from "traditional" to "modern" ways of life. This meant that they changed their homes, jobs, ways of acting, experiences, expectations, and personal habits and needs, including the need for new types of group affiliations and new images of personal identity. Cumulatively, these changes influenced and transformed mass political behavior.

The pound sterling, the franc and the dollar, the cocoa pod and the coffee bean, palm oil and peanuts, the telephone, the telegram,

---

[31] A. K. H. Weinrich, *Black and White Elites in Rural Rhodesia* (Manchester: Manchester University Press, 1973), pp. 224–25. James S. Coleman divides anticolonial manifestations into modernist, traditionalist, and syncristic movements and lumps together all spontaneous movements of resistance to the initial European occupation as "primary resistance," making no effort to determine their class nature ("Nationalism in Tropical Africa").

and the post office, the growth of new governmental agencies, cooperatives and the Department of Cooperation—all these brought together formerly separate peoples and ethnic groups into a new, constantly more intensified contact. From the bush farms and forest villages of Brong-Ahafo, Casamance, Busoga, and the Delta the adventurers and the desperate drifted into Kumasi, Dakar, Kampala, and Port Harcourt. Upon rising in the morning they looked out on telephone poles and concrete. They jostled Tergal-suited men in the streets and pushed paper to nylon-stockinged women in offices. They rode rubber-tired buses and walked on plastic sandals. Wolof farmers, Diola laborers, Serer merchants, Tukulor deputies traveled the same roads, sought better prices in the same markets, bought the same tinned tomatoes, and ate the same long-grained rice imported from the United States and Indochina. They sent their children to the same schools, served in the same armies, voted in the same elections, and suffered the same unfair treatment from the colonial authorities. Out of these contacts came a new political unity.

These changes caused an expansion of the politically relevant strata of the population—that is, all of those who had to be taken into account, those who counted for something in political life, not just the elite. In Africa the politically relevant include the growing number of city dwellers, market farmers, the users of money, wage earners, radio listeners, and literates in both rural and urban areas. Isolated subsistence farmers, apathetic villagers—once the overwhelming majority of the population—are not included: policy makers can overlook the politically unaware because ignorance precludes the demanding of accountability from their government.

The growth in the number of those who were politically aware, who were conscious of new needs, resulted in mounting pressures for the transformation of political practices and in the rise of institutions that allowed for their participation in politics. The newly socially militant had no choice. Uprooted from the villages, family, friends, occupations, and traditions that had served generations in every stage of the life cycle, the new urban dwellers and wage earners had new needs for housing, jobs, and aids against sickness and unemployment. How could they educate their children, retrain themselves for new occupations, secure protection against rent gougers and unscrupulous merchants, and find solace in the midst of all the grand buildings, limousines, officials, uniforms, and boulevards that attested to their insignificance and powerlessness? Increasingly, they brought into politics a range of needs qualitatively different from traditional expectations. Who today can truly believe that "that government is best which governs least"? The newly politically aware demanded at least the chance for a decent life for themselves and their children.

Changes in the numbers of those willing to engage in extensive political activity, coupled with expectations for the provision of new government services, creates a qualitatively different type of politics.

Greater numbers of people show up in crowds and at meetings and provide a growing audience for political communications of all types, whatever the medium. They find and join organizations ranging from burial and cultural societies to trade unions and self-help organizations. The consequences of a government's, *any* government's, ineffectiveness are great, for if the government fails to meet these increasing burdens, a growing proportion of the population is likely to become alienated and disaffected from the state.

Out of these processes and movements, this continual search for an answer to new physical needs, and this quest for new psychological and social identities comes the basis for a new type of mass nationalism. By reuniting the population on a new basis, nationalism offers one solution to problems of loosening ethnic identities. A national culture offers patterns of behavior and evaluation that bring together diverse ethnic and parochial elements. The new technology enables the creation of a common system of economic exchange coupled with a common system of new coercive capacity. New leadership groups arise from the university bureaucracies and commercial exchanges to pull it all together — the newly awakened masses, a new technology, the new commercial and political institutions.[32]

By the end of the Second World War, these social changes had created the forces necessary for a radical new type of politics in most African countries. The growing number of highly educated Africans became increasingly resentful of the colonialists' favored position and their own subordinate role. The rise of cities and the breakdown of rural societies, including the loss of authority of the traditional leaders who were reluctant to change, produced a new class of poorly paid and increasingly discontented wage earners. Unbalanced educational systems gave rise to the "semieducated," the "standard VI boys," who, to their chagrin, could not find jobs upon graduation.

The factors that conditioned the development of a particular nationalist movement, however, varied from country to country for a number of reasons, such as conflicts between different tribal peoples and traditional precolonial hostilities that were exacerbated as a result of imperial policies; tensions between groups resulting from unevenness in development; and tensions among the Westernized elite, the traditionalists, and the masses. Differences among the various colonial policies also directly affected the degree of political liberty afforded to nationalist movements, as did their programs of education and their attitudes towards the Westernized elite.[33]

Above all the Second World War emphasized what the other co-

---

[32] Cf. Karl Deutsch, *Nationalism and Social Communications.* See also Deutsch's *The Nerves of Government* (New York: Free Press, 1966); and Ted Robert Gurr, *Why Men Rebel* (Princeton, N.J.: Princeton University Press, 1970). W. A. Cornelius challenges Deutsch's thesis in "Urbanization and Political Demand Making," *American Political Science Review*, 68, no. 3 (September 1974), 1125–46, by arguing that needs are filled on an individual and not a social basis.

[33] On variations in colonial policies before and after the Second World War, see Chapter III.

lonial wars had revealed to the masses of Africans: they were needed; European society could not function without their participation. Once learned, this lesson could not be unlearned. The colonial authorities had told the peoples of their empires that they could not wage war without them; that they needed their peanuts, their palm oil, their cocoa, and their cotton for their enduring prosperity. They had told them all men were entitled to liberty, equality and fraternity; that a great war against fascism had been fought on their behalf; that all peoples were entitled to self-determination. They had told them that political organization was important, that the common peoples ought, by the laws of God and of nature, to participate in the legislatures, parliaments, and assemblies of government. Then they told them that, of course, all this would take a few hundred years. And then, the colonial authorities were surprised when the peoples of Africa became impatient and would not wait.

Mass awareness of the colonial situation spread. Youth movements were born everywhere. Voluntary associations were galvanized into bearers of nationalism. The newly returned university graduates joined with the masses of the discontented and the semieducated to demand immediate independence.

Full-time professional political activists brought new skills into the fray. Organization, self-consciousness, and a new analytical objectivity characterized the new African leaders. In asserting their leadership of the new self-conscious masses, they promised the creation of "new societies" and a "new African man." They claimed to eschew petty cabals and power for personal advantage. They offered systematic, sustained political organization in the service of a vision of the future.[34] They laid bare not only the injustices of colonialism but also its banality. Politics became a full-time occupation. The organization of the population created a new instrument for combat. The new nationalism was radical not only in the speed demanded for social change, but in the effort to extend organization down to the smallest village so as to incorporate the humblest peasant. This mass mobilization, led by groups of political radicals and moved by new and revolutionary ideologies, heralded, as at similar moments throughout history, "the recapture of control by the virtuous over an inimical destiny."[35] Nationalism converted African traditional nonparticipants, inactive individuals, into political actors.[36] In challenging the colonial establishments, these mass leaders created the moment "when all immunities are suddenly cancelled, old patterns of passivity and acquiescence overthrown."[37] They had a ready target in the colonial rulers headquartered in the capital cities.

---

[34] Michael Walzer, *The Revolution of the Saints; A Study in the Origin of Radical Politics* (New York: Atheneum, 1968), pp. 1–2.

[35] Dunn, *Modern Revolutions*, p. 22.

[36] See Daniel Lerner, *The Passing of Traditional Society* (New York: Free Press, 1958). See also the definition of political modernization by Huntington, *Political Order in Changing Societies*, p. 35.

[37] Walzer, *The Revolution of the Saints*, p. 19.

The Further Development of the African Bourgeoisie

Political revolutions do not, and cannot, take place "in countries where political strength is dispersed in a thousand places, and where myriads of men feel personally involved in the continuing problems of a self-governing parish or township and participate in making the rules for the larger unit, county, state or nations."[38] The increasing centralization of the colonial bureaucratic apparatus not only broke down the power of traditional local authorities, it created a new target for political action. Even where large-scale traditional empires had existed, their authority did not normally directly affect each citizen on a steady basis. The state's functions tended to be limited to the provision of a defense system, the preservation of law and order, the upkeep of roads and other essential public works, and the collection of taxes.[39] *In African countries, the concentration and centralization of powers into the institutions of the national government created a double problem for the first African bourgeoisie: at the same time that the bourgeoisie pressured the colonial authorities for the purpose of gaining control over these new institutions, they themselves became a target for the growing numbers of working-class and lower-middle-class Africans, who were mobilized to fill the offices created by the new commercial and bureaucratic apparatus. Nationalism, as a political movement, helped form a new sense of community by bringing together the diversely aggrieved on a new basis: membership in a particular area controlled by indigenous inhabitants.* T. H. Marshall has pointed out that the "inequality of the social class system may be acceptable provided the equality of citizenship is recognized. . . . citizenship has itself become, in certain respects, the architect of legitimate social inequality."[40]

The creation of these new political units—independent nation-states—based upon universal suffrage, in the final analysis served the purpose of the African bourgeoisie. This "self-government" could provide an illusion of participation in a way that European-dominated arrangements never could. This African "elite" undoubtedly valued parliamentary institutions highly and believed truly that they were good for all men and all classes. Yet, regardless of its motivations, the system of rule advocated by the African bourgeoisie functioned especially to buttress its own interest in a manner similar to the functioning of all forms of indirect government.[41]

Until the dominant African classes recognized the potential of "mass nationalism" to further their positions under a veil of universal

---

[38] Frank Tannenbaum, "On Political Stability," *Political Science Quarterly,* 75 (June 1960), 169; quoted in Huntington, *Political Order in Changing Societies,* p. 367.

[39] See e.g. C. E. Black, *The Dynamics of Modernization* (New York: Harper & Row, 1966), p. 13.

[40] T. H. Marshall, *Class, Citizenship and Social Development* (Garden City, N.Y.: Doubleday, Anchor Books, 1965).

[41] Cf. Harvey C. Mansfield, "Hobbes and the Science of Indirect Government," *American Political Science Review,* 65, no. 1 (1971) pp. 97–110; and the discussion on African democracy in Chapter VIII.

"participation," they feared for their security. Seeing only the dangers of the short run, they considered the Nkrumahs and Kenyattas as upstarts and rabble-rousers. Great political activity could in fact mask — as it has done in Western capitalist countries — the growth of a "new class" of African bureaucratic and commercial bourgeoisie, who were much wealthier, much more powerful — and much more exploitative — than any previous ruling class.[42]

Mass nationalist movements therefore served *class* interests. By definition, "movements" involve a large variety of individuals, groups, and associations, who coalesce for some common general undertaking; "parties" are more highly structured organizations limited to a more specific purpose. Mass nationalist movements in Africa gathered together peoples of diverse social and ethnic backgrounds under a variety of personalities for the primary purpose of throwing out the colonial regimes.[43] They ostensibly left to a later time decisions about the format and purpose of "African" rule. Yet those decisions had in fact already been shaped by the very format and structure of these movements in the nationalist phase of development.[44]

The problem of consolidating political dominance was exacerbated for the African bourgeoisie when, after the Second World War, the colonial governments enfranchised masses of Africans living in the rural areas. This deprived the indigenous bourgeoisie of its monopoly of political rights. If the past politics of this "handful of urbanites" consisted "largely of attempts to secure, reinforce and extend their privileges within the colonial system, then their work was doubly cut out for them when the electoral rolls were flooded with the new influx of the poorly educated or uneducated."[45] In Ghana, to give one example, "disturbances" in the post–World War II years, including demonstrations against shops and other commercial enterprises of foreigners, marked the advent of a new political force that had to be contained. A major shift of power within Ghanaian society, however, did not occur.[46] Although new social classes entered the political arena, they did so under the leadership of middle-class elements who safely channeled the efforts of the new classes into electoral politics and cooperation with the British administration.

[42] However, Ian Davies arrives at a common, mistaken conclusion when he asserts, "In such countries as Nigeria, the Ivory Coast, Morocco and South Africa, the emergence of powerful economic and political interest groups has produced wide discrepancies between elite living standards and a depressed condition of both wage earners and peasants. The revolutionary potential of such societies does not need to be stressed." (*African Trade Unions* [Baltimore, Penguin, 1966], p. 222). Such societies are not necessarily revolutionary as a result of the *income gap*, because, among other reasons, political participation in a common political system helps fill that gap.

[43] Thomas Hodgkin discusses these differences in his *African Political Parties* (Baltimore, Penguin, 1961).

[44] Wallerstein maintains that "mass nationalist movements were not however, class parties. . . . they could not be in a population most of which consisted mostly of peasants still living partially in a subsistence economy." ("Class, Tribe and Party," in *The History and Politics of Colonialism, 1870–1914*, ed. Duignan and Gann, p. 500).

[45] *Ibid.,* p. 497.

[46] Dennis Austin holds the opposite view in his *Politics in Ghana, 1946–1960* (Oxford: Oxford University Press, 1964), p. 12.

Although hindsight enables us to see how these new social classes were ultimately contained in the years immediately following the war, the significance of their entry into politics must not be underestimated. They offered a strident protest not only against colonial rule but against the existing structure of authority. They represented a "much broader, more popular level than had hitherto been active in national politics."[47] Austin notes of politics in Ghana that "it was not easy (even by 1960) to see the Convention Peoples Party as the vanguard of a clearly defined social class, since the general appeal of independence enabled the leaders to muster a broad front of support. . . . Nevertheless, the demand made by the party for self-government was bound up with a struggle for power which had many of the characteristics of a class struggle."[48]

Government became not only an agency for the control of the "socially mobilized" but a vital instrument for the African bourgeoisie to capture because of its intervention in the economy and promotion of large-scale social trends. As Coleman notes,

> Once the government assumed complete control of the economy, it rendered itself vulnerable to blame for all grievances of an economic nature, whether real or imaginary. As marketing boards set the purchase price for primary products, and as these prices were, for sound economic reasons, usually far lower than could be secured in a free market, the thousands of peasant producers became easy targets for anti-government agitators with a nationalist bent. Government controls also affected unfavorably the activities of middlemen and traders in export products.[49]

Coleman goes on to point out that in Nigeria the most aggrieved classes were the emergent Nigerian entrepreneurs anxious to break into the export-import trade with Europe. By the end of the war, ambitious traders who had made good in the newly expanded cocoa industry as well as in other cash crops had accumulated enough capital to establish direct relations with foreign manufacturers, but were thwarted by government control of licenses and currency. By 1945 they were sufficiently politically conscious, aggrieved, and financially equipped to support and help organize any movement that would aid their "legitimate" economic aspirations and ambitions.[50]

In the French territories, the same combination occurred. Mass political manifestations against widespread abuses accompanied the increasing efforts of upper-class Africans to extend and protect their relatively privileged positions. Difficulties in tropical Africa included

[47] *Ibid.*

[48] *Ibid.,* p. 13.

[49] James Coleman, *Nigeria: Background to Nationalism* (Berkeley and Los Angeles: University of California Press, 1958), p. 252.

[50] See Coleman's account of the founding of the National Council of Nigeria and the Cameroons (NCNC), the leading Nigerian nationalist organization between 1944 and 1957 (*ibid.,* p. 255, particularly pp. 264–265). See Coleman also for a detailed case study of how the Second World War accelerated existing trends.

riots in Cameroun and Senegal, continued strike activities in urban areas, unrest among the nomads of Sudan, Niger, and Mauritania, and the desperate refusal of hundreds of thousands of Africans to pay taxes or to submit to forced labor. In 1947 an uprising in Madagascar led to one of history's bloodiest repressions: the killing of tens of thousands of Malagasians. French forces also violently suppressed nationalist demonstrations in North Africa in 1945. The independence of Tunisia enabled France to concentrate her forces on putting down the popular revolution in Algeria.[51]

The tremendous costs and ferocious intensity of colonial repression in Algeria, Indochina, and Madagascar tore French society apart, brought General de Gaulle back to power through a virtual *putsch* by the Algerian generals, and thoroughly shook French society into reconsideration of its historical attitudes toward Black Africa.

African peasants and lower-class "subjects" suffered absolutely, and also in comparison to the privilege strata, whose special status was recognized by French law. The *indigenat* consisted of those special provisions in the penal code that applied to indigenous "subjects"; Africans resented the *indigenat* not only because of its prejudicial provisions but because French administrators could take speedy, arbitrary, and punitive action involving deportation and imposition of individual or collective fines. Local French administrators presided over "native courts" that could inflict the death penalty or penal servitude for life without due process. To the end of the Second World War, forced labor caused tremendous hardships among the "subjects." During the war, entire villages were encircled and men were brutally separated from their families and taken away to build defense installations, or for other allegedly military purposes.[52] At the end of the war a precipitous decline in the prices of commodities affected all Africans, the burden falling particularly heavily on the poorest cash farmers, who could not afford any diminution of income.

Comparatively, the "citizens" and members of their class did well enough under colonialism to win the growing resentment of the "masses." After the revolution of 1848, French citizenship, conferred en masse upon the inhabitants of the four "communes" of Senegal by a revolutionary, egalitarian-minded government, raised their descendants to a special status. From that time, these "citizens," along with the chiefs, enjoyed preferential access to French education, including the most prestigious French educational institution in Black Africa, the *École Normale William Ponty*, which produced most of the African leaders of modern political movements.

After the war, the privileged class expanded to include in its lower ranks skilled laborers. The liberal *Code du Travail* passed by the French National Assembly on December 15, 1952, although stren-

---

[51] See, for example, Ruth Schacter Morgenthau, *Political Parties in French Speaking West Africa* (Oxford: Clarendon Press, 1964).

[52] Sembene Ousmane vividly depicts the despoilation of village life by colonialism in his film, *Amitai*.

uously opposed by European overseas employers, greatly improved the working conditions of certain categories of laborers, established a minimum hourly wage, included significant social security benefits, and recognized the right to form trade unions. African trade unions, an important force since before World War II, undertook major political actions, including strikes in support of the adoption and implementation of the *Code*.[53]

Lamine Gueye, the first African lawyer trained in France and the founder of the first African political party in French Africa, devoted his entire political career to raising the standard of living and improving the legal position of the African higher civil servants.[54] The law of June 30, 1950, in Africa known as the *Deuxieme Loi Lamine Gueye*, provided these privileged Africans with the same fringe benefits as their French civil servant counterparts, including family allowances and trips to France. Later, the tremendously elevated standard of living of the African civil servants, geared as it was to a metropolitan economy, created one of the heaviest burdens upon the budgets of the new African states.

These African higher civil servants constituted an international elite free to travel throughout the French empire and to take employment whenever an appropriate opening occurred within the French overseas administration.[55] These readily mobile "cultured" *evoulées* manned the transterritorial political parties that rose only in Francophone areas, in marked contrast with the country-bound parties of British Africa. Their occupations and style of life nevertheless rendered them rootless, cut off from any sustained contact with a mass base. The social distance between them and the less privileged increased constantly.[56]

To attempt to handle the rising expectations of both African members of the bourgeoisie and the African masses, the French colonial establishment first tried to buy off dissent with administrative decentralization of territorial local government. Although the "war against fascism" still continued, forty-four French colonial administrators and political and trade union leaders met at the beginning of 1944 at Brazzaville and laid down the broad lines of French postwar colonial policy. They urged that the "territories . . . gradually move towards administrative decentralization and become legal political entities"; in addition, however, they warned that "the aims of the civilizing labors of France in the colonies exclude all possibilities of the development outside of the French imperial system; the eventual for-

---

[53] Lamine Gueye reflects on the political struggles necessary to achieve these ends in his *Itineraire Africaine* (Paris: Presence Africaine, 1966).

[54] On Gueye, see Markovitz, "The Political Thought of Blaise Diagne and Lamine Gueye"; and Johnson, *The Emergence of Black Politics in Senegal.*

[55] The careers of Gabriel D'Arboussier and Felix Eboue exemplify this. See D'Arboussier's *L'Afrique vers l'unite* (Paris: Editions Saint-Paul, 1961); and Brian Weinstein, *Eboue* (New York: Oxford University Press, 1972).

[56] Morgenthau, *Political Parties in French Speaking West Africa*, p. 130.

mation, even in the distant future, of self-government in the colonies must be dismissed."[57] The recommendations of this group also included the eventual cessation of forced labor and the Africanization, without changes in salary or status, of the civil service.

Reforms resulting from the Brazzaville recommendations again raised African expectations and increased the tempo of African political activities. In 1956 a *Loi-Cadre* accepted, for the first time, the principle of autonomy as a legitimate direction for the evolution of the French colonies. The colonial regime created territorial representative assemblies along with local and regional councils. These territorial assemblies provided arenas for the continued political activity of the African bourgeoisie. They became important new devices for political socialization and for the entrapment of dissident political activity. They also brought economic benefits, including payments from the French bureaucracy for the cost of many state services, guaranteed prices and markets for many African commodities, and new investment funds for purposes of economic development.

With these new political and economic instruments, the African bourgeoisie succeeded in maintaining itself in power. During the period of transition to a universal electorate, they built a solidly entrenched position. They used patronage skillfully. They promoted loyal civil servants, built mosques for marabouts, floated loans for merchants, awarded medals to veterans, held festivals for traditional leaders, reserved seats on management boards for local dignitaries, and promised ministries to their most powerful rivals.[58]

The net result, then, of the combination of colonial concessions, potentially disruptive conditions, demands for an increased extension of its privileges by the African bourgeoisie, and the growing politicalization of the farmers and lower middle class was the creation of a vast paraphernalia of niches and crannies that guaranteed points of access to increased thousands of Africans, but *only as individuals,* or only as followers of African "notables"—*not as members of an oppressed class.* In 1958 General de Gaulle gave France's African territories the option of voting for their own independence. Under the type of "elite nationalism" that had developed over previous decades, the results were not surprising. In the French territories, with the exception of Guinea, the black bourgeoisie again triumphed, as it did in many other African countries.

Peasant–Based Nationalism

Most Black African countries did not have to go through a sustained, violent war in order to gain independence. In Ghana, Mali, Nigeria, and Tanzania the most radical nationalist leaders created a mass base.

---

[57] Quoted in *ibid.,* pp. 37–39.

[58] Morgenthau, *Political Parties in French Speaking West Africa,* p. 152.

They extended political organization into the most isolated villages and formed united fronts of multipurpose groups. Then they demanded either immediate self-government or an increase in the tempo of change towards goals already accepted, or readily agreed to, by the colonial powers. Exceptions existed to this pattern: in the Cameroons, a well-organized guerrilla movement conducted extensive military operations against the colonial power until the dissidents were violently suppressed; in Kenya, the Mau Mau uprising was instrumental in forcing a basic change in British policy towards the multiracial territories.[59] Barrington Moore has noted that where peasants have revolted, "there are indications that new and capitalist methods of pumping the economic surplus out of the peasantry had been added while the traditional ones lingered on or were even intensified."[60]

Among the Kikuyu who formed the base of the Mau Mau movement, this type of situation certainly existed: The colonial government had responded to the demands of its "kith and kin," a large European permanent settler community, similar in status to that in Algeria. Labor and land regulations restricted the most fertile lands to Europeans and effectively created a reservoir of cheap, unskilled labor.[61]

The colonial regime squeezed the Kikuyu so hard that internal differences disappeared, and this absence of internal differences facilitated political organization: "This 'leveling' effect of European settlement, i.e., the creation of a relatively uniform and impoverished peasant mass, when coupled with the intensifying struggle for scarce fertile land against the economically and politically dominant white settler elite, greatly increased the likelihood of unified political action among the Kikuyu."[62]

One of the most remarkable features of the "Land and Freedom Army" drawn up by the Kikuyu guerrillas was the absence of an "intelligentsia" or anyone educated beyond the primary school level. In 1952 and early 1953 the British arrested the entire leadership, including the middle-level ranks, of the only organized African political party in the country, the Kenya African Union. The colonial government and the European settlers tried to break the back of the African nationalist movement in this major effort. When the recognized leadership disappeared, new cadres emerged out of the "humble men and women who felt passionately for the cause they struggled for. They were the true heroes of the years of forest fighting."[63]

---

[59] On the Cameroons, see Levine, *The Cameroons;* Willard Johnson, "The Integrative Backlash of Insurgency," in *Protest and Power in Black Africa,* ed. Robert I. Rotberg and Ali A. Mazrui (New York: Oxford University Press, 1970), pp. 671–94; Weiss, *Political Protest in the Congo;* and Carl G. Rosberg, Jr. and John Nottingham, *The Myth of Mau Mau: Nationalism in Kenya* (New York: Praeger, 1966).

[60] Moore, *Social Origins of Dictatorship and Democracy,* p. 473.

[61] For a discussion of land hunger and other economic factors as causes of the rebellion, see the *East Africa Royal Commission 1953–1955 Report,* CMD 9475 (London: Her Majesty's Stationery Office, 1961). But see also Rosberg and Nottingham, *The Myth of Mau Mau.*

[62] Barnett and Njama, *Mau Mau From Within,* p. 35.

[63] *Ibid.,* p. 10.

Although the peasant revolution of the Kikuyu lasted for more than three years, from 1953 to 1956, it was ultimately defeated militarily, like the revolution in Algeria. But as in the case of Algeria, military defeat heralded political victory: the official end of the state of emergency in January, 1960 coincided with British agreement to an African majority in the Kenya Legislative Council and to eventual independence for Kenya under African rule, which came on December 12, 1963. After independence, a new Kenya nationalism had to bring together the Kikuyu and many other ethnic groups in a modern nation-state. However, the new nationalism in Kenya overcame only partly the tribal divisions that British administrative policy had exacerbated. After independence, although the new African government did achieve stability and the Africanization of the bureaucracy, the bourgeoisie was able to reassert its significance and position of preeminence, and the peasant base of the original revolutionary movement disintegrated.

In Portuguese Guinea, Amilcar Cabral attempted to create not only the type of political organization, but also the type of social organization, that would ultimately enable guerrillas to become responsible officials. He aimed at meeting the material needs of the moment as well as awakening a new psychological consciousness. Cabral wrote:

> In order to further the important task of consolidating independence and insuring progress, the PAIGC is organizing an extensive program for the training of cadres (administration, production, health, tourism, etc.) and is putting it into effect as far as circumstances permit. It is eager to avail itself of every possible opportunity to proceed as rapidly as possible with the training of a large body of personnel, particularly at the intermediate level, so that there will be African civil servants ready to go into action immediately following liberation.[64]

Cabral recognized the existence of a "new class" and pondered the practicality of demanding that a group commit "class suicide." Cabral argued that this was possible. The Guinean bourgeoisie held a vanguard role in the creation of a more humane community. A common interest in membership as "persons" in a nonexploitative society would bind them together with all the other people. An increasingly politically aware mass following would in any event hold them responsible for their actions. The sons of the bourgeoisie may indeed be willing, therefore, to slough off their privileges.

Significantly, Cabral considered his greatest victories in the fight for the liberation of the people of Guinea not military defeats of Portuguese armies or squads, but rather the increased political awareness of the African masses, "who had never before been permitted to exercise those essential functions of man—political thought and action."

[64] Amilcar Cabral, *Revolution in Guinea* (London: Monthly Review Press, 1969), p. 44. Cf. Cabral's *Return to the Source, Selected Speeches* (New York: Monthly Review Press, 1973). A fine study of Cabral's thoughts and developments in Guinea is Lars Rudebeck, *Guinea-Bissau: A Study of Political Mobilization* (Uppsala: Scandinavian Institute of African Studies, 1974).

Like Fanon, Cabral felt that the greatest virtue of the guerrilla struggle was the intensification of unity and the overcoming of differences of long duration among ethnic groups. Also like Fanon, Cabral felt that the anticolonialist movement created a new sense of self and civic pride:

> Gradually overcoming the complexes engendered by colonial exploitation, it has enabled the 'marginal' human beings who are the product of colonialism to recover their personality as Africans. It has reawakened among the Africans of Guinea in general a feeling of confidence in their future.[65]

The murder of Cabral in early 1972 did not prevent the arrival of independence. The PAIGC declared the existence of the Republic of Guinea-Bissau on September 24, 1973. Eighty-one nations—sadly, the United States not among them—immediately granted recognition.[66]

With the assumption of power, a new page turns in the history of African nationalism. Every one of the nationalist movements in each of the territories had internal conflicts. As control over the formal institutions of political power increased, so did the intensities of the rifts between various factions representing diverse social classes and ethnic groups. Yet, hopefully, out of the sustained conflict of all those bloody years may come more responsive and socially effective governments. The important question to ask of postindependence Africa is whether Cabral's goals will be achieved, or whether bloody encounters such as Biafra and the domination of an organizational bourgeoisie will become routine. These problems were especially acute in the areas of the most prolonged fighting in Africa, but they faced all African governments in their postindependence efforts to consolidate power and to put the new institutions of self-rule on a firm footing.

[65] Cabral, *Revolution in Guinea*, p. 45.
[66] See the *New York Times*, January 22, 1972, p. 1 for a report of Cabral's association. For a discussion of the report and the impact of the death of Cabral, see John Marcum, "Amilcar Cabral: The Meaning of an Assassination," *Africa Report*, March-April, 1973, pp. 21–23; and, in the same issue, Justin Mendy, "The Struggle Goes On." Cf. George M. Houser, "Backing Guinea-Bissau," *New York Times*, April 6, 1974, editorial page.

Chapter VI

THE CONSOLIDATION OF POWER: *Rise of the Organizational Bourgeoisie*

Describing the impact of the French Revolution, de Tocqueville noted that although "no nation had ever before embarked on so resolute an attempt as that of the French in 1789 to break with the past, to make, as it were, a schism in their lifeline and to create an unbridgeable gulf between all that they had hitherto been and all that they now aspired to be," he was convinced that, unknowingly, they took over from the old regime "not only most of its customs, conventions and modes of thought, but even those very ideas which prompted our revolutionaries to destroy it; that, in fact, although nothing was further from their intentions, they used the debris of their old order for building up the new." This process involved two distinct phases: "one in which the sole aim of the French nation seemed to be to make a clean sweep of the past; and a second, in which attempts were made to salvage fragments from the wreckage of the old order."[1]

A similar process seems to have occurred in the establishment of the new orders in African countries after independence. Even where mass revolutionary nationalist movements did occur, they too frequently abandoned their euphoric aspirations to make a clean sweep of the past in their effort to create systems of state institutions: they sought above all to consolidate and take a firm grip on power. The new ruling classes either jumped to create much more powerful mechanisms of coercion than those of their colonial predecessors, or they found themselves quickly overthrown by other African challengers. These rivals of similar social origin, equally anxious to grasp power, threatened to be still more resourceful in the manipulation of the new techniques of mass persuasion, organization, the military arts, and bureaucratic control.[2]

Before coming to power, the African "organizational bourgeoisie" committed itself to the general principles of social justice,

[1] Alexis De Tocqueville, *The Old Regime and the French Revolution* (New York: Doubleday, Anchor Books, 1955), pp. vii, viii.

[2] See, for example, Obaro Ikime, ed., *Leadership in 19th Century Africa: Essays from Tarikh* (London: Longman, 1974), particularly pp. 103–76. Cf. Jean-Pierre N'Diaye, *Elites Africaines et culture Occidentale: assimilation ou resistance?* (Paris: Presence Africaine, 1969).

constantly lambasting the "privileges" of the established order. Basing itself on an essentially egalitarian and populist set of premises, it demanded a more perfect social organization, freedom based upon material equality, and a selfless community of citizens. But once this group gained power, its thirst for social justice weakened, as compromise followed compromise, and the contrast between its concepts and those of the old colonial elite dimmed. In many countries, disillusionment with this class became widespread. The hero of the Ghanaian writer Ama Ata Aidoo's short story "For Whom Things Did Not Change" states, "When the white people were here, and they were our masters, it was only understandable that they should have electric lights and water closets and give us, the boys, latrine pails and kerosine lamps. But now we are independent they are going to make this house new. My own people will give me a closet and an electric light."[3] After independence, when African "big men" are in charge and there are no electric lights and no lavatory, the hero discovers, "I did not know I wanted these things so much until I knew I was not going to get them. They have taken the old pail and given me a new one. My own people who are big men do not think I should use these good things they use. Something went out of me then which has not returned since. I do not understand why I was so pained and angry, but I was."[4] Wole Soyinka laments, "We were sent the wrong people. We asked for statesmen and we were sent executioners."[6]

In one of the strongest denunciations of these new rulers, Ayi Kwei Armah demands,

> How long will Africa be cursed with its leaders? There were men dying from the loss of hope, and others were finding gaudy ways to enjoy power they did not have. We were ready here for big and beautiful things, but what we had was our own black men hugging new paunches scrambling to ask the white man to welcome them onto our backs. These men who were to lead us out of our despair, they came like men already grown fat and cynical with the eating of centuries of power they had never struggled for, old before they had even been born into power, and ready only for the grave.[5]

Armah is particularly cynical of the ideologues, who preached socialism while practicing capitalism: "The man when he shook hands was again amazed at the flabby softness of the hand. Ideological hands, the hands of revolutionaries leading their people into new sacrifices, should these hands not have become even tougher than they were when their owner was hauling loads along the wharf?"[7]

Cabral tells us that

---

[3] Ama Ata Aidoo, *No Sweetness Here* (Garden City, N.Y.: Doubleday, Anchor Books, 1972), p. 32.
[4] *Ibid.*, p. 33.
[5] Wole Soyinka, *A Dance of the Forests* (London: Oxford University Press, 1963), p. 30.
[6] Ayi Kwei Armah, *The Beautiful Ones Are Not Yet Born* (New York: Collier, 1969), p. 79.
[7] *Ibid.*, pp. 129–30.

in spite of their armored forces, the imperialists cannot do without traitors; traditional chiefs and bandits in the times of slavery and of the wars of colonial conquest, gendarmes, various agents and mercenary soldiers during the golden age of colonialism, self-styled heads of state and ministers in the present time of neo-colonialism. The enemies of the African peoples are powerful and cunning and can always count on a few faithful lackeys in our country since quislings are not a European privilege.[8]

This is not to say, however, that the new African rulers are either entirely corrupt or homogeneous. Cabral divides what he calls the "petty bourgeoisie" into three subgroups in terms of their relationship to the "national liberation struggle." If part of the petty bourgeoisie became compromised with colonialism, another part became revolutionary and increasingly nationalist. In between are those who have not been able to make up their minds to choose finally between the Portuguese and the national liberation struggle. This revolutionary bourgeoisie, according to Cabral, is:

> honest, i.e., in spite of all the hostile conditions, it remains identified with the fundamental interest of the popular masses. To do this it may have to commit suicide, but it will not lose; by sacrificing itself it can reincarnate itself, but in the condition of workers or peasants. . . . What I mean by honest, in a political context, is total commitment and total identification with the toiling masses.[9]

During the time of the greatest struggle with the Portuguese colonial establishment, Cabral stated, "Our problem is to see who is capable of taking control of the state apparatus when the colonial power is destroyed."[10] Proceeding then to an analysis of the class structure of the Guinean population, Cabral rejects the possibility of the peasantry or working class coming to rule. He concludes that the "African petite bourgeoisie" is the only stratum capable of controlling, or even utilizing, the institutions of rule that the colonial state had created:

> In Guinea the peasants cannot read or write, they have almost no relations with the colonial forces during the colonial period except for paying taxes, which is done indirectly. The working class hardly exists as a defined class, it is just an embryo. There is no economically viable bourgeoisie because imperialism prevented its being created. What there is is a stratum of people in the service of imperialism who have learned how to manipulate the apparatus of the state—the African petite bourgeoisie.[11]

---

[8] Amilcar Cabral, *Revolution in Guinea*, p. 16.

[9] *Ibid.*, p. 72.

[10] *Ibid.*, p. 68.

[11] *Ibid.*, p. 69. Other examples of class analysis may be found in: Charles Elliott, *Patterns of Poverty in the Third World* (New York: Praeger, 1975), especially pp. 17–59 and 84–144; Sylvia Brandel-Syrier, *Reeftown Elite: Social Mobility in a Black African Community in the Johannesberg Reef* (New York: Africana Publishing, 1971); Michael A. Cohen, *Urban Policy and Political Conflict in Africa: A Study of the*

The Legacy of Colonialism

Cabral worried that the bourgeoisies might find colonialism so comfortable that they might never take their countries to independence. He was also concerned with the way in which they guided the people and conducted their revolutionary activities.

Paulo Friere, a Brazilian educator and nationalist, has argued that "it is necessary to trust in the oppressed and their ability to reason . . . not even the best intended leadership can bestow independence as a gift. The liberation of the oppressed is the liberation of men not things."[12] Friere worried constantly that the "downtrodden," conditioned by the values of the dominant culture, would simply reproduce patterns of domination should they come to power:

> Almost always during the initial stage of the struggle, the oppressed, instead of striving for liberation, tend themselves to become oppressors of "sub-oppressors." The very structure of their thought has been conditioned by the contradictions of the concrete, existential situation by which they were shaped. Their ideal is to be men; but for them, to be men is to be oppressors. . . . Their vision of a new man is individualistic. . . . It is not to become free men that they want agrarian reform, but in order to acquire land and thus become land owners—or more concisely, bosses over other workers.[13]

Along similar lines, Julius Nyerere warns the nationalist leadership not to think itself so far above the masses that it need not listen to the "uneducated," and he warns the uneducated that if they are fearful of asserting themselves on the grounds that their minds are empty, they will find the same condition true of their pockets:

Ivory Coast (Chicago: University of Chicago Press, 1974), especially pp. 430–35. See also B. Ameillon, *La Guinée, bilan d'une indépendance* (Paris: Maspero, 1964). In an extremely bitter attack against the alleged perversion of the leadership's original ideals of socialism, Ameillon introduces the concept of "la rente racial," absorbed originally by the European establishment and then taken over and used for their own benefit by the members of the bureaucratic bourgeoisie.

   Cf. John J. Johnson's discussion of the rise of the new classes in Latin America. As late as 1958, Johnson still had to *argue* not only that the urban middle groups were vitally important but that they existed. (*Political Change in Latin America: The Emergence of the Middle Sectors* [Stanford, Calif.: Stanford University Press, 1958]). Johnson's discussion of the changing character and social composition of the urban middle group in Latin America over time is particularly valuable. Interesting case studies can be found in Seymour Martin Lipset and Aldo Solari, eds., *Elites in Latin America* (New York: Oxford University Press, 1967). See also the analysis of class structure in Ladislav Holy, *Social Stratification in Tribal Africa* (Prague: Acadamia, 1968); Majmout Diop, *Contribution a l'étude des problemes politiques en Afrique Noire* (Paris: Presence Africaine, 1958); and B. Delbard, *Les dynamismes sociaux au Senegal: les processus de formation de classes sociales dans un état d'Afrique de l'Ouest* (Dakar: Institut de Science Economique Appliqué, 1966).

[12] Paulo Friere, *Pedagogy of the Oppressed* (New York: Herder & Herder, 1968), p. 53.

[13] *Ibid.*, pp. 29–30. Because Western liberalism has ranked "individualism" among its most highly prized values, the attack by African and other third world leaders has been difficult to comprehend and bitterly resented. See, for instance, the onslaught by Frantz Fanon in his *Wretched of the Earth* (New York: Grove Press, 1968); C. B. Macpherson, in his *The Political Theory of Possessive Individualism* (New York: Oxford University Press, 1962), shows how in the West, individualism was always associated with competitive capitalism. Pierre Teilhard de Chardin distinguishes between the "individual" as an isolated, self-seeking atom and "the person" who needs the community for his complete self-realization, in *The Phenomenon of Man* (New York: Harper & Row, 1961). Richard Sennett and Jonathan Cobb, in *The Hidden Injuries of Class* (New York: Vintage, 1973), reveal the persistence of "conflicts in personality developed under the guise of individualism."

If we do not abolish the two classes of masters and servants from our society, clever people will emerge from among us to take the place of the Europeans, Indians and Arabs. These clever people will continue to exploit our fear for their own benefit. . . . The work of removing colonialism will be used to maintain other cleverer Africans capable of oppressing the people more than the colonialists. . . . You will even lose your property; it will be taken by those who are clever among you. Suddenly you will discover that your area commissioner has a farm of 3,000 acres. You will be surprised to hear that even Julius has a 3,000 acre farm. . . . Yesterday we were all poor. . . . I agree that Tanzania is a large country with a small population. But is it true that our country is big enough for each of us to own 3,000 acres of land? The answer is no.[14]

Andrew MacGuire, in his analysis of political development in Tanzania, noted that "the new administrators are African rather than European and they are representatives of the same TANU [the Tanzania African National Union] which had widespread popular support during the struggle for independence. Yet, in important respects, the current governing elite are to the locality and people they serve very much as were the colonial administrators who preceded them."[15] And Ruth First argues that "if there was any training and adaptation before independence it was a schooling in the bureaucratic toils of colonial government, a preparation not for independence, but against it."[16] First maintains that this could not be otherwise because colonialism, based as it was on authoritarian command, was incompatible with any preparation for self-government.

Kwame Nkrumah describes how the significance, even the existence, of this organizational bourgeoisie in Africa at first was overlooked because the preeminence of race made the face of power of the colonial regime more visible and diverted attention away from the essentially economic and political base of the overlords:

In this colonialist situation, African workers regarded the colonialist, foreign firms and foreign planters, as the exploiters. Thus their class struggle became in the first instance anti-imperialist, and not directed against the indigenous bourgeoisie. It is this which has been responsible in some degree for the relatively slow awakening of the African worker and peasant to the existence of their true class enemy—the indigenous bourgeoisie.[17]

Nkrumah applied the same line of analysis to the concept of the third world, alleging that race too frequently clouded over matters that required class analysis, and that simply having been a colony was not

---

[14] Julius Nyerere, *Uhuru na Ujamaa: Freedom and Socialism, A Selection from Writings and Speeches, 1965–1967* (Dar es Salaam: Oxford University Press, 1968), pp. 140–41.

[15] G. Andrew Maguire, *Toward "Uhuru" in Tanzania* (Cambridge: Cambridge University Press, 1969), p. 363.

[16] Ruth First, *Power in Africa* (New York: Pantheon, 1970), p. 40. Cf. David Hapgood, *Africa: From Independence to Tomorrow* (New York: Atheneum, 1965).

[17] Kwame Nkrumah, *Class Struggle in Africa* (New York: International Publishers, 1970), p. 15.

sufficient ground to determine a country's political position or ideological direction:

> The developing world is not a homogenous block opposed to imperialism. The concept of the "Third World" is illusory. At present, parts of it lie under imperialist domination. The struggle against imperialism takes place both within and outside the imperialist world. It is a struggle between socialism and capitalism, not between a so-called "Third World" and imperialism. Class struggle is fundamental in its analysis.[18]

That Nkrumah's ideas evolved over time and that he changed his emphasis on the relative role of class and other factors in the African struggle for independence should also be noted.

One final contribution of colonialism to the development of organizational bourgeoisies came, paradoxically, from the metropolitan establishment's belated efforts, as independence neared, to Africanize the bureaucracy. "Africanization," in the sense of Africans controlling their own political and administrative structures, must be distinguished from the "Africanization" that took place within the framework of continued overseas dominance. The intent of the latter program was to perpetuate an overseas perspective on problems of government and development. Responding primarily to the pressures from elements of the African organizational bourgeoisie, and hoping to maintain stability and to create bonds that would endure after formal independence, the colonial regime willingly continued its policy of admitting an infinitesimal portion of Africans into a privileged stratum despite the impact this would have on the society as a whole. According to Giovanni Arrighi, "Africanization, because of the principle of equal pay for equal work—brings about a huge gap between the incomes of high level manpower (the African elite and sub-elite), and the incomes not only of unskilled labor but also of semi-skilled and skilled labor."[19] Arrighi goes on to point out that as the demands of civil servants escalate because of their political clout, government officials are reluctant to thwart their rising expectations, even though not doing so creates an even larger gap between a class that is privileged to begin with and the mass of the population.[20]

Towards a Definition of the Organizational Bourgeoisie

Abdoulaye Ly, one of the first African nationalists to warn against African "privileges," declared, "The question of the hour is to know for the

---

[18] *Ibid.*, p. 83.

[19] Giovanni Arrighi, "International Corporations, Labor Aristocracies and Economic Development in Tropical Africa," in *Imperialism and Underdevelopment: A Reader,* ed. Robert I. Rhodes (New York: Monthly Review Press, 1970), p. 236.

[20] *Ibid.*, p. 233. Cf. Giovanni Arrighi and John Saul, *Essays in the Political Economy of Africa* (New York: Monthly Review Press, 1973). Wallace S. Sayre and Herbert Kaufman, in *Governing New York City: Politics in the Metropolis* (New York: Norton, 1965)—written prior to Abraham Beame's adminis-

benefit of which social strata, however united in the anti-imperialist battle, will the apparatus of the state be transformed. . . . A real peril exists: the usurpation of the apparatus of the indigenous state by reactionary social classes who had previously participated in the exploitation of the peasant masses. . . ."[21] In one of his last books, written after his overthrow from power, Kwame Nkrumah stated:

> For too long social and political commentators have talked and written as though Africa lies outside the mainstream of world historical development. . . . Class divisions in modern African society became blurred to some extent during the pre-independence period when it seemed there was national unity and all classes joined forces to eject the colonial power. This led some to proclaim that there were no class divisions in Africa, and that the communalism and egalitarianism of traditional African society made any notion of a class struggle out of the question. But the exposure of this fallacy followed quickly after independence, when class cleavages which had been temporarily submerged in the struggle to win political freedom reappeared, often with increased intensity.[22]

In one of the toughest attacks ever made against this class, Nkrumah invited a comparison to the situation in southern Africa by arguing, "Africa has in fact in its midst a hard core of bourgeoisie who are analogous to colonialists and settlers in that they live in positions of privilege—a small, selfish, money-minded, reactionary minority among vast masses of exploited and oppressed people."[23] According to a Western commentator,

> everywhere . . . African development has been held to ransom by the emergence of a new, privileged, African class. It grows through politics, under party systems, under military governments, from the ranks of business, and from the corporate elites that run the state, the army and the civil service. In some countries, its growth is virtually free. . . . In other countries, policy is opposed to its very existence, but it persists all the same.[24]

What are the characteristics of this organizational bourgeoisie? Its members are distinguishable by their strategic locations in society, from which they make major decisions that affect the life chances of thousands of their compatriots; they are located in agencies that enable them to derive their livelihood from the "national income," from the productive efforts of others; they are distinguishable by their general health, height,

---

tration—argued that it was impossible for any city government, regardless of its party label, to turn down wage-increase demands by city employee unions because of the lack of any effective political payoff in so doing, compared with the enormous organized political dangers. Under what circumstances could there be a "payoff" in the refusing of wage increases in poor countries—under a more stringent socialism? Under fascism?

[21] Abdoulaye Ly, *L'etat et la production paysanne* (Paris: Presence Africaine, 1958), pp. 76–77 (my translation).

[22] Nkrumah, *Class Struggle in Africa*, pp. 16–17.

[23] *Ibid.*, p. 12.

[24] First, *Power in Africa*, p. 10.

and weight, the chances of survival of their children, their manner of speech, their leisure activities, their eating habits—the food they consume as well as the manner of its consumption—their means of transportation, the games they play, the conversation of their wives, the work habits and values they attempt to inculcate in their children—every aspect of their existence.[25]

The organizational bourgeoisie are the first beneficiaries of economic growth. Supplementing and surpassing the prerogatives of the traditional rulers, they enjoy the luxuries of "Western civilization." In Senegal, for example, the winds of *hivernage* had always blown the fine red dust into the cavities of kitchen, bed, home, and person, but it had always done so democratically. Now that window glass, hardwood doors, air conditioners and insulation protect the houses of the privileged, the very dirt of the earth irritates as it never has before.[26] The contrast between the living circumstances of the organizational bourgeoisie and those of their fellow "citizens" creates, in Disraeli's sense, "two nations" in every African country.

Barbara Lloyd has presented us with one of the best descriptions of the development of class identification in her account of the Yoruba. Unlike the traditional Yoruba family, which groups together fathers, sons, wives, and children in a lineage-based compound, "the elite nuclear family" she tells us, "lives in employer-provided quarters isolated from relatives, or in modern houses in the newer residential parts of Ibadan." Not only are children of "elite" parents isolated from their "common" relatives, but "parents take pains to see that their children play only with other children from 'good homes,' and they point out that children learn bad habits easily by imitation. Thus, naughty, stubborn, rude, obscene and dirty children must be avoided." In a traditional compound, all the children play together and are expected to get along well with one another: "A mother who tried to choose her child's companions would be considered unsociable and rude." Whereas the traditional child is seldom alone and is constantly preoccupied by relatives and neighbors, "the elite child . . . is actively encouraged by his parents to learn to play by himself. Elite mothers believe solitary play gives a child time to think, to learn skills such as drawing or painting, and perhaps, most importantly, from a mother's point of view it teaches him not to fret when there is no one about who can play with him." And whereas uneducated mothers "have difficulty verbalizing their educational and

---

[25] Peter Lloyd uses Western education and wealth as criteria in defining "the African elite" in his (ed.) *The New Elites of Tropical Africa* (London: Oxford University Press, 1966), pp. 2–3, and 130. See also Lloyd's *Classes, Crises and Coups* (London: MacGibbon & Kee, 1971). For glaring instances of inequalities in wealth and ownership, see First, *Power in Africa*, pp. 98–99; the divisions studied by Irma Adelman and Cynthia Taft Morris, *Economic Growth and Social Equity in Developing Countries* (Stanford, Calif.: Stanford University Press, 1973); and Rene Dumont, *False Start in Africa*, 2nd rev. ed., trans. P. N. Oh (New York: Praeger, 1969). See also Donald N. Levine, "Class Consciousness and Class Solidarity in the New Ethiopian Elites," in *The New Elites of Tropical Africa*, ed. Lloyd, p. 315; and the definition of elites in F. H. Agblemaghon, "Masses et elites en Afrique Noire: le cas du Togo," in *Ibid.*, p. 125. Cf. International Bank for Reconstruction and Development, *Senegal: Tradition, Diversification and Economic Development* (Washington, D.C., 1974), p. xiii.

[26] Cf. M. B. Lukhero, "Social Characteristics of an Emerging Elite in Harare," in *The New Elites of Tropical Africa*, ed. Lloyd, p. 133.

occupational aspirations for their children, and are ignorant of the expanding educational opportunities available in Nigeria," elite mothers not only have a very precise image of their children's entire futures in mind, but know precisely what is necessary for their children's upbringing as well as the procedural steps necessary for the accomplishments of their objectives.[27]

Grindal tells us how in northern Ghana the Sisla inculcate attitudes of hard work and initiative through a "differential upbringing and training of the illiterate."

> Most parents, whether culturated or unculturated, admit that they raise their illiterate and literate sons differently. While the discipline in training the school boy is left largely to his teachers, that of the illiterate remains in the hands of his father or fathers. He is expected to do farm work and no allowances are made for the fact that his literate brother does not have to engage in manual labor. The illiterate son is usually closer to his father than his educated brother, and if his father is an artisan, he often works closely with him and thereby learns a trade.[28]

The "style" of the organizational bourgeoisie, from the brands of cigarettes they smoke to the child-rearing practices they follow, comes from abroad. Seydou Badian denounces "our cadres" who are "more integrated in the economy of our former metropoles than in those of their own countries. Their needs, the habits that they acquired, their taste — all these constitute a weight that crushes our states. To bring all to a certain level might be theoretically easy, but it doesn't happen by a wave of a magic wand. . . ."[29] But more disturbing than the style of life and "foreign" alignments that separate the organizational bourgeoisie from the mass of the population is the crushing burden of this bourgeoisie upon the nations' economies, a burden that has weighed ever more heavily.

Who Gets What: Government Expenditures on the New Class

The steady growth of the "public sector," the continual expansion of government expenditures for administration, and the rising costs of maintaining political officialdom at ever higher levels of "comfortable" living are among the most striking phenomena of the postindepen-

---

[27] Barbara Lloyd, "Education and Family Life in the Development of Class Identification Among the Yoruba," in *The New Elites of Tropical Africa*, ed. Lloyd, pp. 165–72. Cf. John C. Caldwell, *Population Growth and Family Change in Africa: The New Urban Elite in Ghana* (New York: Humanities Press, 1968); Christine Oppong, *Marriage Among a Matrilineal Elite: A Family Study of Ghanaian Senior Civil Servants* (London: Cambridge University Press, 1974); Marion Kilson, *African Urban Kinsmen: The Ga of Central Accra* (New York: St. Martin's, 1974); and Elliot P. Skinner, *African Urban Life: The Transformation of Ouagadougou* (Princeton, N.J.: Princeton University Press, 1974). All provide evidence of class-related differences in life style.

[28] Bruce T. Grindal, *Growing Up in Two Worlds: Education and Transition Among the Sisla of Northern Ghana* (New York: Holt, Rinehart & Winston, 1972), p. 96.

[29] Seydou Badian, *Les dirigeants d'Afrique Noire face a leur peuple* (Paris: Francois Maspero, 1965), p. 89 (my translation).

dence period. In a searching look at the budgets of new states, Gerard Chaliand reveals that almost half (47.2 percent) of Senegal's budget for 1964–1965 was devoted to administrative salaries; not a single dollar was spent on direct investment. The administration in the Cameroons absorbed eighteen times as much money as capital expenditure. The civil service in the Central African Republic absorbed 81 percent of the budget. In Congo-Brazzaville, the almost 11,000 state employees among the population of 826,000 received 62 percent of the budget. In the Ivory Coast in 1964, 15,000 civil servants, less than 0.5 percent of the total population, absorbed 58 percent of the national budget. Dahomey, which spent 64.9 percent of its budget on civil service salaries, holds the record. Between 1959 and 1962, administrative costs rose 80 percent in Guinea, 60 percent in Mali, and a comparable percentage in Ghana.[30] In December, 1974, Nigeria increased the wages of its civil servants by as much as 133 percent in order "to combat the effects of inflation."[31]

First reveals that in one year, six times as much was spent in importing alcoholic beverages as in importing fertilizer in the fourteen former French colonies; perfume and cosmetics absorbed half as much as machine tools; and five times as much was spent on importing private cars as on importing agricultural equipment. She noted that "the resources of the new states were being devoured by a tiny group whose demands distorted the budgets and the economies of the states they governed. . . . the cost of African presidential and ministerial establishments was probably higher, in relation to national income, than the cost to France of the Court of Louis XVI in 1788."[32]

Who are the members of this tiny privileged class? In this book, I use the term *organizational bourgeoisie* to refer to a combined ruling group consisting of the top political leaders and bureaucrats, the traditional rulers and their descendants, and the leading members of the liberal professions and the rising business bourgeoisie. Top members of the military and police forces are also part of this bureaucratic bourgeoisie. Over time, leading elements in this coalition change.[33] Al-

[30] See Gerard Chaliand, *Armed Struggle in Africa* (New York: Monthly Review Press, 1969). Braudel tells us that from the fifth millennium B.C. and the arrival of cultivated cereals, history becomes divided into "two opposing species of humanity: the rare meat-eaters and the innumerable people who fed on bread, gruel, roots and cooked tubers. In China in the second millennium 'the administrators of the great provinces were termed . . . meat-eaters.' In ancient Greece it was said that 'the eaters of barley gruel have no desire to make war.' " (*Capitalism and Material Life, 1400–1800* [New York: Harper & Row, 1973], p. 68).

[31] *New York Times*, December 29, 1974.

[32] First, *Power in Africa*, p. 110. See also Dumont, *False Start in Africa;* Coumba M'Doffene Diouf et al., *La question des salaires au Senegal* (Dakar: Afrique documents, 1965); and Martin Staniland, "Frantz Fanon and the African Political Class," *African Affairs*, 68, no. 270 (January 1969), 4–25.

[33] If it is true (1) that in broad outline the stratification systems of contemporary industrial societies are similar (see, for example, Joseph Kahl, ed., *Comparative Perspectives in Stratification* [Boston, Little, Brown, 1968], p. ix; and S. M. Lipset and Rhinehard Bendix, *Social Mobility in Industrial Society* [Berkeley and Los Angeles: University of California Press, 1959], pp. 11–13); and (2) that in new African countries a predominant role is taken by political leaders and members of the organizational bourgeoisie, then an important generalization that appears to fit the African case is that by Robert

though the bureaucratic and political components have dominated until now, they have had to seek a social base. Increasingly in West African countries, as in independent countries everywhere on the continent, a developing commercial and business class provides that base.

Arthur Lewis has stated that "West Africa is simply not a class society on Marxist lines. In a class society political power resides in a few people who own the instruments of production."[34] Lewis is correct to the extent that in Africa political power does not reside simply in "a few people who own the instruments of production." Yet he errs grievously in finding the key to the political problems of the new African states in the "personalities" of their leaders. The organizational bourgeoisie is not simply a collection of individuals. Its members derive their power from organization. They are located at pivotal points of control in those overarching systems of political and economic power analyzed by Hobbes, Marx, and Weber—the nation-state and capitalism. These systems incorporate the most diverse, parochial, and isolated elements in rationalizing organizations that stop only tangentially at the national boundaries.

The Yugoslavian philosopher and nationalist political leader Milovan Djilas originated the term "new class" to describe a "historically unique" ruling class that gained its power from its relationship to the political apparatus, in contrast with the Marxian claim that power was rooted in the relationship of classes to the means of production: Marx and Engels maintained that government constituted part of "superstructure." Considering the situation of a poor country attempting to industrialize after a social and political revolution, Djilas argues,

> It is the bureaucracy which formally uses, administers, and controls both nationalized and socialized property, as well as the entire life of society. . . . Ownership is nothing other than the right of profit and control. If one defines class benefits by this right, the communist states have seen, in the final analysis, the origin of a new form of ownership or of a new ruling and exploiting class.[35]

However, the organizational bourgeoisie is more than a "new class" in Djilas's sense, more than either a "bureaucratic" or "state" bourgeoisie because it includes elements of private business as well as managers of

---

Presthus: "In communities with limited leadership and economic resources the power structure will be more likely to be dominated by political leaders, whereas in those with more fulsome internal resources it will probably be dominated by economic leaders" (*Men at the Top: A Study in Community Power* [New York: Oxford University Press, 1964], pp. 410–11). (Cf. a contrary view in Anthony Giddens, *The Class Structure of Advanced Societies* [New York: Harper & Row, Torchbooks ed. 1975], p. 181.) Over the long run, that is to say, economic leaders will become more powerful insofar as their basis of resources is more stable and enduring and insofar as those that control the political apparatus must eventually seek sustenance in the economic base of the society.

[34] W. Arthur Lewis, *Politics in West Africa* (New York: Oxford University Press, 1966), pp. 16–17.

[35] Milovan Djilas, *The New Class* (New York: Praeger, 1957), p. 35. See also the critique of Djilas by Nico Poulantzas, *Political Power and Social Classes* (London: Sheed & Ward, 1973).

public enterprises and top state officials. The organizational bourgeoisie is also more than a "managerial bourgeoisie"[36] or "elite" because they not only manage, they exploit: they are willing to innovate
in their own interest, they increasingly *do* create wealth-producing enterprises, and they are as hungry as any previous ascending class.

The organizational bourgeoisie are the major decision makers —
those whose impact is nation-wide. Not all businessmen, for example,
would be members of the national business bourgeoisie. Other elements of the organizational bourgeoisie — high government, military,
and administrative officials — are similarly located in offices of control
or ownership of either the means of production, distribution, and exchange or of the mechanisms of the state and bureaucracy. Relations
between these elements of the organizational bourgeoisie change.
Control over the state budget, for example, can be used to stimulate
the growth of business, which can then create a clientele with roots so
strong that "the state bourgeoisie" finds itself more dependent on an
increasingly powerful social class.

To draw sharp distinctions among the administrative bourgeoisie, the politicians, and the businessmen can be misleading because power and class are not necessarily matters of individuals, but
of families. The same men can play many roles and take part in politics, administration, and commerce. Their brothers, cousins, fathers,
and sons can do the same. The result is a web of relations that brings
the holders of power into overlapping and sustained contact. How
tight the web, how much room for new strands, and how much flexibility will vary from country to country and from time to time.

Thinking in terms of family units also better enables us to picture the continuities between traditional leaders and their offspring.
Descendants of the ancient ruling classes do not have to possess power
in the same *form* as their elders in order to make crucial decisions.
Some members of the traditional ruling families may continue to bear
ancient titles and positions, but other presumptive heirs of power will
have availed themselves of the special opportunities of their traditional positions by catapulting themselves into the points of control
over the new institutions. Using their connections, accumulated
wealth, and extraordinary access to "Western" education and technological and "scientific" training, they enter the ranks of the new African prime ministers, capitalists, colonels, and permanent secretaries.

Can this African organizational bourgeoisie be independent? Will
it be simply the tool of imperial interests? The degree of autonomy
from external manipulation by foreign governments and multinational corporations matters enormously. But we should also empha-

---

[36] Richard Sklar uses the term "managerial bourgeoisie" rather than "entrepreneurial bourgeoisie"
because he maintains that in "newly developing countries" this class manages the production and
distribution of wealth rather than creating new wealth-producing enterprises (*Corporate Power in an
African State: The Political Impact of Multinational Mining Companies in Zambia* [Berkeley and Los Angeles: University of California Press, 1975], p. 199).

size that a "true" nationalist bourgeoisie as well as a comprador class will have enormous power over the life chances of their fellow citizens in any event, and may be the instrument of their despair. In reality, a dichotomy between a comprador class and a national bourgeoisie has not developed in Africa. The same businessman may play multiple roles or different roles over time. The manager trained by Lever Brothers starts his own canning corporation. The independent printer gladly prints textbooks as well as order forms for the United African Company.

Indigenous business and international business may competitively pressure "independent" African governments. The success of each force will vary over time and from country to country. Policy outcomes will depend on the commodities produced, the quality of leadership, the cohesiveness and resources of the organizations involved, and the nature of the political systems, including their ideological commitments.

The organizational bourgeoisie, therefore, coheres around certain fundamentals: the nation-state and capitalism, individual gain and profit. The organizational bourgeoisie acts as a class in pursuit of an interest that is in conflict with the interest of other classes.

A wide variety of arguments has been marshaled to disprove the significance of class in both traditional and modern African society.[37] Among the arguments advanced concerning modern societies are the following:

1) Land rights are still held predominantly by villages and descent groups and this minimizes the development of rural stratification.

2) Wage earners still have roots in the rural areas and can return there at will to find sustenance. Thus, they are neither bourgeoisie nor proletariat in the strict sense of these words.

3) Classes, in the sense of exploitative conflict groups, would exist only if it could be demonstrated that the privileged position of the ruling class retarded a rise in the standard of living of the masses or impeded their development.

4) Classes tend to be hereditary groups; but in Africa "the elite is characterized by the number of its members who have come from humble homes."[38] Moreover "the network of kinship ties, involving obligations towards members of the extended family at all social levels, prevents the formation of rigid class barriers."[39]

5) Class consciousness is minimal or nonexistent, since movement from the underprivileged to the privileged class is easy and frequent.

6) Because the attainment of independence has been so recent,

---

[37] For a discussion of class in traditional society, see Chapter IV.

[38] Lloyd, ed., *The New Elites of Tropical Africa*, pp. 56–57.

[39] David Kimble, *A Political History of Ghana* (Oxford, England: Clarendon Press, 1963), p. 137.

"the continued evocation of nationalist sentiments is a further factor inhibiting the development of class consciousness."[40]

7) Traditional leaders are not part of a new class because their influence has remained largely confined to their areas of traditional jurisdiction and they have gained very little influence nationally.[41]

8) The most violent conflicts are "between ethnic and religious groups and not between socio-economic classes."[42]

9) Society is stratified in complex ways. First, for example, has maintained that "there has been no necessary congruence between wealth and economic power, or between economic and political power."[43] She goes on to maintain that "no bourgeoisie, in the style of Europe's early nation-states, has found the power to govern alone."[44]

Aristide Zolberg summarizes some of the main contentions of the anticlass position when he argues that "it is not very useful to speak of socio-economic classes in Africa because differentiations are very recent, often visible in one generation only, and there is as yet little evidence of intergenerational transmission of status in the modern sector. . . ." Zolberg then goes on to state that nevertheless, "certain categoric groups stand out as sources of political opposition based on education, occupation, and source or amount of income. They include especially civil servants: railroad, harbor and construction workers; and cash crop farmers."[45]

Although Lloyd remains one of the strongest anticlass critics, he admits that

> the well-educated and wealthy elite is tending to become a predominantly hereditary group. . . . The use of the term elite itself is spreading among Africans, and may well aid them in identifying the

[40] Lloyd, *Africa in Social Change: Changing Traditional Societies in the Modern World* (Baltimore: Penguin Books, 1967), p. 316.

[41] Lloyd, *Classes, Crises and Coups* (London: MacGibbon & Kee, 1970), p. 131.

[42] *Ibid.*, p. 13; see also Joan Davies, *African Trade Unions* (Baltimore: Penguin Books, 1966), pp. 130–32.

[43] First, *Power in Africa*, pp. 96–97.

[44] *Ibid.*, p. 97. Cf. the analysis of Peter Worsley, which began with a radical perspective attacking those "ideologists of the new states" who maintained that their societies were "homogeneous, that they lacked antagonistic class divisions of the Euro-American world." He eventually found that he had "to agree that the evidence [that African societies were homogeneous] shows up to be largely correct." (*The Third World: A Vital New Force in International Affairs*, 2nd ed. [Chicago: University of Chicago Press, 1970], p. 164). Later in his book, however, Worsley states that "sharpening class struggle is the order of the day in the more advanced countries, and is not too far distant in even the less advanced" (*Ibid.*, p. 219).

[45] Aristide Zolberg, *One-Party Government in the Ivory Coast*, rev. ed. (Princeton, N.J.: Princeton University Press, 1969), p. 71. Cf. Suzanne Keller, who advances a counter-theory based upon "strategic elites" to replace the theory of the "ruling class." She objects that many of the definitions of the ruling class are "either tautological, as when the ruling classes are said to consist of those who dominate the population," or so inclusive that all sorts of diverse groups are lumped together (*Beyond the Ruling Class* [New York: Random House, 1968], pp. 50–51). According to Keller "strategic elites differ from the ruling class in their manner of recruitment, internal organization, and degree of specialization" (*Ibid.*, p. 59).

group. . . . Those Africans who have struggled to obtain an affluent
Western style of life are not likely to relinquish these privileges soon after their acquisition. . . .[46]

Moreover, he contends, "the elite are certainly conscious of their position in their society, and of the power and responsibility that has be-
fallen them. Many members tend to be disparaging in their references
to the illiterate farmers and the craftsmen of their country. . . ."[47]

Although always in the shadow of the colonial power, indigenous
African controlling groups made powerful internal decisions that affected the life outcomes of millions of Africans.[48] Under colonialism,
overseas decision makers by and large did not occupy themselves with
day-to-day matters of government or with most areas of jurisdiction.
Every indigenous ruling group possessed tremendous autonomy. To
inflict colonialism with omniscience and omnipotence too easily relieved African rulers of tremendous responsibilities. Although no necessarily exact congruence between economic and political power
existed, a growing coincidence of interest was certainly apparent. If
what ultimately counts are policy outcomes—that is, who gets what—
there is little doubt who benefits in the new state. This remains true even
if we cannot predict which groups will benefit simply on the basis of the
social background of the decision makers.[49]

An important challenge to class interpretations comes from those
who emphasize ethnic identity or communal solidarity. In the African
context, class models must certainly be modified by factors of cultural
values and communal concern, as well as those of race and ideology.
In Kenya, for example, the history of racial domination provides an
essential background for understanding why the objectives of Kenyan
socialism have been drastically modified: the idea of racial equality
possesses such high saliency that the government can unblinkingly
claim the necessity of supporting black businessmen as well as black
professors and prime ministers to demonstrate racial equality.[50]

From a different perspective, Richard Sklar argues, "To be sure,
communal and class values may coexist; but in principle they are in-
consistent, the former implying a conception of the community as corporate and functionally integrated, while the latter signifies the frag-

---

[46] Lloyd, ed. *The New Elites of Tropical Africa*, pp. 57–60.

[47] *Ibid*, Lloyd, *Africa in Social Change* p. 316.

[48] First downgrades the significance of class in analyzing African politics by contending that "indigenous ownership in controlling groups have been able to grow only in the shadow of colonial
power" (*Power in Africa*, p. 97).

[49] See, for example, Lipset and Bendix, *Social Mobility in Industrial Society;* the controversy over "who
governs" between C. Wright Mills and Robert Dahl and their adherents. An interesting contribution
that eschewed focusing on who governs and instead studied policy outcomes may be found in Edward C. Hayes, *Power Structure and Urban Policy* (New York: McGraw-Hill, 1972). T. B. Bottomore
has pointed out that one may use the concept of the ruling class, like any other model, as an ideal
type, and ask simply how closely the relationship in a particular society approaches the ideal type of
a ruling class and subject classes. For a range of possible arguments based on a ruling class and "political elites," see Bottomore's *Elites and Society* (Baltimore: Penguin, 1964), p. 44.

[50] Cf. *African Socialism*, Sessional Paper No. 10 (Nairobi: Government Printing Office, 1965).

mentation or division of the community into groups of conflicting (perceived) interest."[51] In principle, however, a group of people can also exhibit different types of behavior, behavior that is motivated by diverse forces and activated under varying circumstances. Conceiving of an either-or situation, thinking in terms of class and community as mutually exclusive categories is the normal and historical logic of both common sense and the social sciences. Yet the political facts of the real world indicate the need for a different logic or a more subtle formulation. Modern science was shaken profoundly by the discovery that all matter can exhibit wave as well as particle activity—two modes of behavior that are irreconcilable in terms of *visualizing* a substance that has these properties, and yet experimentally these properties exist. Physics still does not understand the underlying structure of this phenomenon, but it happens. Sometimes a given population will act in unity on the basis of a perceived common identity at other times "a people" will split into clashing classes. In this study we emphasize the class correlates of group activity and attempt to understand the class aspects of communal solidarity. Appeals to ethnic or tribal loyalties can be another device that the organizational bourgeoisie employs to strengthen its rule.

No matter how greatly stratified a particular ethnic group might be—no matter what its internal differences in style, prestige, privilege, and preferential treatment—differences in wealth might not be at the expense of their fellow ethnics, but from commercial relations with outsiders. This is one example of what makes possible a peaceful, tight-knit community. Communal solidarity will also be more apparent than class divisions when (1) the economy is in the process of rapid expansion, (2) foreign aid represents a major source of new wealth, and (3) cheap outside ethnic labor is available. When conflicts are couched in communal terms, they often assume a bitterness that is absent in the more prosaic economic concerns of give-and-take pork-barrel politics because the existence of the suprahuman community is at stake. Sometimes, however, class interests may be salient but disguised in communal concerns. Many of the major clashes in Africa that appeared to be tribal conflicts—for example, the Biafran-Nigerian War—were in reality conditioned and precipitated by economic forces.[52]

Defining an organizational bourgeoisie has also been attacked on the grounds that "office" cannot be transferred from father to son in

---

[51] Richard Sklar, *Nigerian Political Parties: Power in an Emergent African Nation* (Princeton, N.J.: Princeton University Press, 1963), p. 477. Robert Melson and Howard Wolpe, "Modernization and the Politics of Communalism," *American Political Science Review*, vol. 64, no. 4, December 1970 takes a similar view.

[52] See Chapter VII. David R. Smock and Audrey C. Smock, in *The Politics of Pluralism: A Comparative Study of Lebanon and Ghana* (New York: Elsevier, 1975), argue the primacy and saliency of ethnicity and communalism. John W. Cole and Eric R. Wolf, in *The Hidden Frontier: Ecology and Ethnicity in an Alpine Valley* (New York: Academic Press, 1974), brilliantly analyze the relation between ecology, ethnicity, and politics. Edouard Bustin's *Lunda Under Belgian Rule: The Politics of Ethnicity* (Cambridge, Mass.: Harvard University Press, 1975), contains a fine study of how ruling families have survived from precolonial times to the postindependence era, even though their objectives have changed.

the way that private property can. Nevertheless, a high degree of "social self-recruitment" can be accomplished through time, not only by the legal transfer of property and wealth to family descendants, but through other kinds of advantages—the most obvious among them being higher education—that can assure the offspring of the new rulers a privileged social position.[53] From the earliest contacts between Africans and Europeans, an African establishment developed and enjoyed precisely these educational advantages. Providing for the special education of their offspring has been a central preoccupation of every indigenous bourgeoisie in every country throughout the continent.

The Rooting of the African Organizational Bourgeoisie

As early as the middle of the nineteenth century, a modern self-conscious African elite had begun to emerge. David Kimble tells us that in 1843, when the Crown took over the Gold Coast forts and settlements from the London Committee of Merchants, British governors had already established a tradition of appointing various prominent indigenous citizens to public office. James Bannerman, the son of a Scottish father and an African mother, and an outstanding member of the local establishment, was appointed justice of the peace in 1820 and civil commandant at Christiansburg in 1850, and later rose to the position of lieutenant governor. That Bannerman's position, though outstanding, was not unique is attested by various dispatches gathered by Kimble that claimed that educated Africans enjoyed "all privileges and advantages of the white merchant traders." In 1853, the secretary of state for colonies "affirmed the equality of white and colored people before the law, warning the governor against 'implying or of seeming to imply that the former had the right to different treatment for similar offenses.' "[54]

According to Weber and Boahen, by 1860 a greater percentage of children were attending school in Sierra Leone than in England:

> This magnificent effort was achieved by the cooperation of the government, the missionary societies and the Creoles, many of whom went into debt to educate their children. . . . The educational system poured forth a stream of teachers, clergymen, doctors, lawyers and writers producing many of the "first" of the professional class of West Africa: John Thorpe, the first African lawyer (1850), J. B. Horton, the first doctor (1859), S. A. Crowther, the first bishop, (1864), Samuel Lewis, the first knight (1896), as well as the first newspaper editor and owner and the

---

[53] See also, Frank Parkin, *Class Inequality and Political Order* (New York: Praeger, 1971), pp. 153–54. In a critique of the "multi-dimensional" approach particularly those that define attributes such as age and sex as elements of stratification, Parkin notes, "Such an approach tends to obscure the systematic nature of inequality and the fact that it is grounded in the material order in a fairly identifiable fashion" (*Ibid.*, p. 17).

[54] Kimble, *A Political History of Ghana,* p. 65.

first to be granted Cambridge and Oxford degrees. . . . In 1872 when Creoles held almost half of the senior civil service posts, Governor Pope-Hennessy maintained that there were enough qualified Creoles to replace the entire European staff.[55]

From the time of the institution of the Supreme Court in the Gold Coast in 1853, educated Africans began to specialize in court cases, and six or seven Gold Coasters were licensed to practice in 1864. The legal profession offered both political independence and an income that was exceptional by any standard. In 1888, Awoonor Renner turned down a senior governmental appointment on the grounds that he was already making over a £1,000 a year from his private practice. From this time on, Kimble notes, "it was noticeably the lawyers who took the lead in political movements, protest, deputations, and petitions. Their legal training and drafting ability, the wealth they had to contribute and their leisure to organize were invaluable assets in the early days of the nationalist movement."[56]

Along the western coast there was by 1900, according to Webster and Boahen, a "sizeable number of educated people—called the elite—who through their newspapers and associations acted as watchdogs of colonial rule, protesting against its abuses."[57] Members of this class went to school together at the famous William Ponty of Senegal in the Francophone areas, or at Freetown, Cape Coast, or Lagos in the English-speaking territories, became "old boys," and maintained close associations. They intermarried. They had interlocking trade relations. Lawyers and merchants moved freely in both English and French areas from one metropolitan colony to the other in the course of their work. This elite thus formed a West African community and thought of themselves as West Africans, rather than Nigerians or Gold Coasters. The West African press shared this cosmopolitan attitude. Although generally unprofitable, this press was an important device for keeping this class in touch and for spreading their influence.[58]

Although strongly self-assertive, leading members of this developing class did not stint in their general support for their "mother countries," even while denouncing imperialism's worst abuses. African coastal merchants echoed the cries of their European counterparts in demanding colonization of the interior in order to bring in new business. African Christians often were no less ardent than their white counterparts in desiring salvation for their pagan brethren. Anglophone Africans felt that if they were to be conquered they would rather be under the egis of Europeans whose languages they understood: "Against the French and German foreigners they began to feel their cultural affinity with the British. 'We black Englishmen, who have been so large benefited by English benevolence and justice can-

[55] J. B. Webster and A. A. Boahen, *History of West Africa* (New York: Praeger, 1970), p. 136.
[56] Kimble, *A Political History of Ghana*, p. 96.
[57] Webster and Boahen, *History of West Africa*, pp. 274–75.
[58] *Ibid.*

not sit still and see her (England) robbed of the well-earned fruits of her sagacity, enterprise and good will.' "[59] Africanus Horton articulated most clearly the position held by this rising bourgeoisie: the British government should extend its responsibilities in West Africa not only for the purpose of introducing civilization to "backward peoples" but because the bourgeoisie would be the chief beneficiaries, using British law and administration to make the country theirs. Horton's biographer interprets this desire as stemming from the bourgeoisie's image of themselves "as pioneers carving out their own empire under the protection of the British flag, like their white compatriots in Australia, New Zealand, or the Canadian West."[60] Referring specifically to the African intelligentsia in Sierra Leone, Fyfe attempts to explain their attitudes towards the English administration:

> As British subjects they had the rights and privileges of free Englishmen. . . . They were in any case inclined to feel grateful towards those who had liberated them from slavery and had given them the opportunity of leading a new life. Government, therefore, did not appear to them as a machine of colonial repression. They did not feel themselves in a "colonial situation." They identified with their British rulers, and felt the same kind of basic loyalty to the British crown that Englishmen felt in England. This basic loyalty runs counter to what is usually perceived as the current of African nationalism. It has been interpreted as servile acceptance of the colonial master. But Sierre Leoneans were no more servile in their attachment to the British crown than were their white contemporaries in Canada or Australia. Like the Canadians and Australians they were proud of their place as free citizens of the British Empire.[61]

The outstanding French colonial governor Felix Eboué, born in Guiana December 26, 1884, traced his descent from a noble house in the Igbo-speaking areas of the Ivory Coast or Nigeria. When asked his views of independence, Eboué responded, "We are Frenchmen and we are loyal to France." One of his biographers, in examining the point of view of the "African masses of French Equatorial Africa," states: "For most of his career Eboué was seen by them as another administrator who happened to be dark in color 'c'etait un Martiniquais de France,' they often said. Eboué had never called himself their brother or urged them to rise in revolt against European authority, for to do so would have been to encourage revolt against himself."[62] As a final tribute, the French government interred Eboué in the Pantheon.

Wesley Johnson, in one of the best accounts of the development of an African elite in the Francophone areas, writes:

[59] *Ibid.,* p. 225.

[60] Christopher Fyfe, *Africanus Horton, West African Scientist and Patriot* (New York: Oxford University Press, 1972), p. 45. See also Fyfe's account of the wealth accumulated by Horton (*Ibid.,* p. 134).

[61] *Ibid.,* p. 10.

[62] Brian Weinstein, *Eboué* (New York: Oxford University Press, 1972), p. 10.

When politics first began in St. Louis and Gorée, in the late 18th century, urban Africans developed an interest in who would become mayors and counsellors. This interest grew in the years that followed, especially after the 1848 decree authorized the servant class to vote for the colony's deputy. Gradually, an African political elite, definable in terms of law, was created in the Four Communes. This group did not by any means include all the municipal inhabitants.[63]

Johnson goes on to point out that although there were no class or caste restrictions on membership in the political elite, it was rare indeed to find lower-caste names among the candidates. Johnson also tells us that as early as 1872 the *originaires* had become aware of themselves as an elite, and that they tried to perpetuate their status by various techniques, including seeing to it that only their friends were admitted to the electoral lists. The *originaires* enjoyed their unique place in Senegal's political and economic world—"as middlemen between big business and small enterprise in the bush, and as mediators between the French and Creole elites and the African masses." The urban elite jealously defended their privileges "in the face of rural envy," and by 1900 there was a sharp division between communal and interior interests.[64]

In Central Africa, even though European agricultural interests and the prices for African agricultural produce had fallen drastically by the early 1920s, a small minority of wealthy Ndebele cattle owners could afford to buy large areas of ranch land. Also, an increasing number of Africans established themselves as "progressive farmers" and built market-gardening businesses near the cities, despite the racially restrictive policies of the government and the British South African Company. This small group of African land purchasers also succeeded in rising to dominant positions of control in the various semipolitical, semilegal associations thrown up by Africans confronting the European ingress. This group of Africans, combining both economic and political leadership, have continued to occupy pivotal positions up to the present time.[65]

In parts of East Africa the development of an African organizational bourgeoisie was at first delayed even more than in Central Africa, because of the presence of a permanent European settler community. As Kilson points out, Kenya's first African lawyer did not begin practice until 1956, whereas by the late 1920s the Gold Coast could already boast of sixty African lawyers.[66]

[63] G. Wesley Johnson, Jr., *The Emergence of Black Politics in Senegal* (Stanford, Calif.: Stanford University, Press, 1971), pp. 84–85.

[64] *Ibid.*, pp. 86–87.

[65] T. O. Ranger, *The African Voice in Southern Rhodesia* (London: Heinemann, 1968), pp. 112–14.

[66] E. C. Quist, later knighted, was named Crown counsel in 1914. By the 1920s, Nigeria and Sierra Leone had a significant number of indigenous attorneys. (Martin Kilson, "The Emergent Elites of Black Africa, 1900 to 1960 in *Colonialism in Africa, 1870–1960*, ed. Peter Duignan and L. H. Gann, Vol. 2, *The History and Politics of Colonialism, 1914–1960*, ed. Duignan and Gann [Cambridge: Cambridge University Press, 1970], p. 352.) See also Kilson's estimates of the number of Africans engaged in elite occupations in the Gold Coast in the 1940s, as well as of the number of graduates from various significant elite schools, such as the William Ponty School (*Ibid.*, p. 354).

By the turn of the century, however, the colonial establishment in the British and French territories had begun to exert great pressure on the privileges of this African bourgeoisie. Demands for egalitarian treatment of this class figured prominently from that time until the advent of mass nationalism at the end of the Second World War. In English-speaking Africa, Hutton Mills, Casely Hayford, H. C. Bankole-Bright, and Dr. F. V. Nanka-Bruce, urged that Europeans and Africans submit to the same qualifying examinations, that all appointments be made on the basis of civil service lists, and that discrimination be ended against African doctors and men of all professions. In the Francophone territories, men such as Blaise Diagne and Lamine Gueye devoted themselves perhaps even more strongly to the same end. Gueye was particularly effective in establishing equal rights for African civil servants.[67]

If this new African bourgeoisie suffered its reverses, particularly during the 1920s and 1930s, it nevertheless succeeded in establishing its preeminence: it negotiated with the external world of the colonial establishment; it mediated the economic system; and it developed linkages with the vast masses whose destiny it dominated and would continue to dominate in the postindependence period. In commenting on contemporary politics in Senegal, for example, Lucy Behrman notes: "Citizens do not feel themselves participant in a democratic governing process; rather, they recognize the authority of paternalistic, authoritarian, regional and national rulers who head clans and brotherhoods. . . ."[68] In the same way that the French negotiated with outstanding indigenous leaders, "Senghor [the present president of Senegal] promised different kinds of aid to the individual council members quietly tying them to his government separately and dividing them from each other. His policy was nothing more than the old, but successful, colonial policy."[69] Perhaps the unkindest summary of all of the development of this early bourgeoisie and its persistence over time was delivered by First: "Yet if the political vigor of the old elite faded, its tradition of exclusiveness from the people of the interior, the uneducated, the poor and contemptible, did not die. It persists in present-day educated African prejudices and unconcern for the plight of the undistinguished mass."[70]

Educational Continuities in the Organizational Bourgeoisie

Members of the organizational bourgeoisie take care that their children receive the best available advanced education. University stu-

[67] See my "The Political Thought of Blaise Diagne and Lamine Gueye," in *Black Leaders of the Centuries*, S. O. Mazu and R. Desar, eds. (Buffalo, Black Academy Press, 1971).

[68] Lucy Behrman, *Muslim Brotherhoods and Politics in Senegal* (Cambridge, Mass.: Harvard University Press, 1970), p. 7.

[69] *Ibid.*, p. 82.

[70] First, *Power in Africa*, p. 63.

dents are an infinitesimal proportion of the total population. Although they appear to be among the most radical-sounding groups, their training prepares them to accept gracefully a standard of living and style of life that not only sets them aside from over 95 percent of the population, but also convinces them that they are entitled to these benefits because of their inherent merits. In Senegal, a country with an average annual income per head of $170 and a total population of 4 million, one tenth of one percent of the total population is enrolled in the University; in Ghana 0.08 percent of the population is enrolled on her campuses, and the per capita income is comparable in that of Senegal; in Tanzania 0.02 percent attend the University, and the per capita income is $80; in the United States 1.9 percent of the population attends college, and the per capita income is almost $4,000.[71]

The development of educational institutions and the training of the children of the organizational bourgeoisie in Ghana is typical of educational experience elsewhere on the continent. Missionaries first brought Western education to the Gold Coast. By 1881 they taught over 5,000 pupils in over 139 primary schools—a number that increased constantly until, by the First World War, over 200 missionary schools existed—and had expanded into secondary education. Missionary pupils went into teaching and the church at first; increasingly, however, they entered commerce, the administration, and politics. According to Kilson, "They thereby broadened their experience, acquired new habits and began to play new roles in society. They also took good care that their offspring should get on in life. Sons of mission trained men were sent to college wherever their fathers could afford the required expense."[72]

Considering the development of an African bourgeoisie, Nkrumah noted the peculiar composition of the students at the universities in Ghana:

> In 1953, before Ghana's independence, out of a total of 208 students in the University College, 12% of the families of students have an income of over £600. a year; 38% between £250. and £600.; and 50% about £250. The significance of these figures is seen when it is realized that it was only in 1962, after vigorous efforts in the economic field, that it was possible to get the average annual income per head of the population up to approximately £94.[73]

---

[71] *Africa Report*, December 28, 1973, p. 55. Abdou Moumouni relates education and class structure in *L'education en Afrique* (Paris: Francois Maspero, 1964). See also Ruth Sloan Associates, *The Educated African*, ed. Helen Kitchen (New York: Praeger, 1962); L. Gray Cowan, James O'Connell, and David G. Scanlon, eds., *Education and Nation-Building in Africa* (New York: Praeger, 1965); and *Black Civilization and Education*, special issue of *Presence Africaine*, No. 87, 3rd quarter (1973).

[72] Kilson, "The Emergent Elites of Black Africa," *The History and Politics of Colonialism, 1914–1960*, ed. Duignan and Gann, p. 351.

[73] Nkrumah, *Class Struggle in Ghana*, p. 38. In a more recent study, David J. Finlay makes much the same point: "Although the range of socio-economic backgrounds among Legon students is broad, a disproportionate number come from urban, high-income, educated families," in *Students in Revolt*, ed. Seymour Martin Lipset and Philip G. Altbach (Boston: Beacon Press, 1970), p. 382. See also Benoit Verhagen, "Sociology of a Student Strike in the Congo," *Presence Africaine*, No. 52 4th Quarter (1964), pp. 135–137.

Philip Foster analyzes preparatory education in Ghana and notes the socioeconomic background of the school population:

> There is a definite association between paternal occupational character-
> istics and access to secondary school education which is even more strik-
> ing for girls than it is for boys. Although professional, higher technical,
> and clerical workers constitute only 7% of the Ghana adult male labor
> force, they supply 34% of our male students and no less than 66% of
> the female students. Whereas farmers and fishermen, who account for
> over 62% of the employed adult male population, provide only 37%
> and 12% of these respective samples.[74]

Foster goes on to argue, however, that although "findings show a degree of constriction in patterns of selectivity, they also indicate a remarkable degree of fluidity and access into the schools"; it is "important to not overlook that over one-third of [the students] are the
offspring of farmers and fishermen."[75]

To assume, however, that being the son of a farmer means coming from a humble home is to assume too much. Recruitment by the
universities remains confined to the most privileged social strata, even
though it may appear that a large proportion of students come from
humble homes because they list their fathers' occupation as "farmer."
"Farmers" may be quite wealthy. According to a most optimistic interpretation of the social background of students in Ghana, only 32.5
percent of the parents were farmers, compared with 63 percent of the
working population. But as G. E. Hurd points out in a statistical
analysis, there is considerable internal differentiation within the farming category: "Some farmers are very wealthy and command high
prestige; others scrape a bare subsistence. On the whole cocoa farmers
are more wealthy than farmers who grow food crops, and they are
certainly more involved in the cash crop economy of modern Ghana
and consequently are less likely to be traditionally oriented." Hurd
then shows that most of the students with a farming background
"come in fact from the wealthier and more modern cocoa farmers, although such farmers constitute rather less than one-third of the farming community in Ghana. Only a quarter of (the students) from farming families come from subsistence farms, although this type of
farming accounts for more than two-thirds of the farmers of Ghana."[76]
He then shows that over half of the ninety-eight fathers in his sample

---

[74] Philip Foster, *Education and Social Change in Ghana* (Chicago: University of Chicago Press, 1965), p. 240.

[75] *Ibid.*, p. 241. See also David J. Finlay et al., who also equate "those coming from families of lower economic status with the children of farmers and manual workers." ("Ghana," in *Students and Politics in Developing Nations*, ed. Donald K. Emmerson [New York: Praeger, 1968], pp. 64–102).

[76] G. E. Hurd, "Education," in *A Study of Contemporary Ghana*, Vol. II, *Some Aspects of Social Structure*, ed. Walter Birmingham et al. (London: Allen & Unwin, 1967), p. 238. See also the table on p. 79 in Emmerson, ed., *Students and Politics in Developing Nations*, which depicts the level of educational attainment of parents of students enrolled at the University of Ghana from 1953 to 1966. See the dis-
tinctions among different types of farmers made by Polly Hill in her *The Migrant Cocoa Farmers of Southern Ghana* (Cambridge: Cambridge University Press, 1963).

who were farmers own three or more farms, so in terms of the amount of land they own as well as the crops they grow, they are likely to represent the better-off segment of the farmers. To conclude from the presence in schools and universities of so many children of farmers that African society is basically egalitarian is therefore most erroneous. As Hurd summarizes, "This combined with the virtual absence of the children of semi-skilled and unskilled workers from the schools and from universities, leaves us to conclude that the open nature of Ghanaian secondary education is yet to be demonstrated."[77]

Even those who believe that universities are open to youth from all social strata recognize that this "doesn't mean students identified with the common man."[78] Almost all of the secondary schools are boarding schools, so students are forced to live in isolation from their families and villages for up to seven academic years, a time span extended by attendance at the university in an atmosphere of elitest attitudes and amenities. Thus, "isolation and a sense of privilege create a relatively homogeneous body of students."[79]

A similar situation exists in Nigeria. According to a newspaper report, a regional government found itself faced with a rumor campaign that was calculated to discredit the state's education policy "and so caused disaffection and disorder." The administrator claimed that those spreading the rumor were annoyed because there were now no segregated grade A schools for their children: "Because they found their children attending the same schools with those of truck pushers and lowly placed citizens, they think that the heavens will fall."[80]

One of the ostensible objectives of the new African governments was to eradicate class differences. The training of a ruling class at African universities is very European. Pierre Van den Berghe writes that social classes at a university he studied are "distinct and unambiguous in their membership; they are self-conscious and act corporately through a variety of institutions and voluntary organizations."[81] No matter what background he might have, no matter which ethnic group he belongs to, no matter what his political philosophy,

> the student knows that the university degree is his passport to elite status, even though the returns on the educational investment tend to decline over the years as the number of university graduates increases steeply. Thus, the student, while often from a background of poverty or near poverty and frequently in severe financial straits during his stay at the university, is also an heir presumptive to elite status. He knows that only three years and his final examinations stand between him and lifelong security and comfort. This ambiguous situation of temporary in-

---

[77] Hurd, *op. cit.,* p. 238.

[78] Finlay et al., "Ghana," in *Students and Politics in Developing Nations,* ed. Emmerson, p. 80.

[79] *Ibid.*

[80] *West Africa,* February 11, 1972, p. 169.

[81] Pierre L. Van den Berghe, *Power and Privilege at an African University* (London: Routledge & Kegan Paul, 1973), p. 72.

digence combined with the high likelihood of future affluence accounts for much of the collective behavior and attitudes of students.[82]

Following the models of the European universities, the African colleges functioned above all as institutions of class training: "The halls were to be breeding grounds for young gentlemen, where students would acquire wisdom and social graces, and learn their places in society by being relieved of all demeaning manual labor and being waited upon by a small army of servants."[83]

With economic development, expanding administrative bureaucracies and business concerns require ever more higher-trained personnel. Although possessing a university degree, even graduates—the most privileged members of their societies—function increasingly not as policy makers but simply as the troops of advancing economies, the cannon fodder who are needed in order that organizational requisites may be met. In industrial societies, the great expansion of state and urban universities (even going to Harvard isn't enough; what matters is which Harvard—the Harvard of the dorms and public schools or the Harvard of prep school alumni and private clubs) means that a college degree does not automatically secure a "good living." In African states as well, greater economic development and the ability of the "lower classes" to send their children to college result in more subtleties in university attendance patterns: organizational bourgeoisie families send their children to university at a much earlier age, and, increasingly, they educate their girls as well as boys. Above all, parental status strongly influences which "faculty" a student will enroll in. According to Van den Berghe,

> children of professionals and semi-professionals make up 43.8% of the prestigious, expensive, and potentially most remunerative faculty of medicine, and only 12.0% of the low-prestige faculty of education; children of farmers, on the other hand, constitute only 18.0% of the medical students and 59.0% of the education students. The other faculties fall in between, in order of their respective status with science near the medicine end of the continuum and social sciences second to bottom before education.[84]

Julius Nyerere considers the type of educational system created by a new state to be essential in determining the nature of the society molded by its leaders. He worries about the development of social and personal values that stem from so apparently necessary components of a public education as competition for grades, and notes the connection of these values with the emergence of a class-conscious new governing group:

[82] *Ibid.*, p. 75. Cf. Joel D. Barkan, *An African Dilemma: University Students, Development and Politics in Ghana, Tanzania and Uganda* (Nairobi: Oxford University Press, 1975) who concludes that African education promotes class divisions, p. 188.

[83] *Ibid.*, p. 173.

[84] *Ibid.*, pp. 153–55.

It [public education] induces among those who succeed a feeling of superiority, and leaves the majority of the others hankering after something they will never obtain. It induces a feeling of inferiority among the majority, and can thus not produce either the egalitarian society we should build, nor the attitudes of mind which are conducive to an egalitarian society. The school is always separate; it is not part of the society. It is a place children go to and which they and their parents hope will make it unnecessary for them to become farmers and continue living in the villages. . . . If they are lucky enough to enter Dar es Salaam University College they live in comfortable quarters, feed well, and study hard for their degree. They may also have the desire to serve the community, but their idea of service is related to status and salary which the university education is expected to confer upon its recipient. The salary and the status have become a right automatically conferred by the degree. He does not really know what it is like to live as a poor peasant. He will be more at home in the world of the educated than he is among his own parents.[85]

One of the most intensely held and prevalent notions about university students in developing countries, particularly in Africa, is that they are antiestablishment and devoted to fundamentally altering capitalist economies and existing governments. In his assessment of the contrast between African student ideologies and career ambitions, Hapgood has noted that

African students are "radical." This is the conventional assumption. . . . But when the students are looked at in African terms, the radicalism of most of them dissipates in hot air. The proclaimed Marxist-Leninist is, in his behavior, supremely bourgeois. His real interests are not the reading of Marx and Lenin but the acquiring of natty clothes, transistor radios and cars or motor bikes. . . . "help for the peasant masses," students may say, but they do not demand the drastic reduction in elite power that such help requires. Certainly they do not demand a reduction in their own privileges. They are able, in fact, to seek an increase in those privileges while denouncing the waste in the government. . . . In fact, students and governments have a great deal in common. Both believe in rule by the educated elite, and therefore neither really questions the privileged position of ministers or students. It would be suicidal for the students to attack the system whose privileges they expect to inherit. . . . Still the students, like the elite itself, are influenced by ideals of social justice. Neither callous nor ignorant, the students would like to see themselves as revolutionaries dedicated to modernizing their continent — though they also want the privileges to which they have become accustomed.[86]

Students in the Congo professed concern with their job prospects and with their present living conditions as well. In a strike by the General Association of Students of Lovaniun University in the Congo in March, 1964, the students demanded the improvement of

---

[85] Nyerere in Ujamaa, p. 55.
[86] David Hapgood, *Africa: From Independence to Tomorrow* (New York: Atheneum, 1965), pp. 196–99.

education through the hiring of internationally respected professors, the joint administration of the university by students and staff, and the substantial betterment of their own material conditions. Jean Claude Williame reports that

> the students worry a great deal about their future careers, hoping for employment from a regime with almost absolute powers whose leaders may be highly suspicious of intellectuals. ... as the students move through their university years, gaining the experience needed to leave their peers, their increasing uneasiness about the future causes them to abandon radical opinions because they know such views may be ill-regarded by the adult political leaders on whom their professional hopes depend.[87]

African students, despite their rhetoric, appear to follow their elders in their career aspirations and material ambitions, even though they cloak them in a more radical rhetoric. Whereas in Western industrialized society the gap between fathers and sons is much talked about (but in reality lacks much substance), Finlay et al., studying

> the influence of parental political interest and opinion [in Africa,] find no evidence of "generational revolt." On the contrary, in several studies patterns of generational continuity and political orientations emerge, while others suggest that parental and student participation in politics are not related. The student who adopts a given political position solely or even largely because it is contrary to his father's views seems to be a rare creature indeed.[88]

What emerges clearly, above all, are the continuities between those in power and their heirs. The educational mechanism unites father and son by providing both the skills necessary for the perpetuation of rule, and the attitudes and values that continue to insulate Africa's organizational bourgeoisie from the rest of the population by reinforcing their self-righteous conviction of superiority and hence legitimacy.[89]

The Organizational Bourgeoisie
in Radical Regimes

Even under those regimes most committed to egalitarianism and the creation of a "socialist" society, the power of the organizational bour-

---

[87] Jean Claude Williame "The Congo," in *Students and Politics in Developing Nations,* ed. Emmerson, p. 53. Student attitudes towards Nkrumah and his objectives and ideology are interesting to note in sketching the conservative bias of this Ghanaian elite. See Finlay et al., "Ghana," in *Students and Politics in Developing Nations,* ed. Emmerson, p. 82. Finlay et al., also make the most interesting point that students at the university had the civil service and educational system as alternative models for emulation. (Cf. Walter Schwarz, *Nigeria* [London: Pall Mall, 1968], p. 357).

[88] Finlay et al., "Ghana," in *Students and Politics in Developing Nations,* ed. Emmerson, p. 396.

[89] For comparative data from India on continuities in education and position of generations of civil servants, see Samuel J. Eldersveld et al., *The Citizen and the Administrator in a Developing Democracy* (Glenview, Ill.: Scott, Foresman, 1968).

geoisie persists. The bureaucracy in Guinea, for example, has been criticized for overcentralization, the "fetishism of the directive," and a drying up of initiative. Initiative tends to disappear as policy makers demand the right to make every decision within their fief, no matter how insignificant it might be, and as the middle and lower civil servants decline all responsibility whatsoever, referring each case to their immediate chiefs. In a country where all the vital services are nationalized, the impact of this phenomenon is particularly severe. Claude Rivière maintains that

> from hyperpoliticization and hyperbureaucratization are born the curse of a new type of class statism and a monopolization of the national income by a politico-administrative bourgeoisie. . . . Ten years after independence in spite of constant propaganda efforts and repeated calls to vigilance, a clear decline of civic spirit coinciding with a whole series of disappointments is perceived by no matter what analyst.[90]

This lack of civil spirit can eventually be the undoing of the whole pursuit. In his assessment of Guinea, Riviere nevertheless maintains a basically optimistic assessment:

> On the political and social level, Guinea has already advanced over its revolution. She has kept her independence in the face of powerful interests eager to reestablish their hegemony; she has broken with certain archaic mental structures, from oppressive ethics, family and religion patterns; she has put her nationals in charge of their own administration; she has distilled among the people an authentically African culture and a progressive education.[91]

An optimistic beginning also accompanied Tanzania's independence: in a measure virtually unique in Africa, the government under President Nyerere conducted a preindependence salary review that introduced significant decreases in the basic salary scales. This did not, however, prevent the rapid rise of persons with Western styles of life and consumption. In 1966 and 1967, another series of measures strove to redress the situation. Included in the steps taken was compulsory national service for those with high school and higher education; further cuts in salaries of senior civil servants and politicians; and taxation measures designed to shift the demand in consumption patterns from imported to domestic goods and from luxury to amenity or mass market goods.[92]

[90] Claude Rivière, *Mutations Sociales en Guinée* (Paris: Marcel Riviere et Cie, 1971), p. 397.

[91] *Ibid.*, p. 401. For less optimistic assessments about Guinea's future, see Victor Du Bois, "Guinea" in *Political Parties and National Integration in Tropical Africa,* ed. J. S. Coleman and C. G. Rosberg, Jr. (Berkeley and Los Angeles: University of California Press, 1964). Du Bois strongly criticizes Sekou Touré's government in two series of reports, *The Decline of the Guinean Revolution* and *The Rise of an Opposition to Sekou Toure,'* American Universities Field Staff Reports, West African Series, Vol. 8 and Vol. 9 (New York, 1965, 1966).

[92] Reginald Green, "Political Independence and the National Economy," in *African Perspectives,* ed. Christopher Allen and R. W. Johnson (Cambridge: Cambridge University Press, 1970), p. 313.

One small example of this reinvigorated policy was the imposition of a far-reaching and complicated sales tax. In industrialized countries, sales taxes are generally recognized to be regressive because the same tax rate is applied to everyone, no matter what their income. In Tanzania, because the sales tax did not apply to basic foodstuffs and certain other goods consumed primarily by peasants and low-income workers, and because it replaced a head tax, it involved shifting a tax burden of about 16 million shillings from rural citizens to urban and other salaried employees. Consumption of manufactured and imported goods was virtually a monopoly of the organizational bourgeoisie so the sales tax was a form of indirect taxation of "the elite." In Tanzania, the biggest single source of national revenue was import and excise duties, which accounted for 51 percent of the total national collection in 1963; the second major source of national revenue was the income tax on corporate and personal income, which accounted for 23 percent of national revenue even though collected from less than 1 percent of the population.[93]

Despite all these stringent measures, the rise of an organizational bourgeoisie in Tanzania, as elsewhere, has proved very hard to prevent. As Reginald Green points out, a university professor requires books and time to read them; an airline pilot needs privacy for rest and relaxation. If these basic requirements are not met, levels of graduate competence and airline safety will deteriorate catastrophically. However, the line between what is objectively necessary for the proper functioning of the society and what are only the imperious demands of the strategically located minority are often difficult to make.[94] Yet, as Samir Amin declared in his study of the Maghreb,

> this does not mean that the poor prospects for growth are inherent in the nature of statism . . . the "liberal" course taken by Morocco has not given better results than the "socialist" policies adopted by Algeria and Tunisia. The reason, perhaps, is rather that the "administrative elites," which have assumed the responsibilities of power have gone no further than establishing and defending the special interest of their own "new class." . . . That is why the differences between the three countries seem to us, in the last analysis, very small. . . .[95]

What ultimately can be expected if this line of evolution continues? Not necessarily revolution, but at least a growing disillusion on the part of the "masses" with their leaders, and a growing, cutting cynicism on the part of the organizational bourgeoisie towards the people. Crawford Young, in his study of the Congo, notes that a crucial factor reconciling the lower strata to the system was a belief in the

---

[93] Clyde Ingle, *From Village to State in Tanzania* (Ithaca, N.Y.: Cornell University Press, 1972), pp. 206–8. See also Eugene Lee, *Local Taxation in Tanzania* (London: Oxford University Press, 1965); and Issag Shivji, "Tanzania: The Silent Class Struggle," *Pan-African Notes*, 4, no. 1 (Winter 1974), 14–43.

[94] Green, "Political Independence and the National Economy," in *African Perspective*, ed. Allen and Johnson, pp. 312–13.

[95] Samir Amin, *The Maghreb in the Modern World* (Baltimore: Penguin, 1970), pp. 245–46.

possibility of mobility for either themselves or their children. However,

> intense was the bitterness when, after independence, the [Congolese] youth found that the unlimited horizons of the campaign for independence had suddenly contracted. Boundless hope was replaced by unrelieved despair. It was in this setting that judgment was passed against the members of the new elite who had found fulfillment in independence. It is within this context that the social logic of the extraordinary violence unleashed by the rebellions against "intellectuals" becomes clear, as does the appeal of a call for a second independence.[96]

Young goes on to describe how awareness of the growing gap between the political administrative class and labor's unemployed and the peasantry had become general by 1962. He also shows how massive unemployment combined with an inflation that impoverished those "lucky" enough to have jobs. He concludes that "the vexations of the deprived were multiple."[97]

During the horrible drought in 1974, accusations of the most cynical behavior were hurled against members of the organizational bourgeoisie. Repeated accusations of misconduct—that Ethiopian administrators were more concerned with national pride than with alleviating the suffering of their countrymen; that the government was inept in transporting foodstuffs to the affected areas; that corrupt officials forced starvation on rent-gouged peasants and sold them at high prices medicines donated by international agencies—accompanied widespread movements of insurrection in Ethiopia. In Niger, Lieutenant Colonel Seyni Kountche justified his overthrow of the government of Hamani Diori on April 15 by stating that although drought and famine had been responsible for many of the nation's current problems, "the indifference of former officials had added to the gravity of the situation."[98] In Chad, the government of Ngarta Tombalbaye was believed to have mismanaged the relief effort for reasons of "incompetence, apathy and participation in or toleration of profiteering on the part of persons close to the national leadership."[99] Chadian transporters with a truck monopoly held the government hostage by enforcing the highest ton-per-mile rate in the world and kept the cheaper, faster, and larger Nigerian trucks from carrying grain to starving farmers. Reportedly, key members of the govern-

[96] Crawford Young, "Rebellion and the Congo" in *Protest and Power in Black Africa*, ed. Robert I. Rotberg and Ali A. Mazrui (New York: Oxford University Press, 1970), p. 981.

[97] *Ibid.*, p. 980. See also Young's table illustrating the rise in salaries by social category between 1960 and 1965. This table demonstrates the tremendous improvement in the standard of living of the "organizational bourgeoisie." (*Ibid.*, p. 979) A good historical study by Roger Anstey shows how in the Congo "by the end of the 2nd World War a sufficient number of *évolués* had emerged for them properly to be termed a class" ("Belgian rule in the Congo and the aspirations of the *évolue* class," in *The History and Politics of Colonialism, 1914–1960*, ed. Duignan and Gann, pp. 196–97).

[98] *New York Times*, April 23, 1974.

[99] Henry Kamm, "Chad's Hungriest See Little of Food Given by World," *New York Times*, October 10, 1974. Cf. Jack Shepherd, *The Politics of Starvation* (New York: Carnegie Endowment for Inter-

ment had an interest in truck ownership, either directly or through close relatives, including President Tombalbaye's wife.

All this points to the need to investigate further the role of African business in the consolidation of political power of the organizational bourgeoisie and in their growing strength as major beneficiaries of independence and economic growth.

national Peace, 1975), who shows that the Imperial Ethiopian Government of Haile Selassie ignored the existence of a major disaster, the drought, and knowingly denied the needed relief to its people, hundreds of thousands of whom were suffering and dying. This partially explains the 1973–74 coup, but not the absence of an international outcry.

Chapter VII

THE CONSOLIDATION
OF POWER:
African Business

Not large or powerful by Western standards, African traders and merchants have nevertheless affected the life chances of their countrymen. They bought groundnuts and sold millet, hired labor and loaned money. They profited where they could, and they resented interference from the *bours* and *emirs* as well as from the *préfets* and district commissioners.

Within the framework of an emerging world capitalist system, African businessmen shook their societies. They played a crucial role as part of world-wide revolutionary forces, and were in turn instruments and victims.

Capitalism battered down the walls of Kano and Gao with its heavy artillery of cheap commodities. It shattered the shell of isolation that surrounded subsistence farmers and thrust forward the peddlers and merchant princes who challenged the power of established monarchs with their Birmingham cloth, bicycles, and sewing machines. Capitalism flooded the cities with self-seekers, engulfed already inadequate public facilities with those who would be clerks and scribes, and heaved from the depths of old societies new captains of commerce. The gods of Oyo and Benin died; believers converted to new religions. Maxim and Gatling guns shredded men's bodies in colonial conquests. Taxes and *corvée* labor drove Africans into unwanted work and occupations. Things fell apart.

Or they seemed to. As we have seen throughout this study, African leaders, representing at times conflicting social classes, have hammered out a new economic, social, and political order. African business — not simply a bureaucratic bourgeoisie, but a business bourgeoisie — played an important part in this process and shows signs of playing an even greater role in the future.

This chapter seeks, above all, to establish the *fact* of African business, to give an indication of its size, scope, and historical development. Beyond that, we will inquire into the dialectical relationship between African business and the overseas powers; investigate the role of African business in achieving new political stability during both the struggle for independence and the postindependence period; and assess the entrenchment of African business in advantageous establishment positions.

The Emerging Importance of
African Business

African businesses come in many sizes, shapes, and forms. Governmental policies toward African business, including those of the traditional political authorities, have varied over time. As African societies have evolved, the political role, function, and significance of indigenous business have been altered greatly. Although it has sustained reverses, African commercial activity has moved in the direction of greater cohesion and greater significance in policy making. We must also see the rise of African business in the context of the rise of its political and bureaucratic allies in the organizational bourgeoisie. Indeed, to a large extent postindependence politics revolves around the search for a social base and a more solid economic foundation by this class, and commercial interests have hastened to step forward to be discovered.

The colonial attitude towards the development of African business changed drastically from the time of the first European contacts. At first, the British and French considered indigenous entrepreneurs natural allies in their mercantile ventures, vital middlemen in integrating the colonies into the international capitalist market. During this period, great African merchant princes accumulated enormous wealth and organized their own far-flung network of lesser African merchants throughout the countryside, a network that extended to the remotest corners of the bush.

About 1900, however, both France and Britain enacted a new policy cutting back on the employment of all Africans who acted as middlemen with the mass of the population. African functionaries and civil servants, who had considered themselves the bearers of Christian civilization, were hard-hit. Imperial business undermined whatever independence the indigenous traders possessed. Overseas corporations incorporated lesser African agents ever more tightly into their bureaucratic frameworks and replaced Africans with Lebanese and *petits blonds* whenever possible. African merchants, nevertheless, with new vigor, self-consciousness, and well-articulated demands, constituted a major force in the rise of nationalism after World War II. After independence, despite occasional setbacks by ideologically committed African leaders and parties, African business grew markedly, even under "socialist" regimes. Under military-led regimes of the organizational bourgeoisie they acted forcefully to help sweep away institutions.

Surprisingly, commentators of virtually every political persuasion have accepted as axiomatic the proposition that the African business class is of little political significance. Kwame Nkrumah, one of Africa's most radical leaders, stated in a class analysis of Ghanaian society written after his overthrow:

> As a result of colonialism and neo-colonialism, there has been comparatively little development of an African business elite. . . . The African businessman is, in general, not so much interested in developing industry as in seeking to enrich himself by speculation, black marketeering, corruption. . . . The African capitalist thus becomes the class ally of the bourgeoisie in the capitalist world. He is a pawn in the immense network of international monopoly finance capital.[1]

That Nkrumah should so judge the role of African business is ironic, given the great role played by the market women in his rise to power, and the subsequent burgeoning of an indigenous business bourgeoisie facilitated by the policies of his government and party politics.[2]

The Polish sociologist Chodak denies that we may describe African entrepreneurs as capitalist, on the grounds that they rarely employ many workers or engage in large-scale industrial activities:

> African businessmen engage in retail trade, transportation or small construction work. They own small work shops. They usually prefer to invest their money in a number of smaller enterprises bringing modest profits in a short time rather than in bigger ventures, the outcome of which is difficult to anticipate. They employ, as a rule, only a few employees and most often recruit for the job their distant relatives.[3]

Chodak maintains that African entrepreneurs "imitate the life style of a middle class rather than being a middle class." Yet Chodak's own description indicates a wide variety of important commercial activities and the mode of operations characteristic of any fledgling bourgeoisie struggling to assert itself against formidable external powers.

Still another objection comes from a Western sociologist: " 'Business,' . . . despite its being strongly represented in the higher councils of the new nation, is not a self-conscious organized grouping displaying classic capitalist attitudes. . . ."[4] On the one hand, Worsley al-

[1] Kwame Nkrumah, *Class Struggle in Africa* (New York: International Publishers, 1970), p. 33.

[2] Richard Wright vividly depicts the political role of the market women in his *Black Power* (New York: Harper & Brothers, 1954). Other students of Ghanaian politics, such as David Apter and Dennis Austin, have noted the eminence of these women. Peter Abrahams presents a fascinating fictional account of women in African politics in his *A Wreath for Udomo* (New York: Collier, 1971).

[3] Szymon Chodak, "Social Stratification in Sub-Saharan Africa," *Canadian Journal of African Studies*, 7, no. 3 (1973), 401–17.

[4] Peter Worsley, *The Third World*, 2nd ed. (Chicago: University of Chicago Press, 1970), p. 143. See also Hugh H. Smythe and Mabel M. Smythe, *The New Nigerian Elite* (Stanford, Calif.: Stanford University Press, 1960), pp. 83–85, for a similar contention about the lack of self-consciousness on the part of the Nigerian "business elite."

leges that business is in fact strongly represented in the "higher councils"; at the same time, he denies that business plays a "self-conscious organized" role. This ambiguity is characteristic of many commentators. The American political scientist Bretton, after having noted that "to be sure, the trend, particularly in non-socialist countries, seems to favor increased allocation of resources to indigenous enterprise," goes on to say that "actually, the odds against the African entrepreneur developing the economic punch necessary to alter public policy in his favor are lengthening. . . ."[5] And Chodak, after his denial of the significance of the African entrepreneur as capitalist, eventually admits that "the role of the African businessmen is growing. They are the men who will take over sooner or later when the European and Asian entrepreneurs are gone. They are the clients of the men in power. In complementing one another, the two groups constitute the embryo of the ruling class of future Africa."[6]

How, then, can these commentators maintain their arguments that the African business class has little political significance? Bretton, in finding the rise of the African entrepreneur "agonizingly, irritatingly slow," argues that the African bourgeoisie will not amass significant wealth because as a pressure group it is likely to remain "organizationally fragmented, scattered in direction and purpose, and generally ineffectual." In remaining "tied to the apron strings either of dominant foreign capital or of the state," it will not be able to gather "the social force that propelled [its] counterparts in early European systems to hold their rulers for ransom."[7] Describing further the mechanics by which this dependency of African capitalism takes place, Samir Amin relates how in the Western experience capital did not come originally from the profits of investments but from the exploitation of noncapitalist sectors. This "primitive accumulation" was syphoned off in the relations between developed countries and underdeveloped countries by mechanisms such as traffic and marketing arrangements that worked for the benefit of dominant foreign capital and "the possibilities of developing local capital" were thereby limited. Therefore, Amin maintains, every third world bourgeoisie whose development is "grafted on to the international markets to which its country adheres" must be a "peripheral bourgeoisie."[8] Amin goes on

[5] Henry L. Bretton, *Power and Politics in Africa* (Chicago: Aldine, 1973), p. 215.

[6] Chodak, "Social Stratification in Sub-Saharan Africa," p. 414.

[7] Bretton, *Power and Politics in Africa*, p. 215.

[8] Samir Amin, "La politique coloniale Francaise a l'egard de la bourgeoisie commerçante Senegalaise (1820–1960)," in *The Development of Indigenous Trade and Markets in West Africa*, ed. Claude Meillassoux (London: Oxford University Press, 1971), pp. 374–75. Amin has also declared that "the real bourgeoisie is absent and lives in Europe" (*Neo-Colonialism in West Africa* [New York: Monthly Review Press, 1973], p.64); that "the urban pseudo-bourgeoisie lacks the resources for investment . . ." (*Ibid.*) and that "only now is a bourgeoisie forming at a time when its possibilities have been exhausted" (*Ibid.*, p. 14). John Hargreaves puts the problem perhaps the most charitably when he asks, "How many innovating capitalists are needed to create a modernizing capitalism?" (*West Africa Partitioned*, Vol. I, *The Loaded Pause* [Madison, Wisc.: University of Wisconsin Press, 1974], p. 10) Ikenna Nzi-

to say, however, "Then politics inevitably intervene." An African in-digenous capitalist class grows in numbers and in economic resources by gaining control of the political apparatus.

Through political power, the indigenous entrepreneurs can gain added leverage in their dealings with overseas firms. They can seek to have the government protect their enterprises through fiscal, invest-ment, and taxation policies like those that Alexander Hamilton pushed through George Washington's government. Or they can ar-range to be paid off at a high price in much the same way as capital-ists in France, Switzerland, and Germany, who accept the takeover of their corporations by American firms when they find no harm done to their own incomes and profits.

Indigenous capitalism might have suffered monetarily and mo-mentarily at the beginning of the century, when foreign capitalism in-tervened more strongly to take over local markets. But African entre-preneurs did not disappear. Their energies poured out in a number of simultaneous directions—the economic bureaucracies as well as those of politics and administration—eventually resulting, in absolute terms, in vastly greater power and wealth for this tiny indigenous bourgeoisie. A common set of mental images pictures a succession of African *beaux idéals* over time: "the chief" is replaced by "the trader," and "the politician" by "the soldier." This conception misleads. Rather, we must focus on the continuities that occurred as members of the traditional ruling families found outlets and allies in power po-sitions that were created by capitalism and centralized administration.

The vibrant markets of rural centers—evident on the most casual tour of any African country—and the huge number of vendors on the streets of every city on the continent would, on a common-sense basis, belie allegations of a lack of indigenous entrepreneurs or the absence of "business skills and values." Available statistics reinforce these im-pressions. In the remote Malian town of Kita in 1903, for example, twenty-one European firms were doing business and over 20,000 Afri-can traders came to engage in commerce.[9] In 1960, over 320,000 traders in Ghana accounted for one seventh of the employed popu-lation, or two fifths of the nonagricultural sector. More than a quarter of a million women, over one fourth of the entire female labor force, were employed in petty trading. This was almost half as many women as were engaged in agriculture.[10] In 1966, Lawson estimated the num-ber of market traders, street sellers, and hawkers of food in Accra to

---

miro, on the other hand, flatly declares that "the indigenous bourgeoisie are merely a comprador class" ("The Political and Social Implications of Multi-National Corporations in Nigeria," in *Multi-National Firms in Africa*, ed. Carl Widstrand [Uppsala: Scandinavian Institute of African Studies, 1975], p. 234).

[9] Nicholas S. Hopkins, *Popular Government in an African Town* (Chicago: University of Chicago Press, 1972), p. 38.

[10] Walter Birmingham et al., eds. *A Study of Contemporary Ghana*, Vol. II, *Some Aspects of Social Struc-ture* (London: Allen & Unwin, 1967), p. 67.

be from 13,000 to 15,000 women—one out of every twelve women in Accra above the age of fifteen.[11]

Obviously, not all of these traders conform to the picture of the businessman held by Western economists or American consumers. For the most part, the tens of thousands of traders in Ghana and elsewhere in Africa are part-time entrepreneurs without stores or fixed capital investment of any type who merely break down commodities and resell them in quantities as small as a package of cigarettes, a dozen tomatoes, or a few pounds of red pepper. Several studies have divided merchants into a variety of categories, including petty traders, petty artisans, small-scale retailers, small-scale industrialists, larger retail traders, and specialized entrepreneurs.[12] A growth in the scale of operations and the amount of capital invested is noticeable everywhere, not only in the emergence of large supermarkets, warehouses, and factories but also in the expansion of the sidewalk sitters into street-side stalls.[13]

Because of the growing attractiveness of the pursuit of profit, politicians and civil servants engage ever more frequently and ferociously in business, either as a sideline or as a full-time occupation. In Zambia, for example, a country where capitalism had always occupied an uneasy and ambiguous position, a change in the status of the African businessman has occurred because commercial pursuits have proved so lucrative. A worker finds that his income is much greater when he enters trade; a civil servant gains more as a specialized entrepreneur.[14]

In the years before and immediately following independence, the greatest proportion of African students overseas took up the lib-

[11] Rowena M. Lawson, "The Supply Response of Retail Trading Services to Urban Population Growth in Ghana," in *The Development of Indigenous Trade and Markets in West Africa*, ed. Meillassoux, p. 387.

[12] See, for example, Andrew Beveridge, "Varieties of African Businessmen in the Emerging Zambian Stratification System," mimeographed (paper presented at the African Studies Associates Meeting, Syracuse, N.Y., October-November 1973); Beveridge, "Economic Independence, Indigenization and the African Businessman," *African Studies Review*, 17, no. 3 (December 1974), 477–92; Peter Marris and Anthony Somerset, *African Businessmen: A Study of Entrepreneurship and Development in Kenya* (London: Routledge & Kegan Paul, 1971); Peter C. Garlick, *African Traders and Economic Development in Ghana* (London: Oxford University Press, 1971); Jean Charbonneau and René Charbonneau, *Marchés et marchands d'Afrique Noire* (Paris: La Colombe, 1961); and Theodore Geiger and Winifred Armstrong, *The Development of African Private Enterprise* (Washington, D.C.: National Planning Association, 1964).

[13] Lawson, "The Supply Response," in *The Development of Indigenous Trade and Markets in West Africa*, ed. Meillassoux, p. 387.

[14] Marris and Somerset report: "There are signs that some quite high-status civil servants are now being attracted towards business. This probably does not represent a different pattern of motivation, but rather the same pattern at a higher level of sophistication. Now that the Africanization of civil service is largely completed, the prospects of pay and promotion are becoming less satisfying. Correspondingly, opportunities for sophisticated businesses are growing. Highly educated men now have the confidence to challenge the predominance of expatriate firms in these markets, and a greater frustration in their civil service prospects. As the African secretary of the Chamber of Commerce remarked to us: 'we want to show that Africans can compete on an equal foot with foreigners. It is a matter of respect.' " *African Businessman*, p. 66.

eral arts and law. During the period of consolidation of power by the new states, they turned to the sciences and technical occupations. Today, growing numbers of African students study business.[15]

Origins of African Business:
Early Trade and Traditional Encouragement

To discover that so many Africans trade, barter, and engage in a vast variety of other commercial activities should surprise no one with an acquaintance of African history. Seldom was the village, or even the smallest tribe, a self-contained economic unit completely isolated from external influences. Prefeudal, predominantly subsistence-based economies engaged in exchange that antedates all written records. When the first outside explorers, the Carthaginians, came to West Africa, they found a system of "silent trade" already established. Gold Coast Africans developed very early their most "durable, portable, and universally acceptable commodity," gold dust, into the equivalent of currency.[16]

In northern Katanga in the Lower Congo, a complex political system integrated a well-developed commerce over a common territory by building upon the complex culture that had existed there since at least the eighth century. Vansina tells us that "by the twelfth century long-distance trade in copper was under way, differences in wealth between poor and rich had increased, and chiefs or kings ruled over larger areas than earlier."[17]

By 1750, the Lunda had created an empire of over one million inhabitants and had established transcontinental trading routes from Angola to Mozambique, and were trading slaves, ivory, copper, salt, and European goods, as well as items of local produce. With the differences between social classes brought by the new wealth of an expanding trade in Lunda, internal confrontations developed. With the subsequent advent of the Portuguese, the rise of powerful traders of commoner origin further exacerbated these tensions.[18]

In West Africa, the rise of the coastal trade was not a substitute for the trade across the savanna and the Sahara: "the development of Dakar or Lagos did not necessarily spell the decline of Jenne or Kano."[19] Out of this new commerce, there again arose a strengthening

---

[15] See the recent reports on education cited in 70–72 Chapter VI.

[16] David Kimble, *A Political History of Ghana: The Rise of Gold Coast Nationalism, 1850–1928* (Oxford: Clarendon Press, 1963), p. 3.

[17] Jan Vansina, "Inner Africa," in *The Horizon History of Africa*, ed. Alvin M. Josephy, Jr. (New York: American Heritage, 1971), pp. 267–69.

[18] Cf. David Birmingham, who analyzes the development of these tensions in his *Trade and Conflict in Angola* (Oxford: Clarendon Press, 1966).

[19] Colin W. Newbury, "Prices and Profitability in Early 19th Century West African Trade," in *The Development of Indigenous Trade and Markets in West Africa*, ed. Meillassoux, p. 104.

of merchant and business classes, and the links between traders and the political ruling classes became ever tighter. For a long period these economic interests pursued their goals independently; a final link could take place successfully only in the postindependence period, when the new territories of the modern nation-states were forged.

Some of the ancient centers of trade either have disappeared — Kong, Buna, Bunduku, all destroyed by Samory Touré — or, like Djenne and Timbuktu, have lost their significance. However, other urban areas — Bamako and Mopti on the Niger, Bouake, Gagmoa, Ibadan, and Kumasi — remain prosperous centers for trade in dried fish, cattle, cola nuts, and other traditional items. The expansion of the capitalist economy, far from undercutting this ancient trade, has facilitated its spread through the widespread use of money, the introduction of the mail, railways, roads, and banking facilities, and the growth of urban populations.

Although there is some argument as to whether trade was always encouraged by state systems, the bulk of the evidence reveals numerous ways in which state protection and expansion encouraged commercial undertakings. Warfare in the most centralized of the states endangered the merchants' need for stability, but the merchants were far from pacifists, being eager, then as now, for those conflicts that brought new areas and customers into their potential reach and jurisdiction. As African states expanded, and as their administrative organization became increasingly complex, the state intervened more directly in trade. Rulers appointed special officials for its control, and allocated privileges and monopolies. Sometimes they assumed direct control over certain commerce.

Samory Touré, to give one example of the relationship between the great African rulers and trade, allegedly interfered "arbitrarily and willfully" in the minutest commercial transactions; he led wars that created consistent turmoil over huge areas of West Africa. Yet, by eliminating great numbers of small states with their persistent customs, other tax charges, and harassment, his empire created a market never before known. Although the merchants may have chafed under the tight economic control Samory's officials maintained over agriculture and markets, they profited immensely, as have merchants everywhere, by the demands for raw materials.[20] Touré relied upon the long-distance network of traders for the economic wherewithal with which to wage his campaigns, as well as for information with which to conduct his enormously successful international diplomacy. Pearson concludes, not surprisingly, that "the empire was dependent on the massive loyalty of the traders to the imperial organization and upon a strong sense of personal loyalty to Samori."[21]

[20] J. B. Webster and A. A. Boahen, *History of West Africa* (New York: Praeger, 1970), p. 45.

[21] Yves Pearson, "Samori and Resistance to the French," in *Protest and Power in Black Africa*, ed. Robert I. Rotberg and Ali A. Mazrui (New York: Oxford University Press, 1970), p. 90.

No wonder that African socialist leaders from coastal areas, educated in Western universities and unfamiliar with this past, underestimated the strength of resistance to their egalitarian and communal policies. They did not understand how over hundreds of years African traditional rulers and merchants had created the most sophisticated alliances of politics and commerce.[22]

---

[22] Abner Cohen goes beyond the clichélike formula that Islam and trade were associated, to argue that the reason for this association was that Islam "provided a blueprint for the establishment of networks of communities" ("Cultural Strategies in the Organization of Trading Diasporas," in *The Development of Indigenous Trade and Markets in West Africa*, ed. Meillassoux, p. 277). The creation of these trading networks required not only the mobilization of "a variety of types of social relationships" but also the "utilization of different kinds of myths, beliefs, norms, values and motives, and the employment of various types of pressure and of sanctions. If one takes all these needs and puts them together the result is an ideology embodied within a social system. What is true of Islam also characterizes Christianity and African traditional religions with their congruent patterns of religious behavior and modes of earning a livelihood." (*Ibid.*, p. 278)

In examining the economic development of an indigenous trading class and the political relations between the rulers of Asante and the Muslims, Ivor Wilks points out that historically non-Muslim traders had "little hope of penetrating the extraordinarily complex network of commercial relations that the Muslims had built up over the centuries throughout West Africa and the desert" ("Asante policy towards the Hausa trade in the nineteenth century" in *The Development of Indigenous Trade and Markets in West Africa*, ed. Meillassoux, p. 133). Wilks cites the example of Abu Bakr al-Sibbiq of Timbuktu and Jenne, branches of whose immediate family were located in Bornu, Katsina, Massina, Kong, and Buna.

Faced with this situation, one of the legendary founders of the Asante state, Osei Bonsu, decided to encourage Muslim settlement in Kumasi itself in order to encourage trade with the North. Around 1830, under a new king, the Asante expelled the Muslim merchants when disturbances occurred at Salaga. Trade was then reorganized more directly under the administration of the Asante political leaders, and a more influential place was accorded to Asante traders. The Asante state acted in a classical vein as the protector of a national commerce in driving out foreign merchants. Virtually the same situation occurred in late 1969, when, to the great benefit of indigenous merchants, the Ghana government under Dr. Busia deported on short notice all non-Ghanaians who did not possess residence permits.

The Asante traditional ruling class at first feared the development of an Asante merchant class because of the latter's growing wealth and revolutionary potential. Strangers, in contrast, were not only encouraged to establish businesses, but were also granted various privileges, including tax relief: "I cannot tell them to give me gold," stated Osei Bonsu, "when they buy and sell the goods," (quoted in *Ibid.*, p. 133). Only much later did Asante kings reverse this policy and encourage indigenous merchants, going so far as to carry on a number of extensive wars in the eighteenth century to secure free passage for Asante merchants attempting to drive to the sea to incorporate the ports that gave access to European venturers. See K. Y. Daaku, *Trade and Politics on the Gold Coast, 1600–1720* (Oxford: Clarendon Press, 1970), pp. 144–76. The first Asante rulers were, therefore, concerned with stimulating a new enterprise, whereas the later kings sought to maximize the Asante interest in an already developed ongoing commerce. See Wilks, "Asante policy towards the Hausa trade in the nineteenth century" in *The Development of Indigenous Trade and Markets in West Africa*, ed. Meillassoux, p. 136. Nkrumah, the first modern Ghanaian national leader, also feared the power of indigenous business. Ghana's present leaders seek Africanization of commerce and invest in its development.

An entirely different pattern of development of indigenous merchants in a traditional African state occurred in Dahomey, where merchants existed not as a separate class but simply as agents of a centralized economy controlled and taxed by the king. When the slave trade was ended, a most striking changeover was effected by the ruling class: privileges once accorded the king for the capture and sale of slaves were now granted for the exploitation and selling of palm oil.

Entrepreneurs also distinguished themselves in the nonempire traditional societies. Among the Masai, for example, a small group of merchants devoted most of their energies to trade and made exceptionally large profits. A study of these entrepreneurs revealed that their success depended on having contacts throughout Masailand so that caravans could be conducted with relative safety and goods could be disposed of rapidly. Success was not simply an individual matter but, as with the Muslims, was related to a network of entrepots and communications; success, in other words, was a matter of families, in which leadership in trade tended to pass from father to son. See

Early Modern African Businessmen and the Development of the New Class Under Colonial Policy

As early as 1787 Paul Denis, an African who could neither read nor write, conducted economic ventures that rivaled the King's Company in the amount of commerce engendered. In the French colonies, African merchants received their greatest official boost under the governorship of General Faidherbe, the "founder of modern Senegal." In addition to founding a special bank in St. Louis to provide local credit and reduce the dependence of local merchants on French financiers, Faidherbe's regime consistently encouraged the trading activity of the Creoles. Wesley Johnson tells us that "the cornerstone of Faidherbe's success in Senegal was his policy of linking the commercial interest of the St. Louis merchants with those of the Senegal river peoples. This inaugurated a cordial relationship that lasted centuries; and many Africans became trusted auxiliaries developing a real loyalty to the French."[23]

The largest commercial houses of Marseilles and Bordeaux did not hesitate to consign tens of thousands of dollars worth of merchandise to these Africans. Johnson also tells us that the overseas French corporations took over every aspect of the disposal of peanuts once they were sold at the provincial market, and the same African merchants could only retail goods such as imported cloth, rice, sugar, tobacco, and hardware, purchased from the same Bordeaux importers. African merchants could only dominate the local markets in fresh food, fish, and cola nuts that were produced and consumed entirely by Africans. This does not mean that African traders were mere servants. As K. Y. Daaku points out, it was they who dictated the terms of trade by insisting on modification of European goods to local speci-

---

Marris, and Somerset, *African Businessmen*, p. 37.

    In West Africa, investigations in recent years have revealed the emergence of a class of rural capitalists contrary to the usual view of West African traders as an "amorphous" group of peasants and fishermen. See Chapter VIII, the discussion of Polly Hill's findings about West African cocoa farmers. In a fascinating study of Anlo fishermen in Ghana, Hill revealed that whereas in the past most Anlo men owned nets of one sort or another, nowadays the ownership of the main seafishing net, the costly *yevudor*, is concentrated in a few hands and many active fishermen have given up aspiring to own one (*Studies in Rural Capitalism in West Africa* [Cambridge: Cambridge University Press, 1967], p. 39). Hill goes on to demonstrate not only how a hereditary class is developed, but also how the net owners have expanded their possessions; many net owners own many more than one net.

    Still another type of African traditional trading class may be found in the Mouride Brotherhood, whose wealthy marabouts became shrewd businessmen. Some of these marabouts ran large plantations, their *talibes* furnishing the labor; others turned more to trade and became rich merchants from the conations of their *talibes* as well as their commercial efforts. See Cheikh Tidaine Sy, *La confrerie Senegalaise des Mourides* (Paris: Presence Africaine, 1969); Lucy Behrman, *Muslim Brotherhoods and Politics in Senegal* (Cambridge, Mass.: Harvard University Press, 1970); Irving Leonard Markovitz, "Traditional Social Structures, the Islamic Brotherhoods and Political Development in Senegal," *Journal of Modern African Studies*, 8, no. 1 (1970), 73–96; and Donal Cruise O'Brien, *The Mourides of Senegal* (New York: Oxford University Press, 1971).

[23] G. Wesley Johnson, Jr., *The Emergence of Black Politics in Senegal* (Stanford, Calif.: Stanford University Press, 1971), p. 28. See also R. Delavignette's essay on Faidherbe in Ch.-Andre Julien, ed., *Les Technicians de la Colonisation* (Paris: Presses Universitaires de France, 1947), pp. 93–111.

fications in terms of color and quality.[24] Perhaps more important, no matter how much the Europeans tried, the Africans could not be displaced in the retail business, for Europeans could never for long venture into the inland states, and certain local industries in the interior continued to produce for a wide African market.

The steamship was one great Western invention that facilitated the rise of small merchants: unlike the clippers owned by the dominant European export-import firms, the steamers offered a faster, cheaper service to anyone who could pay the freight rates and was willing to accept produce and deliver merchandise in smaller lots than before. Kimble tells us that after the African Steamship Company began a regular service from Plymouth to West Africa in 1852–1853, small-scale businessmen entered the direct import-export trade in increasing numbers. This, coupled with an expansion of the credit system, resulted in a new class of traders. So many new African merchants entered the scene that F. Fitzgerald, the London editor of the *African Times,* enthusiastically declared, "We want a race of *native capitalists* in West Africa . . . and we will do our best to help in the creation."[25]

A new group of Africans rose to become true "merchant princes." Many of them first served an apprenticeship in the service of the European traders and learned how to take advantage of the modern credit and transportation facilities of international capitalism. They went on to become powerful and influential, exerting an extensive impact on the political and economic life of their own states, as well as on other colonies on the coast. Robert Hutchison of Ghana, for example, claimed to be worth £60,000 in 1855.[26] Other able and prosperous merchants included the Akrosan brothers of Fetu, Asomani of Akwamu, John Kabes of Komenda, and John Konny of Ahanta. Again, we must emphasize the connections between the traditional leaders and these influential Africans, who could go as emissaries to the courts of Europe as well as inaugurate local industries.

In 1656, the merchant prince John Claessen, one of the most important Africans on the whole coast, turned down the opportunity to become the king of the important regional state of Fetu because the duties of overlordship would have made it impossible for him to carry on his trade. Custom in Fetu forbade the king to view the sea; this, coupled with his other responsibilities, would have precluded a continuation of his contact with the European merchants on the coast.

[24] Daaku, *Trade and Politics on the Gold Coast, 1600–1720,* p. 24. Margaret Priestly shows the relations among Europeans, traditional rulers, merchants, and early nationalists in her *West African Trade and Coast Society* (London: Oxford University Press, 1969).

[25] Quoted in Kimble, *A Political History of Ghana,* p. 5. Cf. Edward Reynolds, *Trade and Economic Change on the Gold Coast, 1807–1876* (London, Longman, 1974), especially pp. 103–38.

[26] Kimble, *A Political History of Ghana,* p. 5. K. O. Dike, in *Trade and Politics in the Niger Delta, 1830–1885* (Oxford: Clarendon Press, 1956), analyzes the rise of African traders and emphasizes that well into the nineteenth century "the sovereignty of the African state was unimpaired by the presence of Europeans" (p. 8).

Claessen preferred his acquired position as a prosperous trader to that of political head of one of the most powerful chieftaincies in the region. No one doubted, however, that Claessen would continue to maintain great influence in the state, "where he was feared and respected by African and European traders alike."[27]

Nicholas Hopkins provides us with an excellent description of the role of African middlemen and bush traders in Kita, a small town in Mali. He points out that peasants grew the peanuts in isolated fields that were hard to find and hard to reach because of the poor road network, so the buyer had the problem of locating the peanuts and the peasant had the problem of transporting them to some collection point. Peasants much preferred to sell their crops on the spot or in their local village rather than incurring the expense of transporting them to some central point. Since the Europeans were hardly prepared to scour the bush, this facilitated the rise of African middlemen.[28]

Second-Class Citizens: Discrimination and the Reaction of African Business

Although they were willing partners in every aspect of European commerce, including the slave trade (African merchants strongly protested its abolition in 1807[29]), even the greatest of African merchant princes were treated as second-rate citizens, if not by the European governors and officers in charge, then more humiliatingly by their subordinates. The West African merchant Andrew Swanzy, for example, complained that too many colonial officials were ignorant of commercial affairs, were generally opposed to the traders, and considered themselves "specially appointed to protect the natives against them."[30] In the French colonies membership in the chambers of commerce, created in 1869, was reserved for French citizens. Although in theory urban Africans of the Four Communes were eligible, in fact only lower-level memberships were open to them. Because categories of membership were based on personal assets and volume of trade, few Africans could match the French and the Creoles. The chambers' statutes also stipulated that the directing members could come only from the upper categories. Membership in a chamber of commerce

[27] Quoted in Daaku, *Trade and Politics on the Gold Coast, 1600–1720*, p. 109. In Nigeria a comparable figure was Chief Nana of Olomo, who, like many other extremely powerful African leaders, functioned both as chief and merchant and was responsible for the shipment of thousands of slaves overseas. Appointed governor of the district by the British, he later was overthrown when the colonial power felt he had become too strong. See Ikime's brilliant analysis in his *Niger Delta Rivalry: Itsekiri-Urhobo Relations and the European Presence, 1884–1936* (New York: Humanities Press, 1969), pp. 69–126.

[28] Hopkins, *Popular Government in an African Town.*

[29] An argument advanced by Casely Hayford against the abolition of the slave trade was that abolition seriously affected commercial prosperity by discouraging trade from the interior, since traders found that their slave carriers deserted them upon reaching the coast (quoted in Kimble, *A Political History of Ghana*, p. 2).

[30] Kimble, *A Political History of Ghana*, p. 13.

was important for business, for this organization, unlike its American equivalent, was a quasi-legal agency that governed trade.

Over the entire economic life of British and French West Africa, three great European corporations (the *Compagnie Francaise de l'Afrique Occidentale*, founded in 1887, the *Societé Commerciale de l'Ouest Africain*, 1906, and Unilever, whose African branch was the United Africa Company—itself a combine fashioned in 1929) dominated wholesale and retail trading. They controlled the banking, currency, and transportation systems, and the buying of colonies' entire crops. These great combines fixed prices so as not to compete with one another; repatriated most of their profits, investing little in the local area; and, with their hundreds of branches and trading centers, made profits ranging from 90 percent in good years to 25 percent in poor.[31] Ghana and Nigeria witnessed the growth of farmers unions that attempted to protect their members against the repeated efforts of *grands comptoirs* to fix cocoa prices. In 1914, 1916, 1921, 1928, and 1930, Ghanaian farmers tried to hold back their cocoa crops in a demand for higher prices. Finally, in 1937 they succeeded in breaking the back of a price-fixing agreement organized secretly by the United Africa Company.[32]

Colonial government consistently aided the European firms and acted to protect them from African competition. One way in which they guarded the interests of the great European firms between the 1890s and the Second World War was to encourage the immigration of rootless Syrians and Lebanese.[33] Often, the African merchant princes were crushed between the developing great combines and the incoming Syrians and Lebanese.

During the nineteenth century the protest of the African merchants did not take on a nationalist character, for they could still make common cause with locally based European businessmen and settlers in demanding greater local political representation. African merchants shared a common policy position and joined in support of their European colleagues' grievances over questions of customs, duties, and other economic matters. By the Second World War, however, they had had enough. As A. G. Grant, the Sekondi timber merchant, told the Watson Commission in 1948, "We were not being treated right, we were not getting the licenses for the import of goods, also we were not pleased with the way our Legislative Council handled matters, because we had not the right people there. At one time, we had the Aborigine's Rights Protection Society who were taking care of the country. Later on, they were pushed out . . . thereby we keep on losing."[34] James Coleman tells us that in Nigeria, "aspiring

---

[31] See Jean Suret-Canale, *Afrique Noire*, 2 vols. (Paris: Editions Sociales, 1961, 1964).

[32] See the discussion of farmers in Chapter VIII.

[33] Virginia Thompson and Richard Adloff, *French West Africa* (Stanford, Calif.: Stanford University Press), pp. 429–31. Cf. R. Bayley Winder, "The Lebanese in West Africa," *Comparative Studies in Society and History*, 4 (November 3, 1962), 296–333.

[34] Quoted in Dennis Austin, *Politics in Ghana, 1946–1960* (Oxford: Oxford University Press, 1964), p. 51.

entrepreneurial groups in Nigeria felt themselves denied opportunities they regarded as theirs, and the responsibility for such denial was projected first upon the alien oligopoly and later upon the British administration, and . . . the entrepreneurial groups were strong and active in their support—both verbal and financial—to the nationalist movement."[35]

Consistently discriminated against, thwarted in their growing ambitions, shaken by European depressions, faced with growing numbers of Lebanese and Syrian small businessmen, and pressed by the ever expanding multilevel entrepreneurial activities of the larger European firms, Nigerian merchants were nevertheless capable and powerful enough to organize their own bank and financial institutions. (The National Bank of Nigeria was founded in 1933, and several others appeared immediately after World War II.) The ability of Nigerian entrepreneurs to establish such institutions belies the pessimistic assessments by Western commentators who exaggerate the admittedly enormous difficulties of African businessmen.[36]

The designation by the British of a European bank as the official bank of the government of Nigeria particularly aroused the ire of Nigerian big businessmen, for this denied working capital to indigenous entrepreneurs. Not only were the African-owned banks major contributors to the Nigerian nationalist movements, they received a substantial share of government business soon after African governments took power. Nigerian big businessmen, antagonized by the denial of hundreds of thousands of pounds of investment funds, provided great financial help for the developing nationalist movements. The hundreds of thousands of petty traders, particularly the women in the urban centers—who were equally aggrieved over a long line of colonial abuses and the commercial policies of the overseas firms—lent their energies to the nationalist movement. These petty traders demonstrated a remarkable capacity for organization and unity of action.[37]

Nigerian business interests were particularly strong in the Action Group, the dominant political party in the former Western Region. Characterized as an "oligarchy of leading chiefs, businessmen and politicians," the core element in the Action Group, according to Richard Sklar, was "a business group of impressive size and affluence . . . prob-

[35] James Coleman, *Nigeria: Background to Nationalism* (Berkeley and Los Angeles: University of California Press, 1958), p. 82.

[36] For example, Immanuel Wallerstein has maintained that "very few Africans still remain as middle-sized merchants [after the turn of the century], and their rise within the colonial framework to the rank of large-scale commercial or agricultural entrepreneurs—to say nothing of industrial entrepreneurs—was clearly out of the question. This was perfectly obvious not only to those who, despite everything, persisted as merchants, but also to that larger group of clerks and teachers who cherished such aspirations or who made few attempts to pursue such inclinations." ("The Colonial Era in Africa: Changes in the Social Structure" in *Colonialism in Africa, 1870–1960*, ed. Peter Duignan and L. H. Gann, Vol. 2, *The History and Politics of Colonialism, 1914–1960*, ed. Duignan and Gann [Cambridge: Cambridge University Press, 1970], p. 415) In a footnote, Wallerstein cites the vivid description by Odinga in his autobiography of the difficulties of a business career for Africans under colonial rule. However the most remarkable aspect of Odinga's career, according to his account, is that despite these difficulties he did succeed in becoming extremely wealthy and successful. See Oginga Odinga, *Not Yet Uhuru* (New York: Hill & Wang, 1967).

[37] Coleman, *Nigeria*, pp. 180–83.

ably the largest and wealthiest compact business group of Africans in Africa."[38]

Before independence, wealthy sections of the Yoruba middle class donated over £12,000 at a single meeting to build the party headquarters in Ibadan.[39] The strength of Yoruba "big business" in the cities was reinforced by its connection with its agents and small businessmen in small towns and rural areas. Throughout Africa, as traditional forms of local government were replaced by elected officials, these "representative" councils were taken over by "subelites" consisting sometimes of school teachers but more frequently of cash-crop farmers, middle-size traders, and shopkeepers.[40]

Action Group businessmen in the preindependence period demanded regional separatism, and advocated a policy of confederation. The Northern Peoples Congress (NPC) in 1953 and "conservative" parties in other countries of the continent strongly supported similar measures because they wished to safeguard their positions of domination and to avoid the risk of taxation and development policies that would transfer funds to other parts of the country.[41]

In Northern Nigeria the major premilitary political party, the Northern Peoples Congress, clearly represented the interests of the traditional ruling class, the *emirs*, and acted as their instrument. The entrepreneurs were predominantly of commoner origin. According to Sklar,

in 1958, 27% of the National Executive Committee of the Northern Peoples Congress and 17% of the executive members of the party in eight major Emirates were engaged in entrepreneurial activity. Nearly all of them were men of non-aristocratic and non-Fulani descent. It may be inferred that the hard core of the NPC comprises an economic elite of humble origin in addition to the Emirate functionaries.[42]

Northern businessmen created the Northern Amalgamated Merchants Union in 1956 to pressure the government into providing opportunities for businessmen of Northern origin. The Northern Con-

---

[38] Richard Sklar, *Nigerian Political Parties: Power in an Emergent African Nation* (Princeton, N.J.: Princeton University Press, 1963), p. 263.

[39] John P. Mackintosh, *Nigerian Government and Politics* (Evanston, Ill.: Northwestern University Press, 1966), p. 439.

[40] Martin Kilson, in a survey in 1964–1965, found that the Agona local council in central Ghana comprised three cocoa brokers, six cocoa farmers, and one lorry owner; the Nsawan-Aburi local council in the eastern region included one cocoa broker, two cocoa farmers, one contractor, two clerks, two merchants, one ex–civil servant, and three unidentified individuals. The composition of other local councils was similar. See Kilson's "The Emergent Elites of Black Africa, 1900–1960" in *The History and Politics of Colonialism, 1914–1960*, ed. Duignan and Gann, p. 370.

[41] Sklar, *Nigerian Political Parties*, p. 264; cf. the program of the National Liberation Movement during the same period described in my "Ghana Without Nkrumah," in *African Politics and Society: Basic Issues and Problems of Government and Development* (New York: Free Press; London: Collier-Macmillan, 1970), pp. 252–65. Sklar goes out of his way to emphasize that the desire for national independence on the part of the most prominent Yoruba businessmen was not contingent upon their anticipations of private gain; on the contrary, he felt that the majority of them, if need be, would have sacrificed their fortunes for the national interest. No doubt General Motors feels similarly about the United States.

[42] Sklar, *Nigerian Political Parties*, p. 335.

tractors Union lobbied successfully for the adoption of regional laws that would discriminate against non-Northerners in awarding government contracts.

Although "subdued antagonism" existed within the Northern Peoples Congress between members of the higher administration who were primarily men of aristocratic birth, and the commercial leaders of more common ancestry, and although the merchants might have resented the tradition that obliged them to "kowtow to the titled functionaries," Sklar suggests that "it is a paradox of Northern social development that traditional class consciousness mitigated the intensity of modern class struggle."[43] The merchants remained traditional commoners despite their affluence and upward mobility. They tended, therefore, to be sympathetic to the feelings of the people among whom they lived. However, their high position and activity on behalf of the NPC counteracted the more radical Northern Elements Progressive Union's appeal for a radical alteration of the existing social structure. Before the coup d'etat, the new Northern big businessmen were already well on their way to being assimilated into the old ruling class of the North.[44]

Today, the policies followed by African businessmen in Rhodesia strikingly parallel the actions taken by businessmen during the pre-independence nationalist phase of the 1950s in the black countries of West Africa. A recent survey in Rhodesia by Weinrich reveals that most of the African businessmen interviewed were "nationalistically inclined" and resented the leadership positions given by the European-controlled government to the chiefs. As elsewhere, business formed a particularly significant segment of the African political movement. Their possession of cars and trucks, for example, enabled businessmen to transport villagers to rallies. Entrepreneurial skills were also turned towards political organization. Affluence meant that businessmen enjoyed not only strong economic but also political influence in their area of origin: in the eyes of the peasants they occupied prominent positions and were objects "if not of admiration, then at least of envy."[45] Weinrich sums up the political feelings of African merchants by stating that

> businessmen do feel dissatisfied with their position. Government regulations impose restrictions on them while limiting their credit facilities and regulating when they may open their stores. When African businessmen compare their own opportunities with those of Europeans, they often feel discriminated against. Many can see only one way out of their difficulties: an African government. Whereas economic rewards tie higher civil servants to the establishment, economic needs spur many African store owners to support nationalistic movements.[46]

[43] Ibid.

[44] Mackintosh provides a detailed account, including the names, occupations, and political role of numerous Northern entrepreneurs, in Nigerian Government and Politics, p. 402.

[45] A. K. H. Weinrich, Black and White Elites in Rural Rhodesia (Manchester: Manchester University Press, 1973), pp. 203–4.

[46] Ibid., p. 204. For a similar assessment of Kenyan businessmen before that country reached inde-

Although dissension occurs among South Africa's merchants, a sizable black bourgeoisie exists that services the African community. This class is comfortable in its affluence and does not wish to rock the boat. It therefore follows an "Uncle Tom" policy comparable to that advocated in the past by the black bourgeoisie in the American South.[47]

The Political Role of African Merchants in the Postindependence Period

While the new African-led governments of the postindependence period were consolidating their power, the African business class continued to pursue its own interests vigorously. Often, black merchants found themselves in head-on conflict with a leadership that they had helped install. Bretton describes the position of these African businessmen:

> Their opposition to their own governments was not difficult to understand. Not only did their own leaders—they mistakenly regarded them as such—fail to produce the largesse popularly associated with independence, not only did they seem to welch on the promise of transfer of economic power into African hands, but all too soon they also allowed a rapidly expanding public sector to strangle the embryonic private sector. Weak to begin with, African private enterprise could not hope to maintain its precarious hold on its rather minute share of the national wealth, let alone carve out new opportunities and improve its overall position, if checked and opposed by the overwhelming resources at the disposal of the directors of the public sector.[48]

Mali

In an analysis of the connections between pre- and postindependence Malian politics, Nicholas Hopkins shows how, for political purposes, the essential occupational distinction, even in remote villages, lay between the salaried workers on the one hand, and the merchants who depended upon market conditions on the other. During the struggle for independence, merchants and civil servants could unite in their expectation of material gains: the merchants sought the commercial positions of the French and Lebanese; the civil servants, in addition to their ideological commitments, hoped for greater wage gains and higher office. Conflicts in Mali after independence, according to Hopkins, arose primarily when the civil servants tried to strengthen their grasp on the economy by putting it under state control and reducing the role of private merchants. Those civil servants not actively in favor of socialism still stood to benefit only by state-run enterprises. The

pendence, see J. M. Kariuku, *Mau Mau Detainee* (Baltimore: Penguin 1963), pp. 44, 135. See also Odinga, *Not Yet Uhuru.*

[47] See Leo Kuper, *An African Bourgeoisie* (New Haven: Yale University Press, 1965).

[48] Bretton, *Power and Politics in Africa*, p. 216.

merchants, on the other hand, considered state hegemony a life-and-death threat to their livelihood and the welfare of their families. They bitterly resented this move by an African government, following as soon as it did upon their contribution of much money and energy to the independence struggle.[49] When an army coup overthrew President Modibo Keita on November 19, 1968, the young officers promised, above all, to redress economic grievances and put the finances of the country in order. Almost immediately, the new government transferred most of the wholesale business sector, formerly a state monopoly, to private concerns. Also, they restored retail trade almost wholly to private hands, despite the survival of a state distribution circuit. Business picked up rapidly, particularly in luxury goods and investments in large apartment houses and other real estate.[50]

Senegal

The African business class in Senegal, rather than help stage a coup d'état, acted in its own best interest by supporting the prevention of one. After crises in 1958 over the referendum for independence and in 1960 over the rupture of the Mali Federation, President Mamadou Dia was overthrown in 1962. Although the overt issue was the struggle for political domination between Dia and Leopold Senghor, foremost among the underlying problems were different concepts of the role of the political party and methods of economic development. African commercial classes strongly opposed socialization of the economy, particularly nationalization of the peanut trade and the use of "rural animation" as an instrument of mass mobilization. The strong alliance between African businessmen and the marabouts (Muslim religious leaders)—sometimes the same individuals—controlled the allegiance of the mass of rural dwellers and strongly affected the outcome of this struggle.[51]

The postindependence demands of a class ever growing in numbers and organized strength were articulated clearly and vociferously in June, 1968, when

> some 2,600 representatives of small Senegalese business enterprises assembled in Dakar to consider ways to improve their lot. The theme of the Congress was frankly stated by the keynote speaker: "the nationals of the former colonial power who have stayed on have lost none of their privileges which, on the contrary, are reinforced through the free play of economic power." The principle resolutions the Congress adopted were even more pointed. They called for numerous economic activities to be restricted to Senegalese citizens, including practically all retail commercial establishments and distributorships, a wide range of services from realtors and insurance agencies to drug stores, printing

[49] Hopkins, *Popular Government in an African Town*, p. 71.

[50] For a discussion of political and economic changes in Mali after the coup, see Noel Ngouo-Ngabissio, "Mali: douloureuse desocialisation," *Jeune Afrique*, No. 593 (May 20, 1972), 40–43.

[51] See Irving Leonard Markovitz, *Leopold Sedar Senghor and the Politics of Negritude* (New York: Atheneum, 1969; London: Heinemann Educational Books, 1970); and Donal Cruise O'Brien, *The Mourides of Senegal* (New York: Oxford University Press, 1971).

plants and laundries and various light manufacturing fields, such as furniture and garment making and construction material. In addition, they sought assistance for Senegalese to accede to wholesale dealerships, to be accorded bank credit, and to attain positions of influence in businessmen's associations.[52]

This rising demand by indigenous enterprise that the government sever or in some way limit its support for the scope of activities of foreign business has become characteristic of all new African countries in the postindependence period. The African governments of the organizational bourgeoisie find themselves in a somewhat paradoxical situation, in that they originally rose to power with support from the colonial establishment.

In Senegal, the French business community responded quickly to the demands of this Union Congress by organizing a rival business group supported by the Senegalese government. However, in a further effort to disguise French economic dominance, the semiofficial Dakar Chamber of Commerce changed its regulations for membership in 1969 for the first time, in order to allow greater participation by African *commerçants*, and named a Senegalese as its President.

In recent years, the Senegalese government has taken additional measures to aid indigenous enterprise. For example, during 1971 a law was passed requiring that managerial posts in private firms be held by Senegalese within ten years. To assist domestic control of capital, the government pledged to take up shares in private foreign firms for the purpose of reselling them to Senegalese.[53]

The Ivory Coast

No country has aided the development of African business more actively than the Ivory Coast. Indeed, President Houphouet-Boigny, virtually alone among African leaders, has written pamphlets advocating African capitalism.[54] The Ivory Coast government established the Office for the Advancement of Ivorian Enterprise and the Fund to Guarantee Credits to Ivorian Enterprises, which provide technical assistance and bank credits for companies with majority Ivorian ownership.[55]

Kenya

Over the years, official Kenyan policy has veered sharply from an original commitment to African socialism to increasing sponsorship of an expanding African capitalist class. In a policy paper entitled *African Socialism*, the Kenyan government specified exactly how procapi-

---

[52] Edward M. Corbett, *The French Presence in Black Africa* (Washington, D.C.: Black Orpheus Press, 1972), p. 93.

[53] *West Africa*, July 9, 1971, p. 792. Other measures involved the creation of special credit facilities and new banking institutions; see *Jeune Afrique*, No. 572 (December 25, 1971), 44.

[54] Felix Houphouet-Boigny, *Discours et allocutions* (Paris: Information Service of the Ivory Coast, 1956).

[55] See Samir Amin, *Le developpement du capitalisme en Cote d'Ivoire* (Paris: Editions de Minuit, 1967).

talist it had become. The paper explained that whereas Africans had made their mark in politics and the liberal professions, the colonial past had prevented Africans from becoming a major force in commerce, and this racial heritage had to be overcome in order for the essential equality of Kenyans to be realized.[56]

Marris and Somerset found that Kenyan businessmen had characteristically been active in the struggle for independence, but as African governments came to power, the part these businessmen played in political life seemed to become less meaningful and they "transferred their patriotism to entrepreneurship."[57] In a strongly procapitalist interpretation, Marris and Somerset state:

> Europeans and Asians still dominated commerce and industry. African society was still backward, and desperately needed to create more employment, widen its industrial base, and generate the income to provide more education. As economic and political development evolved into distinct tasks so they claimed different leadership, and different talents. . . . So they transmuted African nationalism into African capitalism. To build up a business until its headquarters stood proudly in a main street of Nairobi besides the European companies; to provide employment and encourage its workers to build their own enterprises; to develop the township with shops, hotels, industries—these were national as well as political ambitions.[58]

That these Kenyan businessmen had indeed been active in nationalist movements may be seen in the significant number of the ICDC (International and Commercial Development Corporation)-supported merchants who had been detained as Mau Mau sympathizers, some having spent up to eight years in jail, others having been regarded by the colonial regime as hard-core political organizers and "forest fighters." A businessman's political past certainly does not hurt him today; many former activists are able to facilitate the negotiation and granting of loans through political contacts.[59]

Although the demands of enterprise left little time for outside activities, significant numbers of Kenyans who had been active in the struggle for independence have remained party officials. They devote much energy to local party committees, and function as town or country counselors. Only 14 percent of these former activists withdrew entirely from politics, and even they continued to give money to Kenya African National Union (KANU) and maintained their allegiances—they just didn't run for office.[60]

---

[56] "Kenya White Paper," in *African Socialism*.

[57] Marris and Somerset, *African Businessmen*, pp. 67–68.

[58] *Ibid.*, p. 69.

[59] Marris and Somerset state that one quarter of the businessmen they interviewed had facilitated the negotiation of their ICDC loan by political contacts, and they claim that although they did not obtain more money, or obtain it on better terms, they on the whole were able to obtain it more quickly (*Ibid.*, p. 68).

[60] *Ibid.*, p. 67.

The active role taken by African merchants against colonial regimes elsewhere in Black Africa was even more understandable in Kenya, given the racial composition and stringent discriminatory policies of the colonial government there. Industry, like everything else, was segregated. According to the government, the economic role of the Europeans was to engage in commercial agriculture and to operate subsidiary mills, dairies, bakeries, food processing factories, and so forth. They were to have their own urban centers with banks and commercial agencies. The role of the African was to work as subsistence farmers, live as squatters, and provide labor for the European economy. By law, Africans could not own land in European settlements or grow valuable export crops on their own lands; the African reserves were to be simply a source of labor. The European regime justified these policies by maintaining that eventually the entire "community," including the mass of Africans, would benefit. European agriculture would sustain the economy, and "as Africans were drawn into a money economy, as their standard of living rose and industries established themselves in an expanding market, so the groundwork of a progressive modern state would be laid."[61]

In reality, an expanding European economy benefited only a very small percentage of the European ruling class, which based its power upon exploited labor today and "pie in the sky" for tomorrow. In some respects, the present Kenyan government acts similarly: it promises African socialism for some remote future yet promotes the organizational bourgeoisie, which is dominated by an expanding commercial bourgeoisie and a growing capitalist class of larger farmers.[62]

The European political and economic domination in Kenya collapsed in the eleven years between the declaration of the State of Emergency in 1952 and Kenyan independence. In 1953, African farmers were permitted for the first time to grow coffee. Ten years later, a quarter of a million small holders owned half the total coffee acreage in the country. The same thing happened with tea, the second largest export crop; by 1964, the African share of the tea acreage had reached almost 25 percent. After land ownership in the "white highlands" was opened to Africans on the eve of independence in 1962, government settlement schemes enabled the transfer to African farmers of one third of these acres; another half million acres were bought by Africans as individuals or cooperatives, and about 300,000 acres were acquired by local or national governments.[63] Although these figures tell us nothing about the distribution of land among the African population, they do indicate the explosion of commercial farming and the readiness and willingness of Africans to capitalize agriculture once the opportunity became available.

---

[61] *Ibid.*, p. 6.

[62] For a contrary view, see Henry Bienen, *Kenya: The Politics of Participation and Control* (Princeton, N.J.: Princeton University Press, 1974).

[63] John C. de Wilde, *Experience With Agricultural Development in Tropical Africa*, Vol. 2 (Baltimore: Johns Hopkins, 1967).

Government aid to African business in Kenya has been an important factor in its rapid development. In 1956, a fund of £230,000 was made available for loans to enterprising African shopkeepers selected by local boards, and for the organization of business courses for traders. In 1964, the Industrial Development Corporation began granting loans and extending credit guarantees to African shopkeepers so that they could compete with Asian rivals. The government also established the Kenya National Trading Corporation as a subsidiary of ICDC to promote the interest of Africans in wholesale trade.[64] Soon after independence, the government redirected the bulk of the wholesale sugar distribution to African concerns, and forced Asian retailers for the first time to buy an essential commodity from African suppliers. In response to political pressures, the breweries and cigarette manufacturers also turned from Asian to African distributing agencies. By 1966, Asian shopkeepers were withdrawing from the rural market centers.[65]

In 1968, a list of the "top fifty" company directors in Kenya included nine Kenyans and two Ugandians; the rest were British and Irish. Considering the brief amount of time Africans could legally engage in major business enterprises, this figure is remarkable. In 1967, sixty-two companies, with net assets of £67 million, were quoted on the Nairobi stock exchange. Three had a majority of African directors, but over half had entirely European boards. In all, 14 percent of 376 directorships in these companies were held by Africans and 5 percent by Indians. Again, considering the amount of time since independence, these figures indicated remarkable progress on the part of Africans.[66]

In the postindependence period, paradoxically, European enterprise increasingly appeared comparatively "progressive." The organization of large European industries, the Federation of Kenya Employers (FKE), took the lead in supporting a rise in the statutory minimum wage; it also demanded equal pay for equal work. The reasons for this are not hard to discern: the FKE's major objective was that infant African companies and giant European ones should be treated equally under labor law; a government-enforced minimum wage serves to protect large industry from small, nonunionized competitors. The FKE also set up courses and experts to train "progressive" African entrepreneurs in scientific personnel administration and business administration.[67]

[64] Marris and Somerset, *African Businessmen*, pp. 10–11.

[65] *Ibid.*, p. 11.

[66] *Ibid.*, p. 12. Marris and Somerset, however, draw very different conclusions from these figures, arguing that the percentages demonstrate the limited role of Africans in business.

[67] Alice H. Amsden, *International Firms and Labour in Kenya, 1945–1970* (London: Frank Cass, 1971), p. 166.

Sierra Leone

In Sierra Leone in the mid 1850s a group of Creole merchants formed the Sierra Leone Mercantile Association (SLMA), which functioned not only to improve business practices but also to lobby the colonial government for favorable trade policies. Despite occasional reorganizations, the indigenous Sierra Leone businessmen have to the present day remained a well-organized interest, and the government has turned to its recognized spokesmen whenever its advice was required.[68] One goal that brought Sierra Leone businessmen into early conflict with "the natives" was their desire for the British to annex the "hinterland" for the "advancement and protection of trade." Precipitated by colonial encroachments during the "hut tax war," Mende tribesmen killed many Creole merchants and their families. These events have affected the evolution of Sierra Leone political parties to the present day. Although by the turn of the twentieth century lawyers, doctors, journalists, teachers, and other members of the liberal professions had begun to replace merchants as the leading spokesmen for African interests,[69] merchants continued to play an important role, as their children joined them after college and attained new professional status. In addition to the pressure exerted by big imperialist firms against their African competitors, the professional classes possessed more leisure and education, which equipped them to formulate demands in ideological terms and then to promulgate these demands in newspapers and other media.

Since Africans gained control of their governments during the late 1950s, they have adhered vigorously to the declaration made in 1957 by the Sierra Leone Peoples Party Minister of Trade and Commerce, I. B. Taylor, that "it is government's policy to encourage private enterprise."[70] From that time to the present, extensive assistance has been given African businessmen, including the resale of manufacturing machinery to African industrialists at less than original cost, tax holidays under the Development Ordinance of 1960, and special import privileges designed to bring in the necessary goods and materials for the establishment of industries, plantations, and other enterprises.

In 1972, after a series of coups d'etat and administrative changes, government beneficence towards business does not seem to

---

[68] Kilson discusses the history of diverse business associations from the 1850s to the present in "The Emergent Elites of Black Africa, 1900–1960" in *The History and Politics of Colonialism, 1914–1960*, ed. Duignan and Gann, pp. 351–98.

[69] Kilson points out that between 1863 and 1903, nine out of twelve of the educated Africans nominated to the Sierra Leone Legislative Council were merchants. But by 1911, lawyers and doctors were preeminent among the African representatives. A similar situation occurred in Ghana and elsewhere in West Africa. (*Ibid.*, p. 377)

[70] Quoted in Martin Kilson, *Political Change in a West African State: A Study of the Modernization Process in Sierra Leone* (Cambridge, Mass.: Harvard University Press, 1966).

have abated. In 1972, the government commissioned a special report by Dr. N. A. Cox-George and the Bank of Sierra Leone, entitled "Capital Availability and Sierra Leonean Entrepreneurship." The report did not mince words in its very pessimistic assessment of the difficulties facing local concerns:

> As a result of an extremely classical educational tradition and other historical factors, most Sierra Leoneans do not consider business as a worthy vocation. . . . Coupled with extreme individualism and buttressed by an outmoded company law, a very restricted market of only about two and a half million people, political instability, inertia, widespread bribery, corruption and general dishonesty, render Sierra Leonean businessmen helpless in the face of expatriate competition.[71]

Immediately, however, the report then indicates that "effective demand" by purely Sierra Leonean ventures for additional capital and bank loans is on the increase, and that, furthermore, there is every expectation for capital funds to be made available. Little doubt seems to exist in the mind of the authors of the report that business will continue to expand in Sierra Leone and that significant aid from the government will be forthcoming.[72]

Nigeria

Since the end of the Nigerian-Biafran civil war the government has taken steps to guarantee that, in the words of the Federal Commissioner for Finance, Al Haji Shehu Shagari, indigenous interests occupy "all the commanding heights of the Nigerian economy." In Nigeria, as the newsweekly *West Africa* points out, this does not necessarily mean the nationalization of the foreign enterprises that have dominated these heights for so long. It does mean that the government will provide the finances to enable Nigerian businessmen to take over foreign-owned enterprises or increase Nigerian participation in them. To a large extent, this policy is due "to the existence in Nigeria of a thriving commercial class, who have no more enthusiasm for socialism than their counterparts in Europe. . . ." Also, it is due partly to those foreign firms that began issuing shares to the Nigerian public some time ago, and partly to "a realization that there are limits to what governments can or should do in the economic field," a realization that relates to a long-standing belief of leading government officials in "liberalism" rather than socialism.[73]

To effect this policy of "indigenization," the Supreme Military Council passed the Nigerian Enterprises Promotion Decree of 1972, which excluded foreigners totally from certain types of enterprise. Af-

---

[71] *West Africa*, June 2, 1972, p. 707.
[72] *Ibid.*
[73] *West Africa*, April 21, 1972.

ter March 31, 1974, aliens were to be excluded totally from twenty-two types of enterprises—including retail trade, certain light industries, and services such as laundering and road transport—and were permitted only limited participation in such areas as wholesale distribution, interstate bus services, shipping, and the state agencies. Foreigners had to sell all ownership and could participate only in enterprises in which capital exceeded £200,000 or in which turnover exceeded £500,000 annually. Even so, Nigerians had to maintain an "equity holding" of at least 40 percent.[74] A further measure provided for the systematic replacement of expatriates in the management of the remaining large foreign-controlled corporations as more Nigerians qualified.[75] A special body, the Nigerian Enterprises Promotion Board, was to advise on the effectuation of this policy of indigenization. From the beginning, the government was convinced that enough private capital was available in Nigeria to buy or buy into these enterprises, even though a huge sum, over £100 million, had to be raised by Nigerians—an accomplishment that underlines the enormous growth in a short time of Nigerian entrepreneurs.[76]

In 1968, non-Nigerians controlled 70 percent of the nation's 625 largest manufacturing establishments.[77] Depending upon one's perspective, this is either a pessimistic or an optimistic figure. One could argue that it is remarkable that in only a very short period over 30 percent of the country's largest establishments are now controlled by Nigerians, and that the trend is growing constantly in this direction. The capacity of Nigerian business must be viewed especially in terms of recent discoveries of huge pools of crude oil that give Nigeria at least a two-million-barrel-a-day production capacity.

Nigerian business has proved so attractive that the Nigerian Chamber of Indigenous Contractors, in an open letter to the head of state and to all military governors, warned of the growing involvement of high-ranking public officers in private businesses, including partnerships with foreign companies, a trend that threatened the government's indigenization policy. The president-general of the Chamber called for the Decree of 1972 to ban all high-ranking public officers from participating in any type of private business.[78]

Ghana

In Ghana, even under Nkrumah and the "radical" Convention Peoples Party, the government went out of its way to aid private busi-

---

[74] *West Africa*, March 10, 1972, p. 301.

[75] *Africa Digest Guide*, No. 3 (June 1972).

[76] *West Africa*, April 21, 1972, and March 17, 1972, p. 307.

[77] Thomas A. Johnson, "Nigeria Moves Boldly to Gain Control of Her Economy," *New York Times*, September 1, 1972.

[78] *West Africa*, February 4, 1972, p. 135.

ness.[79] A hardening of this attitude toward indigenous entrepreneurs did not occur until 1960. Even then, Nkrumah declared that the economic structure still remained divided into four sectors: that owned by the state, joint state-private enterprise, the cooperative sector, and the truly private area. For the first time Nkrumah declared that the "government intends to place far greater emphasis on the development of Ghanaian cooperatives rather than encourage Ghanaians to start private business enterprises." According to Nkrumah, "In the past, the government has given considerable assistance to Ghanaian private enterprise but the result has been negligible and disappointing." Nkrumah went on to announce that the government intended to foster cooperatives in the retail distribution area and force private Ghanaian enterprise to "stand on its own feet." He also emphasized that his government intended to develop a socialist pattern of society.[80] Nevertheless, institutions created by his regime, such as the guaranteed corporation and the small-loan section of the Industrial Development Corporation, supported the expansion of indigenous business. Numerous grants to contractors and the awarding of all sorts of other contracts to Ghanaians also indicated a contrary intent.[81]

During the 1960s, businessmen were among those imprisoned under Ghana's Preventive Detention Act. Business spokesmen became increasingly vocal in their warnings that government policies had created confusion in the commercial life of the country, and in their opposition to various tax and compulsory savings schemes. The consistent ambiguity of the government's position was revealed when the government continued to give business contracts even to former deputies who had been deposed from the National Assembly and imprisoned.[82] Even in an April 8, 1961 speech in which he announced a more militant political position, Nkrumah said, "Any party member of parliament who wishes to be a businessman can do so, but he should give up his seat in parliament."[83]

A major crackdown on private Ghanaian enterprise came with the establishment of the Ghana National Trading Corporation and the purchase by the government of the Commonwealth Trust Limited, which owned forty-five stores in late 1961. This indicated that the state was entering the international trading field as a serious participant. The Convention Peoples Party (CPP) Draft Program for the period 1963–70 stipulated in no uncertain terms that private Ghanaians would be prohibited from participating in large-scale corporations. The government crackdown on import licensing, the tightening of exchange-controls, and announced plans for government-con-

[79] See Garlick, African Traders and Economic Development in Ghana.

[80] Ibid., p. 124. See also Scott W. Thompson, Ghana's Foreign Policy, 1957–1966 (Princeton, N.J.: Princeton University Press, 1969).

[81] Cf. Bob Fitch and Mary Oppenheimer, Ghana: End of an Illusion (New York: Monthly Review Press, 1966).

[82] Garlick, African Traders and Economic Development in Ghana, p. 124.

[83] Kwame Nkrumah, "Dawn Broadcast to the Nation" (Accra: Government Printing Office, 1961).

trolled wholesaling and retail cooperatives indicated a dim future for private enterprise of any size. Simultaneously, however, the government actively sought foreign aid and established the Capital Investment Board and the Ghana National Investment Bank in 1963 to provide long-term financing for approved development projects run by foreign capitalism.

One of Nkrumah's most uncompromising and hostile statements on the government's attitude toward Ghanaian business was articulated on March 11, 1964, on the occasion of the launching of the Seven-Year Development Plan: "Mr. Speaker, we would be hampering our advance to socialism if we were to encourage the growth of Ghanaian private capitalism in our midst. This would, of course, be in antipathy to our economic and social objectives."[84] Nkrumah went on to say that certain Ghanaians possessed vast entrepreneurial energies that should be utilized to operate state and socialist undertakings. Two types of businesses that had grown up in recent years had to be distinguished. The first type, which the government intended to continue to encourage, was the small businessman employing his capital in an industry or trade that fulfilled a public need. The second type, which consisted of a class of Ghanaian businesses modeled on colonial exploitation, was the purchase and resale at high prices of basic commodities such as fish and salt that were in demand by the people and could be distributed by other means. Nkrumah maintained, therefore, "The initiative of Ghanaian businessmen will not be cramped, but we must take steps to see that it is channeled toward desirable social ends and is not expended in the exploitation of the community."[85] Ghanaian participation in foreign enterprises, according to Nkrumah, had proved to be simply a front for the manipulation of Ghanaian commerce by colonial business ventures; therefore, such participation would be prohibited in the future.

No wonder, then, that the government-sponsored economic survey of 1965 reported, "Business confidence has suffered in the past few years as a result of government's attitude towards private enterprise. . . . The year 1965 was no exception. Business confidence was low throughout the year."[86]

Despite Nkrumah's official policy, private enterprise continued to expand. Among the reasons for this were, first, that anticapitalist government initiatives often backfired. For example, stress on the cooperatives forced diamond and timber men to join forces, yet this only facilitated their carrying on their activities much as before, aided, however, both by increased mutual cooperation and by government technical assistance. A second reason was the bureaucracy circumvented Nkrumah's announced intentions. Along the chain of command there were points with neither strong enough discipline nor

---

[84] Quoted in Garlick, *African Traders and Economic Development in Ghana*, p. 126.

[85] Quoted in *Ibid.*

[86] Quoted in *Ibid.*

sufficient political will. Third, despite a period of low cocoa prices and the declining confidence of the business community, the absolute level of economic activity and the rise in the gross national product continued to increase, thereby benefiting business in general.

After the overthrow of Nkrumah, the new government indicated that it would open a new era for private enterprise, both domestic and foreign. As one commentator described the attitude of African businessmen, "There is little doubt that in general their rejoicing at his downfall was genuine."[87] Against the auspicious background of the highest cocoa prices in over ten years, General Afrifa's National Liberation Council government announced a new policy on July 5, 1968, one that promoted Ghanaian business. As with the Nigerian decree of 1972, this legislation delineated certain types of business activities in which foreigners were not allowed to participate, and outlined financial, managerial, and advisory assistance.[88]

Dr. K. A. Busia came to power as a result of the victory of the Progress Party in the August 29, 1969 election. His Ghanaian Business Promotion Act of July, 1970[89] followed closely the policy of the previous military administration. In promoting Ghanaian enterprises, this law forbade foreign ownership of wholesale or retail trading enterprises—again, similar to the Nigerian legislation—with a turnover of less than 500,000 new cedis a year, and listed several additional fields of economic activity reserved for Ghanaians. The government also established a credit-guarantee scheme under the Bank of Ghana in order to help Ghanaian businessmen buy the businesses foreigners were compelled to give up under the act. The act also set up the Office for Business Promotion in order to assist Ghanaians in their further business ventures. All of this, of course, represented a complete change of policy from that of the Nkrumah regime.

Astonishingly, in contrast with the pan-African philosophy of the Nkrumahists, the Busia government on November 19, 1969 required all aliens without residence permits to leave Ghana within two weeks. Overnight, thousands of non-Ghanaian Africans, in addition to other foreigners, had to dispose of their businesses, most of which were small.[90] Tens of thousands of refugees choked the roads to the bor-

---

[87] *Ibid.,* p. 129.

[88] Under the Ghanaian Enterprises Decree, December 31, 1968, retroactive to July 1, 1968, a special sixteen-man committee was to compile a list of those foreign-controlled businesses that were to cease operation. Before Busia came into power, over 200 firms were ordered under this law to cease their activities. (*Ibid.,* p. 130)

[89] "Ghanaian Business Promotion Act" (Accra: Government Printing Office, July, 1970). The government of President Mobutu Sese Seko of Zaire passed a similar decree in March 1973 that ordered most of the smaller foreign-owned businesses to sell out to citizens of Zaire. This decree sharply accelerated the growth of an indigenous business class. See the articles by Thomas A. Johnson in the *New York Times,* July 4, 1974 and November 15, 1974.

[90] See also the pamphlet, *Burning Questions: Ghanaian Business Promotion Act (Act 334)* (Tema, Ghana: Ghana Publishing Corporation), p. 3, which indicates the direct connection between this act and the policy of the National Liberation Council. The booklet also provides details on the fields of business restricted to Ghanaians and the alien enterprises affected. The only difference between this act and the NLC Decree for the Promotion of Ghanaian Business Enterprises is that the Busia government committed itself to becoming more involved and active in the promotion of Ghanaian business. An

ders, particularly Togolese and Nigerians struggling fearfully to depart. No storm of protest rose in the West—as occurred when Nkrumah acted harshly against his political opponents—to greet this action, which meant untold suffering for so many. Peter Garlick offers the modest assessment that the "legislation in 1968 and 1970 indicates a strong belief on the part of the post-Nkrumah leadership in the capacity of private Ghanaian enterprise."[91]

Under the present military regime, Colonel Acheampong—after stating that previous governments had neglected agriculture and that the present emphasis should be on the country feeding itself, as well as on replacing imported raw materials for factories with local materials—has articulated very clearly his philosophy towards private Ghanaian investors. Categorizing the states of development of Ghanaian policy towards business from the beginning, Acheampong noted:

> In the fifteen years since Ghana attained independence, we have gone through two separate and diametrically opposite phases of development. There was a period when all development was, so to speak, invested upon the state. From 1966, however, an attempt was made to reverse this and in the past three years, we saw a government which believed in total reliance upon the private sector and a free market economy.
>
> Since January 13th [1972] the question has been asked often as to what the principle of economic development will be. My answer is simple. I have said that my aim is to use state power to capture the commanding heights of the economy and to control it in such a way that its development will not go to benefit only a few handfuls of well-placed Ghanaians.[92]

Since this pronouncement, the basic characteristic of the Acheampong regime has been a devoted commitment to nationalism and to the furthering of Ghanaian concerns of every type. Considering itself basically pragmatic, the regime, though stating specifically that it does not condemn the 1966 coup, has resurrected the reputation of President Nkrumah because of his nationalist ideals and aspirations. Insofar as business is Ghanaian, the government has also extended the aid of its bureaucracy and banks, as well as its general support. Under this regime, business, though still suffering from certain disabilities, continues to advance and prosper.[93]

---

indication of the popularity of the expulsion of foreigners and of which interests benefited may be seen in the petition of the market women in Sekondi-Takoradi to the City Council not to reallocate stalls to aliens. The women alleged that after the coup some aliens, mainly Nigerians, attempted to reclaim businesses they had occupied before the Busia government's measure. The army was also asked to intervene in Kumasi to stop a quarrel between Ghanaians and Nigerians who were making the same effort. See *West Africa*, February 11, 1972, p. 166.

[91] Garlick, *African Traders and Economic Development in Ghana*, p. 148.

[92] *West Africa*, June 23, 1972, p. 781.

[93] Consider, for example, the Capital Investments Act, which prescribes investment incentives and leaves no doubt as to the government's intentions towards private capital. See *West Africa*, April 14, 1972, p. 462.

Conclusion

Despite the changing policies of imperial regimes, African business not only managed to endure but went on to play an active role in nationalist movements. Before colonialism, African business made its peace with traditional ruling classes. Despite a wide variety of African precolonial political systems, African business succeeded in becoming an integral part of these societies, a close partner to the governors, and beneficiaries of both war and peace. During the postindependence period, after military coups toppled the first generation of committed radical leaders and so much ideology of African socialism proved rhetorical, African business rose anew and achieved unprecedented heights of prosperity and governmental power.

Although concerned observers worry about the growing power of the multinational corporations, the apparently dominant trend is for the nationals of African countries to run their own local businesses as well as the local branches of giant enterprises, and in general to manage their own economic affairs. In this effort, African businesses have enlisted the aid of their governments. African businesses prosper because the MNCs act more as boosters than competitors. The MNCs' tremendous power provides them with an enormous resiliency in the face of untoward developments. Many traditional expectations about the helplessness of underdeveloped countries in the face of large firms, the social significance of nationalization, and the limited creativity of African businesses have proved unwarranted.

For example, five years ago no international oil expert would have predicted that by 1976 most major oil-producing countries would nationalize their oil industries. Yet the success of the Arab oil embargo, the fivefold price increase of 1973–74, and the cartellike behavior of the Organization of Petroleum Exporting Countries (OPEC) have not diminished either the power or the profits of the multinational corporations. Again demonstrating their resiliency, the MNCs changed the meaning of nationalization from a threatening act, a radical purging of foreign devils with much oratorical floggings, to a mutually satisfactory deal with the indigenous organizational bourgeoisie. The monetary might of the MNCs has not declined as a result of nationalization because the host governments rather than the taken-over companies become responsible for capital investments. Those nations anxious for the MNCs to remain as investors of complete takeovers reluctantly travel "the 100 percent route."

Without the negotiated consent of the MNC, the nationalizing country runs the immense risk of losing the technical and management expertise of the MNC as well as the marketing of its products, particularly if there is a world overcapacity of those products. What matters, however, for the MNCs is their ability to continue to make a profit on the product they sell. The oil companies considered that OPEC had created "quite a constructive atmosphere" when its members questioned whether the 20-to-25-cent profit per barrel was high enough to keep the oil companies "active" in the OPEC countries over the long run.

The ability to provide an orderly market and maintain the traditional buffer role between consumers and producers is a trump card the MNC will always have, despite nationalizations. Thus, "nationalization" can mean merely "participation": the MNCs remain entwined in operations, provide technical assistance, establish markets, and continue in a difficult-to-dissolve relationship that supposedly benefits both the MNC and the host country.

Nigeria, Ghana, Tanzania, and most other African governments have declared their intention to capture the "commanding heights of the economy." Whatever their ultimate power in the matter, states controlled by the organizational bourgeoisie have at least succeeded in insisting on the expanded training and employment of their nationals. As Ghana's Investment Policy warns, "In the field of complete foreign ownership, the foreign investor is advised in his own interest to be associated with citizens of Ghana as they are familiar with Ghanaian business and customs."[94] African governments, as we noted above, increasingly reserve areas of their economy and enterprise that do not require large amounts of capital or complicated technology for their nationals. The result is maximum encouragement for indigenous business.

In this discussion of business, examples have been taken from East, West, and Central Africa. In every country and in every instance, the general conclusion must be that the number, size, and extent of influence of African business everywhere on the continent is growing; at the same time, virtually every government in every country, whether military or civilian, has increasingly sought the support of business as a political interest group and is continuing through its bureaucracies, institutions, practices, and policies to support the active expansion of national enterprises. Backed by the armed strength of the new states and girded in the tightly tailored mantle of nationalist legitimacy, African business must be counted a basic force in the consolidation of power and in the continuing struggle for the determination of policy.

In Western historical development the rise of business threatened to impoverish the industrial wage-earning class. In Africa however skilled labor has prospered. African business found unexpected allies.

---

[94] "Ghana's Investment Policy of Today," advertisement of the Capital Investments Board in the *New York Times*, February 4, 1973. Cf. "Panel (of Ghanaian Businessmen) Discuss Africanization," in the same issue.

Chapter VIII

THE CONSOLIDATION OF POWER:
African Labor, Peasants, and Farmers

Although the wage-earning class in Africa constitutes a much smaller proportion of the labor force than farmers, numbers alone do not give an adequate indication of its significance and strength. Because of its strategic location in the cities as well as in the economy, because of its organization, because of the involvement of labor leaders with the governing bourgeoisie, and because of the growing importance of the expanding commercialized sectors of the economy, organized labor counts heavily in the formation of policy in postindependence Africa. As everywhere, many gradations occur within labor's ranks, but a fundamental division exists between white-collar workers — mainly civil servants — and manual laborers, as well as between skilled and unskilled labor. A further division occurs between labor leaders and the rank and file of the unions.

Although labor unions are, according to one popular image, among the most radical social forces in Africa, here as elsewhere they have concerned themselves primarily with bread-and-butter issues. They have not hesitated to involve themselves in politics when they perceive a direct connection between politics and these matters. In the past labor leaders pressured the French National Assembly to pass legislation ending discrimination in regard to the salaries of African and European civil servants. They did not occupy themselves with politics in the abstract or for broad political objectives. They were much less committed than expected to political independence as an ideological goal. Moreover, unions in many countries did not affiliate with nationalist political movements until virtually the advent of self-government.[1]

---

[1] See William H. Friedland, *Unions, Labor and Industrial Relations in Africa: An Annotated Bibliography* (Ithaca, N.Y.: Center for International Studies, Cornell University, 1965), for the best biographical summary of the literature. See also Ioan Davies, *African Trade Unions* (Baltimore: Penguin, 1966), for a good historical summary. Sembene Ousmane, *God's Bits of Wood* (Garden City, N.Y.: Doubleday, 1962), is one of the best fictional portrayals of a strike in Black Africa, and emphasizes the growing sense of communal solidarity. Numerous excellent studies of countries are available, including Robert H. Bates, *Unions, Parties and Political Development: A Study of Mine Workers in Zambia* (New Haven: Yale University Press, 1971); Alice H. Amsden, *International Firms and Labour in Kenya, 1945–1970* (London: Frank Cass, 1971); H. J. Simons and R. E. Simons, *Class and Color in South Africa, 1850–1950* (Baltimore: Penguin, 1969); Guy Pfeffermann, *Industrial Labor in the Republic of Senegal* (New York: Praeger, 1968); and Richard Sandbrook, *Proletarians and African Capitalism: The Kenyan Case, 1960–1972* (Cambridge: Cambridge University Press, 1975).

Authorities and governments anxious to minimize the extent of unemployment maintain that most of the people who call themselves workers are actually farmers in disguise or, at most, migrant laborers, either because they still retain certain rights to land in the countryside or because "psychologically and socially" the African worker "still belongs to the tribal society."[2] Although many workers can indeed return to their village of origin in times of crisis or periodically to visit relatives, the generosity of the extended family system must not disguise the fact that Africans do move to the city with the intention of seeking permanent employment and settling down to a new way of life.

The Emergence of Employed Labor and the Size of the Working Class

The evolution toward wage labor in the countryside as well as in the city accompanied the expansion of the export market, the improvement of communications, and the general commercialization of agriculture. African cash farmers everywhere began to employ labor on an increasing scale. In the countryside, share-cropping arrangements facilitated the expansion of holdings beyond the size that could be worked economically by one family. In Ghana, for example, such an arrangement was called the *abusa* system: laborers received a one-third share of the proceeds. Then, as marketing arrangements became more standardized, a new system of payment on a piecework basis became widespread. Migrant workers received a fixed sum per load of cash crop harvested. Only at a later stage of development did farmers pay employees by the hour. These three systems coexist today. Wage-earning employment, stimulated originally by the operations of overseas firms, continues to grow in private industries such as mining and in government construction of railways, docks, and other public works.

The size of the wage force varies enormously from country to country: 65 percent of the males in Zambia are employed as wage earners, 29 percent in Congo and Gabon, 19 percent in the Ivory Coast, and less than 4 percent in Togo, Upper Volta, Niger, and Mali.[3] It is easy to underestimate the strength of a wage force that represents a low percentage of the total work force. In Nigeria, for example, the 4 percent of the able-bodied males employed as wage earners comprises over a million workers. Assuming that most wage earners live in towns, about one fourth of the urban population of Nigeria sold their labor on the marketplace.[4] In 1945 and again in June, 1964, general strikes brought the economic life of the country to a

[2] Szymon Chodak, "Social Stratification in Sub-Saharan Africa," *Canadian Journal of African Studies,* 7, No. 3 (1973), 415.

[3] Davies, *African Trade Unions,* pp. 24, 130.

[4] Robert Melson, "Nigerian Politics and the General Strike of 1964" in *Protest and Power in Black Africa,* ed. Robert I. Rotberg and Ali A. Mazrui (New York: Oxford University Press, 1970), p. 773.

standstill. Millions of man-days of labor were lost during these strikes. All essential services and industrial enterprises screeched to a halt.

Because they are organized, workers throughout the continent have an enormous impact on politics.[5] The mine workers union of Zambia, with a membership of over 20,000—over 60 percent of the mine workers—and a monthly income of tens of thousands of dollars, is one of the largest and richest unions in Africa.[6] Membership in trade unions can rise dramatically when a struggle is under way and the workers see the possibilities of definite results from collective enterprise. In Conakry, Guinea, a series of strikes in 1953, including one that lasted for sixty-six days under the leadership of Sekou Touré, galvanized the population so that union membership rose from 4,000 in early 1953 to 20,000 in 1954 to 55,000 in 1955.[7]

To have gained even 4,000 members, however, involved a bitter struggle. Trade unionism in Africa has a long history. Manifestations of deep discontent and manifold grievances, spontaneous violence, and wildcat strikes erupted prior to the creation of formal organizations. As early as 1874, African dock workers went on strike in Freetown, Sierra Leone. Strikes that occurred throughout 1919 and 1920 in South Africa brought the docks and railroads there to a stop. Between the wars, railway strikes occurred across West Africa—in Sierra Leone (1919–1926), in Nigeria (1921), and all along the Thies-Niger Railway (1925). Protests broke out among mine workers in the Gold Coast and dock workers at Baththurst, Gambia in 1930. Among the best-organized strikes were those along the copper belt in Northern Rhodesia in 1935 and 1940.

These first militant workers, having no formal organization to back them up, suffered mortal danger. The Kings African Rifles massacred 150 Africans at a general strike in Kenya organized by the young Kikuyu Association. The colonial situation, the attitude of the various business administrations as well as of the government, made the formation of trade unions, difficult under any industrial circumstance, doubly so. The government of Sierra Leone, for example, in equating industrial agitation with rebellion, as was commonly done, described the 1926 railway strike as "a revolt against the government by its own servants."[8] Colonial troops broke the strike by shooting demonstrators, throwing African leaders into prison, and dismissing and exiling workers.

Over the long run, however, repeated conflicts strengthened a sense of solidarity. Often, trade unions built upon the work of "tribal improvement associations," frequently the first form of organization to represent African workers. These associations constituted urban responses to new problems. They brought together people who came from the same home area. Foreign labor movements, mainly the in-

[5] *Ibid.*, p. 771. See also Chapter VI.
[6] Bates, *Unions, Parties and Political Development*, p. 22.
[7] Davies, *African Trade Unions*, p. 88.
[8] *Ibid.*, p. 72.

ternational wings of metropolitan labor unions, provided minor aid. After the Second World War, they brought the rivalries of Christian, socialist, and communist internationals into Africa.[9] Particularly in East Africa, the AFL–CIO of the United States provided help.

After the Second World War, the change to more radical governments in France and Great Britain brought more liberal administrations to the colonial areas.[10] These administrations encouraged the formation of labor and other political organizations. Above all, however, the continual and remarkable solidarity of workers after numerous strikes and confrontations provided the major impetus to trade union organization. A prolonged railway strike involving the whole of French West Africa—from October, 1947 to March, 1948—was the first major industrial action organized by African unions. It succeeded in winning a unified code on working conditions that stipulated equal treatment for Africans and Europeans.

Despite the existence of tribal improvement associations, trade unions overarched previous divisions created by ethnic or tribal origin by substituting a new class interest. A. L. Epstein provides an account of this development in his analysis of a strike in the copper belt in 1940.[11] The mine owners in conjunction with the government, after having organized the workers in teams and barracks on the basis of tribal affiliation and place of origin, imported traditional elders from the rural compounds and installed them as a court to review and settle disputes. The miners' grievances stemming from their work situation, combined with their desire for higher wages, precipitated a wildcat strike and the emergence of new African labor leaders. The tribal elders revealed themselves to be the tools of the company owners when they urged the workers to return to their jobs. The workers turned against the elders and repudiated them completely. They then formed a new association that was appropriate to their common class interest, the trade union. This organization overrode previously salient traditional concerns and ethnic animosities by forming new types of commitment and bases of unity.

The Unions as Organizations of the Privileged

Union leaders, who were almost always from the white-collar strata, considered themselves heirs presumptive to the Europeans' privileged positions. Later, they did indeed fill those jobs. Although they made

[9] In discussing the historical development of the African labor movement, Amsden states, "The establishment of trade unions became little less than a crusade in Kenya after World War II. The labor government in Britain, the British TUC, the American AFL–CIO, the International Confederation of Free Trade Unions, and the World Federation of Trade Unions all took the interest of the African laborer to heart and fastened on trade unions as his salvation." (*International Firms and Labour in Kenya, 1945–1970*, p. 30.) Cold war concerns played at least as much a part in this "crusade" as did the good-heartedness of international trade unionists.

[10] Ruth Schachter Morgenthau, *Political Parties in French Speaking West Africa* (Oxford: Clarendon Press, 1964), and Pfeffermann, *Industrial Labor in the Republic of Senegal*, discuss differences among the Francophone trade unions.

[11] A. L. Epstein, *Politics in an Urban African Community* (Manchester: Manchester University Press, 1958).

speeches about marching toward a more egalitarian society, they embodied the qualities of a rising middle class in their life styles and aspirations even as they led movements of increasing militancy. In French Africa, the labor unions won landmark victories that typified their objectives, the Lamine-Gueye Law in June, 1950 and the Overseas Territories Labor Code in December, 1952. These laws sought to guarantee equal privilege for equal work.[12] In their campaign, the unions never challenged the legitimacy of the colonial order; they never demanded independence or even self-government. Instead, they cried out for equal rights *as Frenchmen*. They claimed as their aim the goals of French civilization promised in the slogan of the Revolution, "Liberty, Equality, and Fraternity." The Lamine-Gueye Law raised the standard of living of thousands of African civil servants concentrated in the major cities of West and Equatorial Africa. The labor and produce of Africans living in the rural areas paid for those wages and fringe benefits. Between 1949 and 1952, African wages rose from 39 percent to 87 percent in the major cities. During this time, the price of consumer goods fell, thereby producing a substantial rise in real income. African working classes in the cities increased their militancy while enjoying what constituted an incentive to maintain the basic political and economic structure.[13] No wonder, then, that Frantz Fanon asserted, "The workers are in fact the most favored section of the population and represent the most comfortably off faction of the people. Any movement starting off to fight for the bettering of living conditions of the doctors and workmen would not only be very unpopular but would also run the risk of provoking the hostility of the disinherited rural population."[14]

Terence Ranger, in his case study of the rise of a labor force in Southern Rhodesia, points out that the early "elite positions"—those of mine clerk, storekeeper, foreman, and so forth—were filled "by the 'proto-intellectuals' of Nyasaland, men who formed a self-conscious elite, maintaining contact with each other from mine to mine but not attempting to establish contact with indigenous political movements." Ranger goes on to describe various campaigns over bread-and-butter issues, including the price of bread and butter and other foods, wages, and working conditions in the mines. As early as 1919 a successful boycott forced local shopkeepers to lower their prices. In 1922 the Southern Rhodesian Chamber of Mines inquired of the government whether it considered the activities of such societies as tribal associations and burial societies as a prelude to trade unionism. The

---

[12] Lamine Gueye, *Itineraire Africaine* (Paris: Presence Africaine, 1966).

[13] Cf. Pfeffermann, *Industrial Labor in the Republic of Senegal*, Samir Amin, in his *Neo-Colonialism in West Africa* (New York: Monthly Review Press, 1973), presents a different interpretation than either that of Pfeffermann or this chapter.

[14] Frantz Fanon, *Wretched of the Earth* (New York: Grove Press, 1968), pp. 122–23, see also pp. 107–47. In contrast, Sandbrook, in his *Proletarians and African Capitalism*, maintains that unionized workers can still sympathize with the peasantry. Cf. stimulating set of essays in Sandbrook and Robin Cohen, ed. *The Development of an African Working Class* (London: Longman, 1975) which deny Fanon's labor aristocracy thesis.

government was terrified by the possibility of "the ways of fanaticism, ways that will eventually dash them [the African workers] against the rocks of Bolshevism and strikes."[15] When in 1927 and 1928 a labor union blazed up to the surprise of black and white establishment figures, it emerged as a "radical working man's organization, critical of the timidity of the elite." This new organization was the Independent Industrial and Commercial Workers Union of Rhodesia. In 1935, and again in 1940, when African miners struck in support of wage demands, the police did not hesitate to shoot, killing over fifty men and wounding many others.[16]

The unions in the Sudan and Nigeria, which were composed of industrial and manual workers, in contrast with the white-collar composition of the unions in French West Africa, emphasized the concerns of a "developing proletariat." In these two countries, trade-union leaders were absorbed less easily into government posts. In the Sudan, they formed an opposition first against the bourgeois parties and later against the military regime. In Nigeria, even the white-collar movements—for example, the Nigerian Union of Teachers—did not affiliate with the major nationalist political movements, such as the National Council of Nigeria and the Cameroons (NCNC). Although ethnic considerations played a part and differences of personality mattered, trade-union leaders hesitated above all to cross swords with the colonial government, which had strongly opposed *political* activity by labor. Because of their commitment to gain more, they hesitated to endanger their relatively comfortable situation.[17]

From the point of view of the nationalist parties, trade unions offered a formidable organizational weapon. Yet whether the parties actually sought labor's aid depended on the class composition and on the ideology of the political party. According to Davies, parties led by

> chiefs, religious leaders or the more wealthy middle-class elements were inclined to discount the unions as a significant source of strength. The Northern Peoples Congress in Nigeria or the Kabaka Yekka in Uganda drew their power from the established tribal order, and the leaders were already secure in their positions of authority; they did not need the unions to bolster their claim to legitimacy and given their internal organization and conservative ideology, had little room for unions even as convenient recruiting grounds. ... The history of the earlier bourgeois parties—the United Gold Coast Convention, the Kenya African Union, or the Tunisian Destour—show that parties led mainly by the petty bourgeoisie or businessmen had little interest in workers' organizations unless they aimed also to create parties with a mass following, professional party workers and elaborate local networks.[18]

---

[15] T. O. Ranger, *The African Voice in Southern Rhodesia: 1898–1930* (London: Heinemann. 1970), p. 148.

[16] See Ranger's detailed account of the further development of unions in Southern Rhodesia and their relation to the development of nationalist parties in the 1950s (*Ibid.*).

[17] James S. Coleman, *Nigeria: Background to Nationalism* (Berkeley and Los Angeles: University of California Press, 1958), p. 265.

[18] Davies, *African Trade Unions*, p. 93.

Davies points out that the unions participated fully in radical nationalist political parties only in the Sudan, Mali, and Guinea. In these countries, the unions' only alternative was the French-sponsored parties of the chiefs.[19]

The history of labor unions in Ghana illustrates the way governments of different class composition have handled the unions. *All* Ghanaian governments have attempted to control unions. Independent labor organizations in Ghana began joining the Convention Peoples Party as allies against the colonial regime. Over time, however, Nkrumah rationalized, unified, and centralized labor organizations into a powerful tool, and then used that tool for his own purposes. Dr. Busia, on the other hand, tried to destroy the organizational power of labor so that no one could use it. In 1971, Busia's government passed an industrial relations act that abolished the Trade Union Congress. The Congress had previously mounted a vociferous campaign against Busia's Progress Party's budget and his National Development Levy, which required all persons earning over $35 per month to contribute between 1 percent and 5 percent of their wages towards "development." Dr. Busia stated publicly that he saw the role of trade unions as a training ground for good citizens rather than as champions of the workers. Labor did not welcome this point of view. When the unions walked out in a general strike at Takoradi and Accra, Busia's government dismissed 300 workers. Under pressure from the police, the Takoradi Council of Labor called off the strike.[20]

In the postindependence period, trade unions helped precipitate political crises throughout the continent. In the Sudan, a general strike brought the downfall of the Abboud regime; in Nigeria, a general strike stimulated a head-on clash between the state and the workers; in Dahomey, Congo-Brazzaville, Upper Volta, the Central African Republic, the Ivory Coast, and Guinea, trade unions were linked with efforts to overthrow governments.[21] Nowhere, however, were trade unions the only support of African governments.[22]

Trade unions, even where successful in their immediate demands, have also sometimes paved the way for a military dictatorship, as in Upper Volta and Dahomey. Historically, well-established nationalist governments confronted by union action have commonly absorbed the unions more tightly into their party machinery. Such an arrangement exists now in Guinea, Tanzania, Tunisia, Egypt, Algeria, the Ivory Coast, Mali, and Senegal.

Yet even when unions have not been in a position to dictate policy, most governments have bent over backwards to satisfy the expectations of a power block certainly more potent than the disorganized peasantry

---

[19] *Ibid.*, p. 87.

[20] *West Africa*, October 1, 1971, p. 1133. Cf. U. G. Damachi, *The Role of Trade Unions in the Development Process: With a Case Study of Ghana* (New York: Praeger, 1974).

[21] Davies, *African Trade Unions*, p. 10. See also Victor Le Vine, "The Coups in Upper Volta, Dahomey and the Central African Republic," in *Protest and Power in Black Africa*, ed. Rotberg and Mazrui, p. 1070.

[22] Possible past exceptions were Congo-Brazzaville and Mali. See Davies, *African Trade Unions*, p. 10.

or the permanently unemployed of the cities. Thus, when a far-from-radical government in Upper Volta tried to reduce the salaries of local civil servants, which had previously been set at the level of French administrators, the unions resisted strongly. In Tanganyika in 1963, the unions demanded pay raises that would have absorbed all incoming foreign assistance. In Senegal, the government chose to bolster the economy by increasing the price of rice and bread.[23] In Nigeria, following a pattern that occurred throughout Anglophone Africa, a government commission of inquiry recommended wage increases of from 10 to 20 percent for civil servants. This again increased the income gap between urban and agricultural workers and helped the rising cost of living, especially of housing, continue to spiral.[24]

Among the most sophisticated postindependence governments in its handling and co-optation of labor has been Kenya. From the 1950s, the business associations in Kenya have deliberately encouraged the development of a bread-and-butter trade-union movement in order to preempt radical political change.[25] The major business organization, the Federation of Kenya Employers (FKE), pragmatically accepted the rise of Africans into power and discounted the rhetoric of African socialism. Pivoting its position on government cooperation, the FKE has sought to encourage a trade-union movement that it can live with. According to Amsden, "the reciprocal strength which the employer and labor movements derive from each other is the basic theme in Kenya's industrial relations. The interplay of these variables helps explain how the FKE has managed to forge a coherent empire of impressive proportions in a relatively small underdeveloped country."[26] After noting that the orientation of the industry-wide unions in Kenya is "decidedly economist," that action and ideology are geared towards winning higher wages and better working conditions, Amsden states that "this orientation is in large part attributable to employers. . . . The FKE produced something positive that worked: a model of unionism and a system of collective bargaining."[27]

Robert H. Bates has noted that union leaders have not only worked closely with management, but have appeared to profit "unduly" from this relationship. In a survey of rank-and-file members he found that "rather than obtaining respect as the champions of the workers' demands, the leaders instead appear to function as a privileged group attempting to evoke cooperation from the workers in exchange for personal benefits."[28]

If the workers are an aristocracy in comparison with the peasantry, the trade union leaders are an aristocracy vis-à-vis the rank and

---

[23] *West Africa,* August 20, 1973, p. 1171.
[24] *Africa Digest,* No. 3 (June 1972).
[25] Amsden, *International Firms and Labour in Kenya, 1945–1970,* p. 162.
[26] *Ibid.,* p. 85.
[27] *Ibid.,* p. 104.
[28] Bates, *Unions, Parties and Political Development,* pp. 124–25.

file—a double aristocracy doubly privileged.[29] No wonder, then, that trade union leaders who send their children to the same schools attended by the children of the highest government officials and cabinet members, and who buy their clothing from the same tailors, can become allies of key elements of the organizational bourgeoisie. Clearly, African skilled laborers have not borne the historical burdens of the Western proletariat. That weight has been reserved for Africa's small farmers.

African Farmers: Isolation, Divisions, and the Need for New Organizations

Isolated farmers working mountainous, desert, or grassland plots, twenty miles from a road, hundreds of miles from a seaport, compose the world's poorest peoples—illiterate, removed from doctors or hospitals, still confined by the rigidities of subsistence agriculture.[30] Sixteen of the world's least developed countries, according to a report by the United Nations General Assembly, are located in Central and Southern Africa; the bulk of their populations barely eke out a living. Throughout the continent, peasants and farmers are the most disadvantaged part of society.[31]

In subtropical areas, where over 90 percent of the gross national product is derived from agricultural produce, the leisure, health, and conspicuous consumption of the organizational bourgeoisie originate in the labor of the peasant. Too often, all the grandiose theories of economic development boil down to differences of method in further impoverishing those already on the verge of starvation. Not that the situation in Africa differs from historical developments elsewhere. After surveying the experiences of systems as diverse as those in England and the Soviet Union, Japan and France, Barrington Moore demands, "Just what does modernization mean for the peasantry beyond the simple and brutal fact that sooner or later they are its victims?"[32]

If in the West the proletariat lay at the bottom of the social heap, in the agrarian societies of contemporary Africa they are, in contrast, a privileged stratum. In Zambia, to take one instance, although the wage force, which is primarily urban, increased its earn-

---

[29] R. D. Grillo, in his *African Railwaymen: Solidarity and Opposition in an East African Labour Force* (Cambridge: Cambridge University Press, 1973), analyzes differences within a labor force in terms of occupation, "grade," income, and position in the industrial hierarchy. He shows how these factors gave rise to inequalities in status and power among the railwaymen.

[30] See Eric Wolf, *Peasant Wars of the Twentieth Century* (New York: Harper & Row), 1969, pp. xiv–xv.

[31] Cf. the report of the Development Assistance Committee of the Organization for Economic Cooperation and Development, *Development Cooperation, 1972* (Paris, 1972).

[32] Barrington Moore, Jr., *Social Origins of Dictatorship and Democracy: Lord and Peasant in the Making of the Modern World* (Boston: Beacon Press, 1966), p. 467.

ings by 32 percent during the period 1964–1968, the peasantry, approximately 80 percent of the population of the country, increased its earnings by an estimated 3.4 percent. President Kaunda warned that the trend represented by these figures, which indicated a dangerously deprived and aggrieved rural sector, threatened to create two nations in Zambia.[33] Elsewhere on the continent, the peasantry has suffered an absolute, not simply relative, decline in its standard of living. Peasants suffer not only in comparison with other classes, but in terms of their previous standards of living. In Senegal, for example, many cash-crop farmers, caught between an inflationary spiral that forced up the cost of imported manufactured goods and a decline in the world market price paid for their peanuts, returned to the subsistence agriculture practiced by their forebears.

As peasants become farmers, their destiny is threatened with tragedy. As Eric Wolf points out, "the peasant is an agent of forces larger than himself, produced by a disordered past filled with wrongs and inequities as much as by a disordered present." Great social dislocations transform the social structure as a whole and the peasantry with it. If the peasant can rise to act on his own behalf, even then "his efforts to undo his grievous present only usher in a vaster, more uncertain future." The peasant's society, as he has known it, cannot endure, and he must take a new role in a wider world. Yet a new hope also arises: "For the first time in millennia, humankind is moving towards a solution of the age-old problem of hunger and disease, and everywhere ancient monopolies of power and received wisdom are yielding to human effort to widen participation and knowledge."[34]

Precisely this combination of hope and frustration throws peasants in many countries on the continent into uprisings against the constituted authorities. The Hutu in Rwanda, the Kikuyu in Kenya, the "middle-belt peoples" in Northern Nigeria during the '50s and '60s and in the Sudan and in Chad during the '70s, and, most dramatically, peasants in Zaire and the Cameroons have risen against their rulers. They have often shown the way to their more educated and economically better placed brethren. Too often, movements of rebellion and revolution are thought to be the work of intellectuals, or other elements from the middle class. Rare but increasing are those studies that emphasize the role of the peasantry in major political undertakings.[35]

For the peasantry to act as a "class for itself" requires the overcoming of formidable obstacles. Social analysts from Marx, who denounced the idiocy of rural life,[36] to Charles Tilly, who analyzed how

---

[33] Bates, *Unions, Parties and Political Development*, pp. 72–73.

[34] Wolf, *Peasant Wars of the Twentieth Century*, p. 301.

[35] See e.g. Herbert Weiss, *Political Protest in the Congo* (Princeton, N.J.: Princeton University Press, 1967).

[36] David Mitrany, in a bitter attack, collected Marx's statements concerning the peasantry in *Marx Against the Peasant* (New York: Collier, 1961).

an aroused peasantry could side with the forces of reaction,[37] have marked these difficulties as overwhelming. To understand when and how a peasantry can be aroused to act in its own interest requires skillful analysis. Frantz Fanon erred in the same way, as Marx, and just as badly, by crying out for the peasantry to revolt because they had nothing to lose but their chains. Fanon expected that the peasantry, as the most downtrodden class in society, would rise up when their material condition became steadily worse.[38] But Marx also pointed out how the isolation of the peasantry from society as a whole affected the internal structure of the class and its organizational potential:

> Their mode of production isolates them from one another instead of bringing them into mutual intercourse. . . . Insofar as there is merely a local inter-connection among these small-holding peasants and the identity of their interest begets no community, no national, and no political organization among them, they do not form a class. They are consequently incapable of enforcing their class interest in their own name. . . .[39]

Georg Lukacs has also commented on the lack of self-awareness of the peasantry: "We cannot really speak of class-consciousness . . . for a full consciousness of their situation would reveal to them the hopelessness of their particular strivings in the face of the inevitable course of events. Consciousness and self-interest are mutually incompatible in this instance."[40] The peasant is doubly assaulted: first, by the difficulties that prevent his awakening; second, by the tragedy of his own helplessness should he by some chance stir.

In isolation and in the loneliness of rural life, nature and society conspire to separate the farmer into his own shell, bound to the sun and to the habits of his animals. The rhythm of his work is not appropriate for fellowship; nor is the back-breaking demand of the mind-numbing shovel, pitchfork, and hoe type of manual labor; nor are the large spaces of field or the thicknesses of forest. In places where the scholar is the man who can read a newspaper, where the merchant-prince is none other than the village grocer, and where the families of "one's betters" have enjoyed high respect from the neighborhood for ages, one discusses the weather, crops, and religion — not politics, exploitation, or revolution.

What, then, has stimulated those peasants who have rebelled in the past?[41] Movements against established authorities never begin

---

[37] Tilly, *The Vendée: A Sociological Analysis of the Counterrevolution of 1793* (Cambridge, Mass.: Harvard University Press, 1964).

[38] Fanon, *Wretched of the Earth,* pp. 108–109.

[39] Karl Marx, "Eighteenth Brumaire of Louis Bonaparte," in Karl Marx and Friedrich Engels, *Basic Writings on Politics and Philosophy,* ed. Lewis S. Feuer (Garden City, N.Y.: Doubleday, Anchor Books, 1959), pp. 338–39.

[40] Georg Lukacs, *History and Class Consciousness* (Cambridge, Mass.: M.I.T. Press, 1971), pp. 60–61.

[41] See James C. Davies, who, in his *Human Nature in Politics* (New York: John Wiley, 1963), explains

when the oppressed are the most downtrodden: "A rebellion cannot start from a situation of complete impotence; the powerless are easy victims."[42] Therefore, according to Wolf, "the decisive factor in making a peasant rebellion possible lies in the relation of the peasantry to the field of power which surrounds it. . . ." Completely dependent upon the landlord for their livelihood, the poorest peasants have no "tactical power," no sufficient resources of their own to fall back upon in a confrontation. The rich peasant with possessions, employees, and power has too much to lose. The major revolutionary element among the peasantry must come from the "middle peasantry"—those with a secure hold on land of their own, dependent only upon family labor, who are in a position to gather strength and prepare for a drastic undertaking. The middle peasant also develops the greatest knowledge of what is happening in the larger society. Whereas the poor peasant or landless laborer breaks all connections with the land upon emigrating to the cities, the middle peasant usually stays to work the family land while sending some of his children to explore the opportunities in the urban areas. New ideas and notions of political behavior travel rapidly along these networks that bring political movements into the countryside.[43]

Wolf points out that peasants in rebellion are natural anarchists insofar as they believe that their social order can run without the state, which they conceive only as an evil dedicated to doing them mischief.[44] Even if peasants organize effectively and local rebellions succeed in bettering local conditions, the peasants must still connect with forces outside the rural areas. They must gain control of the state through the cities, the repositories of control and of the strategic nonagriculture resources of the society. How, then, are the peasants to relate to this larger society? Which outsiders should they trust, and for what reasons? Too many salesmen have assaulted the peasants with shoddy wares. Why trust the city slicker?

Amilcar Cabral, leader of the PAIGC of Portuguese Guinea and perhaps the most successful revolutionary leader on the continent, wrote about this problem with great insight and clarity. How could the Fula peasants, who had a "strong tendency to follow their chiefs," be weaned from their traditional society, given the historical circumstances and general economic conditions?

---

the disappointment of rising expectations in terms of the J-curve phenomenon. See also, for example, Ted Gurr, *Why Men Rebel* (Princeton, N.J.: Princeton University Press, 1970); Crane Brinton, *The Anatomy of Revolution* (New York: Vintage, 1965); and John Dunn, *Modern Revolutions* (Cambridge and New York: Cambridge University Press, 1972).

[42] Wolf, *Peasant Wars of the Twentieth Century*, p. 290.

[43] *Ibid.*, pp. 291–93. Gavin Williams analyzes the Yoruba uprising of October, 1965 as a revolt of middle peasants against the regional government and their "Kulak-type local adherents" ("The Social Stratification of a Neo-Colonial Economy," in *African Perspectives*, ed. Christopher Allen and R. W. Johnson (Cambridge: Cambridge University Press, 1970), p. 247.

[44] Wolf, *Peasant Wars of the Twentieth Century*, pp. 276–302. See also Samuel P. Huntington, *Political Order in Changing Societies* (New Haven: Yale University Press, 1968). Joel S. Migdal, in his *Peasants, Politics and Revolution: Pressures Toward Political and Social Change in the Third World* (Princeton, N.J.: Princeton University Press, 1974), shows how peasants seeking redress from economic crisis can be organized by radical groups who provide better administrative solutions than the governing regimes.

Thorough and intensive work was ... needed to mobilize them. ... The peasantry is not a revolutionary force—which may seem strange, particularly as we have based the whole of our arms liberation struggle on the peasantry. A distinction must be drawn between a physical force and a revolutionary force; physically, the peasantry is a great force in Guinea: it is almost the whole of the population, it controls the nation's wealth, it is the peasantry which produces; but we know from experience what trouble we had convincing the peasantry to fight. ... The conditions of the peasantry in China were very different: the peasantry had a history of revolt but this was not the case in Guinea, and so it was not possible for our party militants and propaganda workers to find the same kind of welcome. ....[45]

Cabral then discusses various ways in which his movement won the trust of the peasantry. First, it was essential that the militants live among the peasants so that they could see who the militants were and that they *did* what they said they were going to do, for only seeing is believing. Before the independence struggle was won, moreover, the PAIGC under Cabral set up schools, dispensaries, and a governing apparatus that involved the lowliest farmers in the decision-making process. In this way, by *doing*, they increasingly won rural adherence to their cause.[46]

Postindependence Problems:
Unemployment, Class Formation, and Land Reform

Problems set in motion well before independence bear ever heavier on the postindependence governments. The organizational bourgeoisie either does not see many of these trends as problems or is reluctant to take the measures necessary to remedy them for fear of undercutting their own power.

Every new regime confronts what looks like overwhelming unemployment. In Nigeria in recent years, only one third of those who sought jobs could find them. In Kenya, the output of the secondary schools in 1968 was 150,000; only 50,000 jobs were available. In Ghana, 20 to 35 percent of the labor force was unemployed in 1970. In Tanzania, which has a population of over 12,000,000, an age group of 250,000 entering the labor force found only 25,000 jobs available.[47] In Senegal, at least 28 percent of those under twenty-five could not find employment.[48] None of these figures, of course, takes into account "hidden unemployment"—that is, make-work jobs that really do not affect the country's productive capacity and would not be missed if eliminated.

[45] Amilcar Cabral, *Revolution in Guinea* (New York: Monthly Review Press), p. 61.

[46] Basil Davidson, "In the Portuguese Context," in *African Perspectives*, eds. Allen and Johnson, p. 345.

[47] Clyde R. Ingle, *From Village to State in Tanzania* (Ithaca, N.Y.: Cornell University Press, 1972), p. 17.

[48] *Recensement Demographique de Dakar, 1955* (Dakar, Senegal: Service de la Statistique, Ministère du Plan et du Developpement, Republique du Senegal, mimeo, 1962), p. 52.

Yet President Nyerere of Tanzania could give an address stating that "unemployment is no problem." According to Nyerere, "We have, and shall have increasingly, people coming out of primary schools who cannot get wage employment. But this does not mean that they have no work they can do."[49] Nyerere denounced the attitude that education means leaving the land and taking a job in an office. In developed countries such as the United States and Germany, university graduates work as farmers. The intent of education is to make a person better able to do whatever job is important and profitable both to himself and his country. In Africa as well, Nyerere argues, great opportunities exist for improving the nation's resources. With the proper type of social reorganization, unemployment would not be a problem. However, governments face major obstacles in persuading the people to change their attitudes towards agricultural work.

In a sense, Nyerere is saying that farming has a bad image, an image that must be changed. But he is saying more. He is warning us that a system that rewards "office work" more than working with one's hands must be changed drastically, along with the values that go with it. Yet the basic social trends appear to exacerbate, and not ameliorate, these problems. From pre-sixteenth-century England to contemporary Tanzania, the intrusion of commerce into a peasant community has set in motion the concentrating of land in fewer hands.[50] In Tunisia, privileged rural classes rose to eminence after settlers were thrown out. The same situation occurred in Algeria, despite prolonged peasant-based revolutionary warfare. In Morocco, large landowners absorbed foreign-owned properties for their own benefit. Increasingly, the old confrontation between European *colons* and Muslim peasants gave way to conflict between the minority of increasingly rich farmers and the mass of the traditional peasantry. Samir Amin maintains that in 1970 the Maghreb showed certain signs of creating a Muslim rural society with much greater social divisions than existed in the colonial period.[51] In Nigeria, the large-scale farmer increasingly dominates. As early as the 1950s, inequality in land distribution resulted in 9 percent of all Nigerian farmers holding more than one third of the cultivated land.[52]

Probably more than any other African country, Guinea under the leadership of Sekou Touré used all its governmental resources to eliminate the preindependence traditional social structure and its in-

[49] Julius Nyerere, *Uhuru na Ujamaa: Freedom and Socialism, A Selection from Writings and Speeches, 1965–1967* (Dar es Salaam: Oxford University Press, 1968), p. 71.

[50] Barrington Moore, Jr., *Social Origins of Dictatorship and Democracy: Lord and Peasant in the Making of the Modern World* (Boston: Beacon Press, 1966), p. 26.

[51] Samir Amin, *The Maghreb in the Modern World: Algeria, Tunisia, Morocco* (Baltimore: Penguin Books, 1970), p. 224.

[52] Henry L. Bretton, *Power and Politics in Africa* (Chicago: Aldine, 1973), p. 24.
    "The Emergence of Agrarian Capitalism in Africa South of the Sahara," a seminar sponsored by the United Nations African Institute for Economic Development and Planning, held in Dakar, December 3–12, 1973, produced a number of important papers. P. Kupriyanov, senior research worker of the Institute of Africa Academy of Sciences of the USSR, almost alone held to the traditional view that before the establishment of the colonial regime, African agriculture consisted almost

herent inequalities. According to the American anthropologist William Derman, the subordination of former serfs to their Fulbe masters was eliminated in Guinea. By government order, traditional social distinctions were not observed: at cooperative labor projects, for example, both former serf and Fulbe nobles worked side by side. The ideology and practices of the Parti Democratique de Guinée (PDG) limited the domination of one group by another and emphasized "the common aspirations and goals of all Guineans."[53]

Even Guinea, however, is confronted with needed changes: first, the transformation of a feudal structure into a society based upon modern technology; and, second, the creation of a new style of African socialism. Although the government has been extraordinarily successful in striking the final blow against traditional structures (which were already tottering because of the innovations introduced by a new technology and a changed economy), it faced even greater obstacles in transforming these structures into a new communalism. In Derman's view, "the transformation of peasants into socialists will be far more difficult than the transformation of serfs into peasants or the transformation of Guinea from colony into independent nation."[54]

In Tanzania, a series of studies sponsored by the Tanzanian government, various government agencies, and the Department of Political Science at the University of Dar es Salaam all revealed growing rural inequality, despite official commitments to a communal philosophy and persistent efforts to put these ideals into practice. Confronted with realities, the leaders of the country consistently faced moral and practical dilemmas. For example, all government measures aimed at opening up rural areas are bound to increase the value of land. The same is true of the introduction of cash crops. Who is to benefit from this increase in value? As a result of government penetration, peasants were recruited to serve in local development agencies. A dis-

entirely of small producers engaged in subsistence farming and disconnected from the rest of the world. See his "Peculiarities of Agrarian Capitalism in Tropical Africa." A number of other analysts noted the connections between contemporary rural capitalism and traditional social structures. M. Keita, for example, in his paper, "Interventions in the Rural Area and Agrarian Capitalism in the Tillabery Region" said that "in the West of Niger, capitalism took over the masking of the domination and exploitation relations which it found. . . . Today we can still observe the survival of a form of sharecropping between the nobles and the captives in which the former ensure the latter the supply and the renewal—if necessary—of seed in exchange for half the product of the harvest." (p. 9) Claude Reboul drew attention to the widening disparity in the incomes of the farmers in the Sine Saloum region of Senegal—part of the rich peanut-producing area. See his "Agrarian Structures and Development Problems in Senegal: The Experimental Units of the Sine Saloum." Levon Debelian, land-tenure and settlement expert of the Economic Committee for Africa, after perusing the well-documented accounts of rural inequalities in Ethiopia, demonstrated how the net impact of mechanization and other processes of modernization was a greater concentration of ownership and a greater impoverishment of the mass of the peasantry ("The Impact of Agricultural Mechanization on the Traditional Society in Ethiopia," p. 20). For similar contentions, see Elaine de Latour Dejean, "The Transformation of the Land Tenure System, Land Appropriation and Formation of the Ruling Class in the Mawri Country (NIGER)"; and Taye Gurmu, "The Development of Agrarian Capitalism in Ghana With Particular Reference to Ejura District."

[53] William Derman, *Serfs, Peasants and Socialists: A Former Serf Village in the Republic of Guinea* (Berkeley and Los Angeles: University of California Press, 1973). Cf. Rene Dumont, who shows how "great families" still control the villages in his *Paysanneries aux abois: Ceylon, Tunisie, Senegal* (Paris: Editions du Seuil, 1972), p. 193.

[54] Derman, *Serfs, Peasants and Socialists,* p. 251. See also Derman's analysis of the Fulbe legend that justifies the caste system (*Ibid.,* p. 174).

proportionate number of these beneficiaries came from the ranks of wealthy peasants.[55] The reason for this was that the staff members of the agencies encouraged the rich peasants, because the wealthier elements could exert power more easily over other peasants and were therefore considered to be better suited to play the role of mobilizing agent.

Allegedly unique elements in Africa's ecology are an abundance of land and a low population density. Yet in Tanzania two thirds of the rural population is compressed into about 10 percent of the total land area that has sufficient rainfall for farming. With population increases, growing inequality is not difficult to anticipate. A study of the Rungwe district, where underdeveloped land is abundant, portends the future. Already, according to Van Hekken, "certain groups among the peasantry do not have sufficient land to cover their daily . . . subsistence requirements." Those fields with exceptionally rich soil are already in the hands of a minority. As a result of the growing land scarcity, frustrations are increasing and becoming more widespread. Farmers note how other peasants became rich. It is particularly disturbing that "wealthy farmers are establishing networks both within their own communities and with powerful persons outside the village to safeguard and expand their interests."[56]

In another regional study—of Kalebezo in Tanzania—University of Tanzania sociologists discovered three groups of rural capitalists. The first consisted of those with large farms cultivated both by cheap labor and tractors. These farmers also have retail stores and sometimes cattle. The second group of rural capitalists have large farms but do not employ labor or machines, cultivating only a small area themselves with the help of members of their family, and renting the rest to newcomers. The third group have large herds of cattle, sometimes over 100 head, and concentrate on selling milk, doing very little cultivation of their own.[57]

No wonder, then, that although agricultural productivity has increased in Tanzania, this has been due primarily to the efforts of individuals who, by and large, were already relatively well off. The stan-

---

[55] P. M. Van Hekken and H. U. E. Thoden Van Velzen, *Land Scarcity and Rural Inequality in Tanzania* (The Hague: Mouton, 1972), p. 115. On rural inequalities in Tanzania and the Tanzanian government's policy on development, see also the special issue of *Africa Today*, 2, no. 3 (Summer 1974), especially the articles by C. K. Omari and Paul Collins; and the articles collected in two books edited by J. H. Proctor, *The Cell System of the Tanganyika African National Union* (Dar es Salaam: Tanzania Publishing, 1971) and *Building Ujaama Villages in Tanzania* (Dar es Salaam: Tanzania Publishing, 1971).

[56] Van Hekken and Van Velzen, *Land Scarcity and Rural Inequality in Tanzania*, p. 114.

[57] In describing the operations of these rural capitalists, E. H. Ntirukigwa notes, "To use [their] land one has to pay rent or promise to pay rent after one has sold the produce. There are numerous exploitative methods which the landlords employ in making land available, in most cases temporarily, to the landless farmers, particularly the new immigrants. . . ." ("The Land Tenure System and the Building of Aijamaa Villages in Geita" in *Building Ujamaa Villages in Tanzania*, ed. Proctor, p. 37). Cf. James R. Finucane, *Rural Development and Bureaucracy in Tanzania* (Uppsala: Scandinavian Institute of African studies, 1974), for a balanced analysis of Tanzania's efforts to overcome "the basic familiar pattern" of an "ensconced elite" and provide the peasant with a "respectable status."

dard of living of the mass of Tanzanian farmers does not appear to have changed substantially. The ability of the ruling political party, TANU, to turn the efforts of the Tanzanian villages to particular developmental tasks necessary for the realization of socialist objectives is still in question.[58]

An important study in East Africa investigated who converts to *commercial* farming.[59] Richards, Sturrock, and Fortt found that chiefs in Buganda went into various businesses when their salaries increased dramatically. For instance, the salary of the Paramount Chief rose from £60 in 1934 to £970 in 1951. The chiefs bought trucks to carry their produce to market, "and though they started by using their traditional rights to tribute labor, most of them ended by paying a few regular laborers." The second category of men who adopted commercial agriculture were copper-belt workers who saved their wages. The resulting system of rural stratification included the tens of thousands of seasonal laborers, sharecropping tenants, and jobbing laborers of local farmers. Sturrock argues that the creation of a class of "relatively affluent farmers" projects "a good image of prosperity rather than [associating] farming with poverty and ignorance . . . fit only for men too unenterprising to find a better occupation."

In Kenya, the government does not attempt to hide its encouragement of rural entrepreneurs. While solidifying European ownership and confining Africans to reserves, the colonial government paid lip service to strengthening "community" control over land, in opposition to the individual land-tenure system. Reaction to such colonial policies constitutes one element in the present situation.

The Mau Mau movement responded to a deep-seated land hunger felt by the Kikuyu, who were forced to leave their overcrowded reserves and seek employment on European farms and in the cities. Eventually, the colonial regime, out of desperation, proposed to create a class of prosperous Kikuyu farmers, hoping that the colonial governor could then counter political agitation by granting the rich farmers title to their plots. These landowners were expected, in turn, to employ most of the landless Kikuyu on their holdings.[60]

After independence, the Kenya government, despite its forensic protest to the contrary, continued much the same practical agricultural policy as had the British, based upon much the same rationale. The net effect was to aggravate the distance between agricultural

[58] Ingle, *From Village to State in Tanzania,* pp. 58–60, 254–57.

[59] Audrey I. Richards, Ford Sturrock, and Jean M. Fortt, eds., *Subsistence to Commercial Farming in Present-Day Buganda* (Cambridge: Cambridge University Press, 1973). See also Oliver V. A. Madu, who points out that farming is no longer seen as a necessarily lower-class or menial occupation: "Nowadays the new African rural bourgeoisie buys his lands, owns his own farms and applies as much technology as possible" ("Problems of Urbanization in Central Africa," *Presence Africaine,* No. 86, 2nd Quarterly [1973], 20–37). See also the description of such changes in John Dunn and A. F. Robertson, *Dependence and Opportunity: Political Change in Ahafo* (Cambridge: Cambridge University Press, 1973), p. 10; and A. G. Hopkins, *An Economic History of West Africa* (London: Longman, 1973), p. 125.

[60] John C. De Wilde, *Experience with Agricultural Development in Tropical Africa,* Vol. 2 (Baltimore: Johns Hopkins, 1967), p. 9.

classes. Rich African farmers devoted a significant proportion of their rising incomes to the employment of outside labor. The gap grew between small farmers and wealthier entrepreneurs. Echoing the experience of Ethiopia, Senegal, and other countries, agricultural modernization in Kenya left the small holders virtually untouched. Less than 10 percent of the total number of farmers have benefited directly from the increased agricultural input sponsored by the government. Absentee landowners allow a surprising amount of land to lie idle. According to a recent study by an outside agriculturalist,

> the development of the last fifteen years has greatly widened the gap between the still small minority of progressive farmers and the balance of the population. Since this gap keeps increasing rather than diminishing, a special effort would seem to be essential to disseminate agricultural progress more widely and, in particular, to devote more attention to the problems of the numerous small holders.[61]

The net result in Kenya today of one of the most violent struggles for independence and land reform on the continent—the Mau Mau movement and the prolonged state of emergency it precipitated—appears to be the resettlement of about 30,000 Africans, a tiny percentage of all Kenyan peasants, on part of the Highlands formerly occupied by less than 1,000 Europeans. According to Ann Seidman, "barely 3,000 landowners—only a few of them African—own estates ranging from an average of 2,500 acres up to 25 square miles and produce the major share of the nation's marketed crops; while unknown numbers of Africans—estimated to run into tens of thousands—are landless many working laborers earn less than 100 shillings a month."[62]

In Ghana by the mid 1950s, 3 percent of the cocoa farmers obtained 16 percent of all cocoa farmers' income and 15 percent of the farmers obtained 40 percent of the income. At the other end of the spectrum, almost 200,000 agricultural laborers and sharecroppers received less than a third of their crops as wages.[63]

Until a path-breaking study by Polly Hill,[64] the prevailing anthropological view of landowning in Ghana—as in most of Black Africa—rejected the existence of Western "in fee simple" patterns of individual ownership. This theory maintained that the land belonged to a community composed of the dead, living, and yet to be born, and was

---

[61] *Ibid.*, p. 82. See also Amsden, *International Firms and Labour in Kenya, 1945–1970*, p. 164, for a discussion of the impact of agricultural developments on the mass of subsistence peasants. Cf. Leys, *Underdevelopment in Kenya*, p. 62 and *passim*.

[62] Ann Seidman, "Old Motives, New Methods: Foreign Enterprise in Africa," in *African Perspectives*, ed. Allen and Johnson, p. 262.

[63] *Ibid.* Seidman also points out that in Uganda during the early 1950s, about 2 percent of the coffee farmers could be characterized as "large"—that is, employing many wage laborers, living in town frequently, and often having various other business activities. At the bottom of the social ladder, 27 percent of the cocoa farmers barely made a living from cocoa sales, and 20 percent earned their living as agricultural wage laborers.

[64] Polly Hill, *Studies in Rural Capitalism in West Africa* (Cambridge: Cambridge University Press, 1970).

therefore inalienable. Hill's surveys of land ownership in Asante — supplemented subsequently by similar investigations in Northern Nigeria and elsewhere — left no doubt as to the existence of a long-standing group of rural capitalists engaged in the production and marketing of cocoa for profit. They were skilled in land trading and were prepared to shift resources to more lucrative businesses when they saw profitable opportunities. This special group of farmers not only marketed the major part of the cocoa crop but also developed the industry. They expanded their operations beyond "the family farm" by buying land, often far from their home areas, and by employing "strangers." Numerous small cocoa farmers existed side by side with these major entrepreneurs. The distribution of ownership of capital in Ghana is therefore highly uneven, but is characteristic of the structure of African agricultural capitalism. In the words of Sidney Hyman, "this key feature of inequality, rather than uniformity in the distribution of wealth, is not unique to cocoa but is a fairly prevalent feature in West African indigenous economies.[65]

The effect of Hill's studies was comparable to the announcement that the emperor wore no clothes. Once it was pointed out, everybody recognized that the origin of cocoa capitalism began with a Ghanaian, Tetteh Quarshie, who in 1879 returned from Fernando Po to the hills behind Accra with a handful of cocoa seeds and succeeded in his first plantings and marketing, thereby stimulating African imitators in a way that European instructors never could. In 1895, the Gold Coast exported 13 tons of cocoa; only ten years later, this figure had risen to 5,000 tons; by 1911, the Gold Coast had become the world's leading producer, with exports of nearly 40,000 tons, a figure that was quickly to double and double again. Half a century ago, the cocoa industry was described before the West African Lands Committee as a unique example of indigenous industry. To this day, whenever African entrepreneurs of great ingenuity and magnitude are discovered by the Western press or investigatory commissions, they are hailed as unique examples of indigenous industry. Yet what is of political import is precisely the extent, organization, and power of this indigenous class which is rooted in the history of virtually every African country. By the time of independence, the cocoa growers already wore the laurels of numerous victories waged against both colonial regimes and imperialist business empires.[66]

Cocoa farming provides an outstanding example of the situation created by rural capitalism. Growing inequalities have pushed ever greater numbers of peasants to the brink of poverty. Yet the poorest peasants do not assert their self-interest or push for a "new deal" in

---

[65] Sidney Hyman, "Introduction" in Still, *Studies in Rural Capitalism in East Africa*, p. xix.

[66] See Martin Kilson, "The Emergent Elites of Black Africa, 1900 to 1960" in *Colonialism in Africa, 1870–1960*, ed. Peter Duignan and L. H. Gann, Vol. 2, *The History and Politics of Colonialism, 1914–1960*, ed. Duignan and Gann (Cambridge: Cambridge University Press, 1970), p. 371; and David Kimble, *A Political History of Ghana: The Rise of Gold Coast Nationalism, 1850–1928* (Oxford: Clarendon Press, 1963), p. 50.

agriculture—even though intellectuals and technicians have argued the necessity of reform.[67]

Even where traditional communal patterns of land ownership did in fact exist, as we have seen, private individual capitalist possession has produced an increasingly sharp division in rural societies. Land reform will again be placed on the historical agenda for many African countries as conflicts between peasants and the new agricultural capitalists sharpen. Attempts to correct the increasingly glaring rural inequities by legislative or administrative fiat do not appear to have been successful. Under the originally militant socialist regime of Gamal Nasser, a series of measures were passed to restrict the acreage that landlords might retain. Similar laws were passed again and again in an attempt to restore the revolutionary impetus and the social goals of land reform. Yet these measures came to little; finally, even their rationale was undercut by the present Sadat regime.[68] No bureaucracy can implement land reform by itself, for its own technical and economic needs will take precedence over the goals of the peasants. The example of Egypt suggests that even a committed political leadership will have its hands full when dealing with the countryside.

To the extent that peasants do not migrate into the cities, they pose a much greater problem as a class than the industrial working class. In a sense, the worker is a newcomer to the modernizing society. Huntington notes: "He participates in the production of new economic wealth." His struggles with the employer revolve about his right to organize collectively so as to be able to effectively demand his share of the new goods produced. In an ever expanding economy, "the worker thus has little or no incentive to be revolutionary." Indeed, it is in his best interest to see to it that the system as a whole works as effectively as possible. The peasant, on the other hand, does not share a common interest with the landlord, for he must struggle over ownership of the means of production, not over a more equitable distribution of the income that results from economic growth. Insofar as "the landlord loses what the peasant acquires," the peasant, "unlike the industrial worker, has no alternative but to attack the existing system of ownership and control." Thus, land reform involves more than simply an increase in the economic well-being of the peasant; "it involves also a fundamental redistribution of power and status, a reordering of the basic social relationships which had previously existed between landlord and peasant."[69]

No rural-based revolution has ever succeeded by itself, although in Algeria, Kenya, the Cameroons, and the Congo movements in the countryside have played important roles in the achievement of independence and in major domestic rearrangements of government. In

[67] Huntington, *Political Order in Changing Societies*, pp. 382–83.

[68] *Ibid.*, p. 380. Ian Clegg demonstrates a similar decline in socialist commitment in Algeria in his *Workers' Self-Management in Algeria* (New York: Monthly Review Press, 1971).

[69] Huntington, *Political Order in Changing Societies*, p. 299.

the future, peasant discontent and a burgeoning social conflict could be major factors in coups d'état, radical shifts of government coalitions, occasional violence, and even prolonged conflict.

Processes of commercial exchange set in motion during the early great African empires and given a giant boost by expanded peasant cash-crop production after the advent of colonialism have increasingly bifurcated rural societies. On the one hand, well-to-do farmers have increased in number, accumulated huge acreages, and hired labor; frequently, they have entered business. In contrast, increasing numbers of peasants who are barely able to earn a living are forced to sell their land, work as agricultural laborers, or join the deepening pools of the unemployed living in the shanty towns of the larger cities. The large farmers thus joined the traditional chiefs, big businessmen, and trade-union leaders as major political forces in the evolving policies of postindependence African government.

At times, these forces felt thwarted in their aspirations by growing mass discontent and by ideologies that they could only consider socialistic, popularistic, demagogic, and expensive. Fearing the instability that would undermine their power, they turned frequently to the military in an effort to reconsolidate or further consolidate their power.

Chapter IX

THE CONSOLIDATION OF POWER:
Definition of the Political Arena

Creon, announcing the purpose of his rule in ancient Greece, declared:

> Times have changed for Thebes. Thebes has the right now to a prince without a history. . . . I have my two feet on the earth, my hands on my hips and since I have been king I have resolved . . . to employ myself very simply, in rendering the order of this world a little less absurd, if it is possible. It isn't even an adventure, it's a job for every day and like all jobs it's not always pleasant. But because I'm here to do my job, I'm going to do it.[1]

After independence all the new African rulers, princes who claimed to be without histories, consolidated their power. They endeavored to establish their authority, and to found their support on an enduring social base for the long pull of humdrum, nonrevolutionary, bread-and-butter activities. *Coups d'état* and the rise of authoritarian regimes echoed the experience of most of the other nations of the world. Nevertheless, independence created prospects for a fuller, better life for most Africans, prospects that still exist even as African Antigones rise to remind their secular lords that authority requires limits if it is not to degenerate into tyranny.

One-Party Rule, Military Coups d'État and Questions of Democracy: Historical Parallels

Any attempt to deal with the trend toward authoritarianism in Africa must proceed beyond the too-simple explanations that point to the "personal love of power" of "paranoiac politicians thrust forward by the highly emotional struggle for independence."[2] All countries have

---

[1] Jean Anouilh, *Antigone* (Paris: Table Ronde, 1949). That Anouilh wrote this play under the eyes of the German occupation rendered the moral problems of the original Antigone all the more poignant and relevant to Africa in the modern world. Sophocles did not include as blunt a statement in his *Antigone;* his reasoning also differed. Cf. the translation of Sophocles by D. Fitts and R. Fitzgerald (New York: Harcourt, Brace & World, 1969).

[2] W. A. Lewis, *Politics in West Africa* (New York: Oxford University Press, 1966), pp. 30–31.

suffered such politicians, but the problems involved in shoring up new regimes lie beyond personalities and can be appreciated only through a historical perspective. Seymour Martin Lipset, in his study of America as a new nation, destroys the popular belief that the thirteen colonies proceeded easily towards democratic political institutions:

> It was touch and go whether the complex balance of forces would swing in the direction of a one or two-party system, or even whether the nation would survive as an entity. It took time to institutionalize values, beliefs, and practices, and there were many incidents that revealed how fragile the commitments to democracy and nationhood really were.[3]

On a global scale, Barrington Moore concluded his study of the making of the modern world most somberly with the declaration, "At bottom all forms of industrialization so far have been revolutions from above, the work of a ruthless minority."[4]

Since the overthrow of King Farouk of Egypt in 1952, over thirty military coups have shaken Africa. Coups have taken place in Algeria in 1965, Burundi in 1956 and 1966, the Central African Republic in 1966, the Congo Republic in 1963 and 1968, in Zaire in 1960 and 1965, in Ghana in 1966 and 1972, in Mali in 1968, in Sierra Leone in 1967 and 1968, in Togo in 1963, and in Uganda in 1971. Libya had a coup in 1969, Nigeria two separate coups in 1966, Rwanda in 1973, Somalia in 1969, the Sudan in 1958 and 1969, and Upper Volta in 1966 and 1973. Dahomey holds the record, experiencing coups in 1963, 1965, 1967, 1968, 1969, and 1972. The government of Hamani Diori was overthrown in 1974, the same year the regime of Haile Selassie finally toppled. In the midst of an open meeting of the Organization of African Unity in July, 1975, General Gowon was informed that dissident army officers had taken power in Nigeria; other heads of state scurried home precipitously. Over twenty other attempted coups during the same period were unsuccessful. Civil wars occurred in Zaire, Nigeria, Ethiopia, Sudan, and Chad.[5]

Yet what has been the experience of other parts of the world? Most Latin American countries gained their independence in the middle of the nineteenth century. John J. Johnson provides a few "by no means atypical" examples to suggest the extent of the difficulties encountered by these countries:

---

[3] Seymour Martin Lipset, *The First New Nation* (London: Heinemann Educational Books, 1963), pp. 15–16.

[4] Barrington Moore, Jr., *Social Origins of Dictatorship and Democracy; Lord and Peasant in the Making of the Modern World* (Boston: Beacon Press, 1966), p. 506.

[5] Keesing's Research Report, *Africa Independent: A Survey of Political Developments* (New York: Scribner's, 1972); Donald G. Morrison et al., *Black Africa, A Comparative Handbook* (New York: Free Press, 1972); and Robert G. Mitchell et al., *Social Change and Nation Building: A Guide to the Study of Independent Black Africa* (New York: Free Press, forthcoming). Aristide Zolberg, in reviewing the causes of military coups, notes that what is surprising is not that military interventions occur but that they have not occurred everywhere. See his "The Military Decade in Africa," *World Politics*, 25, no. 2 (January 1973), 309–31.

Venezuela suffered fifty revolutions during the century following its independence; up to 1903 Colombia had experienced twenty-seven civil wars, one of which claimed 80,000, and another 100,000 lives; between 1830 and 1895 Ecuador lived under eleven constitutions. By 1898 Bolivia had survived more than sixty revolutions and had assassinated six presidents; by 1920 the country had been ruled by seventy-four executives, and by 1952 had undergone a total of 179 revolutions.[6]

And in England and on the Continent during the sixteenth, seventeenth, and eighteenth centuries, only monarchial absolutism and strong one-party rule succeeded in overcoming the civil wars of family, region, and religion. The British Isles, Carl Friedrich tells us, "had seen a greater measure of effective monarchial absolutism than any other country." In the seventeenth century, he contends, "advanced thought was absolutist thought. . . . It was thought which revolved around the central idea that men had the power to mold their social environment by appropriate legislation and policy."[7] For any revolution to succeed, John Dunn points out, those who seize power must solve some of the problems of their societies. They must do more than simply maintain social control, or they fail to establish their legitimacy.[8] Increasingly, Europe from the eighteenth century on sought the foundations of good government not in political forms but in administration, not in "the arrangements and limitations of political power but in the practical arts of administrative efficiency, rooted in practical knowledge."[9] The famous builders of the modern state in seventeenth-century Europe founded their effectiveness, and hence their legitimacy, on "the army and the bureaucracy, the nameless hundreds and thousands of faithful servants of the king and crown who, in those decades, emerged as the core of modern government."[10]

The great lesson that these historical developments offer for an understanding of contemporary Africa is the rapidity with which a new political framework was created. J. H. Plumb, in his important study of the establishment of English democracy, provides an antidote to the fear of incessant violence as the future of African politics:

---

[6] John J. Johnson, *The Military and Society in Latin America* (Stanford, Calif.: Stanford University Press, 1964), p. 4. Johnson notes a pattern, which is in some ways comparable to the African experience, of Latin American countries passing through a cycle from authoritarianism under colonialism to a period of democracy after independence and then back to authoritarian regimes led by indigenous elements (*Ibid.,* p. 17).

[7] Carl Friedrich, *The Age of the Baroque, 1610–1660* (New York: Harper & Row, 1952), pp. 15, 17. Barrington Moore tells us that although the nineteenth century was the age of peaceful transformation, a period when parliamentary democracy established itself firmly, we must consider how the violence of the seventeenth and eighteenth centuries prepared the way for that transformation: "To break the connection between the two is to falsify history. To assert that the connection was somehow necessary and inevitable is to justify the present with an argument that is impossible to prove" (*Social Origins of Dictatorship and Democracy,* p. 29).

[8] Dunn, *Modern Revolutions* (New York: Cambridge University Press, 1972), pp. 12–22.

[9] J. H. Plumb, *The Growth of Political Stability in England, 1675–1725* (Harmondsworth: Penguin, 1969), p. 26.

[10] Friedrich, *The Age of the Baroque, 1610–1660,* p. 15.

There is a general folk-belief, derived largely from Burke and the nineteenth century historians, that political stability is of slow, coral-like growth; and the result of time, circumstances, prudence, experience, wisdom, slowly building up over the centuries. Nothing is, I think, further from the truth. True, there are, of course, deep social causes of which contemporaries are usually unaware making for the *possibility* of political stability. But stability becomes actual through the actions and decisions of men, as does revolution. Political stability, when it comes, often happens to a society quite quickly, as suddenly as water becomes ice.[11]

Earlier in the same book, Plumb points out the vivid contrast between political society in seventeenth- and eighteenth-century England: "In the seventeenth century men killed, tortured, and executed each other for political beliefs; they sacked towns and brutalized the countryside. They were subjected to conspiracy, plot, and invasion. This uncertain political world lasted until 1715, and then began rapidly to vanish. By comparison, the political structure of eighteenth century England possesses adamantine strength and profound inertia."[12] The great accomplishment of the directors of the English political system between 1688 and 1725, according to Plumb, was to "confirm the nature of power within the political system" by giving not only individuals but classes of men their political identity in the pyramid of authority. Once created, that pyramid lasted for centuries, almost to our own day.

This is not, of course, to argue that the foundations of modern states are not profoundly shaken from time to time. Those who would claim, however, that African states are "not ready for self-government," who expect that the "lessons of democracy" are learned through the tutelege of the "more developed" societies, cannot escape their own bloody ancestry. And today, where are the models of "good," "stable," "democratic" societies?[13]

In Africa as in Europe, societies have moved as quickly into stability as into turmoil. This chapter investigates the form "stability" assumed and the social forces that have made it too often of questionable desirability. Although a few tin colonels and bush dictators, like their Western counterparts, have not troubled to conceal their self-serving exercise of naked power, African *statesmen* have worried about the creation of democratic societies—in terms of both theory and practical requisites—even as they have asserted the uniqueness of their conditions and their right to chart original directions. Yet regardless of politicians' forensic commitments, African military men have eased into new eminence. Invariably, they allege themselves the cure for the cancer of corruption, sin, and sometimes socialism. This chapter will also probe the political consequences and social context of corruption, as well as the social basis of the military and its role in the

[11] Plumb, *The Growth of Political Stability in England*, p. 173.
[12] *Ibid.*, p. 13.
[13] See e.g. story by Flora Lewis, "Western Europe Falters," *New York Times*, March 3, 1974.

consolidation of power. Based upon this assessment and the analysis of case studies, we will then attempt to draw some conclusions about the type of regimes that will survive and the social base on which they are founded.

African and Western Democracy: Form and Substance

Virtually all African countries entered independence with Western parliamentary forms of government. The greatest political change since independence has been an apparently universal trend toward one-pary or "no-party" states—sometimes achieved by coups d'etat, sometimes by the formation of coalitions or the passage of legislation.[14] Although during the 1960s debates whirled furiously around "the prospects for parliamentary democracy," today, fortunately or unfortunately, little excitement surrounds the issue. Many Africans were undisturbed by the demise of these early governmental arrangements. One reason for this is that these arrangements were Western forms, part of the *colonial* heritage, something forcefully imposed and formed. Perhaps, they felt, something as good or better—but indigenous—could develop. Second, the realities under the forms, in particular the domination by the organizational bourgeoisie, soon began to reveal themselves clearly. Third, even where formal opposition was permitted, it became increasingly apparent that the opposition, whether "right" or "left," couldn't "make it," and that elections were really a sham. Fourth, there was a spreading general weariness with politicians and politics as corruption became rampant and African countries began to go through their Tammany Hall days, and as economic development did not appear successful and living conditions did not improve according to expectations or, indeed, became worse.

A growing disillusionment with political forms in the '60s and '70s shook the world, not just Africa. In the West, under the poundings of Watergate and long-unsuccessful popular efforts to end the war in Vietnam, elections and party systems appeared more and more a façade behind which Republicans and Democrats increasingly looked alike and seemed to be pawns of the "power elite" or "ruling class." The "new left," sit-ins, peace marches, Vietnam, and Civil Rights direct-action movements all raised into question the efficacy with which representative institutions meet popular demands. A feeling grew that public opinion simply reflected controlled inputs by the mass media. Voting studies revealed an electorate ignorant of issues and candidates, voting seemingly on the basis of the "goodness" or "badness" of the times. The more sanguine democratic pluralists, such

[14] "By the end of 1973, 5 of 34 African states had multi-party systems, 9 military regimes, and 19 single-party systems. Some of the one party systems were veiled military regimes." In early 1974, Ethiopia was still a monarchy without a party system. In the five multiparty systems, one party usually dominated. From the independence of Ghana in 1957 to 1973, thirty-one successful coups took place in eighteen nations. (Mitchell et al., *Social Change and National Building*, p. 1/41)

as V. O. Key, concluded that representative government requires a few oligarchies in order to function efficiently.[15]

Commentators as diverse as Herbert Marcuse and Teilhard de Chardin have argued that the Soviet Union and the United States look more and more like each other.[16] Other analysts maintain that capitalist and socialist ideologies lose their significance in an interdependent age. "Technological determinists" in both academic and governmental circles argue that the development of nations stems primarily from the employment of science and from efficient modes of organization—not from differences in philosophy.[17] Finally, it has become clear that all political systems, no matter what their labels, tolerate dissent only in limited areas: the United States governing establishments would not allow the Communist Party to come into power, just as the Soviets would not allow capitalism to gain a foothold in their heartland or Czechoslovakia to follow a Western path of development. In Africa, the façades of multiparty democracy are nowhere more apparent than in South Africa or Rhodesia, where functioning multiparty systems fulfill most of the formal requirements of democracy; only blacks don't participate.

These considerations have given new cogency and relevance to those who maintain that in order to judge the "democratic" content of a regime, the observer must look at what a government does. My own view, as I have indicated throughout this book, is that governments and particular policies must be judged by whom they benefit, by policy outcomes—but that the mode of ruling, the safeguard of personal freedoms is also of fundamental concern. Given the special conditions of the continent, African political genius would invariably invent special solutions to these problems.

Sekou Touré asserts that the key question posed to governments is not what kind of democracy a country will have but what kind of dictatorship. All regimes ultimately tell their people to "do this" or "do that" under the threat of dire penalties for noncompliance. Just as a state's political independence cannot be real unless it is founded upon economic independence, similarly, according to Touré, a government cannot meet "democratic aspirations" unless it has sufficient power to meet the real needs of the people and to realize the "full development of the human person."[18]

---

[15] V. O. Key, in *The Responsible Electorate* (New York: Vintage, 1966), argues that although the two major political parties in the United States are controlled by closed oligarchies, this is not fatal if the electorate can choose between the two sets of officers and presumably their positions. See also Seymour Martin Lipset, *Political Man* (New York: Doubleday, 1960), *passim*, for a greatly restricted conception of democracy in comparison with the classical Lincolnian model.

[16] Herbert Marcuse, *One Dimensional Man* (Boston: Beacon Press, 1964); Pierre Teilhard de Chardin, *The Phenomenon of Man* (New York: Harper & Row, 1961). Cf. Samuel P. Huntington, *Political Order in Changing Societies* (New Haven: Yale University Press, 1968), p. 11.

[17] See, for example, W. W. Rostow, *The Stages of Economic Growth: A Non-Communist Manifesto* (New York: Cambridge University Press, 1971); Herbert Butterfield, *The Origins of Modern Science*, rev. ed. (New York: Free Press, 1965); and C. E. Black, *The Dynamics of Modernization* (New York: Harper & Row, 1966).

[18] See Sekou Touré, *Guinean Revolution and Social Progress* (Cairo: Société Orientale de Publicité, n.d. [1963], excerpts of which are reprinted in *African Politics and Society*, pp. 219–25). For an account of

In this context, Nyerere makes added sense when he maintains that in new countries everybody will vote for the government party, because of its monopoly of power and alleged legitimacy; in any event, the opposition will naturally atrophy because those in control can outmaneuver, out-promise and out-deliver it. From the start, therefore, those concerned with the substance of democracy should focus on *intra*party competition.[19] What really matters, Nyerere argues, is not the number of parties or their form, but rather their leadership, their policy outcome, their programs, and the class interests they represent and advance.[20]

Like Nyerere, Samuel Huntington has claimed that in political development, "what counts is not the number of parties but rather the strength and adaptability of the party system, i.e., the capacity of assimilating the new social forces produced through modernization."[21] However, we must distinguish two fundamental issues: the theoretical or moral desirability of any particular form of government, on the one hand and the political, cultural, and economic foundations required to make that form possible, on the other hand. African countries cannot choose freely among forms of government, as if democracy were a Camembert cheese to be picked from a supermarket shelf. African leaders are responsible for their actions. They choose,

conditions in Guinea today, see below *Jeune Afrique;* and Victor Du Bois. For additional discussion of various difficulties in the establishment of democracy in Africa, see Immanuel Wallerstein, "The Decline of the Party in Single Party African States," in *Political Parties and Political Development,* ed. Joseph LaPalombara and Myron Weiner (Princeton, N.J.: Princeton University Press, 1966), pp. 201–16; Omolade Adejuyigbe, "The Size of Political States and Stability in Nigeria," *African Studies Review,* 16, no. 2 (September 1973), 157–82; Henry L. Bretton, *Power and Stability in Nigeria* (New York: Praeger, 1962); Nadav Safran, *Egypt in Search of Political Community* (Cambridge, Mass.: Harvard University Press, 1961); B. O. Nwabueze, *Presidentialism in Commonwealth Africa* (New York: St. Martin's, 1974); Bereket H. Selassie, *The Executive in African Governments* (London: Heinemann Educational Books, 1974); Gwendolen M. Carter, ed., *African One Party States* (Ithaca, N.Y.: Cornell University Press, 1962); Peter T. Omari, *Kwame Nkrumah: The Anatomy of an African Dictatorship* (London: C. Hurst, 1970); Jean Ziegler, *La contre-revolution en Afrique* (Paris: Payot, 1963); William Burnett Harvey, *Law and Social Change in Ghana* (Princeton, N.J.: Princeton University Press, 1966); and Leo Kuper and M. G. Smith, eds., *Pluralism in Africa* (Berkeley and Los Angeles: University of California Press, 1971). On the more specific problem of creating unity, see, in addition to the above Donald Rothchild, *Toward Unity in Africa: A Study of Federalism in British Africa* (Washington, D.C.: Public Affairs Press 1960); Victor A. Olorunsula, ed., *The Politics of Cultural Sub-Nationalism in Africa* (Garden City, N.Y.: Doubleday, Anchor Books, 1972); and David R. Smock and Kwamina Bentsi-Enchill, eds., *The Search for National Integration in Africa* (New York: Free Press, forthcoming).

[19] Julius Nyerere, "One Party Rule," *Spearhead* (Dar es Salaam), November, 1961. Compare V. O. Key's arguments for the primary as the focal point of political activity in one-party states in his *Southern Politics* (New York: Knopf, 1949). Andre Gorz argues that the political arrangements of Western systems have become outmoded and that freedom of the individual has been undercut more than ever. See especially his *Socialism and Revolution* (New York: Doubleday, Anchor Books, 1973).

[20] In an argument comparable to Touré's assessment, Harvey C. Mansfield Jr. calls representative government "that modern cloud ... which claims to present man to himself and tries to prevent men from asking what is good for themselves." Cf. "Hobbes and the Science of Indirect Government," *American Political Science Review,* 65, no. 1 (March 1971), 97–110.

[21] Huntington, *Political Order in Changing Societies,* p. 121. Cf. Clement Moore, who, in "The Single Party as Source of Legitimacy," in *Authoritarian Politics in Modern Society,* ed. Samuel P. Huntington and Clement H. Moore (New York: Basic Books, 1970), p. 49, points out that the True Whig Party of Liberia was founded in 1877. This gives it claim to being the oldest establishment party in the world. Longevity and "stability" have not saved it, however, from severe criticisms. See, for example, J. Gus Liebenow, *Liberia: The Evolution of Privilege* (Ithaca, N.Y.: Cornell University Press, 1969); and Robert W. Clower et al., *Growth Without Development: An Economic Survey of Liberia* (Evanston Ill.: Northwestern University Press, 1966).

however, within perimeters that are defined more closely than they appear at first. Their realistic alternatives—if any—might revolve around a one-party system. A choice among one-, two-, or multiparty systems may not be available on the historical menu.[22] Let us, therefore, consider the theoretical case for, first, the Western liberal conception of parliamentary democracy, and, second, the model of African democracy prepared by Nyerere. Both versions maintain that they take into account socioeconomic realities as well as lofty ideals.

The Western Case for Multiparty Parliamentary Democracy

Seymour Martin Lipset offers a definition of democracy that synthesizes basic elements of classic Western conceptions and incorporates both the moral goals and the functional requisites for their realization. According to Lipset, a democracy is

> a political system which supplies regular constitutional opportunities for changing the governing officials. It is a social mechanism for the resolution of the problem of societal decision making among conflicting interest groups which permits the largest possible part of the population to influence those decisions through their ability to choose among alternative contenders for political office.[23]

Lipset spells out the conditions implied by this formula: (1) a system of beliefs that legitimizes these democratic arrangements and specifies the institutions—political parties, free press, and so on—that are accepted as proper by all; (2) one set of political leaders in office; and (3) one or more sets of leaders out of office who act as a legitimate opposition attempting to gain office. Lipset's analysis links the development of democracy with an interrelated cluster of variables, including economic development, Protestantism as the source of a special culture, and various historical factors that have created an aura of legitimacy.[24]

David Apter has also called for an active, recognized political opposition in new nations, and has argued that such an opposition performs many useful functions, even for the regime in power. He bemoans the fact that new governments rarely see the necessity for a regular opposition party or accept the idea of opposition as a normal

[22] Cranford Pratt, *The Critical Phase in Tanzania 1945–1968* (London: Cambridge University Press, 1976), pp. 242–64, offers the best defense of Nyerere's strategy for the transition to socialism and powerful arguments that democracy is not a dead issue in a poor country.

[23] Seymour Lipset, "Some Social Requisites of Democracy," *American Political Science Review*, 53, no. 1 (March 1959). See also Chapter II of Lipset's *Political Man*.

[24] For a critique of Lipset's methodology, see, for example, Jonathan Sunshine, "The Economic Basis and Consequences of Democracy," mimeographed (Washington, D.C.: American Political Science Association Conference, 1972). See also Deane Neubauer, "Some Conditions of Democracy," *American Political Science Review*, 61, no. 4 (December 1967), 1002–9; Dankwart A. Rustow, "Transitions to Democracy: Toward a Dynamic Model," *Comparative Politics*, 2 (1970), 339–42; and John V. Gillespie and Betty A. Nesvold, eds. *Macro-Quantitative Analysis, Conflict, Development and Democratization* (Beverly Hills, Calif.: Sage Publications, 1971). Cf. T. H. Marshall, *Class, Citizenship and Social Development* (New York: Doubleday, Anchor Books, 1965).

feature of government. Third world leaders and Western analysts from Asoka Mehta to Julius Nyerere and Robert Dahl to C. B. Macpherson and Apter himself have explained this failure to accept the opposition as legitimate, citing among their reasons:

1) The recent attainment of independence, which leaves the nationalist leaders in possession of a monopoly of political loyalties: Apter, for example, cites Nkrumah's statement, "Until independence there is only one political position, that of independence, and I happen to be holding it."[25]

2) The antigovernment reflex of the opposition: in new countries, political action is aimed at changing the fundamental character of the country rather than accepting well-established rules of political life and working within them.

3) Special difficulties faced by new nations after independence: these range from the building of adequate medical, educational, transportational, and other services to the improvement of housing, the food supply, and other necessities—all of which indicate that the basic struggles are not over when independence has been won.

4) New and "higher" objectives: industrialization and the integration of a single nation out of many smaller units continue to pressure new leaders.

5) Irresponsibility: governmental fears that opposition will increase factionalism, corruption, and separateness at a time when the major necessity is to create a new social solidarity are too often well founded.

6) The threat of counterrevolution: one must certainly contend with the possibility that the opposition will bring the whole structure tumbling down.

Under these circumstances, an opposition might indeed appear academic at best and traitorous at worst.

Apter maintains, however, that a political opposition is neither a luxury nor a danger. An organized opposition represents interests overlooked by the majority party, alleviates discontent, holds out the long-run prospect of equal treatment for all, promotes compromise, provides information for rational decisions as well as feedback on public reaction to official policy, and prevents the transformation of competition between groups over pork-barrel demands into value conflicts that would challenge the foundations of society as a moral order.[26] Apter is perfectly correct in maintaining that if an opposition

---

[25] David Apter, "The Role of a Political Opposition in New Nations," in *African Politics and Society,* ed. Markovitz, pp. 226–241.

[26] For additional functions of the opposition, see Apter, "The Role of a Political Opposition in New Nations," in *African Politics and Society,* ed. Markovitz, pp. 226–41; Angela Burger, *Opposition in a Dominant Party System* (Berkeley and Los Angeles: University of California Press, 1969); Asoka Mehta, *Democratic Socialism* (Bombay, Bharatiya Vidya Bhavan, 1959); and C. B. Macpherson, *The*

performs its functions well, it provides crucial services to the government in its day-to-day, bread-and-butter politics, and helps determine the success or failure of efforts to solve diverse problems.[27] Obviously, these objectives are highly desirable. But are they possible?

An Alternative Conception of Democracy

Julius Nyerere offers an alternative model of democracy, one that is based upon African history and practical necessities. He points out that to the Greeks, democracy meant "government by discussion among equals." The people discussed issues, and when they reached agreement, the result was a "people's decision." Nyerere refers to an account of traditional African democracy in Malawi that describes the elders as sitting around a tree and talking until they reached agreement. This talking "until you agree," according to Nyerere, is the essence of the traditional African concept of democracy: government by discussion, as opposed to government by force; discussion between the people or their chosen representatives, as opposed to government by hereditary clique. Nyerere writes that

> to minds molded by Western parliamentary tradition and Western concepts of democratic institutions, the idea of an organized opposition group has become so familiar that its absence immediately raises the cry of "dictatorship." It is no good telling them that when a group of 100 equals have sat and talked together until they agreed where to dig a well (and "until they agreed" implies that they will have produced many conflicting arguments before they do eventually agree), they have practiced democracy. Proponents of Western parliamentary traditions will consider whether the opposition was organized and therefore automatic, or whether it was spontaneous and therefore free. Only if it was automatic will they concede that here was democracy![28]

Nyerere maintains that pure democracy is too clumsy a way of conducting the affairs of a large modern state, and that a system of government by discussion does not necessitate an opposition group. Two-party systems, Nyerere goes on, may or may not be democratic, but they represent only one form of democracy. The Anglo-Saxon model reflects societies bifurcated by a struggle between the haves and the have-nots: one party represents wealth and the status quo, and the other represents the masses and change. Nyerere argues that there were no such ready-made decisions within African society. The patri-

Real World of Democracy (New York: Oxford University Press, 1972). Cf. Robert A. Dahl, who, in his *Political Opposition in Western Democracies* (New Haven: Yale University Press, 1966), p. 348, identifies at least seven major conditions that help account for differences among patterns of opposition in Western nations. Among the primary conditions he discusses are the constitutional structure and electoral system, shared cultural premises, specific subcultures, the record of grievances against the government, and social and economic differences.

[27] Apter, "The Role of a Political Opposition in New Nations," in *African Politics and Society*, ed. Markovitz, p. 230.

[28] Nyerere, "One Party Rule," p. 186.

otic struggle for independence united all elements and left no room for internal differences. Once freedom was achieved, the real task of building the economy and raising the standard of living began. The low economic level required maximum effort and total unity; again, therefore, there was no room for differences or division. The post-independence period, according to Nyerere, is "our time of emergency," a period comparable to that of a country at war or in the midst of a depression, when all differences are obliterated by a common effort.

The essentials of democracy, Nyerere maintains, are the freedom and the well-being of the individual. Freedom alone is not enough, however, for it can imply, as in Western democracy, the freedom to starve. There must also be freedom from bondage, discrimination, indignities—all the things that hamper a people's progress: "Where, then, you have the freedom and well-being of the individual, who has the right freely and regularly to join with his fellows in choosing the government of his country, and where the affairs of the country are conducted by true discussion, you have democracy."[29]

In the past, colonial governors were preoccupied with law and order. Nyerere points out that the new tasks assumed by the modern indigenous regime are much wider, and that no government today finds it easy to fulfill all its responsibilities to the people:

> The very success of the nationalist movements in raising the expectations of the people, the modern means of communications which put the American and British worker in almost daily contact with the African worker, the 20th century upsurge of the ordinary man and woman—all these deprive the new African governments of those advantages of time and ignorance which alleviated the growing pains of modern society for the governments of older countries.[30]

The rising demands of Africans are confronted by severe shortages of money, trained personnel, and time. This produces a situation of great urgency, which requires that any opposition act responsibly. Any government has the right to self-defense against sabotage and the duty to safeguard unity against attempts to divide and weaken it. Too often, the demagogic and the irresponsible take advantage of freedom to exploit democracy for their own benefit. A constructive opposition party can well be tolerated, but, Nyerere demands, where is it? A responsible opposition with a definite, sincerely held alternative policy might reasonably attempt to persuade the electorate to reject the existing government at the next election, but "that sort of mature opposition is rare indeed in a newly independent state." A country in its vital early years cannot afford the same degree of tolerance a long-established democracy can safely allow. A genuine and responsible opposition can arise in time and will be welcome. Until then, Nyerere

[29] *Ibid.,* p. 187.
[30] Nyerere, "One Party Rule," p. 187.

concludes, there is no reason why government by discussion, and hence democracy, cannot be continued.[31]

Obviously, not all one-party systems are alike. Nyerere's claims for democracy need not be accepted automatically, but, like the claims for all other systems, they should be examined critically. C. B. Macpherson, for example, in a generally sympathetic assessment, points out that whether a single party can be called democratic "in a strict sense" depends on three criteria:

1) intraparty democracy — that is, how much control the rank and file within the party have over the leaders;

2) how open membership is in the party;

3) how strenuous a degree of activity is required as the price of membership in the party — that is, how far beyond men's willing cooperation this price is.[32]

Over time, Nyerere developed an institutional mechanism to implement his philosophy of African democracy in Tanzania. This mechanism was a type of electoral competition in which the people chose between two TANU (Tanzanian African National Union) candidates. This system was designed to eliminate the apparent conflict between, on the one hand, freedom in choosing the representative, and, on the other hand, the necessity of preserving national unity.[33]

Exercising criticism and providing alternatives — specific and detailed critiques within the framework of the overall value consensus of the society — are classic functions of the opposition. Despite Nyerere's arguments against interparty "organized" opposition, he has attempted to institutionalize a process of *intra*party opposition to serve many of the same ends. In seeking first to assure that "the opposition" will not overthrow Tanzania's system of government, Nyerere acts no differently — as pointed out above — than leaders of all other systems.

Nyerere welcomes a system of opposition within a stipulated consensus for practical as well as philosophical consideration. This assumes that public debate will bring out more of the facts, that bureaucrats and officials will be less able to hide their faults and inequities, and that popular participation in government will result in increased popular support of the government.

Although Nyerere wishes to create a government based on popular participation, some observers have raised the question of whether his objectives — even though extended to encompass the "good of the

---

[31] *Ibid.*, p. 188. Compare Nyerere's doubts about opposition with George Washington's attack against factions and organized parties in his Farewell Address. Washington inveighed against parties on the grounds that they promoted corruption, conflict, divisiveness, and inefficiency; hence, they encouraged political instability and made the state vulnerable to external influence.

[32] Macpherson, *The Real World of Democracy*, p. 27.

[33] Nyerere elaborates this point in his *Uhuru na Ujamaa: Freedom and Socialism: A Selection from Writings and Speeches, 1965–1967* (Dar es Salaam: Oxford University Press, 1968), p. 29.

people"—have resulted from input from the illiterate and quiescent mass of the population. To insure that self-government serves the "right purposes" produces what Andrew Maguire calls the "Rousseauist dilemma" of Nyerere's administration: "how to reconcile democratic popular participation and self-government by a predominantly unsophisticated citizenry with the requirements for unity and nation building which are clearly received and understood in terms of specific policies only by the governing elite and which, therefore, seem to require a centrally directed effort that can only with difficulty not be described as authoritarian."[34] This problem cuts to the heart of the relationship between leaders and followers within a party.

A discussion of Nyerere's conceptions of democracy—although crucial because he is head of state as well as of government—should not convey the impression that these are his ideas alone: they have the support of TANU's leaders. A survey indicated that most of the TANU party leaders considered democracy the most desirable form of government for their country. Sensitive to criticisms of the one-party state, they volunteered defenses of the government's institutions, they emphasized the popular and democratic character of the Tanzanian political system, and they indicated trust in the ability of the average person to choose good leaders.[35]

One of the biggest drawbacks to Tanzania's claim for democracy, according to Raymond F. Hopkins—who questions whether Tanzania is democratic at present, using criteria that he admits differ from those of the political rulers in Tanzania itself—is that only one candidate may stand for president, and there are no provisions for write-ins. This system was designed as President Nyerere's response to the demands for stability, demands similar to those that impelled many of the founding fathers of the United States to propose George Washington as president for life. Although Hopkins, a major critic of this system, maintains that "a closed style of politics has emerged in Tanzania and is becoming institutionalized in the political system" he also notes that opposition candidates and policies are not forcibly suppressed.[36] By "closed" Hopkins means the absence of procedures "for channeling alternative policies and candidates into a public area." "Alternative policies and candidates" are those that fall outside the framework of consensus or that have not been accepted, for a variety of reasons, by the pillars of the establishment. "Outsiders" in every political system feel the same way, of course. Nyerere has stated bluntly that he feels no obligation to help his opponents gain power, and, indeed, where is it written that this is a requirement for a democracy? Hopkins himself, after presenting a variety of criticisms, concludes:

[34] Andrew Maguire, *Toward "Uhuru" in Tanzania* (Cambridge: Cambridge University Press, 1969), p. 366.

[35] *Ibid.*, p. 363.

[36] Raymond F. Hopkins, *Political Roles in a New State: Tanzania's First Decade* (New Haven: Yale University Press, 1971), p. 234.

In spite of these characteristics Tanzania is certainly not a monolithic one-party state or a radical mobilization system in which political control is used as a tool to transform social and economic practices. Democracy and democratic institutions are highly valued by most members of the elite and the rights of criticism and freedom of thought are widely accepted.[37]

The structure and objectives of TANU have evolved over time. Part IV of the Arusha Declaration called for a shift of emphasis in party membership from mere size to "quality"; "greater consideration" was to be given to a member's commitment to the beliefs and objectives of the party and to its policy of socialism. How far this change will carry the party into an "elitest vanguard" as opposed to a mass party remains to be seen.[38]

On balance, even Tanzania's severest critics conclude that despite the possibility of authoritarian development in the future, Tanzania has managed to institute a unique and functioning form of democracy in its postindependence period of consolidation of power. Indeed, postindependence political parties, almost regardless of their ideological content and class basis, have declined in power and effectiveness in virtually every country on the continent, with a few notable exceptions besides Tanzania. Why should this be the case?

The Decline of Political Parties

Historically, political parties linked masses of people without great material possessions or social position into an organizational weapon capable of realizing the philosophical goals of "democracy." Yet in our own time, parties have declined everywhere in their efficacy in reaching political goals and in their ability to retain the deep loyalties of the masses. In Africa, this phenomenon has led to the decline of multi-party systems and the rise of one-party, "no-party," and military rule. Less striking but nevertheless increasingly evident, similar processes of disintegration affect Western political parties. Samuel Huntington

---

[37] *Ibid.*, p. 241.

[38] In a debate comparable to that between Apter and Bretton over the nature of the Convention Peoples Party, William H. Friedland, in his "The Evolution of Tanganyika's Political System," Program of East African Studies, Syracuse University Occasional Paper No. 110, n.d., p. 55, argued that TANU has become "an institution which pervades and dominates all other institutions and society," whereas Henry Bienen, in *Tanzania: Party Transformation and Economic Development* (Princeton, N.J.: Princeton University Press, 1970), maintained that the party had little power to affect decisions and behavior at the local level. Hopkins attempted to reconcile these conflicting positions by arguing that TANU is the predominant institution relative to other national organizations, but nevertheless is limited in its ability to induce integration or development at the local level (*Political Roles in a New State*, p. 31). Cf. Clyde Ingle's discussion, in his *From Village to State in Tanzania* (Ithaca, N.Y.: Cornell University Press, 1972), of citizen participation in the nation-building process. Ingle concludes that TANU succeeded in stimulating virtually every village to create a self-help project, and succeeded "in creating a sense of urgency and involvement in the minds of Tanzania's millions": school buildings, community centers, dispensaries, and countless TANU office buildings sprang up through these efforts (p. 62; also, see especially pp. 63, 259–60).

points out that a bureaucracy based upon a complex organization and merit system is more up-to-date in its inherent logic than the political party that operates on the bases of patronage, influence, and compromise.[39]

Walter Dean Burnham argues that in the United States, political parties have failed to cause political development, and have declined as instruments of action since 1900. Fortunately, Burnham points out, material and cultural circumstances in the United States have been favorable to rapid socioeconomic development, and if this continues, there is no apparent reason why profound transformations of the political system should ever occur. Therefore, the essence of the American "political system . . . has been the maintenance of a high wall separation between political conflict on one side and the socioeconomic system on the other." Economic development has been a quasi-automatic process, expanding with an energy and thrust unparalleled in modern history, while "the political system from parties to policy institutions has remained astonishingly little transformed in its characteristics and methods of operation."[40] Although political parties have struggled to win elections and manage tensions among the various groups of the coalition of which they are composed, they have not acted as forces for collective purposes and action. Indeed, Burnham maintains, elections have become "candidate image affairs for which only the very wealthy or those close to the very wealthy need apply." As long as economic growth is not seriously undercut by depression, the "pursuit of middle-class individualist political values" will intensify, thereby eroding even further the function of the party as an action organization. Contrary to popular assumptions, therefore, political modernization, defined as "systematic transformation toward greater rationalization of government structures and processes," has been "conspicuous by its absence."[41]

In Africa, the most startling phenomenon has not been the development of one-party states, but rather the rapid loss of support and disintegration of the organizations that were powerful at the time of independence. Immanuel Wallerstein has claimed that "in effect the one-party state in Africa has become in many places the no-party state."[42] Among the special reasons for this decline of party systems in Africa — in addition to the reasons affecting party organizations around the world — *the loss of revolutionary momentum after the achievement of independence* ranks foremost. In any society enthusiasm for participation in mass movements can be maintained only for relatively short periods of time; mass and then even cadre boredom set in. Wallerstein points out that at the level of the village, the very success

---

[39] Huntington, *Political Order in Changing Societies*, p. 91.

[40] Walter Dean Burnham, *Critical Elections and the Mainsprings of American Politics* (New York: Norton, 1970), pp. 176–79.

[41] *Ibid.*, p. 177.

[42] Wallerstein, "The Decline of the Party in Single Party African States," in *Political Parties and Political Development*, ed. LaPalombara and Weiner, p. 203.

of political leaders in incorporating traditional establishment figures meant a change in the function of the party from a weapon of reform to a defense mechanism for local interests.[43]

Along these lines, Western voting studies show the independent effects of "party" and "class" on voting. The emphasis in American voting studies has always been that party identification is a much more important factor than class in influencing and predicting votes. Yet at the same time, the theory of class polarization holds that "class" varies in saliency over time, even though the general direction of change in American politics has been away from class and toward party. With the expansion of trade unions during the Great Depression, class polarization reached its height. With the movement toward affluence and industrial peace, class consciousness declined.[44]

In undeveloped societies, although class factors were always present, the first great crisis of achieving independence placed a premium on creating national unity. Afterwards, with the return to "normalcy," material concerns bearing upon class interest became much more important.

With the development of mass electorates, all parties that sought governing power through the polls claimed to represent all the people. All wanted to become institutionalized, strongly articulated, increasingly disciplined. All used organization as a weapon, were led by educated men, legitimized formal structures of government, and attempted to integrate the population in one fashion or another.[45] In Africa, as in Europe, weakly articulated parties of the "patrons" belong to the days when politics was simply an affair of a small handful of middle-class intellectuals who sat in legislative councils as a result of appointment by the governor or election by restricted or indirect franchises.[46] Universal suffrage made all parties in every country democratic—at least in the sense that popular opinion could no longer be ignored, but had to be fashioned or manipulated in one way or another—even if they did not fulfill the real needs of the people. In seeking the differences between political parties, we err if we assume that elite parties are always content simply to reflect the structure of society as it is or as it used to be, that "conservative" parties are those opposed to change. What party in the past has opposed change that

---

[43] *Ibid.*, p. 207.

[44] Angus Campbell et al. discuss class polarization in *The American Voter* (New York: John Wiley, 1964).

[45] Aristide Zolberg, in his analysis of the history of African parties, distinguishes between the parties' "initial organizational spurt" that occurred in the Ivory Coast (around the period 1947–1949), Senegal (1948–1951), Ghana (1949–1951), and Guinea and Mali (1944–1956) and their slowing down to normal business (*Creating Political Order* [Chicago: Rand McNally & Co., 1966], p. 134). This historical evolution explains why competent observers came to greatly different conclusions about the same phenomenon, as did, for example, Henry Bretton, in *The Rise and Fall of Kwame Nkrumah* (New York: Praeger, 1966), and David E. Apter, *Ghana in Transition*, 2nd rev. ed. (Princeton, N.J.: Princeton University Press, 1972), in their assessments of the Convention Peoples Party.

[46] Thomas Hodgkin distinguishes between mass and patron parties in his *African Political Parties* (Baltimore: Penguin, 1961), as does Ruth Schachter Morgenthau, in her "Single Party Systems in West Africa," *American Political Science Review*, 55, no. 2 (June 1961). A "patron" party is a type of elite party.

improves its material well-being or political control! Change is opposed when it is seen as threatening, not because there is a philosophical predisposition to remain static. Conservative parties throughout the world have revealed their capacity to develop economically, to industrialize, to continue to manipulate a mass electorate under their hegemony. The fundamental difference between parties, then, must be sought not so much in their attitude towards change but in their class composition.

The history of the major political party in the Ivory Coast illuminates these propositions. The rise of antigovernment activity followed ultimately by a falling of political interest did not in this case result in disintegration, because of the nature of the class interests involved and because of the constraints of the colonial system.

Plantations and Communists in the Ivory Coast: A Case Study

The dominant party in the Ivory Coast, the *Parti Democratique de la Cote d'Ivoire* (PDCI), founded in 1946, had its social base in an organization of African planters, the *Syndicat Agricole Africain*, which played a role in the PDCI comparable to that of the trade union in the single-party system of Guinea.[47] The planters of the *Syndicat* were men of substance and property, yet they were driven to radical measures by the peculiar circumstances of the Ivory Coast. A small group of French settlers dominated the administration and used its political leverage to discriminate against African entrepreneurs. Between 1949 and 1951, a series of violent clashes between the PDCI and the French administration almost resulted in guerrilla warfare. In the French National Assembly, Houphouet-Boigny joined a group of African deputies in an association with the French Communist Party.

The Vichy government undertook a policy of systematic discrimination against the African planters, who had previously paid migrant workers wages as low as those paid by Europeans, and who indeed took advantage, when possible, of forced labor. In addition to cutting off indigenous employers from all labor, the French paid Africans lower prices for their coffee and subsidized Europeans for shipping their crops to France. Government inspectors often destroyed African plantations on the ground that they harbored crop parasites. They drafted all African subjects, including planters, for forced labor. No wonder, then, that in contrast with their class counterparts in Ghana, for example, the Ivory Coast planters took the initiative in their struggle against the colonial regime after the Second World War. Because of the similarity of the traditional social structure of the Asante and of the Baule, as well as of their modern organization as

[47] On political developments in the Ivory Coast, see Aristide Zolberg, *One-Party Government in the Ivory Coast*, rev. ed. (Princeton, N.J.: Princeton University Press, 1969); and Michael A. Cohen, *Urban Policy and Political Conflict in Africa: A Study of the Ivory Coast* (Chicago: University of Chicago Press, 1974).

cocoa farmers and coffee planters in Ghana and the Ivory Coast, respectively, a comparison of their political roles is especially interesting. At the end of 1951, with the change of government in metropolitan France and the coming into power of the PDCI in the Ivory Coast, Houphouet-Boigny undertook a new policy of cooperation with the metropole that has continued to the present. This policy resulted in the rapid development of an urban administrative bourgeoisie possessing a strong basis of support among a wealthy and successful commercial farming class in the rural areas.

Yet if political activity in the Ivory Coast declined, the PDCI did not disintegrate. Nor was the government overthrown by a military coup. The masses never did play a dominant role in politics, but the regime seemed to have found a secure social base. Elsewhere in Africa the most prominent governments and personalities, many of whom were famous for their radical past, fell or were overthrown. What were the further causes of this decline? Aside from Tanzania and a small number of other African states, corruption has been blamed for both the disintegration of political parties and for military coups.

Corruption and the Erosion of Civility

The corruption of politicians and the decline of public morality figure prominently in postindependence African politics. Every major and colonel who can command a microphone after having seized a palace announces that the conspirators were motivated by the desire to end corruption, inefficiency, and anarchy. After the first Nigerian coup, for example, Major Nzeogwu said, "We wanted to get rid of rotten and corrupt ministers, political parties, trade unions and the whole clumsy apparatus of the federal system." And his cohorts announced over Lagos radio, "The military has taken over to bring an end to gangsterism and disorder, corruption and despotism."[48]

In Guinea, tribunals were set up in each of the various districts for the purpose of judging cases of corruption among the ruling party and government officials. Touré spoke on Radio Conakry of "serious lapses" among officials.[49] Volumes of special commission reports poured out of the Ghanaian printing office; almost as detailed as the Watergate Hearings, they announced the extent of the official and unofficial dippings into the till. Why even radical regimes could not develop a communitarian and revolutionary ethos is a key question to an understanding of contemporary African politics.

In probing this problem, we must ask whether corruption was the *cause* of the overthrow of the old regimes or merely a symptom of a more basic social phenomenon. Huntington, for example, relates corruption to his basic theme of stability, arguing that "the absence of stable relationships among groups and of recognized patterns of au-

---

[48] Quoted in N. J. Miners, *The Nigerian Army, 1956–1966* (London: Methuen, 1971), p. 177.
[49] *West Africa*, no. 27, 1972, p. 1606.

thority enables corruption to thrive on disorganization." "Corruption varies inversely with political organization" because "the machine" or the party enables organized group interests to effectively exercise legitimate authority, thereby transcending the interests of individuals and social groups and reducing the opportunity for corruption.[50] Even before Watergate, any salesman in the United States who had tried selling something to state or local governmental agencies or who had learned the hard way the correct method of approaching the buyer's agents of even the largest corporations, might have questioned these propositions seriously. After Watergate and in the self-told success stories of the Magruders and Hunts, it has become increasingly apparent that corruption extends beyond matters of organization and stability.

De Tocqueville undoubtedly comes closer to the truth when he assesses how the competitive system that replaced feudalism, a society of "place," promoted greed and a desperate isolation:

> For in a community in which the ties of family, of caste, or class, and craft fraternities no longer exist people are far too much disposed to think exclusively of their own interest, to become self-seekers practicing a narrow individualism and caring nothing for the public good. ... It immures them, so to speak, each in his private life and taking advantage of the tendency they already have to keep apart, it estranges them still more. ... Since in such communities nothing is stable, each man is haunted by a fear of sinking to a lower social level and by a restless urge to better his condition. And since money has not only become the sole criterion of a man's social status but has also acquired an extreme mobility—that is to say it changes hands incessantly, raising or lowering the prestige of individuals and families—everybody is feverishly intent on making money or, if already rich, on keeping his wealth. ...[51]

Although De Tocqueville wrote to decry the loss of "true" aristocracy and to express his terror of the rising "tyranny of the majority," his sensitivity to the sickness of self-seeking spurred by a rising capitalism resounds in the tales of Chinua Achebe, Wole Soyinka, Kwesi Armah, Sembene Ousmane, and a host of other African writers. Achebe's *No Longer at Ease* tells of a civil servant living beyond his means who ultimately disgraces himself. Half a decade later, when Achebe wrote *A Man of the People*, Nigerian society had become so corrupt that the man who disgraced himself in the earlier novel became the honest person who seemed too dumb to take advantage of available opportunities like everybody else.[52]

Not all regimes suffer equally from corruption. For example, Barrington Moore points out that in any preindustrial society, extracting enough resources from a subsistence-level population to pay the

---

[50] Huntington, *Political Order in Changing Societies*, p. 71.

[51] Alexis De Tocqueville, *Democracy in America*, Vol. I (New York: Vintage, 1960), p. xiii.

[52] Chinua Achebe, *No Longer at Ease* (New York: Fawcett, 1969); *A Man of the People* (New York: Anchor Books, 1967).

salaries of a burgeoning large-scale bureaucracy is very difficult. How the rulers manage to solve this difficulty has a tremendous impact on the whole social structure. If the French solution was to sell offices and the Russian solution was to consolidate a new serfdom, the ancient Chinese imperial solution was to permit more-or-less open corruption.[53] The African experience seems to indicate that any government in which the civil service is a major pillar courts the same development.

James C. Scott, in a brilliant analysis, points out that the normal effect of corruption is "to cement together a conservative coalition and hold back or cancel out the effects of growing collective actions."[54] Quoting V. O. Key's statement, "Much of what we consider as corruption is simply the 'uninstitutionalized' influence of wealth in a political system,"[55] Scott argues that in a radical egalitarian regime there are few, if any, legitimate ways for wealth to buy power. In the absence of large firms and business groups that operate legally and directly as pressure groups for legislation, conducting expensive public relations campaigns and contributing to candidates, affluence almost automatically spills illegally into the political and bureaucratic arenas.[56] Corruption foments conservative tendencies, and especially damages socialist regimes by undermining egalitarian principles of property distribution and undercutting the liberal democratic assumptions of majority rule and the universal distribution of civil and social rights.

In underdeveloped countries, another factor in corruption is the difference in status and education between civil servants and their clients. The African bureaucrat, a high school or university graduate, leads a style of life that puts him on a different plane from the illiterate peasant or laborer, for whom government appears remote and terrifying in its regulations: "In approaching a civil servant the peasant is not generally an informed citizen seeking a service to which he is entitled but a subject seeking to appease a powerful man whose ways he cannot fathom; where the modern citizen might demand, he begs or flatters."[57]

The Kafkaesque entanglements of an unemployed Senegalese with an unmovable bureaucracy are depicted brilliantly in Sembene Ousmane's film *Mandabi,* an account of a poor illiterate trying to cash a money order. As in his other film, *Borom Sarat,* a morality tale that brings us into contact with a series of poor people of the city, he depicts exploitation and corruption by the organization bourgeoisie of those not in a position to control the forces of the modern state.

---

[53] Moore, *Social Origins of Dictatorship and Democracy,* pp. 172–73.

[54] James C. Scott, *Comparative Political Corruption* (Englewood Cliffs, N.J.: Prentice-Hall, 1972), p. ix.

[55] *Ibid.*

[56] Scott maintains that giving wealth a legitimate, not to say prominent, place within political systems marks a decline of corruption because the influence of wealth has been institutionalized. There is no reason to assume a priori, however, that corruption as a supplementary weapon in the arsenal of business will decline or disappear, even though it is untidy and possibly a nuisance in the rational calculations and predictions involved in planning.

[57] Scott, *Comparative Political Corruption,* p. 15.

Ousmane's films are a warning against those who seek stability through the creation of a Tammany-type political machine.[58] Those who are willing to tolerate "a little corruption" to grease the wheels of the political machine in the interests of efficiency fail to see, or do not honestly acknowledge, the political implications of this type of system.[59] In corruption involving the poor and the rich;

> The poor trade their potential electoral power for wealth or security in the form of employment, help with the police, welfare and bribes. The patronage and bribes distributed to the unorganized poor represent a "side payment," moreover, which all but precludes basic structural change that might improve the *collective* access of the poor to economic opportunities and make those opportunities less ephemeral.[60]

In countries such as Ghana, Scott notes, the political party developed its most profitable relations with large foreign firms, but the essence of the transaction remained unchanged: the ruling party gained a substantial portion of its income from the private sector, in exchange for protection and favorable decisions on policy, contracts, and administrative matters.[61]

Corruption, then, results in the loss of liberty and the death of idealism. The blight spreads so that nothing remains exempt from manipulation, nothing remains that cannot be perverted by the rulers and the governing class. By paying for doing things that should be done anyhow, by suffering policy decisions manipulated by those with wealth and influence, by crushing faith in the capacity of popular agencies to bring real changes, by freezing the individual in his own possessiveness, and by disintegrating unity, corrupt governments disinherit the poor and obliterate the dreams of communal societies.

Military Coups: Captains of Industry, and the Industry of Creating Captains

To what extent, then, do military leaders step in to end the corruption of politicians in order to purify their societies and ready them for

---

[58] Among those who advocate old-fashioned machine politics are Huntington, in *Political Order in Changing Societies;* Zolberg, in *Creating Political Order;* and Henry Bienen, in "One Party Systems in Africa," in *Authoritarian Politics in Modern Society,* ed. Huntington and Moore, pp. 99–127. Huntington can rest his conscience on the belief that "to the extent that corruption builds parties, it undermines the conditions of its own existence" (p. 71). As indicated above, this is a highly dubious proposition; more likely, as parties become less politically significant, corruption follows power elsewhere. According to Zolberg, "machines lack dignity and tend to be corrupt. But what is usually called corruption in this context can be viewed, under certain circumstances, as a fairly rational distributive system which is based on other than rational-legal norms and hence is better adapted than bureaucracy to societies of this type" (p. 159).

[59] Scott, *Comparative Political Corruption,* pp. 150–51.

[60] *Ibid.,* p. 149.

[61] *Ibid.,* pp. 125–217. Cf. Maxwell Owusu, *Uses and Abuses of Political Power: A Case Study of Continuity and Change in the Politics of Ghana* (Chicago: University of Chicago Press, 1970); and Victor T. Le Vine, *Political Corruption: The Ghana Case* (Stanford, Calif.: Hoover Institution Press, 1975).

higher objectives, and to what extent do the guns of the soldiers simply enable them to be first at the trough? Why has the military been able to intervene so easily in Africa but not in the United States or, ordinarily, in most industrialized countries? Does the military really have something special to offer, or is it simply a group of civilians with guns? Can army-based regimes endure for a long time, and will a pattern of substantive policy decisions emerge from them? What role does the military play in the consolidation of power of the new indigenous governments?

A fundamental reason for the ease of the military takeovers throughout the continent was that the politicians represented only a handful of the privileged. They were not based firmly either on the propertyless or on indigenous business. Ruth First is right when she claims that in the absence of a socially rooted, economically productive base, "power lies in the hands of those who control the means of violence. It lies in the barrel of a gun, fired or silent."[62] The means of violence do not appear out of thin air; however, they must be produced and paid for. Ultimately, therefore, the military must seek alliances with those who control the means of production.

Two recent trends in the development of a social base are apparent in Africa. By far the stronger social movement favors the protection of the interests of the new African entrepreneurial class. For example, many governments have enacted legislation against foreign small businesses—Indians in East Africa and Lebanese in West Africa—and even against nonnational Africans, such as the Nigerian Hausa traders in Ghana. The other trend appears now to have its greatest potential in a peasant-based guerrilla army and popular uprising, as in Guinea-Bissau, where originally Amilcar Cabral, and now his brother and the first president, Louis Cabral, and the PAIGC have carried out a social revolution in the midst of an armed struggle against the Portuguese.

Some background will help in reaching an understanding of these developments. To gain some perspective on the surprise with which the first military coups were greeted, consider the size of African armies at the time of independence. Togo, with 250 men, had the smallest West African army; the Nigerian military, numbering 7,500 at independence, was proportionately no larger.[63] In comparison, Argentina, with half Nigeria's population, possessed an army of 120,000. Miners points out that African armies at independence not only were without tanks, heavy artillery, and other sophisticated military equipment, they also had little public prestige, because they were created originally by the colonial powers not to defend the inhabitants against foreign attack, but to help foreigners conquer the country. The rank-and-file soldiers had been enlisted from the remote areas for the most

[62] Ruth First, *Power in Africa* (N.Y.: Pantheon, 1970), p. 6. See also D. E. H. Russell, who argues that no mass rebellion can succeed without the defection of the regime's armed forces (*Rebellion, Revolution and Armed Force* [New York: Academic, 1974]).

[63] Miners, *The Nigerian Army, 1956–1966* p. 2.

part, and although they were "excellent soldiers, loyal to their comrades, their regiment and (perhaps) to the British Empire or the French Republic [they] were quite ready to suppress rebellions against Colonial rule that might arise elsewhere."[64] The French African troops had been used to put down national uprisings in Indochina and in Algeria. Clearly, at the beginning of the period of the consolidation of power they were not national armies, and had played no part in the struggle for independence.

Patterns of political behavior of the African military have both varied from and shared certain common elements with the patterns of political behavior of other elements of the organizational bourgeoisie, as well as with those of military establishments elsewhere. Most observers have called attention to the distinctive military format, and the military's control of the instruments of violence. Armies differ in their social cohesion, which in turn affects the ability of officers to intervene in domestic politics and produce stable leadership. Janowitz points out that the military establishments in new nations differ markedly in their social cohesion because "of differences in training, indoctrination, operational experience, and inter-generational cleavages."[65]

Skills and abilities of the officers also vary, which frequently imposes severe limitations on the military's capacity to bargain and communicate politically with clients and publics outside of the military. Certain themes characterize the professional and political ideology of the officers, although they do not necessarily constitute a single unified ideology of all military regimes. Among the recurrent characteristics articulated are a strong sense of nationalism, a puritanical outlook, a willingness to extend government control when "necessary" over widespread areas of the economy and society, a disdain of politicians, and a suspicion of "politics."[66]

Huntington presents a portrait of the military mind motivated by a philosophy of "conservative realism":

> The military ethic emphasizes the permanence, the irrationality, weakness, and evil in human nature. It stresses the supremacy of society over the individual and the importance of order, hierarchy, and division of function. . . . it exalts obedience as the highest virtue of military men. The military ethic is thus pessimistic, collectivist, historically inclined,

---

[64] *Ibid.*, p. 2.

[65] Morris Janowitz, *The Military in the Development of New Nations* (Chicago: University of Chicago Press, 1964), p. 29.

[66] *Ibid.*, pp. 27–28. See also John Ellis's *Armies in Revolution* (New York: Oxford University Press, 1974), a series of case studies, from Cromwell's Army of 1642 to the Chinese Civil War of 1926–49, that focuses on the role of ideology in the consolidation of a military organization. Janowitz's proposition that the military has tended not to displace the single mass-party authoritarian political regimes is difficult to evaluate, for although military coups have occurred in countries that once were governed by such regimes, by the time the coups occurred their mass base had probably withered away. Janowitz's further proposition that after takeover the military regime must develop mass support for its programs is more doubtful, because the military is generally much more inclined to resort to "technocratic innovations" or to "engineering from above."

power oriented, nationalistic, militaristic, pacifist, and instrumentalist in
its view of the military profession. It is, in brief, realistic and conservative.[67]

To enable us to understand why the military intervenes in politics,
Huntington explains that "just as war serves the ends of politics, the
military profession serves the ends of the state. Yet the statesman
must recognize the integrity of the profession and its subject matter.
The military man has the right to expect political guidance from the
statesman."[68] Presumably, then, a higher morality impels the military
to enter the fray.

Many commentators have depicted the soldiers who stage *coups*
as progressive forces whose entry into politics is to be commended,
rather than condemned as the usurpation of civilian authority. They
argue that the continuing modernization of military organization and
weaponry has instilled in the officers the belief that their societies
ought also to be modernized. Allegedly, the military also acts as an effective agent of socioeconomic change because of its close connection
with the "new middle class." Eric Nordlinger, however, believes that
authors who support this position have presented remarkably little
evidence for their arguments, and that other factors, which over-
shadow the officers' possible modernizing dispositions, have been ignored. Indeed, Nordlinger maintains that "the officer politicians are
commonly unconcerned with the realization of economic change and
reform, and where there are civilian organizations or strata pressing
for such changes the officers purposely oppose them."[69] Nordlinger
immediately modifies this assertion by adding that "soldiers in mufti"
sometimes allow or even encourage economic modernization within
social and political contexts in which workers and peasants have not
been politically mobilized and in which there is hardly a "middle class"
to speak of. What counts above all in accounting for the officer-
politicians' conservative tendencies in protecting or failing to alter the
economic and social status quo are their "determined pursuance of
their corporate interest in combination with their deeply inculcated
military values that assign overriding importance to the preservation
of a particular type of political stability, and [their] attachments to
their middle-class interests and identities."[70]

Thus, military regimes may effect modernizing changes as much
as certain civilian governments, but the key variable is the officers' corporate interest and military values. Even though in modern times all
army officers must claim to be "card-bearing reformers," when they
lack a constituency to which they are responsible they will act much

[67] Samuel Huntington, *The Soldier and the State* (New York: Vintage, 1957), p. 79.

[68] *Ibid.*, pp. 71–72.

[69] For a critical review of the literature that depicts the military in new countries as "progressive," see
Nordlinger's "Soldiers in Mufti: The Impact of Military Rule Upon Economic and Social Change in
the Non-Western States," *American Political Science Review,* 64, no. 4 (December 1970), 1131–48.

[70] *Ibid.*, p. 1134.

more like the country's most powerful "trade union" than like the revolutionary vanguard of the masses:

> And as is true of most unions, the military act to maintain or increase their wealth and prerogatives even when these values conflict with the aspirations and interest of larger segments within the society. In countries suffering from economic scarcity, and in the absence of internal or external threats, funds devoted to military expenditures hinder the rate of economic growth and limit the size of progressive social service, health and welfare programs.[71]

Janowitz maintains that in comparison with Western European professional armies, in new nations there is a marked absence of a history of feudal domination; as a result, the military profession does not have strong ties with or allegiance to an integrated upper class.[72] In Africa, although the data are unclear, there are serious grounds for questioning this proposition. Afrifa, for example, states with obvious pride his connections with the ruling house of Asante.[73] In Northern Nigeria many, if not all, of the officers are the sons of the traditional ruling emirs. On the other hand, there is reason to suspect that in countries that have suffered a series of military coups, subsequent coups leaders are more likely to come not only from the lower ranks but also from strata lower in the social hierarchy. The background of the present military council under Colonel Acheampong in Ghana is particularly interesting in this respect.[74]

The majority of officers may have middle- and lower-middle-class backgrounds; some may even have originated in the lower social strata; the officers may have come from opposed aristocratic, feudal, and landowning strata; yet all of this will not necessarily lead to support for the lower classes or to concern with progressive socioeconomic change. Frequently, Nordlinger points out, the poverty and degradation experienced by many of the soldiers before entering the military simply provide an impetus for individual mobility; they do not necessarily instill a broader concern for the plight of other disadvantaged strata.[75] Although at the time Nordlinger wrote he specifically exempted African armies from his generalizations, on the ground that their military establishments were small ones, subsequent events have borne out the truth of these statements. In Ghana five years after the 1966 coup, for example, military allocations totaled New Cedis 40.4 million, compared with New Cedis 1.8 million allocated to the Ministry of Labor and Cooperation.[76]

---

[71] *Ibid.*

[72] Janowitz, *The Military in the Development of New Nations*, p. 30.

[73] A. A. Afrifa, *The Ghana Coup, 24th February 1966* (London: Frank Cass, 1966), Chap. I.

[74] See the analysis in Dennis Austin and Robin Luckham, eds., *Politicians and Soldiers in Ghana* (London: Frank Cass, 1975).

[75] Nordlinger, "Soldiers in Mufti," p. 1134.

[76] Bretton, *The Rise and Fall of Kwame Nkrumah*, p. 230.

Nun maintains that the military establishment is inseparable from the society surrounding it. In new countries today, military interventionism does not threaten the "middle class" as it might in "liberal" Western systems. Rather, "it tends to represent that class and compensate for its inability to establish itself as a well-integrated hegemonic group."[77] Those who expected that increased "professionalization" of the army would induce officers to withdraw from politics by placing a barrier between them and the rest of society made the mistake of considering social phenomena in isolation. European armies became professionalized only at the end of the nineteenth century, as a result of deliberate government policy dictated by the interests of self-preservation:

> The bourgeois state had experimented with various formulae for the control of the armed forces — examples of which are the unsuccessful French and American attempts to have the highest posts of command submitted to popular election — until the logic of capitalist society eventually dictated the solution. In the framework of a general tendency towards fragmentation and the division of labor, the exercise of violence was also converted into a specialized field calling for high professional qualifications. . . . Professionalization is therefore the means by which the armed forces are incorporated into a determined place in the structuralization of society as a whole, and it is this, and not professionalism as such, that explains the apparent political neutrality of the army in the Western democracies.[78]

In African as well as in other preindustrial societies the process of professionalization, therefore, produces different results. In contrast with the preexisting hegemony of the bourgeoisie in Europe, what seems to be occurring in Africa — as Nun points out, what has already occurred in Latin America — is that a struggling fledgling class, characterized by its own organizational weakness, is welcoming an alliance with a sector that possesses "a remarkable degree of institutional cohesion and articulateness."

Regis Debray maintains that regardless of which social forces initially supported a government brought to power by a coup, "a lightening action at the top" necessarily tends to the "right," because in the absence of mass organization the coup must base itself upon establishment institutions:

> Compelled to obtain immediate success in order to win the support of the expected masses, it has to base itself on the institutions which already exist — established economic interests, the bureaucracy, the majority of the army. Since the masses lack political consciousness or organization — things which can only be acquired in a long and difficult revolutionary experience — on whom can the government base itself?

---

[77] Jose Nun, "The Middle Class Military Coup," in *Imperialism and Underdevelopment: A Reader,* ed. Robert I. Rhodes (New York and London: Monthly Review Press, 1970), p. 344.

[78] *Ibid.,* pp. 328–29.

How can it ask for the sacrifices which a real policy of national independence would demand, if the peasantry and above all the working class are not convinced of the need for them?[79]

Whether the masses are as expectant as Debray believes is debatable. Luttwak, in what is reportedly a parody on how to conduct a coup, describes the situation of a preindustrial society on the eve of one:

All power, all participation, is in the hands of the small educated elite. This elite is literate, educated, well fed and secure, and therefore radically different from the vast majority of their countrymen, practically a race apart. The masses recognize this and they also accept the elite's monopoly of power, and unless some unbearable exaction leads to desperate revolt they will accept its policies. *Equally they will accept a change in government whether legal or otherwise.* After all, it is merely another lot of "them" taking over. . . . This lack of reaction is all the coup needs on the part of the people in order to stay in power.[80]

The "them" so removed from the people consist of leaders in the army and key members of the organizational bourgeoisie.

The Army and the Organizational Bourgeoisie

After every African coup, the military has turned naturally to the civil servants for immediate aid in sustaining its rule. Although recourse to the bureaucracy is necessary to maintain basic functions and to keep the country running, and although severe limitations on the size and training of the relatively tiny officer corps make such an alliance a necessity, the ideological and temperamental affinities of the officers with the higher civil servants extend beyond practical exigencies. Both groups consider themselves more suitable rulers than the politicians;

[79] Debray, *Strategy for Revolution* (New York: Monthly Review Press, 1970), p. 29. See also Debrays, *Revolution in the Revolution* (New York: Monthly Review Press, 1970).

[80] Edward Luttwak, *Coup d'Etat* (New York: Knopf, 1969), p. 22. Eric Wolf's findings support Debray's contentions about the conservative nature of military coups. Comparing societies in which the dominance of the party and the army vary, Wolf found that in Mexico and Algeria, where the army was dominant, these two societies continued to operate on the basis of the market, with fundamental control being exercised over the society rather than the economy: "The army furnishes the organizational pivot for the social order, but the economy is left unencumbered to develop according to the dictates of the market" *Peasant Wars in the Twentieth Century* (New York: Harper & Row, 1969), p. 299. In Russia, China, Vietnam, and Cuba, on the other hand, where both society and economy remain under the control of the party, "the market is abrogated, and ideological considerations and appeals take the place of the 'invisible hand' in moving men to action" (*Ibid.,* p. 299).

See also First, *Power in Africa;* Ian Clegg, *Workers' Self-Management in Algeria* (New York: Monthly Review Press, 1971); and David and Marina Ottaway, *Algeria: The Politics of a Socialist Revolution* (Berkeley and Los Angeles: University of California Press, 1970), who point out that the highly organized and professional army of the exterior took over real power in Algeria after independence and seven years of sustained internal war based upon a peasant rural revolt and fired by workers, students, and intellectual militants in the cities. After independence, in a contest of elite groups, the professional officer corps of the career army managed to acquire political and economic vantage points and impose a "highly centralized, authoritarian and bureaucratic armed structure" (First, *Power in Africa*, pp. 95–96).

both enjoy membership in an organizational hierarchy that places the greatest emphasis on order, rationality, predictability, competitive progress, and personal ability; both enjoy a life style far beyond the capacities of the mass of the population. Technical competence provides not only a skill salable to the highest bidder, but the basis for an ideology justifying the rule of experts over the ignorant masses. In this respect, the style of command of army officers and technocrats of the civil service are strikingly alike: both groups depend on direct orders or manipulation from above; both are concerned with persuading the people to do what the experts know is "best for them," and neither is concerned with the opinions of the uneducated.[81]

The African officer corps and the upper civil service speak differently, dress differently, eat differently, play differently, intend different career patterns for its children, walk differently, and are healthier than the mass of the people over whom they rule. They differ in their outlook on life, in their political philosophy, in their self-confidence, and in their moral and political outlook from the politicians they replaced. Exhibiting a manipulative attitude toward the rural groups and urban lower classes, they make an effort to identify with these "commoners" only when they are useful for their work, not out of political or moral conviction. Claiming no interest in ideology or indoctrination, the military bureaucrats hold themselves to be practical men interested only in "getting the job done."

In East Africa, the military bureaucrats, known as *Wa-Benz*, "the people of the Mercedes Benz," worry openly about obstacles to their career advancement and berate politicians for insufficiently funding their armies and departments. What they demand, more than simple increases of salaries or emollients—although these are quickly forthcoming from frightened or generous civilian politicians—is control over the state, so that they can rule directly on the basis of criteria that they feel are legitimate.[82]

African armies differ in their origin from the ruling political parties: socialized in British and French military traditions, they also inherited British and French pay scales, "which made them a very expensive institution and a privileged, well-armed minority."[83] A European feudal heritage, compounded by a colonial division between white officers and black enlisted men, resulted in sharp internal divisions within African armies. A huge gap separated the pay of officers

---

[81] See my article, "Ghana Ten Years After Independence: The Development of Technocracy-Capitalism," *Africa Today*, 14, no. 3 (1967), 6–12.

[82] John H. Johnson, who, in describing the development of the Latin American military into a "profession," discusses the developing identity of interest between the military and the higher civil servants "Professionalization meant bureaucratization. As bureaucrats the new officers, in contrast with the civilian-warriors of an earlier period who moved in and out of uniform frequently and often used rank solely for political ends, had a continuing personal and institutional interest in the services. They were concerned with the attitudes of civilian politicians toward security, salaries, pensions, and privileges and with armed forces budgets, armaments, and new barracks." (*The Military and Society in Latin America*, p. 73).

[83] Anton Bebler, *Military Rule in Africa* (New York: Praeger, 1973), p. 111. See also Leo Hamon, ed., *Le role extra-militaire de l'armee dans le Tiers Monde* (Paris: Presses Universitaires de France, 1966).

and that of enlisted men. The officer corps possessed multiple amenities, including special housing, servants, and a style of life suitable to "gentlemen." African armies maintained these sharp divisions between officers and enlisted men. In addition to the ethnic differences in most African armies, enlisted men come predominantly from hinterland areas, whereas officers are recruited from coastal and urban areas, which are generally places of greater opportunity and wealth.

As Lee has pointed out, "a brutal fact about the allocation of state resources is that the army seems to be in the best position to exploit whatever is available."[84] Even before coups, fear of what the army might do has led to the maintenance of European pay scales after independence. Yet the gap between officers and enlisted men has continued. Indeed, in Sierra Leone a coup against a coup was staged by a group of warrant officers and enlisted men against commissioned officers in April, 1968, because of the latter's insensitivity to the needs and pleas of the foot soldiers for pay raises to compensate for sharp increases in the cost of living. In justifying the takeover, a spokesman gave these reasons: "It has since March 23, 1967 become absolutely clear that most of the so-called national reformation council members only wanted to benefit their selfish ends; the rank and file of the army and police have been ignored. All that was practiced in both the army and the police were nepotism and blatant victimization."[85] It should be kept in mind, however, that although the pay of the noncommissioned officers and enlisted men was closer to the prevailing pay of civilians, as a general rule it was still several times higher than the gross national product per capita. Military intervention in Ghana, Mali, Dahomey, Upper Volta, and other countries followed, within a period varying from several days to several months, the implementation of new austerity measures by civilian governments.[86] Generally severe economic difficulties alone did not precipitate coups, even in a country such as Guinea, where the economic situation had been quite miserable for a long time. Another important consideration was that members of the officer corps of diverse African countries were joined together through the "old boy" network of veterans of colonial armies, and this proved to be the strongest source of contagion, setting off a chain reaction of coups.[87]

Even though the ultimate causes of African coups are indigenous, external interventions must not be overlooked. Dependence upon outside powers by new states that possess virtually no capacity for the manufacture of modern armaments becomes necessary for any major operation—civil wars as well as foreign enterprises. Zolberg

[84] J. M. Lee, *African Armies and Civil Order* (London: Chatto & Windus, 1969), p. 89.

[85] Quoted by Claude Welch in *The State of the Nations*, ed. M. F. Lofchie (Berkeley and Los Angeles: University of California Press, 1971), p. 225. See also Welch's *Soldier and State in Africa* (Evanston, Ill. Northwestern University Press, 1970).

[86] Bebler, *Military Rule in Africa*, p. 115.

[87] First, *Power in Africa*, pp. 22–23. See also Robert Pinkney, *Ghana Under Military Rule, 1966–1969* (London: Methuen, 1972).

points out that the experience of Zaire from 1960 to 1965 and of Nigeria from 1966 to 1970 demonstrate quite clearly the connection between domestic and international politics. Sifting through scattered evidence, Zolberg finds indications that United States military advisors contributed to the success of loyalist elements in putting down an attempted coup in Ethiopia in 1960. Great Britain intervened to quell mutinies in Tanganyika, Uganda, and Kenya in 1964, a year in which all three of these East African states could be viewed as "moderate," but she did not act to prevent the overthrow of the Obote government, which had evolved a more radical policy. The French military acted to restore the Gabon government in 1964, and intervened on numerous other occasions during the 1960s.[88] In discussing the role of European regimes in the political evolution of the Congo, Zolberg maintains that

> Western powers welcomed and probably encouraged the first Mobutu referee intervention in 1960; the United States and Belgium later invested heavily in the building of an A.N.C. [Armée Nationale Congolese] as a relatively cohesive force and it is likely that they encouraged Mobutu to take over in 1965. Surely his survival since that date—and, more abstractly, the sudden passage of the Congo from the unstable to the stable category of African states—cannot be understood without reference to the intentions of external powers.[89]

A closer look at the causes of the Nigerian Civil War will illuminate the generalizations discussed above and show how African military coups arise above all out of domestic political situations.

A Case Study of Civil War in Nigeria: The Consolidation of Power, Coups d'Etat, Corruption, and the Organizational Bourgeoisie

In Nigeria after independence, tangible benefits long promised by politicians (more schools, better roads, electricity, pure water, more jobs) had all failed to materialize. These unfulfilled promises contributed to a growing popular disillusionment with the civilian establishment. In no other country of Africa was corruption practiced so blatantly, the poor becoming poorer and the politicians growing more ostentatiously rich.

Ruth First maintains that a quarrel over spoils lay at the bottom

---

[88] Zolberg, "The Military Decade in Africa," p. 327. Today, the attitude of the French towards various regimes might be more significant in determining whether or not the African military will intervene in some French-speaking countries and not in others: "Indeed, there is good reason to believe that in some countries, including Gabon, the Ivory Coast and Senegal, the message from Paris to the barracks has long been clear: 'stay out.' On the other hand, at various times France probably adopted a much more neutral stance towards the survival of civilian governments in such countries as Upper Volta, Congo, Brazzaville, or Dahomey." *Ibid.,* p. 327.

[89] Colin Legum, *Pan-Africanism: A Short Political Guide* (New York: Praeger, 1962), and Conor C. O'Brien, *To Katanga and Back* (New York: Grosset & Dunlap, 1962), on the role of the United States and Western powers in the Congo.

of the Nigerian political crisis. Led by those politicians who "abandoned their electorates as they devoted themselves to their bank balances and their businesses," the conflict took place at two levels:

> The first was the rivalry of the regions, which competed against each other for a larger share of the federal revenue and of the export trade, etc. . . . On the second level of the quarrel, there was competition—often called tribalism—for jobs, for promotion, for vice-chancellorships of universities and chairmanships of corporations.[90]

Whereas in the early days of independence the competition was fought out mainly between Yoruba, and Ibo, in the South by the late 1960s Northerners also began to assert their claims to plums in the federal government and employment. Each job could affect more than the applicant and his immediate family First points out, for each post, especially the higher ones "benefited a host of kinsmen, a local community, a region." Job competition was exacerbated when immediately after independence commodity prices, especially that of cocoa fell on the world market, foreign capital did not arrive as anticipated, new "school leavers" came onto the labor market and the supply of jobs dried up. Desperate competition between the new graduates, the previously unemployed and a deluge of migrants to the towns, drove urban unemployment up to at least 30 percent of the labor force. University graduates were not exempt; in 1968 an estimated 1,000 B.A.'s could not find adequate positions.[91] This growing competition for jobs masked by a growing ethnic hostility formed the essential background for the Biafran-Nigerian conflict.

The prelude to the Civil War was set by the first military *coup* of January, 1966 which quickly brought General Ironsi, an Ibo, to power. The original instigators of the *coup* killed the North's leading politicians including several Emirs and a number of Southerners, but no Ibo leaders. Nevertheless, there were Yorubas and Hausas as well as Ibos who supported this first takeover which had among its objectives, greater unity under a more socialist government. Many Northerners however, considered the *coup* to be a "devilishly cunning Ibo plot" even though most of the young Ibo officers who had originated the plot were arrested by General Ironsi. Ironsi geared his actions specifically to rewinning the support of the traditional Northern leaders.

However, on May 24, 1966, General Ironsi, with the full support of Northern *military* leaders, issued "decree No. 34." This decree abolished the regions and created a single federal public service. The Northern organizational bourgeoisie, the civil servants, university students and school teachers, felt their interests threatened by these measures with the decree depriving them of the privileges guaranteed by the old federal system. Constituting no more than 1 percent of the total number of civil servants in the federal public service then, the

---

[90] First, *Power in Africa*, p. 58.
[91] *Ibid.*, p. 59.

Northerners believed their only chance for success lay in the Northern regional public service that excluded Southerners. B. Dudley points out that, "thus Northern university students, particularly those at the Ahmadu Bello University, saw their chances of an automatic entry into the administrative class of the Northern civil service dwindling away."[92] In a unified bureaucracy, these new graduates would have to face competition from far larger numbers of Southern graduates. A few days after the passage of this decree, on May 29, 1966, well organized pogroms in Zaria, Kaduna, Kano, Jos and Katsina, resulted in the murder and mutilation of hundreds of Ibos. In panic the Ibos began to flee to the Eastern region, only to be stopped by the pleas of the Eastern region's military Commander-Governor. Colonel Ojukwu, soon to be the head of the State of Biafra, in what he later lamented as a horrible mistake, urged the Ibos to remain in the North and to work for a United Nigeria.

On July 29th the Northerners succeeded in their counter-*coup*, killing General Ironsi. They placed a Northerner, a non-Moslem, Colonel Gowon, into a position of dominance as head of the government. This second *coup* precipitated a second even larger massacre of Ibos in the North. Most Ibos nevertheless remained at their jobs and businesses. Finally, at the end of September, with no apparent precipitant, the worst holocaust of all sent the Ibos fleeing to the South by the millions. The Ibos, once the strongest proponents of a unified, strongly centralized Nigeria, withdrew into the redoubts of their embattled homeland and prepared to—in their eyes—defend themselves as "a nation wrought out of their own sufferings."[93]

How are these pogroms to be explained? The Ibos lived in the North as petty traders, small shopkeepers, civil servants and technicians. In making their homes where they made their living they, like the Indians in East Africa, the Chinese in Southeast Asia, the overseas Chinese in Southeast Asia, the Lebanese and the Jews, in Toynbee's phrase, were "in society but not of it." According to Colin Legum:

> Like all petty traders the world over, they exploited their customers and ignored their resentment. The hatred that grew up around them was dismissed as jealousy fanned by the Northern Emirs. They were the sharpest, shrewdest, most successful, and most pushful element in a slow-moving society. . . . While the peasants complained of exploitation, the educated Northerners spoke of the Ibos as vermin, criminals, money grabbers, and sub-humans without genuine culture. 'Their god is money,' they said.[94]

---

[92] B. J. Dudley, *Parties and Politics in Northern Nigeria* (London: Frank Cass, 1968), p. x.

[93] Cf. Colin Legum, "The Tragedy in Nigeria," in *African Politics and Society,* ed. Markovitz, pp. 248–51. See also Eric Ayume Opia, *Why Biafra?* (San Rafael, Calif.: Leswing Press, 1972); Frederick Forsyth, *The Biafra Story* (Baltimore: Penguin, 1969); John M. Ostheimer, *Nigerian Politics* (New York: Harper & Row, 1973); Kenneth Post and Michael Vickers, *Structure and Conflict in Nigeria, 1960–1966* (London: Heinemann Educational Books, 1973); and Joseph Okpaku, ed., *Nigeria: Dilemma of Nationhood: An African Analysis of the Biafran Conflict* (New York: Third Press, 1972).

[94] Legum, "The Tragedy in Nigeria," p. 249.

Legum goes on to point out that, under certain conditions, the unfortunate fact is that all peoples are capable of brutal massacres: "one is struck by the obvious parallels between the Armenians and the Ottoman Empire, the Jews in Europe, the Chinese in Indonesia (and, tomorrow, it may be the Indians in East Africa), and the fate of the Ibos."[95]

In order for mass killings to occur two conditions are necessary: first, the host community must feel itself threatened by the "outsiders"; secondly, a state of great tension exists because of depression or war.[96] In sum, a pogrom requires both a particular social situation and the exploitation of that situation by a politically organized group. Northern entrepreneurs, civil servants, students, contractors, and ex-politicians of the Northern Peoples Congress provided that leadership and organization. Even though anti-Ibo resentment was widespread, an organizational mechanism was still necessary for wholesale butchery. The massacre started only when established authorities allowed the spread of the belief that they would promote, or at least condone, attacks against Ibos. Thus, the pogroms and warfare in Nigeria, though they involved the death and maiming of tens of thousands, represented far more than simply a rekindling of ancient tribal animosities.

The difficulties of creating a unified Nigeria cannot be underestimated. The federal authorities had to consolidate sufficient power to prevent the continued massacre of minority groups. Although following the coup of January, 1966 the military had led the movement for a more unified form of government, by July, 1966 the army itself had become a casualty of the schisms that wrecked the society. It ceased to be a cohesive force obeying a single command, and, thus, in some ways similar to the army in Zaire, it ceased to be a force for the integration of the country as a whole.[97] The July coup unleashed widespread political demands for regional autonomy that endangered Nigeria's very existence and resulted in a twofold disintegration of the army. First, a mutiny by Northern troops resulted in the systematic slaughter of close to 200 Ibo officers and men, including General Ironsi. Nearly all the surviving Ibo soldiers and others of Eastern origin sought refuge in their home areas; consequently, Northern troops decamped from the Eastern region. Second, the chain of army command became disrupted when, among others, Ojukwu, military governor of the Eastern region, did not recognize the legitimacy of Lt. Colonel Gowon's succession of General Ironsi as supreme commander.[98]

[95] *Ibid.*, p. 250.

[96] *Ibid.*, p. 251. See also Ted Robert Gurr, who argues that "political violence can provide the discontented with a sense of community" that makes men aware of "their common discontents, or the worthiness of their group organization, and of their potential for cooperative action against their oppressors" (*Why Men Rebel* [Princeton, N.J.: Princeton University Press, 1970], p. 208).

[97] For a comparison of the Nigerian and Congolese civil wars, see Crawford Young, *Politics in the Congo* (Princeton, N.J.: Princeton University Press, 1965).

[98] S. K. Panter-Brick, ed., *Nigerian Politics and Military Rule* (London: Athlone Press, 1970), pp. 24–25.

One of the most striking features of the two coups of 1966, Luckham points out, was the cohesiveness of the participants in terms of age and rank: the majors of January and the lieutenants of July. Friendship and a sense of solidarity developed within groups of military peers who went through training together.[99] Although after the military came into power the focus of the struggle appeared to shift toward ethnic and regional issues, Luckham believes that *ethnicity was used to disguise assaults against particular personalities and at the same time to protect the army as an ongoing system:* "To make a direct attack on senior officers would be to challenge the entire authority systems of the army. In contrast, hostilities of other kinds, such as that between different ethnic groups, do not run up against the same kind of constraint and this may help to explain why antagonisms in the army gravitated during 1966 towards ethnic and regional conflicts in so freewheeling a manner."[100] Luckham argues that tribal and regional ties were never the most powerful factor in differentiating groups within the army. Although tribe and ethnicity were salient at times, the characteristics of the army "as a total institution, its internal cohesion as well as doctrinal commitments against tribalism counteracted these tendencies quite effectively."[101] What Luckham does maintain is that differences in rank and generation, combined with ethnic cleavages, sharpened the conflict without necessarily being its main source. Only with the sudden destruction of the higher officers did discipline suffer a fatal blow. Once this happened, mutinous troops took the lead in the slaughter of Ibo civilians.[102]

Nigeria Today

After one of the bloodiest civil wars on the continent, a conflict marked by mass starvation and charges of genocide, the Biafran forces surrendered on January 15, 1970. Fears of massive retaliation by federal troops proved unfounded. Under the leadership of General Gowon, the federal government achieved a remarkable policy of reintegration and reconciliation with the previously opposing factions. The ruins and wounds of the war are still evident everywhere in the old Eastern region. Yet in the brief period since the end of the war the Ibos, with the aid of the federal government, have rebuilt every one of their major industries. A substantial number of Ibos have returned and become re-integrated into towns throughout the country.

---

[99] A. R. Luckham, "The Nigerian Military: Disintegration or Integration?" in *Nigerian Politics and Military Rule*, ed. Panter-Brick, p. 61. The "majors of January" considered themselves a corporate group to such an extent that while knowing that officers of higher rank, such as Lt. Col. Ojukwu, would be sympathetic to their plans, they excluded them from direct participation in the inner circle (*Ibid.*, p. 67).

[100] *Ibid.*, p. 68.

[101] *Ibid.*, p. 72. Sources of differentiation among officers from the North, such as religion, tribe, and subregional origin, appeared about as important as what they had in common. See also Luckham's refutation of Martin Dent's argument that it was a *combination* of ethnic and regional cleavages that was important (*Ibid.*).

[102] *Ibid.*, p. 75. See also Miners, *The Nigerian Army, 1956–1966*, p. 217.

The federal government reinstated almost all of the Ibo civil servants who joined the secession, including army officers. Ibo businesses expanded their activities in the Phoenix-like cities of Onitsha, Aba, and Port Harcourt and resumed funneling vast amounts of commerce through their marketplaces into the interior. Many technicians, former army officers, and politicians, forced to forsake their former professions, turned their energies and talents with great success to entrepreneurial activities. Predictions that economic development will continue to gather steam come from many of "the talented, the educated and the lucky," despite the struggle of many thousands of Ibos who live at the subsistence level. But with peace and the resumption of enterprise, old class divisions have emerged with a new vigor. State officials have expressed concern about the growing antagonism exhibited by many of the poor towards local officials. Here is what one state worker had to say: "The old Biafran super-structure is still intact with the civil servants mostly still at their posts. The little man—especially when he is suffering—is beginning to say 'there goes that official with the big house and with the Mercedes talking about one Nigeria now. He is the same man who led me into secession, war and death. Now he is back on top, and we are suffering.' "[103] To eliminate these conditions, Brigadier Murtala Muhammed maintained, was a major reason for the coup he led on July 29, 1975 to overthrow Gowon's regime.[104]

Despite the federal government's breaking up of the former Eastern region into what are now the East Central, South Eastern, and Rivers states, despite its depriving the Ibos of the nation's rich oil fields and refineries, and despite its forcing them into a geographically restricted area, the often predicted massacres by the conquering army did not occur. By the standards of any nation recuperating from a civil war, the new unity and reconciliation of Nigeria must be reckoned one of the major modern successes of African regimes attempting to consolidate power. This case study also reveals that the military and other elements of the organizational bourgeoisie can use "tribalism" to further their rule. Above all, the experience of Nigeria demonstrates that even bitter civil war will not bar the creation of modern nation-states.

Conclusion

Which regimes will endure? Whose interests will they serve? What methods of rule will they use? On the basis of the experiences of Afri-

---

[103] Quoted in Thomas A. Johnson, "In What Was Biafra, Business is Booming Amid Harsh Poverty," *New York Times*, January 29, 1973, p. 8. The remarkable persistance of class structure during the civil war is portrayed by Achebe in his *Girls at War* (Greenwich, Conn.: Fawcett, 1974). He depicts top Ibo civil servants and entrepreneurs continuing to enjoy expensive foodstuffs, parties, and chauffeured limousines while the mass of the population was starving.

[104] Cf. Levi A. Nwachuka, "Why Gowan Fell," *Africa Report*, September-October, 1975, pp. 8–11. Brigadier Murtala Rufai Mohammed was assassinated in an attempted coup on February 14, 1976. The military council peacefully appointed a new head of government, Lt. Gen. Olusegun Obasonjo, and the system as a whole did not appear shaken.

can nations thus far, as well as in terms of the historical evolution of nation-states throughout the world, two types of systems are now establishing roots. In one, the African business classes, the civil service, technocrats, the liberal professions, and the army and police are in power. This kind of society exists, for example, in Ghana, Senegal, and the Ivory Coast. In the other, efforts are made to create a mass following. For instance, in Tanzania a peasant-based movement is led by a highly articulate, ideologically sophisticated vanguard; in Zambia, the skilled workers of the copper mines have aligned themselves with small farmers in a regime that seems to be furthering its objectives of economic and social development.

The most unstable regimes, one would suspect, are those in which the government is still seeking a social base. Thus, military regimes can be unstable, despite their guns, if they do not accommodate some of the major interests in their countries. In Congo-Brazzaville, in Mali, and in Ethiopia this still seems to be the case.

The key factor in determining stability, therefore, is not whether a government is supported by "traditional" or "modern" elements. The government in Northern Nigeria can be perfectly stable even with the emirs as the major political interest, if it can convert the economic basis of power to twentieth-century, technico-industrial, competitive capitalism, as did the nobility of England and Japan, who brought their subjects into the twentieth century and managed to maintain their relative positions of domination.

Among the greatest difficulties of radical states must be reckoned the dilemma that once the condition of the formerly oppressed individuals and classes is improved, they become most anxious to protect their gains rather than continue the revolution. They therefore become conservative, interested primarily in consolidating the establishment. This is true of nations and of classes: of the Soviet Union, where the first Marxist-Leninist socialist revolution occurred; and of the working class in the United States, whose unions lead the ranks of the most avid defenders of the American capitalist system.

Among the remaining radical African regimes, two directions and models appear in the making. To some degree, the model that has provided some lessons for Tanzania is China, not in terms of the role of its army or its ideology of Marxism-Maoism, but in the involvement of the peasantry as a mass base; in its cultural revolution; in its conflict of "Reds," or ideologically committed, versus "experts," or technicians; and in its anticorruption drive. Not long ago, students were running around the streets of Dar es Salaam waving "the little green book" with the sayings of Julius Nyerere. More significantly, the Arusha declaration against corruption was followed up with legislation that curtailed the ownership of property and the holding of outside positions by civil servants. This constituted part of a major effort to curtail the development of a new class. The cultural revolution TANU seeks, unlike that sought by Senegal and Zaire, is not founded on doctrines such as negritude or "authenticity" but on an African version of the Puritan ethic, on a philosophy designed to instill the honesty and hard work necessary to achieve the socialist revolution desired by the leaders of the country.

Guinea, though not seeking to emulate the Soviet model, nevertheless shows unfortunate signs of an evolution along the lines of an elitist vanguard party through the process of conversion of a mass party to a tighter and tighter circle of close followers of the leader.[105] From an organization that sought its support in the peasantry and town-workers to a terror-ridden system of bureaucratic domination, Guinea has survived but has radically altered its intended humanistic, democratic, participatory program. Although the internal dynamics of party policy and factional disputes must place the responsibility on the shoulders of those in power, external events exerted tremendous pressures on Guinea. In 1958, when Guinea alone of all the Francophone states "opted for independence," France cut off all financial aid and technical assistance. The giving, and then the withdrawing, of Soviet aid resulted in an isolation of Guinea from the East as well as the West. Remarkably, given the regime's philosophy, the United States — not the Soviet Union, not China, but the "paragon of imperialism" — has today replaced France. Although Guinea's fears of foreign invasion by major European powers were dismissed as propaganda, the Portuguese invasion stunned foreign observers, who had believed even imperial countries capable of more sophisticated techniques. As the pressures against the regime increased, and as the government became more repressive, opposition hardened. Exile groups strove to bring down the government. This, in turn, resulted in retightened security and pressures against dissent by the government. All of these events have taken place in a country not nearly as developed as the Soviet Union was at the time of its great revolution at the beginning of the century. In the absence of a great wage-labor force, in the absence even of a market-based agricultural labor force, the reservoir of conscious political militants the party could draw upon was indeed small. The lack of resources meant that any policy involving major investments could be undertaken only at great cost to the population: the curtailing of consumption by people already at a subsistence level. These events have indeed come to pass, and, already, many more purges have occurred in Guinea than in the Soviet Union at a comparable stage of evolution. In desperation, the regime has petitioned France to resume diplomatic relations and has sought, unsuccessfully, to put its financial affairs in order. The present government has practically turned her major bauxite and iron reserves over for development by consortiums of leading American companies in the hope that sufficient capital and expertise will be gained by Guineans to enable them to proceed with their own economic advancement. Far

---

[105] K. S. Karol discusses his concern with the Cuban system in his *Guerrillas in Power* (New York: Hill & Wang, 1970). Herbert L. Matthews challenges Karol's interpretation in his *Revolution in Cuba* (New York: Scribner's 1975).

from embodying a classic Marxist-Leninist doctrine, the regime in Guinea still seems to be seeking desperately for a new identity and ideology. In the meantime, it appears to rest increasingly upon terror.

Terror or Cooperation

Governments may invest their energies in creating mechanisms of coercion. They can institutionalize and organize the process of terror on a steady and rational basis. If it is willing to pay this price, such a government may overcome resistance and secure cooperation of a kind. In the words of E. V. Walter

> Fortified by terror, men have invented a way to escape the eternal problems of unity and division and have also built their rulers a monumental defense against the pains of justice, limits, and renunciation. But this stronghold is only one of the ramparts that societies have raised in many terrible shapes throughout human history. It is the cruelest form of the common barrier that marks the difference between what men need and what they get.[106]

Certainly, terror is not the only way that a consolidation of power for humanistic and socialist objectives can succeed. The example of Guinea and other dictatorial regimes does indicate that in the consolidation of power and in the final determination of who gets what, when, where, why, and for what reasons in African countries, questions of means as well as of ends are still of the greatest relevance.

With the decline of political parties, African leaders of all persuasions have turned more expectantly to their new bureaucratic organizations. Through administrators and technocrats, through the civil service and the new organizations, they have sought the remolding, the "encadrement" of their populations. They have, at least, become convinced that economic development is necessary, if not inevitable.

---

[106] E. V. Walter, *Terror and Resistance* (New York: Oxford University Press, 1969), p. 343.

Chapter X

PROCESSES OF ENCADREMENT:
Bureaucratic Development and Economic Growth

Providing a good standard of living for all the peoples of Africa requires more than simple economic growth. The alleviation of tremendous poverty requires that those at the bottom of the social structure benefit by receiving part of the product of growth. Two problems of equal importance are: first, the necessity of changing the lifestyles of people and the economic forces of production that have existed for centuries; and, second, the creation of the appropriate political apparatus to guarantee a more equitable distribution of the new goods that are produced.

Encadrement comes from the French term *cadre*, and refers to the necessity of reorganizing people, materials, and mentalities in order for development "to take." The major modern instruments necessary for psychological and technical modernization, for a new sense of self and society, and for conveying the necessary seeds and fertilizer to the farmers are governmental and administrative bureaucracies. They constitute the institutional apparatus for whatever political will is manifest. These developmental bureaucracies provide the organizational mechanism that links modern science, isolated farmers, the ruling decision makers, and the promise of a new life. The motivations of the civil servants who man these organizations and the ideologies of the political rulers, as well as their class nature, are most important in determining who gets what, when, where, how, and why.

Robert S. McNamara, president of the World Bank, in emphasizing the need to design development strategies that will bring greater benefits to the poorest groups in the developing countries, observed that "the basic problem of poverty and growth in the developing world can be stated very simply. The growth is not equitably reaching the poor. And the poor are not significantly contributing to growth."[1] McNamara pointed out that it is common in developing countries for the upper 20 percent of the population to receive 55 percent of the national income while the lowest 20 percent is receiving 5 percent, "a very severe degree of inequality—considerably greater

[1] Robert S. McNamara, *Address to the Board of Governors, Nairobi, Kenya, September 25, 1973* (Washington, D.C.: International Bank for Reconstruction and Development, 1973), p. 10.

than in most of the advanced countries."[2] As poor countries have developed economically, income mal-distribution has increased—despite rosy images of communal societies, particularly in the rural areas. While industry and mining have increased their output, the productivity and income of the small farmer has stagnated.

McNamara describes absolute poverty as

> a condition of life so degraded by disease, illiteracy, malnutrition, and squalor as to deny its victims basic human necessities. . . . A condition of life so limited as to prevent realization of the potential of the genes with which one is born; a condition of life so degrading as to insult human dignity—and yet a condition of life so common as to be the lot of some 40 percent of the peoples of the developing countries. . . .[3]

Given this situation, in which the poorest 40 percent of the population receive only 10 to 15 percent of the national income, McNamara directly confronts the "trickle-down theory" of economic growth by demanding, "Is it a really sound strategy to devote a significant part of the world's resources to increasing the productivity of small-scale subsistence agriculture? Would it not be wiser to concentrate on the modern sector in the hopes that its high rate of growth would filter down to the rural poor?"[4] The president of the World Bank, former president of the Ford Motor Company and former United States Secretary of Defense, replies that the answer to this question is no:

> Experience demonstrates that in the short run there is only a limited transfer of benefits from the modern to the traditional sector. Disparities in income will simply widen unless action is taken which will directly benefit the poorest. In my view, therefore, there is no viable alternative to increasing the productivity of small-scale agriculture if any significant advance is to be made in solving the problems of absolute poverty in the rural areas.[5]

The productivity of small-scale holdings, McNamara points out, is not, contrary to widespread economic opinion, inherently low. Not only does the overwhelming evidence of Japan disprove that proposition,

---

[2] *Ibid.*

[3] In describing conditions of life of absolute poverty, McNamara pointed out: "20% to 25% of [these people's] children die before their fifth birthdays. And millions of those who do not die lead impeded lives because their brains have been damaged, their bodies stunted, and their vitalities sapped by nutritional deficiencies. The life expectancy of the average person is 20 years less than in the affluent world. They're denied 30% of the lives those of us from the developed nations enjoy. In effect, they are condemned at birth to an early death." *Ibid.*, p. 7.

[4] *Ibid.*, p. 13. For a contrary view, see Elliot Berg, "Socialism and Economic Development in Tropical Africa," *Quarterly Journal of Economics*, 67, no. 4 (November 1964). Berg maintains that it is ridiculous to distinguish between economic growth and economic development, because without economic growth economic development is impossible, and because everybody will benefit eventually if sufficient economic growth does take place.

[5] McNamara, *Address to the Board of Governors*, pp. 13–14. McNamara is, of course, also aware that millions of poverty victims live in urban slums and that their social and economic advance depends on an acceleration of the pace of development.

but recent studies in Guatemala, the Republic of China, India, and Brazil demonstrate that, small farms can be as productive as large farms, given the proper conditions. On this basis, McNamara maintains that the ultimate solution to world poverty in the developing areas must come from "new forms of rural institutions and organizations that will give as much attention to promoting the inherent potential and productivity of the poor as is generally given to protecting the power of the privileged."[6]

Whether the structural changes McNamara proposes are politically possible is another question. McNamara believes that land and tenancy reforms are imperative. He claims that despite resistance by members of the political power structure who own large holdings, this ruling class will recognize that "an increasingly inequitable situation will pose a growing threat to political stability." This expectation of rationality, typical of other believers in the efficiency of technical innovation, such as W. W. Rostow, remains to be proved.[7]

The extent of Africa's economic vulnerability, as well as the enormity of the political obstacles to her development, was demonstrated vividly by the catastrophic drought of recent years. Famine, disease, and desiccation scourged every country on the edge of the Sahara, from Mauritania to Ethiopia. The drought also dramatized how even under conditions of immense tragedy, the rich grow richer and the poor poorer. Government action could have alleviated much more suffering and prevented more deaths. Yet from their own point of view, "reasonable" men did not act irrationally in preferring to line their own pockets at the expense of others—hardly something new, yet another caution and reminder that in every major economic event, the distribution of benefits and losses occurs not randomly, but within a framework of power relations. In this case, peasants and subsistent villagers were the chief victims.

In Ethiopia alone, famine swept at least two million farmers and herdsmen, killing uncounted thousands. In the Wallo and Tigre provinces of northern Ethiopia, famine and cholera have taken an estimated 50,000 to 100,000 lives.[8] In the Sudan, north of Ethiopia, as well as in Chad, Upper Volta, Niger, Mali, Mauritania, and Senegal, the toll in livestock and agriculture has rendered residents of the

---

[6] *Ibid.,* p. 17. Brazil's "economic miracle" was denounced by the Roman Catholic bishops of Brazil in a signed declaration that accused the present military regime of "repression, colonialism, and manipulation of an economic policy to benefit only 20% of the population." According to a report in the *New York Times* of May 19, 1974, "The thirty-page document, signed in Recife on May 6th, immediately banned by the authorities, tells of starvation wages, unemployment, hunger, illiteracy and high infant mortality in the Northeast and decries Brazil's so-called economic miracle as merely a means to 'make the rich richer and the poor poorer.'"

[7] See Rostow's *The Stages of Economic Growth,* 2nd ed. (New York: Cambridge University Press, 1971), and *Politics and the Stages of Growth* (New York: Cambridge University Press, 1971). On the dangers of new agricultural technology, see I. G. Stewart, ed., *Economic Development and Structural Change* (Edinburgh: Edinburgh University Press, 1969), especially pp. 1–12 and 83–103. See also Celso Furtado, *Obstacles to Development in Latin America* (Garden City, N.Y.: Anchor Books, 1970).

[8] Martin Walker, "Famine South of the Sahara," *New York Times,* February 24, 1974.

stricken rural regions destitute for more than four years. Millet, maize, and other grains have withered under a burning sun that has dried up lakes, rivers, and ponds, depriving the cattle of fodder and water and killing them in the tens of thousands. Hundreds of thousands of refugees have streamed into the towns of the Sahel, searching for food; authorities have set up refugee camps where supplies could be distributed.

The drought also illustrates the *complexities* of economic development in Africa. The success of aid organizations in providing pump-driven wells, vaccination programs, and minimal health care helped double the number of cattle and people in the Sahel between 1959 and 1966. But as the cattle overgrazed the sparse desert grass and uprooted trees as food, the Sahara began to creep south, in one year alone advancing up to fifty miles, destroying thousands of villages in the two-thousand-mile belt from Dakar to Lake Chad which had survived on subsistence crops, and forcing the nomad herds of the Sahara ever further south.[9] Farmers desperate for food sold what little land they owned, adding still further to the concentration of land ownership, which in many areas already is the greatest single political and social problem. Even in the absence of the drought, employment for the rural population had become more and more difficult; now, resettlement forced by the drying up of the land delayed ever further the time when meaningful employment would become possible.[10] In addition, profiteering by merchants and the failure of government agencies to mobilize national resources effectively were fundamental causes of the widespread failure to distribute equitably whatever foodstuffs were available.[11]

Africa's poorest classes have also been hit the hardest by the soaring world inflation. According to the United Nations Economic and Social Council, 68 million, or 25 percent, of Africa's 273 million people are fed insufficiently. Soaring food prices, instead of contributing to the national income of primary producing countries, made still more difficult the ability of poorer countries and poorer people to meet their basic needs. Lester Brown, an economist with the Overseas Development Council, declared, "Hundreds of millions of people in the developing world cannot pay higher food prices. Their only way

[9] Roger Morris and Hal Sheets document the extent of the tragedy in their *Disaster in the Desert: Failures of International Relief in the West African Drought* (Washington, D.C.: Carnegie Endowment for International Peace, 1974). The decline in annual rainfall has, of course, spread beyond Africa to affect countries in the same line of latitude around the earth, from Nicaragua through West Africa and Ethiopia and into India's Maharashtra province. Cf. *Drought Damage and Famine in Sub-Saharan Africa*, Dept. of State Publication 8792, African Series 58, W19. (Washington, D.C.: Government Printing Office, 1974).

[10] On how famine encourages the capitalist transformation of the drought-stricken areas, see Claude Meillassoux, "Development or Exploitation: Is the Sahel Famine Good for Business?" and Lionel Cliffe, "Capitalism or Feudalism? The Famine in Ethiopia," *Review of African Political Economy*, No. 1 (August-November 1974), pp. 27–33 and 34–40, respectively.

[11] See Walker, "Famine South of the Sahara"; and David Binder, "One Hundred Thousand Deaths in Africa Linked to Drought Neglect," *New York Times*, March 4, 1973.

to adjust is to eat less. Their governments—already under heavy burdens of short-term import debts—cannot very long provide loan subsidies to hold down domestic prices of rice or other cereal imports."[12] To give one example, the price of rice, a staple in Africa, recently rose to nearly $600 a metric ton, compared with $136 in mid 1972. The rise in energy and fertilizer costs, coming on top of the skyrocketing of grain prices, Mr. Brown noted, has seriously disrupted food economics. As Richard Flaste has pointed out, "The cost of poverty, like everything else keeps going up."[13]

Optimistic Assessments:
Material and Historical Perspectives

There is nevertheless a rational basis for an optimistic assessment of future economic development in Africa. Fears that economically underdeveloped parts of the world were incapable of growth or that their political problems would be overwhelming have not been well founded.[14] Economic growth in many of the developing countries—as the Pearson Commission, for example, pointed out—has proceeded at faster rates than the industrialized countries ever enjoyed at a similar stage in their history. Between 1850 and 1950, the United States and Europe saw their income per head rise by an average of 2 percent per year, "a rate which multiplied incomes by seven in that century and produced dramatic changes in standards of living."[15] Technological and economic change throughout the nineteenth century was confined largely to Europe and the United States, and later Canada and Australia; the only notable Asian participant was Japan. Between 1950 and 1967, the "new countries," many of whom had gained formal independence only after World War II, increased their total production of goods and services by an annual average rate of 4.8 percent. Even discounting the acceleration of population growth—a rate as high as 2.5 percent per year, this per capita income growth vastly outshone all

---

[12] *New York Times,* July 6, 1974.

[13] *New York Times,* February 4, 1974.

Even before the drought and the rise in oil prices, the rich nations were becoming richer and the poor poorer. Crawford Young presents us with the sobering thought that the annual budget of Uganda is significantly less than that of the University of Wisconsin. "Agricultural Policy in Uganda," in *The State of the Nations,* ed. Michael F. Lofchie (Berkeley and Los Angeles: University of California Press, 1970), p. 163.

When 200 million Americans use more energy for air conditioning alone than China's population of 700 million use for all purposes, it is time to begin considering whether any country has a permanent right to a disproportionate share of the world's resources. This was the demand of Maurice F. Strong, Executive Director of the United Nations Environment Program. *New York Times,* November 21, 1973. See also Robert Theobald, *The Rich and the Poor* (New York: Mentor, 1960); L. J. Zimmerman, *Poor Lands, Rich Lands: The Widening Gap* (New York: Random House, 1965); Josue DeCastro, *The Black Book of Hunger* (Boston: Beacon Press, 1967); and G. O. Nwankwo, "Malthus in Africa," *West Africa,* August 18, 1972, pp. 1077–79.

[14] Lester B. Pearson, *Partners in Development: Report of the Commission on International Development* (New York: Praeger, 1969), p. 10.

[15] *Ibid.,* p. 25.

previous gains.[16] By any historical standard of comparison, then, third world countries are showing "a remarkable acceleration."[17]

William Hance, in his study of African economic development, agrees that the list of impediments facing economic advance in Africa is formidable, but he asserts that "most of the factors catalogued are subject to amelioration or elimination and the future should see accelerating progress in this direction." Most encouraging are advances in education and training, the prerequisites to the solution of so many of Africa's problems. According to Hance, "there is no justification for pessimism regarding the future of many [African] countries; there is need for greater realism, and it is realistic to aim towards far higher standards than prevail today."[18]

Surendra Patel, in another forward-looking analysis, emphasizes the enormous potential of the continent. The amount of arable land in Africa is more than twice that of Latin America or China. It is nearly one and a half times that of India, and Africa has only half of India's population and a climate ideally suited to growing all kinds of crops, both for human consumption and for industrial raw materials. The land that is usable for the grazing of cattle, the unlimited opportunities for fishing, and the rich forest resources await tapping. Although the continent already produces nearly one seventh of the world's minerals almost every day brings major new discoveries. The Sahara, for example, has turned out to be dry of water but rich in oil. With oil and gas in the north, coal in the south, and hydro-power in the center, with Africa's mighty rivers accounting for 40 percent of the world potential hydroelectric power, the continent's energy potential appears unlimited. Nevertheless, with 8 percent of the world population, the continent can boast of only 2 percent of world production, less than half that of the United Kingdom. With a per capita income of little more than $100 per year, or one twelfth that of industrial countries—and one fourth of this received by a tiny minority of non-Africans—the internal market is severely limited.

Even today, however, Patel suggests that the per capita agricultural output of the industrial countries is only twice as high as that of Africa; "the agricultural distance between these two areas is much narrower than is commonly imagined." Focusing on the nonindustrial sector, Patel goes on to argue that "this distance could be covered if an annual per capita growth rate of 1.5 percent to 2 percent were maintained for some forty to fifty years. Thus, the distance that now separates agricultural scarcity in Africa from surplus in industrial countries is not very large nor very difficult to cover."[19] Indus-

---

[16] *Ibid.,* p. 27.

[17] *Ibid.,* pp. 12–13.

[18] William A. Hance, *African Economic Development,* rev. ed. (New York: Praeger, 1967), p. 30.

[19] Surendra J. Patel, "Economic Transition in Africa," *Journal of Modern African Studies,* 2, no. 1 (1964), 329–49; reprinted in *African Politics and Society: Basic Issues and Problems of Government and Development* (New York: Free Press; London: Collier-Macmillan, 1970), p. 319. Included in Patel's essay is a historical analysis of economic changes over the last century that parallels Pearson's analysis. Pa-

trialization, though presenting qualitatively greater difficulties, does not constitute an overwhelming obstacle:

> The gap in the industrial field is very wide—output being thirty-two times as high in the industrial countries. This appears formidable, but it could be overcome in only forty to fifty years if industrial output per capita were raised annually at a rate of 7 percent to 9 percent (that is, a growth rate of about 9 percent to 11 percent per total industrial output). This is a high rate, but many countries have obtained it in recent years. . . . It would require a per capita growth rate of 5 percent maintained for forty to fifty years, or only an adult's life time. The growth rate is neither forbiddingly high, nor the period unbearably long. There is thus little basis for the pessimist's pathetic patience to postpone the possible—the very rapid elimination of want and poverty.[20]

Confirmation of this optimistic assessment has come from some of the traditionally most conservative agencies. For example, according to the annual report of the International Monetary Fund, the developing countries enjoyed their best balances of payment on record in 1972 and early 1973 as a result of the boom in the industrialized countries, soaring commodity prices, and heavy inflows of private capital.[21]

Nevertheless, reminders of the gravity of the economic situation in African countries abound. A few years ago, in Senegal, for example, the price of peanuts—which accounted for 70 percent of the value of Senegal's exports—fell so low that thousands of farmers returned to the growing of foodstuffs and to subsistence agriculture.[22] Although the international market situation precipitated this decline, the peasants protested Senegalese governmental policies. From the time of the French, most of the small farmers had suffered an exploitative market situation that guaranteed their perpetual debt.[23] After independence, with an explosion in the monies spent on the bureaucracies and with the rise in power of the Senegalese merchants, the condition of the small farmers worsened.[24] The political obstacles

---

tel points out that many inventions existed by 1850 but that their adoption was restricted mainly to Great Britain, and even there mostly on a small scale except in the textile industry. "The muscles of men and animals provided 95% of the energy available for men in 1850. . . . Over one half of the population in Western Europe still could not decipher the magic of the written word. . . . The world output of steel as late as 1870 was only 700,000 tons, or less than one-fifth of India's in 1961." (p. 314) See also Bert F. Hoselitz, ed., *The Progress of Underdeveloped Areas* (Chicago: University of Chicago Press, 1952); and Alexander Gerschenkron, *Economic Backwardness in Historical Perspective* (Cambridge, Mass.: Harvard University Press, 1962). For an account of the technological basis of economic development in agricultural countries, see Lester R. Brown, *Seeds of Change: The Green Revolution and Development in the 1970's* (New York: Praeger, 1970).

[20] Patel, "Economic Transition in Africa," in *African Politics in Society*, ed. Markovitz, p. 320.

[21] Edwin L. Dale, Jr., "Monetary Fund Reports Four Nations Have Gained," *New York Times*, September 10, 1973.

[22] See also the tables showing the growth rate of GNP per capita, taken from the *World Bank Atlas, 1972*, in *Africa Digest*, April, 1973, p. 44.

[23] For an explanation of the system of "le traite," see Felix Brigaud, *Histoire traditionnelle du Senegal* (St. Louis, Senegal, I.F.A.N., 1962).

[24] See B. Ameillon, *La Guinée: bilan d'une independence* (Paris: Francois Maspero, 1964); Chapter VI of the present text.

to equitable economic development remained formidable and fundamental.

To Create a New Society: to Make a System of Production

As economic development begins to "take," the pulling together of populations leads to greater interdependence and the prospect of ever tighter unity. However, as Wallerstein has pointed out, "functional inter-dependence leads to greater integration only if the citizens are aware of how inter-independent they have become. And the nation in its economic network must become 'visible.' "[25] To create a nation out of a new interdependent economy is to reverse the experience of previous ages. The Hammonds said of the industrial revolution in England, "The age had turned aside from making a society to make a system of production."[26] This is not to deny that the state played a key role in these developments—just as African governments lead in their nation's planning.

Beginning with the mercantilism of the seventeenth century, the European state aided mightily in the expansion of economic activities. At that time, Carl Freidrich points out, the first attempts were made to ascertain, "the basic data of national life, and this new science was given, characteristically, the name of 'statistics.' Men concerned with these matters of state were likewise called 'statists.' All thought of public life revolved, in short, around the idea of the state."[27] The state matters because of the overwhelming problems of interest and reorganization that require for their resolution force and persuasion. Denis Goulet points out that development "proposes images of the good society, prescriptions for obtaining it, and symbols for generating enthusiastic allegiance to it," but "above all it deals with power. . . ." No wonder, then, that "underdevelopment is experienced as vulnerability."[28] Those countries that have gained "a victory over space and time have also won privileged access to the world's resources."[29]

Moreover, all governments agree, no matter what their political complexion, that if development is to take place, people's attitudes towards themselves, their community, and especially their environment must change. Above all, the notion must spread that the environment can be manipulated, that people can change their surroundings, that people's destinies are not immutable, that the laws of nature can be rightly understood and taken advantage of for the benefit of man,

---

[25] Immanuel Wallerstein, *Africa: The Politics of Independence* (New York: Vintage, 1961), p. 91.

[26] "The Industrial Revolution: The Rulers and the Masses," in *The Rise of Modern Industry*, ed. A. J. Taylor (London: Methuen, 1925), p. 40.

[27] Carl Friedrich, *The Age of the Baroque, 1610–1660* (New York: Harper & Row, Torchbook ed., 1962), p. 3.

[28] Denis Goulet, *The Cruel Choice: A New Concept in the Theory of Development* (New York: Atheneum, 1971), p. 59.

[29] *Ibid.*, p. 19.

that the life cycles of generations can be interrupted and the life chances of future generations improved through self-effort.

To distinguish the natural from the supernatural and to provide the courage to use newly found levers of science and technology, appear as tasks so simple as to be axiomatic, yet every regime in every developing country wrestles with the effort. Indeed, one basic division in African countries is between the areas where people's attitudes have already changed so that they demand self-improvement, and the places where the stimulation of this desire is still an issue. This is one great difference between Senegal and Ghana. In Senegal, a major task of administrative agencies is to "animate" the countryside, to shake people loose from their traditional moorings and inculcate a sense of necessity for fundamental change. Ghana faced the same problem in 1948, when the first mass education drives began; community development organizers introduced the notion of "self-help," and the people of the countryside were induced to think about and articulate their "self-needs."

In China an important word in the vocabulary introduced by the Chinese revolution was *fanshen:*

> Literally, it means 'to turn the body,' or 'to turn over.' To China's hundreds of millions of landless and land-poor peasants it meant to stand up, to throw off the landlord yoke, to gain land, stock, implements, and houses. But it meant much more than this. It meant to throw off superstition and study science, to abolish 'word blindness' and learn to read, to cease considering women as chattels and to establish equality between the sexes, to do away with appointed village magistrates and replace them with elected councils. It meant to enter a new world.[30]

In Senegal the same necessities were marked by the introduction of the nation's national plan, which stated:

> Changes in behavior and an improvement in the attitudes of the population that favor the prospects of development do not require simply superficial action or organization of social and economic structures. . . . To obtain these changes, it is first necessary that the concept of 'development' have a real meaning, and one that is right for the Senegalese. Secondly, there must exist means for the propagation of new ideas and methods of organization, education, and information, arranged so that they reach the masses of the population and create a revolution in depth. Finally, it would be advantageous if dynamic groups existed within the country that could provide the ferment for this revolution.[31]

Among the most important attitudes that were to be overcome were

> the ascendency of the environment over the individual. . . . an unfavorable attitude towards technical progress and better ways of doing

[30] William Hinton, *Fanshen* (New York: Monthly Review Press, 1966), p. vii.

[31] *Rapport general sur les perspectives de developpement du Senegal*, Vol. 2, 2nd ed. (Dakar, 1960), reprinted in *African Politics and Society*, ed. Markovitz, p. 293.

things; attitudes of fatalism and discouragement. Persuaded that he is exploited and subject to the dictates of nature, rural man is convinced that his fate cannot be improved, an attitude that is not negative but passive. [Traditional man] remains convinced that "progress" does not concern him.

. . . Four outstanding ideas that should be at the heart of the educational programs and initiatives undertaken by the political and educational officials for the development of Senegal are (1) the idea of progress; (2) the idea of responsibility; (3) the idea of a dynamic community; (4) the idea of the nation. If these key ideas are taken up by all the great corporate groups that make up the nation (the political party, the administration, the different religious groups, etc.), it is possible that they will provide myths necessary for development.[32]

In contrast with a traditional society, in which the idea of "progress" rarely exists, and in which the basic objective of the whole educational apparatus is to inculcate in the young the notion "that their economic and social role in the village is to imitate everything their elders [do] and in the same manner," in a developing society

a new role for individuals must be learned. The ideas of change and progress must come to be considered as great values, while feelings of helplessness, satisfaction with the status quo, and fatalism are abolished. The greatest difficulty is demonstrating to the people that progress is possible; that the advantages to be gained are worth the effort involved in making the changes necessary to rise out of ignorance.[33]

Under these circumstances, the state must first promote "a certain climate of feeling, a certain type of ambience"; second, it must construct the necessary structures and organizations; and, third, it must provide the proper education. "Together, these aims will enable the individual alone and with his fellows . . . to march towards progress."[34]

---

[32] *Ibid.,* pp. 294–95.

[33] *Ibid.,* p. 295.

[34] *Ibid.,* p. 293. For literature dealing with similar political problems in Africa's economic development, see C. C. Onyemelukwe, *Problems of Industrial Planning and Management in Nigeria* (New York: Columbia University Press, 1966); Reginald Green and Ann Seidman, *Unity or Poverty? The Economics of Pan-Africanism* (Baltimore: Penguin, 1968); Osende Afana, *L'economie de l'Ouest-Africain: perspectives de developpement* (Paris: Francois Maspero, 1966); Archibald Callaway, "Educational Planning and Unemployed Youth in Africa," in *Approaches to Employment Problems in Africa and Asia* (London: Commonwealth Secretariat, 1973); Naomi Caiden and Aaron Wildavsky, *Planning and Budgeting in Poor Countries* (New York: John Wiley, 1974); James R. Sheffield, ed., *Road to the Village* (New York: African-American Institute, 1974); African-American Institute, *The Absolute Poor: Report of Donor Agencies Meeting on Rural Development in Africa* (New York: Interbook, 1974); Edgar Owens and Robert Shaw, *Development Reconsidered: Bridging the Gap between Government and People* (Lexington, Mass.: Heath, 1972, Lexington Books ed., 1974); Andrew M. Kamarck, *The Economics of African Development,* rev. ed. (New York: Praeger, 1971); Abdoulaye Wade, *L'economie d'Ouest Africaine: unite et croissance* (Paris: Presence Africaine, 1964); Pierre Fougeyrollas, *Modernisation des hommes: l'example du Senegal* (Paris: Flammerion, 1967); Hance, *African Economic Development;* David E. Carney, *Government and Economy in British West Africa* (New Haven: College and University Press, 1961); William J. Barber, *The Economy of British Central Africa* (Stanford, Calif.: Stanford University Press, 1961); *Employment, Incomes and Equality: A Strategy for Increasing Productive Employment in Kenya* (Geneva: International Labour Office 1972); Olufemi R. Ekundare, *An Economic History of Nigeria, 1860–1960* (London: Methuen, 1973); and Ann Seidman, "Key Variables to Incorporate in a Model for Development: The African Case," *African Studies Review,* 17, no. 1 (April 1974), 105–21.

Creating and carrying out a national development plan appropriate to these purposes requires more than an inventory of resources and a list of objectives. Not only must a plan be considered within its historical and social context, but full awareness of the political implications and pressure groups involved is necessary to facilitate the plan's implementation.[35]

Barriers Between the Technocrats and the Masses

In the final analysis, the realities of African politics are reflected in the determination of how monies will be spent, not in the advice of foreign experts or other technicians who are drawing up the national plans. As David Hapgood has pointed out, the real political decisions are made *after* the writing and adoption of the plan: "The money goes where the power is, which, in Africa today means that it goes to satisfy the desires and interests of the elite, not the powerless peasantry."[36]

Too frequently, the phenomenon of planning for planning's sake gained currency. "The Plan" acquired an independent reality and became a substitute for actual work in the real world instead of an instrument to aid it:

> Plan and reality can therefore go their separate ways. The plan calls for concentration on rural development; the elite spends the money on palaces or airlines or universities. . . . No strain in rationalizing is needed to explain the new rulers. They are catering to their political clientele. If the money is spent in the capital, it is because the clientele of the regime is mainly urban. . . . They are the people who supplied the membership of the pre-independence political parties and they are the main supports of the regime after independence. They are the class that is being 'taken care of' when the new governments dot the countryside with new (and by African standards, luxurious) housing for the thousands of new employees they have put on the state payroll—which is why the administrative part of the plan is over-fulfilled.[37]

The new science and technology that many economists and social scientists see as the key to development, Hapgood points out, "will be funneled through the tiny, educated class that holds power in the capitals of independent Africa." Does this group really want to innovate? Do they really desire "progress" if a rise in the standard of living of those in rural areas would threaten their own way of life, their own positions in society?

[35] Cf. Cranford Pratt's analysis of the difficulties of planning in Tanzania, "The Administration of Economic Planning in a Newly Independent State," *Journal of Commonwealth Political Studies*, 5, no. 1 (March 1967), pp. 38–59, reprinted in abridged form in *African Politics and Society*, ed. Markovitz, pp. 332–47.

[36] David Hapgood, *Africa: From Independence to Tomorrow* (New York: Atheneum, 1965), p. 65.

[37] *Ibid.*, pp. 65–66.

Communications between African governors and farmers are necessary for progress and rural development. An increase in agricultural production requires sustained effort, systematic organized activities, and trust between technicians and farmers. The new techniques must not only be demonstrated; farmers must utilize them on a systematic basis—not just in pilot studies, but in their actual production. The lack of roads, the low rate of literacy, and poorly developed systems of exchange are fundamental obstacles to communication between the mass of the farmers and the technicians. A more subtle barrier rises from the huge gulf between the culture of the "new" organizational bourgeoisie and that of the "newly mobilized."[38]

In African countries, where up to 90 percent of the population can be illiterate, the simplest distinction that separates mass from nonmass is the ability to read and write. Carlo M. Cipolla reminds us that "for thousands of years the craft of reading and writing remained the sacred monopoly of the small elite. By 1750 at the dawn of the Industrial Revolution, almost 5000 years had elapsed since the first rudimentary appearance of the art of writing. Yet more than 90 percent of the world's population had no access to the art."[39] Cipolla substantiates at length the following contention: "It is not easy to analyze in detail the motivations that prompt a society to train its members adequately, but it is easy to prove that failure to do so is always a sinister omen of impending disaster for a country."[40]

Historically, the rise of bureaucracy and the rise of literacy have gone hand in hand in the formation of the modern state. Marc Bloch points out that the practice of writing and the growing interest in its potentialities enabled states to form those archives without which there could be no real continuity of government:

> Lists of feudal services due from fiefs [and] innumerable memoranda of various kinds made their appearance, from the middle of the twelfth century, in the Anglo-Norman state and the Norman kingdom of Sicily and, towards the end of the same century or in the course of the thirteenth, in the kingdom of France and most of its great principalities. Their emergence was the premonitory sign that there was arising a new power, or at least one that had hitherto been confined to the great churches and the papal courts, namely the bureaucracy.[41]

Although the bureaucracy functioned as a formidable weapon in the molding of the new states, most bureaucrats—as today in Africa—concerned themselves primarily with the rote work that produces paychecks at the end of the month. Periodically, however, technocrats came to the fore who desired to institute in society those principles of rational organization characteristic of bureaucracies themselves. They

---

[38] *Ibid.,* pp. 4–5.

[39] Carlo M. Cipolla, *Literacy and Development in the West* (Baltimore: Penguin, 1969), p. 8.

[40] *Ibid.,* p. 22.

[41] Marc Bloch, *Feudal Society* (Chicago: University of Chicago Press, 1961), p. 422.

wished to employ as a social science, managerial techniques and the latest rationalistic discoveries. The economists of eighteenth-century France and the *cientificos* in Mexico in the twentieth century share with the technician of modern Africa certain similarities in attitude, method, and approach toward economic development, the use of the state machinery, and the manipulation of the "unlettered."

Sons of the establishment, the economists of pre-1789 France considered themselves carriers of Reason and wished to reorganize and rationalize their feudal-bound society along the lines of their new science. Yet their method was not mass revolution but, instead, manipulation from above by the most reasonable elements of the society—themselves. De Tocqueville described them as follows:

> [They] saw no hope of erecting the revolutions they had in mind with this obsolete machinery [of the Estates General] and the idea of recognizing the nation as sole arbiter of its own destinies and entrusting to it the execution of their plans was little to their taste. For how could a whole nation be persuaded to accept and to put through a program of reform so vast and so intricate? To their thinking the simplest, most practical solution was to enlist the support of the royal power.[42]

African technicians, similarly distrustful of what they consider to be the ability of a nation of functional illiterates, would create a state even more powerful than the colonial regime to carry out their policies.[43]

John Womack described the *cientificos* in Mexico who believed it a natural law that the nation could progress only through their control and for their benefit: "From the early 1890's on they lectured Mexico about the authority their special science entitled them to, and they eventually convinced great sections of the public of their infallibility."[44] A number of African technicians and administrators considered Nkrumah's advice, "Seek ye first the political kingdom and all other things will be added unto you," as an "adolescent attitude to politics long abandoned in mature societies." According to W. Arthur Lewis,

> mature societies rely for good government on having a trained civil service rather than on the vagaries of politics. West Africa will not begin to make real progress until its peoples realize that politics is marginally im-

---

[42] Alexis De Tocqueville, *The Old Regime and the French Revolution* (New York: Doubleday, Anchor Books, 1955), p. 161.

[43] See Irving Leonard Markovitz, *Leopold Sedar Senghor and the Politics of Negritude* (New York: Atheneum, 1969; London: Heinemann Educational Books, 1970), Chap. VIII.

[44] John Womack, Jr., *Zapata and the Mexican Revolution* (New York: Vintage, 1970), p. 10. When upon the death of President Porfirio Diaz the *cientificos* had a chance to enter practical politics, their policies proved "naive, treacherous, and incompetent" and in a short time "their fashionable order collapsed" (*Ibid.*). For a discussion of the conflict between the technocrats and reformers in contemporary Latin America, see Ernest Feder, *The Rape of the Peasantry* (Garden City, N.Y.: Doubleday, Anchor Books, 1971). For an interpretation of history from a technocratic point of view, see Herbert Butterfield, *The Origins of Modern Science: 1300–1800*, rev. ed. (New York: Free Press, 1965).

portant to the quality of government; reduce the political temperature; debunk the pretentions of politicians; and establish good administrative frameworks. Too much politics is the curse of West Africa.[45]

But are the administrators any less "political" than the politicians? Theodore Lowi has argued that modernization has meant the replacement of "old machines with new machines":

> The new machines are the professionalized administrative agencies that now run the cities. The career bureaucrat is the new Boss. He is more efficient, honest and rational than the old amateur boss. But he is no less political. If anything the bureaucrat with his new machine is more political because of the enormously important decisions we entrust to him.
>
> ... There are many new machines where there used to be only one or two old machines. They are functional rather than geographic in their scope. They rely on formal authority rather than upon majority acquiescence. ... the new machines are machines because they are relatively irresponsible structures of power. That is, each agency shapes important public policies, yet the leadership of each is relatively self-perpetuating and not readily subject to the controls of any higher authority. The new machines are machines in that the power of each, while resting ultimately upon services rendered to the community, depends upon its cohesiveness as a small minority in the midst of the vast dispersion of the multitude.[46]

In his indictment of these new machines of the technocrats, Lowi distinguishes between "management" and "governing":

> The modern city is now well run but badly governed because it is now comprised of *islands of functional power* before which the modern mayor stands impoverished. No mayor of a modern city has predictable means of determining whether the bosses of the new machines—the bureau chiefs and the career commissioners—will be loyal to anything but their agency, its works, and related professional norms.[47]

African civil servants hold up the standards of "a higher training" to legitimate their failure to follow the dictates of constituted political authority. Not only do "professional standards" act as a barrier against the intrusions of politicians, they also become an important weapon in justifying the manipulation of mass constituencies. A professor of sociology at the University of Ghana once expounded on the "necessity of raising standards"—meaning university training—for rural community development and social welfare workers: politicians and the government did not understand that rural folk were not so dumb; they were tricky and obstinate, and so it took a high order of

---

[45] W. Arthur Lewis, *Politics in West Africa* (New York: Oxford University Press, 1966), p. 78.

[46] Theodore Lowi, *The End of Liberalism* (New York: Norton, 1969), pp. 200–201.

[47] *Ibid.,* p. 201.

skill to learn how to manipulate them into doing what was really good for them. This is what really justified the existence of the "educator" and other technocrats: they were needed to provide the training to manipulate the country bumpkins. Building up the sophistication of the farmers added to the self-importance of those insightful enough to see "the complexities of the situation."

In Defense of Class Interests

Despite this ideology of "expertise" and high, nonpolitical standards, the professionals have always organized to defend their material and class interests. Among the first of the organizations formed by civil servants was the Sierra Leone Civil Servants Association, established in 1909, which described its role as "a medium whereby representations can be made to government on all matters affecting the interests of the African staff . . . and to insure that mutual improvement and support of its members are maintained."[48] Founded in 1921, the Southern Nigeria Civil Servants Union sought higher wages for its members and more government clerkships for Africans. The African Civil Servants Association in Nyasaland, organized in 1930, acted similarly. In the Francophone areas as well, African civil servants, considerably before the Second World War, had founded cultural and social organizations with economic and political concerns such as the *Mutuelle des Fonctionnaires* in Ouagadougou and the *Comité d'etudes Franco-Africaines* in Dakar, Abidjan, and other capital cities.[49]

When African governments came into power, they sought quickly to Africanize the civil service because of nationalistic and political reasons and because they required the support of an indigenous mass base. They also feared the resistance and constant sabotage experienced by European administrators. Nkrumah, for example, stated in his autobiography:

> It happened too often for it to be a coincidence that whenever government policy was to be put into effect, the officials either dilly-dallied or saw that nothing was done about it. Again, I could at one time almost guarantee that if there was any movement afoot against the government, every attempt was made on the part of the civil service to enhance the opposition against the government.[50]

Almost two decades later, Kenneth Kaunda, President of Zambia, analyzed the causes for the overthrow of Nkrumah and wrote, "The sys-

[48] Quoted in Martin Kilson, "The Emergent Elites of Black Africa, 1900–1960," in *Colonialism in Africa, 1870–1960*, ed. Peter Duignan and L. H. Gann, Vol. II, *The History and Politics of Colonialism, 1914–1969*, ed. Duignan and Gann (Cambridge: Cambridge University Press, 1970), p. 367.

[49] Cf. Ruth Schacter Morgenthau, *Political Parties in French Speaking West Africa* (Oxford: The Clarendon Press, 1964) p. 18.

[50] Kwame Nkrumah, *Ghana* (London: Nelson and Sons, 1957), p. 151.

tem and not the people dominated all aspects of life."[51] Even after Africanization, it was difficult to recruit individuals with the appropriate motivation and resources. If at the time of independence the major problem was to Africanize the civil service, the problem since then has been to make it work effectively and efficiently. But effectively and efficiently by whose standards?

Samuel Huntington, among others, has pointed out how "an indifferent bureaucracy can make reform a nullity." He describes how the failure of land reform in several districts in India was caused in large part by the negative attitude of government officials at state, district, and village levels who made no effort to enforce enacted land-reform legislation. The government of India did not attempt to mobilize a substantial bureaucratic force to implement the reform in the countryside. In addition to the requirement of a substantial mobilized bureaucracy, the second organizational requirement of land reform would have been the organization of the peasants themselves: "Concentrated power can enact land reform decrees but only expanded power can make those decrees into reality. While peasant participation may not be necessary to pass legislation, it is necessary to implement legislation."[52]

Yet African civil servants have not on the whole shown a great tendency to organize the peasantry or to rally around their causes. On the contrary, they have sought to associate themselves with the style of life and political interest of those who are the most powerful. In this, of course, they are not unique but merely follow a well-trodden historical path. Samuel Eisenstadt, in his study of empires, has pointed out the historical tendencies of bureaucracy towards self-aggrandizement:

> This was connected in general with the tendency by the bureaucracy itself—the very instrument of power of the rulers—to "aristocratize" itself, to acquire symbols of aristocratic status, and to ally itself with aristocratic forces. In such cases the bureaucracy very often displaced its goals of service to the rulers for those of self-aggrandizement; its members used their positions for enriching themselves and their families, thus becoming a growing burden on the economy and losing their efficiency.[53]

Today in Africa, the great symbol of aristocratic status is neither a scepter nor robes of ermine but rather the Mercedes-Benz. Wage and salary differentials in Africa today are among the highest in the world and are growing. Even middle-level "functionaires" earn more

---

[51] Quoted in B. B. Schaeffer, "The Deadlock in Development Administration," in *Politics and Change in Developing Countries*, ed. Colin Leys (Cambridge: Cambridge University Press, 1969), p. 201.

[52] Samuel P. Huntington, *Political Order in Changing Societies* (New Haven: Yale University Press, 1968), p. 389.

[53] Samuel N. Eisenstadt, *The Political Systems of Empires* (New York: Free Press, 1963), p. 401.

in a month than farmers do in many years.[54] After independence and after every coup d'état, the disparities between the civil servants and the rest of the population increased. Practically every African country has established a commission to review wages and salaries, and practically all of these blue-ribbon government-sponsored committees, composed of the most prominent citizens, have brought back recommendations for higher wages and better working conditions.[55]

Again, the question arises as to who in the new African societies will benefit from economic growth. After the achievement of independence and the consolidation of power, will the restructuring of society, the creation of great new organizations, the enormous movement of people and their fundamental changes in attitude result only in the growth of despair for the many?

In this chapter, we have analyzed the material potential for the betterment of conditions of existence for the majority of people. African governments have either already overcome the difficulties they encountered in creating the necessary organizational machinery for these purposes, or — to the surprise of the cynics and pessimists — they have demonstrated that nothing fundamental will block their achievements in the foreseeable future. But who will share in the expected increases?

African political leaders of every ideological complexion seek, as part of the encadrement process, a *prise de conscience* of their countrymen — that is, a snapping awake to the possibility that everybody, personally, can do something about changing their physical environment. This is essential for progress. But government leaders want their people to engage themselves and to awaken as *individuals* who seek their own success and advancement.

Prise de conscience is not the same as "class consciousness." Yet, objectively, as this study has shown time and again, classes — not merely strata or "socio-technical status groups" — exist in every African society. Only rare African governments seek to convert this "class-in-itself" to a "class-for-itself." Participation by African millions, as individuals, in the new, technically sophisticated, bureaucratically organized societies can result, therefore, only in a new deadening of political consciousness. The people perceive their felt needs only in terms of values and a social structure that is already loaded against them.

The ideology of the technocrats, their mode of operation, and their class interests — in conjunction with the political alliances of other

---

[54] See Rene Dumont, *False Start in Africa*, 2nd rev. ed. (New York: Praeger, 1969); and Reginald Green, "Political Independence and the National Army," in Christopher Allen and R. W. Johnson eds., *African Perspectives* (London: Cambridge University Press, 1970), p. 312.

[55] See the report in *West Africa*, November 19, 1971, p. 1345, on the Wages and Salaries Review Commission of Nigeria. See also J. R. Nellis, "Is the Kenyan Bureaucracy Developmental? Political Considerations in Development Administration," *African Studies Review*, 14, no. 3 (December 1971), 389–402; and Raymond Apthorpe, "The Introduction of Bureaucracy Into African Politics," *Journal of African Administration*, 12 (July 1960), 125–34.

elements of Africa's organizational bourgeoisie—threaten the interests of the dispossessed. What a tragedy if encadrement ends only in the firmer entrenchment of the bureaucrats in their offices. Foremost among the political obstacles to real economic development, therefore, may well be "the developers" themselves. Who indeed will not only "guard the guardians" but also develop the developers?

Chapter XI

CONCLUSION:
Development and Diversity

Americans do not believe in the inevitability of human perfection, nor in the possibilities of social harmony, nor in universal happiness. Most people in our society, nevertheless, are children of the Enlightenment insofar as they are confident that at least the *material* condition of all men in all societies will improve. We believe in the necessity and in the inevitability of "equality"—some rich, fewer and fewer poor, all power to the middle class. Our own experience, as well as the history of Western civilization, provides us with evidence for this optimism. Despite world wars, epidemics, even backslidings into prolonged economic slumps, at the very least we can feel sanguine that the history of our world has been a history of the rise in the universal standard of living. We all share what Ortega y Gasset called a sense of living at the "height of the times." In our own country we knew of the existence of "poor people," but, although jarring, these were the exceptions that proved the rule; they were "gaps," "pockets of poverty." Because the wealth of American capitalism provided a good living to organized labor—pounding on the banks built of marble in the 1930s, trading shares on the New York Stock Exchange in the 1970s—we assumed that it was only a matter of time before blacks, Puerto Ricans, Chicanos, sharecroppers, migrant workers, rednecks in Alabama, and drunks on the Bowery would all eventually participate in the American Dream.

With confidence, therefore, we turned to the rest of the world. Our presidents addressed African presidents, our professors and technicians spoke to African professors and technicians—and told them that if only they had a little bit of patience, they would, they could, become just like us.

From this perspective, Fernand Braudel, in his apparently matter-of-fact effort to describe and summarize the basic facts of people's ordinary material existence in Europe from the fifteenth to the nineteenth centuries, delivers one of the most shocking, one of the most challenging statements to confront the "common-sense" image of Western development that most of us share. Braudel informs us that from the middle of the sixteenth century almost to our own times, most people in the West suffered a decline in their standard of living, and that from 1350 to 1550

> Europe probably experienced a favorable period as far as individual life was concerned. Following the catastrophes of the Black Death, living conditions for workers were inevitably good as manpower had become scarce. Real salaries have never been as high as they were then. In 1388, Canons in Normandy complained that they could not find anyone to cultivate their land "who did not demand more than what 6 servants made at the beginning of the century." The paradox must be emphasized since it is often thought that hardship increases the farther back towards the middle ages one goes. In fact the opposite is true, as far as the standard of living of the common people—the majority—is concerned. Before 1520–40, peasants and craftsmen in Languedoc (still little populated) ate white bread. The fact cannot be misleading. The deterioration becomes more pronounced as we move away from the "autumn" of the middle ages; it lasted right up to the middle of the nineteenth century. In some regions of Eastern Europe, certainly in the Balkans, the downward movement continued for another century, to the middle of the twentieth.[1]

If we find it difficult to believe that the real salaries of workers and farmers in Western Europe have "never been as high as they were then," the Senate Select Committee on Nutrition and Human Needs informed us recently that the "needy" in the United States are "hungrier and poorer than they were four years ago despite great increases in spending on food programs, rising world agricultural output, etc."[2] Elsewhere, in one of the countries often held as a model for the development possibilities of the third world, the result of what was known as "Brazil's economic miracle" was a halving of the real income of the poor in a decade.[3]

In Africa, Panglossian scholars can point to the "take-off" of the economy of countries such as Liberia, which, during the decade preceding 1961, had a rate of expansion higher than that of almost any other country of the world. Between 1950 and 1960, money income in Liberia soared more than 400 percent; government revenues rose more than 8 times, imports quadrupled, the export of rubber expanded over 30 percent, and iron ore shipping rose to almost three million long tons per year. With leading production income series averaging about 15 percent per annum, Liberia enjoyed a rate of growth surpassed in the whole world only by that of Japan.[4]

[1] Fernand Braudel, *Capitalism and Material Life, 1400–1800* (New York: Harper & Row, 1973), p. 129.

[2] William Robbins, "U.S. Needy Found Poorer, Hungrier than Four Years Ago," *New York Times,* June 19, 1974.

[3] Marvin Howe, *New York Times,* December 14, 1974. Howe reports, for example, that in the last decade Brazil's gross national product rose 56 percent while the real value of the minimum wage dropped 55 percent. Official figures from the same period show a substantial drop in the proportion of the national budget devoted to health, education, and other social services.

[4] Robert Clower et al., *Growth Without Development: An Economic Survey of Liberia* (Evanston, Ill.: Northwestern University Press, 1966), p. 23.

Yet Robert Clower and his associates concluded in their study of Liberia's economy that all of this rapid growth in production had "little developmental impact on Liberia or Liberians." The enormous growth in primary commodity production was unaccompanied by any "structural" or "institutional" changes designed "to diffuse gains in real income among all sectors of population."[5] The net result was that a relatively large proportion of wage and salary income went to a small number of people; according to Clower et al., less than 5 percent of the working population received more than 90 percent of the "total domestic income in money and in kind."[6]

Clower et al. make no effort to disguise their conclusion that the root obstacle to the changes necessary for the development of Liberian society and its economy is the political control exercised by Liberia's traditional rulers:

> Like the Portuguese in Angola and the Afrikaners in the Republic of South Africa, the rulers of Liberia are descendants of an alien minority of colonial settlers who were free Negros from the U.S. and are known as Americó-Liberians. These families, which comprise some 5% of Liberians, control the country and govern the tribes (about 95% of the population) on a colonial pattern and through direct rule. . . . because the traditional policies and ruling group remain unchanged in the new economic environment [despite] massive iron mines and rubber plantations, Liberia is growing but not developing. The over-riding goal of Liberian authority remains what it has been for the past 150 years; to retain political control among a small group of families of settler descent and to share in the material benefits of economic growth among its own members. The politics and society, and not the economics of Liberia are what remain arcane and problematical.[7]

The gist of the present study has been to argue in similar fashion that an understanding of African politics must deal not only with whether there is a problem of an increase in the gross national product, but also with the central question of who benefits and for what reasons.

Besides issues concerning the best strategy for achieving the most rapid growth and guaranteeing that it be distributed most equitably, African politics also involves fundamental concerns about basic values of people and civilization. What type of world should be created? What should be the purpose of man's existence? What can motivate people to take an active role in creating new societies?

Development does not signify simply an increase in material goods; it involves the development of, in Leopold Sedar Senghor's felicitous phrase, "the whole man and all men."[8] Yet, as the experi-

---

[5] *Ibid.*, p. vi.

[6] *Ibid.*, p. 65.

[7] *Ibid.*, p. 5. Cf. Merran Fraenkel, *Tribe and Class in Monrovia* (London: Oxford University Press, 1964), pp. 197–229. See also J. Gus Liebenow, *Liberia: The Evolution of Privilege* (Ithaca, N.Y.: Cornell University Press, 1969).

[8] Irving Leonard Markovitz, *Leopold Sedar Senghor and the Politics of Negritude* (New York: Atheneum, 1969; London: Heinemann Educational Books, 1970), p. 156.

ence of Senegal itself has revealed, transposing words into actions sometimes requires more political imagination and diligence than appears necessary at first. In this work, I have attempted to clarify, underline, and dramatize some of the problems involved in this type of endeavor.

Despite the length of this work and the apparent weight of its scholarly apparatus, it remains a personal essay, in the sense that I have attempted to present a consistent point of view united by an admittedly "special" perspective, even at the expense of simplification. Sometimes this was necessary to emphasize "the significant"; sometimes material for a more nuanced position simply was not available. In this sense, as with any essay, I will have succeeded if I maintained a reasoned argument and provided a reasonable framework for analysis. Many problems cry out for further investigation.

Nevertheless, at a minimum we have seen that the threat of anarchy—unfurled like a banner by those cold war warriors for law and order who shed false tears for the torn and battered—is unfounded. Stability in Africa, as elsewhere, is in the interest of those who control power and of those who receive a disproportionate share of benefits made possible by collective effort and social organization.

Furthermore, conflict and classes exist despite the best efforts of Africa's most dedicated political leaders to create community. In order to realize dreams of unity and long-thwarted aspirations for a more humane society, these obstacles must be recognized and overcome. Insofar as class polarization becomes greater in times of crisis, African states are still undergoing a time of great stress.[9] Most societies are now at the stage of political development where their governments are undertaking the consolidation of state power. This involves determining the basic institutions of politics and learning their practical functions. Class interests emerge more markedly under these circumstances. Moreover, less-developed economies mean fewer industrial and productive sectors. This results in a quantitatively and qualitatively small economic "establishment"—not that internal conflicts don't exist, but by the nature of the case there must be fewer of them. More united, the establishment is more visible, the contrast between the "we" and the "them" more pronounced. As political commentators from Aristotle to Seymour Martin Lipset have pointed out, the gap

[9] Members of a class are not always either "self-conscious" or united on any particular line of policy or set of objectives. Class unity varies over time. Classes break down into a wide variety of components, with many internal divisions. Polarization between ruling and nonruling classes occurs primarily at moments of crises—for example, during depressions or prolonged economic slumps. Class polarization lessens when productivity expands and real living standards rise—even when wages climb slower than profits. During such periods of relaxation in inter-class tensions, internal disagreements within both ruling and nonruling elements become most vociferous. The absence of perfect knowledge upon which to base economic calculations, will always also produce a basis for disagreement. The demands of diverse sectors of an economy can be compounded further by the conflicting requirements of various regional interests. New business and industries can spurt forth from new inventions and discoveries. Arguments can occur over what is best in "the short run" and "the long run." Competing factions in the political or military establishments can be determining in the making of certain policies at different times. No wonder, then, that the discernment of patterns of consistent "class" interest becomes difficult.

between ruling and nonruling classes in less-developed countries is made more visible and emphatic by the absence of a "middle class." Coupled with the absence of the "cloud of representative government," the fact that most people do not count in the formation of politics stands out emphatically. No wonder, then, that Eric Wolf states that in underdeveloped countries, classes are not abstractions but conflict groups that have very real meaning to the people involved.

But as we have also seen in this study, class differences are nothing new in African societies. Indeed, the continuities between Africans' past leadership groups and those of the present were among the most striking and important political phenomena investigated.

A previous generation of political analysts discussed the disintegration of ancient societies and the decline in the power of the traditional rulers as if this had already happened. This study has emphasized how much alive those rulers and their descendants are today. No longer mystical guardians of the land, the Asantehenes and Bours acquire ownership and interests in shoe factories, shipping lines, and phosphate mines and send their sons to Oxford and Harvard to become Ministers of Planning and Economic Development.

We also cannot accept the "common-sense" categorization currently in vogue in social science literature of the so-called "conflict" between "the traditionalists" and "the modernizers." By and large, issues do not revolve around either the maintenance of tradition or innovation, for their own sake. Substantive matters of power and the authoritative distribution of benefits emerge consistently as focal points of dispute. A key point of this study has been to argue the ready adaptability of "ancient" ruling groups to new economic, administrative, and political systems.

With the expansion, strengthening, and centralizing of the government, the bureaucracy, and the economy, the heirs of the traditional rulers can join the higher civil servants, the powerful politicians, and the merchant princes in the consolidation of an organizational bourgeoisie, a class that is potentially richer and more powerful than any class known before.

In this study we have also considered the impact of imperialism on Africa's historical development. Braudel's assessment of the decline in the material conditions of the majority of men in the West astounds us because we find it difficult to believe that such a deterioration could have occurred simultaneously with the burgeoning industrial output that was supposed to have heralded a new age of abundance.

Trickle-down imperialism served African peoples far worse than trickle-down capitalism benefited Europe's downtrodden. Western social scientists may speak of the benefits of Newtonian Science and the unfolding of the processes of social change that allegedly bring "individualism" and "parliamentary democracy." Yet our evidence is of great civilizations crushed, inventions lost, traces of pre-European contacts with Egypt, China, and the New World all but covered — it is the archeologists who stand to have benefited.

Yet with the transition to independence, Africans shook the old structures and rattled their bonds. Everywhere on the continent there was a stirring of new hopes and desires—some noble, others banal—that assumed many different political forms.

These stirrings remind us, in concluding this overview of African politics, of one additional, all-important fact: the inevitability of diversity in the future political development of African states. Even as the Sahara sifts through the streets of Noukchott threatening to bury the artifacts of one civilization, tens of billions of dollars never before available to a Black African nation spurt out of Nigeria's oil wells to fuel an economy in full expansion—the Texas of the continent.

In Benin (Dahomey), President Mathieu Kerekeu, after declaring the establishment of a "Marxist-Leninist state," ordered the setting up of "watchdog committees" to "protect the revolution from sabotage."[10] Yet from up the western coast of the continent, the Ghanaian writer Ayi Kwei Armah denounces "the socialists of Africa, fat, perfumed, soft with the ancestral softness of those who have sold their people, and who are celestially happy with the fruits of the trade."[11]

Students in Ethiopia stirred by egalitarian ideologies venture to remote mountain villages to tear down the "vestiges of feudalism" (and are sometimes shot by "unself-conscious peasants" who mistake them for yet another city-led invasionary force); motivated by different ideals, students at Ibadan go out on strike for better maid service, improved restaurant meals, and larger scholarships. Zaire holds herself open to the invasion of reporters, publicists, and shoddy entrepreneurs for the world boxing championship; Portuguese soldiers without invitation sweep into Guinea frantically seeking the head of Sekou Touré. Somalia girded herself to treat drought victims with special facilities, doctors, and thousands of volunteers; Chad's newly overthrown profiteers used their political position to gouge enormous profits out of the selling of relief foods meant to relieve the misery of the starving.

Yet in Tanzania and in Angola, in Namimbia and in the Republic of the Congo, in Guinea-Bissau and Mozambique, in Ethiopia and in Somalia, in politics, economics, literature, and in the arts, many people in many places struggle to forge more human, more creative societies. Who is to say that they cannot succeed?

[10] *New York Times,* December 15, 1974.
[11] Ayi Kwei Armah, *The Beautiful Ones Are Not Yet Born* (New York: Collier, 1969), p. 130.

SELECTED BIBLIOGRAPHY

ABDEL-MALEK, ANOUAR, *Egypt: Military Society.* New York: Random House, 1968. Originally published as *Egypte: societe militaire.* Paris: Editions du Seuil, 1962.

ABOYADE, O., *Foundations of an African Economy: A Study of Investment and Growth in Nigeria.* New York: Praeger, 1966.

ABRAHAM, W. E., *The Mind of Africa.* Chicago: University of Chicago Press, 1962.

ABRAHAMS, PETER, *Mine Boy.* New York: Collier, 1946; 2nd edition, 1970.

———, *A Wreath for Udomo.* New York: Collier, 1956; 2nd edition, 1971.

ABSHIRE, DAVID, AND MICHAEL SAMUELS, eds., *Portuguese Africa, A Handbook.* New York: Praeger, 1967.

ACHEBE, CHINUA, *Things Fall Apart.* Greenwich, Conn.: Fawcett, 1958, 1969.

———, *No Longer at Ease.* New York: Fawcett, 1969.

———, *A Man of the People.* Garden City, N.Y.: Doubleday, Anchor Books, 1967.

———, *Girls at War and Other Stories.* Greenwich, Conn.: Fawcett, 1974.

ADAM, HERIBERT, *Modernizing Racial Domination: South Africa's Political Dynamics.* Berkeley and Los Angeles: University of California Press, 1971.

ADELEYE, R. A., *Power and Diplomacy in Northern Nigeria, 1804–1906.* New York: Humanities Press, 1971.

ADU, A. L., *The Civil Service in the New African States.* New York: Praeger, 1965.

AFANA, OSENDE, *L'economie de l'Ouest-African: perspectives de developpement.* Paris: Francois Maspero, 1966.

AFRICA RESEARCH GROUP, *Race to Power: The Struggle for Southern Africa.* Garden City, N.Y.: Doubleday, Anchor Books, 1974.

AFRIFA, A. A., *The Ghana Coup, 24th February 1966.* London: Frank Cass, 1966.

AGBODEKA, FRANCIS, *African Politics and British Policy in the Gold Coast, 1868–1900.* London: Longman, 1971.

AIDOO, AMA ATA, No Sweetness Here. Garden City, N.Y.: Doubleday, Anchor Books, 1972.

AJALA, ADENKUNLE, Pan-Africanism: Evolution, Progress and Prospects. New York: St. Martin's, 1974.

AJAYI, J. F. ADE, AND MICHAEL CROWDER, eds., The History of West Africa, Vols. I and II. New York: Columbia University Press, 1972, 1973; London: Longman, 1972, 1974.

AJAYI, J. F. ADE, AND JAN EPSIE, eds., A Thousand Years of West African History. Ibadan: Ibadan University Press, 1965.

ALLEN, CHRISTOPHER, AND R. W. JOHNSON, eds., African Perspectives. Cambridge: Cambridge University Press, 1970.

ALPERS, EDWARD A., Ivory and Slaves in East Central Africa. Berkeley and Los Angeles: University of California Press, 1975.

AMEILLON, B., La Guinée, bilan d'une independence. Paris: Francois Maspero, 1964.

AMERICAN SOCIETY OF AFRICAN CULTURE, Africa Seen by American Negroes. Paris: Presence Africaine, 1959.

————, Pan-Africanism Reconsidered. Berkeley and Los Angeles: University of California Press, 1962.

AMIN, SAMIR, Le developpement du capitalisme en Cote d'Ivoire. Paris: Editions de Minuit, 1967.

————, The Maghreb in the Modern World: Algeria, Tunisia, Morocco. Baltimore: Penguin, 1970.

————, Neo-Colonialism in West Africa. New York: Monthly Review Press, 1973. Originally published as L'Afrique de l'Ouest bloquée. Paris: Editions de Minuit, 1971.

AMSDEN, ALICE H., International Firms and Labour in Kenya, 1945–1970. London: Frank Cass, 1971.

ANDREWS, WILLIAM G., French Politics and Algeria. New York: Appleton-Century-Crofts, 1962.

APTER, DAVID E., Ghana in Transition, 2nd rev. ed. Princeton, N.J.: Princeton University Press, 1972.

————, The Political Kingdom in Uganda: A Study in Bureaucratic Nationalism. Princeton, N.J.: Princeton University Press, 1961.

————, The Politics of Modernization. Chicago: University of Chicago Press, 1965.

————, Some Conceptual Approaches to the Study of Modernization. Englewood Cliffs, N.J.: Prentice-Hall, 1968.

ARMAH, AYI KWEI, The Beautiful Ones Are Not Yet Born. New York: Collier, 1969.

ARNAULT, JACQUES, Du colonialisme au socialisme. Paris: Editions Sociales, 1966.

ARIKPO, OKOI, The Development of Modern Nigeria. Baltimore: Penguin, 1967.

ARRIGHI, GIOVANNI, *Political Economy of Rhodesia*. The Hague: Mouton, 1967.

ARRIGHI, GIOVANNI, AND JOHN SAUL, *Essays on the Political Economy of Africa*. New York: Monthly Review Press, 1973.

AUSTIN, DENNIS, *Politics in Ghana, 1946–1960*. Oxford: Oxford University Press, 1964, paperback ed., 1970.

AUSTIN, DENNIS, AND ROBERT LUCKMAN, eds., *Politics and Soldiers in Ghana*. London: Frank Cass, 1975.

AWOLOWO, OBAFEMI, *Path to Nigerian Freedom*. London: Faber & Faber, 1947.

_____, *The Peoples Republic*. Ibadan: Oxford University Press, 1968.

AYANDELE, E. A., *The Missionary Impact on Modern Nigeria, 1842–1914*. New York: Humanities Press, 1967.

AZIKIWE, NNAMDI, *Zik, a Selection from the Speeches of Nnamdi Azikiwe*. London: Cambridge University Press, 1961.

BADIAN, SEYDOU, *Les dirigeants d'Afrique Noire face a leur peuple*. Paris: Francois Maspero, 1965.

BALANDIER, GEORGES, *Ambiguous Africa*. New York: Pantheon, 1966.

_____, *Sociology of Black Africa*. New York: Pantheon, 1970.

BARBÉ, RAYMOND, *Les classes sociales en Afrique Noire*, Paris: Economie et Politique 1964.

BARBER, WILLIAM J., *The Economy of British Central Africa*. Stanford, Calif.: Stanford University Press, 1961.

BARKAN, JOEL D., *An African Dilemma: University Students, Development and Politics in Ghana, Tanzania and Uganda*. Nairobi and London: Oxford University Press, 1975.

BARNETT, DONALD L., AND KARARI NJAMA, *Mau Mau from Within: Autobiography and Analysis of Kenya's Peasant Revolt*. New York: Monthly Review Press, 1966.

BARRY, BOUBACAR, *Le royaume du Waalo: Le Senegal avant la conquete*. Paris: Francois Maspero, 1972.

BASCOMB, WILLIAM, AND MELVILLE HERSKOVITS, eds., *Continuity and Change in African Cultures*. Chicago: University of Chicago Press, 1959.

BASTIDE, ROGER, *African Civilizations in the New World*. New York: Harper & Row, Torchbook ed., 1971. First published as *Les Ameriques Noires*. Paris: Editions Payot, 1967.

BATES, ROBERT H., *Unions, Parties and Political Development: A Study of Mineworkers in Zambia*. New Haven: Yale University Press, 1971.

BAUER, P. T., *West African Trade*. Cambridge: Cambridge University Press, 1954.

BAULIN, JACQUES, *The Arab Role in Africa*. Baltimore: Penguin, 1962.

BEBLER, ANTON, *Military Rule in Africa: Dahomey, Ghana, Sierra Leone and Mali*. New York: Praeger, 1973.

BEHRMAN, LUCY, "The Political Significance of the Wolof Adherence to Muslim Brotherhoods in the Nineteenth Century," *African Historical Studies,* (1968), 60–78.

————, *Muslim Brotherhoods and Politics in Senegal.* Cambridge, Mass.: Harvard University Press, 1970.

BENNETT, GEORGE, AND CARL ROSBERG, *The Kenyatta Election: Kenya 1960–1961.* New York: Oxford University Press, 1961.

BENNETT, NORMAN ROBERT, *Mirambo of Tanzania, 1840–1884.* Oxford: Oxford University Press, 1971.

BENSON, MARY, *South Africa, The Struggle for a Birthright.* New York: Minerva Press, 1969. First published as *The African Patriots.* London: Faber & Faber, 1963.

BENVENISTE, GUY, AND WILLIAM E. MORAN, JR., *Handbook of African Economic Development.* New York: Praeger, 1962.

BIENEN, HENRY, *Tanzania: Party Transformation and Economic Development.* Princeton, N.J.: Princeton University Press, 1970.

————, *Kenya: The Politics of Participation and Control.* Princeton, N.J.: Princeton University Press, 1974.

BIRMINGHAM, DAVID, *Trade and Conflict in Angola.* Oxford: Clarendon Press, 1966.

BIRMINGHAM, WALTER, PAUL BOHANNAN, AND GEORGE DALTON, *Markets in Africa.* Evanston, Ill.: Northwestern University Press, 1962.

BIRMINGHMAM, WALTER, I. NEUSTADT, AND E. H. OMABOE, eds., *A Study of Contemporary Ghana,* Vol. I, *The Economy of Ghana,* Vol. II, *Some Aspects of Social Structure.* London: Allen & Unwin, 1966, 1967.

Black Civilization and Education, special issue of *Presence Africaine,* no. 87, 3rd quarterly (1973).

BOHANNAN, PAUL, AND PHILIP CURTAIN, *Africa and Africans,* rev. ed. Garden City, N.Y.: Natural History Press, 1971.

BONNAFÉ, PIERRE, *Nationalismes Africaines.* Paris: Fondation Nationale des Sciences Politiques, 1962.

BOVILL, E. W., *The Golden Trade of the Moors,* 2nd ed. New York: Oxford University Press, 1968.

BRANDEL-SYRIER, SYLVIA, *Reeftown Elite: Social Mobility in a Black African Community in the Johannesberg Reef.* New York: Africana Publishing, 1971.

BRAUSCH, GEORGES, *Belgian Administration in the Congo.* London: Institute of Race Relations, 1961.

BRETT, E. A., *Colonialism and Underdevelopment in East Africa: The Politics of Economic Change, 1919–1939.* New York: Nok Publishers, 1973.

BRETTON, HENRY L., *Power and Stability in Nigeria: The Politics of Decolonization.* New York: Praeger, 1962.

————, *The Rise and Fall of Kwame Nkrumah*. New York: Praeger, 1966.

————, *Power and Politics in Africa*. Chicago: Aldine, 1973.

BRIGAUD, FELIX, *Histoire traditionnelle du Senegal*. Saint-Louis, Senegal, C.R.D.S., 1962.

BROCKWAY, FENNER, *African Socialism*. London: Bodley Head, 1973.

BROKENSHA, DAVID, *Social Change at Larteh, Ghana*. Oxford: Clarendon Press, 1966.

BROOKS, LESTER, *Great Civilizations of Ancient Africa*. New York: Four Winds Press, 1971.

BUELL, RAYMOND LESLIE, *The Native Problem in Africa*, 2 Vols. New York: Macmillan, 1928.

BUNTING, BRIAN, *The Rise of the South African Reich*. Baltimore: Penguin, 1964.

BURKE, FRED G., *Local Government and Politics in Uganda*. Syracuse: Syracuse University Press, 1964.

————, *Tanganyika: Preplanning*. Syracuse: Syracuse University Press, 1965.

BUSIA, K. A. *The Position of the Chief in the Modern Political System of Ashanti*. London: Oxford University Press, 1951.

————, *The Challenge of Africa*. New York: Praeger, 1962.

BUSTIN, EDOUARD, *Lunda under Belgian Rule: The Politics of Ethnicity*. Cambridge, Mass.: Harvard University Press, 1975.

BUTLER, JEFFREY, ed., *Boston University Papers in African History*, 2 vols. Boston: Boston University Press, 1964, 1966.

BUTLER, JEFFRY, AND A. A. CASTAGNO, eds., *Boston University Papers on Africa: Transition in African Politics*. New York: Praeger, 1967.

CABRAL, AMILCAR, *Revolution in Guinea*. London: Monthly Review Press, 1969.

————, *Return to the Source, Selected Speeches*. New York: Monthly Review Press, 1973.

CALDWELL, JOHN C., *Population Growth and Family Change in Africa: The New Urban Elite in Ghana*. New York: Humanities Press, 1968.

————, *African Rural-Urban Migration: The Movement to Ghana's Towns*. New York: Columbia University Press, 1969.

CARNEY, DAVID E., *Government and Economy in British West Africa*. New Haven: College and University Press, 1961.

CARTER, GWENDOLEN M., *The Politics of Inequality: South Africa since 1948*. New York: Praeger, 1958.

CARTER, GWENDOLEN M., ed., *African One Party States*. Ithaca, N.Y.: Cornell University Press, 1962.

————, *Five African States*. Ithaca, N.Y.: Cornell University Press, 1963.

————, *National Unity and Regionalism in Eight African States.* Ithaca, N.Y.: Cornell University Press, 1966.

CARTER, GWENDOLEN M., and WILLIAM O. BROWN, eds., *Transition in Africa.* Boston: Boston University Press, 1958.

CARTER, GWENDOLEN M., THOMAS KARIS, AND NEWELL STULTZ, *South Africa's Transkei: The Politics of Domestic Colonialism.* Evanston, Ill.: Northwestern University Press, 1967.

CHALIAND, GERARD, *L'Algerie est-elle socialiste?* Paris: Francois Maspero, 1964.

————, *Armed Struggle in Africa: With the Guerrillas in "Portuguese" Guinea.* New York: Monthly Review Press, 1969. Originally published as *Lutte armé en Afrique.* Paris: Francois Maspero, 1967.

CHARBONNEAU, JEAN, and RENÉ CHARBONNEAU, *Marches et marchands d'Afrique Noire.* Paris: La Colombe, 1961.

CHARPY, JACQUES, *La fondation de Dakar.* Paris: Larose, 1958.

CHILCOTE, RONALD H., ed., *Protest and Resistance in Angola and Brazil.* Berkeley and Los Angeles: University of California Press, 1972.

CHINWEIZU, *The West and the Rest of Us: White Predators, Black Slaves and the African Elite.* New York: Random House, Vintage Books, 1975.

CLARK, J. DESMOND, *The Prehistory of Africa.* New York: Praeger, 1970.

CLARK, LEON E., ed., *Coming of Age in Africa.* New York: Praeger, 1969.

CLARK, MICHAEL K., *Algeria in Turmoil.* New York: Grosset & Dunlap, 1960.

CLEGG, IAN, *Workers' Self-Management in Algeria.* New York: Monthly Review Press, 1971.

CLIFFE, LIONEL, ed., *One Party Democracy: The 1965 Tanzania General Election.* Nairobi: East African Publishing, 1967.

CLIGNET, REMI, AND PHILIP FOSTER, *The Fortunate Few.* Evanston, Ill.: Northwestern University Press, 1966.

CLOWER, ROBERT W., GEORGE DALTON, MITCHEL HARWITZ, A. A. WALTERS et al., *Growth Without Development: An Economic Survey of Liberia.* Evanston, Ill.: Northwestern University Press, 1966.

COHEN, ABNER, *Custom and Politics in Urban Africa: A Study of Hausa Migrants in Yoruba Towns.* Berkeley and Los Angeles: University of California Press, 1969.

COHEN, DAVID WILLIAM, *The Historical Tradition of Busoga.* Oxford: Clarendon Press, 1972.

COHEN, MICHAEL A., *Urban Policy and Political Conflict in Africa: A Study of the Ivory Coast.* Chicago: University of Chicago Press, 1974.

COHEN, WILLIAM B., *Rulers of Empire: The French Colonial Service in Africa.* Stanford, Calif.: Hoover Institution Press, 1971.

COLEMAN, JAMES S., *Nigeria: Background to Nationalism.* Berkeley and Los Angeles: University of California Press, 1958.

COLEMAN, JAMES S., AND CARL ROSBERG, JR., eds., *Political Parties and National Integration in Tropical Africa.* Berkeley and Los Angeles: University of California Press, 1964.

COLLINS, ROBERT O., ed., *Problems in African History.* Englewood Cliffs, N.J.: Prentice-Hall, 1968.

CONRAD, JOSEPH, *Heart of Darkness.* New York: Signet, 1950.

COPANS, J., PH. COUTY, J. ROCH, AND G. ROCHETEAU, *Maintenance sociale et changement economique en Senegal doctrine economique et pratique du travail chez les Mourides.* Paris: Travaux et Documents de L'ORSTOM, 1972.

CORBETT, EDWARD M., *The French Presence in Black Africa.* Washington, D.C.: Black Orpheus Press, 1972.

CORNEVIN, ROBERT, *Histoire du Congo-Leo.* Paris: Editions Berger-Levrault, 1963.

COWAN, L. GRAY, JAMES O'CONNELL, AND DAVID G. SCANLON, eds., *Education and Nation-Building in Africa.* New York: Praeger, 1965.

CROWDER, MICHAEL, *Senegal: A Study in French Assimilation Policy.* London: Oxford University Press, 1962.

————, *A Short History of Nigeria,* rev. ed. New York: Praeger, 1966.

CROWDER, MICHAEL, ed., *West African Resistance: The Military Response to Colonial Occupation.* New York: Africana Publishing, 1971.

CROWDER, MICHAEL, AND OBARO IKIME, eds., *West African Chiefs.* New York: Africana Publishing, 1970.

CRUISE O'BRIEN, CONOR, *To Katanga and Back.* New York: Grosset & Dunlap, 1962.

CRUISE O'BRIEN, DONAL B., *The Mourides of Senegal.* New York: Oxford University Press, 1971.

————, *Saints and Politicians: Essays in the Organization of a Senegalese Peasant Society.* Cambridge: Cambridge University Press, 1975.

CRUISE O'BRIEN, RITA, *White Society in Black Africa: The French of Senegal.* London: Faber & Faber, 1972.

CURTIN, PHILIP, *The Atlantic Slave Trade: A Census.* Madison, Wisc.: University of Wisconsin Press, 1969.

————, *Economic Change in Precolonial Africa: Senegambia in the Era of the Slave Trade.* Madison Wisc.: University of Wisconsin Press, 1975.

DAAKU, KWAME YEBOA, *Trade and Politics on the Gold Coast, 1600–1720.* Oxford: Clarendon Press, 1970.

DAMACHI, UKANDI GODWIN, *The Role of Trade Unions in the Development Process: With a Case Study of Ghana.* New York: Praeger, 1974.

DAVIDSON, BASIL, *The Lost Cities of Africa*. Boston: Little, Brown, Atlantic Monthly Press, 1959, 1970.

———, *The African Slave Trade: Pre-Colonial History, 1450–1850*. Boston: Little, Brown, Atlantic Monthly Press, 1961.

———, *A History of West Africa to the Nineteenth Century*. Garden City, N.Y.: Doubleday, Anchor Books, 1966.

———, *The African Past: Chronicles from Antiquity to Modern Times*. New York: Grosset & Dunlap, 1967.

———, *The African Genius*. Boston: Little, Brown, Atlantic Monthly Press, 1969.

———, *The Liberation of Guinée*. Baltimore: Penguin, 1969.

———, *In the Eye of the Storm: Angola's People*. Garden City, N.Y.: Anchor Books, 1972, 1973.

DAVIES, IOAN, *African Trade Unions*. Baltimore: Penguin, 1966.

DECALO, SAMUEL, *Coups and Army Rule in Africa: Studies in Military Style*. New Haven and London: Yale University Press, 1976.

DELAVIGNETTE, ROBERT, *Freedom and Authority in French West Africa*. New York: Oxford University Press, 1950.

DELBARD, B., *Les dynamismes sociaux au Senegal: les processus de formation de classes sociales dans un état d'Afrique de l'Ouest*. Dakar: Institut de Science Economique Appliqué, 1966.

DELCOURT, ANDRE, *La France et les établissements Francais äu Senegal entre 1713 et 1763*. Dakar: Memoires de l'Institut Francais d'Afrique Noire, 1952.

DELF, GEORGE, *Asians in East Africa*. New York: Oxford University Press, 1963.

DE KIEWET, C. W., *A History of South Africa*. London: Oxford University Press, 1941.

DERMAN, WILLIAM, *Serfs, Peasants and Socialists: A Former Serf Village in the Republic of Guinea*. Berkeley and Los Angeles: University of California Press, 1973.

DE WILDE, JOHN C., *Experience with Agricultural Development in Tropical Africa*, Vol. 2. Baltimore: Johns Hopkins, 1967.

DIA, MAMADOU, *The African Nations and World Solidarity*. New York: Praeger, 1961. Paris: Presses Universitaires de France, 1960.

DIAMOND, STANLEY, AND FRED G. BURKE, eds., *The Transformation of East Africa*. New York: Basic Books, 1966.

DIKE, K. O., *Trade and Politics in the Niger Delta, 1830–1885*. Oxford: Clarendon Press, 1956.

DINESEN, ISAK (KAREN BLIXEN), *Out of Africa*. New York: Modern Library, 1952.

DIOP, ABDOULAYE BARA, *Societé Toucouleur et migration*. Dakar: Institut Francais d'Afrique Noire, 1965.

DIOP, CHEIKH ANTA, *Nations nègres et culture*. Paris: Presence Africaine, 1955.

————, *L'unité culturelle de l'Afrique Noire*. Paris: Presence Africaine, 1959.

————, *Les fondements culturels, techniques et industriels d'un futur état federal d'Afrique Noire*. Paris: Presence Africaine, 1966.

————, *Anteriorité des Civilisations Nègres*. Paris: Presence Africaine, 1967.

————, *The African Origin of Civilization: Myth or Reality*, ed. and trans. Mercer Cook. New York and Westport, Conn.: Lawrence Hill, 1974.

DIOP, MAJHEMOUT, *Contribution a l'étude des problemes politiques en Afrique Noire*. Paris: Presence Africaine, 1958.

DIOUF, COUMBA N'DOFFENE, GEORGE VERMOT-BOUCHY, AND CHARLES FRANCOIS BRUN, *La question des salaires au Senegal*. Dakar: Afrique Documents, 1965.

DOUGLAS, MARY, AND PHYLLIS M. KABERRY, eds., *Man in Africa*. Garden City, N.Y.: Doubleday, Anchor Books, 1971. Originally published in London: Tavistock, 1969.

DOWSE, ROBERT E., *Modernization in Ghana and the USSR*. London: Routledge & Kegan Paul, 1969.

Drought Damage and Famine in Sub-Sahara Africa, Department of State Publications 8792, African Series 58. Washington, D.C.: Government Printing Office, 1974.

DU BOIS, W. E. B., *The World and Africa: An Inquiry into the Part Which Africa Has Played in World History*. New York: International Publishers, 1946; enl. ed., 1965.

DUDLEY, BILLY J., *Parties and Politics in Northern Nigeria*. London: Frank Cass, 1968.

DUFFY, JAMES, *Portuguese Africa*. Cambridge, Mass.: Harvard University Press, 1959.

DUIGNAN, PETER, ed., *Guide to Research and Reference Works on Sub-Saharan Africa*. Stanford, Calif.: Hoover Institution Press, 1971.

DUIGNAN, PETER, AND L. H. GANN, eds., *Colonialism in Africa, 1870–1960*, Vol. 1, *The History and Politics of Colonialism, 1870–1914*, ed. Duignan and Gann. Cambridge: Cambridge University Press, 1969.

————, *Colonialism in Africa, 1870–1960*, Vol. 2, *The History and Politics of Colonialism, 1914–1960*, ed. Duignan and Gann. Cambridge: Cambridge University Press, 1970.

————, *Colonialism in Africa, 1870–1960*, Vol. 3, *Profiles of Change: African Society and Colonial Rule*, ed. Victor Turner. Cambridge: Cambridge University Press, 1971.

DUMONT, RENÉ, *False Start in Africa*, 2nd rev. ed., New York: Praeger, 1969. Originally published as *L'Afrique Noire est mal partie*. Paris: Editions du Seuil, 1962.

————, *Paysanneries aux abois: Ceylon, Tunisie, Senegal.* Paris: Editions du Seuil, 1972.

DUMONT, RENÉ, WITH MARCEL MAZOYER, *Socialism and Development.* New York: Praeger, 1973. Originally published as *Developpement et socialismes.* Paris: Editions du Seuil, 1969.

DUNN, JOHN, AND A. F. ROBERTSON, *Dependence and Opportunity: Political Change in Ahafo.* Cambridge: Cambridge University Press, 1973.

DUVIGNAUD, JEAN, *Change at Shebika: Report from a North African Village.* New York: Vintage, 1972. Originally published as *Chebika.* Paris: Editions Gallimard, 1968.

EKUNDARE, R. OLUFEMI, *An Economic History of Nigeria, 1860–1960.* London: Methuen, 1973.

ELIAS, T. OLAWALE, *Nigerian Land Law and Custom.* London: Routledge & Kegan Paul, 1953.

EMMERSON, DONALD K., ed., *Students and Politics in Developing Nations.* New York: Praeger, 1968.

EPSTEIN, A. L., *Politics in an Urban African Community.* Manchester: Manchester University Press, 1958.

Ethiopian Students Union in North America, *Repression in Ethiopia.* New York: Africa Research Group, 1971.

EZERA, KALU, *Constitutional Developments in Nigeria,* 2nd ed. New York: Cambridge University Press, 1964.

FAGE, J. D., *A History of West Africa,* rev. ed. Cambridge: Cambridge University Press, 1969.

FAGE, J. D., ed., *Africa Discovers her Past.* London: Oxford University Press, 1970.

FALLERS, LLOYD A., *Bantu Bureaucracy.* Chicago: University of Chicago Press, 1956, Phoenix Books ed., 1965.

————, *Inequality: Social Stratification Reconsidered.* Chicago: University of Chicago Press, 1973.

FANON, FRANTZ, *A Dying Colonialism.* New York: Grove Press, 1965.

————, *Black Skins, White Masks: The Experiences of a Black Man in a White World.* New York: Grove Press, 1967.

————, *Toward the African Revolution.* New York: Grove Press, 1967. Originally published as *Pour la Revolution Africaine.* Paris: Francois Maspero, 1964.

————, *The Wretched of the Earth.* New York: Grove Press, 1968. Originally published as *Les damnes de la terre.* Paris: Francois Maspero, 1961.

FEIT, EDWARD, *African Opposition in South Africa: The Failure of Passive Resistance.* Stanford, Calif.: Hoover Institution, 1967.

FIELD, M. J., *Search for Security: An Ethno-Psychiatric Study of Rural Ghana.* Evanston, Ill.: Northwestern University Press, 1962.

FILESI, TEOBALDO, *China and Africa in the Middle Ages.* London: Frank Cass, 1972.

FINUCANE, JAMES R., *Rural Development and Bureaucracy in Tanzania: The Case of Mwanza Region.* Uppsala: Scandinavian Institute of African Studies, 1974.

FIRST, RUTH, *Power in Africa.* New York: Pantheon, 1970.

FIRST, RUTH, JONATHAN STEELE, AND CHRISTABEL GURNEY, *The South African Connection: Western Investment in Apartheid.* London: Temple Smith, 1972.

FISHER, ALLAN G. B., AND HUMPHREY FISHER, *Slavery and Muslim Society in Africa.* Garden City, N.Y.: Doubleday, 1971, Anchor Books ed., 1972.

FITCH, BOB, AND MARY OPPENHEIMER, *Ghana: End of an Illusion.* New York: Monthly Review Press, 1966.

FOLTZ, WILLIAM, *From French West Africa to the Mali Federation.* New Haven: Yale University Press, 1965.

FORDE, DARYLL, AND P. M. KABERRY, eds., *West African Kingdoms in the Nineteenth Century.* London: Oxford University Press, 1967.

FORTES, MEYER, AND E. E. EVANS-PRITCHARD, eds., *African Political Systems.* London: Oxford University Press, 1940.

FOSTER, PHILIP, *Education and Social Change in Ghana.* Chicago: University of Chicago Press, 1965.

FOSTER, PHILIP, AND ARISTIDE R. ZOLBERG, eds., *Ghana and the Ivory Coast: Perspective on Modernization.* Chicago: University of Chicago Press, 1971.

FOUGEYROLLAS, PIERRE, *Modernisation des hommes: l'exemple du Senegal.* Paris: Flammerion, 1967.

FRAENKEL, MERRAN, *Tribe and Class in Monrovia.* London: Oxford University Press, 1964.

FRIEDLAND, WILLIAM H., *Unions, Labor and Industrial Relations in Africa: An Annotated Bibliography.* Ithaca, N.Y.: Center of International Studies, 1965.

FRIEDLAND, WILLIAM H., AND CARL G. ROSBERG, JR., eds., *African Socialism.* Stanford, Calif.: Stanford University Press, 1964.

FYFE, CHRISTOPHER, *Africanus Horton, West African Scientist and Patriot.* New York: Oxford University Press, 1972.

GAILEY, HARRY A., *History of Africa from Earliest Times to 1800.* New York: Holt, Rinehart & Winston, 1970.

GANN, L. H., AND PETER DUIGNAN, *Burden of Empire: An Appraisal of Western Colonialism in Africa South of the Sahara.* New York: Praeger, 1967.

GARLICK, PETER C., *African Traders and Economic Development in Ghana.* London: Oxford University Press, 1971.

GEIGER, THEODORE, AND WINIFRED ARMSTRONG, *The Development of African Private Enterprise.* Washington, D.C.: National Planning Association, 1964.

GENDZIER, IRENE C., *Frantz Fanon: A Critical Study.* New York: Pantheon, 1973.

GIBSON, RICHARD, *African Liberation Movements.* New York: Oxford University Press, 1972.

GIDE, ANDRÉ, *Travels in the Congo.* Berkeley and Los Angeles: University of California Press, 1962. Originally published as *Voyage au Congo* and *Le Retour du Tchad.* Paris: Librarie Gallimard, 1927, 1928.

GLUCKMAN, MAX, *Rituals of Rebellion in South East Africa.* Manchester: Manchester University Press, 1954.

———, *Custom and Conflict in Africa.* New York: Barnes & Noble, 1956, 1967.

———, *Order and Rebellion in Tribal Africa.* New York: Free Press, 1963.

———, *Politics, Law and Ritual in Tribal Society.* New York: New American Library, 1965.

———, *The Ideas in Barotse Jurisprudence,* New Haven: Yale University Press, 1965; Manchester: Manchester University Press, 1972.

GOODY, JACK, *Technology, Tradition and the State in Africa.* London: Oxford University Press, 1971.

GOUILLY, ALPHONSE, *L'Islam dans l'Afrique Occidentale Francaise.* Paris: Larose, 1952.

GREEN, M. M., *Ibo Village Affairs.* New York: Praeger, 1964.

GREEN, REGINALD H., AND ANN SEIDMAN, *Unity or Poverty?: The Economics of Pan-Africanism.* Baltimore: Penguin, 1968.

GREENFIELD, RICHARD D., *Ethiopia: A New Political History.* New York: Praeger, 1965.

GRILLO, R. D., *African Railwaymen: Solidarity and Opposition in an East African Labour Force.* Cambridge: Cambridge University Press, 1973.

GRINDAL, BRUCE T., *Growing Up in Two Worlds: Education and Transition Among the Sisala of Northern Ghana.* New York: Holt, Rinehart & Winston, 1972.

GRUNDY, KENNETH, *Guerrilla Struggle in Africa.* New York: Grossman, 1971.

GUEYE, LAMINE, *Etapes et perspectives de l'union Francaise.* Paris: Editions d'Union Francaise, 1955.

———, *Itineraire Africaine.* Paris: Presence Africaine, 1966.

GUTTERIDGE, WILLIAM, *The Military in African Politics.* London: Methuen, 1969.

HAILEY, LORD, *An African Survey,* rev. ed. London: Oxford University Press, 1957.

HALIBURTON, GORDON MACKAY, *The Prophet Harris: A Study of an African Prophet and his Mass Movement in the Ivory Coast and the Gold Coast, 1913–1915.* New York: Oxford University Press, 1973.

HALPERN, MANFRED, *The Politics of Social Change in the Middle East and North Africa.* Princeton, N.J.: Princeton University Press, 1963.

HAMON, LEO, ed., *Le role extra-militaire de l'armée dans le Tiers Monde.* Paris: Presses Universitaires de France, 1966.

HANCE, WILLIAM A., *African Economic Development,* rev. ed. New York: Praeger, 1967.

HANNA, WILLIAM J., AND JUDITH L. HANNA, *Urban Dynamics in Black Africa.* Chicago: Aldine; New York: Atherton, 1971.

HAPGOOD, DAVID, *Africa: From Independence to Tomorrow.* New York: Atheneum, 1965.

HARDY, GEORGES, *La mise en valeur du Senegal de 1817 a 1854.* Paris: Emile Larose, 1921.

HARGREAVES, JOHN D., *West Africa Partitioned,* Vol. I, *The Loaded Pause, 1885–1889.* Madison, Wisc.: University of Wisconsin Press, 1974.

HARRIS, JOSEPH E., *Africans and Their History.* New York: New American Library, 1972.

HARVEY, WILLIAM BURNETT, *Law and Social Change in Ghana.* Princeton, N.J.: Princeton University Press, 1966.

HERSKOVITS, MELVILLE, AND MITCHELL HARWITZ, eds., *Economic Transition in Africa.* Evanston, Ill.: Northwestern University Press, 1964.

HESS, ROBERT L., *Ethiopia: The Modernization of Autocracy.* Ithaca, N.Y.: Cornell University Press, 1970.

HILL, POLLY, *The Migrant Cocoa Farmers of Southern Ghana.* Cambridge: Cambridge University Press, 1963.

————, *Studies in Rural Capitalism in West Africa.* Cambridge: Cambridge University Press, 1970.

HISKETT, MERVYN, *The Sword of Truth: The Life and Times of Shehu Usuman Dan Fodio.* New York: Oxford University Press, 1973.

HODGKIN, THOMAS, *Nationalism in Colonial Africa.* New York: New York University Press, 1957.

————, *African Political Parties.* Baltimore: Penguin, 1961.

HOGBEN, S. J. AND A. H. M. KIRK-GREENE, *The Emirates of Northern Nigeria.* London: Oxford University Press, 1966.

HOLY, LADISLAV, *Social Stratification in Tribal Africa.* Prague: Acadamia, 1968.

HOOKER, JAMES, R., *Black Revolutionary: George Padmore's Path from Communism to Pan-Africanism.* New York: Praeger, 1967.

HOPKINS, A. G., *An Economic History of West Africa.* London: Longman, 1973.

HOPKINS, NICHOLAS S., *Popular Government in an African Town.* Chicago: University of Chicago Press, 1972.

HOPKINS, RAYMOND, *Political Roles in a New State: Tanzania's First Decade.* New Haven: Yale University Press, 1971.

HORWITZ, RALPH, *The Political Economy of South Africa.* London: Weidenfeld & Nicolson, 1967.

HOUPHOUET-BOIGNY, FELIX, *Discours et allocutions pronounces par Monsieur le Ministre Houphouet-Boigny.* Paris: Information Service of the Ivory Coast, 1956, 1957.

HOVET, THOMAS, *Africa in the United Nations.* Evanston, Ill.: Northwestern University Press, 1963.

HUNTINGTON, SAMUEL P., AND CLEMENT H. MOORE, eds., *Authoritarian Politics in Modern Society: The Dynamics of Established One Party Systems.* New York: Basic Books, 1970.

HUNTON, W. ALPHAEUS, *Decision in Africa*, rev. ed. New York: International Publishers, 1960.

IKIME, OBARO, *Niger Delta Rivalry: Itsekiri-Urhobo Relations and the European Presence, 1884–1936.* New York: Humanities Press, 1969.

IKIME, OBARO, ed., *Leadership in 19th Century Africa: Essays from Tarikh.* London: Longman, 1974.

INGLE, CLYDE R., *From Village to State in Tanzania.* Ithaca, N.Y.: Cornell University Press, 1972.

International Bank for Reconstruction and Development, *Senegal: Tradition, Diversification and Economic Development,* Washington, D.C., 1974.

International Institute of Differing Civilizations, *Development of a Middle Class in Tropical and Sub-Tropical Countries.* Brussels, 1956.

International Labour Office, *Employment, Incomes and Equality: A Strategy for Increasing Productive Employment in Kenya.* Geneva, 1972.

————, *The Promotion of Balanced Rural and Urban Development.* Geneva, 1973.

————, *Employment, Status and Conditions of Non-National Workers in Africa.* Geneva, 1973.

ISAACMAN, ALLEN F., *Mozambique: The Africanization of a European Institution.* Madison, Wisc.: University of Wisconsin Press, 1972.

JABAVU, NONI, *Drawn in Colour.* London: Murray, 1960.

JOHNSON, G. WESLEY, JR., *The Emergence of Black Politics in Senegal.* Stanford, Calif.: Stanford University Press, 1971.

JOHNSTON, H. A. S., *The Fulani Empire of Sokoto.* London: Oxford University Press, 1967.

JOSEPH, HELEN, *Tomorrow's Sun: A Smuggled Journal from South Africa.* New York: John Day, 1966.

JOSEPHY, ALVIN M., JR., ed., *The Horizon History of Africa.* New York: American Heritage, 1971.

JULIEN, CH.-ANDRE, *Les techniciens de la colonisation.* Paris: Presses Universitaires de France, 1947.

JULY, ROBERT W., *The Origins of Modern African Thought.* New York: Praeger, 1967.

KAMARCK, ANDREW M., *The Economics of African Development,* rev. ed. New York: Praeger, 1971.

KANE, CHEIKH HAMIDOU, *Ambiguous Adventure.* New York: Collier, 1969. Originally published as *L'Aventure ambigue.* Paris: Rene Julliard, 1962.

KANZA, THOMAS, *Conflict in the Congo: The Rise and Fall of Lumumba.* Baltimore: Penguin, 1972.

KARIUKI, JOSIAH MWANGI, *Mau Mau Detainee.* Baltimore: Penguin, 1963.

KAROL, K. S., *Guerrillas in Power.* New York: Hill & Wang, 1970.

KARUGIRE, SAMWIRI RUBARAZA, *A History of the Kingdom of Nkore in Western Uganda to 1896.* Oxford: Clarendon Press, 1971.

KASFIR, NELSON, *The Shrinking Political Arena: Participation and Ethnicity in African Politics.* Berkeley and Los Angeles: University of California Press, 1976.

KAY, G. B., ed., *The Political Economy of Colonialism in Ghana.* Cambridge: Cambridge University Press, 1972.

KENNEDY, GAVIN, *The Military in the Third World.* New York: Scribner's, 1974.

KENYATTA, JOMO, *Facing Mt. Kenya.* London: Secker & Warburg, 1938. Reprinted by Random House, New York, n.d.

————, *Suffering Without Bitterness.* Nairobi: East African Publishing House, 1968.

KILSON, MARION, *African Urban Kinsmen: The Ga of Central Accra.* New York: St. Martin's, 1974.

KILSON, MARTIN, ed., *New States in the Modern World.* Cambridge, Mass.: Harvard University Press, 1975.

KILSON, MARTIN, *Political Change in a West African State.* Cambridge, Mass.: Harvard University Press, 1966.

KILSON, MARTIN, AND ADELAIDE C. HILL, eds., *Apropos of Africa: Afro-American Leaders and the Romance of Africa.* Garden City, N.Y.: Doubleday, Anchor Books, 1971.

KIMAMBO, I. H. AND A. J. TEMU, eds., *A History of Tanzania.* Nairobi: East Africa Publishing House, 1969.

KIMBLE, DAVID, *A Political History of Ghana: The Rise of Gold Coast Nationalism, 1850–1928.* Oxford: Clarendon Press, 1963.

KIMBLE, G. H. T., *Tropical Africa,* 2 vols. New York: Doubleday, 1960.

KIWANUKA, M. S., *A History of Buganda.* New York: Africana Publishing, 1972.

KLEIN, MARTIN A., *Islam and Imperialism in Senegal, Sine-Saloum, 1847–1914.* Stanford, Calif.: Stanford University Press, 1968.

KRITZECK, JAMES, AND WILLIAM H. LEWIS, eds., *Islam in Africa*. New York: Van Nostrand-Reinhold, 1969.

KUPER, LEO, *Passive Resistance in South Africa*. New Haven: Yale University Press, 1957.

———, *An African Bourgeoisie: Race, Class and Politics in South Africa*. New Haven: Yale University Press, 1965.

KUPER, LEO, AND M. G. SMITH, eds., *Pluralism in Africa*. Berkeley and Los Angeles: University of California Press, 1971.

LANGWORTHY, H. W., *Zambia Before 1890: Aspects of Pre-Colonial History*. London: Longman, 1972.

LAST, MURRAY, *The Sokoto Caliphate*. New York: Humanities Press, 1967.

LEAKEY, LOUIS S. B., *Mau Mau and the Kikikuyu*. London: Methuen, 1952.

———, *Defeating Mau Mau*. London: Methuen, 1954.

———, *The Progress and Evolution of Man in Africa*. London: Oxford University Press, 1961.

———, *Olduvai Gorge 1951–1961*, 2 vols. London: Cambridge University Press, 1965–1967.

LEE, EUGENE, *Local Taxation in Tanzania*. London: Oxford University Press, 1965.

LEE, J. M., *African Armies and Civil Order*. London: Chatto & Windus, 1969.

LEFEVER, ERNEST W., *Spear and Scepter*. Washington, D.C.: Brookings Institution, 1970.

LEGUM, COLIN, *Pan-Africanism: A Short Political Guide*. New York: Praeger, 1962.

LEVGOLD, ROBERT, *Soviet Policy in West Africa*. Cambridge, Mass.: Harvard University Press, 1970.

LE VINE, VICTOR T., *The Cameroons: From Mandate to Independence*. Berkeley and Los Angeles: University of California Press, 1964.

———, *Political Corruption: The Ghana Case*. Stanford, Calif.: Hoover Institute Press, 1975.

LEVTZION, NEHEMIA, *Ancient Ghana and Mali*. London: Methuen, 1973.

LEWIS, HERBERT S., *A Galla Monarchy*. Madison, Wisc.: University of Wisconsin Press, 1965.

LEWIS, I. M., ed., *Islam in Tropical Africa*. New York: Oxford University Press, 1966.

LEWIS, W. ARTHUR, *The Theory of Economic Growth*. Homewood, Ill.: Richard D. Irwin, 1955.

———, *Politics in West Africa*. New York: Oxford University Press, 1966.

LEWIS, WILLIAM H., ed., *French Speaking Africa: The Search for Identity*. New York: Walker and Co., 1965.

LEYS, COLIN, *European Politics in Southern Rhodesia*. Oxford: Clarendon Press, 1959.

———, *Underdevelopment in Kenya: The Political Economy of Neo-Colonialism: 1964–1971*. Berkeley and Los Angeles: University of California Press, 1974.

LEYS, COLIN, ed., *Politics and Change in Developing Countries*. London: Cambridge University Press, 1960.

LIEBENOW, J. GUS, *Liberia: The Evolution of Privilege*. Ithaca, N.Y.: Cornell University Press, 1969.

LITTLE, KENNETH, *West African Urbanization: A Study of Voluntary Associations in Social Change*. New York: Cambridge University Press, 1965.

———, *African Women in Towns*. London: Cambridge University Press, 1973.

LLOYD, P. C., *Africa in Social Change*. Baltimore, Md.: Penguin, 1967

———, *Classes Crises and Coups*. London: MacGibbon & Kee, 1971.

———, *The New Elites of Tropical Africa*. London: Oxford University Press, 1966.

LLOYD, P. C., A. L. MABOGUNJI, AND B. AWE, eds., *The City of Ibadan*. London: Cambridge University Press, 1967.

LOFCHIE, MICHAEL, *Zanzibar: Background to Revolution*. Princeton, N.J.: Princeton University Press, 1965.

LOFCHIE, MICHAEL, ed., *The State of the Nations*. Berkeley and Los Angeles: University of California Press, 1971.

LOW, D. A., *Buganda in Modern History*. Berkeley and Los Angeles: University of California Press, 1971.

LUGARD, LORD, *The Dual Mandate in British Tropical Africa*. Edinburgh: Blackwood & Sons, 1922; reprinted by Frank Cass, London, 1965.

LUMUMBA, PATRICE, *My Country*. New York: Praeger, 1962.

LY, ABDOULAYE, *Les masses Africaines et l'actuelle condition humaine*. Paris, Presence Africaine, 1956.

———, *Mercenaires Noirs*. Paris: Presence Africaine, 1957.

———, *La compagnie du Senegal*. Paris: Presence Africaine, 1958.

———, *L'etat et la production paysanne*. Paris: Presence Africaine, 1958.

McCALL, DANIEL F., *Africa in Time-Perspective*. New York: Oxford University Press, 1969.

McKAY, VERNON, ed., *African Diplomacy*. New York: Praeger, 1967.

MACKENZIE, W. J. M., AND KENNETH ROBINSON, eds., *Five Elections in Africa*. Oxford: Oxford University Press, 1960.

McKINLEY, EDWARD H., *The Lure of Africa: American Interests in Tropical Africa, 1919–1939*. Indianapolis and New York: Bobbs-Merrill, 1974.

MACKINTOSH, JOHN P., *Nigerian Government and Politics.* Evanston, Ill.: Northwestern University Press, 1966.

MAGUIRE, G. ANDREW, *Toward "Uhuru" in Tanzania.* Cambridge: Cambridge University Press, 1969.

MAINGA, MUTUMBA, *Bulozi under the Luyana Kings: Political Evolution and State Formation in Pre-Colonial Zambia.* London: Longman, 1973.

MAIR, L. P., *Native Policies in Africa.* London: Routledge and Sons, 1936.

MAITLAND-JONES, J. F., *Politics in Africa: The Former British Territories.* New York: Norton, 1975.

MAKONNEN, RAS, *Pan-Africanism from Within.* New York: Oxford University Press, 1973.

MAMDANI, MAHMOOD, *Politics and Class Formation in Uganda.* New York: Monthly Review Press, 1976.

MAQUET, JACQUES, *Power and Society in Africa.* London: Weidenfeld & Nicolson, 1971.

————, *The Premise of Inequality in Ruanda.* London: Oxford University Press, 1961.

MARAN, RENE, *Batouala.* Rockville, Md.: New Perspectives, 1973. Originally published by Editions Albin-Michel, Paris, 1921.

MARCUM, JOHN, *The Angolan Revolution,* Vol. I, *The Anatomy of an Explosion 1950–1962.* Cambridge, Mass.: M.I.T. Press, 1969.

MARKAKIS, JOHN, *Ethiopia: Anatomy of a Traditional Polity.* Oxford: Clarendon Press, 1974.

MARKOVITZ, IRVING LEONARD, *Leopold Sedar Senghor and the Politics of Negritude.* New York: Atheneum, 1969; London, Heinemann Educational Books, 1970.

MARKOVITZ, IRVING LEONARD, ed., *African Politics and Society: Basic Issues and Problems of Government and Development.* New York: Free Press; London: Collier-Macmillan, 1970.

MARRIS, PETER, AND ANTHONY SOMERSET, *African Businessmen: A Study of Entrepreneurship and Development in Kenya.* London: Routledge & Kegan Paul, 1971.

MARSH, ZOE, AND G. W. KINGSNORTH, *An Introduction to the History of East Africa.* London: Cambridge University Press, 1965.

MARSHALL, D. BRUCE, *The French Colonial Myth and Constitution-Making in the Fourth Republic.* New Haven: Yale University Press, 1973.

MAZRUI, ALI, *On Heroes and Uhuru-Worship: Essays on Independent Africa.* London: Longman, 1967.

MBEKI, GOVAN, *South Africa: The Peasants Revolt.* Baltimore: Penguin, 1964.

MBOYA, TOM, *Freedom and After.* London: Andre Deutsch, 1963.

MEEK, C. K., *Law and Authority in a Nigerian Tribe: A Study in Individual Rule.* London: Oxford University Press, 1937.

MEILLASSOUX, CLAUDE, *Urbanization of an African Community: Voluntary Associations in Bamako.* Seattle: University of Washington Press, 1968.

MEILLASSOUX, CLAUDE, ed., *The Development of Indigenous Trade and Markets in West Africa.* London: Oxford University Press, 1971.

MEZU, S. OKECHUKWU, AND RAM DESAI, *Black Leaders of the Centuries.* Buffalo: Black Academy Press, 1970.

MIDDLETON, JOHN, AND DAVID TAIT, eds., *Tribes Without Rulers.* London: Routledge & Kegan Paul, 1958.

MILNER, ALAN, ed., *African Penal Systems.* London: Routledge & Kegan Paul, 1969.

MINER, HORACE, ed., *The City in Modern Africa.* New York: Praeger, 1967.

MINERS, N. J., *The Nigerian Army 1956–1966.* London: Methuen, 1971.

MINOGUE, MARTIN, AND JUDITH MOLLOY, eds., *African Aims and Attitudes, Selected Documents.* Cambridge: Cambridge University Press, 1974.

MINTER, WILLIAM, *Portuguese Africa and the West.* Baltimore: Penguin, 1972.

MONDLANE, EDUARDO, *The Struggle for Mozambique.* Baltimore: Penguin, 1969.

MONTEIL, VINCENT, *L'Islam noir.* Paris: Editions du Seuil, 1964.

MOORE, CLEMENT HENRY, *Politics in North Africa: Algeria, Morrocco and Tunisia.* Boston: Little, Brown, 1970.

MOREL, EDMUND D., *King Leopold's Rule in Africa.* New York: Funk & Wagnalls, 1955.

MORGAN, E. PHILIP, ed., *The Administration of Change in Africa.* New York: Dunellen 1974.

MORGENTHAU, RUTH SCHACHTER, *Political Parties in French Speaking West Africa.* Oxford: Clarendon Press, 1964.

MORRIS, ROGER, AND HAL SHEETS, *Disaster in the Desert, Failures of International Relief in the West African Drought.* Washington, D.C. Carnegie Endowment for International Peace, 1974.

MORRISON, DONALD G., ROBERT C. MITCHELL, JOHN N. PADEN, AND HUGH M. STEVENSON, *Black Africa, A Comparative Handbook.* New York: Free Press, 1972.

MOUMOUNI, ABDOU, *L'education en Afrique.* Paris: Francois Maspero, 1964.

MPHAHLELE, EZEKIEL, *Down Second Avenue.* London: Faber, 1959.

———, *The African Image.* rev. ed. New York: Praeger, 1974.

MTSHALI, OSWALD MBUYISENI, *Sounds of a Cowhide Drum.* New York: The Third Press, 1972.

MURPHY, E. JEFFERSON, *History of African Civilization.* New York: Thomas Y. Crowell, 1972.

MWASE, GEORGE SIMEON, *Strike a Blow and Die,* ed. Robert I. Rotberg. Cambridge, Mass.: Harvard University Press, 1967, 1970.

NAIR, KANNAN K., *Politics and Society in South Eastern Nigeria 1841–1906.* London: Frank Cass, 1972.

N'DIAYE, JEAN-PIERRE, *Elites africaine et culture occidentale: assimilation ou resistance?* Paris: Presence Africaine, 1969.

NELLIS, JOHN R., *A Theory of Ideology: The Tanzanian Example.* London: Oxford University Press, 1972.

NGUGI, JAMES, *Weep Not, Child.* London: Heinemann Educational Books, 1964.

————, *The River Between.* London: Heinemann Educational Books, 1965.

NKOSI, LEWIS, *The Rhythm of Violence.* London: Oxford University Press, 1964.

NKRUMAH, KWAME, *Ghana: The Autobiography of Kwame Nkrumah.* London: Nelson and Sons, 1957.

————, *I Speak of Freedom.* London: Heinemann, 1961.

————, *Africa Must Unite.* London: Heinemann Educational Books, 1963.

————, *Consciencism.* London: Heinemann Educational Books, 1964.

————, *Neo-Colonialism: The Last Stage of Imperialism.* New York: International Publishers, 1965.

————, *Challenge of the Congo.* New York: International Publishers, 1967.

————, *Dark Days in Ghana.* New York: International Publishers, 1968.

————, *Class Struggle in Africa.* New York: International Publishers, 1970.

————, *Revolutionary Path.* New York: International Publishers, 1973.

NWABUEZE, B. O., *Presidentialism in Commonwealth Africa.* New York: St. Martin's, 1974.

NYAKATURA, J. W., *Anatomy of an African Kingdom: A History of Bunyoro-Kitara.* ed. Godfrey N. Uzoigwe. Garden City, N.Y.: Doubleday, Anchor Books, 1973.

NYERERE, JULIUS, K., *Ujamaa — Essays on Socialism.* New York: Oxford University Press, 1968.

————, *Uhuru na Ujamaa: Freedom and Socialism, A Selection from Writings and Speeches, 1965–1967.* Dar es Salaam: Oxford University Press, 1968.

————, *Freedom and Development: A Selection from Writings and Speeches 1968–1973.* New York: Oxford University Press, 1973.

NZIMIRO, IKENNA, *Studies in Ibo Political Systems.* Berkeley and Los Angeles: University of California Press, 1972.

OBENGA, THEOPHILE, *L'Afrique dan l'antiquite: Egypte pharaonique-Afrique Noire.* Paris: Presence Africaine, 1973.

OBICHERE, BONIFACE I., *West African States and European Expansion: The Dahomy-Niger Hinterland, 1885–1898.* New Haven: Yale University Press, 1971.

ODINGA, OGINGA, *Not Yet Uhuru.* New York: Hill & Wang, 1967.

OKPAKU, JOSEPH, ed., *Nigeria: Dilemma of Nationhood: An African Analysis of the Biafran Conflict.* New York: Third Press, 1972.

OKUMA, THOMAS, *Angola in Ferment: The Background and Prospects of Angolan Nationalism.* Boston: Beacon Press, 1972.

OLIVER, ROLAND, AND ANTHONY ATMORE, *Africa Since 1800.* New York: Cambridge University Press, 1967.

OLIVER, ROLAND, AND BRIAN M. FAGAN, *Africa in the Iron Age, 500 B.C. to A.D. 1400.* London: Cambridge University Press, 1975.

OLORUNSOLA, VICTOR A., ed., *The Politics of Cultural Sub-Nationalism in Africa.* Garden City, N.Y.: Doubleday, Anchor Books, 1972.

OLORUNTIMEHIN, B. O. *The Segu Tukulor Empire.* New York: Humanities Press, 1972.

OMARI, T. PETER, *Kwame Nkrumah: The Anatomy of an African Dictatorship.* London: C. Hurst, 1970.

OMER-COOPER, J. D., *The Zulu Aftermath: A Nineteenth Century Revolution in Bantu Africa.* Evanston, Ill.: Northwestern University Press, 1964.

ONYEMELUKWE, C. C., *Problems of Industrial Planning and Management in Nigeria.* New York: Columbia University Press, 1966.

OPPONG, CHRISTINE, *Marriage Among a Matrilineal Elite: A Family Study of Ghanaian Senior Civil Servants.* London: Cambridge University Press, 1974.

OSTHEIMER, JOHN M., *Nigerian Politics.* New York: Harper & Row, 1973.

OTTAWAY, DAVID, AND MARINA OTTAWAY, *Algeria: The Politics of a Socialist Revolution.* Berkeley and Los Angeles: University of California Press, 1970.

OUOLOGUEM, YAMBO, *Le devoir de violence.* Paris: Editions du Seuil, 1968. Translated as *Bound to Violence.* New York: Harcourt Brace Jovanovich, 1971.

OUSMANE, SEMBENE, *God's Bits of Wood.* Garden City, N.Y.: Doubleday, 1962.

OWUSU, MAXWELL, *Uses and Abuses of Political Power: A Case Study of Continuity and Change in the Politics of Ghana.* Chicago: University of Chicago Press, 1970.

OYONO, FERDINAND, *Houseboy.* London: Heinemann Educational Books, 1966. First published as *Une Vie de Boy.* Paris: Editions Julliard, 1960.

PADEN, JOHN N., AND EDWARD W. SOJA, eds., *The African Experience,* 3 vols. Evanston, Ill.: Northwestern University Press, 1970.

PADMORE, GEORGE, *Pan-Africanism or Communism.* London, 1956.

PANKHURST, RICHARD, *An Introduction to the Economic History of Ethiopia from Early Times to 1800.* London: Sidgwick & Jackson, 1961.

PANTER-BRICK, S. K., ed., *Nigerian Politics and Military Rule.* London: Athlone Press, 1970.

PARIN, PAUL, et al., *Les blancs pensent trop: 13 entrentiens psychoanalytiques avec les Dogon.* Paris: Payot, 1966.

PATTERSON, SHEILA, *The Last Trek: A Study of the Boer People and the Afrikaner Nation.* London: Routledge & Kegan Paul, 1957.

PAULME, DENISE, ed., *Women of Tropical Africa,* University of California Press, Berkeley and Los Angeles, 1971. Translated from the French, *Femmes d'Afrique Noir,* Mouton and Co., The Hague, 1960.

PELISSIER, PAUL, *Les paysans du Senegal.* Saint-Yrieix, France: Imp. Fabregue, 1966.

PERLMUTTER, AMOS, *Egypt: The Praetorian State.* New Brunswick, N.J.: Transaction Books, 1974.

PETEREC, RICHARD J., *Dakar and West African Economic Development.* New York: Columbia University Press, 1967.

PFEFFERMANN, GUY, *Industrial Labor in the Republic of Senegal.* New York: Praeger, 1968.

PINKNEY, ROBERT, *Ghana Under Military Rule, 1966–1969.* London: Methuen, 1972.

PLOTNICOV, LEONARD, *Strangers to the City.* Pittsburgh: University of Pittsburgh Press, 1967.

POPE-HENNESSY, JOHN, *Sins of the Fathers: A Study of the Atlantic Slave Traders, 1441–1806.* New York: Knopf, 1967; New York: Capricorn Books, 1969.

POST, KENNETH, *The New States of West Africa,* rev. ed. Baltimore: Penguin, 1968.

POST, KENNETH, AND GEORGE D. JENKINS, *The Price of Liberty: Personality and Politics in Colonial Nigeria.* London: Cambridge University Press, 1973.

POST, KENNETH, AND MICHAEL VICKERS, *Structure and Conflict in Nigeria, 1900–1966.* London: Heinemann Educational Books, 1973.

POTHOLM, CHRISTIAN P., AND RICHARD DALE, eds., *Southern Africa in Perspective.* New York: Free Press, 1972.

PRATT, CRANFORD, *The Critical Phase in Tanzania, 1945–1968.* London: Cambridge University Press, 1976.

PRICE, ROBERT M., *Society and Bureaucracy in Contemporary Ghana.* Berkeley and Los Angeles: University of California Press, 1975.

PRIESTLY, MARGARET, *West African Trade and Coast Society: A Family Study.* London: Oxford University Press, 1969.

PROCTOR, J. H., ed., *The Cell System of the Tanganyika African National Union.* Dar es Salaam: Tanzania Publishing, 1971.

QUINN, CHARLOTTE A., *Mandingo Kingdoms of the Senegambia-Traditionalism. Islam and European Expansion,* Evanston, Ill.: Northwestern University Press, 1972.

RANGER, T. O., *The African Voice in Southern Rhodesia.* London: Heinemann Educational Books, 1968.

RANGER, T. O., ed., *Emerging Themes of African History.* Nairobi, East African Publishing, 1968.

RATTRAY, R. S., *Ashanti.* London: Oxford University Press, 1923.

————, *Religion and Art in Ashanti.* London: Oxford University Press, 1927, 1954.

————, *Ashanti Law and Constitution.* London: Oxford University Press, 1929, 1956.

REYNOLDS, EDWARD, *Trade and Economic Change on the Gold Coast, 1807–1874.* London: Longman, 1974.

RICHARDS, AUDREY, I., FORD STURROCK, AND JEAN M. FORTT, eds., *Subsistence to Commercial Farming in Present-Day Buganda.* Cambridge: Cambridge University Press, 1973.

RIVIERE, CLAUDE, *Mutations sociales en Guinée.* Paris: Marcel Riviere et Cie, 1971.

RIVKIN, ARNOLD, *Nation-Building in Africa.* New Brunswick, N.J.: Rutgers University Press, 1969.

RIVKIN, ARNOLD, ed., *Nations by Design.* Garden City, N.Y.: Doubleday, Anchor Books, 1968.

ROBINSON, RONALD, AND JOHN GALLAGHER, WITH ALICE DENNY, *Africa and the Victorians: The Climax of Imperialism.* New York: St. Martin's, 1961.

RODNEY, WALTER, *West Africa and the Atlantic Slave Trade,* Historical Association of Tanzania Paper No. 2. Nairobi, 1967.

————, *How Europe Underdeveloped Africa.* London: Bogle-L'Ouverture Publications; Dar es Salaam: Tanzanian Publishing, 1972; Washington, D.C.: Howard University Press, 1974.

ROSBERG, CARL G., JR., AND JOHN NOTTINGHAM, *The Myth of Mau Mau: Nationalism in Kenya,* Praeger, New York, 1966.

ROTBERG, ROBERT I., *A Political History of Tropical Africa.* New York: Harcourt, Brace, and World, 1965.

————, *The Rise of Nationalism in Central Africa.* Cambridge, Mass.: Harvard University Press, 1965.

ROTBERG, ROBERT I., AND ALI MAZRUI, eds., *Protest and Power in Black Africa.* New York: Oxford University Press, 1970.

ROTHCHILD, DONALD, *Toward Unity in Africa: A Study of Federalism in British Africa.* Washington, D.C.: Public Affairs Press, 1960.

ROUX, EDWARD, *Time Longer Than Rope: A History of the Black Man's Struggle for Freedom in South Africa.* London: Victor Gollancz, 1948; Madison, Wisc.: University of Wisconsin Press, 1964.

RUBIN, LESLIE, AND BRIAN WEINSTEIN, *Introduction to African Politics: A Continental Approach.* New York: Praeger, 1974.

RUDEBECK, LARS, *Guinea-Bissau: A Study of Political Mobilization.* Uppsala: Scandinavian Institute of African Studies, 1974.

RUSSELL, D. E. H., *Rebellion, Revolution, and Armed Force: A Comparative Study of Fifteen Countries with Special Emphasis on Cuba and South Africa.* New York: Academic, 1974.

RUTH SLOAN ASSOCIATES, *The Educated African,* ed. Helen Kitchen. New York: Praeger, 1962.

RWEYEMAMU, JUSTINIAN, *Underdevelopment and Industrialism in Tanzania: A Study of Perverse Capitalist Industrial Development.* Nairobi: Oxford University Press, 1973.

SACHS, BERNARD, *The Road from Sharpeville.* New York: Marzani & Munsell, 1961.

SAFRAN, NADAV, *Egypt in Search of Political Community.* Cambridge, Mass.: Harvard University Press, 1961.

SAMKANGE, STANLAKE, *On Trial for My Country.* London: Heinemann Educational Books, 1966.

SAMPSON, MAGNUS J., *Gold Coast Men of Affairs.* London: Dawsons of Pall Mall, 1937, 1969.

SANDBROOK, RICHARD, *Proletarians and African Capitalism: The Kenyan Case, 1960–1972.* Cambridge: Cambridge University Press, 1975.

SANDBROOK, RICHARD and ROBIN COHEN, eds., *The Development of an African Working Class.* London: Longman, 1975.

SANKALE, MARC, L. V. THOMAS, P. FOUGHYROLLAS et al., *Dakar En Devenir.* Paris: Presence Africaine, 1968.

SCHNAPPER, BERNARD, *La politique et le commerce Francais dans le Golf de Guinee de 1838 a 1871.* Paris: Mouton, 1961.

SCHUMACHER, EDWARD J., *Politics, Bureaucracy and Rural Development in Senegal.* Berkeley and Los Angeles: University of California Press, 1975.

SCHWAB, GEORGE, *Tribes of the Liberian Hinterland,* Vol. 31. Cambridge, Mass.: Peabody, 1947.

SCHWARTZ, FREDERICH A. O., JR., *Nigeria: The Tribes, the Nations or the Race — The Politics of Independence.* Cambridge, Mass.: M.I.T. Press, 1965.

SCHWARZ, WALTER, *Nigeria.* London: Pall Mall, 1968.

SCOTT, MICHAEL, *A Time to Speak.* New York: Doubleday, 1958.

SEGAL, RONALD, *Political Africa.* London; Stevens & Sons, 1961.

SELASSIE, BEREKET H., *The Executive in African Government.* London: Heinemann Educational Books, 1974.

SENGHOR, LEOPOLD, *African Socialism*. New York: Praeger, 1957.

———, *Les fondements de l'Africanité ou Negritude et Arabité*. Paris: Presence Africaine, 1967.

SHAMUYARIRA, H. M., ed., *Essays on the Liberation of Southern Africa*. Dar es Salaam: Tanzania Publishing, 1971.

SHEPHERD, JACK, *The Politics of Starvation*. New York: Carnegie Endowment for International Peace, 1975.

SHINNIE, P. L., *The African Iron Age*. Oxford: Clarendon Press, 1971.

SHIVJI, ISSA G., *Class Struggle in Tanzania*. New York: Monthly Review Press, 1976.

SIMONS, H. J., AND R. E. SIMONS, *Class and Color in South Africa, 1850–1950*. Baltimore: Penguin, 1969.

SITHOLE, NDABANINGI, *African Nationalism*, 2nd ed. New York: Oxford University Press, 1968.

SKINNER, ELLIOT P., *The Mossi of Upper Volta*. Stanford, Calif. Stanford University Press, 1964.

———, *African Urban Life: The Transformation of Ouagadougou*. Princeton, N.J.: Princeton University Press, 1974.

SKLAR, RICHARD L., *Nigerian Political Parties: Power in an Emergent African Nation*. Princeton, N.J.: Princeton University Press, 1963.

———, *Corporate Power in an African State: The Political Impact of Multinational Mining Companies in Zambia*. Berkeley and Los Angeles: University of California Press, 1975.

SLADE, RUTH, *King Leopold's Congo*. London: Institute of Race Relations, 1962.

SMITH, M. G., *Government in Zazzau, 1800–1950*. London: Oxford University Press, 1960.

SMITH, ROBERT S., *Kingdoms of the Yoruba*. London: Methuen, 1969.

SMITH, STEWART, *U.S. Neocolonialism in Africa*. New York: International Publishers, 1974.

SMITH, WILLIAM EDGETT, *Nyerere of Tanzania*. London: Victor Gollancz, 1973.

SMOCK, DAVID R., AND AUDREY C. SMOCK, *The Politics of Pluralism: A Comparative Study of Lebanon and Ghana*. New York and Amsterdam: Elsevier, 1975.

SMYTHE, HUGH H., AND MABEL M. SMYTHE, *The New Nigerian Elite*. Stanford, Calif.: Stanford University Press, 1960.

SNOWDEN, FRANK M., JR., *Blacks in Antiquity*. Cambridge, Mass.: Harvard University Press, 1970.

SOYINKA, WOLE, *A Dance of the Forests*. London: Oxford University Press, 1963.

———, *The Lion and the Jewel*. London: Oxford University Press, 1963.

STAVENHAGEN, RODOLFO, *Social Classes in Agrarian Societies.* Garden City, N.Y.: Doubleday, Anchor Books, 1975.

STEWARD, JULIAN H., ed., *Three African Tribes in Transition,* Vol. I of *Contemporary Change in Traditional Societies.* ed. Steward, Urbana, Ill.: University of Illinois Press, 1967, Illinois Books ed., 1972.

STILLMAN, CALVIN, ed., *Africa in the Modern World.* Chicago: University of Chicago Press, 1955.

STRIDE, G. T., AND C. IFEKA, *Peoples and Empires of West Africa: West Africa in History, 1000–1800.* New York: Africana Publishing, 1971.

SURET-CANALE, JEAN, *Afrique Noire,* 2 vols. Paris: Editions Sociales, 1961, 1964.

SY, CHEIKH TIDIANE, *La confrerie Senegalaise des Mourides.* Paris: Presence Africaine, 1969.

TAMUNO, T. N., *The Evolution of the Nigerian State: The Southern Phase, 1898–1914.* London: Longman, 1972.

TESSLER, MARK A., WILLAIM M. O'BARR, AND DAVID H. SPAIN, *Tradition and Identity in Changing Africa.* New York: Harper & Row, 1973.

THIAM, DOUDOU, *La portee de la citoyennete Francais dans les territoires d'outre-mer.* Paris: Societé d'Editions Africaines, 1953.

THIAM, MEDOUNE, *Cheickh Ahmadou Bamba, fondateur du Mouridisme 1850–1927.* Conakry: Imprimerie Nationale, 1964.

THOMPSON, LEONARD, *Politics in the Republic of South Africa.* Boston: Little, Brown, 1966.

THOMPSON, LEONARD, AND MONICA WILSON, *Oxford History of South Africa,* 2 vols. Oxford: Oxford University Press, 1969, 1971.

THOMPSON, W. SCOTT, *Ghana's Foreign Policy, 1957–1966.* Princeton, N.J.: Princeton University Press, 1969.

THOMPSON, VIRGINIA, AND RICHARD ADLOFF, *French West Africa.* Stanford, Calif.: Stanford University Press, 1957.

TOURÉ, SEKOU, *Guinean Revolution and Social Progress.* Cairo: Societe Orientale de Publicité, n.d. [1963].

TRAORE, BAKARI, MAMADOU LO, AND JEAN-LOUIS ALIBERT, *Forces politiques en Afrique Noire.* Paris: Presses Universitaires de France, 1966.

TRIMINGHAM, J. SPENCER, *A History of Islam in West Africa.* London: Oxford University Press, 1962.

TUDEN, ARTHUR, AND LEONARD PLOTNICOV, eds., *Social Stratification in Africa.* New York: Free Press, 1970.

TUTUOLA, AMOS, *The Palm-Wine Drinkard.* New York: Grove Press, 1953.

UCHUMI Editorial Board, ed., *Towards Socialist Planning.* Dar es Salaam: Tanzania Publishing, 1972.

UNESCO, *Social Implications of Industrialization and Urbanization in Africa South of the Sahara*. Paris, 1956.

United Nations Institute for Economic Development and Planning, *The Emergence of Agrarian Capitalism in Africa South of the Sahara*. Dakar, 1973.

VAN DE BERGHE, PIERRE, *South Africa: A Study in Conflict*. Middletown, Conn.: Wesleyan University Press, 1965.

_____, *Power and Privilege at an African University*. London: Routledge & Kegan Paul, 1973.

VAN HEKKEN, P. M., AND H. U. E. THODEN VAN VELZEN, *Land Scarcity and Rural Inequality in Tanzania: Some Case Studies from Rungwe District*. The Hague: Mouton, 1972.

VANSINA, JAN, *Kingdoms of the Savanna*. Madison, Wisc.: University of Wisconsin Press, 1966.

VINCENT, JOAN, *African Elite: The Big Men of a Small Town*. New York: Columbia University Press, 1971.

WADE, ABDOULAYE, *Economie de l'Ouest Africain, unité et croissance*. Paris: Presence Africaine, 1964.

WALKER, ERIC, *A History of South Africa*. London: Longman, 1964.

WALLERSTEIN, IMMANUEL, *Africa: The Politics of Independence*. New York: Random House, Vintage Books, 1961.

_____, "Africa in a Capitalist World," *Issue*, 3, no. 3 (Fall 1973), 1–11.

_____, *The Road to Independence: Ghana and the Ivory Coast*. Paris: Mouton, 1954.

WALSHE, PETER, *The Rise of African Nationalism in South Africa: The African National Congress, 1912–1952*. Berkeley and Los Angeles: University of California Press, 1971.

WARD, W. E. F., AND L. W. WHITE, *East Africa: A Century of Change, 1870–1970*. New York: Africana Publishing, 1971.

WASTBERG, PER, ed., *The Writer in Modern Africa*. New York: Africana Publishing, 1969.

WEBSTER, J. B., AND A. A. BOAHEN, *History of West Africa*. New York: Praeger, 1970.

WEINRICH, A. K. H., *Black and White Elites in Rural Rhodesia*. Manchester: Manchester University Press, 1973.

WEINSTEIN, BRIAN, *Eboue*. New York: Oxford University Press, 1972.

WEISBORD, ROBERT G., *Ebony Kinship: Africa, Africans and the Afro-American*. Westport, Conn.: Greenwood Press, 1973.

WEISS, HERBERT, *Political Protest in the Congo*. Princeton, N.J.: Princeton University Press, 1967.

WELCH, CLAUDE E., JR., ed., *Soldier and State in Africa*. Evanston, Ill.: Northwestern University Press, 1970.

WELLS, F. A., AND W. A. WARMINGTON, *Studies in Industrialization: Nigeria and the Cameroons.* London: Oxford University Press, 1962.

WHEARE, JOAN, *The Nigerian Legislative Council.* London: Faber & Faber, 1950.

WHITAKER, C. S., JR., *The Politics of Tradition: Continuity and Change in Northern Nigeria, 1946–1966.* Princeton, N.J.: Princeton University Press, 1970.

WIDSTRAND, CARL, ed., *Multinational Firms in Africa.* Uppsala: Scandinavian Institute of African Studies, 1975.

WIEDNER, DONALD L., *A History of Africa South of the Sahara.* New York: Random House, 1962.

WIGHT, MARTIN, *The Gold Coast Legislative Council.* London: Faber & Faber, 1947.

WILLETT, FRANK, *African Art: an Introduction.* New York: Praeger, 1971.

WILSON, FRANCIS, *Labour in the South African Gold Mines, 1936–1969.* Cambridge: Cambridge University Press, 1972.

WILSON, HENRY S., ed., *Origins of West African Nationalism.* New York: St. Martin's, 1969.

WILSON, MONICA, AND LEONARD THOMPSON, eds., *Oxford History of South Africa.* New York: Oxford University Press, 1969.

WODDIS, JACK, *Africa: The Roots of Revolt.* New York: Citadel Press, 1960.

WOLFF, RICHARD D., *The Economics of Colonialism: Britain and Kenya, 1870–1930.* New Haven: Yale University Press, 1974.

WORONOFF, JON, *West African Wager: Houphouet versus Nkrumah.* Metuchen, N.J.: Scarecrow Press, 1972.

WRIGHT, RICHARD, *Black Power.* New York: Harper & Brothers, 1954.

YOUNG, CRAWFORD, *Politics in the Congo.* Princeton, N.J.: Princeton University Press, 1965.

ZIEGLER, JEAN, *La Contre-revolution en Afrique.* Paris: Payot, 1963.

ZOLBERG, ARISTIDE, *Creating Political Order.* Chicago: Rand McNally and Co., 1966.

————, *One-Party Government in the Ivory Coast,* rev. ed. Princeton, N.J.: Princeton University Press, 1969.

INDEX

A

Abboud, Ibrahim, 269
Aborigine Rights Protection Society, 243
Aboyade, O., 85n
Abrahams, Peter, 233n
Accra, Ghana
  general strike in, 269
  women traders in, 235–36
Acheampong, Ignatius K., 259, 309
Achebe, Chinua, 303, 319n
Action Group (Nigeria), 163, 244–45
Adansi, 178n
Adelahu, Adegoke, 163n
Adeleye, R. A., 159n
Adelman, Irma, 8, 206n
Adloff, Richard, 62n, 243n
Adowa, battle of (1896), 30, 48
Afana, Osende, 132n, 333n
AFL-CIO, 266
Afonja (slave leader), 150
African Civil Servants Association, 338
African Socialism (policy paper), 249–50
African Steamship Company, 241
African Times, 241
Africanus, Leo, 143
Afrifa, A. A., 156–57, 258, 309
Agblemaghon, F. H., 206n
Agbodeka, Francis, 61n
Aidoo, Ama Ata, 200
Ajayi, J. F. Ade, 31n, 47, 142n
Akans, 178n
Akilu, Alhaji Ali, 162
Akrosan brothers, 241
al-Bakri, 143
al-Sibbiq, Abu Bakr, 239n
Algeria, 282
  army in, 311n
  coup in, 286

Algeria *(cont.)*
  elites in, 156n, 227
  revolution in, 15, 192, 196
  rural inequalities in, 276
  trade unions in, 269
Alibert, Jean-Louis, 160n
Allen, Christopher, 226n, 274n, 275n,
    280n, 340n
Almoravids, 42–43
Alpers, Edward A., 74n, 148n, 171n
Altbach, Philip G., 220n
Alula, Ras, 48
Ameillon, B., 202n, 330n
Americo-Liberians, 345
Amhara, 122n–23n
  feudalism in, 140
Amin, Idi, 170
Amin, Samir, 58n, 89–90, 227, 234–35,
    249n, 267n, 276
Amsden, Alice H., 252n, 263n, 266n, 270,
    280n
Ancient kingdoms, 28–32
Angola, 72, 109n
  foreign investment in, 96
Angrand, A. P., 124n
Ankole, 101
Anlo, 240n
Anokye, Okonfo, 38
Anouilh, Jean, 285n
Anstey, Roger, 228n
Apter, David, 19n, 39n, 105n, 170, 233n,
    292–94, 298n, 300n
Apthorpe, Raymond, 138n, 340n
Arabs:
  slave revolts and, 150
  slave trade by, 143–44
Armah, Ayi Kwei, 200, 303, 348
Armstrong, Winifred, 236n
Arrighi, Giovanni, 204